FULLY COVERS **NEW** SPECIFICATION

KEN BROWNE

SOCIOLOGY

FOR A2 AQA

Jonathan Blundell, Pamela Law and Margaret Whalley

polity

First published in 2009 by Polity Press

Polity Press
65 Bridge Street
Cambridge CB2 1UR, UK

Polity Press
350 Main Street
Malden, MA 02148, USA

ISBN-13: 978-0-7456-4189-8
ISBN-13: 978-0-7456-4190-4(pb)

A catalogue record for this book is available from the British Library.

Typeset in 9.5 on 13 pt Utopia Regular
by Servis Filmsetting Ltd, Stockport, Cheshire
Printed and bound in China by 1010 Printing International Ltd

The publisher has used its best endeavours to ensure that the URLs for external websites referred to in this book are correct and active at the time of going to press. However, the publisher has no responsibility for the websites and can make no guarantee that a site will remain live or that the content is or will remain appropriate.

Every effort has been made to trace all copyright holders, but if any have been inadvertently overlooked the publishers will be pleased to include any necessary credits in any subsequent reprint or edition.

For further information on Polity, visit our website: www.politybooks.com

Contents

Detailed Contents

Acknowledgements

Ken Browne wrote chapters 1, 3, 5 and 6, and undertook general editing and compilation of the book; Jonathan Blundell wrote chapter 2, Margaret Whalley wrote chapter 4 and Pam Law wrote chapter 7. We would all like to thank Penny Halliday and Eirene Mitsos, and the various anonymous readers approached by Polity, who provided us with several ideas for activities and improvements, and some very constructively critical and supportive comments, many of which have been incorporated into the finished text.

We would all like to thank the staff at Polity, particularly Emma Longstaff, who has once again proven to be a brilliant, supportive and understanding editor, and Jonathan Skerrett, who put in a lot of hard nurturing work and kept the show on the road. Clare Ansell and Breffni O'Connor did great jobs in producing and marketing the book, and Sarah Dancy once again demonstrated high levels of skill and knowledge in copy-editing the typescript.

We would like to thank all those who gave us permission to reproduce copyright material. The source of copyright material is acknowledged in the text. Should any copyright holder have been inadvertently overlooked, the author and publishers will be glad to make suitable amendments at the first possible opportunity.

Illustration Credits

The publisher would like to acknowledge permission to reproduce the following images:

Chapter 1:
Lee Pettet/iStock; Stan Rohrer/iStock; © Ken Pyne; © Photosbyash | Dreamstime. com;Jon Larson/iStock; Aidar Ayazbayev/iStock; Blackbeck/iStock; Huriye AKINCI/ iStock; Lisa Thornberg/iStock; Jeremy Richards/iStock; CWLawrence/iStock; Churches Advertising Network; © Tektite | Dreamstime.com; Trevor Norman/iStock; Dennis Guyitt/iStock; Juanmonino/iStock; The Salvation Army; manuel velasco/ iStock; Jean Burnett/iStock; narvikk/iStock; Steven Allan/iStock; Edward Shaw/ iStock; Christian Research; diego cervo/iStock; Robert Kohlhuber/iStock; Rejesus

Chapter 2:
Raido Väljamaa/iStock; Jerry Koch/iStock; William Walsh/iStock; helloyiying/iStock; David Joyner/iStock; Lee Jordan; © Beisea | Dreamstime.com; Anna Pustovaya/ iStock; Sieto Verver/iStock; aguirre_mar/iStock; Ricardo Stuckert/PR; Anutik/iStock; Konstantin Sutyagin/iStock; Slobo Mitic/iStock; oneclearvision/iStock; luoman/ iStock; Raysonho; William Walsh/iStock; José Luis/iStock; Don Bayley/iStock; U.S. Signal Corps; Steven Jones/iStock; Eric Weijers/iStock

Chapter 3:
Aldo Murillo/iStock; esemelwe/iStock; Stefan Schulze; © Ken Pyne; bubaone/iStock; Horst Gossmann/iStock; US Navy; Drazen Vukelic/iStock; Ted Foy/iStock; Joseph C. Justice Jr./iStock

Chapter 4:
Liv Friis-Larsen/iStock; Jean Nordmann/iStock; Brian Pamphilon/iStock; Stephanie Horrocks/iStock; 1001nights/iStock; Eileen Hart/iStock; Eduardo Jose Bernardino/ iStock; Tomaz Levstek/iStock; Pavel Losevsky/iStock; Andy Medina/iStock; dagmar heymans/iStock; Chris Schmidt/iStock; Hanne Melbye-Hansen/iStock; Denise Ritchie/iStock; Vasiliki Varvaki/iStock; Peeter Viisimaa/iStock; Bryan Myhr/iStock; Jonathan Smith; Clavedoc/Dreamstime; Andrea Booher/ FEMA News Photo

Chapter 5:
Winston Davidian/iStock; Giles Angel/iStock; © Ken Pyne; Adivin/iStock; Sandra O'Claire/iStock; Daniel Bobrowsky/iStock; Brasil2/iStock; Oleg Prikhodko/iStock;

Sean Locke/iStock; webphotographeeer/iStock; Jerry Koch/iStock; Erik Reis/iStock; Rich Legg/iStock; Exkalibur/iStock; Mehmet Salih/GuleriStock; olaf loose/iStock; Pei Lin Shang/iStock; Pali Rao/iStock; Valentin Casarsa/iStock; Chris Schmidt/iStock; Davorin Pavlica/iStock; digitalskillet/iStock; Scott Griessel/iStock

Chapter 6:
Sascha Burkard/iStock; Monika Gniot/iStock; Simonmcconico/iStock; Alphone Bertillon; Mark Strozier/iStock; Howard Becker; Douglas Freer/iStock; Linda Steward/iStock; Uffe Zeuthen/iStock; Denis Jr. Tangney/iStock; RT Images/iStock; Jami Garrison/iStock; John Tomaselli/iStock; kelvin wakefield/iStock; Peeter Viisimaa/iStock; Jeff Dalton/iStock; Mark Evans/iStock; Brasil2/iStock; ©Victoo/Dreamstime; Denis Jr. Tangney/iStock; Stefan Witas/iStock; 1001nights/iStock

Chapter 7:
Nicholas Monu/iStock; Chris Schmidt/iStock; dra_schwartz/iStock; asiseeit/iStock; William Murphy/iStock; Paul Piebinga/iStock; © Ken Pyne; Franky de Meyer/iStock; acilo/iStock; Duncan Walker/iStock; asiseeit/iStock; Silvia Jordan/iStock; Nicholas Sereno/iStock; Juanmonino/iStock; Thomas Schoch; Izvorinka Jankovic/iStock; Jean Schweltzer/iStock; Erich Spieldiener/iStock; Christoff/Dreamstime; bubaone/iStock; Marko Radunovic/iStock; Paul Kline/iStock; Lajos Repasi/iStock; Tomaz Levstek/iStock; Kenneth C. Zirkel/iStock; Tomas Levstek/iStock; alvarez/iStock; larkyphoto/iStock; Ami Beyer/iStock; starfotograf/iStock; Alberto Pomares/iStock; Danish Khan/iStock; Studio/Dreamstime.com; g-studio/iStock; Eric Hood/iStock

A2 Sociology

This book provides comprehensive coverage of all units of the AQA A2 Sociology specification, and is designed as a companion volume to the book covering the AS specification. It aims to give students the knowledge and understanding necessary successfully to achieve an A-level qualification in Sociology, and to help in the development of the skills of interpretation, application, analysis and evaluation – though these skills are often best developed in the classroom, through discussion and individual or group activities. There is a range of activities to develop these skills in the main chapters covering the various subject areas. This book aims to provide a readable approach to subject content, while still maintaining the integrity of the subject and recognizing some of its complexities.

The A2 specification

The AQA A2 specification involves the following units.

Unit 3

Any *one* from these:

- Beliefs in Society
- Global Development
- Mass Media
- Power and Politics

Choose <u>one</u> of the four topics. Answer one compulsory question *and* one essay question from a choice of two. The compulsory question is a stimulus response/structured question consisting of either two or three parts, and carries 27 marks. The essay question carries 33 marks.
Total marks = 60, worth 20 per cent of the total A level marks. Exam is 1 hour 30 minutes.

Unit 4

Either
- Crime and Deviance
Or
- Stratification and Differentiation
And
- Theory and Methods

This book covers all the subject requirements for the A2 exam, but students only have to study a minimum of one subject area for each unit, plus 'Theory and Methods' in Unit 4. This gives students a complete choice of areas on each paper.

Assessment

At A2 Sociology, students are assessed on two main objectives:

Knowledge and understanding

This involves sociological theories, concepts and research, an understanding of how sociologists use a range of methods and sources of information, and the practical, ethical and theoretical issues arising in sociological research.

Knowledge and understanding are likely to be tested in questions by the use of words like:

- Outline . . .
- Explain . . .
- Examine . . .
- Describe . . .
- Discuss. . .
- Give reasons for . . .

Application, interpretation, analysis and evaluation

This involves things like being able to recognize and criticize sociologically significant information, to 'make sense of' data, recognize the strengths and weaknesses of sociological theories and evidence, and reach conclusions based on the evidence and arguments presented.

The skills of *application* and *interpretation* are likely to be tested in questions by the use of words like:

- Identify . . .
- Illustrate . . .
- Give an example . . .
- Suggest . . .
- How might . . . ?
- In what ways . . . ?

The skills of *analysis* and *evaluation* are likely to be tested in questions by the use of words like:

- Assess . . .
- Evaluate . . .
- To what extent . . .?
- How useful . . .?

- Critically discuss . . .
- Compare and contrast . . .
- . . . for and against the view . . .

To show the examiner that you are using the skill of *analysis*, you might consider using the following words and phrases:

- the relevance of this is . . .
- this indicates . . .
- this is similar to/different from . . .
- so . . .
- therefore . . .
- this means/does not mean . . .
- hence . . .
- a consequence of . . .
- the implication of . . .
- the contrast between . . .
- put simply . . .

For *evaluation skills*, you might use the following words and phrases:

- a strength/weakness of this . . .
- an argument for/against . . .
- an advantage/disadvantage of . . .
- the importance of . . .
- this is important because . . .
- this does not take account of . . .
- however . . .
- alternatively . . .
- a criticism of this is . . .
- others argue that . . .
- a different interpretation is provided by . . .
- on the other hand . . .
- the problem with this is . . .
- this does not explain why . . .
- to conclude . . .
- this argument/evidence suggests . . .

Two themes

There are two themes or threads that run through the whole AS- and A-level course:

1 Socialization, culture and identity
2 Social differentiation, power and stratification

These are not expected to be taught as specific subjects, but, rather, are themes that should be referred to throughout the course. For example, in the 'Beliefs in

Society' unit, you might consider the socialization of children into religious beliefs, inequalities of power and status between men and women in religious organizations, or religion as a source of identity in minority ethnic groups. In the 'Mass Media' unit, you might consider issues like the role of the media in socializing people into the dominant ideology, or the way the media supports the interests of the powerful in society, or their role in socializing people into gender or other identities.

How to Use this Book

Each chapter of this book is designed to be more or less self-contained, and to cover the knowledge and skills required to achieve success in A-level Sociology.

Important terms are highlighted in colour in the text, and defined in the page margins. These are normally explained in the text, and also listed at the end of the chapter. In addition, they are included in a comprehensive glossary at the end of the book. Unfamiliar terms should be checked in the glossary or index for further explanation or clarification. The contents pages or the index should be used to find particular themes or references. The References include all research referred to in the book in case you should wish to explore any of the studies further. There are activity-based sections on research at the end of chapters 6 and 7; these should help to prepare you for that part of the examination question in unit 4 which asks you to apply your knowledge of research methods to particular issues in crime and deviance or stratification and differentiation.

Chapter summaries outline the key points that should have been learnt after reading each chapter. These should be used as checklists for revision – if you cannot do what is asked, then refer back to the chapter to refresh your memory. The glossary at the end of the book also provides both a valuable reference source and a revision aid, as you can check the meaning of terms. A typical examination question is included at the end of the chapters. Students should attempt these under timed conditions, both as practice and to gauge how ready they are for the examination in that unit.

Websites

The Internet is a valuable source of information for sociologists, and for exploring the topics in this book. However, there is a lot of rubbish on some Internet sites, and information should be treated with some caution. As a general rule, Google provides one of the best search engines. Try this for any research topic – putting 'UK' at the end usually helps – for example, 'church attendance uk'. There are some useful websites referred to throughout this book, but you can find more, and other resources, at:
www.politybooks.com/browne

Beliefs in Society

KEN BROWNE

Contents

1

Beliefs in Society

Beliefs are ideas about things we hold to be true

Beliefs are ideas about things we hold to be true. There is a very wide range of beliefs in society, but this chapter will focus primarily on religious beliefs. These concern themselves mainly with beliefs in supernatural powers or forces of some kind, and deal with ideas about fundamental issues of human existence, like the meaning and purpose of life, the place of human beings in the cosmos, whether there is a soul, whether there is some kind of spirit or life force either within ourselves or watching over us, and what happens after we die. Religious beliefs include those found in the world's most common religions, such as Christianity, Hinduism, Islam, Judaism, Sikhism and Buddhism, but also a wide diversity of other beliefs and groups which concern themselves with similar issues, such as witchcraft (Wicca), paganism and Satanism. Religious beliefs are often also taken to include a range of activities that generally fall outside the framework of the world's established mainstream religions. These include beliefs in things like faith healing, astrology, horoscopes and fortune telling, superstitions of various kinds, magic, and a vast range of New Age beliefs, such as the spiritual or life force dimensions of crystal healing, meditation, massage, aromatherapy and even beliefs in alien abduction and UFOs.

This chapter will focus on the social significance of religious beliefs, the roles they perform in society, the organizational forms they take, their relationship to particular social groups and whether or not religious beliefs are of declining significance in contemporary society.

Before defining and exploring religion itself, it is first necessary to examine how religious beliefs differ from two concepts with which they have, at various times, been entangled: science and ideology.

Ideology

The term ideology is used in a wide variety of ways; it is most commonly regarded as a set of ideas and values shared by a social group that:

- provides a particular vision or way of seeing and interpreting the world;
- presents only a partial, incomplete or false view of reality;
- expresses and justifies (legitimizes) the interests of particular social or political groups.

> **Ideology** refers to a set of ideas, values and beliefs that provides a means of interpreting the world, and represents the outlook, and justifies the interests, of a social group.

Different conceptions of ideology

There are many different types of ideology within this general definition, in part reflecting the wide range of ways in which the concept has been used.

Pluralist ideology

Pluralism is a view that sees the exercise of power in society as reflecting a broad range of social interests, with power spread among a wide variety of competing interest groups and individuals, with no single one having a monopoly on power.

Pluralist ideology is a view of the world which suggests that there are many different types of social group, each with its own ideologies, or sets of ideas and means of interpreting the world, which live alongside each other. None has any claim to be the only right way of seeing the world or has a privileged position of dominating or suppressing others, and there is no single dominant ideology that reflects the interests of a particular social group. However, pluralist ideology falls into the trap of itself claiming a form of superiority over other ideologies, as it aims to persuade people that the prevailing ideas in society reflect those of a broad range of social groups, with no single dominant ideology, and this is something to be approved of and welcomed. But in doing this, it is denying that there may be an unequal distribution of power in society, and that not all social groups are equally able to influence those with power or get their views accepted as part of the prevailing vision in society. In effect, the pluralist ideology tries to conceal the fact that there is an unequal distribution of power in society by trying to persuade us that this isn't the case.

> **Pluralism** is a view that sees power in society spread among a wide variety of interest groups and individuals, with no single one having a monopoly on power.

> **Pluralist ideology** is the set of ideas reflecting the pluralist view of the distribution of power, with no one particular ideology able to dominate others, with the prevailing ideas in society reflecting the interests of a wide range of social groups and interests.

Marxism: dominant ideology and hegemony

Marxists believe that the ideas that people hold are formed by their position in society, and ideology is therefore seen very clearly as the ideas of particular social groups reflecting their interests. The Marxist view is most associated with the view that there is a dominant ideology in society. This is a set of ideas and beliefs of the most powerful groups and, in particular, of the ruling class in society. Mannheim, in *Ideology and Utopia* (1985, originally published 1929) generally associated the dominant ideology with the deliberate obscuring of facts in order to conceal the inequalities of capitalist society and to preserve existing patterns of inequality, the privileged position of the dominant class, and to prevent any social change that might threaten their interests. Althusser (1971) suggested the dominant ideology was spread through a series of ideological state apparatuses – social institutions like the family, the education system, the mass media, the law and religion, which spread the dominant ideology and justify the power of the dominant social class.

The Italian Gramsci further developed the Marxist view of ideology with his development of the concept of hegemony. Hegemony refers to the process whereby the ruling class, through the dominant ideology, maintains its power by persuading other social classes, and particularly the working class, to adopt ruling class ideology as part of their own beliefs and values, and therefore consent to the rule of the dominant class rather than being forced to obey. An example of this, as will be considered later in this chapter, is the way Marxists regard religion as part of the dominant ideology, establishing the hegemony and justifying the power of the ruling class.

Other forms of ideology

There are two other forms of ideology that you may come across in your reading, which are briefly described below.

Patriarchal ideology   Feminist writers have identified a patriarchal ideology, which is a set of ideas that supports and tries to justify the power of men in a patriarchal society. As will be seen later in this chapter, some feminists regard many contemporary religions and religious organizations both to be patriarchal in structure and to reflect a patriarchal ideology. Many feminists would suggest that a wide range of other ideologies are also patriarchal, as they are much more concerned with promoting and protecting the interests of men than they are those of women.

Political ideologies   Political ideologies are those held by political parties, like the Conservative, Labour, Green or Liberal Democrat parties in the UK. Political ideologies are sets of ideas and aims offering an interpretation and analysis of the world, how they think it works, and how it should be changed. These ideas may themselves be borrowed from a range of other ideologies, but, like all ideologies, political ideologies are usually aimed at protecting and promoting the interests of particular social groups.

The **dominant ideology** refers to the set of ideas and beliefs of the most powerful groups in society, usually associated with Marxist ideas of the ruling class.

Ideological state apparatuses are agencies that spread the dominant ideology and justify the power of the dominant social class.

Hegemony refers to the dominance in society of the ruling class's set of ideas over others, and acceptance of and consent to them by the rest of society.

Patriarchal ideology is a set of ideas that supports and justifies the power of men.

There are a host of other ways that the term ideology has been used, and a vast array of ideologies in society. If you want to find out more, go to www.google.com and do a search on ideology. The fact that there are nearly 800,000 pages in English gives some insight into the diversity of ways that the concept of ideology has been used and interpreted.

Ideology and religion

Religion, like ideology, also offers a vision of and a means of understanding, interpreting and explaining the world. However, unlike ideology, religious beliefs are not necessarily tied to the interests of a particular social group, and as Giddens (2006) put it, religion involves 'shared beliefs and rituals that provide a sense of ultimate meaning and purpose by creating an idea of reality that is sacred, all-encompassing and supernatural'. There are three main aspects to religion:

1 *Belief in the spiritual and supernatural* – a person, entity or other extra-worldly spiritual forces or being of some kind, which ultimately provide a sense of meaning and a means of interpreting and explaining the world.
2 *Faith on the part of believers* – a strong sense of trust and conviction in a person or entity that is not based on observable, testable or falsifiable evidence.
3 *A body of unchanging truth.* Religions usually contain certain fundamental and unchangeable beliefs, like Christ being the son of God, or Mohammed being Allah's Prophet, and new discoveries are fitted into these existing frameworks.

Religion differs from ideology in that ideologies are not necessarily based on faith in supernatural beliefs, but on the interests of social groups. However, religion may become part of an ideology, as a social group may seek to use religion for its own ends, such as promoting and protecting its own interests. Marx, for example, regarded religion as part of the ideology of the dominant class in society (what he called the dominant ideology), forming part of the worldview and helping to justify the interests of that class, and acting like the drug opium to dull the senses and pain of those that it exploited. This will be considered later in the chapter.

More recently, fundamentalist Christians in the United States, and increasingly in Europe, have transformed some religious beliefs into a campaigning ideology called Intelligent Design (sometimes also called Creative Design). Intelligent Design is a religious belief that the universe and living things, including the human race, are not products of the scientifically accepted process of natural evolution, but are, rather, created by an intelligent force (God). This religiously based ideology is aligned to conservative American politicians and seeks to remove the teaching of the scientific theory of evolution in schools.

Activity

If you want to learn a bit more about Intelligent Design, and why it might be regarded more as an ideology or religious faith than a science, you can explore it on the following websites:

- www.intelligentdesignnetwork.org/ – Intelligent Design
- www.actionbioscience.org/evolution/nhmag.html – an article from the Natural History magazine debating Intelligent Design theories
- www.venganza.org/ – the site of the Church of the Flying Spaghetti Monster, which has developed the Pastafarian creation theory. This spoof site challenges Intelligent Design theories through absurdity, showing how its own made-up theories are no different, in the sense of being unscientific, from those of Intelligent Design.

As a result of your investigations, explain why Intelligent Design might be regarded more as a religious faith or an ideology than as what most would regard as a scientific explanation.

Science

For a very long time, science was so mixed up with religious beliefs, superstition, and magic that it bore little relationship to the systematically collected research evidence, experimentation and rational argument we associate with science today. Even now, science and religion are often seen as competing ways of explaining the world.

What is science?

Objectivity means approaching topics with an open mind, avoiding bias, and being prepared to submit research evidence to scrutiny by other researchers.

Although there are differing views of science, it is generally accepted that, unlike religion and ideology, it aspires to objectivity and value-freedom, and is based on research methods producing explanations that are based on empirical evidence.

Popper (2002) suggests the scientific method involves:

Value-freedom is the idea that the beliefs and prejudices of a researcher should not influence the way research is carried out and evidence interpreted.

1 *Hypothesis formation*: forming ideas or informed guesses about possible explanations for some phenomena, which are capable of being tested against evidence derived from systematic observation and/or experimentation.
2 *Falsification*: the aim of testing hypotheses against the evidence is to try to prove them wrong, as just one exception can prove a hypothesis false.
3 *Prediction*: through establishing cause and effect relationships rooted in evidence, precise predictions of what will happen in the same circumstances in future can be established.

Empirical evidence is observable evidence collected in the physical or social world.

4 *Theory formation*: if the hypothesis is capable of being tested against evidence and cannot be shown to be false, and predictions appear sound, then there can be some confidence that the hypothesis is probably true. This may then become part of a scientific theory.
5 *Scrutiny*: a scientific theory will be scrutinized by other scientists, and will stand only until some new evidence comes along to show the existing theory is false.

The application of the scientific method means that ideas and theories in science are not unquestionably accepted as an act of faith as they are in religion, but are subject to constant challenge, change, correction and improvement as more and better evidence is collected.

Science as a social product

Popper's principle of falsification suggests researchers should aim not to prove their hypotheses true, but to falsify them, or prove them wrong. This is because no hypothesis can ever finally be proven true, as there is always the possibility of some future exception. However, a hypothesis can easily be proven false, as just one observation to the contrary can disprove it. The more a hypothesis stands up to such attempts, the more likely it is to be a 'scientific truth'.

However, Kuhn's book *The Structure of Scientific Revolutions* (1962) challenges whether scientists really do in practice set out to collect evidence with the specific aim of attempting to falsify their hypotheses. Kuhn argues that, on the contrary, scientists work within a **paradigm** – a set of values, ideas, beliefs and assumptions about what they are investigating which is not called into question until the evidence against them is overwhelming.

A **paradigm** is a set of values, ideas, beliefs and assumptions providing a model or framework within which scientists operate and guidelines for the conduct of research. These are rarely called into question until the evidence against them is overwhelming.

Paradigms and scientific revolutions

A paradigm is really a set of values, like a pair of coloured lenses through which scientists look at the world. The paradigm colours their views of the nature of the problem or problems to be investigated, the 'approved' methods which should be followed to tackle these problems, and what should count as proper and relevant scientific evidence.

Kuhn argues that when scientists test their hypotheses through observations and experiments, they try to fit their findings into the existing paradigm, rather than attempt to falsify their hypotheses. The power of the paradigm may mean that scientists focus on what they are looking for, and overlook or fail to see evidence which doesn't fit the paradigm. When findings do not fit into the existing paradigm, they are likely to be dismissed as having resulted from experimental errors or freak conditions. This suggests that what passes for scientific truth may often be more an act of faith in scientific values than of scientific rigour. Only when there are so many anomalies, or things the existing paradigm can't explain, will the established paradigm change, as scientists begin to question their basic assumptions and produce a new paradigm which explains what the old paradigm could not. Kuhn therefore argues that science changes in dramatic leaps, resulting in 'scientific revolutions', as one scientific paradigm breaks down when a series of discoveries cannot be fitted into the dominant paradigm, and another comes along to take its place.

Activity

Try to think of times in your own science lessons at school when you got the 'wrong' result. Did you immediately question the validity of the theory or just assume that you had, for example, a dirty test-tube or did something wrong? Did you investigate the new finding – or stick with the paradigm, and keep trying until you got the 'right' result?

Social influences on the nature and direction of scientific research

There is a range of other factors suggesting that scientific research is not as 'objective' as it claims to be. For example:

- the values and beliefs of researchers will influence whether or not they think issues are worth studying;
- the career aspirations of scientists lead to an understandable desire to prove their own hypotheses right, for experiments to succeed, to publish scientific papers showing their successes, and to research what are seen as cool or lucrative research areas;
- the search for funding may determine which research is carried out and how it is approached – for example, research for military or defence purposes will attract funding more readily than research into help for disabled people;
- objectivity may be limited by the institution or funding constraints within which the scientist is working – for example, medical research on the effects of smoking funded by the tobacco industry, or research on genetically modified crops funded by the biotechnology industry.

The points above suggest that science may in some respects be itself a form of ideology, and that it is not always as objective, value-free and independent of prejudices and social pressures as scientists might like to claim. Scientists do not always ruthlessly pursue evidence to attempt to falsify their theories, as Popper believes they should, but often protect favoured theories and fit their findings into the prevailing scientific ideology (or paradigm) of the time – an approach more akin to religion or ideology than the ruthless pursuit of truth associated with the scientific method.

> **Activity**
>
> Drawing on the material in the previous sections, answer the following questions:
> 1 Identify and explain three ways that science differs from ideology.
> 2 Identify and explain three ways that a scientific understanding of the world differs from a religious one.
> 3 Identify and explain three reasons why religion might be seen as an ideology.
> 4 Identify and explain three reasons why scientific knowledge might be regarded as socially constructed.

Science and religion

There is still a great deal in the world that remains unexplained, and certainly science has not provided all the answers to questions that religion answers by appeals to faith. However, Bruce (2008) argues that it is the scientific method rather than specific scientific discoveries that has provided the greatest challenge to religion as a belief system. This challenge to religion from the scientific method grew as society moved towards **modernity**, and also as a result of the growing concern with evidence-based causes and effects rather than the search for meanings.

Science as a product of modernity

Modernity refers to the period of the application of rational principles and logic, including scientific method, to the understanding, development and organization of human societies. It was the development of modernity that brought with it science as we know it today. Aldridge (2007) describes Comte's view of how the transition to modernity through three stages changed human understanding from a more religious to a more scientific explanation of the world:

1   *The theological stage*, where phenomena are explained as arising from the actions of spirits, gods or other supernatural beings.
2   *The metaphysical stage*, where the supernatural element of the previous stage is diminished, and phenomena are explained as arising from the action of more natural, though abstract, entities and forces, like the power of Nature.
3   *The positive or scientific stage*, where theological and metaphysical explanations are displaced by rational scientific explanations based on evidence derived from observation and experimentation, logical thought and reasoning. It is at this stage that there is what Weber (1993, originally published 1920) called a growing '**disenchantment** with the world'. By this, Weber meant that the magical and mystical elements of life – the province of religion – are displaced by science and scientific explanation. Deciding whether a particular understanding of the world was true or not would no longer be based on appeals to religion, faith, intuition, tradition and superstition, but on evidence and rational argument.

Bruce suggests that in modernity religious explanations and superstitions are gradually displaced by scientific explanations as many religious beliefs are shown to be wrong. For example, science proved that the earth moved around the sun and not vice versa as religion once taught, and the theory of evolution displaced the biblical account of the creation given in the Book of Genesis in the Christian Bible.

When phenomena occur that are hard to explain or understand– such as strange lights in the night sky, paranormal events like ESP (extra-sensory perception) or psychokinesis (moving objects with the mind), apparently 'miraculous' cures, an attack of disease or an accident – we are now more likely to look for scientific explanations than explanations based around supernatural beliefs, like the power of god or gods, the devil, witches, spirits and so on. An example of this is the so-called miraculous cure that put the Catholic Mother Teresa on the track towards sainthood in 2003. Dr Ranjan Mustaphi, one of the doctors treating the patient whose tumour was allegedly cured in 1998 after Mother Teresa's divine intervention, was astonished at the Vatican's belief that Mother Teresa ever performed a miracle. He described the allegation that it was a miracle as a farce, and claimed that it was scientifically proven that the tumour was linked to tuberculosis and that the so-called 'miracle' was simply a patient responding to anti-tubercular drug treatment.

Modernity refers to the period of the application of rational principles and logic to the understanding, development and organization of human societies.

Disenchantment refers to the process whereby the magical and mystical elements of life are eroded, as understandings of the world based on religion, faith, intuition, tradition, magic and superstition are displaced by rational argument, science and scientific explanation.

Scientific explanations have replaced many religious ones, as with the theory of evolution displacing the biblical account of the creation given in the book of Genesis in the Old Testament

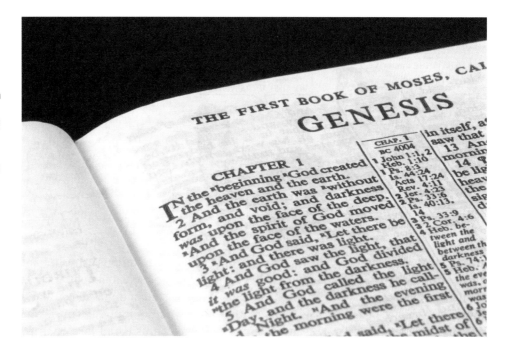

If we accept Popper's approach to the scientific method – that a hypothesis must be capable of being falsified by empirical research and observation or experimentation – then science might be expected gradually to displace religion, as there is no evidence that can prove or disprove the existence of God, nor that Christianity, Islam, Buddhism, Hinduism, Sikhism, Judaism or any other religions are 'true'.

Has science displaced religion?

The sections above suggest that the growth of a scientific understanding of the world in modernity might be expected to relegate religion to the position of a relic of a pre-modern, non-rational age. Nonetheless, this has not happened. Many millions of people identify themselves with the great religions of the world, such as Islam, Judaism, Christianity, Hinduism, Sikhism and Buddhism, and all manner of religious and supernatural beliefs and superstitions continue to have extraordinary power over human behaviour. In 1978, for example, 913 members of the People's Temple religious sect, including more than 270 children, committed suicide, and in the first decade of the twenty-first century, hundreds of religiously motivated people killed themselves as suicide bombers, including those who killed 3,000 people in the attack on the World Trade Center in New York in 2001. Buddhist monks led an unsuccessful uprising against the military dictatorship in Burma in 2007, and in 2008 Britain and the USA were engaged in a war in Afghanistan against an Islamic fundamentalist-inspired Taliban movement. Islamic fundamentalism is a significant force in the world, and Christian fundamentalists have substantial political influence in the United States.

Fundamentalism means a return to the literal meaning of religious texts and associated behaviour.

Explain how the cartoon suggests that science, ideology and religion differ from one another. What arguments might you give that the cartoon is oversimplifying these differences?

Many individuals hold beliefs in some abstract, unseen, mysterious extra-human forces with the capacity to intervene in life for individual or social benefit, including those who may not see themselves as religious in any conventional sense. Many continue to cling to beliefs in magic, superstition, ghosts, demonic possession, extra-sensory perception, the tarot, séances, spells, potions, chants, good luck charms, fortune telling, horoscopes and so on. Whichever way you look at it, religious beliefs of some kind remain significant features of life in many contemporary societies.

Ideology, science and religion in the postmodern age

Postmodernism, which is discussed in more depth in chapter 5, argues that society is now changing so rapidly that it is marked by chaos and uncertainty. No longer can the world be interpreted or understood through the application of what Lyotard (1984) called **metanarratives** – general theories or belief systems that try to provide comprehensive explanations and knowledge of the world.

For postmodernists, religion, science and ideology are all metanarratives, claiming to provide comprehensive explanations of the world, and often also claiming a monopoly on truth. Postmodernists like Lyotard suggest such metanarratives can no longer (if they ever could) be held up as the truth, and each is now just one 'story' among others giving different versions of 'the truth'. Science can no longer lay claim to the superiority of its scientific method, as it repeatedly fails to rise to the challenges it faces. Creutzfeldt-Jakob ('Mad Cow') disease, antibiotic resistant superbugs (e.g. MRSA), global warming and climate change, environmental pollution and weapons of mass destruction are all products of science, and science has failed to provide cures for many of the killer degenerative diseases in Western societies, such as cancer and heart disease. Many scientists have shown themselves to be serving the interests of wealthy corporations and governments, rather than pursuing objective and value-free research. Such circumstances mean that science has lost its authority in society, and some claim that belief in the superiority of science is as much an act of faith as belief in a god or gods, or other supernatural forces, or any ideology.

A **metanarrative** is a broad, all-embracing 'big theory' or explanation for how the world and societies operate.

> **Activity**
>
> 1 Suggest three ways that religious interpretations of the world might differ from scientific ones.
> 2 Suggest two ways in which science might differ from ideology.
> 3 Identify and explain two ways in which the development of science might have displaced religious explanations of natural phenomena.
> 4 Explain in your own words what postmodernists mean when they suggest science, religion and ideology are all metanarratives.
> 5 Suggest reasons why religious and other supernatural beliefs and superstitions continue to be held by many people in contemporary society.

Defining religion

Defining religion is quite important, as the definition adopted will decide what should be examined as a religious phenomenon and what should not, whether society is becoming more or less religious or whether religious belief is simply changing the forms it takes.

The sacred and the profane

Durkheim (2001 [1912]), defined religion as 'a unified set of beliefs and practices relative to sacred things, that is to say, things set apart and forbidden'. Durkheim contrasted this with the 'profane' – the everyday, mundane world. Durkheim's view of religion will be discussed shortly, but his notion of the 'sacred' has been questioned as a useful definition of religion, since many people hold as sacred and 'set apart and forbidden' a range of things that most would not really regard as religious in any conventional sense of the word. This very broad view of religion as 'all things held sacred' is part of what is known as the functional and inclusivist definition, which is generally contrasted with what is called the substantive and exclusivist definition

The functional and inclusivist definition of religion

This is a very broad definition of religion, which covers a wide range of beliefs to which people give a religious or sacred quality, but which does not necessarily include beliefs in a supra-human, supernatural being. This definition, seen in Durkheim's approach, focuses on the function of beliefs in society, and the way in which things that people regard as sacred can, for example, bind societies or groups together through shared values. As well as conventional religious beliefs, this wide definition might also include beliefs that many would not regard as religious. For example, interests in football, music, the lives of celebrities and royalty take on an almost sacred quality for some people, and play a similar role in their lives to conventional religions. For most sociologists, and for the purposes of this chapter, the main definition of religion that will be used is the substantive and exclusivist definition, which is discussed below.

The substantive and exclusivist definition of religion

This definition focuses on what religion actually is (its substance or content), and involves supernatural, supra-human beliefs of some kind. It therefore excludes those views that suggest that anything that people regard as 'sacred' can be regarded as a religion. This definition fits with what most people would regard as religion, such as Islam, Christianity, Buddhism, Sikhism and Hinduism, though it also includes non-conventional supernatural beliefs like Wicca (witchcraft), paganism and Satanism.

It is this definition, with a supernatural dimension, that is one adopted by most sociologists. Bruce (1995), for example, defines religion as 'beliefs, actions and institutions which assume the existence of supernatural entities with powers of action, or impersonal powers or processes possessed of moral purpose'. Berger (1990) views religion as a 'sacred canopy' or shield providing supernatural protection against, and explanation of, random and apparently meaningless events (this is discussed later in the chapter).

Features of religion

In accordance with the substantive and exclusivist definition, religions are likely to include all or some of the following five features:

1 *Beliefs*: Beliefs in the supernatural and/or incomprehensible powers (often some sort of belief in God or gods) or in symbols which are in some way regarded as sacred and representing these supernatural or incomprehensible powers, such as a cross, totem pole or holy water.
2 *Theology*: A set of teachings and beliefs, usually based on some holy book, such as the Bible or the Qur'an.
3 *Practice*: A series of rituals or ceremonies to express religious beliefs, either publicly or privately. For example, most religions contain religious ceremonies of worship, and rituals such as getting on your knees to pray, covering your head in places of worship, singing, fasting, ritual washing or lighting candles.
4 *Institutions*: Some form of organization of the worshippers/believers, such as by priests or religious leaders, and buildings like churches, mosques and temples.
5 *Consequences*: A set of moral or ethical values that are meant to guide or influence the everyday behaviour of believers.

Activity

Refer to the five features of religion above.
1 If you wanted to carry out research into the strength and extent of religious belief in a society, suggest two indicators for *each* feature you might use to measure this (excluding the following examples). For example, for the religious practice dimension, you might use the number of times a week a person visits their local mosque, church or temple; and for theology, you might devise questions about holy books, religious history or doctrines.
2 Suggest reasons why the indicators you have identified may not provide a valid, or true, genuine and authentic, picture of the strength and extent of religious belief in a society.

Theories of religion

Sociological theories of religion are primarily concerned with religion's role for individuals and society. These theories can be broadly divided into two main debates:

1 *Religion acting as a conservative force.* Seeing religion as a conservative force involves three aspects:
    - building and maintaining social solidarity and social stability;
    - protecting traditional values and the existing state of affairs in society (but see the next point); *or*
    - changing society to restore traditional values and ways of life that may be at risk of disappearing or have already disappeared.
2 *Religion acting as a force for social change.* This is concerned with how religious beliefs and organizations can change society and move it forward, rather than simply acting as a conservative force or moving society backwards to the way it was at some previous time.

Religion as a conservative force 1: the functionalist perspective

The functionalist perspective sees religion as mainly a conservative force, promoting social harmony, social integration and social solidarity through the reinforcement of the value consensus – a widespread agreement around the main values of a society which is the basis of social order. The functionalist perspective is essentially concerned with analysing the role of religion in meeting the functional prerequisites or basic needs that society has in order to survive. For example, society can only survive if people share at least some common beliefs about right and wrong behaviour. Religion is seen by functionalists as part of the culture or way of life of a society, and it helps to maintain cultural traditions and establish the basic rules of social life.

Durkheim

Durkheim (2001 [1912]) believed that social order and stability could only exist if people were integrated into society by a value consensus. He saw religion as an important element in achieving this, by providing a set of beliefs and practices which united people together.

Durkheim argued that all societies divide the world into the 'sacred' and the 'profane'. The 'sacred' refers to things that members of society regard as special, as 'set apart and forbidden', that are spiritual, religious, or holy and that are in some ways extraordinary, inspiring awe, reverence, fear and so on. The 'profane' refers to the ordinary, everyday, non-sacred, non-spiritual, non-religious or unholy aspects of life. Religion relates to the sacred aspects of a society. Durkheim emphasizes that the sacred does not necessarily have to be a god, spirits or other supernatural

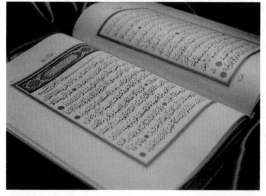

Images of the sacred. Durkheim said that anything can be held sacred. The photos above show, left to right: a sacred rock (Uluru or Ayer's Rock); a river (the Ganges); places (Mecca and Glastonbury); a book (the Qur'an); a person/symbol (crucified Christ on the cross); an animal (a painted cow in India); a building (a temple).

phenomena, but can be anything that people regard as sacred – such as a stone, a tree, a place, a river, a book, a person or an animal.

> **Activity**
>
> 1 In your own words, explain Durkheim's distinction between the 'sacred' and the 'profane', using examples from contemporary society.
> 2 Look at the photographs opposite, and explain how and why each of the items might be regarded as sacred according to Durkheim – use the Internet to find out if you're not sure.
> 3 Suggest examples of things beyond conventional religion in contemporary Britain that might fit Durkheim's view of the sacred.

Durkheim studied the practice of totemism among the central Australian Arunta tribe of aborigines. He argued that totemism – the practice of worshipping a sacred object, known as a **totem** (usually named after the name of a tribe or group) – represented religion in its most basic form.

A **totem** is a sacred object representing and having symbolic significance and importance for a group.

Durkheim argued that the totem is created by society and is so sacred because it is a symbol of the group or society. When worshipping the totem, people are really worshipping society. Religious beliefs, such as totemism, and accompanying ceremonies and rituals, act as a kind of social glue, binding people together and building bonds between them. By sharing beliefs, giving them a sacred quality and worshipping together, people develop moral ties between themselves, and a sense of shared identity, commitment and belonging – what Durkheim called the **collective conscience**. This collective conscience exists outside of individuals, but controls individual behaviour and regulates how members of a community relate to one another.

The **collective conscience** refers to the shared beliefs and values which form moral ties binding communities together, and regulating individual behaviour.

For example, in minority ethnic communities in contemporary Britain, religious beliefs and customs are often a means for these groups to maintain their own cultural identity and traditions, and provide guidelines on how individuals should conduct themselves in their daily lives. Sikh and Hindu temples and Muslim mosques often play an important role in integrating such communities, acting as focal points of community life as well as religious life.

Although Durkheim saw religion playing a key role in building the collective conscience, he believed that the supernatural dimensions of religion would eventually disappear, and that other 'civil religions' might take on this role in people's lives. Civil religion suggests that sacred qualities are attached to aspects of society itself, with non-religious rituals and ceremonies performing similar functions as religion, though not necessarily having any link with the supernatural. Examples of this idea of civil religion might include the devotion some people display towards royalty, the lives of celebrities, popular music or football in contemporary Britain. However, once we abandon the link between religion and some form of belief in supernatural forces, then it is questionable whether we are still really talking about religion at all, rather than just the various other non-religious ways that people are socialized and integrated into the societies to which they belong.

Malinowski

Like Durkheim, Malinowski (2004 [1926]) saw religion as reinforcing social norms and values and promoting social solidarity. However, Malinowski also saw religion as providing explanations for events that were hard to explain and security in the face of uncertainty. Religion fulfils a need for emotional security and relieves situations of emotional stress which threaten social stability and solidarity. Events such as death, serious illness, suffering, accidents and disasters, as well as other life crises like divorce or unemployment, can produce anxiety and tensions which may threaten social solidarity as people experience bitterness, disillusionment, uncertainty or loss of meaning as they encounter events which they can't fully control, predict, explain or understand. Religion can provide a source of comfort, explanation and meaning for individuals when faced by such crises. Funeral services, for example, act as a source of comfort for the bereaved – either with beliefs in life after death, or by the support gained in such moments of stress through the gathering of friends and relatives. Church attendances soar during wartime.

Parsons

Parsons emphasizes the role of religion in providing and underpinning the core values of any culture, and the social norms which regulate people's behaviour. The set of moral beliefs and values in religion may become so deeply ingrained through socialization that it may have an effect on the everyday behaviour of believers and non-believers alike. For example, if the social rules about killing, stealing and adultery are broken, most individuals will experience a guilty conscience about doing something wrong, and this is a powerful socializing and controlling influence over the individual. Like Malinowski, Parsons also sees religion giving meanings and explanations to, and thereby enabling people to make sense of, otherwise inexplicable and uncontrollable life crisis events which might threaten order and stability in society. He argues that religion provides what he called a 'mechanism of adjustment', providing a means of emotional adjustment in the face of the various crises that occur in life, and providing a means of returning to some sense of normality.

For the functionalists Durkheim, Malinowski and Parsons, religion reinforces social solidarity and restricts both deviance and social change, because the existing social and moral order is regarded as 'sacred'. It provides stabilizing and regulating influences for both individuals and society. Religion is therefore acting as a conservative force – maintaining the status quo and keeping society as it is. Figure 1.1 provides a summary of the functionalist view of religion.

> ### Activity
>
> 1 Suggest ways that religion might provide guidelines for everyday conduct.
> 2 Suggest two ways, with examples, that religion might act as a 'mechanism of adjustment' helping people to adjust to crises in life.
> 3 How do religious rituals help to control situations of stress and anxiety?
> 4 In what ways do these religious rituals strengthen social solidarity?
> 5 Give examples of any contemporary rituals which might strengthen social solidarity.

Figure 1.1 The functionalist view of religion

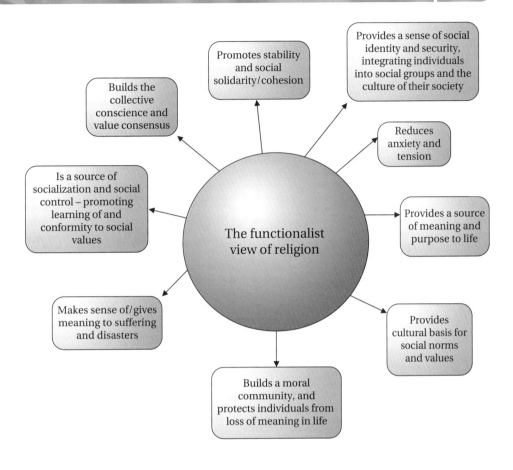

Promotes stability and social solidarity/cohesion

Provides a sense of social identity and security, integrating individuals into social groups and the culture of their society

Builds the collective conscience and value consensus

Reduces anxiety and tension

Is a source of socialization and social control – promoting learning of and conformity to social values

The functionalist view of religion

Provides a source of meaning and purpose to life

Makes sense of/gives meaning to suffering and disasters

Provides cultural basis for social norms and values

Builds a moral community, and protects individuals from loss of meaning in life

Criticisms of the functionalist view of religion

Downplaying social change

The functionalist perspective sees religion as a conservative force, promoting social harmony and protecting the status quo. However, this downplays the role that religion can sometimes play in social change, as discussed later.

Declining religiosity and secularization

Religiosity refers to the extent of importance of religion, religious beliefs and feelings in people's lives.

Religion can only fulfil some of the functions that functionalists claim if people actually hold and practise religious beliefs. However, there is diminishing **religiosity** and growing **secularization** in many Western European countries.

Secularization is the process whereby religious thinking, practice and institutions lose social significance.

Religious thinking, practice and institutions are becoming less important both in the lives of individuals and in society as a whole, and those involved are a declining group. This is shown, for example, by dramatic declines in attendance at services in all the main Christian churches in the UK; less than half of the population now say they believe in God. This secularization issue is considered extensively in the final section of this chapter.

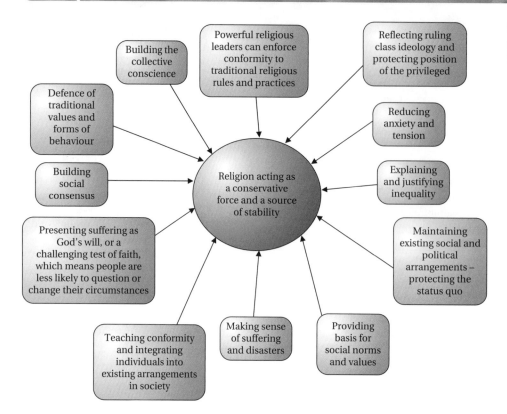

Figure 1.2 Religion as a conservative force

The diagram shows the following boxes connected to a central circle labelled "Religion acting as a conservative force and a source of stability":

- Building the collective conscience
- Powerful religious leaders can enforce conformity to traditional religious rules and practices
- Reflecting ruling class ideology and protecting position of the privileged
- Defence of traditional values and forms of behaviour
- Reducing anxiety and tension
- Building social consensus
- Explaining and justifying inequality
- Presenting suffering as God's will, or a challenging test of faith, which means people are less likely to question or change their circumstances
- Maintaining existing social and political arrangements – protecting the status quo
- Teaching conformity and integrating individuals into existing arrangements in society
- Making sense of suffering and disasters
- Providing basis for social norms and values

Religion can be a disruptive and socially divisive influence

While it is possible to see a common religion bringing people together, establishing a value consensus and integrating small-scale communities, it is hard to see how it can perform this role in contemporary societies, where there is a wide diversity of different beliefs and faiths. Indeed, religion can often, and perhaps more often than not, do the opposite. Different religions and religious beliefs and values can tear people and communities apart, and pose threats to social order and stability.

Historically, religion seems to have played a far greater role in dividing people than in uniting them, as can be seen in countless religiously based wars or community conflicts. It is often the case that the stronger the religious belief, the stronger is the sense that other religious beliefs are wrong, heretical or evil and need to be defeated, as found among Christian and Islamic fundamentalists.

Examples of religion causing conflict and instability might include:

- *Conflicts within the same religion*, like Protestant and Catholic Christians in Northern Ireland over hundreds of years, disputes in the Anglican Church over homosexuality, and between Sunni and Shia Muslims in Iraq.
- *Conflicts between religions.* In the Indian subcontinent, warfare between Muslims and Hindus was in part responsible for the division of a once united India into two separate countries, India and Pakistan. In the 1980s and 1990s, these divisions were added to by conflicts between Hindus and Sikhs. In the 1990s, the former Yugoslavia disintegrated into warring factions of Serbs, Croats

and Bosnians, often aligned on religious lines. In contemporary Britain, there are growing tensions with the Muslim community, and internationally there are links between terrorism in the predominantly Christian West and Islamic fundamentalism.

Religion as a conservative force 2: the traditional Marxist perspective

Marx saw religion as part of the dominant ideology – the ideas or belief system of the ruling class which shape people's view of the world and reproduce and reinforce the false class consciousness (or lack of understanding) by the working class of the fact that they are being exploited. The French Marxist Althusser saw religion as an ideological state apparatus – an institution spreading the dominant ideology and manufacturing what Gramsci called hegemony – consent and acceptance by people that their positions were unchangeable and inevitable.

Marx thought religion did two main, interrelated things:

1 It acted as the 'opium of the people', cushioning the pain of oppression and exploitation in unequal societies.
2 It legitimized and maintained the power of the ruling class.

Religion as the 'opium of the people'

Marx regarded religion as 'the sigh of the oppressed creature, the heart of a heartless world, and the soul of soulless conditions' and, most famously, as 'the opium of the people', acting like a hallucinatory, pain-relieving drug creating illusions among the oppressed which helped to maintain the power of the dominant class. Religion eased the pain produced by poverty, exploitation and oppression in unequal class societies, and helped to overcome the effects of the **alienation** (lack of control, fulfilment and satisfaction) of individuals in capitalist society by providing some control, purpose and meaning in their lives.

The Marxist approach suggests that religion eases the pain of oppression and exploitation in three main ways:

Alienation refers to the lack of power, control, fulfilment and satisfaction experienced by workers in a capitalist society, where the means of producing goods are privately owned and controlled.

1 Religion promises an eventual escape from suffering and oppression in this life with promises of an ecstatic future in life after death. Some religions make a virtue of suffering and poverty on this earth. If people believe that what happens to them is God's will, and possibly a test of their faith to be rewarded in the afterlife, they are more likely to accept, or even welcome, their fate and not try to change or improve their circumstances. For example, the Christian Bible promises that 'the meek shall inherit the earth'.
2 Religion sometimes offers hope of supernatural intervention to solve problems on earth. For example, the Jehovah's Witnesses believe that God will intervene to destroy the wicked and eliminate the present system of things on earth in the

battle of Armageddon – the showdown between God and Satan. Survivors, along with millions of others who will be resurrected, will form a new paradise on earth where they will live forever ruled by a heavenly government. This promise for the future, found in many of the world's religions, can encourage people to accept their position and not act to change society.

3   Religion provides a religious explanation and justification for inequality. For example, the Hindu religion provides a religious justification for the inequalities of the Indian caste system and an individual's position in the social hierarchy. In the caste system, there are strict rules about how people should behave, what they should wear and eat, the jobs they can do and who they can and can't marry. People have obeyed these rules because they believe in reincarnation, and if they don't obey the rules of their caste they will be reborn on a lower level. This has kept the caste system in place for over 1,000 years; it is still found in contemporary India, despite efforts to remove the system, because people still hold the religious beliefs that underpin it.

Religion and the power of the ruling class

Traditional Marxists see religion as an instrument of social control and oppression, used by the ruling class to legitimize (justify) their power and material wealth. Inequalities of wealth, income and power are presented as God-given and therefore legitimized and inevitable. The inequalities between rich and poor can't be challenged or changed without questioning the authority of religion or God itself. The Hindu caste system referred to above is one example of this, which protects the position of those in the highest castes. In the past, religion has justified the power of kings through a doctrine called the 'divine right of kings', which suggested it was the will of God that gave monarchs the right to rule. Religion has even turned kings into gods – for example, the Pharaohs of ancient Egypt.

Criticisms of the Marxist view of religion

Like any drug, religion can only act like opium, performing an hallucinating and pain-relieving role, if people actually take it. In other words, religion can only perform the role Marxists suggest both if people believe and if religion has some institutional power – neither of which is true of the majority of people in Britain or most contemporary Western capitalist societies.

Furthermore, religion can act as a form of resistance to the powerful, and as an agent of social change, and not simply as a conservative force, as the following examples suggest:

1   Some early Christian sects opposed Roman rule.
2   Islam, particularly Islamic fundamentalism, is often a vehicle for resisting the global influence of Western **cultural imperialism**, fighting the Americanization of the world's culture, and resisting the dominance of Western corporations in the world economy.

Cultural imperialism refers to the way in which Western, and especially American, cultural values are forced on non-Western cultures, with the consequent undermining of local cultures.

3   In Iran, Islam produced revolutionary change, with a revolution led by Ayatollah Khomeini leading to the overthrow of a dictatorial monarchy (the shahdom) and the establishment of an Islamic republic in 1978–9.

4   In South America in the 1960s and 1970s, Roman Catholic priests – followers of a doctrine mixing Communism and Catholicism called Liberation Theology – played major roles in fighting against political dictatorships and poverty. Liberation Theology sought to present an image of Christ portrayed more as a reforming revolutionary than the passive peacemaker presented in mainstream Catholicism.

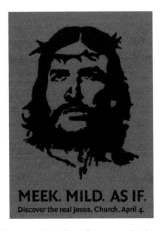

MEEK. MILD. AS IF.
Discover the real Jesus. Church. April 4.

Portraying Christ as a revolutionary, like Che Guevara, is the sort of image that Liberation Theology wanted to promote in the 1960s.

Functionalism and Marxism compared
- Both explain the origins and functions of religion in terms of social factors.
- Both see religion as a human creation, with the supernatural having no reality.
- Both see religion as a conservative force, integrating society and maintaining the status quo.
- Functionalists see religion's role as necessary and justified, while Marx saw religion as repressive – an ideology legitimizing the power of the dominant class, misleading ordinary people into conforming to, rather than challenging, societies in which the majority are exploited by the minority.

Religion as a conservative force 3: the interpretivist perspective

Structuralist theories, like Marxism and functionalism, tend to see religion as an external force, working on people to mould them into social conformity. Interpretivist approaches, by contrast, study the meanings and interpretations of people in order to understand their behaviour. They therefore look at the way religion is used by followers to create meanings and interpretations of the world, and to understand the meanings sacred symbols have for individuals, such as crosses, rivers, places, people, statues and items of clothing. The Shroud of Turin, for example, is an old piece of cloth, and in itself has no value, meaning or importance. However, some attach sacred meanings to it, as they believe it to be the burial shroud of Christ, with his face revealed on it.

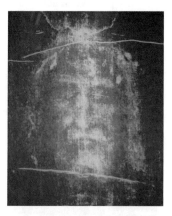

Some believe that the Shroud of Turin is the cloth in which Jesus Christ was buried, and, because people give it this meaning, it is regarded as a sacred object. Can you think of other examples in which people place a high value on objects because of the meanings they give them?

A universe of meaning, theodicy and the sacred canopy

Berger (1990) argues that religion provides what he calls a '**universe of meaning**'. This is a set of ideas and values about the meaning of life which helps people make sense of the world, and enables them to give life some focus, order and meaning.

The universe of meaning provided by religion gives individuals a sense of meaning and explanation in the face of a chaotic world. As part of this universe of meaning, religion provides a **theodicy**, a religious framework that gives meaning to and makes sense of seemingly inexplicable and fundamental questions about human existence, such as the meaning of life and death, and why poverty, injustice and inequality, accidents, disease, suffering, pain, evil and death exist in the world.

Berger sees religion as a kind of sacred canopy stretching over society, providing a shield that protects people from the uncertainties, meaninglessness and pointlessness of life, by helping them to interpret and make sense of the world and their position in it.

By suggesting that religion provides universes of meaning and theodicies to explain the darker sides of daily life, interpretivists are arguing that it is contributing to the maintenance of social stability. To that extent, therefore, they are allied with functionalists and Marxists in that they all see religion acting as a conservative force in society.

A **universe of meaning** is a set of ideas and values about the meaning of life which helps people make sense of and give meaning to the world, and enables them to give life some focus, order and meaning.

A **theodicy** is an explanation for the contradiction between the existence of a God who is assumed to be all-powerful and benevolent, and, at the same time, the prevalence of widespread suffering and evil in the world.

Does religion still provide a universe of meaning and a sacred canopy?

Berger argues that in modern (and postmodern) societies, religion is losing its role for most people as the provider of a universe of meaning. This is because, as discussed earlier, reason, logic and science have largely replaced faith and superstition in people's consciousness as the means of understanding and making sense of the world, and there is growing secularization and disenchantment with the world. In a media-saturated, globalized, postmodern society, there is increasing diversity and fragmentation of beliefs and lifestyles, and religion is losing its validity as a universe of meaning and as a theodicy giving meaning to human suffering. Berger suggests that the sacred canopy of religion has therefore been lost, and that religion no longer provides a source of meanings and morality, or the sacred shield against life's insecurities and uncertainties.

Activity

1 Identify ways in which religion creates universes of meaning that enable people to give some focus to life, and order and meaning to inexplicable events like pain, accidents, suffering, death, disease and disasters. Try to draw on examples from a range of religions.
2 To what extent do you think this role of religion is still significant in contemporary society? Explain your answer.
3 What other sources of meaning are available to people, apart from religion?

Religion as a conservative force 4: religion as a compensator

Stark and Bainbridge's (1996) theory of religion echoes the concerns of Berger, as well as functionalists, as they examine the meaning and the functions of religion for individuals in society. Stark and Bainbridge see religion meeting the needs of individuals when their sense of social order is disrupted by economic hardship, loneliness, grief, accidents, death, disease and ill-health. They argue that belief in God, religion and religious organizations provides a means for individuals to make sense of and come to terms with such events, as well as answering universal fundamental questions – for example: Why are we here? Why is there suffering in the world? What is the purpose of life? Stark and Bainbridge see religion acting as a general compensator – a belief that if individuals act in a particular way, they will eventually be rewarded. Providing hope for life after death is an important compensator, with the promise of future rewards in an uncertain world. Stark and Bainbridge therefore suggest that religion in some form or another will never disappear, as it provides answers to universal questions – much like Berger's universes of meaning – and offers general compensators meeting universal human needs.

Stark and Bainbridge suggest that religion, by acting as a compensator, is contributing to the maintenance of stability in social life, and to that extent it is acting as a conservative force in society.

Religion and social change

Is religion always a conservative force?

While most sociologists agree that, in general, religion helps to maintain the status quo and that changes in society lead to changes in religion, there is an alternative view which argues that religion can also cause social change, and therefore doesn't always or necessarily act as a conservative force. Some of the criticisms in the previous sections have already shown how religion can act to challenge the powerful and change society.

Max Weber

Weber (1864–1920) was a social action theorist, who believed that to understand human behaviour, it was necessary to examine the meanings people give to events and ideas. People's ideas and beliefs, which make up their worldview or image of the world, can have important consequences for the way they think and act. Religion is often an important component of this worldview, and Weber attempted to show that the evolution of new religious ideas can stimulate social and economic change as people act in terms of their beliefs.

Through cross-cultural analysis of the links between religion and social change in a number of societies, Weber sought to explain why capitalist industrialization developed first in Western Europe rather than in other parts of the world, even when they had similar levels of technological development. Weber's analysis was explored in *The Protestant Ethic and the Spirit of Capitalism* (2001), which was first published in 1904.

The Protestant Ethic and the Spirit of Capitalism

Weber studied the rise of Calvinism in Europe. Calvinism is a form of ascetic Protestantism (Puritanism) characterized by austerity and self-denial, with strong self-discipline to maintain these. Weber's study showed that Calvinist religious beliefs had an important influence on the development of an industrial capitalist economy and the emergence of a capitalist class.

Weber argued that for capitalism to develop, both the normative conditions (the necessary values) and the material conditions (factories, technology, etc.) were needed. He saw Calvinism, which developed in seventeenth-century Western Europe, producing the normative conditions – the set of ideas, ethics and values making up the Protestant ethic – which provided the 'spirit of capitalism' that encouraged capitalist development.

Weber emphasized the following features of Calvinism and the Protestant ethic:

1   Calvinists believed in predestination – followers believed that their fate was already decided by God. However, a believer had no way of knowing whether he or she was one of the 'saved' or 'chosen ones'.
2   The solution to this problem of not knowing one's destiny was to become involved in 'intense worldly activity', since hard work and material success

were seen as religious virtues and a likely sign of being one of God's chosen.

3   The Protestant ethic emphasized values and virtues like hard work, thrift, trade, profit, modesty and punctuality and the avoidance of idleness, time wasting, excessive sleep and self-indulgence. Living life according to these values, with hard work leading to material success, became signs of God's grace and an indication that the individual was 'chosen'.

4   Weber argued that this Protestant ethic was a major reason why capitalist industrialization developed first in Western Europe rather than elsewhere. The Protestant ethic valued the pursuit of wealth and making money, which was something people had always done and did in a wide range of societies with different religions. But the Protestant ethic also promoted as virtues the reinvestment of profits back into the business – rather than spending them on luxuries, conspicuous, self-indulgent consumption and high living – and working regularly with self-discipline rather than erratically and whenever you felt like it. Hard work, self-discipline and self-denial, and making money to reinvest and expand a business, were therefore not just part of good capitalist business practice, but also good religious morality.

5   Weber therefore came to the conclusion that Calvinism, alone of all the religions, provided the rationality and religious ideology and ethics which encouraged the development of capitalist industrialization first in the Protestant countries of Europe.

Weber's study of religion and the Protestant ethic led him to conclude that religion could be an important force in social change, including economic change, and this contrasts with those functionalist and Marxist theories that emphasize the conservative roles of religion.

Evidence that religion can act as a force for social change

There is abundant evidence that religion can act as a force for social change, rather than simply maintaining the status quo. A number of examples of this have been mentioned previously (see criticisms of Durkheim and Marx above), including those of Northern Ireland, Liberation Theology in South America and the Iranian revolution in 1979–80. A good contemporary example is presented by the world growth in Islamic fundamentalism. Bruce (2008) suggests that Islamic fundamentalism consists of ideas based on the literal meanings of the words in the Qur'an and a belief in and a return to the true form of religion that existed in some earlier time, such as seventh-century Mecca and Medina for Islam. Islam became a major international force for social change in the late twentieth century, and the present spread of Islamic fundamentalism has attempted to forge social changes in much of the Islamic world, and even beyond the Islamic world based on literal interpretations of the Qur'an. The terrorist attacks on the Twin Towers of the World Trade Center in New York on 11 September 2001, the bombings in London on 7 July 2005 and the wars in Afghanistan and Iraq have all been, at least in part, motivated by

Islamic fundamentalism and its opposition to Western values, culture and global dominance.

Activity

To what extent do you think Islamic fundamentalism is an example of religion acting as a force for social change, or an example of religion acting as a conservative force, for example as it tries to maintain or restore traditional values and resist change?

Religion: conservative force or a force for social change?

There is a range of evidence that can be used to support the Marxist and functionalist views that religion acts as a conservative, stabilizing and integrating force, promoting social stability and protecting the status quo in society. However, many sociologists accept that religion is not necessarily or always a conservative force; it can also act as a destabilizing source of social division and conflict, and, as the Weberian approach suggests, a means for radical change. There is a danger of overstating the importance of religion, whether in the context of conservatism and social stability or in the context of social change, as there are often a number of other social, economic and political factors which also influence the nature and extent of religion's role in society.

McGuire (2001) and Robinson (2001) suggest that there are four major interrelated factors which influence whether religion acts as a conservative force or a force for social change:

1 *The nature and extent of religious beliefs.* If most people in a society hold religious beliefs and a religious view of the world, and these beliefs have strong moral codes which conflict with some features of existing society, then religion is more likely to lead to criticism of society, and attempts to change it.
2 *The significance of religion in a society's culture.* If religion is a central part of the culture and everyday life of a society, as with Catholicism in many Latin American countries, or many countries where Islam is the main religion, religion is more likely to be used as a means of justifying behaviour and change. Examples might include the role of Catholicism in Ireland, where the Catholic religion is embedded in the culture, and where Catholicism has historically been aligned with Irish Republicanism in the fight against British rule in Ireland. In Islamic countries, reference to Islam is often very important in justifying social changes. By contrast, in the UK, religion is fairly marginal and irrelevant in most people's lives, and so plays little role in social change.
3 *The extent of the social involvement of religion.* In societies in which religious organizations, priests and other religious figures are close to and involved with the people and play important roles in the political and economic life of societies, then religion is more likely to influence social change. An example might be the role of Islam in contemporary Iran or Saudi Arabia, or the Catholic Church

in the Middle Ages, when religion had a major influence on social and political decision-making. This aspect of the social involvement of religious organizations in affecting social change is likely to become of even greater importance in societies which lack democracy, where protest and change have to be fed through religion as other means are blocked by the political power of governments. This is what occurred with Liberation Theology in Latin America, in countries where Catholicism was very deeply embedded and where Roman Catholic priests attempted to lead protest and change against dictatorships when the dictators themselves claimed to hold Catholic beliefs. This social involvement of religion meant the church was able to exercise influence in a way that was almost impossible for ordinary people.

4 *The degree of central authority in religious organizations.* In societies where religious organizations have strong central authority, religion is in a much better position to either promote change or prevent it. This is most apparent in Islamic countries like Saudi Arabia or Iran, where Islam has very strong centralized authority, and this authority is effectively used to influence the extent of changes in society.

> A **typology** is a generalization used to classify things into groups or types according to their characteristics, which do not necessarily apply in every real world example.

Activity

1 Suggest two examples illustrating ways in which religion has undermined stability in society.
2 Suggest two examples illustrating ways in which religion has promoted social change.
3 On the basis of your work so far on religion, do you consider religion to be mainly a conservative force or a force for social change? List the arguments for your view, backing them up with examples drawn from contemporary societies, and preferably from a number of different religions.

> An **ideal type** is a model of 'pure types' that contain the essential features of something, like a religious organization, but which don't exist in the real world in their pure form. They provide a measuring rod that enables the researcher to compare particular examples and identify the extent to which they are similar to or different from the ideal type.

Religious organizations

There have been various attempts made to categorize the different types of organization through which people express and practise their religious beliefs, to provide a basis for comparing different kinds of group. This categorization, or **typology**, is based on factors like their organizational structure, their relationship with the state, their attitudes to the wider society around them and other religious beliefs, their size and type of membership, and the commitment required from members. There are four main categories: church, denomination, sect and cult.

The four categories are summarized in table 1.1, drawing on the work of Weber (1993 [1920]), Niebuhr (1957 [1929]), Troeltsch (1992 [1931]) and Wallis (1984). These typologies are really generalizations or **ideal types**, with features that apply in many, but not all, cases, and no religious group will conform exactly to the categories outlined. Any particular religious organization may combine aspects of each type, and may develop and change in character over time. Much of the work on these categories is based on Western Christian religions, and therefore they do not necessarily apply to other faiths like Islam or Hinduism.

Table 1.1 includes Wallis's categorizations of organizations as world-rejecting, world-accommodating or world-affirming. Although Wallis developed these in relation to the new religious movements which have developed since about 1945, they can also be usefully applied to older traditional religious organizations.

Table 1.1: Religious organizations: churches, denominations, sects and cults		
	Churches	Denominations
Example	Church of England; Roman Catholic Church.	Methodists & religious organizations in countries where there is no established (official) church.
Organizational structure	Bureaucratic, hierarchical power structure with paid officials – often large, wealthy, with powerful leaders.	Hierarchy of paid officials & bureaucratic structure, but some division of authority roles and higher degree of democratic participation (more lay preaching).
Attitude to wider society and the state	WORLD-ACCOMMODATING Conservative – likely to accept dominant norms and values of society & in general tend to support status quo. Often close links with the state e.g. Britain's Queen is head of the Church of England.	WORLD-ACCOMMODATING Generally accept dominant norms & values, though perhaps some minor differences and restrictions on members e.g. alcohol and gambling by Methodists. More concerned with spiritual behaviour & everyday morality than 'other worldly'. Often no links with the state.
Commitment required – demands on members/followers	Integrate with the social & economic structure of society. Few demands or restrictions on members, who play full part in social life and not expected to withdraw from society. Accept the social environment in which they exist.	Integrate with the world. Accept secular culture. No rejection of the wider society. Members often disillusioned members of established churches, other denominations or sects, but live conventional and conforming lives outside their religious activities.
Membership	Universalist and inclusive – embraces all members of society, and don't have to demonstrate faith to be a member. Often born into it, and all members of society assumed to be members unless opt out.	Members recruited by self-selection (conversion) or family tradition. Open membership.
Social base	Members drawn from all social classes, but higher status groups tend to be over-represented in membership.	Hardly ever a social majority. Membership drawn from all levels of society but less closely identified with upper classes than a church, and lower working class least likely to be represented.
Attitude to other beliefs/religions	Tend to be intolerant of other groups and claim monopoly of religious truth.	Tolerant of other groups and religions, and don't claim monopoly of truth. See themselves as one denomination among many.

Table 1.1 (continued)

	Sects	Cults
Example	People's Temple; ISKCON (International Society for Krishna Consciousness – the Hare Krishnas); Unification Church (the Moonies); Jehovah's Witnesses.	Transcendental Meditation, Scientology.
Organizational structure	Often no hierarchy of paid officials or bureaucratic structure. More egalitarian power structure. Tightly-knit community, often under control of single charismatic leader.	Loosely structured, tolerant and non-exclusive. Often lack some of features associated with a religion e.g. religious buildings, collective rituals of worship, developed theology, ethics.
Attitude to wider society and the state	WORLD-REJECTING Radical – in opposition to or in tension with the world. Many involve a radical rejection of the wider society and its institutions, including the state. Reject many dominant norms and values & replace them with alternative beliefs and practice. Some may face state disapproval and/or persecution.	WORLD-AFFIRMING Accept world as it is, offering individuals special knowledge, personal insight, and access to either spiritual powers within themselves and/or supernatural powers, providing the opportunity to be more successful, secure and happy in existing society. No opposition to or links with the state, but some may face state disapproval and/or persecution e.g. Scientology.
Commitment required – demands on members/followers	Strict entry criteria, with members required to demonstrate strong involvement and commitment, change their lifestyles, and sometimes expected to withdraw from/make sharp break with conventional life outside sect (but some contact with outside world allowed for recruitment & fundraising). Tight social control of members, and risk of expulsion if fail to conform.	Often 'followers' rather than formal members, who carry on normal lives, with little social control over them by the cult.
Membership	Members recruited by self-selection or family tradition. Voluntary adherents. Small, elitist, exclusive, close-knit closed membership; initiation ceremonies. Hostile to non-members.	Cults are non-exclusive and open to all. Many are highly individualistic, selling services to individuals, with use of these services, 'salvation' or other rewards a purely personal matter.
Social base	Often a small, exclusive dispossessed or alienated minority, drawn from groups who experience relative deprivation, and/or are marginalized and/or drawn from poorer social groups.	Followers often have above average incomes, who feel something is lacking in their otherwise successful lives. Less likely to have deprived members or followers since cult services are often for sale (at high prices) and purchased by supporters.
Attitude to other beliefs/religions	Claim a monopoly of the truth, and only members have access to the religious knowledge that offers the only true path to salvation, which is reserved for this 'saved' or chosen minority. Intolerant of other religious groups and those outside sect.	Tolerate existing religions, and coexist alongside them. Followers may belong to/support and buy services from other religious organizations or cults.

World-rejecting, world-accommodating and world-affirming groups

- *World-rejecting* groups are in opposition to the world, and reject many of the dominant norms and values of society, and replace them with alternative beliefs and practices. Members are likely to live their lives in different ways to other members of society.
- *World-accommodating* groups generally accept the dominant norms and values of society, and members will live similar lifestyles to other members of society.
- *World-affirming* groups accept society as it is, and offer individuals the opportunity for self-improvement within it. Members are likely to live similar lives to other members of society, apart from their interest in what many regard as deviant, bizarre, esoteric or obscure matters.

Churches and denominations

Churches and denominations have relatively minor differences between them, other than their size, influence and relationship to the state. Churches and denominations both have a bureaucratic structure, which means they have a hierarchy of officials with different amounts of authority. For example, the Pope is the head of the Roman Catholic Church, presiding over a bureaucracy of cardinals, archbishops, bishops and so on, down to the local priest, with clearly spelt out rules and regulations about the form that services and rituals should take, the dates of important events, appropriate forms of dress and literature and so on.

Is the concept of the church now obsolete?

Bruce (1996) suggests that the concept of 'the church' is really outdated in most Christian countries now, and should only be applied in cases where a single religious organization really does dominate society and can reasonably claim to be administering to all members of society. Such examples might include Roman Catholicism in medieval Europe, when the Catholic Church was all-powerful and the only major religion, or where particular religions have state support and legal privileges, such as the Orthodox Church in contemporary Greece, the Roman Catholic Church in Ireland, Spain or Italy, or Islam in countries such as Iran, Saudi Arabia and Pakistan.

Many Western societies are now experiencing **religious pluralism**, with a wide diversity of minority interest religions and religious organizations. This is accompanied by growing secularization (a decline in religious belief and practice), and many churches and denominations do not either expect or get a high degree of commitment. Bruce (1995) argues that the Church of England, for example, although it is still the established or 'official' church in England, now commands such little support among the population as a whole that it really only has the status of one denomination among others. Churches and denominations are becoming more alike, more tolerant of other groups and beliefs, and coexist quite happily alongside other churches and denominations. The idea of a church-type organization may therefore

Religious pluralism refers to a situation where there are a variety of different religions, different groups within a religious faith, and a range of beliefs of all kinds, with no one religious belief or organization reasonably able to claim to hold a monopoly of truth or to have the support of most members of society.

Should the term 'the church' now only be applied to societies where a single religious organization dominates society and has legal privileges, as with the Greek Orthodox Church in contemporary Greece?

now be obsolete, with the term 'denomination' more accurately describing the major religious organizations in societies where there is religious pluralism.

Sects and cults

Whereas churches and denominations are generally seen as fairly respectable and mainstream organizations, sects and cults tend to be seen as more deviant – involving beliefs and behaviour that are seen as odd, weird or bizarre, or as a threat to existing society. Somewhat confusingly, the terms 'sect' and 'cult' are often used interchangeably, with the same group sometimes classified as a sect and sometimes as a cult. For the sake of clarity, sects and cults are defined differently and kept clearly separate here (see table 1.1).

Barker (1989) has suggested that the terms 'sect' and 'cult' have such a stigmatized and pejorative (strongly negative) meaning attached to them that they have been abandoned altogether. This is because mass media treatment of sects and cults has meant they are associated in the popular imagination (often quite unfairly) with groups seen as evil, controlling, extremist and manipulative, as brainwashing their members into unthinking robots, and as harmful to both their own members and the wider society.

Sects

Wilson (1982) suggests that sects have the following main features:

- they exist in a state of tension or conflict with the wider society, frequently rejecting that society and its values;

- they impose tests of merit on would-be members, who claim elite status as alone having access to what they regard as the only route to salvation;
- they exercise stern discipline, regulating the beliefs and lifestyles of members and using sanctions against those who deviate, including the possibility of expulsion;
- they demand ongoing and total commitment from members, overriding all other interests;
- they are often led by a charismatic leader – a person with a powerful, imposing and 'magnetic' personality that gives them power over other group members.

Cults

Wallis (1974) and Bruce (1995) see cults differing from sects in that, whereas sects are very tightly knit, closed groups, with strong demands on the commitment of members and strong internal discipline, cults are often very loosely knit groupings, open to all and highly individualistic. Giddens (2006) suggests that the focus on the individual, and individual expression and experience, are the main features distinguishing a cult from a sect. There is often little discipline or commitment demanded of members. Cults generally don't claim any monopoly on the truth, and often lack the clearly defined and exclusive belief systems associated with sects. Aldridge (2007) suggests that cults see themselves offering just one route to self-realization or salvation out of a choice of others, with followers making individual choices and drifting in and out of cults depending on what works best for them at the time.

Cults can embrace a wide range of beliefs, some of which may not appear as religious in any accepted sense. These include things like alternative medicine and therapies, belief in UFOs, occult beliefs and practices and, as Aldridge suggests, for most people, they are more like therapies than religions, used as relaxation and stress-busting techniques. Many cults sell their services to individuals.

Audience cults, client cults and cult movements   Stark and Bainbridge (1985) identify three types of cult:

1   *Audience cults* provide little beyond information services of some kind for individuals, and there is little if any organization or involvement of followers. The service is often consumed individually and spread by the media, through the Internet, books and magazines, for example. Such cults might include New Age ideas (discussed below) such as astrology, horoscopes, interest/belief in UFOs, and reincarnation.
2   *Client cults* have more organization, and offer services to followers such as therapy and courses, which are often sold to clients by practitioners. Examples include spiritualism offering contact with the dead, or various forms of alternative medicine and treatments.
3   *Cult movements* are more organized, involving a wider range of activities, support and personal involvement and commitment. Scientology is an example of a cult movement, which is very highly organized and commercial, claiming to offer its followers a route to improved mental health.

From audience cult to cult movement – the example of Scientology

Scientology originated in 1950 as an *audience cult*, primarily focused on the marketing of founder Ron Hubbard's books on mental health, then developed into a *client cult*, as it began to form networks and provide counsellors to sell clients therapeutic services and courses based around Hubbard's concept of Dianetics (his 'science of mental health'). From the late 1950s it developed into a *cult movement*, as it grew to become the highly organized and wealthy global Church of Scientology it is today. For further information on Scientology, go to www.scientology.org/home.html.

Activity

1 Refer to Table 1.1 and the sections above on churches, denominations, sects and cults. Mark the following statements as true or false:
- churches are world-rejecting institutions
- cults are world-affirming movements
- denominations have close links with the state
- sects are large, world-accommodating organizations
- sects are often controlled by people with powerful personalities
- churches are intolerant of other religions and beliefs
- cults often appeal to the more 'well off' sections of society
- sects are often hostile to or suspicious of those not belonging to the sect
- cult members can carry on with their existing religious beliefs if they want to
- denominations tend to be a bit more critical than churches of the present state of society

2 Explain, with an example of each, the difference between world-rejecting, world-accommodating and world-affirming religious organizations.

New religious movements

New religious movements (NRMs) are those that have emerged in the period since the end of the Second World War in 1945, and particularly since the 1960s. Many have little in common with established churches, denominations or religious sects, although, as Wallis pointed out, many of them draw upon traditional Christian or other religious faiths, like Hinduism and Buddhism. NRMs are mainly sects and cults, and as Aldridge (2007) notes, although they consist of a very diverse range of groups, they contain some of the most controversial social movements in the modern world, posing threats both to the lives of their own members and to the wider society. Some of these, like Heaven's Gate, the Branch Davidians and Scientology, are described shortly. The mass media frequently attack and stereotype NRMs for being bizarre, weird and sinister, and for brainwashing, controlling, abusing and harming individuals, as in the People's Temple or Heaven's Gate. However, some NRMs, like Transcendental Meditation, have support from highly respectable people and business corporations.

The features of NRMs

Eileen Barker (1989) suggests that new religious movements have some or all of the following features:

1. They are religious in so far as they are often concerned with spirituality and/or the supernatural, and with similar questions shared with mainstream religions – for example: Why am I here? What is the meaning of life? Is there a God? Is there life after death?
2. They are most likely to find supporters among young adults, who are first-generation converts, rather than born into the sect or cult.
3. There is a high turnover of members, suggesting that the need fulfilled by new religious movements is temporary.
4. They are likely to be led by a charismatic leader – a person with a powerful, imposing and 'magnetic' personality that gives them power over other group members.
5. They are certain that they hold the only correct 'truth', and that they are the 'chosen' ones.
6. There is frequently a sharp divide between 'us' – the 'good and godly' group – and 'them' – the 'bad' and, perhaps, 'satanic' outsiders.
7. There is often suspicion or hostility from wider society, particularly the mass media.
8. Many are short-lived or transient, particularly world-rejecting sects, as the heavy commitment required is hard to maintain, and younger people grow older and look to more normal lives, or support dwindles when the leader dies.

There are many different new religious movements, with wide differences in beliefs, membership, organization and rituals. Wallis developed his threefold typology of world-accommodating, world-rejecting and world-affirming groups, which was discussed earlier, in relation to the NRMs, though he recognizes that no group will conform exactly to the categories he outlines. Wallis notes that the ideas and beliefs of most NRMs are hybrids, in that they combine ideas from different belief systems into a new hybrid belief system of their own.

World-rejecting NRMs

These are among the most controversial groups, and are often targeted by so-called anti-cult de-programming groups who attack them for brainwashing. World-rejecting NRMs are typically hostile to the wider society and often receive hostility in return, from the media and sometimes from state authorities too. They have the characteristics of sects, and examples include the Unification Church (the Moonies), the International Society for Krishna Consciousness (ISKCON or Hare Krishna), the People's Temple and Heaven's Gate (see the box below). Some of these groups have very high levels of control and discipline over their members, who are expected to show uncritical obedience to leaders. Membership often entails a sharp break with conventional life and significant lifestyle changes, like diet, hairstyles and dress, and sometimes involves communal/group living.

Millenarianism is the belief that existing society is evil, sinful or otherwise corrupt, and that supernatural or other extra-worldly forces will intervene to completely destroy existing society and create a new and perfect world order.

World-rejecting NRMs sometimes hold millenarian beliefs – that some form of extra-worldly or supernatural intervention will change the world rapidly and suddenly, in what Aldridge calls 'an imminent apocalyptic collapse of the existing world order and its replacement by a perfect new dispensation' (2007: 31).

The Branch Davidians (see the box below) were an example of a Christian-based millenarian NRM. They believed that the second coming of Christ to earth was imminent, and would be accompanied by the Apocalypse and the final battle of Armageddon mentioned in the Bible. Aldridge cites the example drawn from Islam of the millenarian belief in the reappearance of the Mahdi – the 'hidden imam' who will establish a world in accordance with the will of Allah.

Despite the threats to society that the mass media sometimes allege these NRMs pose, they generally have a tiny membership, and, as Barker (1984) found, they are very bad at holding on to members – there is very high turnover, due in part to the harshness of the regimes they are expected to follow.

World-accommodating NRMs

These are mainly denominations or offshoots of mainstream Christian churches and denominations. They are more concerned with rediscovering a spirituality thought to have been lost, and revitalizing the spiritual life of their members, than with everyday worldly affairs. Religion is seen as a personal matter, with their typically white, well-educated middle-class membership living conventional and conforming lives outside their religious activities. Examples include neo-Pentecostalism and the charismatic movement, which involve themselves in things like speaking in tongues, faith healing and exorcism.

World-affirming NRMs

Wallis sees these as mainly cults. They often lack many of the features associated with traditional religions or religious organizations, such as having religious buildings, religious services and rituals, and ethical and moral codes. Many are more like therapy groups than religious organizations, and they claim to be able to provide the techniques and knowledge that will enable individuals to access spiritual powers within themselves, to unlock their human potential, meet their personal needs and solve their problems. This helps people to remain or become successful in terms of existing society and its values. Examples include Scientology and Transcendental Meditation, both of which claim to provide access to the techniques and knowledge enabling personal growth and problem-solving.

Aldridge notes that most of the people who use the services of world-affirming movements do so as consumers, buying services that are for sale to anyone who can afford them, with commercial marketing of courses, conferences, books, therapies and so on. Followers of world-affirming NRMs live otherwise conventional lives, and the services they buy are meant to help them to do this more successfully than ever. Aldridge points out that although these groups are world-affirming and generally the most in tune with the contemporary world, the services they offer can come into conflict with established professional groups, such as the medical profession. Scientology, for example, is uncompromisingly hostile to modern psychiatry, and campaigns against the use of mood altering psychoactive drugs like Prozac.

Seven new religious movements

The following organizations, and all other religious organizations mentioned in this chapter, can all be explored further at www.religioustolerance.org/.

Heaven's Gate

A *world-rejecting sect* which believes that UFOs contain extra-terrestrial beings, and whose members believe that, by committing suicide together at the correct time, they will themselves be reborn as extra-terrestrials. In March 1997, when the Hale Bop comet, which members believed had a spaceship behind it to offer them rebirth, was at its nearest to earth, 39 men and women voluntarily committed suicide.

The People's Temple

A *world-rejecting sect*, founded by Jim Jones in the United States, but based finally in Guyana. Jones developed a belief called *Translation*, by which he and his followers would all die together in a mass suicide, and would move to another planet for a life of bliss. Following a shooting in 1978 carried out by the Temple's security guards, with 11 wounded and 5 killed, including a US Congressman on an inspection visit, Jones initiated a group suicide. In all, 638 adults and 276 children died, with most dying after drinking a grape drink laced with cyanide.

The International Society for Krishna Consciousness (ISKCON or the Hare Krishnas) (www.iskcon.com)

A *world-rejecting sect* this has around one million members worldwide, and follows, with some exceptions, much of conventional Hinduism. While some members live in temples and ashrams (monasteries) as monks and nuns, most ISKCON members practise Krishna consciousness in their own homes, and congregate in temples for worship. Hare Krishna monks are often seen in public places, and are highly visible when spreading their message – dressed in brightly coloured robes, chanting, playing drums, selling their literature and incense; the men's heads are distinctively shaven.

Church of Scientology (www.scientology.org/home.html)

A *world-affirming cult*, founded by science fiction writer L. Ron Hubbard in the USA in the 1950s, this claims a membership of about eight million worldwide. It has been widely persecuted, but has now become more accepted. It believes that individuals can improve their lives through the application of the philosophy of Dianetics, and the removal of 'engrams' which cause mental health problems through 'auditing' by a member of the clergy using an 'e-meter'.

The Unification Church (the 'Moonies') (www.unification.org)

A *world-rejecting Christian-based sect*, this was founded in 1954 in Korea by the Revd Sun Myung Moon (hence the nickname the 'Moonies'). Membership estimates range from one to three million in more than 150 countries. Many of their beliefs are similar to those of other Christian groups, though the Moonies also believe that the Revd Moon has been asked by God to complete the work that Jesus Christ started, and to unite all Christians into a single body.

Transcendental Meditation (TM) (www.tm.org)

A *world-affirming cult* founded by Maharishi Mahesh Yogi in India and brought to the West in the 1950s. This merges a simplified form of Hinduism with science, and believes that meditation can develop human potential and intelligence, and provide better health and career success; it is believed that individuals are eventually able to develop paranormal powers, such as levitating or flying in mid-air (yogic flying). Well over a million people have taken basic TM courses, and there are estimated to be tens of thousands of members worldwide.

The Branch Davidians

This *world-rejecting Christian sect* was led by David Koresh, and believed in the imminent second coming of Christ to earth. This would only occur when at least a small group of Christians had been 'cleansed' by David Koresh, who was sent by God to do this. Koresh and 75 followers, including 21 children, died in a shoot-out with the FBI in 1993 in Waco, Texas, USA, believing that the beginning of the Apocalypse and the final 'battle of Armageddon' mentioned in the Bible was beginning at their compound.

Activity

Refer to the box on 'Seven new religious movements', the features of new religious movements identified on pages 36–8, the differences between world-accommodating, world-rejecting and world-affirming organizations outlines on page 32, and audience cults, client cults and cult movements on pages 34–5.

1 Explore two of the new religious movements, or two of your own choosing, using a Google search – www.religioustolerance.org/ or the websites mentioned in the box.
2 Identify those aspects of each group that fit the features of a new religious movement, and the reasons they may be classified as either sects or cults
3 Classify them as world-accommodating, world-rejecting or world-affirming, and explain your reasons.
4 Explain in your own words, with an example of each (use the web), the difference between an audience cult, a client cult and a cult movement. Explain how your examples show the form of cult you identify.

New Age groups

The term 'New Age' is used to refer to a wide diversity of mind-body-spirit ideas, interests and therapies from across the globe that first began to become prominent in the 1980s. New Age ideas draw on and combine religious and occult traditions from the fairly conventional to the obscure, esoteric and bizarre. Many of the ideas have little to do with the supernatural dimension which is normally seen as a defining feature of a religion. Heelas (1996) sees the New Age consisting of a range of beliefs

The Hare Krishnas.
Founder of the Unification
Church, the Revd Moon,
with his wife.

in self-spirituality in which everyone becomes their own spiritual specialist, dipping into whatever beliefs and practices they fancy.

What is New Age religion?

Bruce (2002a) suggests New Age religion consists of five main features:

1 *The emphasis is on the self*, and freeing the 'self within', which is seen as essentially good and divine.
2 *Everything is connected.* This involves a holistic approach, with the mind, body and spirit all connected, and individuals connected to the environment and the supernatural.
3 *The self is the final authority.* There is no authority higher than the individual, and no single truth: the truth is what the individual believes and what works for them. Personal experience is the only test that matters.
4 *The global cafeteria.* There is a vast range of beliefs, therapies and techniques drawn from across the globe, and people can mix these as they choose.

5 *Therapy*. New Age ideas are designed to be therapeutic: to make you more successful, healthier and happier.

The box below lists a range of things that might reasonably be included in the broad category of the New Age. The New Age also has its own music associated with it. This is gentle, relaxing, other-worldly inspirational music, created with medieval instruments like the flute, harp and lute, with the human voice used for chanting and humming. It is used for relaxation therapy and to accompany meditation, healing and massage.

What's included in the New Age?

UFOs, extra-terrestrials (aliens), and alien abductions
astrology
clairvoyance
crop circles
Eastern and native American mysticism
Feng Shui
Gaia (Mother Earth) as a living entity
green and environmental issues
herbalism
hypnosis
ley lines
magic and spells
massage
meditation

natural healing and alternative remedies/medicine
near-death experiences
organic foods
paganism
reincarnation
spirit guides
Tai Chi
the energizing and healing power of crystals
the i-ching
the tarot
traditional therapies
WICCA (witchcraft)
wizards and fairies

Stonehenge is a place that has significance for some New Age followers. Search the Internet to find out why.

A New Age window display (left), and a typical menu of services available outside a New Age shop (right). Is the New Age just another part of mainstream consumer culture?

Is there a New Age movement?

Sutcliffe (2003), suggests that the New Age refers to such a diverse range of ideas and lacks features like premises, leaders, and shared beliefs and rituals that it can't be regarded as being a movement or movements. He suggests it is more a means for individuals to pursue their own self-development and explore their inner spirituality. The nearest it comes to an organizational form is perhaps the loose network of like-minded individuals, who might keep in touch through the Internet and social networking sites, or the occasional meeting, workshop or conference.

New Age ideas are mainly spread through the mass media and through specialized New Age shops, such as those selling rock crystals and various Eastern and Native American Indian artefacts and services, found in many towns and cities. The New Age requires very little commitment by those who are interested, and really just involves buying products or magazines and books. The New Age is therefore best understood to combine the concepts of Stark and Bainbridge and Wallis, as either one or many world-affirming audience or client cults, rather than a movement or movements.

Activity

1. To find out the range of ideas included under New Age spirituality, go into a local bookshop and browse the shelves on 'New Age' or books on the mind, body and spirit.
2. Visit the Kendal Project at www.kendalproject.org.uk. This explores religion in one town in Britain, which contains an array of findings about religion, including new age spirituality, and discussion of methods on how to explore it.

(a) Find out and explain what is meant by the 'Holistic Milieu'.

(b) Go to the Holistic Milieu questionnaire and identify five groups or therapies listed as part of this milieu.

3 Using ideas from the Kendal Project, devise and carry out a small survey among your fellow students to explore the following:

(a) What, if anything, do people understand by New Age ideas?

(b) To what extent is there belief in or support for New Age ideas?

(c) Are there any differences in terms of age, gender, ethnicity, or social class in understanding of and support for New Age beliefs?

(d) Analyse your findings and suggest explanations for them.

Reasons for the appeal and growth of sects and cults

Why do people get involved in sects and cults, including the new religious movements and New Age spirituality?

Churches and denominations are predominantly part of mainstream conformist life, and why people attend them does not require much explanation, since for many it is simply an aspect of the socialization process as they grow up seeing going (or not going) to church/mosque/temple/synagogue etc. as part of normal adult life. However, what does need explaining is why people join or support deviant religious sects and cults, and particularly the world-rejecting ones, like some of the new religious movements and the New Age audience and client cults. This can't simply be explained as a result of the stupidity or gullibility of individuals, as most people can be persuaded to support something only if it fulfils some need or offers them some reward. This section provides a range of reasons for the appeal and growth of sects, cults and New Age ideas. How these explanations apply will vary between more traditional religious sects and the NRMs, and whether they are world accommodating, world-rejecting or world-affirming. These explanations should therefore be regarded as a kind of tool-kit, with different combinations necessary to understand any particular religious group.

Practical or pragmatic reasons

1 *The key to success.* Heelas (1996) suggests that what he calls 'self-religions' – world-affirming NRMs and New Age ideas – appeal to more affluent, university-educated, socially integrated and generally successful middle-class groups, whose members nonetheless find something missing in their lives. They seek techniques to recapture their inner selves, and they also have the money to pay for the services on offer. Wallis suggests that world-affirming movements like Transcendental Meditation and Scientology are likely to appeal to such groups for various reasons: they claim to offer knowledge, techniques and therapies that enable people to unlock spiritual powers within themselves, helping them to reduce stress and anxiety at work, find career and financial success and a happier personal and spiritual life – making them better people in both work and personal terms.

2   *Escape.* Some groups may provide short-term practical solutions for those escaping from some difficult family, personal or work circumstances. In her study of the world-rejecting Unification Church (the Moonies), Barker (1984) argued that the sect offered a type of substitute family, providing support and comfort.

Secularization

Weber saw the modern world as one in which there had been what he called a 'disenchantment with the world'. By this, he meant that the spiritual, magical and mystical aspects of life had diminished or disappeared, and the world had become more rational, or planned and predictable. Secularization (discussed later in this chapter) is part of this growing rationality and disenchantment, with developments in science and technology undermining religious beliefs.

Many traditional churches and denominations have watered down their beliefs to accommodate a more secular world, and have become more worldly, less spiritual and lacking firm beliefs and commitment. Giddens (2006) suggests that 'people who feel that traditional religions have become ritualistic and devoid of spiritual meaning may find comfort and a greater sense of community in smaller, less impersonal new religious movements'. Bruce (1996) sees the growth of New Age ideas and cults as a consequence of some people's loss of faith in traditional religious leaders and beliefs. He suggests the attraction of world-affirming groups lies in the techniques they offer to bring spiritual dimensions otherwise lacking into people's lives.

Traditional religious sects and new religious movements, and New Age ideas, may attract those turned off by mainstream religion, and provide a refuge for those seeking the spiritual and supernatural, and firm beliefs and commitment, in a secular society.

Filling the 'vacuum of meaning' in postmodern society

Linked to the secularization discussion above is the view of Lyotard (1984) that in postmodern society there has been a loss of faith in metanarratives – the all-embracing 'big' theories which try to explain everything, such as science and what Berger called the universes of meaning provided by traditional religious ideas. Bauman (1992) suggests there is now a 'crisis of meaning' in postmodern society, and Heelas (1998) believes the rise of New Age ideas might be seen as a means for individuals to fill what he calls a 'vacuum of meaning'. Joining sects or following cults may therefore provide new sources of meaning and purpose for individuals.

Identity formation in postmodern society

Postmodernists suggest that traditional sources of identity, like social class, gender and ethnicity, have become more fragmented in contemporary societies, and people increasingly form their own identities through the lifestyles they build and their consumption patterns, and this includes the various beliefs they buy into. Joining a sect or following a cult, as well as providing a sense of meaning and purpose for individuals, may therefore also meet their personal needs in terms of identity formation and lifestyle choices.

Globalization and the mass media

Globalization, particularly in the mass media, including the Internet, has meant that people now have access to a huge range of ideas from around the globe.

We now live in what Baudrillard called a 'media-saturated society', and people are able to pick and choose, and mix and match beliefs from across the world. The NRMs are able to communicate with larger numbers of people than ever before through the media, especially the Internet, and this has raised the visibility and profile of these groups, particularly among younger people.

Social deprivation, marginality and theodicies of disprivilege

Weber (1993 [1920]) argued that sects are most likely to emerge among marginal groups in society. These are people who are pushed to the edges or margins of society, and are not integrated into mainstream society. Wilson (1970) suggests that a variety of factors may lead to marginalization, such as economic deprivation, including poverty, homelessness and unemployment, racism, or because people are in trouble, lonely, have personal or family problems or are disillusioned or alienated from wider society for some reason. Weber suggests that religious sects appeal to these groups by providing what he called a '**theodicy of disprivilege**'. This is a religious explanation and justification provided by sects for the social marginalization (or disprivilege) of their members.

Sects also sometimes turn social deprivation and poverty into a virtuous test of faith, and offer compensation for suffering in this world. Stark and Bainbridge, for example, saw many of the world-rejecting NRMs acting as what they called 'compensators' to help deal with problems of marginality, particularly as the secularization of mainstream religions has meant they are less able to perform this role. Pentecostalist sects among African Caribbeans in the UK, or those like the Jehovah's Witnesses or the Branch Davidians, provide access to a close-knit group of members in a similar position, a sense of security, clear values and the reward of being one of the chosen few who will achieve salvation either in the afterlife or in a future new heaven on earth.

Wallis suggests that many well-educated middle-class young people were attracted to world-rejecting new religious movements in the 1960s and early 1970s because they felt marginalized and disillusioned following the failure of the radical student and hippie movements and their challenge to dominant norms and values. Also, such young people, as Barker found among those in the Moonies, can afford to 'drop out' for a while, with their backgrounds giving them reasonable prospects of re-entering conventional society after their temporary break.

Status frustration

Status frustration means that people are frustrated at their lack of status in society. Marginality, discussed above, may cause status frustration, but it is particularly associated with young people going through the long period of transition from childhood to full independent adult status, brought about by longer periods in education and their lack of work and family commitments. Wallis (1984) suggests this may explain

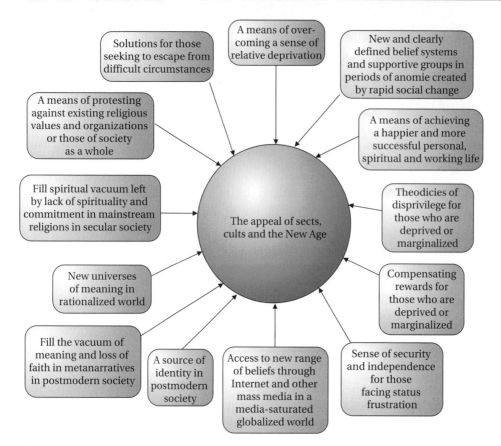

Figure 1.3 The appeal of sects, cults and the New Age

why new religious movements are most likely to appeal to young people, as membership can provide some support for an identity and status independent of school or family, and overcome the sense of status frustration. Barker suggests that the fact that young adults often lack the responsibilities of work, paying rent or a mortgage, or looking after children gives them the time and freedom to get involved should they so choose. Both Barker and Wallis argue that world-rejecting groups appeal to such unattached young people, as it joins them together in a supportive community of others facing similar experiences, bringing them both companionship and a sense of independence.

However, such periods of status frustration are generally short-lived, and Wallis concluded that 'the new religious movements involve only a very small proportion of the population . . . and even then often for only very brief periods during the transition to adulthood'.

Relative deprivation

Membership of sects and cults is not exclusively limited to the socially deprived, the marginalized or the status-frustrated young, and sometimes those from more advantaged, middle-class social groups join them. Stark and Bainbridge suggest that the concept of **relative deprivation** may help to explain this.

Relative deprivation is the sense of lacking something compared to the group with which people identify and compare themselves.

This refers to the subjective feeling of being deprived or lacking something compared to those in the social group with which individuals identify and compare themselves. This may be a sense of status or income, but could be a sense of spiritual or emotional inadequacy compared to others, even if there is no material deprivation. The ideas and support derived from sect membership or cult following may help to overcome this.

Social change

Wilson (1982) argues that periods of sudden or rapid social change can provide fertile ground for the growth of sects. Such periods may create what Durkheim called **anomie**. This refers to a sense of normlessness, or uncertainty and insecurity over social guidelines for behaviour, as rapid change undermines or disrupts traditional norms and values and universes of meaning.

Sects and cults may provide solutions to such periods of uncertainty, by providing new and clearly defined belief systems and close-knit supportive social groups – a sense of certainty in an uncertain world. Wilson (1970) suggests that the rise of Methodism, which began as a sect in eighteenth- and nineteenth-century Britain, was a response to the rapid social change and insecurity of life in the new industrial towns. Similarly, the rise of NRMs might be seen as a response to the uncertainties generated by rapid social change since the 1960s.

Anomie refers to a sense of normlessness, confusion and uncertainty over social norms, often found in periods of rapid social change and other disruptions of the routines and traditions of everyday social life.

Protest

Glock and Stark (1965) suggest that sects emerge as a form of religious or social protest of some kind, as many embody elements of protest against existing society. They may therefore appeal to those who find that their values, for a variety of reasons, are at loggerheads with those of the existing society around them, or of other religious groups, which they see as watered down or corrupted. Examples might be the Nation of Islam in the USA, which is a religious group for black people embodying protest against white society, or Pentecostalist sects. The growth of NRMs in the 1960s is sometimes seen as part of the protest movement among young people against existing society and their disillusionment with it, and the search for new alternative beliefs and lifestyles.

Activity

Refer to the toolkit of explanations above.

1 Suggest reasons why individuals might join
   - a world-rejecting group
   - a world-accommodating group
   - a world-affirming group
2 Suggest reasons why new religious movements are more likely to be supported by young people, and why membership is often only for short periods.
3 Suggest arguments and evidence for *and* against the view that the growth of new religious movements might be a response to the secularization of modern society.

The dynamics of sects and cults

The dynamics of sects and cults is concerned with how and why they may change over time. Some suggest that sects tend to be short-lived, as they will, over time, either turn into denominations or disappear altogether. For example, both the Quakers, or Society of Friends, and the Methodists originally began as world-rejecting religious sects, with members living distinctive lifestyles in opposition to existing society. However, both have long abandoned their world-rejecting features, and have evolved from sects into the highly respectable world-accommodating and tolerant denominations they are today. On the other hand, some sects, like the Jehovah's Witnesses, have retained their features as world-rejecting sects over a long period of time, while others, like the People's Temple, have completely disappeared. What influences whether a sect is short-lived or long-lived, whether it turns into a denomination or whether it disappears?

Why are sects thought to be only short-lived?

Many writers have argued that sects are short-lived and transient, and that there is little possibility of a sect surviving for long periods of time. There are a number of reasons given for this.

1   *The problem of maintaining commitment and fervour.* Barker (1989) suggested that, particularly in world-rejecting new religious movements, the heavy commitment required is hard to maintain. Niebuhr (1957 [1929]) thought the enthusiastic fervour and commitment of sect members is hard to sustain after the first generation – the commitment of parents who converted to the sect is hard to keep going in their children. Either the sect will then gradually wither away, or it will need to become less of a protest movement and modify its beliefs and practices to accommodate, and be more tolerant of, mainstream society and other beliefs. This would then allow its members to live more normal lives, and give it a better chance of retaining members, but this entails the sect becoming more settled and denomination-like. Becker (1950) identified this process, when he described a denomination as 'a sect that has cooled down', as it loses some of its initial fervour, and becomes more tolerant, world-accommodating and 'respectable'.
2   *The loss of charismatic leaders.* Sects that are founded and led by a single charismatic leader, whose inspirational personal magnetism and leadership attracted people into the sect, may lose support and disappear once the leader dies.
3   *The changing circumstances of members and appeal of sects.* The variety of personal reasons and social circumstances that were discussed earlier, and which originally attracted people to the sect, may, after a period of time, disappear. For example, original reasons for joining, such as social deprivation, marginality, anomie and the search for meaning, may cease to be relevant. This is particularly likely in generations following the first generation of converts.

Barker suggests that, in new religious movements, as younger people grow older, the reasons that drove them into the sect diminish, and they begin to look for more normal lives. This may mean that the sect disappears, or that is loses its world-rejecting features and becomes more like a denomination.

4   *Religious diversity in postmodern societies.* Postmodern societies are characterized by a fragmentation of belief and a wide diversity of religious, spiritual and other beliefs. Postmodernists tend to see the beliefs people hold as purely a personal matter, and they can go spiritual and religious shopping, picking, choosing and changing beliefs as freely as they might chop and change washing liquids in their local supermarkets. There is greater tolerance of all beliefs today, and this may mean that religious sects have a short shelf-life as consumer tastes and current fads change.

Are all sects necessarily short-lived?

Are disappearance or denomination the only options for sects? Aldridge (2007) argues that the suggestion that sects must over time either disappear or turn into denominations is false. He points out that:

- many sects have existed a long time while still retaining their features as sects;
- not all sects depend on charismatic leadership;
- many sects have been successful in socializing their children into acceptance of the sect's beliefs and practices, while also converting adults;
- sects can maintain strict standards of conduct, including expelling those who fail to conform to these standards, over long periods of time.

Aldridge points to sects like the Jehovah's Witnesses and the Amish to illustrate this (see the box overleaf).

Wilson (1959) has also rejected the view that the disappearance of a sect or its becoming a denomination are the only alternatives, pointing to the Jehovah's Witnesses and the Seventh Day Adventists as examples of long-standing groups that have retained their sect-like features and not become denominations. Wilson suggests that what will affect whether a sect can retain its status or will turn into a denomination will depend on what its members see as being required in order to be 'saved'.

Conversionist sects

Wilson suggested that what he called 'conversionist' sects were the most likely to develop into a denomination. These are sects which think that the best way to save the world is not to be hostile to and isolated from it, but to be engaged with it, and to try to change or convert individuals by spreading the religious message and 'saving souls'. Should they be successful, and win a lot of support, they may turn into a denomination, but this doesn't prevent them carrying on as they were when they were a small sect. The Salvation Army is an example of a small former conversionist sect that has turned into a conversionist denomination.

The Amish are a Christian sect found predominantly in Pennsylvania in the USA. They have no interest in converting others to their way of life and have cut themselves off from the modern world, both physically and socially. They live in their own rural communities modelled on communities in the past, and reject features of modern life like TV, cars and modern technology. They live according to their own principles, based around spiritual experience, self-discipline and self-control, and have distinctive styles of dress and speech.

Jehovah's Witnesses are a worldwide world-rejecting Christian millenarian sect, and have managed to survive as such and maintain their religious fervour, despite not completely isolating their members from contact with wider society, or being led by charismatic leaders; they are also fairly wealthy and very bureaucratic. They try to protect their members, including children, from 'evil' – birthdays and Christmas are ignored. They encourage friendships to be formed only with other Witnesses, but their children attend the same state schools as other children. They are most famously known in Britain for refusing blood transfusions under any circumstances, and for going round in pairs knocking on doors and attempting to convert people.

The Amish are an example of a long-standing world-rejecting sect. Members wear distinctive clothing and reject modern transport, using their own horse-drawn carriages.

The Salvation Army is an example of a former small conversionist sect that has been transformed into a highly respectable worldwide conversionist denomination.

Introversionist and Adventist/revolutionary sects

There are two types of sect that Wilson saw as not being able to survive in denominational form – the introversionist and the Adventist or revolutionary sects.

Introversionist sects are those, like the Amish, which believe that the only route to salvation involves total withdrawal from the corrupting influences of the world and becoming inward-looking (introverted). Such sects can only succeed and last by keeping apart from the world. Trying to convert people by going outside the sect to preach is likely to be a polluting and corrupting experience, and would compromise and destroy the fundamental beliefs of the sect. Such sects therefore cannot survive in denominational form.

Adventist or revolutionary sects are those, like Jehovah's Witnesses, who hold millenarian beliefs that suggest there is going to be some form of imminent, sudden, dramatic and catastrophic change in the world, brought about by the Second Coming (advent) of Christ, Judgement Day, Armageddon or other revolutionary divine interventions. This will destroy the evil and ungodly world, and only the exclusive few selected members of the sect will be saved. Like Jehovah's Witnesses, they may try to spread their beliefs, but there can be no question of compromise with the world, watering down of beliefs, or tolerance of other beliefs, as otherwise they would be counted among the sinners and cast aside when Judgement Day arrives. Such sects cannot take on denominational form and compromise with other beliefs without abandoning the very beliefs and values and exclusivity on which their own sect is founded.

Gender and religion

Feminist approaches to religion

Most feminists focus on the way in which many existing religions are patriarchal, with writers like de Beauvoir (1953) and El Saadawi (1980) seeing religion and religious ideology playing a part in maintaining the male domination over women that is found in many aspects of contemporary social life. This is achieved by religious ideas that seek to control women's sexuality, and that emphasize their once-traditional roles as partners of men, mothers and carers in the family.

Feminists differ in their attitudes to religion, depending on their more general beliefs:

1   *Liberal feminists* are likely to aim for more equality for women within existing religions, by seeking to remove obstacles that prevent them from taking on positions of authority, such as priests or religious teachers and leaders.
2   *Radical feminists* tend to see most existing religions as existing for the benefit of men, and either present a fundamental challenge to religion altogether or seek to reshape it by recapturing the centrality of women in religion from early times.
3   *Marxist feminists* tend to emphasize the Marxist view that religion acts as 'the opium of the people', focusing on the way religion acts as a means of compensating women, particularly working-class women, for their double exploitation through their status as being both working class and women.

Patriarchy and religion

Most, but not all, mainstream contemporary religions and religious organizations tend to be patriarchal, and women and men are rarely treated equally. Evidence for this is shown by a number of things:

1   *Religious scriptures.* Women are either invisible or occupy subordinate positions to men in most religious scriptures. For example, in the Christian Bible, Eve is formed from a rib taken from a man, and it was Eve the evil temptress who led Adam astray and laid the basis for original sin in Christianity and Judaism. God is always seen as male, Jesus is male, Christ's 12 apostles were all men. In Islam, Mohammed is a man. Aldridge (2007) notes that, in the Qur'an, women are legally inferior to men, lacking the same rights as their husbands, to whom they must submit. De Beauvoir (1953) argues that most scriptures in most religions suggest that 'man is master by divine right'.
2   *Barred from the priesthood.* Women are excluded from the priesthood (or equivalent) in Roman Catholic and Orthodox Christianity, in Islam and Hinduism. In Buddhism, female nuns are always given less status than male monks. In Orthodox Judaism, only males are allowed to take a full part in ceremonies. Even in Sikhism, where all religious offices are theoretically equally open to men and women, only a small minority of women take on important positions. When women have been able to become priests, as in the Church of England since 1992,

this has been accompanied by bitter controversy, and only after long and difficult campaigns to achieve it.

3   *The (stained) glass ceiling.* Within religious organizations, women are often found at the bottom of the career ladder, facing the same 'glass ceiling' that they face in many other organizations – an invisible barrier of prejudice and discrimination that stops them from rising higher up the hierarchy. For example, although the Church of England ordained its first woman priest in 1994, there are no female bishops in the Church of England, even though women make up around one fifth of all full-time Anglican priests. Despite legal obstacles to the appointment of female Anglican bishops being removed in 2005, there is deep opposition within the Church of England to women becoming bishops, and women face what has been called the 'stained glass ceiling', barring their progress to positions of authority in the church.

4   *Patriarchal religious doctrines.* Feminist writers like Walby (1990) and de Beauvoir suggest that the doctrine (or teachings) of many of the world's religions contain an ideology of the family, emphasizing women's traditional roles as wives and mothers in the family. For example, in Christianity, respect for the Virgin Mary as a submissive mother is widespread, particularly in Roman Catholicism. Barrett (1977) and Pryce (1979) suggest that Rastafarianism, a religion that appeals mainly to African-Caribbean men, involves an assumption that women will take on the traditional roles of housewife and mother in the family, which Rasta men believe will protect women from racial and sexual harassment by white society. However, such an apparent defence of women in effect gives power to men, by discouraging women's more active engagement and participation in society. Writers like Holm and Bowker (1994) point out that many religious fundamentalist movements, such as 'Born Again' (New Right) Christianity and Islamic fundamentalism, seek to return women to their traditional roles in the family, as wives and mothers. In some Islamic countries, like Iran and Saudi Arabia, women may face very serious punishments for violating traditional gender roles, such as wearing unapproved clothing, make-up and being out in public in the company of a man who is neither their husband nor a close relative.

5   *The veiling of women.* Aldridge notes the veiling of women (hijab) in some Islamic cultures has been interpreted as a powerful symbol of patriarchy, keeping women invisible and anonymous (but see below for an alternative view of this).

6   *The portrayal of women as morally polluting and corrupting, and as sexual predators.* Women's bodies, menstruation and sexuality are often portrayed as being 'polluting' by many of the world's religions. Aldridge notes that sexual pleasure, particularly for women, is disapproved of or condemned outright in many religions. Sexuality is often presented as something that should be linked only to reproduction, and non-reproductive sexual acts are strongly discouraged in Roman Catholicism, and are regarded by most Muslims and conservative Jews as forbidden. This explains, for example, Roman Catholic opposition to the use of artificial methods of contraception, and reinforces women's primary roles as a mother. Women are often, too, presented as sexual predators, with endless desires, who are out to seduce and snare men, diverting them from their proper

religious duties. As Holm (1994) notes, women's menstruation is nearly always regarded as polluting, and Hindu and Muslim women, for example, are generally forbidden from entering sacred places (like a mosque) or touching sacred objects (like the Qur'an or a family shrine) during their monthly periods.

Are all religions patriarchal?

Although women are subordinate within most religions, this has not always been the case, and it is not true of all religious denominations or faiths. In many ancient religions, like those of ancient Egypt or Greece, in Hinduism, and in modern New Age religions, like the pagan witchcraft-based Wicca, there are female goddesses. Three examples are shown in the images below. While these goddesses have mainly been replaced by monotheistic (single God) religions such as Judaism, Christianity and Islam, with patriarchal teachings, beliefs and practices, Aldridge suggests that gender equality can be found among contemporary groups like the Society of Friends (the Quakers), the Unitarians, the Baha'is and some spiritualist movements.

The Egyptian goddess Isis was the patron of women, mothers, children, magic, medicine and the Ritual of Life.

The Greek Aphrodite (Roman name, Venus) was the goddess of love, beauty and fertility.

Kali is a Hindu goddess associated with death and destruction, here shown with her foot on the male God Shiva. Kali is now highly regarded as a benevolent mother-goddess in contemporary New Age spirituality.

Do you think the wearing of the veil (hijab) by Muslim women – either the headscarf or full body covering with chadors or burqas – reveals patriarchy, or is a form of resistance to it? Is it a means of asserting an independent identity and freedom from male harassment? Does it make a difference if the wearing of the veil is imposed on women, or whether they choose to wear it?

Writers like Leila Ahmed (1992) and Helen Watson (1994) argue that the veiling of women in some Muslim communities in Britain and some Islamic countries can be interpreted as a form of resisting patriarchy, by providing an independent female identity and freeing women from male harassment. The veil can also be seen as a symbol of female and ethnic identity, and as a sign of Muslim pride in resistance to a patriarchal Western culture which treats women as sex objects

Gender and religion: the facts

Given the patriarchal nature of many of the world's religions, it is perhaps surprising that women remain the biggest consumers of religion. Although in much of Europe, most men and women don't participate in organized religion, women are more likely than men to have religious beliefs and to practise their religion, and this appears to be true across all faiths and religious organizations, including the New Religious Movements and New Age spirituality. The only exception appears to be Islam, where men seem to show greater commitment and involvement than women. Compared to men, women are more likely:

- to express a greater interest in religion, to have stronger personal faith and belief in life after death, and have a stronger personal religious commitment;
- to involve themselves more in religious rituals and worship – e.g. they are more likely to attend religious services, do so more often and more regularly, and they participate more in religious life generally;
- to see private prayer as important, and to practise it;
- to join or involve themselves with new religious movements and New Age movements, as Bruce (1996) found.

Why are women more religious than men?

It is ironic that, despite the patriarchal nature of many of the world's religions, with women relegated to the margins or lower levels of many religious organizations and given minor or subordinate positions in many religious beliefs and texts, women do appear to be more religious than men. There have been a number of possible explanations for women's greater religiosity and religious participation.

Socialization, motherhood and femininity

Men and women in many societies continue to be socialized into different roles. Miller and Hoffmann (1995) suggest that gender socialization means females are brought up to be more submissive, passive, obedient and nurturing than males, and more involved with feelings, cooperation and caring. These factors may explain women's greater involvement in religion in the following ways:

1   *Guardians of family life.* Women are often expected to be the guardians of family life, defenders of tradition in the family and to take on the major responsibilities for looking after the home, family and children. Halman and Draulans (2006) note that these roles give women a greater focus on the family, and it is women, rather than men, who are more likely to feel it necessary to take charge of their children's moral development and to introduce them to approved social values, including religious beliefs.
2   *Visions of God.* Davie (1994) suggests that women associate God with love, comfort and forgiveness, which are linked with traditional femininity and family roles. In contrast, men associate God more commonly with power and control. The fact that women lean more to people-orientation than to concerns with power may explain their greater involvement in religion.
3   *Nurturing.* Bruce (1996) suggests that women's socialization into the nurturing aspects related to traditional femininity together with their child-bearing and rearing experiences make them less confrontational, less aggressive, less goal-oriented, less domineering, more cooperative and more caring. This would explain their greater involvement not just in the mainstream denominations, but also in religious sects, and the New Age ideas which were discussed earlier in this chapter. These include ideas such as Gaia (Mother Earth as a living entity), natural solutions and therapies associated with well-being – like herbalism, yoga and meditation, homeopathy, aromatherapy and massage, horoscopes, astrology, fortune-telling and tarot, which Glendinning and Bruce (2006) found appealed far more to women than men.
4   *Life, death and the changes in life.* Greeley (1995) suggests that caring tends to be associated with a more religious outlook, and Walter and Davie (1998) see women as more exposed than men to the ups and downs and changes of life. This is because of their biological involvement through childbirth, and through their greater participation in paid caring jobs, for example as teachers, nurses, social workers and care assistants, and as informal carers of children, the elderly, the disabled and the sick and the dying in the family. Davie (1994) suggests that these factors give women a closer association with birth and death than men, and these are also central issues for many religions. They make women more aware of the vulnerability of human life, and more attuned to the spiritual dimensions of human existence.

Greater life expectancy

Women live longer than men, and this means they are more likely to be widowed and living on their own as they grow older. They may therefore turn to religion as a source of support and comfort, and as a means of building support networks in their communities.

Social deprivation, marginality and theodicies of disprivilege

Women are more likely than men to face social deprivation and marginality, and may experience more disillusionment and alienation from wider society. Compared to men:

- women are more likely to experience poverty;
- women are likely to experience personal or family problems more acutely (for the reasons suggested above);
- women are often less self-confident, sometimes marginalized, and they are therefore more likely to seek self-improvement, perhaps through New Age cults and new religious movements;
- women are more likely to be less powerful than men in a patriarchal society, particularly working-class women and women who are isolated in the home and not in paid employment.

These circumstances mean that women may seek and find some solace in religious groups, and particularly in religious sects and new religious movements which provide theodicies explaining their feelings, as well as solutions and support.

Status frustration

Status frustration may be experienced by some women, who lack personal fulfilment or status as a result of being confined to the home by the constraints of housework and childcare, or are in unsatisfying lower-middle-class jobs, which are mainly done by women. Religious participation, particularly in religious sects or New Age cults, may help to overcome or compensate for this.

Activity

1 With reference to the sections above, suggest reasons why:
  (a) older women might be more likely to participate in religious activities than younger women
  (b) men are less likely to hold religious beliefs and participate in religious activities than women
  (c) women with children might be more likely to participate in religion than those without
  (d) women in full-time employment might be less likely to participate in religious activities and to hold religious beliefs than those who are not.
  (e) women might be more likely than men to participate in new religious movements or New Age spirituality.

2 Devise a questionnaire to test the extent of people's religious beliefs, such as whether or not they believe in God, the extent of their participation in religious activities, such as whether they attend church, mosque, temple, etc., how often they attend and what religion means to them.

3 Use this questionnaire to carry out a small survey in your school, college or community, using equal numbers of males and females, to see if there are any differences between men and women. Analyse and suggest explanations for your findings.

Ethnicity and religion

Ethnicity refers to the shared culture of a social group which gives its members a common identity in some ways different from other social groups. A minority ethnic group is a social group which shares a cultural identity which is different from that of the majority population of a society, such as African-Caribbean, Indian Asian and Chinese ethnic groups in Britain. An ethnic identity is one where individuals assert their identity primarily in terms of the ethnic group and culture to which they belong.

Table 1.2: The UK by religion, 2001 census data*

Response	Thousands	Percentage
Christian	42,079	71.6
Buddhist	152	0.3
Hindu	559	1.0
Jewish	267	0.5
Muslim	1,591	2.7
Sikh	336	0.6
Other religion	179	0.3
All religions	45,163	76.8
No religion	9,104	15.5
Not stated	4,289	7.3
All 'no religion'/not stated	13,626	23.2

*Respondents were asked 'What is your religion?', and tick-boxes were provided for six of the main world religions. A write-in box was provided for any non-specified religion and respondents could also tick that they had no religion

Source: UK census, ONS 2001

Table 1.3: The UK population by religion, British Social Attitudes Survey*

	1996 (%)	2006 (%)
Christian		
Church of England/Anglican	29.3	22.2
No denomination	4.7	9.6
Roman Catholic	8.9	9.0
Presbyterian/Free-Presbyterian/Church of Scotland	3.8	2.5
Baptist/Methodist	3.0	2.4
United Reform Church (URC)/Congregational	0.8	0.1
Brethren	0.1	–
Other Protestant/other Christian	2.2	1.7
Non-Christian		
Islam/Muslim	1.8	3.3
Hindu	0.6	1.4
Jewish	0.3	0.5
Sikh	0.2	0.2
Buddhist	0.5	0.2
Other non-Christian	0.4	0.4
No religion	42.6	45.8
Refusal / not answered / didn't know	0.8	0.6

*Respondents were asked 'Do you regard yourself as belonging to any particular religion?' and those who said 'Yes' were asked which religion.

Source: British Social Attitudes Survey, National Centre for Social Research, *Social Trends 38*

An important element of the identity of minority ethnic groups in the UK is their religious faith. As a result of immigration, mainly from Pakistan, India, Bangladesh and the Caribbean in the 1950s and 1960s, Britain is now characterized by religious pluralism, with a diversity of religious faiths and forms of religious practice, as shown in tables 1.2 and 1.3.

The 2001 census collected information for the first time about religious identity, asking the single question 'What is your religion?', which assumed that everyone had one, and without making any distinction between practice, belief or religious background (see table 1.2). Table 1.3, based on research carried out in 2006, asked people whether they regarded themselves as belonging to any particular religion, producing rather different results.

Activity

Refer to tables 1.2 and 1.3

1　What percentage of the UK population reported having a religion in 2001?
2　After Christianity, which was the most common faith in 2001?
3　What percentage of the UK population said they had no religion in 2001?
4　In 2006, what percentage of the population said they did not regard themselves as belonging to a particular religion?
5　Suggest reasons why in 2001 the percentage of people saying they were Christian was so much higher than in 2006.
6　Drawing on the two tables, how might the evidence be used to show that religious commitment is higher in minority ethnic group religions than in the majority ethnic group Christian religion?

Minority ethnic group religions

African Caribbeans

The main religion among African Caribbeans is Christianity, and African Caribbeans made up about 17 per cent of all those attending Christian churches on an average Sunday in 2007. Many African Caribbeans were Christians before they originally came to Britain, but often encountered racism in the established Christian churches. Their Christianity had developed mainly in the Pentecostalist and charismatic tradition (see box), and they found the established British churches rather boring, with a preponderance of older women, an emphasis on doctrine and teachings and with very passive congregations – quite different from what they were used to. Consequently, they began to establish their own churches.

Pentecostalism is today the largest Christian group among British African Caribbeans. According to Christian Research, congregations in half the Pentecostal churches in England are predominantly black, and Pentecostalism is the fastest growing group within Christianity, globally and in the UK, and is in third place behind Catholics and Anglicans in terms of attendance. Rastafarianism is another faith that is found in the African Caribbean community, particularly among young men, and often gives them very distinctive group identities (see below).

African Caribbeans are generally well assimilated into mainstream British society. Modood et al. (1994) found that, unlike in Asian communities, religion amongst African Caribbeans, as in the white population, is much less important to their ethnic identity, and is mainly a matter of individual choice.

Pentecostalism (including the charismatic movement)

This is a Christian denomination that places an emphasis on experience rather than teaching doctrine and dogma. Religious services are very vibrant, family-centred and have high entertainment value. They involve elements like call-and-response interaction between the priest and the congregation, shouting and clapping, singing and dancing, fainting, trances, prophesying, speaking in tongues, impromptu healing and praying, and exorcism.

Rastafarianism

Rastafarianism emerged in Jamaica among working-class and peasant black people in the early 1930s. It regards Haile Selassie I, the former Emperor of Ethiopia, as a god figure, with the Jamaican black separatist Marcus Garvey seen as a prophet. It is associated with the spiritual use of cannabis and dreadlocks, and became widely known across the world through reggae music, particularly that of the Jamaican singer and songwriter Bob Marley, who has become an icon of Rastafarianism.

Asian religious groups

While those originally coming from the Caribbean were entering a country with which they shared the dominant Christian beliefs, those from Pakistan (and, later, Bangladesh) and India had non-Christian backgrounds and had to establish their own temples, mosques and other places of worship, as there were none already in existence. The main religions are Islam, Hinduism and Sikhism.

In contemporary Britain, young people from minority ethnic groups are being brought up in a society with equal opportunity laws, including equal rights for men and women and gay people, and laws against sex discrimination in work and education. This means some of the values associated with these religions are under pressure and difficult to sustain. For example, the caste system, which is rooted in Hindu religious beliefs, has religious rules about the kind of work that can be done, who one can eat with and who one can marry. Similarly, Islam sees it as desirable for men and women to be educated and raised separately, and treated differently. Arranged marriages, when couples are matched by parents in terms of social suitability rather than necessarily through a love match, are encountering resistance among some younger people. All these things can be difficult to sustain in a society where human rights and equality legislation exist.

Religious commitment in the minority ethnic groups

Research has repeatedly shown that the major minority ethnic groups in Britain (African Caribbeans, Bangladeshis, Indians and Pakistanis) are, in general, significantly more religious than the white ethnic majority, though they share some similarities in that younger people are less religious than older people, and women show more commitment than men (though the opposite is the case among Muslims).

Evidence for the greater religious commitment among minority ethnic groups is shown by the following:

1   In 2007, while only around 6 per cent of the British population went to a Christian church on an average Sunday, around one in six of them were African Caribbeans – around three times their proportion in the population.
2   Research in 1997 showed Muslim men over the age of 35 visited a mosque at least once a week, and this is growing among younger people. The white ethnic majority shows very little commitment to religion at all. On current trends it is likely that practising Muslims will soon outnumber practising Anglicans.

Since 1969, the number of mosques in Britain has grown to almost the same number of Anglican churches that have closed.

3   There is a growth of mosques and temples, while Christian churches are closing. In 1961 there were just seven mosques, three Sikh temples and one Hindu temple in England and Wales, compared with nearly 55,000 Christian churches. By 2005 the number of churches had fallen to 47,600, with another 4,000 likely to disappear over the next 15 years, according to Christian Research. Between 1969 and 2005, 1,700 Church of England churches were closed – the same as the number of mosques there now are in Britain.

4   There are growing demands for state-funded faith schools for minority ethnic religions, as are already provided for Church of England and Roman Catholic faiths. Demands are particularly strong for Muslim schools, where girls and boys can be educated separately according to Muslim religious principles. These are very controversial, and a *Guardian* ICM poll in 2005 showed 64 per cent of people were opposed to any kind of faith schools, as they were seen as a threat to social cohesion. There are currently around 7,000 faith schools in England, making up 36 per cent of primary and 17 per cent of secondary schools. The vast majority (99 per cent) are Christian, with 36 Jewish, five Muslim and two Sikh schools.

Activity

1   Consider the reasons why the establishment of new faith schools is very controversial, particularly the establishment of Muslim schools, when there are already many Church of England and Catholic schools.
2   In two columns, list all the arguments you can think of for and against faith schools, and discuss these in your group.

Why are minority ethnic groups more religious?

Many of the reasons for higher levels of religious commitment in minority ethnic groups have been considered throughout this chapter, in both the theories of religion and in the section on religious organizations, so they will only be briefly outlined here.

Community identity and cohesion

Functionalist writers, following in the steps of Durkheim, emphasize the role of religion in social integration, in building group solidarity, shared values and identity. Davie (1994) suggests that higher levels of religiosity help to maintain tradition, group cohesion and community solidarity. She links this to other aspects of ethnic identity, such as art, marriage, cooking, diet, dress, dress codes and language. Mosques and Sikh temples, for example, are community centres as well as places of worship, and provide a focus for social life as well as a means of protecting and promoting cultural values and traditions which may be seen as under threat by the dominant white culture. Modood et al. (1994) found that religion was important in the lives of minority ethnic communities as a source of socialization, and as a means of maintaining traditional morality, such as conceptions of mutual responsibility, trust, and right and wrong. It also helped to cope with the worries and pressures in life, perhaps arising from the hostility and discrimination arising from racism in the wider society which many from minority ethnic groups encounter.

Social deprivation, marginality and status frustration

Social deprivation and marginality, as well as the sense of dissatisfaction with a lack of status in society (status frustration), may account for higher levels of religiosity. People may turn to religion as a secure and solid source of identity, status and community, which they find lacking in mainstream society. Many older Asian women, particularly, may feel marginalized in mainstream society, as they often have a poor grasp of English.

Pakistani and Bangladeshi households are the poorest in Britain: 63 per cent of them were living in poverty in 2005–6. Many African Caribbeans face higher levels of unemployment, and racism affects all black and Asian ethnic minority groups. Marx's view of religion – as the 'opium of the people' providing comforting diversion from attacking the causes of their poverty and the racism they encounter – might explain higher levels of religiosity. Religion may also provide a 'theodicy of disprivilege', as Weber suggested, and the compensators that Stark and Bainbridge identified. This may explain the Pentecostalism found among African Caribbeans, and the Rastafarianism among alienated young black men.

Family pressures

Family structures are much tighter knit in Asian communities, with strong extended families. This, combined with generally closer-knit communities, may result in pressure to conform to religious values and behaviour.

Social identity

Religion in minority ethnic groups can provide individuals with many markers of identity, such as their customs, dress and food, and also rituals and festivals, such as Divali (Hindus and Sikhs) or Ramadan and Al-Hijra (the Muslim new year). By asserting an identity drawn from religious elements of their cultures, members can resist the denial of status and the devaluing of their own culture by racism.

Johal (1998) suggests that many younger British Asians have forged a single new hybrid identity, which he calls 'Brasian', derived from blending both British and Asian cultures. This involves establishing an identity by adopting *selective* elements of the religion of their parents, with strong dimensions of personal choice. For example, the religious beliefs of Brasians might be important to them, but they might expect to marry whomsoever they wish, rather than have an arranged marriage or a partner from the same ethnic or religious group, and they may not necessarily follow traditional religious customs, such as constraints over diet, drinking alcohol or dress. Butler's (1995) interviews with 18–30-year-old Muslim women in Bradford and Coventry came up with similar findings. While these young women had some attachment to the religious values of their culture, and saw religion as important in shaping their identities, they also challenged some of the restrictions that traditional Asian Muslim culture imposed on them and wanted more choice and independence in their lives.

Jacobson (1998) explored the issues of religion and identity among young British-born Pakistanis in the East End of London. She found that a Muslim identity, rather than just an Asian or Pakistani identity, appealed to young people, as it provided them with stability, security and certainties when they faced much uncertainty in other aspects of their lives.

Islam and identity in the UK

The discussion above explains a number of possible reasons for the greater religiosity among the minority ethnic religions. However, the growing commitment and fervour and the public controversy that have surrounded Islam in the 2000s in Britain deserve further discussion.

Since the attacks on the World Trade Center in New York in 2001 and the London bombings of July 2005, both of which were carried out by Muslim extremists, the media reporting of the activities of a tiny minority of Muslims in Britain have formed the basis for the stereotyping in the popular imagination of all Muslims. The word 'Muslim' all too often conjures up images of terrorism and extremist preachers. As a result, Islam has become an important, and growing, marker of identity for many in the Muslim community in Britain – whether they want it to be or not. Media reporting has also meant that being identified as 'Muslim' has become almost a **stigmatized identity**, bringing with it harassment and fear for the vast majority of Muslims who have no sympathy with extremists or terrorism of any kind.

Growing numbers of young male and female Muslims in the UK, but especially young men, are choosing Islam as their prime marker of identity. Islam and its symbols and values have become central features in building a positive identity

A **stigmatized identity** is an identity that is in some way undesirable or demeaning, and stops an individual or group being fully accepted by society.

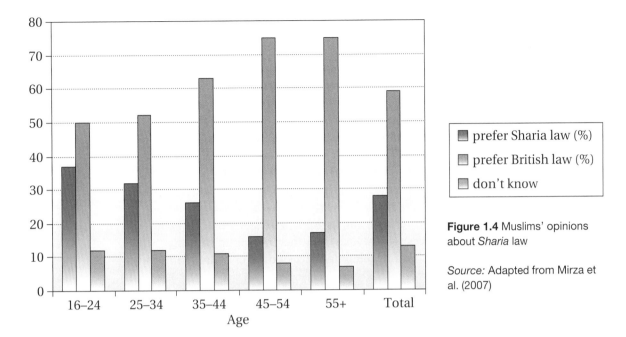

Figure 1.4 Muslims' opinions about *Sharia* law

Source: Adapted from Mirza et al. (2007)

Islamophobia is an irrational fear and/or hatred of or aversion to Islam, Muslims or Islamic culture.

which they see as otherwise denied to them by a white, racist, **Islamophobic** British culture. About 70 per cent of British Muslims are under the age of 25, so this pattern is likely to signal long-term trends, as the young Muslims of today are the parents of tomorrow.

The rise of religiosity and a specific Muslim identity among young British Muslims was explored by Mirza et al. (2007) and Mirza (2008). Mirza found an increase in religiosity and identification with Islam among young second and third generation Muslims, shown by things like more younger Muslim women wearing the headscarf (hijab), greater identification with the worldwide Muslim community, and growing membership of Islamist political groups and youth associations. There were also growing demands among the young for education, financial and legal arrangements that complied with Islamic (Sharia) law. Although well over half of all British Muslims in all age groups say they'd rather live under British law than Sharia law, around 35 per cent of 16–24-year-olds expressed a preference for Sharia law, as shown in figure 1.4.

Mirza suggests that the rise of a Muslim identity among the young might be to do with three main factors:

1 *British foreign policy.* Many Muslims saw British foreign policies in the 2000s, such as the invasions of Iraq and Afghanistan, as anti-Islamic acts.
2 *The decline of other sources of identity*, like political parties, nationality, trade unions, or social class and ethnicity. This drives young Muslims, whose status is more insecure than older ones, to seek new sources of meaning, identity and belonging by asserting an Islamic identity.
3 *Multicultural policies.* These policies are found in many areas of life in British society, and have been a major feature of the British education system for many years. These policies are based on the idea that it is important to recognize, learn

about and respect the cultural differences between ethnic groups. Such policies involve treating groups differently as a mark of respect for their cultures, and to make them feel included, rather than excluded and marginalized, in mainstream society. Mirza suggests that these policies have led to Muslims demanding things like more faith schools, laws against blasphemy (insulting references to God) and permission to wear traditional dress at work – for example, allowing Muslim women police officers the option of wearing the hijab instead of the traditional uniform cap. Mirza suggests that multicultural policies, which are designed to include and protect Muslims, may have had the opposite effect. This is because they make Muslims feel different and excluded from mainstream society. At the same time, they generate hostility among the white ethnic majority, and possibly other minority ethnic religious groups, as Muslims are seen as being unreasonable in getting special treatment, and unwilling to adapt to mainstream British society. This hostility then drives young Muslims further into embracing an Islamic identity, as they are constantly reminded of their difference, and increasingly lack other sources of identity.

Although Mirza is primarily concerned with explaining the growth of extremism among some young Muslims, much of what she says offers general explanations for the growing assertion of a Muslim identity among all young Muslims, the vast majority of whom are neither extremists nor terrorists. Mirza's work may also provide some general explanations for the importance of religion as a marker of identity among other minority ethnic groups.

Activity

1 Identify and explain three reasons why levels of religious commitment and participation are generally higher among minority ethnic groups.
2 Explain the meaning of the following concepts, and how they might explain greater levels of religious commitment among minority ethnic groups:
   - social cohesion
   - identity
   - status frustration
   - theodicy of disprivilege
   - marginalization
3 Suggest reasons why some of the rules and beliefs associated with minority ethnic group religions, like arranged marriages, might be under pressure and hard to sustain in contemporary Britain. Give examples of at least three rules or beliefs (use the Internet if you want to explore the rules of different religions).
4 Explain why 'Muslim' has tended to become a stigmatized identity in contemporary Britain.
5 Design a small survey in your class to explore whether people claim to have a religion, their level of commitment to it, and what it means to them. If possible, try to get answers from a range of ethnic and religious groups, drawn from different ages and both sexes. Analyse your findings, and identify and discuss any significant findings, such as any differences between men and women, ethnic groups and age. Suggest explanations for your findings.

Age and religion

In general, people seem to develop a greater attachment to religion as they grow older. Belief in God is lowest among those under 34, and highest among those over age 55. Young people are not only less likely to participate in mainstream religious activity than older people; more than half of them say they don't regard themselves as religious at all, as shown in such studies as the British Social Attitudes survey and the European Values study. This contrasts with only about 2 per cent of those over the age of 65 who make this claim. Bruce (2001) found that the age gap between church-goers and non-churchgoers had widened in all Christian denominations over the past 25 years. Christian Research suggests that the age gap among those who do go to church is already very wide, and will continue to increase if current trends continue, as shown in table 1.4.

Table 1.4: Proportions of Sunday churchgoers in each age group, Great Britain, 2000–50			
Age group	2000 (%)	2025* (%)	2050* (%)
Under 15	19	5	1
15–19	5	1	0
20–29	9	5	2
30–44	17	12	7
45–64	25	25	18
65 and over	25	52	72
Base (=100%) All churchgoers	4.4 million	2.3 million	0.9 million
Average age of churchgoers	47	59	67
Average age of population	40	42	44

*Estimate
Source: Christian Research

Activity

Refer to table 1.4:
1 Describe, giving figures, what the table shows about the relationship between church attendance and age groups in 2000.
2 Identify two trends that are shown in the table.
3 How many people are there estimated to be attending Christian churches in 2050?
4 What proportion of churchgoers are estimated to be under the age of 30 in 2050?
5 Suggest reasons for the pattern of churchgoing identified in the table.

Older people and religion

The attachment of older people to religion is often explained by three main factors:

1   *Disengagement.* Disengagement means that, as people get older, they become detached from the integrating mechanisms of society, such as participation in workplaces through paid employment. Older people may face a growing privatization of their lives, with increasing social isolation as partners and friends die. Participation in religious organizations provides a form of social support in this situation, and a network of people to relate to.
2   *Religious socialization.* Older people are more likely to have had a greater emphasis placed on religion through the education system and socialization in the family when they were younger. This may have laid seeds that flower as they grow older, as they rediscover a religiosity they may previously have ignored.
3   *Ill-health and death.* Older people tend to be faced with declining health, and death looms on the horizon. These are the very things that religion concerns itself with. The ageing process and disengagement from society may therefore generate an engagement with religion for comfort, coping, meaning and support.

Are young people less religious than older people?

Young people are undoubtedly less religious in terms of their expressed religious belief in surveys and their participation in the mainstream Christian religions,

Religion deals with the fundamental questions of the meaning of life and death, and this may explain the greater religiosity of older people.

although this is not true among young Muslims. As discussed earlier, young people seem more attracted to New Age spirituality and new religious movements, but the vast majority do not participate in either. This does not necessarily mean that young people are lacking all spirituality or religious feeling and belief. The explanations suggested below for the apparent lower religiosity and religious practice of young people may be because these are simply being expressed in new, private ways which are difficult to record in statistical surveys.

The declining attraction of religion

The mainstream religious organizations are very unattractive to most young people. In many cases, they find services to be boring, repetitive and old-fashioned, full of old people, and out-of-touch with the styles and attitudes of younger people. Controversies in religion over issues like abortion, contraception, the ordination of women priests and bishops, gay priests and gay rights in general, sex before marriage and so on seem bizarre to many young people, and alien to the values they hold. A former Archbishop of Canterbury, George Carey, said in 1991 that he saw the Church of England as like 'an elderly lady, who mutters away to herself in a corner, ignored most of the time'. If even the head of the Church of England saw it that way, then it is perhaps not surprising that many young people see mainstream Christianity as 'uncool', and stay away.

The expanded spiritual marketplace

Lynch (2008) suggests that young people may be turning away from conventional ideas of religion as there is now what Roof (2001) called an 'expanded spiritual marketplace'. This involves growing exposure and accessibility to a wide diversity of religious and spiritual ideas. This includes the religions that have become more significant as a result of immigration, such as Islam, Hinduism, Sikhism and Buddhism, but also the wide diversity of new religious movements and New Age spirituality, like Wicca and paganism, to which young people are more likely to be exposed as the greatest consumers of the mass media and the Internet. These have opened up new avenues for exploring religion and spirituality. Lynch suggests that these have meant there are now more sources for young people to draw on to build religious and spiritual beliefs, identities and lifestyles, and these may be finding expression outside traditional religions and religious organizations.

The privatization of belief – believing not belonging

Young people may be choosing to treat their religion, of whatever faith or mix of beliefs, as a private matter. Even if they have some general spiritual or religious beliefs, they may not feel they belong to any particular religion, or hold any specific religious belief. They may prefer not to make any public display of whatever they believe through involvement in religious organizations, or admit to them in surveys. Davie (1994) expressed this in the words 'believing without belonging'.

Secular spirituality and the sacred

Lynch suggests that, although young people may be diverted from religion as normally conceived, they may be finding religious feelings inspired in them by aspects of

To what extent do you think that the fervour and commitment shown by some young people towards things like clubbing have replaced traditional religious ideas, and are new forms of expression of spirituality and religiosity?

what are generally regarded as non-religious or secular life. He develops an argument along the lines of Durkheim's conception of the 'sacred' and the inclusivist conception of religion discussed at the beginning of this chapter. He argues that when people become particularly attached to objects, experiences, other people or things – such as celebrities, clubbing, football or music stars, nature or the environment – these can take on the form of the 'sacred' in their lives. This may cause them to reflect on the meaning of their lives and the ways they live them. Lynch suggests, then, that young people may not have lost all religiosity, but that it is simply finding new forms, many of which are associated more with the secular and non-religious world than with religion as it is presently understood by most people.

Secularization and the decline of metanarratives

As discussed earlier, secularization is concerned with the general decline of religious thinking, practice and institutions, and growing disenchantment with the world. Postmodernists like Lyotard (1984) suggest that metanarratives like religion have lost their power to influence how people think about, interpret and explain the world. Young people may be becoming less religious simply because they no longer believe the old religious explanations, and they can pick, mix or reject any beliefs they choose.

Declining religious education

Bruce points out that the Church of England is increasingly unable to recruit young people by socializing them into religious thinking through such things as church Sunday schools or religious education. Sunday schools are in a state of terminal decline – Christian Research says that a century ago over half of all children attended a Sunday school, but by 2000 this had reduced to just 1 in 25 children. If the current rate of decline continues, there will be hardly any Sunday schools left by 2016. Although secondary schools are meant by law to hold assemblies of a broadly Christian character, most generally resort to a kind of secular moral or personal education, or ignore it altogether. This means that the majority of young people don't get any religious education at all, but it also reflects the fact that most of them don't want it.

Pragmatic reasons

There is also a range of possible more practical or pragmatic explanations for the decline of religious belief and commitment among the young. Leisure has become a much bigger part of life, and shops, clubs and pubs all open for very long hours, including Sundays. Young people have more demands on their time, and they may simply have more interesting and enjoyable things to do. It is also seen as very 'uncool' to be religious in many young peer groups, which exerts social pressure not to be religious. Former prime minister Tony Blair, a committed Christian, admitted in 2007 that while he was prime minister he had to play down his religious beliefs for fear of being seen by the public as a 'nutter'. It is perhaps not surprising, then, if young people choose to do the same.

Activity

As a student, you are probably young, and you may or may not hold some kind of religious or spiritual beliefs. You should therefore have some insights and views on the issues above. Apply them to the following:

1. Study the various explanations offered here for the lower levels of religious belief, commitment and participation by young people. Put them in order of those you think are the most and least convincing, and explain your reasons.
2. Identify and explain any other reasons you can think of why younger people might, in general, be less religious than older people.
3. We have suggested that 'controversies in religion over things like abortion, contraception, the ordination of women priests and bishops, gay priests and gay rights in general, sex before marriage and so on seem bizarre to many young people and alien to the values they hold'. Do you agree or disagree? Explain your reasons, or discuss it in your group.
4. Lynch (2008) 'decided to explore the hard-house and techno dance scene to see if the people involved in it saw it as having any kind of religious or spiritual significance'. To what extent do you agree or disagree with Lynch's suggestion that young people may

be finding spirituality or having mystical or religious experiences by giving a 'sacred' quality to secular activities like clubbing and football and to their engagement with the lives of celebrities? Explain your reasons, including how you think they relate to religion.

The secularization thesis

A contested concept

The word 'secular' means 'non-religious'. The secularization thesis is the suggestion that religious beliefs are becoming less plausible (believable) and less appealing to those who might once have believed in them, and religion is therefore of declining importance both in society and for the individual. Secularization is an extremely contested concept, in the sense that there are deep and controversial theoretical and methodological debates over what it is, how to measure it, and whether or not it is occurring.

Defining secularization

The definition of secularization given by Wilson (1966) is one of the clearest: 'the process whereby religious thinking, practice, and institutions lose social significance'.

- *Religious thinking* refers to the influence of religion on people's beliefs and values, such as the importance of religion in their lives, whether they see themselves as a religious person, whether they believe in things like God, spirits, good and evil, and life after death.
- *Religious practice* refers to the things people *do* to carry out their religious commitment, such as the extent to which they actively participate in acts of religious worship and devotion, like attending church, mosque or temple.
- *Religious institutions* refer to the extent to which religious institutions have maintained their social influence in wider society, and how far they are actively involved and influence the day-to-day running of society.

Activity

Fox (2005, p. 354) describes the following exchange in a doctor's waiting room between a mother and her 12-year-old daughter, as they fill in a medical form and come to the religion question:

DAUGHTER: 'Religion? What religion am I? We're not any religion are we?'
MOTHER: 'No, we're not, just put C of E.'
DAUGHTER: 'What's C of E?'
MOTHER: 'Church of England.'
DAUGHTER: 'Is that a religion?'
MOTHER: 'Yes, sort of. Well, no, not really – it's just what you put.'

1 What does the mother–daughter conversation above tell you about the difficulties of measuring religious belief?
2 Take each of the three aspects of secularization – religious thinking, religious practice and religious institutions – and in each case suggest two ways you might measure whether secularization is occurring.
3 Using the measures you have drawn up, suggest two ways in each case that the indicators may *and* may not provide reliable evidence of a decline of religion in society.

Inclusivist and exclusivist definitions of religion

There are theoretical problems in defining secularization. One key theoretical issue is how religion is defined in the first place, as the definition of religion will influence the methodological indicators used to measure it, and therefore the extent of secularization. The following definitions were discussed at the beginning of this chapter (see pages 13–14), and you may wish to refer back for more detail.

1 *The exclusivist definition* sees religion as involving beliefs in some supernatural, supra-human being(s) or forces of some kind.
2 *The inclusivist definition* does not necessarily require beliefs in a supra-human, supernatural being or force, but may include a wide range of beliefs and activities, including conventional religion, to which people give a 'sacred' quality. These might include beliefs and activities that many would not regard as religious, such as New Age therapies and inner-directed spirituality, as well as, for example, football, clubbing or the lives of celebrities, which seem to have a sacred quality for some people. Such a wide definition means that religion is never likely to decline, as alternative activities which replace religion in people's lives simply become redefined as religious. As Aldridge (2007) suggests, such all-embracing evidence for the continued existence of religion is not telling us anything about the world, but is a 'mere trick of definition'. The following discussion of secularization will focus primarily on the exclusivist definition of religion.

Measuring secularization – methodological problems

Measurement and interpretation are major difficulties in the secularization debate, as they depend heavily on the researcher's definitions and judgements of what religion and religiosity are. Three important methodological issues include:

1 *Validity.* Do the findings of research on religion actually provide a true, genuine or authentic picture of what is being studied? Do they show what they claim to show?
2 *Reliability.* Would another researcher achieve the same results? Does the way statistics are gathered mean that different researchers can get different answers? Does the way questions are asked change the information obtained? Do different religious organizations use the same methods of counting membership?

3   *Representativeness.* Can the results obtained from surveys of religion be general-
    ized or applied to the whole population?

Some examples of these methodological difficulties are considered below.

Measuring decline: was there ever a 'Golden Age of Faith'?

Secularization means that religion is declining in some ways compared to the past,
so supporters of secularization need to show that society was once more religious
than it is now. Often, this is based on assumptions about some past 'Golden Age of
Faith', when nearly everyone believed in God and went regularly to church, most of
which were generally packed out. However, there are problems with this reference
to the past:

- historical records about the strength of religion in the past are sparse;
- data collection methods weren't as reliable and didn't use the sophisticated survey methods used today;
- there were no opinion polls or interviewers carrying out surveys to explore
  whether people believed in God, whether they attended church voluntarily or
  because it was expected, and what religion meant to them;.
- most people even 150 years ago couldn't read or write, so the few records that do
  exist are based on the views of a small privileged section of the population, and
  probably tell us little about the religiosity of ordinary people.

   Such records may therefore lack validity, reliability and representativeness, and the
Golden Age of Faith from which a decline is said to have occurred may well be exaggerated. Even in the first Census of Religion carried out in 1851, in England and Wales
only 40 per cent of the adult population attended church.

The meaning and interpretation of evidence

The evidence collected may not give a full picture of what is really happening, and
deciding whether or not secularization is taking place will depend on how that evidence is interpreted, as the following examples suggest:

1   *High participation doesn't mean strong belief.* Even if church attendance remains
    high, it doesn't necessarily mean people still believe in religious ideas, but may
    attend for non-religious reasons, like social support or being seen as socially
    respectable. Martin (1969) argues, for example, that in Victorian Britain church
    attendance was a socially necessary part of middle-class respectability. High
    levels of church attendance in the contemporary United States are, as Aldridge
    (2007) points out, part of the American way of life, based on the secular – not reli-
    gious – values of fitting into the community. Church attendance requires only a
    superficial commitment, with few demands placed on those who go.
2   *Low participation doesn't mean lack of belief.* People might have strong religious
    beliefs but prefer to treat them as a private matter and never go near a religious
    institution, and so won't be recorded in attendance statistics, despite their
    religiosity.

3   *Quantitative versus qualitative data.* Quantitative data, like statistics on church attendance and other forms of participation in religious ceremonies and acts of worship, may suggest that religion is in decline, but qualitative data gained through in-depth interviews exploring people's religious beliefs and thinking may give a very different impression.

Asking questions about religion

Questions about religious belief involve quite personal and sensitive issues, and when questioned by opinion pollsters about their religious beliefs and activities, people may exaggerate or lie, perhaps because of a sense of guilt or because they feel they should give what they see as approved answers. What people say may therefore not be what they really believe, and may in any case have no influence over their behaviour.

Surveys are also very vulnerable to the wording of the questions being asked, which can affect the reliability and validity of the information obtained. For example, in response to the 2001 census question 'What is your religion?' 72 per cent of people described themselves as Christian (even though most never go anywhere near a church) and 15 per cent said they had no religion. The British Social Attitudes Survey of the same year asked the question, 'Do you regard yourself as belonging to any particular religion?'. This found that 54 per cent of people regarded themselves as Christian, and 40 per cent said they had no religion. The difference might, in part, be explained by the assumption behind the census question that people would have a religion, while the British Social Attitudes question introduced the possibility that they might not have one. In addition, the word 'belonging' may have been interpreted by respondents as requiring membership of a church or other practising faith group, reducing the number identifying themselves as belonging.

Membership, attendance and other statistics on religious practice

Statistics on religious practice are difficult to interpret:

1   What counts as 'practising' a religion may vary between individuals and religious groups. Some sects demand very high levels of commitment to be counted as a practising member, while some mainstream churches demand very little.
2   Information about smaller religious groups is often unavailable, and some sects and cults might wish to overestimate their membership to increase their sense of social importance and give the impression they are more established than they really are.
3   A lot of religious practice may not be recorded at all, so is not taken into account in official attendance statistics. An example is participation in the growing House Church movement, where people meet to worship in private homes.
4   Different denominations use different criteria of membership, so apparently similar types of figures may be recording different things. For example, the Church of England and Catholic Churches use criteria like the number of those who have been baptised and confirmed, whether they attend or not, while sects like the Jehovah's Witnesses include only those who show the high levels of commitment demanded.

Competing evidence on secularization 1: religious thinking and belief

Arguments and evidence for the decline of religious thinking and belief

Declining religious belief and the desacrilization of consciousness Bruce (2002b) suggests the growth of scientific explanations and the application of technology have undermined religious beliefs. Weber thought growing disenchantment with the world would create a **desacrilization** of consciousness – 'a loss of the capacity to experience a sense of sacredness and mystery in life'. Opinion polls seem to confirm this, as they have repeatedly shown a general decline in religious belief. For example, a Eurobarometer survey in 2005 found that only 38 per cent of people in the UK believed there was a god, compared to around 60–70 per cent in polls in the 1980s.

> **Desacrilization** refers to the loss of the capacity to experience a sense of sacredness and mystery in life.

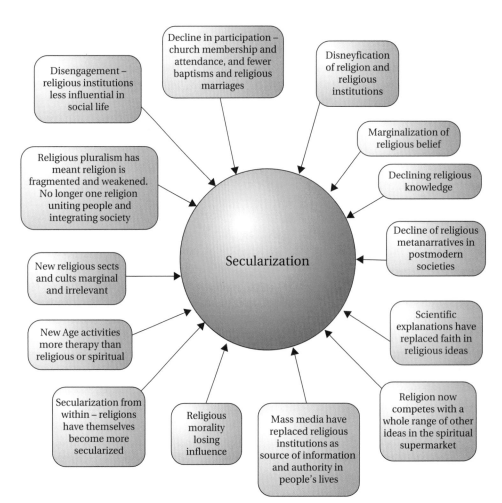

Figure 1.5
Indicators of secularization

The marginalization of religious belief Following from the point above, Bruce (2008) suggests that religion and related beliefs have now been marginalized – they have been relegated to the sidelines of life. Religious beliefs are now, for most people, only a last resort, concerned with those areas of human life over which science and technology have no control, such as incurable illness. As Bruce puts it, 'when we have tried every cure for cancer, some of us pray'.

The declining influence of religious morality Various churches' traditional disapproval of divorce, contraception, abortion, sex outside marriage, illegitimacy and homosexuality appears to have little impact on people's behaviour. The rising number of divorces, lone-parent families, children born outside marriage and couples living together without getting married; the growing acceptance of gays and lesbians, extra-marital sex and the widespread use of contraception among Catholics in direct opposition to Catholic teachings; and rising levels of drug abuse, pornography and violent crime – these are all often used as evidence for the declining importance of the influence of religious beliefs on people's behaviour.

The fragmentation of belief There is no longer one set of beliefs which most people share, but a wide diversity of different religious faiths and organizations, fragments drawn from different faiths, and New Age ideas. Traditional religions now have to compete with tarot cards, paganism, Native American spirituality, self-help therapies, spiritual healing, New Age mysticism, palmistry and horoscopes, astrology, witchcraft and beliefs in the paranormal (like extra-sensory perception).

The decline of metanarratives and the growth of do-it-yourself spirituality in post-modern societies Postmodernists like Lyotard (1984) argue that in postmodern societies, metanarratives like religion have lost their power to influence how people think about, interpret and explain the world; people are taking more control over their own lives and are less willing to be told by religious authorities what to believe. In contemporary consumer-driven societies, people are choosing to create their own 'pick-'n'-mix', do-it-yourself cocktail of beliefs, centred on themselves and construction of their identities, after shopping around in the spiritual supermarket. Religion is now just one form of belief competing with many others.

The emphasis, particularly in New Age spirituality, is now on the quality of experience rather than the truth of the doctrine. Many of these New Age 'spiritual cocktails' have little religious meaning to those involved in them. Bruce (2002a) points out that most involvement is shallow and barely goes beyond reading a few books or listening to a few lectures. The most popular parts of the New Age are mainly secular therapies, like relaxation techniques, meditation, yoga and massage, and not alternatives to traditional religion, like the occult or Hindu philosophies. Bruce points out that 'much of the New Age is not an alternative to traditional religion; it is an extension of the doctor's surgery, the beauty parlour and the gym'.

Declining religious knowledge The evidence suggests that many people now know very little about religion. For example, even those who describe themselves as

Christians, like the 72 per cent of the population in the 2001 census, don't know much about the life of Jesus or the religious meaning of important events like Easter and Christmas. The activity below may help you to test this yourselves.

Activity

1 Devise and carry out a small survey to test people's religious knowledge. Some ideas for types of questions are listed below, but try to devise some of your own, adapted to the group you're in.
   - Which disciple betrayed Jesus for 30 pieces of silver?
   - Name the first book of the Bible.
   - Give three of the Ten Commandments.
   - Who turned water into wine?
   - In which religion is Bar Mitzvah a ceremony?
   - By what name are members of the 'Society of Friends' often known?
   - Which religion has the Qur'an as its sacred book?
   - Who was the founder of Islam?
   - Which is Islam's holiest city?
   - Members of which religions in Britain normally worship in a temple?
   - Name one Hindu god.
   - Which religions celebrate Divali?
   - What does the Christian Easter celebrate?
2 Analyse your findings and draw conclusions, and discuss whether you think it is necessary to have knowledge about a religion in order to be committed to it.

Arguments and evidence against the decline of religious thinking and belief

Many people still show signs of religiosity   Surveys show that although around 70 per cent of the population think that religion is losing its influence, around 70 per cent still claim to believe that there is a soul, and almost as many believe in sin. The 2005 Eurobarometer survey found that just 38 per cent of people in the UK believed in a God, while a further 40 per cent believed in some sort of 'spirit or life force'. This suggests that up to 78 per cent of people still have some elements of religiosity in their thinking.

Secularization and resacrilization: the reorientation of religious belief   In an age of uncertainties and unpredictability, and the decline of traditional religious metanarratives, people are still searching for new meanings and commitment in, for example, New Age ideas, new religious movements and cults like Scientology, in order to re-establish religiosity in their lives and get clues to what their future holds. Heelas et al. (2004), using data gathered in Kendal (see www.kendalproject.org.uk), found there was a 'spiritual revolution' with growing involvement with what they called the 'holistic milieu' – New Age mind–body spirituality of some kind, such as yoga, Tai Chi and alternative therapies. They argued that while there may be secularization in relation to traditional religions, there is, at the same time, a process of

Resacrilization
refers to the renewal and continuing vitality of religious beliefs.

resacrilization – a renewal and continuing vitality of religious beliefs – as people shift from conventional religion to a more individualistic spirituality centred on the self. Such research suggests that religious belief is not disappearing, but is simply being reoriented – taking a new form in which people pick 'n' mix their spirituality from the wide range of beliefs on offer, tailored to what they feel they need and what works for them.

Activity

Go to the site of the Kendal Project (www.kendalproject.org.uk) and answer the following questions:

1 Explain what is meant by the terms 'Congregational Domain' and the 'Holistic Milieu' and explain the differences between them.
2 How was the congregational attendance count carried out?
3 What was the purpose of the street survey, and what method was used? Identify three things it asked about.
4 Go to the Holistic Milieu questionnaire and identify three of the reasons offered in the questionnaire for people attending activities or therapies.
5 Identify any evidence found in the Kendal Project to support the claim of a 'spiritual revolution'.

Traditional religious beliefs remain strong   Various forms of Christian beliefs (and practice) in the UK remain strong. As discussed earlier, Pentecostalist denominations are growing, and Evangelical Christianity is the fastest growing form of Christianity in Britain. Evangelicalism is a broad collection of Christians sharing a fundamentalist belief in the Bible – accepting that the Bible is God's literal word and should be followed strictly. Many Evangelicals believe in the second coming of Christ, faith healing, speaking in tongues, miracles, casting out of demons and possession by evil. They campaign against witchcraft, Satanism, black magic, any form of occult activity, smoking, drinking, sexual promiscuity and homosexuality. The religious fundamentalism this involves cannot be regarded as 'watered-down' religion. Much the same may be said of the commitment required by many new religious movements. High levels of commitment are still shown in the minority ethnic religions in the UK, such as Hinduism, Sikhism and Islam.

Such evidence suggests that religious belief remains high in the UK, but it is even higher in parts of Europe. The 2005 Eurobarometer survey found that four out of five European Union citizens have religious or spiritual beliefs, including belief in God or a spirit or life force. In Malta, 95 per cent said they believe in a God, and in Cyprus, Greece, Portugal, Poland, Italy and Ireland the figure was around 75 per cent.

The continuing vitality of religiously based moral values   Rising rates of crime, divorce, births outside marriage and so on have a wide range of causes, and cannot be explained as simply arising from declining religious beliefs.

Competing evidence on secularization 2: religious practice

Arguments and evidence supporting the view of a decline of religious practice

Whether or not people claim to hold some religious beliefs and values, most do not have much attachment to religious institutions, and nearly every indicator of religious practice in the mainstream religions shows a decline. For example:

1 *There is declining membership* in all the major Christian denominations (see table 1.5), and this decline is progressive: as many existing members grow older, and as they die off, they are not being replaced by younger recruits.

2 *There is declining attendance.* Compared to about 40 per cent in 1851, in 2007 only around 2 per cent of the population attended religious services on most Sundays, and these are mainly older people. Two-thirds of the population attended a religious service (excluding baptisms, weddings and funerals) no more than once a year or less or never. There are also declining attendances at Christmas and Easter – the most important events in the Christian calendar. This trend is likely to get worse, as there is little evidence of religious participation by younger people to replace the present generation of older worshippers.

3 Fewer than a half of marriages now involve a religious ceremony, and fewer than a quarter of all English babies are now baptized, compared with two-thirds in 1950.

4 A century ago, half of all children attended a Sunday school. If current trends continue, Sunday schools will be extinct by 2016.

5 While involvement in new religious movements, religious sects and New Age spirituality has been growing, tiny numbers of people are involved, and this growth is insignificant compared to the membership loss of the major denominations.

Activity

Study table 1.5 and answer the following questions:

1 How many people belonged to Anglican churches in 1995?

2 By how many did the membership of the Catholic Church decline between 1990 and 2002?

3 What percentage of the population belonged to a Trinitarian church in 1995?

4 Identify two trends shown in the membership of non-Trinitarian Christian churches.

5 Which three churches or religions are estimated to increase membership most between 1990 and 2005?

6 How might the evidence in the table be used to show that religion is not necessarily declining in the United Kingdom?

7 There has been a decline in the number of religious marriages in Britain, and more than half of all marriages today are civil ceremonies. Do you think this necessarily means there is a decline in religious belief? What other explanations might there be?

8 Suggest reasons why most surveys on attendance at religious services don't count baptisms, weddings and funerals.

Table 1.5: Membership of churches and other religions: United Kingdom, 1990–2005

Church or religion	1990	1995	2002	2005[a]
Trinitarian churches:[b] thousands				
Anglican	1,728	1,785	1,495	1,549
Catholic	2,205	1,921	1,712	1,631
Presbyterian	1,214	1,099	933	856
Methodist	450	403	334	306
Baptist	232	224	214	209
Pentecostal	167	209	261	280
Other Trinitarian	638	663	729	767
Total Trinitarian	6,634	6,304	5,678	5,598
% of population	11.6%	10.9%	9.6%	9.4%
Non-Trinitarian churches (active members): thousands				
Mormons	160	170	180	188
Jehovah's Witnesses	117	131	128	130
Spiritualists	45	40	34	30
Church of Scientology	75	122	155	165
Other non-Trinitarian	61	55	52	50
Total non-Trinitarian	458	518	549	563
% of population	0.8%	0.9%	0.9%	0.9%
Other religions: thousands				
Muslims	495	632	823	905
Sikhs	125	145	172	184
Hindus	210	242	286	305
Jews	101	94	86	83
Buddhists	31	52	80	92
Others (includes new religious movements)	71	87	113	124
Total other religions	1,033	1,252	1,560	1,693
% of population	1.8%	2.2%	2.6%	2.8%
All religions: thousands	8,125	8,074	7,787	7,854
% of population	14.2%	14%	13.1%	13.1%

[a] Estimate
[b] Trinitarian churches are Christian churches that believe God consists of three persons: father, son, and Holy Spirit
Source: Adapted from Christian Research, *UK Christian Handbook Religious Trends 2003/2004*

Arguments and evidence against the view that a decline of religious practice shows secularization

Belonging without believing Attending religious services does not necessarily mean believing in God. In the past, many people may have attended church regularly only because churchgoing was seen as necessary to achieve respectability in the community. The decline in church attendance today therefore may not necessarily mean that there has been a decline in belief, only a decline in the social pressure to attend church.

Believing without belonging and the privatization of religious practice Believing in God does not necessarily mean having to attend religious services. Davie (2002), looking across a number of European countries, has argued that declining religious attendance has not been accompanied by declining religious belief. She suggests that people are simply becoming 'unchurched' – that is, they don't attend or belong to churches, even though they still claim to hold religious beliefs. Davie (1994) used the words 'belief without belonging' to describe this situation, in which people hold religious beliefs without participating in religious organizations. They may simply be disillusioned with the traditional churches and be choosing to express their beliefs in more private ways, such as in their own homes, in 'house groups' or with services on TV and radio.

Not all denominations and faiths are declining As table 1.5 shows, there has actually been an increase in membership of other Christian groupings, such as the Mormons and the Jehovah's Witnesses, and of other religions, like Islam, Sikhism and Hinduism among the minority ethnic groups. New religious sects and cults, and New Age ideas, are constantly emerging, and more people are getting involved. These may be responding to a deep-seated spirituality that people find lacking in existing religious institutions and faiths.

Despite an overall decline in church attendance, many people continue to make use of religious ceremonies for the 'rites of passage' such as baptism, marriage and death. This suggests they still believe it is important for religion to 'bless' the important stages in their lives. About 90 per cent of funerals involve a religious ceremony.

Competing evidence on secularization 3: religious institutions

Arguments and evidence for the decline of religious institutions

Bruce points out that the church in the Middle Ages was the dominant social institution in Europe, with enormous wealth, power and influence. Church leaders exercised real power in terms of the secular areas of law-making, education, politics and social welfare. Religion therefore affected many aspects of people's lives and was a major influence on the way people viewed the world.

Compared to this, religious institutions today have become increasingly marginalized, as they are no longer directly involved in every important area of social life.

They therefore lose significance and influence, and most people can now live their lives completely untouched by religious institutions, and, by extension, the religious beliefs they seek to spread.

This declining power and significance of religious institutions is demonstrated by the following types of evidence:

1 Church buildings are closing and crumbling today, while in the much poorer society of the past elaborate and ornate cathedrals and churches were built, expensively decorated, well maintained and repaired, and even the poor donated generously to church funds.

2 The status of the clergy is steadily declining; they are poorly paid and hard to recruit.

3 In schools, religious education is more like personal development or social studies, and Sunday schools are on the verge of extinction.

4 Religious institutions are unable to command respect for even the major Christian festivals, like Christmas and Easter. These have little religious meaning to most people in British society and are for most people simply an excuse for a holiday, and/or an orgy of shopping, overeating and excessive drinking.

5 Religious institutions have, as Martin (1969) described it, 'disengaged' from society. This refers to the withdrawal of religious organizations from many areas of life in which they used to be involved. For example, the welfare state and other agencies and experts now provide free state education, social services, the NHS, welfare benefits, care homes for older people and so on, to care for the sick, the poor, the unemployed and other disadvantaged groups that were once a near-monopoly of the church. This reduces the significance of religion in people's lives.

6 There are increasing numbers of alternative sources of knowledge. The development of the mass media, particularly television and the Internet, and free education have now effectively eliminated the monopoly of knowledge once enjoyed by religious institutions. The mass media and the Internet have replaced religion as the main sources of authority and knowledge for many people, and these are likely to have far more influence on people's thinking than religion. The erosion of the influence of traditional religious institutions is accelerated by globalization. This has meant that people are now exposed to a vast array of new doctrines, books, knowledge and ways of thinking by the ever-growing globalized mass media and the Internet. This was confirmed by Halman and Draulans (2006), who found that the more globalized a society, measured in terms of IT facilities (e.g. Internet access), the less religious the people in that country were.

7 The church is no longer closely associated with the state and the machinery of government, with the possible exception of the 26 Bishops (the 'Lords Spiritual') in the House of Lords, and the fact that the Archbishop of Canterbury still crowns the monarch.

8 The church now has little influence over social policies. For example, civil partnerships (gay marriages) are now a legal form of partnership, but the major religions still tear themselves apart when it comes to issues like, for example, appointing a gay bishop.

9   Ceremonies marking the 'rites of passage', such as birth, marriage and death, which were once a church monopoly, can now not only be performed without a religious ceremony of any kind, but in almost any location, like a hotel or pub.

10 The ecumenical movement is a movement among different Christian denominations to achieve greater unity between them. Ecumenicalism is sometimes seen as a sign of the weakness of religious organizations. Once-powerful independent institutions, tossed about aimlessly in a sea of apathy and indifference, are now forced to clutch at the straw of ecumenicalism and compromise with other denominations to try to save themselves from drowning.

11 Institutional religion has become fragmented into a vast and diverse range of competing religions, beliefs and religious organizations, There is no longer one main church or body of shared religious belief around which people are united, but religious pluralism. This means that religion is no longer able (if it ever was) to provide a single 'universe of meaning' nor act as a 'social glue' binding people together, integrating them into society and building social solidarity and social cohesion. As Aldridge (2007) notes: 'The very fact of religious diversity introduces doubt: why should one particular faith be the truth and command our allegiance when there are so many others, each with its own truths, vying for acceptance?'. The fragmentation of beliefs and religious pluralism reduces the power of religious institutions, marginalizes their influence in society and, as a study by Halman and Draulans (2006) found, corrodes religious belief and practice among the population as a whole.

where will you
find him?

myspace.com/isthisjesus

Do you think the fact that religious institutions now promote themselves through advertising and sites like myspace.com is a strength or a weakness of contemporary religion?

Secularization from within: the secularization of religious institutions In order to survive in a secular society, religious institutions have been forced to move away from traditional doctrines and concern with the supernatural, and have compromised and watered down their beliefs and become less religious, and more like the secular society in which they're set. Herberg (1960) called this 'secularization from within'. Examples of this collapse of traditional doctrines and teachings include things like the acceptance of cohabitation as no longer 'living in sin', easier divorce laws, the abolition of Latin in Catholic services, the ordination of women priests and bishops, the growing – though still very controversial – acceptance of lesbians and gay men by the church, and the downplaying of doctrines concerning miracles and literal interpretations of heaven and hell.

Religious institutions are now so weak that they can no longer set trends, but have to follow them. This adaptation of religion to secularization has been the case for years in the USA, as Herberg found. There, membership and attendance of religious organizations is high, but mainly because traditional doctrines and the supernatural/spiritual aspects have been played down. Religious participation has become an almost secular part of the American way of life rather than involving any serious religious belief and commitment.

Religious institutions are becoming Disneyfied Disneyfication is described by Lyon (2000) 'as a process that diminishes human life through trivializing it, or making involvement within it appear less than fully serious'. Lyon argues that in postmodern societies, people want to establish their identities, including the beliefs they hold, by customizing their own personalized packages rather than those formed by social class, gender, ethnicity or beliefs handed down by religious institutions. In postmodern society, religion is forced to market and package itself in many different guises, in order to attract customers by appealing to a wide variety of consumer tastes, as it competes with a whole host of other consumer products and leisure activities. One way religion does this is by trivializing itself and placing an emphasis on fun and amusement, and merchandising (selling) itself like the fantasy-world of the Disneyland theme park. Lyon therefore suggests that religion has been 'Disneyfied', packaged as a commodity like washing powder or Mickey Mouse, for sale in the spiritual supermarket, in which all the other rival belief manufacturers jostle desperately to sell variations of the same product to a declining market.

Arguments and evidence against the decline of religious institutions

The institutional power of churches remains The Church of England (C of E) remains the established (or 'official') church in England, and the British monarch must be a member of the Church of England, is crowned by the Archbishop of Canterbury and, since the time of Henry VIII, has been head of the Church of England, and 'Defender of the Faith'. Church of England bishops continue to have seats in the House of Lords (the 'Lords Spiritual'), despite extensive reform of the House of Lords in the early 2000s. The C of E is extremely wealthy, with investment funds of £3.5 billion in 2002, and it is one of the largest landowners in the country. The Roman Catholic Church is the world's largest Christian denomination, and retains extensive powers and influence over the state in several European countries (for example, Ireland, Spain, Italy and Poland) and in many Latin American countries.

Religious institutions remain very influential in education in Britain Britain has very many C of E and Catholic faith schools, with a growing number being provided by other faiths. This power of religion in education is also shown by the legal requirement for schools to hold a religious act of worship, and religious education is a compulsory part of the National Curriculum.

The strengthening of religious institutions The Church (the main Christian churches, at least) has disengaged from secular society in many ways, but this might also strengthen the place of religion in people's lives. This is because it is now more focused on spiritual matters than at any time in the past, and avoids 'pollution' from involvement in non-religious affairs.

Religious institutions remain very important in the minority ethnic communities Mosques, temples, and synagogues are often a focus of social and cultural life as well as religious life, and are very important symbols of identity in minority ethnic communities. Minority ethnic group religious leaders are becoming increasingly influential, particularly in Muslim communities, and are often consulted by governments in relation to social policies relating to those communities.

Evaluating the secularization thesis

Most sociologists would agree, on the basis of the evidence presented above, that in the UK and much of Europe, traditional religious thinking and beliefs, practice and institutions are declining. However, the extent of this secularization, and whether religion is simply reorienting itself and appearing in new guises, requires weighing up and evaluating the competing evidence for and against secularization. To help your evaluation, it is worth considering the following five 'myths' in the secularization debate, which can, if ignored, lead to misleading conclusions:

(1) The myth of secularization as a universal phenomenon

There is plenty of evidence that the secularization process does not occur equally in all societies, that religion still continues to play a major role in the world, and in some cases is actually growing in strength and commitment.

1   *Religious fundamentalism is a significant force in the world today.* Bruce (2008) suggests that fundamentalism is a rational response of traditionally religious peoples to social, political and economic changes that threaten their religious values.
   - *Christian fundamentalism*, particularly in the United States (as mentioned earlier in this chapter), is politically active in the New Christian Right, and often wields substantial political influence. It has been instrumental in get-

ting the teaching of the theory of evolution banned in some schools, and actively campaigns very vigorously against, for example, abortion, sex before or outside marriage and homosexuality.

- *Islamic fundamentalism* is an important and growing force in the Muslim countries of the world, and among some members of Muslim minority ethnic groups in Western societies. As Bruce suggests, Islamic fundamentalism may be seen as a rational means of defending traditional Islamic beliefs and values threatened with elimination by the combined global influences of Western cultural imperialism, the Americanization of the world's culture and the dominance of Western corporations in the world economy. These bring with them Western values and culture, and Islamic fundamentalism emerges as a means of self-defence against this cultural imperialism.

2 *Religious belief and practice remain high in many Catholic countries of the world.* This is particularly true in countries such as Ireland, Spain, Italy, Portugal and Poland, in many South American countries, and in the Christian Orthodox countries, for example, Greece, Cyprus and Serbia.

3 *Among ethnic minorities in the UK*, as discussed earlier in this chapter, religion often remains strong, though whether this is for reasons of cultural identity and community solidarity rather than religious belief is open to discussion.

4 *Religion still dominates in a number of societies across the world.* For example, in Iran, the Islamic Revolution of 1979 brought political power to religious leaders, which continues today. In Iran, Saudi Arabia and some other Muslim countries, the law is rooted in religious doctrine, and special religious police are used to enforce conformity to it, such as in dress and behaviour. In such societies where religion is so deeply embedded in the culture and the state, it is practically impossible to remain unaffected by religion in everyday life.

(2) The myth of belief without belonging

Davie's claim that people still believe and just no longer belong to religious organizations is mistaken. Voas and Crockett (2005) found that in Britain and many other European countries both belonging *and* believing are falling, and at a similar rate. A majority of those who don't belong (or are 'unchurched', in Davie's words) either do not consider themselves as religious or have no belief in God at all.

(3) The myth of strength through disengagement

The suggestion that religious organizations are becoming stronger as they disengage from secular society (as former functions pass to the welfare state and so on), because they are purer and untouched by secular concerns and so can concentrate on religion, may or may not be true. What certainly is true is that if they are concentrating more on their religious message, there is absolutely no evidence that they are getting through to enough people to offset their loss of influence or people's participation.

(4) The myth of belief in a 'spirit or life force' as an indicator of religiosity

Bruce (2002a) suggests that although many people still claim to believe in a 'spirit or life force', this is an indicator of growing secularization, not of continuing religiosity. It simply represents a halfway house, in which people place themselves as they move away from religious belief, but can't yet bring themselves to admit that they are non-believers.

(5) The myth of resacrilization

The claim that resacrilization is occurring through the growth of new religious movements, religious sects and New Age spirituality is flimsy. The influence of such groups is marginal, and the number of people involved is tiny, particularly compared to the declining membership of, and participation in, mainstream religions. Wilson regards religious sects as the last outposts of religion in a secular society, showing that the only way religious belief can survive is by isolation from the secularizing influences of the wider society. New religious movements and New Age spirituality are of no significance in the lives of the vast majority of people, and almost irrelevant to society as a whole. Some of these activities are in many cases little more than a form of self-indulgent pseudo-religious titillation for society's dropouts, except perhaps when they provide exciting and sensationalized stories in the media. Many of the most popular new movements and activities are, in any case, of the world-affirming type, driven by secular rather than religious concerns, such as self-improvement so individuals can be more successful and get on in their careers.

Glendinning and Bruce (2006) pointed out that the research collected in the Kendal Project, often cited as evidence of a growing reorientation of religiosity and of a 'spiritual revolution', showed that fewer than one in fifty people in the area around Kendal were engaged in New Age activities in a typical week, and fewer than half of them saw these as spiritual activities. They suggest that this is hardly evidence of resacrilization or a 'spiritual revolution'.

Activity

1 Suggest two reasons why globalization might threaten traditional religious beliefs.
2 Identify and explain three reasons why religious ideas may be of declining importance to many people.
3 Identify and explain two reasons why the extent of secularization varies between societies.
4 Explain what is meant by 'religious pluralism', and suggest two reasons why religious pluralism might weaken the influence of religion in society.
5 Identify and explain two reasons why New Age mind-body spirituality:
   (a) might be used as evidence against the secularization thesis;
   (b) might be used as evidence to support the secularization thesis.
6 Write an essay answering the following question: *'Assess the view that Britain is becoming a more secular society.'*

CHAPTER SUMMARY

After studying this chapter you should be able to:

- explain what is meant by religion, ideology and science, and the differences between them;

- outline pluralist, Marxist and feminist accounts of ideology;

- explain different views of science and the scientific method, including the concepts of falsification and paradigms, and the various factors influencing the social construction of scientific knowledge;

- explain the concept of modernity, and examine the extent to which science has displaced religious belief;

- explain the difference between the inclusivist and exclusivist definitions of religion;

- explain and criticize different theoretical approaches to the role of religion in society, including the functionalist, Marxist, interpretivist and Weberian approaches;

- explain, with evidence, the various ways religion can act as a conservative force and as a force for social change;

- identify and explain the factors that influence how and whether or not religion will influence social change;

- explain, with examples, what is meant by the concepts of church, denomination, sect and cult, and the differences between them;

- explain the meanings of world-accommodating, world-affirming and world-rejecting groups, and the differences between them;

- explain the meanings of, and differences between, audience and client cults and cult movements;

- explain, with examples, what new religious movements and New Age groups are, who might support them and why;

- explain and criticize the view that sects are necessarily short-lived organizations;

- examine the evidence and explanations for why, in general, women are more religious than men;

- discuss the view that religious organizations are mainly patriarchal institutions;

- examine the links between minority ethnic groups and religion, and why religiosity appears to be higher in minority ethnic groups;

- examine the extent to which younger people are less religious than older people, and reasons for this;

- explain what is meant by secularization, the theoretical and methodological difficulties involved in defining and measuring it, and examine a range of arguments and evidence both for and against the view that it is occurring, both in the UK and globally;

- explain how postmodernists see religion in contemporary societies, and what is meant by 'pick-'n'-mix' spirituality, the 'spiritual supermarket' and Disneyfication.

KEY TERMS

alienation
anomie
beliefs
collective conscience
conservative force
cultural imperialism
desacrilization
disenchantment
dominant ideology
empirical evidence
ethnic identity
ethnicity

functional prerequisite
fundamentalism
globalization
hegemony
ideal type
ideological state
  apparatus
ideology
Islamophobia
metanarrative
millenarianism
minority ethnic group

modernity
objectivity
paradigm
patriarchal ideology
pluralism
pluralist ideology
relative deprivation
religiosity
religious pluralism
resacrilization
secularization
social solidarity

status frustration
stigmatized identity
theodicy
theodicy of disprivilege
totem
typology
universe of meaning
value consensus
value-freedom

EXAM QUESTIONS

SECTION A: BELIEFS IN SOCIETY

If you choose this Section, answer Question 1 and **either** Question 2 **or** Question 3.

Time allowed: 1 hour 30 minutes   **Total for this section: 60 marks**

1 Read **Item A** below and answer parts (a) and (b) that follow.

Item A

Secularization refers to the declining influence of religious thinking, practice and institutions compared to some 'Golden Age of Faith' in the past when religion had major influences on people's lives. Postmodernists see secularization as part of the general collapse of metanarratives in contemporary postmodern societies. Metanarratives are general theories or belief systems, like religion, ideology and science, that claim to provide comprehensive   5
explanations and knowledge of the world, and superior status over other belief systems. In postmodern society, there is a growing diversity and fragmentation of beliefs and lifestyles, and the metanarrative of religion has collapsed in contemporary British society. Increasingly, people believe in whatever they personally choose to believe in, which is not necessarily what religious institutions would like them to believe.   10

Personalized beliefs have replaced the metanarrative of religion, with secularization relegating religion to the margins of contemporary society. However, despite postmodernist views, many people still regard religion as an important part of their lives.

(a) (i) Identify and briefly explain **two** examples of sociological evidence that might support the view that the 'the metanarrative of religion has collapsed in contemporary British society'. (**Item A**, line 8)   *(6 marks)*

   (ii) Identify and briefly explain **one** way in which religious beliefs differ from scientific beliefs.
                                                                              (3 marks)

(b) Using material from **Item A** and elsewhere, examine the view that religion appears to be of declining significance in people's lives in contemporary Britain.   *(18 marks)*

EITHER

2 Assess the view that religion in most societies contributes more to the creation of social conflicts and divisions than it does to the promotion of harmony and consensus.   *(33 marks)*

OR

3 'Religion can act as both a conservative force and as a force for social change.' To what extent do sociological arguments and evidence support this view of religion in the contemporary world?

                                                                              (33 marks)

Global Development

JONATHAN BLUNDELL

Contents

CHAPTER 2 Global Development

Development: the process by which societies change; a controversial term, with different writers having different conceptions of what processes are involved and what the outcome should be.

The topic of global **development** is about global divisions between the rich and privileged on the one hand and the poor and underprivileged on the other, and about the attempts to eliminate those divisions. The world today is more unequal than ever before.

Activity

To begin to get an understanding of life in poorer countries, try one or all of these:
1 Visit www.guardian.co.uk/katine
   The *Guardian* newspaper is working with an African NGO, AMREF, to see what progress can be made in improving the lives of people in an area of Uganda. You will find a wide range of reports that give you an overview of life in Katine.

2   Visit www.savethechildren.org.uk/kroobay
    Here you can watch 'webisodes' and see the lives of people in a slum area of
    Freetown, Sierra Leone.
3   Visit www.worldmapper.org
    Hundreds of maps of the world, covering many issues and providing you with
    new ways of seeing the world.

Defining and measuring development

What is meant by development?

Development is the most important concept in this area of sociology. The term is used in several different but related ways, which can be summed up as 'good change'. It is the first and third senses – as given in figure 2.1 – of development as an ideal state to be achieved by human effort, which are the most common meanings adopted in this book (Thomas 2000).

What is meant by 'good change'?

First, economic development – or **economic growth** – means that an economy gets bigger, producing more goods or goods of higher value. Economic development involves a change from an economy based on subsistence agriculture and small workshops to factory-based mass production of goods, mass consumption and service industries such as finance and banking. Economic growth means a rise in living standards and less poverty, but not everyone will benefit equally, and some may lose out.

Economic growth: the growth of national income, usually measured by Gross National Product.

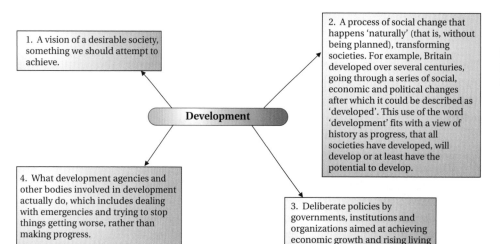

Figure 2.1 The meaning of development

1. A vision of a desirable society, something we should attempt to achieve.

2. A process of social change that happens 'naturally' (that is, without being planned), transforming societies. For example, Britain developed over several centuries, going through a series of social, economic and political changes after which it could be described as 'developed'. This use of the word 'development' fits with a view of history as progress, that all societies have developed, will develop or at least have the potential to develop.

Development

4. What development agencies and other bodies involved in development actually do, which includes dealing with emergencies and trying to stop things getting worse, rather than making progress.

3. Deliberate policies by governments, institutions and organizations aimed at achieving economic growth and rising living standards.

Second, social development covers a range of aspects of social life, including:

- education;
- health;
- democracy;
- human rights;
- gender equality;
- happiness and well-being;
- **sustainability**.

Finally, combining both economic and social aspects is the idea of development as the reduction or eradication of poverty.

Measuring development: how do we know when countries are developing?

Economic well-being

Sustainability means that something can continue at the same level indefinitely; for example, using trees from a forest for fuel is sustainable only if the wood is taken at the rate that the trees grow, so that the number of trees in the forest remains constant.

Gross Domestic Product (GDP) is the total value of goods and services produced by a country in a particular year.

The economic well-being of a society is usually measured either by **Gross Domestic Product** (GDP) or by Gross National Product (GNP). Both measure the total value of goods and services produced in an economy in a year, but the latter also includes net income from abroad and is seen as the more useful. GDP is usually given as a 'per capita' (per person in the population) figure to allow for differences in size of populations between countries, and is given in US dollars. GDP figures reveal the dramatic scale of inequality between the developed and developing worlds.

Changes in GDP from year to year give a measure of economic growth. At the moment, some economies in the developing world, such as China and India, are experiencing rapid growth, faster than developed countries both now and in the past. At the same time, some economies, notably in Africa, have suffered a fall in GDP, from already low levels, over recent years. In 2008, most economies were entering a period of low growth or even recesson.

Sociologists use GDP with caution, and in combination with other measures, for a number of reasons:

1 Economic growth does not cover all the aspects of social development which sociologists are interested in; a rise in GDP per capita does not necessarily mean that education, health and so on are improving.
2 GDP per capita is an average for the whole population, and so conceals inequalities. A high GDP does not necessarily mean a high standard of living for all members of the population. This applies even to developed countries, where a high GDP per capita can conceal significant minorities living in poverty.
3 GDP only counts what happens in the 'official' economy; some important activities are outside the market and are not counted, such as growing food for one's own consumption. These are likely to be more important in developing countries than in developed countries; moreover, they are often activities carried out by women, so that GDP can be seen as a gender-biased measure (Storey 2003, p. 30).

4 Continuous economic growth cannot mean **sustainable development**. A rise in GDP can also be accompanied by problems such as rising crime rates and the loss of community as well as environmental degradation.

Social development

Some commonly used measures include:

1 Education: the percentage of school-age children attending school; and literacy (the proportion of the population who can read and write).
2 Health: child and infant mortality rates; mortality rates in general; maternal mortality rates; the number of doctors and hospitals in relation to population.
3 Democracy: whether there are free and fair elections, in which everyone can vote; whether opposition parties are allowed to organize.
4 Gender equality: differences between males and females in education, health, politics and other measures.

Several measures of development combine different measures of development to create a score for each country. Countries can then be put in rank order, and changes over time can be measured.

The Human Development Index

The most important of these measures is the **Human Development Index** (HDI), produced by the United Nations Development Programme (UNDP). Each country is given an HDI score which is calculated by considering what the UNDP takes to be the three most important aspects of development, covering both economic and social aspects:

1 Material standard of living (measured by GDP per capita).
2 Education (measured by the proportion of the population of relevant age who are in education, and by levels of literacy).
3 Health (measured by life expectancy).

Each country's score is between 0 and 1, with 1 being the highest. Countries can then be ranked in order of HDI score. The 2007/8 Human Development Report, based on statistics for 2005, showed Iceland at the top, with an HDI index of 0.968. The lowest ranking country of the 177 listed was Sierra Leone on 0.336. The HDI also classifies countries as having high, medium or low human development. In 2007/8, 70 countries were classified as having high human development and 22 as having low human development, with the remaining 85 having medium human development. All the countries with low human development were in Africa.

In many developing countries, there are doubts about the accuracy of some of the statistics used because of the difficulties in collecting data; figures are not always available for all countries. It can also be argued that not all important aspects of development can be measured quantitatively. The three measures of development seem rather arbitrary (there are other ways of measuring health and education) and they are equally weighted. Nevertheless, HDI is useful in giving a broad impression of development and of the links between the economy and social well-being.

Sustainable development is development which sustains the natural environment, thereby ensuring that **future generations** can have the same level of development.

The term **'future generations'** means that the concept of sustainable development requires consideration of the future of today's children, and also of people not yet born, even though there is no established way of representing their interests.

The **Human Development Index** is a composite measure of social and economic indicators, giving a statistical value to the level of development.

Table 2.1: Highest and lowest ranking countries, by HDI and by GDP, 2007/8

Highest ranking countries by HDI, 2007/8	Highest ranking countries by GDP, 2007/8
1 Iceland	1 Luxembourg ($60,228)
2 Norway	2 USA ($41,890)
3 Australia	3 Norway ($41,420)
4 Canada	4 Ireland ($38,505)
5 Ireland	5 Iceland ($36,510)
6 Sweden	6 Switzerland ($35,633)
7 Switzerland	7 Hong Kong ($34,833)
8 Japan	8 Denmark ($33,973)
9 Netherlands	9 Austria ($33,700)
10 France	10 Canada ($33,375)
...	11 UK ($33,238)
12 USA	
...	
16 UK	

Lowest ranking countries by HDI, 2007/8	Lowest ranking countries by GDP, 2007/8
168 Congo	165 Zambia ($1023)
169 Ethiopia	166 Yemen ($930)
170 Chad	167 Madagascar ($923)
171 Central African Republic	168 Guinea-Bissau ($827)
172 Mozambique	169 Sierra Leone ($806)
173 Mali	170 Niger ($781)
174 Niger	171 Tanzania ($744)
175 Guinea-Bissau	172 Congo ($714)
176 Burkina Faso	173 Burundi ($699)
177 Sierra Leone	174 Malawi ($667)

In addition, the reports in which the HDIs are published have broadened the scope of development by covering, for example, human rights and political freedoms and sustainability.

Although GDP is included in the calculation of the HDI, it is instructive to compare the two scorings. Countries that are much higher in the HDI table than they are in the GDP table are those where the wealth created is being used for social development. Examples include Cuba, Armenia, Ecuador, Madagascar and Myanmar (Burma). On the other hand, where countries are lower in the HDI table this suggests that the wealth is not being used for social development. Examples include Iran, Saudi Arabia, South Africa and Equatorial Guinea.

The Human Development Report includes three other indices of development:

1 The Human Poverty Index (HPI), which is considered below.
2 The Gender-Related Development Index (GDI), which is essentially the HDI adjusted for inequality between males and females. The greater the gender disparity on the measures included in the HDI, the more the GDI score falls. The GDI is not directly a measure of gender equality, but comparing it with the HDI can show the extent of gender equality.
3 The Gender Empowerment Measure (GEM), which measures the extent to which men and women are equally represented in political and economic decision-making.

Alternative indicators

These represent attempts to broaden what is meant by development to include factors seen to be important but which are difficult to quantify.

Gross National Happiness

In 1972 the King of Bhutan, in response to criticisms of his country's slow economic growth, proposed a plan for development that rejected the pursuit of economic growth as a good in itself and reflected Bhutan's Buddhist values. Gross National Happiness also takes into account spiritual and psychological aspects of development.

The International Institute of Management is attempting a global Gross National Happiness Survey. See: www.iim-edu.org/polls/grossnationalhappinesssurvey.htm

Measuring poverty

The poverty of whole countries can be measured by GDP, but for individuals and households a different measure is needed, because GDP can only give an average. As a criterion for measuring success in achieving the Millennium Development Goal of halving the proportion of people living in extreme poverty by 2015, the World Bank uses income of less than one American dollar a day (increased to $1.25 in 2008), adjusted for purchasing power. On this definition, in 2004, there were 980 million people, almost one in six, living in extreme poverty.

Millennium Development Goals are a set of eight targets created by the United Nations to achieve progress in development.

Having less than a dollar a day to live on is a measure of *absolute* poverty; another way of conceptualizing poverty is by defining it in relation to others – this is called *relative* poverty. For example, poverty might be defined as living on half the mean income in society, or being excluded from full participation in society. The poverty line is set at a higher level for developed countries because it is necessary to have a minimum level of consumer items to take part in what is accepted as normal everyday life.

The Human Development Report measures poverty at the individual level in the Human Poverty Index (HPI). This considers a wider range of factors than simply low income. There are two sets of measures: one for developing countries and another for developed countries. For developing countries, HPI considers the percentage of the population living below the poverty line, the adult illiteracy rate, the probability at birth of not surviving to the age of 40, the percentage of children under 5 who are underweight and the percentage of the population who do not have access to clean water.

> **Millennium Development Goals** are a set of eight targets created by the United Nations to achieve progress in development.

The Millennium Development Goals

Development is also currently being measured by progress towards the Millennium Development Goals (MDGs). These were set by the United Nations as targets for the

> Having less than one dollar a day to live on has very different consequences in different parts of the world, e.g. an industrial city in the UK compared to a slum in South Africa. What sorts of issue need to be considered when measuring relative poverty?

world to achieve; they can be seen as representing agreement by the world's nations on how development can be defined in specific terms. The goals are:

MDG1   To eradicate extreme poverty and hunger; by 2015, to halve the proportion of the world's population living in extreme poverty and hunger

MDG2   To achieve universal primary education

MDG3   To promote gender equality and to empower women

MDG4   To reduce child mortality

MDG5   To improve maternal health

MDG6   To combat HIV/AIDS, malaria and other diseases

MDG7   To ensure environmental sustainability

MDG8   To develop a global partnership for development

These goals, and progress towards them, are considered later in the chapter. Progress has not been as fast as hoped, even though the goals are arguably not that ambitious; Naidoo (2008) calls them, 'Minimalist Development Goals'. For example, the first goal – to reduce extreme poverty and hunger by half – leaves the other half in poverty. Nevertheless, achieving these goals would mean progress towards development far greater than that achieved so far.

MDG1

To eradicate extreme poverty and hunger; by 2015, to halve the proportion of the world's population living in extreme poverty
Between 1990 and 2004, the proportion of the population in developing countries living on less than a dollar a day fell from 31.6 per cent to 19.2 per cent. At this rate, the goal will be achieved, but much of the progress has been in East Asia; Africa and West Asia are making less progress. At the same time, however, in equalities are widening both between and within countries. The poorest quintile (20 per cent) of the population of developing countries actually gets a lower share of national consumption than they did in 1990.

Terminology

There is no agreement about the right terms to use to describe the ways in which the world is divided. Always choose the terms you use carefully for your purpose, and note that the terms used by different writers may indicate assumptions and judgements. In this chapter we have used a variety of terms depending on the context.

Three worlds

Dating back to the period of the Cold War (1948–89), one of the conventional ways of describing differences between groups of countries has been to divide the world into three:

1 First World: the **industrialized** capitalist world – the USA, Western Europe, Japan, Australia, New Zealand
2 Second World: the industrialized communist world – the Soviet Union and its Eastern European satellites (Poland, Bulgaria, Czechoslovakia, Hungary, etc.).
3 Third World: the rest of the world – Central and South America and the Caribbean, Africa, Asia and the Middle East.

Industrialized countries are those whose economies are based on industry rather than on agriculture or extraction.

The terms First and Second World were (and still are) much less used than Third World. The **Third World** covered a vast range of countries in different circumstances and at different stages of development. The idea of a distinct group made sense because many countries saw themselves as having a shared interest against the superpowers, and joined together in a non-aligned movement (that is, not aligned to either the USA or the Soviet Union). Many of these countries actively sought a 'third way' between **capitalism** and communism. In addition, almost all shared the experience of having recently been colonies of European powers.

The **Third World** is a term used to describe the world's poorer countries, distinct from the First World (developed capitalist countries) and Second World (developed communist, or, today, ex-communist countries).

After the collapse of the Soviet Union in the late 1980s there was no Second World, and the term Third World became used less. Around the same time, it became obvious that some Third World countries were developing and others were not; differences within the Third World became more distinct, and it no longer seemed sensible to treat it as a single group. The non-aligned movement also became less important; the Third World acted even less as a unified group.

Capitalism is an economic system in which investment in and ownership of the means of production, distribution and exchange of wealth is made and maintained chiefly by private individuals or corporations, whose primary aim is to make profits.

North and South (and West)

The developed, industrialized countries are mainly in the northern hemisphere and the poorer, undeveloped countries in the tropics or further south. From the 1970s on, the former became referred to as the **North** and the latter as the **South**. The distinction was used by the Brandt Commission, which recommended strategies to reduce world poverty in 1980 (Brandt 1980).

This is a geographical way of distinguishing between countries that involves two groupings rather than three. The term 'West' is also often used as a shorthand way of meaning the most industrialized and wealthiest countries. The main problem with this approach is that not all countries fit neatly into the geographical pattern. For example, Australia and New Zealand are geographically in the south but in terms of development, they belong in the category of North.

The **North** refers to the world's richer countries, those that are developed; sometimes, the 'Global North'.

Majority and minority worlds

These two terms are a more recent attempt to describe more accurately the state of the world, but their use has not become widespread. 'Majority' refers to the Third World and to the fact that two-thirds or more of the world's population live there; 'minority' refers to the rich world, drawing attention to the fact that the living standards of the rich world are available only to a privileged minority of the world's population.

The **South** refers to the world's poorer countries, those that are developing; sometimes, the 'Global South'.

Developed, undeveloped and underdeveloped countries

The difference between 'undeveloped' and 'underdeveloped' is one of perspective. 'Undeveloped' suggests that the poor world is simply further behind and can catch up; it has not yet experienced progress. 'Underdeveloped' suggests that the poor world has been made poor through exploitation by what has become the rich world. The significance of these terms will be explained in the later section on modernization and dependency theories.

MEDCs, LEDCs, LLEDCs

More economically developed countries (MEDCs), less economically developed countries (LEDCs) and least economically developed countries (LLEDCs) are terms used to refer to economic development, with social development being assumed to go with this. Although these terms demonstrate the hierarchical nature of the world today, they inevitably put into the same category countries that are actually very different.

The bottom billion

The economist Paul Collier (2007) has used the term the '**bottom billion**' as a way of acknowledging that many parts of what were once described as the Third World have achieved some degree of development. The remaining problem, Collier argues, is the lack of development in most of Africa and in a fairly small number of other countries (including Haiti, Bolivia, the central Asian countries, Laos, Cambodia, Yemen, Burma and North Korea), which are affected by war and other factors. Collier refers to these 58 countries together as 'Africa plus'. They account for about a sixth of the world's six billion people, though most of the countries are small and, even combined, they have fewer people than either China or India. Collier argues that in India, China and other countries that are achieving some level of development, economic growth will eventually bring progress on social indicators, so the world needs to concentrate its efforts on the countries of the bottom billion, where economic growth is non-existent or too small to make a difference. The Millennium Development Goals, in Collier's view, are misguided, because they measure the progress of five billion people; the focus needs to be on the bottom billion only.

The **bottom billion** is Collier's term for the poorest billion of the world's population – also described as 'Africa plus'.

All the terms discussed above are about differences between countries. However, most countries are in some ways both developed and underdeveloped. There are extremes of rich and poor within as well as between countries. There are people in poor countries who are incredibly wealthy by any standards, while most rich countries have substantial numbers living in poverty. Within all countries there are also structured inequalities of gender and ethnicity.

Theories of development

Modernization theory

The dominant theory of development over the past 50 years has been **modernization theory**; it is related to and overlaps with the broader sociological perspective, functionalism.

Modernization theory arose in the early 1960s, during the Cold War period. It assumed that development means capitalist development and offered the newly independent nations of the Third World a route out of poverty provided they adopted Western, capitalist ways. After the Second World War, in 1947, the USA launched the Marshall Plan to rebuild the shattered economies of Western European countries, including the UK, France, West Germany and Italy, at a cost of $17 billion. The success of the Marshall Plan, which also ensured that the European economies provided markets for the USA's growing manufacturing industries, was seen as a precedent for the Third World. The generosity of the USA and its allies, providing technological and other assistance, would lift the rest of the world out of poverty.

Modernization theory is closely associated with American policies, and its best-known exponent, W. W. Rostow, worked in the US State Department. The theory sets out to explain how, following the example of Western nations, poorer countries could achieve development through economic growth, and also how communism could not be the way to achieve development. The theory needs to be seen in the context of the Cold War, with the USA offering reasons to newly independent countries as to why they should ally themselves with the West and not with the Soviet Union. Rostow subtitled his most popular work 'a non-communist manifesto' and described

Many developing countries model themselves on developed nations with the aim of 'modernization' – such as Shanghai in China following the precedent of New York's skyscrapers.

communism as 'a kind of disease which can befall a transitional society if it fails to organize effectively those elements within it which are prepared to get on with the job of modernization' (1960, p. 164)

Modernization theory is essentially an ethnocentric approach; it argues that the only route to development is to follow the example of the USA, and success is measured by whether the economy is based on mass consumption, as in the USA. The USA and other developed countries are seen as having reached the destination of being modern; the rest of the world is behind, needing to follow the same road in order eventually to catch up – following in the footsteps of the West.

From traditional to modern

For modernization theorists, the process of development meant 'total change': poorer countries had to move from being traditional to being modern. The changes needed included:

1 Technology – from simple and traditional technology to applying scientific knowledge and using more advanced technology.
2 Agriculture – from subsistence farming to commercial production.
3 Industry – from using human/animal power to machines.
4 Geographical – from farm and village to town and city – urbanization.
5 Political – from hereditary chiefs and kings to liberal democracy.
6 Social and cultural – from extended kin groups to nuclear families, from traditional to modern values and attitudes, such as from instant to deferred gratification, and becoming entrepreneurial.

The dichotomy between traditional and modern can also be found in the work of the structural functionalist sociologist Talcott Parsons. For Parsons, the most significant differences between traditional and modern societies were that the former were collective and based on ascribed status, whereas modern societies were individualized and based on achieved status. Parsons argued that societies passed through evolutionary stages, marked by 'evolutionary universals' such as the decline of traditional kinship patterns like the extended family and the emergence of a system of stratification. The dichotomy between traditional and modern is questionable, because some of the supposed characteristics of traditional societies survive even in the most developed societies, and some supposed characteristics of modern societies can be found in less developed societies.

What prevents development?

According to modernization theorists, obstacles to development are internal to the poorer countries, and include:

- having traditional values and attitudes;
- a lack of the necessary modern values and attitudes, especially deferred gratification and what McClelland (1961) referred to as the '**need for achievement**', so that, for example, people would be unwilling to work for longer than necessary or to move to where there were jobs;

Need for achievement refers, in modernization theory, to the desire to be entrepreneurial and to make money, essential for modernization.

- high birth rates and rapid population growth – because of traditional values, people want to have too many children;
- a shortage of people with entrepreneurial skills and a desire to compete and succeed in business;
- a lack of the necessary institutions and organizations for economic growth, such as banks, and lacking capital;
- a lack of the necessary technology.

Differences within modernization theory

Emphasis on economic modernization Rostow (1960) argued that societies need to pass through five **stages of economic growth** (see table 2.2). He suggests that there is a period of about 60 years from take-off to maturity. It was therefore possible to foresee the whole world having achieved American standards by the mid twenty-first century.

Rostow saw the role of the USA as providing assistance to poorer countries, supplying them with some of what they needed in order to modernize – capital, expertise and technology such as tractors – putting them on a 'fast track' to modernization. Generating economic growth would mean people being paid higher wages and the income generated would eventually 'trickle down' to the whole population. Most importantly, the good will towards the USA that this would create would ensure that the countries helped in this way would become American allies in the Cold War.

The **Stages of economic growth** refer, in Rostow's version of modernization, to the five stages through which societies pass as they move from being traditional to fully developed.

Subsistence farming is a system whereby crops and livestock are produced for consumption by the family rather than for sale in the market.

Take-off, in Rostow's five stages of economic growth, is the third stage at which societies achieve a momentum that ensures development.

Table 2.2: Rostow's five stages of development

Stage 1	Traditional societies based on **subsistence farming**. There is limited wealth, and traditional values hold back social change.
Stage 2	Preconditions for **take-off**. Western values and practices begin to take hold, establishing the conditions that are necessary for development. There may be new technologies to modernize agriculture, improvements in infrastructure such as roads and bridges, more education, and money to invest in business. These provide the fuel for 'take-off' in stage 3.
Stage 3	Take-off. The society's economy grows as modern values and practices pay off; the changes become self-reinforcing. A new class emerges which is willing to take risks in investing in business – a sign of traditional values being eroded. The society begins to produce on a large scale, including for export, and the newly created wealth begins to reach the mass of the population.
Stage 4	Drive to maturity. The economic benefits produced in stage 3 continue and investment in education, health services and mass media lead to rising living standards. The society is now becoming modern.
Stage 5	Age of high mass consumption. The society achieves the kind of levels the USA had reached by the 1960s: high mass consumption, high standards of living for most with access to education and health, most people living in cities and so on.

Emphasis on social obstacles Functionalists such as Hoselitz (1952) applied the functionalist model of change to the Third World and argued that developing countries needed to modernize socially and culturally as well as economically. Obstacles to modernization included social systems that impeded social mobility and getting people to accept new patterns of work. They saw the main assets of modern society as being educational opportunity, individual freedom and the rule of law. Other methods suggested for achieving the transition to modern values and attitudes included:

- cities could act as centres of Western values and spread them to rural areas;
- education – not only Western-style schools in the Third World, but also bringing the future rulers of developing countries to schools and universities in the USA and Western Europe so that they would absorb Western values;
- mass media – radio in particular could be used to spread Western ideas.

Modernization theory today

Like functionalism in sociology more generally, modernization theory tends to be dismissed as no longer being of great relevance. Yet, like functionalism, it has laid foundations that prove durable, for example:

1 Communism proved not to be a way to achieve development; China's economic growth under a Communist government has been achieved through capitalism. Western standards of economic growth and of consumption remain the aspiration of many in developing countries.
2 The rich countries continue to use development aid to try to help poorer countries develop.
3 Rostow saw India and China as being at the stage of take-off in the late 1950s; his estimate of 60 years to maturity seems prescient given recent growth rates in those countries.

Dependency theory

Dependency theory developed in the 1970s as a response to modernization theory. In many respects, it is the opposite of modernization theory, although they agree on the importance of economic growth and of state-led industrialization. Like modernization theory, dependency theory originated in the Cold War period. Alternative and revolutionary movements were strong in many parts of the Third World as well as in the West. Dependency theory developed at a time when Marxist and radical theories were strong, and at a time when protest movements, such as that against the war in Vietnam and those for greater rights for women and for minorities, were widespread.

Where modernization theory comes clearly from the developed world, dependency theory takes the perspective of developing countries; it can be seen as 'a view from the South'. Much of it is based on analysis of Latin American economies, such as the work of the best-known dependency theorist, André Gunder Frank (1969). For Frank, development and **underdevelopment** are two sides of the same coin; the underdevelopment of the Third World made possible the development of the West.

Dependency theory is an alternative Marxist-influenced theory to modernization, focused on external factors which impede development, including relationships with developed countries.

Underdevelopment is a term used by dependency theorists to describe the process of exploitation by which the North became and stayed rich at the expense of the South.

Similar conclusions were reached by writers studying other parts of the world – for example, Samir Amin's study of Cote d'Ivoire in West Africa (1976). The title of Walter Rodney's book, *How Europe Underdeveloped Africa* (1972), sums up the dependency approach.

Frank died in 2005 but his website is still accessible: www.rrojasdatabank.info/agfrank.

What prevents development?

Unlike modernization theory, dependency theory sees the obstacles to development as imposed from outside rather then being internal. Third World countries have been forced into a position of dependency on the developed world. The end of **colonialism** did not end exploitation, only bringing in **neo-colonialism**, whereby the exploitation continues but is less direct and obvious. Political independence is not enough to allow poor countries to escape from their dependency. The problem is the world capitalist system, and in order to develop, Third World countries need to break away from this system. Relationships with richer countries are the problem, not the solution; where modernization theorists see a helping hand being offered to the less fortunate, dependency theorists see neo-colonialism and exploitation.

Colonialism is a system in which European powers had direct political control over most of today's developing countries.

Neo-colonialism refers to the continuation of past economic domination of former colonial powers over ex-colonies.

The nature of dependency theory

1 It rejects modernization theory – the problems are not internal to Third World countries, but imposed upon them from outside.
2 It is anti-capitalist – capitalism has spread all over the world, but is a system based on exploitation.
3 The situation today is seen as a direct result of the history of capitalism, world trade and colonialism. This contrasts with modernization theory, which tends to assume that the historical experience of Third World countries is unimportant.
4 The developed capitalist countries benefit by cheap access to raw materials and markets for manufactured goods.
5 Dependency theory led to an emphasis in Third World countries on nationalism, national unity and self-reliance, rather than a reliance on aid.

Metropolis refers, in dependency theory, to the centre of economic activity, profiting from an exploitative relationship with satellites.

How is underdevelopment seen by dependency theorists?

The developed countries have made the poorer countries poor, and it is in their interests to keep them poor – by, in Ha Joon Chang's metaphor, 'kicking the ladder away' (Chang 2003). This happens through a chain of relationships between the **metropolis** or core nations in the rich world and the **satellite** or periphery countries of the Third World. This is called the 'chain of dependency'. The development of the metropolis causes the underdevelopment of the satellite. The metropolis 'buys off' the elites of poorer countries by allowing them a small share of the profits. This ensures that most poor countries are ruled by groups that are involved in exploiting their own people and whose interests involve preventing changes which would benefit the majority of the people. These groups are exactly those that modernization theorists would expect to lead their country's development.

Satellite refers, in dependency theory, to the deformed and dependent economies of the underdeveloped countries.

How did we reach this situation?

Dependency theorists see history as essential to understanding the situation we are in today. They point out that the rich countries were never underdeveloped in the sense of being dominated and exploited; they are better described as having been undeveloped (Frank 1966). The historical experiences of developing countries mean that they are in a very different situation, and cannot follow in the footsteps of the West as suggested by modernization theorists. Moreover, the spread of capitalism will lead to greater underdevelopment, not development.

According to dependency theorists, non-Western societies were often wealthy and economically complex when they first came into contact with the West. They cite, for example, the civilizations of the Aztec and the Inca in the Americas before the arrival of Europeans, and the complexity of Chinese and Indian civilizations. At this time, before about 500 years ago, it was not certain that the European powers would come to dominate the world. What has happened since can be traced through three broad historical periods, which can be seen as stages of dependency and underdevelopment.

Stage 1: Mercantile capitalism   In the fifteenth and sixteenth centuries, merchants in Europe travelled to many parts of the world in search of goods which would command high prices in Europe, such as spices, cloths and jewels. Production in Europe of goods that could be traded increased as well. The merchants were often able to impose favourable terms of trade, threatening or using force, and sometimes what happened was plunder and looting rather than trade. This period also saw the beginning of the **triangular trade** (see figure 2.2 on page 111). Stable and complex societies that were as economically and socially advanced as the Europeans were damaged and sometimes destroyed by contact with the Europeans. Many suffered huge declines in population through war and disease.

> **Triangular trade** refers to the slave trade linking West Africa, Europe and the Americas.

Stage 2: Colonialism   During this period, which occurred at different times in different parts of the world, the European powers, and particularly Britain and France, took direct political control of lands around the world rather than simply trading with them. The colonies were exploited for cheap food, resources and labour; local industries were destroyed to ensure they could not compete, social divisions were encouraged and arbitrary borders imposed. The cash economy was introduced, and people were forced into paid work by the need to pay taxes in cash. Subsistence farming and the cultivation of crops for sale locally were replaced by **cash crops** for export to the colonial power. British people, for example, benefited from tea from India and sugar from the West Indies. These changes led to a lasting legacy of inequality and of economic changes that benefited the colonial powers.

> **Cash crops** are crops grown for sale in the market, and especially for export; colonialism imposed cash crop cultivation as the main form of agriculture in many colonies.

Stage 3: Neo-colonialism   The period of colonialism came to an end for most colonies in the mid-twentieth century, when the European powers had been weakened by the world. People in the colonies had been influenced by Western ideas about freedom, democracy and independence and demanded the right to rule themselves. In some cases, long and bloody wars were fought, as in Malaysia and Algeria, and the colonial powers gradually relinquished their rule. However, according to dependency theorists,

Figure 2.2 The triangular trade

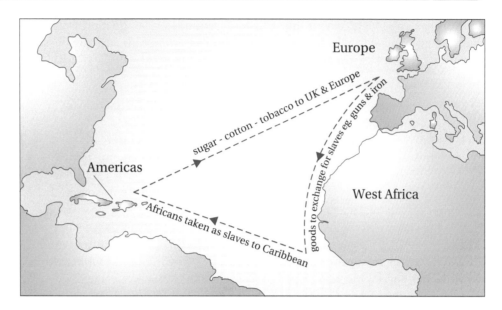

although they gave up direct political control, they did not give up their economic control and the economic dependency of the ex-colonies continued. In other words, the ex-colonies continued to be underdeveloped and remained in a state of dependency.

The legacy of colonialism

Dependency theorists argue that the history of developing countries puts them in a fundamentally different situation from that of developed countries before their development. The following aspects of colonialism have provided a legacy that still has consequences today (Potter 2000a):

1   Policies decided by the government of the colonial power and shaped by the interests of outsiders: this leaves a legacy of vulnerability to outside forces, such as changes in commodity prices.
2   Authoritarian and bureaucratic rule: no experience of participation and democracy.
3   Colonial powers used force, including civilian police, to suppress political opposition, establishing a tradition that some governments today find very useful.
4   The state was involved much more in economic life than in the colonial powers themselves; few countries developed a capitalist class of their own or significant numbers of entrepreneurs. Independence then involved starting from a very low base in industrial and business experience and skills.
5   Colonial rule involved persuading the ruled that the colonial power was both benevolent and invincible, and that colonialism was in their interests. This powerful ideology has to be challenged and replaced.

How can underdeveloped countries develop?

For dependency theorists, underdevelopment appears permanent; the only way out of dependency is for an underdeveloped nation to escape from the capitalist system and the 'master–servant' relationship with poorer countries, taking action itself rather than relying on outside help, though it might be able to work with others in the same situation. Action taken would involve:

1 Development needs to be led by the state itself, because the national or compra-dor bourgeoisie are tied to the interests of the First World, and it would involve keeping out foreign capital.
2 Isolation – e.g. China until the 1980s, North Korea even today and Cambodia under the Khmer Rouge from 1975 to 1979. This involves an attempt to be self-reliant and to have little contact with the rest of the world. This is very difficult, because countries attempting this are poor to start with, their only source of money for capital being their own population's savings.
3 Breaking away at a time when the metropolitan power is weak, such as during war or recession. South American countries were able to do this when the European colo-nial powers such as Spain were weakened by war in the early nineteenth century.
4 'Associate development' or 'dependent development'. Some later dependency theorists suggested that limited development is possible even when remaining locked in the capitalist system. For example, industries developed in Brazil and Argentina. This development remains limited, however.

Dependency theory today

Dependency theory never provided much direct guidance to Third World countries on how to develop, having a pessimistic message that any development would be lim-ited. Even communist countries today, such as Cuba and North Korea, see a role for the market and are not attempting a completely non-capitalist route to development. Today, the theory is seen more as an analysis of some of the obstacles to development rather than as a guide to action; as such, dependency theory has some value.

Traditional Marxism

While dependency theory can be described as a neo-Marxist approach, it is clearly different from a traditional Marxist approach to development. Marx himself saw capitalism as a dynamic system with an unmatchable potential for economic growth. Capitalism was the best way to achieve growth; the problem involved the inequalities that were produced at the same time. The traditional Marxist view is that developing countries need capitalism in order to develop. Economic growth under capitalism is progress, and the wealth created can later be distributed equally under socialism. In many ways, traditional Marxism is similar to modernization theory, except that it expects sudden revolutionary change rather than gradual evolutionary change, and that it foresees a further stage, socialism, beyond fully developed capitalism.

This Marxist view, which is far more optimistic about development than depend-ency theory is, was revived by Bill Warren (1980). Warren claimed to find evidence of industrial growth in Third World economies, indicating that independent devel-opment was possible. Colonialism had introduced capitalism to the Third World where it had taken root. Economic relations with the First World were strengthening independent capitalism, and the absence of growth, or its slow pace in some countries, was more the result of internal factors such as mistaken policies by Third World governments influenced by dependency theory.

World systems theory

The **modern world system** (MWS) refers, in world systems theory, to the global capitalist system.

This is associated with the work of Immanuel Wallerstein from the early 1970s onwards and developed from dependency theory, sharing with it a basis in Marxism. Where dependency theorists tended to focus on the experiences and prospects of individual countries, world systems theory describes the world as consisting of a single unified capitalist system: the **modern world system** (MWS). This comprises a hierarchy of countries from the core (developed), through the semi-periphery (countries such as Brazil and South Africa, with some advanced urban sectors), to the periphery (the least developed). The MWS came into existence as European trade expanded in the late fifteenth and early sixteenth centuries, and, because of its global scale, was a new kind of social system the world had not experienced before. The processes by which underdeveloped countries are exploited are the same as in dependency theory, with an emphasis on economic factors and on external rather than internal factors. However, the MWS is a dynamic system and countries can move up and down the hierarchy. This is because capitalism does not respect national borders; capital will move to wherever money is to be made, so the MWS continually changes as capitalism searches for profit (Wallerstein 2004).

The theory impasse

By the 1980s, both modernization and dependency theories were clearly unable to explain adequately how the world was changing. The certainties that both sides had

Canary Wharf in London is currently the centre of a large part of the world's financial affairs. However, this is only because UK law has made it an attractive base for large companies, which could easily move to another country in the search for more profit – taking their capital with them.

held were challenged. In 1985 David Booth wrote of a 'theory impasse', and within a few years the end of the Cold War and recognition of globalization added to the feeling that the old theories could not hold.

Reasons for the impasse

1   *The failure of development*. In the 1960s and '70s most developing countries made some progress towards economic growth as well as progress on indicators of social development such as life expectancy and literacy. The following decade, however, saw a slowing down or even reversal; the 1980s are now referred to as 'the lost decade' for development. On rates at the time, it would take developing countries many generations to approach Western standards. Modernization theory could not explain the failure to take off, while dependency theory could not explain the significant differences in the situations of developing countries that were becoming evident, notably the rapid growth of the 'Asian tigers' (the newly industrializing countries, such as South Korea, Taiwan, Singapore and Hong Kong; see page 148). The end of communism in Europe also undermined the legitimacy of Marxist and neo-Marxist theories.

2   *Postmodernis*m. Postmodernist ideas in the social sciences began to undermine the 'metanarratives', not only Marxism (which underpinned dependency theory), but also the very idea of development. Postmodernists argued that development and the development theories carried assumptions about social evolution and progress, and were based on Western values. This questioning of the metanarrative of development led some writers to talk of 'post-development'.

3   Social scientists began to discuss *globalization*; not all accepted it as a real phenomenon, but the concept opened up new debates that increasingly overlapped with debates about development. These are discussed in the next section (and see Schuurman 2002).

Neo-liberalism

Neo-liberal economic theory replaced modernization theory as the guiding 'official' approach to development in the 1980s. Like modernization theory, it takes the obstacles to development to be internal, but focuses on economic policies and institutions which are seen as holding back development because they limit the free market. Neo-liberalism insists that developing countries remove obstacles to free market capitalism and allow capitalism to generate development. The argument is that, if allowed to work freely, capitalism will generate wealth, initially for a minority who are successful, for example as entrepreneurs, but eventually for all, as the wealth 'trickles down'. The policies proposed are those that were tried first in Chile in the 1970s, then in Britain under Thatcher's Conservative governments, and elsewhere. They include:

- privatization: selling to private companies industries that had been owned and run by the state – in many countries power, water, telecommunications and broadcasting, etc.;
- getting rid of 'parastatal' institutions, often with names such as 'marketing

Neo-liberal economic theory was dominant in influencing development policies in the 1980s and 1990s, based on a minimal role for states and liberalization of trade to allow the free market (capitalism) to work without restrictions.

Parastatals are state-run organizations such as marketing boards, which played a leading role in the development policies of many states before neo-liberal policies were enforced.

boards', by which governments regulated production, distribution and pricing of particular goods;

- cutting state spending, especially on welfare, so that the state would be less important in the economy;
- cutting taxes: leaving people free to spend their money rather than the government taking a large share and spending it;
- free trade: removing tariffs and restrictions on both imports and exports;
- integration into the global economy.

The **structural adjustment programmes** (SAPs) refer to a set of policies imposing neo-liberal policies on governments used by IGOs, especially the IMF.

Some countries willingly adopted these policies, believing they would work; others were imposed as part of **structural adjustment programmes** (SAPs) created by the **International Monetary Fund** (IMF) and other **international governmental organizations** (IGOs). The agreement by the **World Bank** and IMF on these policies as a development strategy, together with liberal democratic political systems, is referred to as the **Washington Consensus**.

The **International Monetary Fund** (IMF) is a key IGO, giving loans to members, which has spread neo-liberal economic globalization.

Neo-liberalism is now not as widely accepted as being the key to development. Its advocates argue that it has worked in some countries and that opening to the free market is the explanation for the recent economic growth of, for example, China and India, and that where it seems not to have worked this is because the policies have not been fully implemented. Its opponents, however, point out that after 20 years or so of neo-liberal policies, development has proceeded at only a slow pace in most countries. There is also, arguably, a contradiction in that imposing free markets requires a strong state that has to undermine its own role.

International governmental organizations (IGOs) are organizations established by states, such as the IMF, the World Bank and the World Trade Organization (WTO).

Assessing the impact of neo-liberal policies

A report from the Center for Economic and Policy Research (CEPR) compared the period from 1960 to 1980, when most countries had more restrictive, inward-looking economies, to the period 1980 to 2000, the period of neo-liberal policies in trade and imposition of policies by the IMF and World Bank. It considered indicators such as income per person, life expectancy, mortality among infants, children and adults, literacy and education. The report found that progress was greater before 1980, and that there has been a decline since. For example, in poor countries child mortality fell faster and school enrolment increased faster before 1980 than after. The report's authors do not claim that liberalization of trade and capital flows has caused the decline in progress, but they do say that supporters of neo-liberal policies have not yet produced proof for their claims that the Washington Consensus is the way to development (Weisbrot et al. 2001).

The **World Bank** is a key IGO, which gives aid and loans to members to fight poverty; it is often accused of spreading neo-liberal economic globalization.

Globalization

The **Washington Consensus** is a set of neo-liberal policies which were argued to be essential for reforming economies and promoting development.

Globalization is a relatively new term, which quickly became a 'buzz word' – widely used without its meaning and implications always being fully examined. Even within sociology it is always worth asking what a particular writer means by globalization.

The context for globalization is the end of the Cold War and the collapse of the Soviet Union in 1989. Together with rapid changes in communications technology,

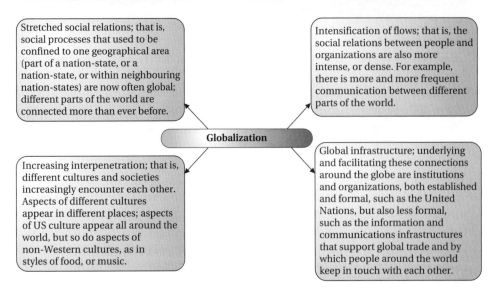

Stretched social relations; that is, social processes that used to be confined to one geographical area (part of a nation-state, or a nation-state, or within neighbouring nation-states) are now often global; different parts of the world are connected more than ever before.

Intensification of flows; that is, the social relations between people and organizations are also more intense, or dense. For example, there is more and more frequent communication between different parts of the world.

Globalization

Increasing interpenetration; that is, different cultures and societies increasingly encounter each other. Aspects of different cultures appear in different places; aspects of US culture appear all around the world, but so do aspects of non-Western cultures, as in styles of food, or music.

Global infrastructure; underlying and facilitating these connections around the globe are institutions and organizations, both established and formal, such as the United Nations, but also less formal, such as the information and communications infrastructures that support global trade and by which people around the world keep in touch with each other.

Figure 2.3 What is meant by globalization?

this made possible the spread of free market capitalism, which has been imposed on many developing countries through structural adjustment programmes and the pressure to get debt relief.

There is a series of debates about globalization, which include questions such as:

- Is it happening or not? (Does the term refer to a new phenomenon, different from earlier social changes?)
- When did it begin?
- Is it irreversible?
- Who benefits from it?
- Is it overall a positive or negative force?

What is meant by globalization?

According to Cochrane and Pain (2004), there is general agreement that what is meant by globalization can be summarized in figure 2.3. Globalization can be seen as having cultural, political and economic dimensions. The following section discusses some of the arguments and evidence that have been put forward for globalization; we then consider the different interpretations of the evidence and arguments which have led to different theoretical positions on globalization.

Evidence for economic globalization

The case for economic globalization, as presented below, is that there is now a single fully integrated global economy.

1　The spread of capitalism (the 'free market') around the world. Even nominally communist countries, such as China and Vietnam, have moved away from state control of the economy and allow capitalist businesses. The adoption by many countries of neo-liberal policies, sometimes under pressure to follow structural adjustment programmes, has extended the market even further, into areas that once were under the control of the state (for example, supplying energy and water).

2 The growth and strength of **transnational corporations** (TNCs). Both production and consumption have been globalized. These giant companies (or their subsidiaries or franchises) make the same products (with local variations) in many countries, and sell them in many countries. The products of companies such as Unilever, Nestlé and Sony are household names around the world. (See page 138.)

3 The ways in which TNCs tend to operate has led to social changes which George Ritzer refers to as **McDonaldization**.

4 Finance and money markets have also been globalized. Financial events on the other side of the world can quickly affect us. Banks and stockbrokers are often transnational operations, and money can be moved very quickly around the world. This became evident with, for example, the 'credit crunch' and recession in 2008, which spread very quickly from one economy to another around the world, showing how closely the economies of different countries were interconnected.

Transnational corporations (TNCs) are large business enterprises which produce and sell globally and have global supply chains.

McDonaldization is Ritzer's term for the ways in which the organizing principles of a fast-food restaurant chain are coming to dominate and standardize many aspects of economic and cultural life globally.

In 2008, problems with home-owners in the US being unable to keep up with their mortgage payments caused ripples throughout the world, leading to a global credit crunch. Northern Rock – a UK bank – was one of the first to be particularly hard hit, resulting in people queuing over several days to withdraw their money.

McDonaldization

Since George Ritzer wrote *The McDonaldization of Society* in the 1990s, the word has caught on and been used in a wide variety of contexts. Many people find it a useful shorthand term for a range of ways in which we can see social life changing, and others have adapted it, talking of 'McJobs', 'McUniversities' and so on. McDonaldization is a global process and an aspect of globalization. Here are Ritzer's dimensions of McDonaldization (Ritzer 2008):

1 *Efficiency*. McDonald's is all about getting customers from hungry to full as quickly as possible. Staff are trained to prepare food and serve customers in a precise series of steps that delivers efficiency.

2 *Calculability*. Quantity replaces quality; a Big Mac's selling point is its size, not its taste.

3 *Predictability*. The restaurants will look the same inside and out, the menus will be the same, the food will taste the same and the staff will say the same things to customers.

4 *Control*. The experience of eating at McDonald's is carefully controlled to ensure that people eat quickly and leave as soon as they have finished. Wherever possible, McDonalidization replaces people with machines.

Evidence for political globalization

Some writers assume that, as capitalism spreads, so will the political system of liberal democracy (based on political parties, regular elections, freedom to speak and vote). A second aspect of political globalization is that nation-states and local political structures become less important compared to TNCs and global or supranational political entities such as the European Union.

Around the world, the number of liberal democracies has grown considerably over the past two decades and there are far fewer dictatorships. Not all political systems and elections are 'free and fair', with the opposition allowed to organize freely, but elections are almost always now observed by international monitors and there are procedures to try to reduce bribery, vote rigging and so on. Having free and fair elections is now often a condition of aid.

National governments increasingly face problems that are too big for them to deal with on their own, for example climate change, pollution, terrorism, the illegal drugs trade, the power of TNCs, AIDS and refugees. The big political questions now require **global decision-making**. This has made governments willing to concede some powers to international organizations like the United Nations and the European Union, and willing to negotiate agreements with other countries. In the long term, the logical outcome would be a world government.

Nation-states have also given up some political power to smaller and more local political structures; for example, in Britain there are now devolved assemblies in Scotland, Wales and Northern Ireland, and there have been calls for English regional assemblies.

New social movements often operate across several countries or even globally; national boundaries no longer restrict political activity. Important global political

Global decision-making refers to states acting together through IGOs to take decisions at a global level.

The major problems of today, such as pollution and climate change, drug-trafficking and nuclear threats, are too large for single nation-states to regulate and require global cooperation.

Non-governmental organizations (NGOs) are non-profit groups which are independent of the state; they are largely funded by private contributions and are mostly involved in humanitarian activities.

'actors' include Greenpeace, the Red Cross, Amnesty International and many **non-governmental organizations**, as well as movements working on environmental and political issues.

Evidence for cultural globalization

Cultural globalization is very closely linked to economic globalization, and includes:

- the existence of world information and communication systems;
- global patterns of consumerism;
- cosmopolitan lifestyles;
- world sport;
- world tourism.

Most of the attention is focused on the spread of highly visible aspects of American consumer culture: McDonald's, Coca-Cola, fast-food chains, baseball caps, jeans, hip hop and rap music and so on, but other aspects include the growth of Christianity, Islam and other religions, the dominance globally of the English language and the spread of Western values regarding families, relationships and so on.

Global sporting events, such as the Olympics, can be evidence for cultural globalization. The slogan of the 2008 Games in Beijing, China, was 'One world, one dream'.

Theoretical perspectives on globalization

According to McGrew (2000), it is possible to distinguish three theoretical accounts of globalization.

(1) The neo-liberals

Neo-liberals (also referred to as positive **globalists** or optimists) see globalization as the worldwide extension of capitalism, or, as they would prefer to call it, the free market. They see this as good because a global free market will lead to economic growth, the eradication of poverty and the spread of democracy all around the world. A new world order is being created which will ensure peace and prosperity. Neo-liberals would say that countries that are embracing the global free market are the ones where development is happening now (for example, India and China), while the continuing problems in Africa are because that continent remains largely outside the global free market. Globalization spreads the benefits of capitalism around the world. Allowing people to use their entrepreneurial skills by liberalizing markets will,

Globalists are those in the globalization debates who argue that globalization is a positive and irreversible force from which all will eventually benefit, and is associated with neo-liberalism.

they argue, produce wealth that will eventually 'trickle down' to the whole population. Liberal democracy tends to be seen as the inevitable accompaniment to the spread of the free market. In the long run, there will be no losers, only winners, from globalization. Cultural globalization involves the spread of Western values, which are essential in a globalized world.

(2) The radicals

Radicals refer to those in the globalization debates who argue that globalization is a powerful negative force; associated with dependency theory and neo-Marxists.

Radicals agree with the neo-liberals in seeing globalization as essentially the global spread of capitalism, but they see this as negative. This position is often associated with Marxism. Economic globalization is seen as spreading globally an economic system which impoverishes many and, because it is based on high consumption, is environmentally not sustainable. Globalization widens the gap between rich and poor – even if some countries benefit, the rich world, or at least the majority there, benefits even more, and the poor are excluded. Globalization creates a global system based on structural violence, condemning parts of the South to poverty and stagnation. Cultural globalization is seen as **cultural imperialism** – that is, it is seen as destroying local cultures through a process of **homogenization**, by which a single global culture based on American or Western culture is created.

Cultural imperialism is the theory, associated with neo-Marxism, that the developed world now exercises control over the rest of the world through exporting its culture.

Homogenization refers to the removal of cultural differences, so that all cultures are increasingly similar.

For the radicals, what is happening now is a deepening or intensification of long-standing trends. Capitalism began its global expansion centuries ago, but is only now completely dominant. What is new is that transnational corporations (TNCs), supported by the IGOs, have replaced the developed nations as the driving force of these changes. The new world order which is emerging seems more like disorder; the North cannot be safe and secure as long as its wealth is based on intensifying the poverty of the South.

(3) The transformationalists

Transformation-alists are those who see globalization as a force the outcomes of which are uncertain, but which can be controlled and used to promote development.

The **transformationalists** see globalization as a very important development, but disagree with both the neo-liberals and the radicals on several grounds:

- globalization may not be unstoppable – it may even slow or go into reverse;
- it may be possible for people and countries to reject some negative aspects of globalization while embracing the more positive aspects;
- far from creating a homogenous global culture, the meeting of different cultures creates new hybrids (**hybridization**) – of peoples, of music, of religions, of languages and so on – which is seen as creating greater diversity, and more vibrant, exciting cultures;
- the world is still unequal, but globalization is transforming the old hierarchies of North/South and First World/Third World.

Hybridization refers to the creation of 'third cultures' when aspects of two different cultures encounter each other.

> **Ankie Hoogvelt and the shape of the globalized world**
>
> Hoogvelt (2005) has argued that globalization has transformed the world social order so that geographic boundaries are no longer relevant. Rich and poor live alongside each

other in the world's great cities, not in different countries. She sees the world order as a three-tiered structure of circles: the affluent and elites (the 'bankable'); the insecure; and the excluded. In the rich countries, she says, the proportions are 40:30:30; in poor countries, 20:30:50; in Africa, more like 10:10:80.

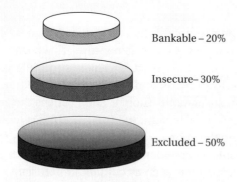

Bankable – 20%

Insecure– 30%

Excluded – 50%

Figure 2.4 The three-tiered structure of the world

How far has economic globalization gone?

It is far from complete. There are still many national companies, and even the largest corporations have clear national bases and so are more properly **multinational corporations** (MNCs) than TNCs. Even if national governments have less control over their economies than in the past, regional groups of governments (like the European Union) can provide some protection for workers and insist on basic rights (such as the Social Chapter), placing limits on the power of TNCs.

Hirst and Thompson (1999) argue that economic globalization is a myth. Outlining ideal types of the international economy and the global economy, they argue that we are still much closer to the former. Nation-states remain important actors, with the ability to control the direction taken by the world economy. Hirst and Thompson see no evidence of a fully developed global system; neo-liberals and radicals both point to evidence of greater global economic activity.

> **Multinational corporations (MNCs)** are enterprises that operate globally but are still clearly based in one nation.

How far has political globalization gone?

Governments still have considerable scope to influence developments and it is national governments that are entering into the agreements that create the international organizations. National governments still wage wars and raise taxes. More countries have adopted the trappings of liberal democracy. Dictators such as Robert Mugabe in Zimbabwe can hold and win elections and claim to be democratically elected even though nothing else has changed there. The USA and its allies still tolerate undemocratic regimes as long as they are on their side (e.g. Saudi Arabia). On the other hand, there has been progress, with a decline in the number of dictatorships or authoritarian regimes and a rise in the number of democracies.

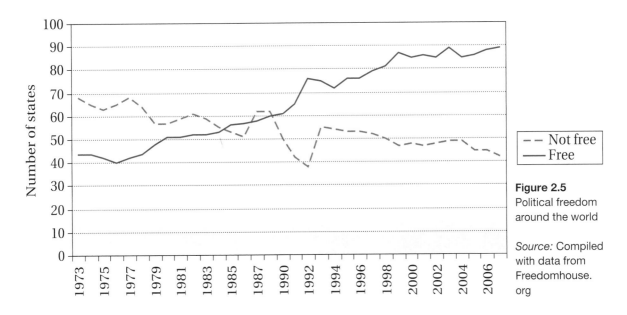

Figure 2.5
Political freedom around the world

Source: Compiled with data from Freedomhouse.org

The transformationalist case has been put forward by McGrew (2004), arguing that although nation-states are not in terminal decline, there is plenty of evidence of a transformation of politics, with the development of global decision-making structures and also a diffusion of power. The ways in which people become active in politics have also changed, with more global and international movements and organizations, at the same time as traditional political activities such as party membership and voting are declining in the North. The problems that people face increasingly require both global and local change, and politics is changing to reflect this.

If economic globalization does mean a much reduced role for nation-states, as neo-liberals claim, then the idea that this also means greater democracy is questionable. While the citizens of more countries may be able to join parties and vote as the number of liberal democracies grows, the politicians they vote for are no longer able to take really important decisions. Those are taken by transnational corporations, whose leaders are not elected and which are accountable only to shareholders.

How far has cultural globalization gone?

Evidence of Western or American culture is hard to avoid anywhere in the world now. The giant media and communications corporations are all based in the North. But not everything American spreads globally: baseball and American football have limited appeal outside the USA (the baseball 'World Series' is always between two North American teams).

The cultural flow is not always one-way from North to South. Bollywood and the Japanese and Hong Kong film industries challenge the supremacy of Hollywood in global cinema. Migration of people means that southern cultures have significant presences within developed countries (for example, Islam in Britain). The cultural

Cultural globalization is not only a one-way phenomenon. Bollywood-inspired cinema is attracting larger audiences in the West, with an associated increased interest in Indian dancing. World music, such as reggae, has been embraced by popular culture, and martial arts from East Asia are commonly practised by children and adults.

products of the developing world are often highly valued (world music, 'ethnic' fashions and jewellery, Eastern religions, 'ethnic' foods and so on).

Some welcome American culture, but others actively resist it. Western culture can be seen as degrading or even as destroying local cultures, and also as creating a generation gap as young people embrace it while the older generation rejects it. Some countries vigorously reject Western cultural values, turning to religious fundamentalism (Iran), or isolationism (North Korea). This in itself can be seen as proof of globalization: globalization so unsettles people that they retreat to old familiar values simply as a way of making sense of a world that seems out of control. However, the meeting of cultures seems often to lead not to the disappearance of the non-Western, but to new hybrids in which the non-Western can survive in a new form. Encounters between cultures create 'third cultures', where aspects of different cultures are

Global tourism can help keep local traditional cultures alive, albeit in a sometimes artificial way. For example, travellers to Thailand are often keen to see the cultures of local tribes, such as the Akha pictured here.

combined. Traditions may also be kept alive, or resurrected, for tourists, many of whom highly value what they take to be an authentic cultural experience. While tourists may only be presented with a simplified version of an aspect of culture, or one removed from its original context, this can still promote a sense of the value of one's own culture and the cultures of others.

Cultural globalization seems to involve an unprecedented level of difference and variety, with the variety extended by hybridization; this can be seen, for example, in the range of foods or types of music available. At the same time, on the other hand, there is an unprecedented level of homogenization.

Who benefits and who loses from globalization?

The neo-liberal case is that in the long run everyone can benefit. Globalization will bring economic growth to the whole world. Initially, this is likely to create inequalities, but eventually living standards will be higher.

The case against globalization is that its negative effects seem to outweigh any advantages. It has failed to deliver peace and prosperity, or even economic stability. Progress towards development has been slow; some countries in Africa have even slipped backwards on some development measures. It is poorer people in poorer countries – Collier's 'bottom billion' – who seem not to be helped by globalization. The winners, from this point of view, are what Sklair (1995, pp. 8–9) has called the '**transnational capitalist class**', the executives controlling TNCs, politicians, bureaucrats and consumer elites, a class no longer tied to national boundaries. It has been questioned, however, whether these people have enough in common to act together as a class. For Naomi Klein (2000) the winners are TNCs; she argues that globalization is a project by TNCs to further their own interests and profits. The neo-liberals respond that the poor are only missing out because they are not yet sufficiently integrated into the global economy.

> The **transnational capitalist class** is associated with the radical view of globalization, which sees globalization creating a new transnational class of business leaders, politicians and others who increasingly share common interests.

Globalization then, whatever its benefits, seems to create two problems:

- a growing gap between rich and poor, or the secure and the excluded;
- growing environmental problems because of the spread of consumerism.

> The **anti-globalization movement** is a loose network of groups and organizations globally opposing neo-liberal economic globalization (but using globalized communications).

There has been an **anti-globalization movement** since at least 1995, a loosely organized coalition of many groups from around the world. They attracted global media attention with demonstrations at the World Trade Organization (WTO) meeting in Seattle in 1999 and then at Genoa in 2001. Because of its disparate nature, the movement lacks a coherent programme, but is broadly in favour of decisions being taken locally rather than imposed by 'experts', and is mainly non-violent. Although opposed to neo-liberal globalization, the groups involved take full advantage of the possibilities of cooperating globally using the Internet and other global telecommunications.

Globalization after 9/11

The terrorist attacks of 11 September 2001 were a setback to optimistic views of globalization. One of the darker realities of globalization, the ability of terrorist networks to organize and operate globally, had become unavoidable. It became clear also that there was considerable hostility to the USA and the rich world more generally. Islamic and other cultures showed no signs of being about to disappear under Western cultural imperialism. The USA then acted without UN support and against strong public opinion in the developed world in invading Iraq in 2003, suggesting a return to international politics dominated by nation-states. Global justice issues were pushed to one side, especially as the anti-globalization movement took time to adjust to face the changed situation. For example, the reaction of condemning the invasions of Iraq and Afghanistan as the actions of an arrogant superpower was too easy; the question of what actions could be taken to help people living under oppressive regimes had also to be faced (Cohen and Kennedy 2007, pp. 454–7).

Kunstler (2005) argues that there is nothing inevitable about globalization, and that it is coming to an end. He sees globalization as a product of two factors: the relative peace of the post-Cold War period and the simultaneous availability of cheap energy sources, especially oil. These two factors are fading: US troops (and others) are currently involved in wars in Iraq and Afghanistan and the West is also under continuing threat from Islamic terrorism; oil reserves are limited and much of the remaining oil is under the control of states that resent or are hostile to the West. Even without considering global warming, the West's oil-led lifestyle has a very limited future. Kunstler therefore expects an imminent end to globalization.

Saul (2004) sees globalization as having reached its high point in the mid-1990s, with the creation of the WTO, but then being challenged by a reclaiming of power by some nation-states from the supposedly all-powerful global economic forces. Malaysia broke all the neo-liberal rules to successfully escape the 1997 Asian crisis; Argentina ignored IMF advice after its economic collapse in 2001, and recovered; India shrugged off WTO pressure to allow genetically modified (GM) seeds; and governments across South America and elsewhere have elected governments opposed to globalization. But Saul sees positive signs of more benign aspects of globalization emerging as neo-liberalism retreats, in non-economic international treaties and the setting up of the International Criminal Court.

Aid

Aid can be classified according to where it comes from:

1 Aid by voluntary agencies and non-governmental organizations (NGOs) such as Oxfam, Christian Aid, World Vision and Voluntary Service Overseas. This form of aid is considered in the section on NGOs.
2 **Official Development Assistance** (ODA): The Organization for Economic Co-operation and Development (OECD) comprises 25 developed countries. Its members have aid budgets – they allocate a part of their resources to ODA. ODA takes the form of grants and 'soft' loans to promote economic development and the welfare of developing countries. ODA can be given directly to a developing country (**bilateral aid**); or to multilateral organizations, such as the United

Aid refers to economic, military, technical and financial assistance given (or loaned) to developing countries.

Official Development Assistance (ODA) comprises the foreign aid programmes of the OECD countries.

Bilateral aid involves only the donor and the recipient, usually government to government.

Nations (UN), World Bank and European Union aid programmes (**multilateral aid**).

> **Multilateral aid** is where donors contribute to a shared fund, from which aid is then given to recipients.

Years ago, the UN agreed that OECD members should aim to allocate 0.7 per cent of their GNP to ODA. In 2007, only four countries met this target: Norway, Sweden, Luxembourg and the Netherlands. Britain gave 0.36 per cent; this works out at $165 per person on overseas aid, compared with $984 on defence (Blanchflower 2008).

The word 'aid' covers grants and loans (which have to be repaid), and also the writing off of debt (so that the recipient country is not receiving aid at all in the expected sense). Aid is often tied – that is, it must be used for a particular purpose specified by the donor. The donor country may also specify that the money be paid to one of its own companies to carry out a particular project, such as building a road or dam or supplying technical equipment. Aid may also be conditional – that is, it will only be given if the recipient country abides by certain conditions. For example, aid may be cancelled if the recipient country fails to hold elections, or to reform its economy.

A recent development is the giving of aid by countries outside the OECD group of rich nations. For example, Venezuela under Hugo Chavez has used some of its oil wealth to give aid to South American governments, and is using this to push an alternative to the Washington Consensus, based on breaking all ties with the IGOs. Bolivia has ended its agreement with the IMF and long-standing structural adjustment programme, compensating for this with loans and aid from Venezuela which come with fewer conditions and can be used for projects involving the state (Forero and Goodman 2007).

The case against aid

The very word 'aid' suggests something positive, yet the arguments against aid, or at least against the way it has usually been given, are strong and come from both sides of the political spectrum – from neo-liberals and neo-Marxists. Emergency aid is usually, though not always, seen as above these criticisms, though it too can create dependency and worsen conditions.

The neo-liberal view: aid creates dependency

The use of the word 'dependency' here points to considerable shared ground between right and left on the subject of aid. Neo-liberals make similar criticisms of aid as they do of the welfare states providing social security in the North: aid is seen as teaching people to be dependent on handouts, taking away their initiative and their ability to help themselves. Countries are seen as poor because of their own failings, such as laziness, corruption or inefficiency, and giving aid does not help overcome these failings and may even encourage them. Third World countries then demand aid as a right just as, from this view, social security 'scroungers' do, and become trapped in a culture of dependency. If a project is viable, it should be able to attract investment so that aid is unnecessary. If it can't attract private sector funding, it can't be worth doing.

A strong and controversial statement of these views was made by Peter Bauer (1995), an economist who popularized these views and became known as Lord Anti-aid in the British media (he was made a baron in 1983 by Margaret Thatcher). The main argument for aid is that it supplies what developing countries do not have, but Bauer argued that aid could not be necessary for development, because Northern countries did not receive aid when they were developing. He suggested that aid implied that the Third World was incapable of achieving what the West had achieved. The term 'aid' is misleading, he said, because it implies something positive; a more neutral term would be 'government to government subsidy'. The term 'aid' allows governments to seem to be doing the right thing; it is hard to avoid calling them 'donors', which is another term loaded with positive connotations. Bauer said that the reality was that aid went to Third World governments, not to people. The aid industry has developed a logic and momentum of its own because it suits some groups in both the North and South.

The neo-Marxist view: aid as imperialism

A good example is the work of Teresa Hayter, whose book is entitled *Aid as Imperialism*. She stresses how aid is conditional – it nearly always comes with strings attached. It is one way in which rich countries exercise power over poorer ones, and, as such, it is a form of **imperialism**. Hayter regards the claim made by Western governments that aid helps the South as hypocritical: most aid doesn't alleviate poverty, because it isn't meant to; its real purpose is to strengthen a system which damages the interests of the poor. Most aid doesn't go to the people or countries who need it, but to those who are of strategic or other importance to the donor country and who arguably don't need it. Aid creates jobs and export markets for the donors. Aid can also be used to win political support: the recipient country gets aid if it agrees to support the donor, perhaps by votes at international conferences, or by allowing its land and air space to be used for military purposes.

> **Imperialism**: the process of empire-building associated with the colonial system.

The middle ground

Aid can work, but it is often inappropriate or inefficient. This is not an objection to all aid, but a recognition that much aid is misdirected and abused, and a desire to see it used well. There have been many examples of aid which has not contributed to development:

- aid that supports corrupt or undemocratic governments, or where the money is wasted through inefficiency;
- aid that is used to strengthen the armed forces;
- projects that are inappropriate and do more harm than good;
- projects that cause damage to the environment;
- projects that employ highly paid foreign experts who have little knowledge of local conditions and ignore the views of local people;
- projects based on ignorance or lack of thought – e.g., sending food to refugees in a war zone; the food is likely to be seized by combatants and will prolong the war and the suffering of the people it was intended to help.

The overriding criticism is that aid doesn't seem to work; 50 years of aid have not led to development. There are two possible conclusions to be drawn from this: either aid does not help development, or the aid given so far has not been enough and more needs to be given.

The case for aid

The justification for aid comes originally from modernization theory: the rich world could provide aid in the form of capital, expertise or technology as a helping hand to those who were behind on the road to prosperity and mass consumption. Although modernization theory has lost its explanatory power, it is still clearly the case that the North has much that can be shared with the South. A similar case to that of modernization theory has recently been put forward by Jeffrey Sachs (2005) who argues for a big push of large-scale, focused and integrated aid to lift developing countries out of poverty.

Aid has not solved the problems of world poverty, but it may have made things better than they would otherwise have been. Collier (2007) estimates that over the past 30 years, aid has added one percentage point to the annual growth rate of the countries of the 'bottom billion'. This does not seem much, but it is significant; these countries would have been poorer without this aid. Aid may not have led to development, but it has stopped the situation being even worse.

Bauer's view of aid has been challenged on ethical grounds. He argues that Third World countries are responsible for their own poverty, but it is chance that leads to an individual being born in the Third World rather than the North. A person born in poverty in Africa does not have the same life chances as someone born in the North, and this is through no fault of their own. It can be argued on grounds of natural justice that giving aid is a moral imperative; not even to try to help is inexcusable. If aid helps improve life chances, it is worth it. This argument has gathered strength with the discourses of globalization and of the environment, which emphasize how we all share one small and fragile planet.

The aid debate today

Sachs vs Easterley

These writers are both on the middle ground, rejecting the extremes of neo-liberalism and neo-Marxism. They share common aims but have very different ideas about what will work.

- Sachs (2005): the 'big push' – aid should be increased, focused and integrated; one big sustained effort by rich nations and the IGOs working together can solve the problem. For example, eradicating infectious diseases that claim millions of lives each year, such as measles, malaria and diarrhoea, would cost $10 billion a year – only $15 from every person in the developed world. The influence of this view can be seen in the Millennium Development Goals, the 2005 G8 summit and the Live 8 concerts.

- Easterley (2006): rejects Sachs's approach because it is a top-down planners' intervention, and these nearly always fail. Aid should involve searching for what will work and supporting home-grown small-scale initiatives, with real accountability to the poor. Rather than raising more money, we should make sure that what we have reaches those who need it. The problem with this view is whether many small initiatives can make a real difference.

Does aid do more harm than good?

A lot depends on the type of aid that is offered. The right kind of aid – small scale, aware of local needs, controlled at a local level, usually given by an NGO – can be very positive, but is not on its own going to transform a country. Aid in a disaster or emergency can be vital, although some aid of this kind has been misdirected and has often been restricted to relief rather than establishing foundations for a more secure future. Overall, however, the net flow of capital is *from*, not *to*, the South; for example, African countries send more money to the West in payment of interest on loans than they receive in aid. Aid needs to be seen in a bigger context, which includes debt and trade. The following sections explore these issues.

The debt crisis

The 'debt crisis' has its origins in the 1970s when banks in the rich world lent money to Third World governments. At this time, modernization theory led many people to believe that, if they were helped, poorer countries would quickly develop and begin to catch up with the rich world. The loans were seen both as good business for the banks and a contribution towards modernization. Interest was to be charged on the loans, but Third World countries took the money, believing that economic growth would mean they could pay the interest and eventually repay the loan.

Some of the money lent went into the pockets of dictators, and a lot was spent on arms, but there was briefly some real development. However, recession in the 1980s in richer countries reduced the export markets of Third World countries – but they still had to repay the interest on their loans. Many countries went deeper and deeper into debt, borrowing even more money to pay off the interest due on earlier loans. When governments were obliged to curtail their spending, they often found it easier to cut health and education budgets than, for example, to reduce spending on arms and the military (which risks a military coup by unhappy soldiers).

By the end of the century, debt had clearly become a huge obstacle to development, though it is impossible in practice to separate the effects of debt from those of globalization, trade and neo-liberal policies.

George (1991) introduced the term 'debt boomerang', arguing that debt was also creating problems for the North, and that action on debt was in the interests of the North as well as being ethically desirable. George's argument is important, because it suggests that debt cancellation is actually in the interests of those to whom the money is owed – it is not charity or compassion, but social and economic sense.

The **debt crisis** refers to the inability (and sometimes refusal) of indebted countries to pay interest on loans or to repay the original loan; debt repayments hold back development by diverting money and resources.

Debt boomerang is George's term to describe the ways in which the debt crisis has negative effects in the developed world

The six boomerangs:

People in developing countries are forced by debt to exploit their natural resources in the most profitable and least sustainable way; for example, cutting down rain forest for timber to export. This leads to climate change, exhaustion of resources and depletion of bio-diversity.

For some countries in debt, the huge demand in developed countries for illegal drugs such as cocaine and heroin provides a tempting market, but with huge social and economic costs in the developed countries.

People in developed countries pay taxes to give banks concessions so they can write off bad debts.

If the indebted countries were better off, they would be able and willing to buy from developed countries, so jobs have been lost for lack of markets.

Migration

Many flee poverty by moving to the North or to other richer countries nearby. Economic migrants are not recognized as refugees.

War

Debt creates social unrest, and can lead to war. Iraq's invasion of Kuwait, which led to the first Gulf War (1990–1), happened partly because Iraq was under pressure to repay a $12 billion loan.

One of George's boomerangs refers to the environment. Developing countries that are home to the world's last great rainforests – for example in South East Asia and South America – are often forced to destroy huge swathes of rainforest to plant crops for fuel or food. This has serious consequences for climate change, which is of concern to the developed world as well as the developing world.

A coalition of agencies and other interested groups set up Jubilee 2000, now the Jubilee Debt Campaign, arguing that the misery caused by debt has dwarfed that caused by slavery. Their original campaign was for the debts of the world's 50 poorest countries to be cancelled by 2000; they estimated this would save 21 million lives. They were partially successful. The pace of debt relief has been slow, with countries having to meet strict qualifications to qualify for the **Highly Indebted Poor Countries Initiative** (HIPC). This is, in effect, a form of structural adjustment programme (see box), through which highly indebted countries can have their debts written off if they follow IMF and World Bank approved economic policies. Britain has been among the countries advocating greater and faster debt relief. While debt relief is welcome, the root causes of the problems that led to debt are not being addressed.

> **Structural adjustment programmes (SAPs)**
>
> These are a form of conditionality. Since the mid 1980s, a condition of aid, loans and writing off of debts has often been that countries adopt neo-liberal economic policies. These SAPs have the long-term aim of helping economies (according to free market economic theories); in a strong economy, it is claimed, wealth will eventually 'trickle down' to the poor.

The main argument for not cancelling the debts completely is 'moral hazard', a term used in the insurance industry referring to when people are not held responsible for what goes wrong as a result of decisions they have made. In this case, cancelling debts rewards those countries that did not use the money well (for example, spending it on a new presidential palace or private jet). Another argument is that banks would probably not loan money to the countries concerned in future. Much of the money is owed to the World Bank and the IMF; debt cancellation would leave them with limited funds to promote development. On the other hand, should people today be expected to repay loans if they didn't benefit from them? Is it their fault if a dictator wasted money 20 years ago, and should not the banks have realized that the money would be wasted?

The writing off of debts has been hampered by so-called 'vulture funds', which buy the debts owed by poor countries at cheap rates and then sue those governments in order to make a profit. In 2007 the IMF found that 11 of the 24 countries in the HIPC initiative had been sued by vulture funds, with a total of £1 billion being awarded to the vultures; in one case, a company called Donegal International bought an old debt owed by Zambia for £3 million, sued for £55 million and was awarded £15.5 million in a British court (Seagar and Lewis 2007).

The **Highly Indebted Poor Countries Initiative** (HIPC) refers to a system by which heavily indebted countries can apply to have debt written off provided they keep to conditions.

Conditionality is the setting of conditions on aid, so that it will be withheld if those conditions are not met.

Trade

The extent and terms of trade between Northern and Southern countries are issues increasingly recognized as essential to an understanding of development. Trade was once seen as a rather dry concern of economists, but has now become the subject of

A fair trade product, displaying the philosophy behind the scheme.

This t-shirt is part of the social economy.

(ask me what that means)

Fair trade is a movement to try to alter the terms of trade so that producers in developing countries receive a higher proportion of the profit.

popular debate and protest. In the last few years, Northern consumers have become aware of some of the issues through the growth of the **fair trade** movement and the availability of fairly traded goods – and the claim implicit in the term itself that normal free trade is not fair. Increased trade is an aspect of globalization; the ratio of exports to GDP, a measure of the extent of trade, has risen significantly for the whole world over the past 50 years, and for most developing countries (Coyle 2001).

The least developed countries are much less involved in world trade than the developed world. The 49 poorest countries, with 646 million people, had only a 0.6 per cent share of world trade in 2002, while the world's top five exporting countries (the USA, France, Germany, the UK and Japan), with 646 million people, had 37 per cent.

Often, smaller countries rely almost entirely on one crop or material, and sometimes on exporting it to a limited number of countries (such as their former colonial power). Coffee accounts for 73 per cent of Burundi's exports, copper for 70 per cent of Zambia's (http://news.bbc.co.uk/1/shared/spl/hi/pop_ups/03/business_trade_and_poor_countries/html/8.stm). This leaves such countries, and the farmers or producers within them, in a very vulnerable situation. They receive only a tiny proportion of the final price of the crop or product, with the main profits being taken by the businesses which ship, process, package and sell – the middlemen. Even this small proportion is at risk, for several reasons:

- prices fluctuate according to supply and demand – if supply rises because more countries are producing a particular crop or material, the price is likely to fall;
- changing tastes and fashions in the North can affect demand;
- crops are vulnerable to severe weather conditions and disease – relying on one or a limited number of crops provides no insurance.

However, because terms of trade and prices of commodities change, developments which are positive for Southern countries can happen in an unplanned way. In 2008, for example, Africa was benefiting as a result of a number of phenomena:

1   *High oil prices.* The Overseas Development Institute estimates that if the price stays high, African oil producers will earn £19 billion a year, more than has been promised in aid.

2   *A dramatic increase in trade with China.* China's rapid industrialization means that it needs raw materials such as minerals which Africa can supply, and the demand is pushing prices up; in return, affordable Chinese goods are increasingly available in African markets;

3   *Falling prices of consumer goods.* As a result, many consumer goods become affordable in Africa – for example, mobile phones (Dowden 2006).

Cocoa farming in Ghana

Ghana once produced a third of the world's cocoa (which is used to make chocolate). But in the late 1970s the world cocoa price fell, and many Ghanaian farmers switched to crops to feed themselves and to sell locally because they could not earn enough from cocoa. The Ghanaian government had relied on tax revenues from cocoa export and found itself in economic difficulty. It accepted a structural adjustment programme from the IMF and World Bank to 'rescue' the economy. This included removing subsidies to cocoa farmers, thereby increasing their difficulties. At the same time, chocolate producers in the West were cutting the cocoa content of chocolate, reducing demand and, as a result, pushing down the prices that Ghanaian farmers could get. Ghanaian chocolate has a reputation for its high quality and is nearly all now fairly traded, and Ghana's hope is that Western consumers will be willing to pay more for a high-quality and ethically sound product (Swift 1998).

For dependency theorists and radicals, trade is one of the ways in which the North ensures the neo-colonial exploitation of the South. Under colonialism, the economies of the colonies were used for the benefit of the colonial power, by providing primary products (raw materials and cash crops). Despite political independence, developing countries remain heavily dependent on the export of these. However, the rich world uses its dominance in the world trade system to ensure that the prices that developing world producers can get are low. The profits from such exports will never be sufficient to fund development, or even to keep many people out of poverty.

For neo-liberals, free trade is fundamental. They favour **trade liberalization** – that is, the opening of national markets to international competition. This will, in theory, ensure that those who can produce goods for which there is a market, and at a price that customers are willing to pay, will do well. Trade liberalization includes the removal of protectionist policies in the developed world, where there are often tariffs on goods imported from the developing world and other barriers such as quotas, technical regulations and health and safety standards. Developed countries also subsidize agriculture and some industries, giving them an advantage in the global market. Agricultural subsidies alone are about six times the value of aid given to poor countries. According to an Oxfam report in 2002, the European dairy industry that year was being subsidized by £16 billion a year. In practice, developed countries are very reluctant to reduce subsidies or to allow in cheap foreign goods that

Trade liberalization refers to the removal of barriers to free trade, such as tariiffs and subsidies.

would undermine their own producers. In other words, they do not practise what the neo-liberals preach. Developing countries, on the other hand, being in a weaker bargaining position, often have no alternative but to accept liberalization.

Mali and the cotton trade

The West African country of Mali grows high-quality cotton, but farmers there cannot sell it at a price that brings them a reasonable income. This is because the price of cotton on the world market is brought down by subsidies that the US government gives to its cotton farmers. American cotton farmers are able to sell cotton at a lower price than Malian farmers. Mali cannot afford to subsidize its farmers. Increasingly, Malian cotton is hard to find even in Mali, and across Africa people wear imported clothing rather than clothes locally made with local cloth. Mali and other West African cotton producers (Chad, Benin and Burkina Faso) have lobbied the WTO to make the USA remove its subsidies, but the stalling of world trade talks prevented this.

Oxfam estimates the cost to the four West African cotton producers through suppressed world prices to be £400m for the years 2001–3 alone (Oxfam 2007) (http://news.bbc.co.uk/1/hi/programmes/panorama/4306219.stm).

Fair trade

Products bearing a Fairtrade label have become more popular in the North, although they still only cover a limited number of types of product and have only a small share of the market. Fair trade is an attempt to alter the terms of trade to give a fairer deal to producers in developing countries.

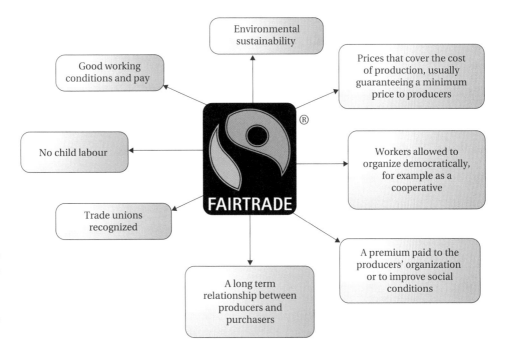

Figure 2.6 Some of the principles of fair trade (Look for the FAIRTRADE Mark on products. www.fairtrade.org. uk.)

Match the writers with their ideas:

Frank	One big push to solve world poverty
Bauer	The rich nations have kicked the ladder away
Hayter	Five stages to modernization
Collier	Aid as government to government subsidy
Rostow	World systems theory
Wallerstein	Focus on the bottom billion
Sachs	The debt boomerang affects the rich too
George	Dependency and underdevelopment
Chang	McDonaldization
Ritzer	Aid as imperialism

Activity

Exam style questions:
1 Identify and briefly explain some of the sociological evidence for cultural globalization. (9 marks)
2 Assess the view that aid primarily serves the needs of the givers, not the receivers. (18 marks)
3 'First World countries and organizations they control are responsible for the lack of or slow pace of development.' To what extent do sociological arguments and evidence support this view? (33 marks)
Advice on question 3: Although the theoretical perspectives are not referred to, this question invites you to compare dependency theory (which agrees with the view in the question) and modernization theory (which emphasizes factors internal to developing countries). Your answer will be stronger if you can include other theories as well.

Agencies of development

Agencies of development are those organizations and institutions that play a part in development. The specification says that you need to know about transnational corporations, non-governmental organizations and international agencies; to give a fuller picture, this section starts by looking at the role of states in development.

States

States are not the same as governments. Governments are in temporary control of some or most aspects of the state, but, for example, the civil service, the military, the police and the judicial and legal systems, which are also part of the state, have greater continuity.

Neo-liberals favour the state being as small as possible; their view of globalization is that states should have a fading role, while transnational actors, such as TNCs, should have a growing role. Neo-liberals argue that states in the developing world have been too big, with over-sized bureaucracies and too much interference in the market. However, even neo-liberals accept that states have the responsibility to create and maintain a stable and secure social situation in which the free market can operate. Countries in which states cease to be able to do this, such as Somalia, are referred to as 'failed states'.

Marxists and dependency theorists are opposed to capitalism and favour development being led by the state – provided it represents the people. In most countries, however, the state is controlled by the ruling class or bourgeoisie, and it therefore acts against the interests of the majority of the population and in favour of the elites of the North. A transformation of the state via revolution is needed.

Broadly speaking, there are three ways in which the state can affect development:

1   The state can itself lead development, setting development as a goal it actively pursues. Many newly independent countries in the 1950s and 1960s attempted this.
2   The state can limit its role to guiding and facilitating capitalist development, by maintaining order, providing infrastructure and making it possible for the market to work
3   The state can be an obstacle to development. It may be corrupt, with politicians and civil servants enriching themselves from aid or from the country's resources.

State-led development

Before the rise of neo-liberalism in the 1970s, it was widely accepted that the state had to play a leading role in development. States ran industries, organized agriculture and bought products for marketing; they were large and employed many people. The state played an essential role in the few examples of successful industrialization and economic growth – for example, the rise of Japan and, later, the Asian 'tigers'. Adrian Leftwich (1995) argues that the common factor in the development success of the past 50 years (Japan and the Asian tigers) has been the presence of what he calls the 'development state' in which the state focuses on development goals and works closely with the private sector. These states tended to be authoritarian, with weak or absent opposition. In the twenty-first century, this is less acceptable, with aid and debt relief often dependent on countries being democratic.

A **development state** is one that sees its main purpose as development and leads the country's development programme.

States blocking development

In other cases, the state did not help development. Large bureaucracies and corruption may actually even have helped prevent development. This is an argument often put by neo-liberals. Many of these cases were in Africa. African states were created by colonialism, when the European powers fixed borders that did not reflect social or ethnic divisions among African people. Many African states have always been weak, sometimes only held together by international insistence that the borders could not be changed in case greater instability was unleashed. African states have struggled to build a sense of national identity, though some achieved this through wars to free themselves of colonial rule or through promotion by governments (Allen and Thomas 2000, pp. 198–9).

An example of a 'predatory state' is Zaire (now the Democratic Republic of the Congo) under Mobutu, where the president and a small group around him became immensely wealthy by preying on the population, with support from rich nations and from the World Bank (Evans 1989, p. 571). Because of Mobutu's arbitrary power, it was impossible for either a civil service implementing agreed rules or a capitalist class investing in business to exist. Mobutu stayed in power for so long because of external support, especially from France and Belgium; if external actors are important, it is possible they can steer a state towards more constructive action instead, which is arguably what the World Bank and other IGOs now try to do.

> A **predatory state** is one that preys upon its own people, through appropriation and corruption, preventing development.

Transnational corporations

The term 'transnational corporation' (TNC) refers to corporations that have globalized their operations; they produce and sell around the world, use global supply chains and employ people in many different countries. As a result of globalization, there are more, and larger, TNCs than ever before. Some writers have argued that, as economic globalization progresses, TNCs are at least as important as nation-states; certainly, some have larger turnovers than the GNPs of the least developed countries. A listing using 2004/5 data of the 120 most important economic units in the world found that 54 were nation-states and 66 were TNCs (Cohen and Kennedy 2007, pp. 180–1). The majority of the world's countries (191 were recognized by the UN in 2005) therefore have economies smaller than the 66 largest TNCs. TNCs clearly have considerable economic power; the question is how that power is used.

A distinction can be made between TNCs and **multinational corporations** (MNCs). The latter operate in different countries but retain a clear base in a particular country; for example, Honda has subsidiaries in Europe and elsewhere but remains clearly a Japanese company. MNCs have not yet become truly global in the way TNCs are. From the point of view of developing countries, the distinction in less important; both TNCs and MNCs are very powerful outside organizations that can affect development for better or for worse.

> A **multinational corporation** (MNC) is one that has some global aspects, but is still clearly based in one nation, though it is sometimes used interchangeably with a TNC.

TNCs exist to make profits for their shareholders; it is not their purpose or aim to help a country develop, although all now accept the idea of corporate responsibility. The question is whether in doing this they can also contribute to development. Most countries actively seek investment by TNCs, setting up special areas where TNCs can operate without the usual restrictions (for example, they may be exempt from tax, planning laws or minimum standards for workers). Such areas are called **Export Processing Zones** (EPZs), but also are known by different names around the world. Countries that set up EPZs assume that the presence of TNCs will eventually have benefits, even if initially the situation seems more like exploitation.

> **Export Processing Zones**: areas in developing countries where the normal workplace regulations, etc. are relaxed to encourage TNCs to invest.

Corporate responsibility

Many companies now have corporate responsibility policies, or try in some way to show that they have social responsibilities, beyond complying with the law, which they take seriously. Some British supermarkets, for example, support community initiatives in developing countries. While sometimes the main aim may be to attract customers who approve of such practices, there can also be practical developmental and environmental gains. Corporate social responsibility (CSR) is voluntary, and can be seen as a way of heading off criticism and preventing regulations controlling what TNCs can do. Despite the popularity of CSR today, TNCs are frequently accused of abuses. These two websites report on alleged wrongdoings of TNCS:

www.multinationalmonitor.org/

www.corporatewatch.org/

Be aware when visiting these sites that they are campaigning against TNC activities; for balance, visit the websites of some TNCs and look for information on their corporate or social responsibility policies and practices.

Applying the theories to TNCs

Modernization theory and neo-liberal approaches see TNCs as essential, able to introduce modern values and to kick-start an economy. Any accompanying abuses are comparable to those that Britain and other now developed countries went through during industrialization – painful but necessary.

Dependency theorists concentrate on the abuses, some of which are listed in table 2.3 under 'Costs'. The presence of TNCs is seen as intensifying dependency, preventing local industry from growing and ensuring that the country stays poor. The overall effect of the growth of the power of TNCs is to weaken workers and strengthen capitalism; for example, if the workforce in a factory proves troublesome by demanding higher wages or better conditions, the company can close its operation and relocate elsewhere, even in another country. Trades unions around the world are beginning to recognize that, faced with transnational employers, they need to cooperate so as to provide a transnational voice for workers.

Table 2.3: Costs and benefits of TNCs

Costs	Benefits
Exploitation of workers: conditions and pay may be low; some TNCs have been implicated in employing children, not allowing trade unions, making overtime compulsory and other abuses. Developing countries compete with each other to attract TNCs, providing ever lower standards. TNC investment goes to those who will accept the lowest wages, least benefits and worst conditions. Charles Kerngahan described this, in his book about Bangladesh, as a 'race to the bottom' (cited in Jones 2006).	TNCs bring in investment in terms of money, resources, technology and expertise and creating jobs, often where local companies are unable to do this.
Exploitation of the environment: using up renewable resources, damaging ecosystems and creating pollution, with negative consequences for local people.	TNCs need trained workers and this should raise the aspirations of local people and encourage improvements in education.

Table 2.3 (continued)

Costs	Benefits
Exploitation of markets: mis-selling of goods (e.g. baby food), dumping of out-of-date goods (e.g. medicines) and selling harmful goods regardless of consequences (e.g. faced with a shrinking market in the North, tobacco companies have turned to developing countries with marketing that plays down the health consequences of smoking).	The jobs and training often provide opportunities for women, who may not have had them before, promoting gender equality.
Jobs created, especially the better-paid ones, may go to expatriates from the developed world rather than to local people.	TNCs bring modern values, which may help development; for example, ideas about gender equality.
Profits are unlikely to stay in the developing country, and the TNC may avoid paying tax, so that the host country does not benefit financially.	TNCs need and will pay for infrastructure such as roads and power lines, from which local people may also benefit.
Products are for export to Western markets, so local people are unable to buy them.	TNCs encourage international trade and open up new markets.
TNCs have little loyalty to particular countries; when supplies of raw materials have dried up, or when labour is cheaper elsewhere, they will move on.	
Bio-piracy: TNCs are able to patent traditional medicines and sources of food, making money from resources that ought to belong to developing countries and also eliminating domestic firms that sold these products.	

Why are TNCs able to act in unethical ways?

Global economic influence   The largest TNCs are more powerful than some developing countries, so they are able to put pressure on individual countries, and also on IGOs such as the World Trade Organization. For example, world trade rules now allow TNCs to patent medicines and foods that have been used for many years in developing countries and should really belong to their people. This is known as **bio-piracy**.

Parent–subsidiary relationship   TNCs often operate through smaller, subsidiary companies. When there is a court case, the subsidiary is prosecuted and the parent TNC is protected, both financially and in terms of publicity and image. For example, chains of clothes shops such as Nike and Gap can claim to be unaware of use of child labour or other unacceptable practices in the factories in which the clothes are produced if they do not own the factories.

Regional economic influence   TNCs hold power within particular countries and regions; they can force or blackmail governments into overlooking what they do. For example, Shell's investment makes up 90 per cent of foreign investment in Nigeria.

Bio-piracy refers to the appropriation, generally by means of patents, of legal rights over indigenous knowledge – particularly indigenous biomedical knowledge – without compensation to the indigenous groups who originally developed such knowledge.

Whose legal system? Where can a TNC be prosecuted? TNCs might break a law in their country of origin but there may not be a law in the developing country (e.g. some countries don't have laws against child labour).

How and who to punish? Where TNCs or their subsidiaries are prosecuted for breaking regulations and laws, fines are tiny as proportions of profits, and in any case the cost can be passed on to consumers. And who at what level in a TNC is responsible? If a chief executive resigns (prison sentences are unusual for corporate crimes), he or she will be replaced by someone with the same outlook following similar practices.

Activity

Research one or more of these allegations against TNCs in developing countries:
- Shell's exploitation of oil in the Ogoni area in Nigeria;
- Nestlé's selling of powdered baby food in developing countries;
- the use of sweatshop labour for branded clothes, such as Primark, Nike and Gap;
- the Bhopal disaster of 1984, involving a factory owned by Union Carbide;
- allegations against Coca-Cola of polluting water supplies in India and of being indirectly responsible for murders of trade unionists in South America;
- allegations against McDonald's in the McLibel trial.

Non-governmental organizations

There is a very wide range of non-governmental organizations (NGOs). These organizations are part of 'civil society', not part of government, or businesses that exist to make a profit. They are essentially organizations of concerned citizens who want to act together for humanitarian and philanthropic ends, though many have grown beyond such small-scale origins and now employ many people and have huge budgets. Many NGOs work on local and domestic issues; this section is concerned only with those that work on global issues, development and the environment, referred to as international non-governmental organizations (INGOs). Some focus on campaigning, others on charitable work via fundraising. Some work locally at grassroots level, others at the national or international level. Some of the best-known INGOs work on issues wherever there is a need; for example, Oxfam has helped people in poverty in the UK as well as in developing countries.

The amount of aid that NGOs can provide is small compared to aid from governments and multilateral aid provided by IGOs. NGOs have for many years had a vital role in emergencies, raising funds from the public for disaster relief. Some of the UK's largest NGOs work together in the Disasters Emergency Committee (DEC) to coordinate fundraising. Although this is the most visible aspect of their work, most also work on development aid. They are growing in importance; because of the many criticisms of other forms of aid, more Official Development Assistance is being channelled through NGOs, allowing donors to claim that the money is benefiting the poor more directly.

Disaster relief work with vulnerable populations is the most visible aspect of NGOs' aid work.

Some NGOs have grown into large organizations which keep expanding and, argu-ably, lose sight of their original idealism. Not all practise as organizations what they are trying to achieve in their development work; ideals about social justice, equality and democracy do not always translate into decent wages for staff or involvement in decision-making. For the public of Northern countries, on whom NGOs rely for most of their income, another concern has been the amount of money absorbed by admin-istration rather than helping people in developing countries directly.

Overall, NGO aid is worthy and often highly successful at a local level, but there is not enough of it to transform the global situation.

Strengths of NGOs

- smaller and more effective than large state bureaucracies;
- continuity (unlike government aid, which can be affected by elections);
- not driven by profit (unlike TNCs);
- able and willing to take risks;
- able to undertake small-scale projects working as partners with local people;
- responsive to donors, on whom they rely for funding.

Criticisms of NGOs

Most of these criticisms apply particularly to the larger INGOs; smaller NGOs are more able to avoid the pitfalls.

- working too closely with governments or relying on government funds;

- having links with TNCs;
- unclear accountability;
- inappropriate spending of funds; for example, flying in experts rather than using the knowledge and experience of local people;
- being too concerned with good publicity and building a successful brand.

The 2005 tsunami

Mari Marcel Thekaerkara, who co-founded the South Indian NGO, Accord, was at first impressed by the response of INGOs to the tsunami in India. Thanks to the unprecedented generosity of people around the world, the INGOs were able to play vital roles, especially in the first few days, delivering money to people that the government failed to reach, providing support to orphaned children and so on. But as time went on, some of the worst aspects of INGOs became evident. Some thought they knew better than local people – for example, building unsuitable temporary houses rather than the traditional coconut palm structures local people would have preferred. They acted as 'disaster tourists', more interested in getting their brand name publicized than in the victims (Thekaerkara 2005),

---

Global civil society

Global civil society (GCS) comprises a loose collection of NGOs, activist groups and others, overlapping with the anti-globalization movement. There is a debate as to whether there is a coherent GCS or whether the organizations are too different and lack any common focus.

The term 'civil society' refers to the networks of groups and organizations that exist in any society, between individuals and families and the state, including municipalities, business, political groups and voluntary organizations of all kinds. The size and vitality of civil society is often seen as a sign of the health of a society. Globalization has meant that a worldwide civil society is emerging, made up of all the groups and organizations whose interests and activities are no longer confined to one state. GCS includes NGOs, both those with permanent staff and large networks of volunteers, and much smaller ones without paid staff.

Many of the activist NGOs and groups focus on working on particular areas of concern – for example, for equality for women or for cancellation of debts – and can be seen as forming clusters working within, or constituting, a global social movement (GSM). These movements have grown in numbers and size as people around the world become disenchanted with traditional politics and the issues it tends to focus on, and seek new ways of expressing themselves and demanding change.

The growth of global civil society and of global social movements has led to the emergence of an anti-globalization (in the sense of neo-liberal globalization) movement, also referred to as the global justice movement, or as globalization from below. Global activists have come together to protest at G8, IMF and WTO meetings, and also at the annual **World Social Forum** (WSF). This is a gathering of tens of thousands of people representing many GSMs and other groups. It acts as a voice for a very wide range of reformist, radical groups, creating a broad coordinating body for those who oppose neo-liberal globalization. It meets annually at the same time as the

Global civil society (GCS) refers to a loose collection of NGOs, activist groups and others, overlapping with the anti-globalization movement.

The **World Social Forum** (WSF) is an annual gathering of the anti-globalization movement.

World Economic Forum, a rather secretive meeting of many of the world's political and business leaders. The WSF, with its inclusive slogan 'another world is possible', seeks to provide a progressive alternative and to demonstrate the strength of feeling globally against neo-liberal globalization.

GCS is, by its nature, very difficult to describe or measure. The Centre for the Study of Global Governance at the London School of Economics publishes a year-book on global civil society which includes a chronological record of GCS events, broadly defined. The information is gathered by people around the world (including students), and tries to record events that have not come to the attention of the main-stream media, without any bias to events in the developed world.

GCS gives a voice to people whose opinions cannot usually be heard. On the other hand, the groups and organizations involved have very different interests, motivations and characteristics, so it remains to be seen whether they have sufficient common interest to work together. There are also emerging differences of opinion. While most are left-leaning, those who see themselves as grassroots organizations are often wary of the involvement at the WSF and elsewhere of the big INGOs, politicians and repre-sentatives of business. Although GCS presents itself as an alternative to undemocratic globalization, many groups are not democratic or accountable (Jones 2006, p. 97).

The **World Economic Forum** is an annual gathering of the world's business and political leaders.

> ### Activity
>
> Here is a list of some well-known large INGOs, and also some smaller ones: Oxfam; Action Aid; Save The Children; Global Rescue Mission Sierra Leone; Tree Aid. Research one or more of these by visiting their websites or requesting their publicity material. Ask yourself these questions:
> 1 What are the main aims of this NGO?
> 2 In the UK, do they work mostly on fundraising or on raising awareness of issues?
> 3 In which developing countries do they work, and on what sorts of projects?
> 4 How effective are they in promoting development?
> Also visit the gateway to INGOs to see the range of organizations: www.uk.oneworld.net

International governmental organizations

States cannot solve problems alone, and so they cooperate to set up a growing number of supra-state organizations, referred to as international governmental organizations (IGOs). The largest and best known of these is the United Nations (UN), founded in 1947.

The UN was set up partly to promote development, but initially its activities in this area were limited by a lack of commitment from developed countries. By the 1960s, many colonies had become independent and had a vote in the UN General Assembly, so voices from the Third World began to be more influential. However, the General Assembly is mainly a debating forum and its votes are not binding. Real power in the UN is with the Security Council, which has 15 members, 5 of whom are permanent members with a veto (China, Russia, France, the UK and the USA). The 10 non-permanent members always include some developing countries. The UN also takes on a peacekeeping role in conflict situations. However, differences of opinion linked to strategic and national interests can hamper the Security Council, as when in 2008 Russia and China vetoed sanctions against Robert Mugabe's government in Zimbabwe.

The UN system comprises a wide variety of programmes and agencies. Many of these take a more radical and pro-South line than the IMF, the WTO and the World Bank, because of the numerical strength of the developing countries when voting is based on one-country-one-vote rather than on economic strength or financial contributions. So, for example, the Human Development Report produced by the UN Development Programme has a more radical interpretation of development than the World Bank's World Development Report.

UN programmes and agencies involved in development include the following:

- United Nations Development Programme (UNDP): provides grants for sustainable development and produces the Human Development Report;
- World Health Organization (WHO);
- World Food Programme (WFP): provides food aid in disaster and emergency situations; the WFP buys food to distribute, but also accepts donations; some Northern countries have used this to dispose of food surpluses, which has sometimes resulted in culturally or nutritionally inappropriate food being distributed;
- Food and Agriculture Organization (FAO): helps improve food production and food security;
- Office of the United Nations High Commissioner for Refugees (UNHCR): provides protection and assistance for refugees, including, increasingly, internally displaced people.

World Bank, International Monetary Fund and World Trade Organization

The three major supranational organizations which run the world economy are the International Monetary Fund (IMF), the World Bank and the World Trade Organization (WTO). They are formally part of the UN system, but are, in practice, separate. A common criticism of them is that they seem to have taken on lives of their own. The first two were established at a meeting of 43 countries in 1944 at **Bretton Woods**. In both cases, voting is based on financial contributions ('dollar-a-vote'), meaning that they are, in effect, under the control of developed countries, especially the USA. The President of the World Bank has always been American and the managing director of the IMF has always been a West European. Neither organization can be held accountable by other parts of the UN system, and the developed countries have rejected attempts to reform the allocation of votes. Both are large bureaucratic organizations in which admirable goals such as poverty alleviation can be lost in internal demands of the organization.

Bretton Woods is the place in the United States where an agreement in 1944 set up the IMF, the World Bank and what became the WTO.

The IMF

The IMF's role was initially to control the system of fixed exchange rates based on gold. This system ended in the early 1970s and the IMF lacked a clear role until the debt crisis began in the 1980s. The IMF then became a sort of financial police for the countries in debt, giving loans provided that the countries adopted an IMF economic programme. By the mid-1990s, many developing countries had such structural adjustment programmes.

Criticisms of the IMF's role in development A number of general criticisms are levelled at the role played by the IMF in development:

- it adheres strictly to neo-liberal policies, despite lack of evidence of their effectiveness;
- it is unconcerned with the human effects of SAPs;
- it imposes the same conditions on all regardless of how far the country has developed or what resources it has – 'one size fits all';
- it deals mainly with short-term economic problems, and is less interested in longer-term development;
- it fails to foresee economic crises, such as that in Asia in 1997.

The verdict on IMF structural adjustment programmes, as presented by a former chief economist at the World Bank, is as follows:

> IMF structural adjustment policies – the policies designed to help a country adjust to crises as well as to more persistent imbalances – led to hunger and riots in many countries; and even when the results were not so dire, even when they managed to eke out some growth for a while, often the benefits went disproportionately to the better-off, with those at the bottom sometimes facing even greater poverty. (Stiglitz 2002, p. xiv)

The World Bank

The World Bank has always had a clearer development role than the IMF. The Bank raises money from finance markets at a much lower rate of interest than governments would be able to, and then passes this rate on to its members. This enables governments of developing countries to borrow at much lower rates of interest than they could get commercially. The Bank also provides International Development Association (IDA) loans to the poorest countries, at zero interest. It has recently focused much more on poverty eradication.

Criticisms of the World Bank's role in development

- in the past, it has been restricted to lending for specific projects, such as dams, which were often inappropriate;
- it works closely with the IMF, so is still associated with SAPs.

The WTO

The WTO was set up largely at the instigation of the USA. Its mission is essentially to push for neo-liberal reforms in the area of trade. Although in theory all its member nations have an equal say, no votes are taken and decisions are reached by consensus. This means that decision-making is often difficult, and WTO talks have recently usually ended without agreement.

Criticisms of the WTO

- undemocratic decision-making, with poorer countries in theory having a vote but in practice excluded from important discussions;
- so far ineffective in making rich nations reduce subsidies and tariffs when they are determined not to;
- giving free trade priority over all other considerations, including sustainable development.

Activity

Visit the websites of the big three IGOs:

- www.imf.org
- www.worldbank.org
- www.wto.org

and of the G8:

- www.g7.utoronto.ca

To what extent do these websites acknowledge the criticisms made of the IGOs? How successfully do they put across their case?

For criticism of the IGOs, see:

- www.brettonwoodsproject.org

MDG8

To develop a global partnership for development

There are several targets embedded in this final Millennium Development Goal:

- to develop an open trading and financial system, including a commitment to good governance, development and poverty reduction;
- to address the needs of the least developed countries, landlocked and small island states;
- to deal with developing countries' debt problems, develop decent and productive work for youth;
- with pharmaceutical companies, to provide access to essential drugs;
- with the private sector, to make new technologies available.

This MDG, unlike the others, lacks benchmarks, targets and timelines; it is also the one that is the responsibility of rich countries' governments. Progress has been mixed. On trade, it has been negligible, with the governments of developed countries unwilling to allow developing countries to use the economic tools they themselves used.

On aid, it seems that billions can be raised quickly to fight terrorism or to rescue banks, but not to tackle poverty. Naidoo (2008) says that this MDG is 'the deal breaker'; the success or failure of the MDG project rests on the willingness of rich countries to meet their obligations. He suggests that global warming, because it requires global action and brings all parts of the world together, offers hope for global action against poverty too.

Activity

Which six three-word acronyms (TWAs) are relevant to global development? What do they stand for? Give a one-sentence explanation of each of them.

NGO	WHO	SAS
GCE	IMF	TNC
SAP	KFC	MBE
DHL	ITV	HDI

What are the six non-global development acronyms? Tie break: can you find any way to link these to global development sociology?

Industrialization

As we have found in our study of modernization and dependency theories, development is usually seen in terms of becoming more like the developed countries, and this involves becoming industrialized. Industrialization refers to the transition whereby the methods of production change, with accompanying social and cultural change.

The industrialization of the West

Britain was the first country to industrialize, with the Industrial Revolution usually dated roughly to the period from 1750 to 1850. Other countries such as France and the USA soon followed. Industrialization involved a 'total change', involving all aspects of society, which Polanyi called 'the Great Transformation'.

Achieving industrialization

In the 1950s and 1960s, many Third World countries tried **import substitution industrialization** (ISI); already aware of the difficulties of breaking into the markets of the developed world, they produced goods for their own domestic market, in competition with imports from the developed world. This usually involved the state setting up industries, and protecting them by putting high tariffs or even complete bans on imported goods. Countries which attempted ISI on a large scale included Mexico, Argentina, Brazil and India. Many expected economic growth to be fast and modernization to be achieved, but it soon became apparent that few countries were 'taking off'. A major problem was that the savings of domestic production of goods was balanced by the costs of importing the necessary raw materials (Hewitt 2000, p. 294).

In the 1970s, there was a shift towards **export-oriented industrialization** (EOI). This had already been achieved by Japan, which produced goods cheaply and succeeded in marketing them in the developed world. A group of other countries followed Japan – notably South Korea, Taiwan, Singapore and Hong Kong, which became known as **newly industrializing countries** (NICs) and also as the 'Asian tigers'. The NICs protected their industries in the early stages and development states provided considerable support to companies. However, the success of Japan and each subsequent

Import substitution industrialization: an industrialization strategy based on domestic production of consumer goods to replace imported ones.

Export-oriented industrialization: an industrialization strategy based on production for export.

Newly industrializing countries: those that seemed to make rapid progress in the late twentieth century, notably the 'Asian tigers'.

Japan, China and Taiwan have all succeeded in export-oriented industrialization, mass producing items for global distribution.

country seems to make it harder for other countries to succeed, because the world market is already under the control of developed countries. There are few opportunities left to exploit.

Agriculture as industry

The strength of most developing countries is in agriculture, not industry, with those especially in tropical zones having good conditions for growing crops for export to the West. Growing crops has also been the main way of life for many, and the export of cash crops was established during the colonial period. So some countries have concentrated not on industry, but on agriculture, though sometimes treating it very much as an industry in order to increase production and to meet the standards required by Western consumers and supermarkets. Production and export is often controlled by TNCs, such as Del Monte and United Fruit. The **green revolution**, which started in the 1960s, was based on new high-yield varieties and enabled production to increase substantially; but it required ever greater use of environmentally damaging fertilizers and pesticides. The growing demand for organic, fair trade and exotic food provides new opportunities for developing countries.

Green revolution: scientific and technological developments that improved agricultural yields, enabling more food to be produced in developing countries but creating some environmental problems because of heavy use of pesticides and insecticides.

New opportunities for industry

Globalization has opened up some new opportunities for developing industries, notably global tourism and using global communications technology to process data or develop software for customers in rich countries, as India has done recently.

Tourism in Africa

International tourism is a huge industry, often regarded as the third largest industry in the world after oil and vehicle production (Cohen and Kennedy 2007, p. 291, citing Sinclair and Tsegaye). Until recently, the main destinations for international tourists were a small number of developed countries, but non-Western destinations have grown in popularity.

The small West African nation of Gambia now relies heavily on tourism. To European visitors, it can oVer winter sunshine, English-speaking staV and guides, and the chance to experience Africa, even though the Gambia lacks the charismatic wildlife species of East Africa (see table 2.4).

Table 2.4: Advantages and disadvantages of tourism to the Gambia

Advantages	Disadvantages
Formal sector employment for Gambians, for example as hotel staff.	Environmental damage, especially to the coast, through hotel building and providing beaches.
Informal sector employment for Gambians, for example selling fruit to tourists on the beaches.	The presence of wealthy tourists encourages begging, prostitution and theft.
Local farmers benefit from selling their crops to hotels.	Tourists sometimes act in culturally insensitive ways.
Tourists bring and spend money, most of which goes into the local economy (though not if spent in a foreign-owned hotel).	Growing inequality between coastal areas benefiting from tourist income and inland areas which do not.
	Tourism is seasonal, leaving people unemployed or underemployed for parts of the year.
	Relying on one industry is risky; a recession, rising costs or attractions of an alternative destination could destroy many people's livelihoods.
	Hotels often import much of the food they serve and the materials they use.

For more information about the problems of tourism in developing countries: www.tourismconcern.org.uk

There is therefore a range of different strategies for developing industries that can be adopted. There are, however, some problems with the whole idea of a country having a development strategy:

- it can involve adopting the latest fashion, whether or not it is appropriate and likely to work;
- it is usually adopted by an elite and its main purpose may even be to line their own pockets;
- any strategy will have different outcomes for different groups, but they are not usually consulted – for example, industrialization needs factory workers who will have to be persuaded to leave their agricultural livelihood, and move to a city.

The social historian Barrington Moore (1967) pointed out that there is no evidence to show that any population anywhere ever wanted industrialization, and plenty to show that many did not want it. Industrialization was favoured by members of the emerging middle classes, who saw opportunities for enrichment and to take power

Informal sector: employment, characterized by lack of regular work and wages, including petty trading, self-employment, casual work and so on; the dominant sector in cities in developing countries.

from the rulers of pre-industrial society. For the masses, there were fewer benefits. In Britain, industrialization was strongly opposed (by the Luddites, in the Swing riots of the 1830s, for example) because it would end traditional livelihoods and would uproot people from their homes and destroy communities. Polanyi described the great transformation as a struggle between those who wanted to establish the market as the organizing principle of society and those who wanted to protect themselves, their land and their livelihoods against the new market forces (in Thomas 2000, pp. 39–40). Industrialization requires one generation to pay a heavy social and environmental price in order that their descendants can (perhaps) benefit.

Is there a new international division of labour?

The 'traditional' division of labour, established in the colonial period, meant that the colonies provided the raw materials for the industries of the colonizing powers. Industries in the colonies themselves were discouraged; in India, for example, the cotton clothing industry was destroyed so that it could not compete with Britain's cotton mills.

From the 1970s onwards, manufacturing production moved away from developed countries and increasingly to developing countries. The spread of TNCs and improvements in global travel and communication changed the earlier pattern. The **new international division of labour** (NIDL) refers to the new situation whereby manufacturing takes place in the developing world, with goods exported to and consumed mainly in the North. This idea is a useful one because it draws attention to the increasing use of cheap labour in poor countries to produce goods for rich countries. In some ways, however, the term is misleading for several reasons:

The **new international division of labour** (NIDL) refers to the new global economic order said to be produced by factory production moving from the developed world to some developing countries.

1 Many poor countries still rely heavily on the export of food and raw material, while rich countries still have some manufacturing industries – so the old division of labour survives alongside the new.
2 Most investment of capital by TNCs continues to be within the developed 'Triad' (Europe, Japan and the USA); less investment goes to Africa and South America than it did 50 years ago.
3 Rich countries also have to compete for TNC investment.

Urbanization

Urbanization: the process by which a growing proportion of people live in towns and cities, and the social and other changes which accompany this process.

For the first time, more than half the world's population (more than 3 billion people), live in cities, a dramatic rise from 13 per cent in 1900. This is the result of **urbanization**. The urban population is expected to grow at 1.8 per cent a year until 2030, nearly twice the rate of growth of the population as a whole. The growth of cities in developing countries will be much faster than that in developed countries. Rural populations are expected to remain stable overall, though with some variation between regions of the world.

Urbanization refers to the process by which the proportion of a country's population living in cities increases and also to the related economic, social and political changes. A city is usually defined as having more than 100,000 inhabitants; mega-cities

Table 2.5: The world's largest cities

2005		2015 (projected)	
City	Population (millions)	City	Population (millions)
Tokyo, Japan	35.2	Tokyo, Japan	35.5
Mexico City, Mexico	19.4	Mumbai, India	21.9
New York, USA	18.7	Mexico City, Mexico	21.6
São Paulo, Brazil	18.3	São Paulo, Brazil	20.5
Mumbai, India	18.2	New York, USA	19.9
Delhi, India	15.0	Delhi, India	18.6
Shanghai, China	14.5	Shanghai, China	17.2
Kolkata (Calcutta), India	14.3	Calcutta, India	17.0
Jakarta, Indonesia	13.2	Dhaka, Bangladesh	16.8
Buenos Aires, Argentina	12.6	Jakarta, Indonesia	16.8

Source: United Nations, World Urbanization Prospects 2005

have more than 10 million inhabitants. Urbanization occurs as a result of migration but also of smaller settlements growing so that they are reclassified as cities.

Historically, many cities were in what is now described as the developing world. For example, in the Middle Ages, China had several cities with populations of more than 1 million people. The phenomenon of most of a country's population living in cities is, however, relatively modern – it dates from industrialization and was first seen in England (in 1800, 20 per cent of the population lived in towns and cities; by 1900 that figure was 74 per cent).

In 1950, there were only two mega-cities: New York and Tokyo; by 2005, there were 20, of which 15 were in developing countries. Tokyo was the largest urban agglomeration in the world in 2005, with 35 million residents. Tokyo is expected to remain the largest metropolis, although its population will not grow substantially. Mumbai (Bombay) is expected to become the second largest mega-city by 2015, with a population of 22 million, followed by Mexico City, São Paulo, New York and Delhi. Most of the world's largest cities are now in the developing world (World Urbanization Prospects 2005, revision).

Modernization theorists, looking back to the model of Western development, see the growth of cities as an essential part of economic growth. Cities provide a labour force concentrated in one place for factories and businesses. They are also important in promoting cultural change, because they remove people from the countryside, where traditional ways are strongest, and expose them to Western values. Modernization theorists would therefore expect that urbanization would be an essential part of the process of cultural and economic change leading to development.

However, there are several ways in which urbanization in developing countries today is different from the process that the now developed world experienced in the past:

1   Third World cities tend to be bigger and fewer. There is often a principal city, much larger than any other cities in the country, where there will be an international airport and other facilities.
2   Urbanization has not been accompanied by industrialization; city-dwellers often make a living from informal sector work rather than being formally employed.
3   The poor in the growing Western cities of the nineteenth century formed a proletariat, working in factories and workshops and often organized in trade unions, Marx saw this industrial working class as the group that would rise in revolution to overthrow capitalism. While traditional Marxists dismissed the urban poor as having no revolutionary potential, Franz Fanon (1963) in *The Wretched of the Earth*, turned this derogatory view around and said that their very marginality made them potentially revolutionary – they had nothing to lose.

Fanon's view is not widely shared when the poor in the cities of the developing world are considered today, because few strong political movements have arisen. Nancy Scheper-Hughes wrote of the people she studied over several years in South America:

> It is too much to expect the people of the Alto to organize collectively when chronic scarcity makes individually negotiated relations of dependency on myriad political and personal bosses in town a necessary survival tactic. . . . Staying alive in the shanty town demands a certain 'selfishness' that pits individuals against each other and that rewards those who take advantage of those even weaker. (Quoted in Beall 2000, p. 441)

Dependency theorists point out that colonialism has made it impossible for developing countries to follow in the footsteps of the developed world. Urbanization in developing countries today is fundamentally different because it is not a response to industrialization. Many cities in developing countries were established or grew dramatically under colonial rule, because they were used as administrative centres and as staging posts in exports of raw materials and cash crops. A two-tiered social system grew up, with the colonial administrators and some of their higher-ranking native allies enjoying a much higher standard of living and access to goods than the mass of the population. Dependency theorists argue that these characteristics have not changed under neo-colonialism, as TNCs have replaced the colonial powers. Cities play a key role in keeping countries underdeveloped by soaking up resources in unproductive ways

Urban housing in developing countries

In developing countries, the number of people in cities far exceeds the number of jobs available, leaving many unemployed or underemployed. The poor usually have

A shanty town in South Africa.

no access to regular housing, so they build their own. The areas they live in exist everywhere under different names: shanty towns, barrios, favelas, bidonvilles, bustees. They are often on illegally occupied land, and governments generally see them as problems, so that the residents live under constant threat of their homes being demolished. The housing is, at least initially, temporary and of low quality, but over time some more permanent features are created, with residents acting together to arrange resources and amenities. For the people who live there, they are often a viable solution to their problems, providing accommodation they can afford close to sources of income. Spontaneous settlements (a more neutral term than 'shanty towns') also offer new arrivals in the city a foothold and can encourage self-help and collective action; they can be, in Lloyd's (1979) term, 'slums of hope'. Not surprisingly, though, access to water, sanitation, education, health and other resources is low. Residents are often unable to vote, because they do not have a legal address, and are vulnerable to exploitation by landlords, politicians, police and criminals (Slatterthwaite 2007).

Migration

Much urban growth is the result of natural population increase, but migration also plays a large part. Migrants tend to be unmarried male adults who move for a variety of **push and pull factors** (see figure 2.7). The pull factors have a negative side, because the influx of large numbers of people without steady incomes contributes to urban squalor. Step migration is common; that is, people move from a rural area to a town to a city, and perhaps on to the developed world. Migration is often seasonal; migrants retain close links with rural family members and may return home to help with the harvest, for example, or they may send money home.

Push factors refer to the disadvantages of rural life which push people into moving to cities.

Pull factors refer to the advantages of city life which attract people to move there from rural areas.

Figure 2.7 Push
and pull factors
involved in
migration

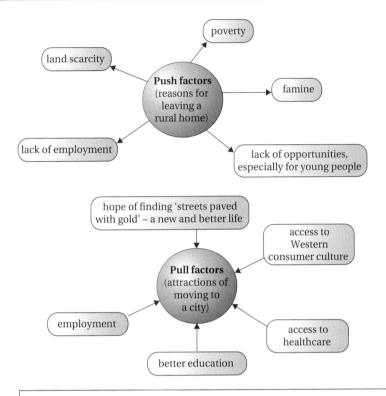

> **MDG7 – target 7c**
>
> *To improve the lives of at least 100 million slum-dwellers by 2020*
> One in three city-dwellers lives in slum conditions, defined as lacking one of three
> basic conditions of decent housing: adequate sanitation, improved water supply and
> durable housing or adequate living space. One in five city-dwellers lives in overcrowded
> conditions, defined as more than three people sharing a bedroom. The rapid expansion
> of the number of city-dwellers will make it hard to reach the goal.

Differences between urban and rural poverty in developing countries

People in cities are usually closer to facilities and services that those living in rural areas
– but that doesn't mean they have access to them. In the cities of developing countries,
the living conditions of the poor are often worse than those who live in rural areas.
Such conditions include overcrowding, contaminated water, poor or absent sanitation, threat of floods/landslides and indoor pollution. In the case of water, supplies are
now privatized in most countries as a result of free market policies and SAPs. In cities,
piped water and sewerage is usually only provided for a minority in affluent areas
(where the company supplying the service can expect to make a profit). Companies
pursuing profit have no interest in providing services to people who cannot pay for
them. So the poor buy their water from vendors – they pay more than their wealthier
fellow citizens do and the water they buy is of a poorer quality (Beall 2000, p. 439). In
rural areas, people are more likely to have access to natural water supplies, which are

generally not privately owned and so are free to all. People in rural areas also benefit from having family members in cities who send home some of their earnings.

Cities and the environment

Cities are often seen as the main source of pollution and greenhouse gas emissions. However, having large numbers of people and industries in one place makes it easier to bring in new environmental regulations and lowers the cost of delivering water, sanitation and healthcare (Slatterthwaite 2007). Cities also provide opportunities to change the way people live more quickly, for example by designs which favour public transport, cycling and walking rather than cars.

The environment

Throughout history human activity has changed the environment. Most of what appears to be natural landscape has in fact been shaped by people. For most of history this was not seen as a problem, but as inevitable and even necessary; to survive and to prosper, people had to use what was around them (Woodhouse 2000, p. 141).

Concern about human effects on the environment can be seen in the Romantic movement in the early nineteenth century, which celebrated nature and deplored the new industrial landscape of factories and cities. By the second half of the twentieth century, it was recognized that pollution of air and water was a serious threat to health. The environment became an important political issue, and one intimately linked to economic growth and development. Within society and sociology, it became clear that human society was part of nature, not separate from and above it.

Economic growth and industrialization, which developing countries are trying to achieve, will cause further environmental degradation if practised in the same way as by the West. China, for example, has large reserves of coal and will use them to meet its citizens' energy needs, despite the contribution to global warming that will accompany this. Green thinking in developed countries can involve, in effect, telling people in developing countries that they should not aspire to the lifestyle that people in the West have enjoyed.

Many environmental issues are now seen as being global, but both the causes and the effects are unequally distributed between regions of the world. The consumerist lifestyle of the developed world and its greater energy and fuel use mean that it creates and worsens many of the problems. The situation of poorer countries means that the effects of such problems are particularly severe, especially for poorer people, who lack the resources to move or to improve their position. For example, it is the poor who live on land that is liable to flooding, or close to sources of pollution, because they cannot afford to move anywhere else.

Global warming refers to the rise in global temperatures now acknowledged to be caused mainly by human activity, likely to lead to severe consequences such as rising sea levels and increased desertification.

Some current environmental issues:

- global warming, attributed mainly to carbon emissions (from factories, power plants, cars, aeroplanes, etc.);

- deforestation, particularly loss of tropical rain forest;
- desertification, involving the loss of farm land;
- loss of biodiversity: extinction of species, depletion of the gene pool of other species and loss of variety of ecosystems to support biodiversity;
- land, air and water pollution, damaging shared resources, including the dumping of waste, especially toxic waste in developing countries by TNCs or Western governments;
- ozone depletion: the only issue on which the world has so far been able to work together and make significant progress, by banning the use of chlorofluorocarbons (CFCs).

Deforestation refers to the fall in the amount of land covered by forest as a result of human activity.

Desertification is the spread of deserts, as land on the edges of deserts loses its vegetation and top soil.

Biodiversity refers to the number and variety of species in ecosystems, threatened by human activity.

Shared resources (also 'public goods') are those resources that are not privately owned and whose use is freely shared – for example air, water (unless you choose to buy bottled water) and parts of the countryside.

Exhaustible resources are those that can be renewed, but can also be exhausted and destroyed if overused, for example, fish stocks and forests.

MDG7

To ensure environmental sustainability

1. Although globally the amount of forested land remained constant from 2000 to 2005, deforestation continues, and is particularly affecting regions that are biologically diverse. The world has lost 3 per cent of the forest it had in 1990 and forest continues to be converted to agricultural land in Africa and South America.

2. Biodiversity: there is a continuing loss of biodiversity, partly due to the overuse of exhaustible resources. More areas are protected, but more species are threatened with extinction. Only 22 per cent of the world's fisheries are now sustainable.

3. Greenhouse gas emissions continue to grow, nearly doubling in the developing world between 1990 and 2005. Global energy consumption has grown by 20 per cent in that period.

4. Ozone layer: the clearest example of progress has been in the reduction of ozone depleting substances; concentration of CFCs in the atmosphere is down, though it will take time for damage to the ozone layer to be reversed. CFCs continue to be produced and traded illegally.

5. Sanitation: half the developing world lacks safe drinking water or basic sanitation (this is part of the environmental MDG because it is pollution that makes water unsafe to drink, and because water is, or should be, a public good).

Environmental problems in developing countries

Environmental problems are not seen in the same way in the North as they are in the South. For the North, at least for those concerned with the environment, the focus is on issues such as global warming, deforestation and conserving habitats, often using the discourse of sharing a small planet. In the South, there is more concern about the effects of TNCs, uneven trade and Western consumerism in making it difficult for developing countries to avoid problems (Cudworth 2003, p. 148). The pressure to attract investment from TNCs leads some developing countries to weaken environmental controls – for example, having less stringent controls on pollution. The use of the best agricultural land by TNCs for cash crop production, employing few workers, pushes small farmers onto marginal land, for example on the edge of forests, and into unsustainable use of the forest and its resources.

Some Southern environmentalists have accused the North of using environmental concerns as a cover for their own interests, with international agreements that appear fair often seeming in practice to allow TNCs to carry on with unsustainable practices. The USA, in particular, seems unwilling to act if there is likely to be any impact on its corporate interests – for example, in refusing to join 160 countries in signing the Kyoto Protocol on the reduction of carbon emissions.

The current emphasis in developed countries on recycling can have a negative impact in developing countries as well. Poorer countries are often dependent on the use of natural resources (timber, mining, etc.). Recycling of scrap materials and the substitution of synthetic materials reduces demand for these.

Clash of interests

Actions to try to protect the environment are political and run the risk of affecting some people adversely. The well-meaning attempts of outsiders may be met with hostility and may create social problems even as they try to solve environmental ones. George Monbiot gives this example:

> The Bambuti Ba'twa tribe of Pygmies who used to live in the low equatorial forests on the border of Rwanda and what is now the Democratic Republic of Congo had their lands designated a national park to protect gorillas. The Pygmies were evicted in the name of conservation and are now found in small groups living in squalor on the edge of the park.
> 'Life was healthy and good, but we have become beggars, thieves and prowlers,' said one chief. 'This disaster has been imposed on us by the creation of the national park.' (Monbiot 2008)

Applying the theories

Neo-liberals

Neo-liberals see the solution to environmental problems in the extension of the free market. Capitalism may have contributed to environmental problems, but its nature as an unprecedented 'growth machine' (Saunders 1999, p. 269) means that it will generate solutions to the problems. So current problems such as the use of high-polluting **non-renewable** fuels for cars and other transport will be solved as costs rise, creating incentives to develop more environmentally acceptable alternatives. Such solutions are referred to as 'technological fixes', and both environmentalists and sociologists tend to be very sceptical about them. Environmental problems have their roots in complex social and economic contexts, so a 'fix' seems too easy. Moreover, the fix has to come from pursuit of greater wealth by individuals or corporations when most environmentalists would prefer a collaborative effort. Neo-liberals also advocate privatization or commodification of public goods, extending the market into areas it has not reached before. The owners would act as custodians and would promote sustainable use because this would make economic sense

Non-renewable resources: those which, once used, are gone forever, such as coal and oil.

Neo-Malthusians

The **neo-Malthusian** view is put forward by those influenced by the writings of Thomas Malthus (explained in more details below, on pages 174–6). They are concerned by the implications for the environment of population growth, especially in developing countries. For neo-Malthusians, those whose damage to their environment most

Neo-Malthusian: modern followers of Malthus's main argument, that population growth will overtake food supply.

needs curbing are poor people in developing countries, especially in rural areas. Their poverty leads them to degrade the environment. Even if they are aware of the long-term problems being created, short-term needs mean they use the available resources. Population growth contributes to this. Growing numbers of people mean that marginal land has to be farmed, with loss of soil and eventual desertification.

Anti-Malthusians

For anti-Malthusians, who are often environmentalists, the people whose damage to the environment most needs curbing are the wealthiest people on the planet, because they consume a far greater share of resources and generate far more waste than poor people do. They would point to the fact that exploitation of the developing world's resources is for the benefit of consumers in the North. A poor family may take firewood from a forest, but it takes a timber company with an export market to devastate large areas of rainforest.

It is not population that is the basic problem, but consumption – not how many people there are, but how much they consume. The unequal global distribution of resources is the real underlying issue. The world can sustain far more people if they have a lifestyle based on low use of resources than it can if they have a lifestyle like that in the West today. Anti-Malthusians argue that developed world consumers must reduce their consumption levels.

Activity

Ten of the words below are concepts used in global development; the rest are not. Find the global development terms and then write one-sentence explanations of each of them:

Panthusian	Modernization	Mint imperialism	Sustainability
Satellites of love	Commodious	Underdevelopment	Malthusian
Cultural imperialism	Desertification	Urbane metropolitans	Malapropism
Dependency	Agribusiness	Herbivorous	Neo-anti-postmodernism
Neo-liberalism	Metropolis	Structural violence	Structural isomerism

---

War and conflict

Structural violence: Galtung's term for the way in which even in an apparently peaceful society, a group (usually distinct because of, for example, its gender, ethnicity, religion or caste) can be exploited by the systematic denial of their rights.

Conflict in the sense of struggles between groups or individuals is an inevitable feature of any complex society. Many sociologists emphasize conflict within societies, as opposed to consensus. If conflict is taken in this wider sense, rather than meaning violence, it can also be seen as necessary and positive, providing the impetus for change and progress. All societies develop ways of managing conflicts; for example, the democratic political process manages changes of government without coups or revolutions. But conflicts can develop into wars.

Rwanda as a structurally violent society

In analyzing the roots of the Rwandan genocide in which more than half a million people died, Uvin (1998) has argued that Rwanda before the genocide was a structurally violent society. Its economy was growing, and many aid agencies were working there.

> But only a small group, the 'state class', was benefiting, and there was growing inequality, with education and health poor following a structural adjustment programme. An apparently peaceful society concealed mounting anger which was channelled into scapegoating of the Tutsi group in the genocide.

The nature of wars today

War can be defined differently depending on the answers to questions such as:

- How many deaths are there and over what period?
- What are the causes of death? (only battle-related, or including disease which has spread because of the war?)
- Are regular armed forces involved?
- Is the purpose to control all or part of a state?

By most counts, there have been around 35–50 wars going on at any one time in recent years. Since the end of the Cold War, and with the exceptions of the US-led invasions of Iraq and Afghanistan, most wars have not been the conventional wars of history between two or more states for possession of territory. States have lost the monopoly on military violence. Most of today's wars are civil wars, and occur in some of the poorest developing countries. Kaldor (1999) calls them 'new wars', arguing that although they appear localized, they involve global 'shadow' economies and global networks such as the arms trade, diamonds and drugs. They are a result of globalization, and to some extent a reaction against it.

Why are there so many civil wars in the poorest countries?

Neo-Malthusians would see uncontrolled population growth and environmental scarcity as the main factors. Countries such as Sierra Leone are those where the struggle to survive is most intense. This is the New Barbarism thesis, which is explained below on page 175.

Mohammed Ayoob (2001) argues that civil wars are part of the process of creating modern states. Medieval and early modern Europe experienced similar wars, with many warlords controlling often small areas and constantly shifting borders and alliances. From this view, related to modernization theory, civil wars will become less common as countries begin to modernize. Peace will come as a result of free trade and democracy.

Contrasted with these views are those, related to dependency theory, which see civil wars in the global context and look at external factors. Amongst the factors contributing to civil wars are:

- relative poverty worsening: some groups in these countries are not benefiting from globalization and development, or are affected by SAPs;
- weak state institutions: the state ceases to be able to provide social goods such as security, health and education, and is less able to resist challenges such as rebellions (Hanlon 2006b, p. 123);

- the presence of unemployed young men who see no future for themselves (for example, being unable to find a wife or support a family);
- changes in terms of trade adversely affecting people; for example, the ending of the International Coffee Agreement by the USA in 1989, which drastically reduced the incomes of Rwandan coffee farmers – the resulting poverty contributed to the 1994 genocide;
- the arms trade: weapons and equipment are easily and cheaply available;
- aid can help create the conditions for war if most of the benefits go to one group and so strengthen inequalities;
- the presence of valuable resources such as oil or diamonds, which can be goals in themselves or can be used to buy arms and military equipment;
- ethnic or other divisions which can be exploited by politicians and others seeking power;
- interference by other countries.

Underlying and uniting all of these, it can be argued, is structural violence on a global scale – 'the deliberate maintenance of a global system based on fundamental and self-reinforcing inequality' (Richard Cornwell, quoted in Hanlon 2006b, p. 124).

Civil wars

Civil wars tend to be marked by shocking brutality. A good example is the practice of Sierra Leonean rebels of cutting off the hands or feet of their victims, most of whom were civilians. This is partly because rules of war such as the Geneva Convention, to which most states subscribe, do not apply.

Most of the casualties in civil wars are civilians, who die because of reduced access to food and healthcare rather than in battle. It is therefore very difficult to calculate

A child solider in South-east Asia. What consequences might there be for a society in which young children are required to fight in wars and conflicts?

how many people have died, especially as civilian casualties may not be counted. People flee from their home areas because of fear, and so wars create refugees. Some will join an armed group as the best survival option.

Women and children are often the main victims of war, but both are also increasingly involved in the fighting too. War destroys families and leaves widows, widowers and orphaned children. It is often easier for a widower to find a new partner, because there are likely to be fewer men than women. A widow without family support may find it difficult to make a living, and to find a new partner, especially if she has been raped or become pregnant. Child soldiers (both boys and girls) have been a visible new feature of some recent wars such as those in Sierra Leone and Uganda.

Intervention in civil wars

Wars often lead to intervention. This may be by a neighbouring country, but is more likely to be a multilateral intervention, by the United Nations or a regional grouping such as the African Union. Intervention can succeed in imposing a ceasefire, but this may just give the combatants time to regroup and rearm. The end of fighting is not the end of the problem; unless the underlying causes of the war are removed, fighting is likely to resume. More than half of all civil wars restart within 10 years.

The purpose of intervention is to stop the killing. This is, however, not always the most desirable outcome. A quick end to a war may bring a bloody dictator to power, with greater loss of life and probably little progress to follow. It may be better for there to be a long war to defend a popular elected government than to allow the government to be overthrown quickly in a coup. Luttwak (1999) has argued provocatively that it can be better to let wars run their course, because they will eventually end with a resolution of political conflict and with peace. Intervention prevents wars from 'naturally' coming to an end, by a decisive victory for one side or through exhaustion of both sides.

The effects of war on development

Only 11 per cent of countries that were ranked in the top half of the Human Development Index in 2003 had experienced an armed conflict in the preceding 10 years. Of the countries in the lower half of the index, 43 per cent had done so (Ware 2006, p. 108).

Although poverty can lead to war, so too does war create poverty, for a number of reasons:

1   War is expensive, absorbing money that could be used for development.
2   War destroys the infrastructure that makes development possible: schools, hospitals and health centres and the roads and bridges that trade relies on.
3   The human costs of war can be enormous – for example, communities, families, homes and businesses are often destroyed, and people are left wounded and disabled as well as homeless.
4   Unexploded munitions and landmines cause deaths and impede agriculture for many years after a war.

5 Environmental costs can be very high, including bomb damage and other arms that destroy or cause damage to, for example, forests, wildlife and agricultural land, from which it may take many years to recover. Such damage might be the direct result of explosions as well as of the release of poisons into air, water and land.

6 Refugees are forced to use whatever is available to survive, resulting in further environmental damage; for example, they need to use any available wood for fires to keep warm, cook and boil water.

War kills after the fighting has stopped

The war in Congo officially ended in 2002. Yet findings from the International Rescue Committee, based on a nationwide survey, found that the crude mortality rate in Congo from January 2006 to April 2007 was 57 per cent higher than the average for sub-Saharan Africa. The committee estimates that from 1998 to 2007 there were 5.4 million excess deaths because of the war, and that more than 2 million of these were after the 2002 peace agreement. Less than 0.5 per cent of recent deaths were from violence; after the war, people were dying from infectious diseases, malnutrition and pregnancy and childbirth-related causes. The social and economic disruption caused by the war, with people displaced, infrastructure destroyed and health services and food supplies weaker, led to higher rates of disease and death. Children accounted for 47 per cent of deaths, but make up only 19 per cent of the total population (Brennan et al. 2008).

The arms trade

Most of the weapons used in wars were produced by the permanent five members of the UN Security Council. Originally, most were sold legally to other states, but increasingly the arms trade involves transnational criminal networks.

Terrorism

Terrorism: in war and conflict, the use of tactics intended to persuade the opponents, or civilians, not to resist.

Terrorism is now an inescapable part of war. In traditional wars, it is used sometimes as a supplementary measure, but in civil wars it has become more important than armed action. Groups that cannot sustain traditional armed action terrorize civilians. The word terrorism was first used for state actions, and many states have used terror tactics against parts of their own population or others or have sponsored terrorism. Although the distinctions between state-directed terror, state-sponsored terror and non-state terror are often blurred, in popular use the term now usually refers to non-state terror.

The US State Department defines terror as 'politically motivated violence perpetrated against non-combatant targets by subnational groups or clandestine agents, usually intended to influence an audience' (Cohen and Kennedy 2007, p. 234). According to this definition, incidents of terrorism fell from a peak of around 660 in 1987 to around 200 in the early 2000s. The Islamic jihadist attacks on the USA on 11 September 2001 came in a context of declining non-state terrorism. The Islamic jihadists comprise a globalized form of terrorism, present in small groups around the world and attacking globally dispersed targets. They also differ from earlier terrorists in not always claiming responsibility for attacks, in having few or no specific demands and in being more indiscriminate. These characteristics may indicate a change in the nature of terrorism; Giddens refers to 'new-style terrorism' (2006, p. 886).

> **Activity**
>
> Find out more about the nature and extent of terrorism, including recent incidents, from the Terrorism Research Centre website: www.terrorism.com.

> **Activity**
>
> Exam-style questions:
> 1 Identify and briefly explain three ways in which TNCs can influence development. (9 marks)
> 2 Assess the view that war and conflict are the main reasons for the lack of development in some parts of the Third World. (18 marks)
> 3 'Population growth is a major problem facing developing countries and if unchecked will lead to food shortages and environmental degradation.' To what extent do sociological arguments and evidence support this view? (33 marks)

Employment

There are many more people in developing countries than in developed countries who are not in full-time regular paid work, but few households where there is no income at all. The issues are different from those in the North, where some house-holds have no paid work at all. Unemployment statistics would not give an accurate picture of work and non-work in the South.

Many people in the South, especially in cities, rely for their income on work in the informal sector. This includes self-employment, micro-enterprises, petty trading, casual and irregular work and personal services. Work in the informal sector is often labour-intensive and unregulated, and may be illegal. Informal-sector businesses are

A roadside fruit and vegetable stall in Guam in the Western Pacific, an example of the informal sector. What other examples of economic production might official figures not take account of?

usually not officially registered and may not pay tax. People working in this sector make a living (just about) in an astonishing variety of ways, which reveal the extent of human ingenuity. But such work is precarious, often temporary, and the problems are especially acute for women, minority ethnic groups and disabled people. In the informal sector people tend to work very hard but productivity is low and they do not get paid well.

In addition, many people in developing countries support themselves and their families through growing food for their own consumption (subsistence agricultural production), or by hunting, fishing and gathering.

Work in the formal sector tends to involve large businesses with fairly stable employment, higher wages and regulated conditions (for example, paid holidays and sick pay), and workers may even be able to organize themselves as trade unions. The formal sector includes those working for TNCs, or for local businesses supplying TNCs. Where these can be described as sweat shops, there are normally regulations on pay and conditions, even if these are not being applied fully. Formal-sector work is in short supply (TNCs only account for about 5–6 per cent of the world's jobs, and many of those are in the developed world) (McGiffen 2002, p. 80) and is highly sought-after in most countries. Despite offering good pay and conditions by local standards, TNCs are still the target of criticism from campaigners because workers receive only a very small proportion of profits in the form of wages and benefits, with most of the wealth created being taken out of the country.

The economy of developing countries therefore consists not only of the formal, recorded economy, but also of the 'informal' economy, which is unrecorded and might include activities like production for own consumption, which replace money and market activities. Taken together, these are the 'real economy' (Wield and Chataway 2000, p. 108). A similar situation exists in developed countries, but there the formal sector is much larger and the other two sectors are smaller. These differences mean that it is very difficult to establish reliable statistics on employment or unemployment.

Where the informal sector is the main way of making money, some groups are in particularly difficult situations, for example:

1 *Children.* Even where schooling is free, time spent in school is time that could be spent earning money, so children may work rather than go to school.
2 *The elderly.* The idea of retirement belongs to the formal sector, and there are unlikely to be state pensions.
3 *People with disabilities.* In the absence of state support, disabled people rely on family and community, or may generate income by begging. In Sierra Leone's civil war, the rebels often cut off the hands or feet of victims; a priority for both government and NGOs has been to train victims in skills that will help them find work.
4 *Women.* In some cultures it is unacceptable for women to work outside the home. Women are often reliant on husbands and fathers to earn money; for women alone, such as widows, making money may be very difficult.

Although more jobs have been created as countries experience economic growth, globally the number of unemployed people has grown and will continue to grow because the number of people of working age will grow. The bigger problem concealed by the figures is the number of people who are underemployed, unable to work to their full potential and unable to work themselves out of poverty.

Globalization and the availability of cheaper international travel have enabled increasing numbers of people from developing countries to work in the North. Some are well trained and qualified, for example as doctors; others are unqualified. Some work legally, others not; some are abroad only for a short period and others stay for many years. In all cases, the big pull of the North is the availability of higher wages. Although to some extent these are absorbed by the higher costs of living, being able to send money home to support families in the country of origin is an increasingly important aspect of many economies; Harris has described it as 'one of the most successful mechanisms for redistributing the world's income in favour of poorer countries' (Harris 1995).

Helping people make a living

One way in which agencies have sought to support the informal sector is through **micro-credit** loans. Poor people are unlikely to be able to borrow money from a bank to start a small-scale enterprise; micro-credit fills this need with small loans, often supported by training, for example in how to track stock and keep accounts. The best-known scheme is the Grameen Bank, launched in Bangladesh by Mohammed Yunus, but such schemes are now widespread across the South and have also been used in developed countries. Micro-credit schemes are not without problems, however. Many loans have been to women, for the best of motives, but not always with awareness of gender relations in the community and wider society, potential conflicts with men, and the potential difficulties of repaying the debt (Pearson 2000, pp. 396–7).

Micro-credit: schemes to allow poor people to borrow small sums of money.

Child labour

Many children around the world work; for example, those aged 14 and over in Britain can do some kinds of part-time work. Such work can be valuable preparation for work later in life, but the law limits the amount and type of work so that the child's education does not suffer.

In developing countries, families have often relied on children to work – for example, helping on the family farm or selling the produce at a market. This has been cited as one reason for families having several children: children who work are an economic asset to the family. The International Labour Organization (ILO) makes a distinction between working children and child labour. The ILO works to abolish child labour, but recognizes that some work by children, depending on age and local conditions such as the availability of schooling, is acceptable and even essential.

Child labour normally refers to children under the age of 15 who work for more than 14 hours a week (and who are usually not attending school). The ILO estimates that in 2004 about 14 per cent of children aged 5–17, about 218 million, were child labourers, more than half of these in hazardous work. The great majority were in developing countries, and there were many more boys than girls. Both the number and percentage of child labourers has fallen in recent years as a result of international campaigns to reduce child labour, and the ILO believes that total abolition is possible, arguing that the cost of eliminating child labour is much lower than the benefits gained in health and education (Hagemann et al. 2006).

Education

Education – and schools in particular – is widely accepted as an essential aspect of development. On achieving independence, countries committed to development often spent highly on education. In the past, boys were more likely than girls to be educated, but there is an increasingly strong emphasis on education for girls, because this is seen as effective not only in getting women into the workforce, but also in raising general education and health standards.

However, many schools and pupils in developing countries face problems, some of which are outlined here:

1 Many countries cannot afford universal primary, let alone universal secondary, education.
2 Teachers are not well paid, so teaching is not an attractive career. It is not unusual for teachers to take on other jobs at the same time in order to supplement their pay. The country may also struggle to train teachers well, or may have to take people on as teachers whose qualifications are not really good enough.
3 Schools are under-resourced – they have access to few textbooks, little science or other practical equipment.
4 Many schools are housed in inadequate buildings with few facilities.
5 Schools may charge fees which parents cannot afford. Parents may decide to keep children out of school so that they can earn a wage or help a family business.
6 Even where there are no fees, parents will be expected to pay for uniform and books. Children whose parents cannot afford this will be unable to go to school unless scholarships or other help are available.
7 The education system and the curriculum are often shaped by the experience of colonialism – for example, English literature is studied rather than the country's own literature.
8 Many African schools, in order to maximize use of buildings and resources, often operate on double shifts: one group of children is educated in the morning, a different group in the afternoon. This is a good use of resources but it means that children do not get a full day of schooling, and teachers who work both shifts will be overworked.
9 War disrupts education.
10 Pupils may have a lot of time off school because of illness, such as bouts of malaria.
11 Even for pupils who do well at primary level, there are often not enough secondary places available. Walking a long distance to school may be necessary.
12 To try to meet the Millennium Development Goals, countries are getting more children enrolled, but the facilities are not always there to ensure a good quality of education. Progress towards the MDG may be achieved, but only with overcrowded classes, poor facilities and untrained teachers.

This community in Zambia recognizes the importance of education in development. But what factors might cause a developing nation such as Zambia to give less priority to education? Could some of these factors also apply to a country like the UK?

Modernization theory

Modernization theorists argue that education is essential to development. They favour a Western-style education system and curriculum, able to spread modern values. Higher education is essential to train future political and business leaders. The level of education required is linked to the country's stage of economic growth; a fully modernized society will need a well-educated general population, The theory of **human capital** argues that investment in education, provided it is tied into developing the skills necessary for industry, can be a basis for modernization, and that human capital can to some extent make up for shortage of money capital. Education is a way to spread modern values, to encourage entrepreneurial skills and break with traditional values that act as a brake on modernization.

Human capital: the theory that a country's people are a potential source of wealth; by educating its people a country can increase its human capital.

Dependency theory

Dependency theorists see education as it is normally practised as a form of cultural imperialism, imposing Western values. Dependency theorists argue that education was one of the main ways colonial powers exercised control over their colonies – existing education systems were replaced by new systems which trained a small elite in the colonial powers' values and rewarded them with jobs. The elite had a stake in the system and would support it. On independence, developing countries inherited inappropriate education systems geared to the needs of a minority. Copying Western-style education systems is today not appropriate, when the situation of developing countries is so different.

Beacon of excellence or a wasteful parody?

Kamuzu Academy in Malawi, Southern Africa, is modelled on Eton. Pupils wear boater hats with a green and gold uniform and have to study Latin and Greek to GCSE level. They have piano lessons and a golf course.

Dr Hastings Banda, President of Malawi from 1961 to 1994, founded the school to ensure that Malawi's brightest children could fulfil their potential, and in so doing to train the country's future leaders. When first set up, it took most of Malawi's education budget, so most other children received no education at all. When Banda died in 1997, the school went through a difficult period but is now doing well, with very good results at GCSE. A small number of poorer children who pass an entrance exam receive bursaries, but most pupils have their fees paid by wealthy parents – so wealthy that if Kamuzu did not exist, they would probably be sent to a boarding school in the UK or elsewhere (Carroll 2002).

Universal primary education

MDG2

To achieve universal primary education

The number of children in primary education is measured by the net enrolment ratio, which is the number of children of primary school age who are enrolled in school as a percentage of the age group. For the whole developing world, the net enrolment ratio is now 88, up from 80 in 1991. There were about 72 million children of primary school age not enrolled in 2005, of whom 57 per cent were girls. The enrolment figure is an underestimate because some children are enrolled but do not attend, or do not attend regularly, and also because figures are usually not available for areas affected by war, where schools are unlikely to be able to work normally. Girls and children from poorer or rural families are the least likely to be in school. One child in five of secondary school age is still in primary school. Starting school late, and slow progress through the grades, perhaps with whole years out because of illness or when parents cannot afford fees and uniform, puts children at a disadvantage and prevents them progressing far in their education.

Overall, there has been progress, but the world is not on course to meet this MDG.

The second MDG makes universal primary education one of the priorities for all countries. For governments of developing countries, though, this is not always accepted as the best use of resources.

Arguments for universal education as a priority

- universal education in the North was associated with economic growth, rising living standards and improvements in health;
- education is the best way of ensuring that there are people with the skills and qualifications needed for the country's development;
- education, especially for literacy and numeracy, is a human right – it gives people some control over their own lives, and makes it more difficult for them to be exploited;

- universal education of girls has positive outcomes in improving the health and nutrition of families, chances of employment and limiting the number of children women have.

Arguments against universal education as a priority

- where a country has limited resources, it may be better to educate a minority for leadership and management posts if the majority do not need an education for their work;
- a country may decide to achieve economic growth first, seeing education as something that cannot yet be afforded;
- education may simply make people more discontented and rebellious if they cannot use their education to improve their lives (through a new career, for example); among the leaders of the rebels in Sierra Leone's civil war were well-educated young men who had come into contact with radical ideas in their education, but could see no future for themselves in Sierra Leone as it was (Richards 1996, pp. 25–7).

Health

There is a broad correlation between a country's per capita income and its levels of health, as measured by life expectancy, infant mortality, overall death rates and incidence of particular diseases. All over the world there has been considerable progress over the past 30 years, notably in increased life expectancy, but in some countries there has recently been a slip backwards.

Causes of death are strongly related to development. In sub-Saharan Africa, about 65 per cent of deaths are the result of infectious diseases and causes related to birth and maternity, but in developed countries only 5 per cent of deaths have these causes. The great majority of deaths in developed countries are from non-infectious medical conditions such as cancers and heart disease (Sutcliffe 2001), both of which are associated with lifestyle factors such as rich and fatty diets, smoking and stress. These diseases are also more likely to occur the longer a person lives. In developing countries, although these 'diseases of affluence' are present, the main health problems are communicable diseases, which are often still big killers: diarrhoea, bacterial and viral diseases such as polio, cholera, hepatitis and typhoid, and also airborne diseases such as tuberculosis, pneumonia, meningitis, whooping cough, diphtheria and influenza. All of these are still found in developed countries, but there they can be treated effectively and are rarely fatal. More specific to the developing world are diseases carried by insects, such as malaria (although this is now returning to Southern Europe), bilharzia, sleeping sickness, elephantiasis and river blindness.

Disease in the South tends particularly to affect children, who are often weakened by malnutrition, and also women, and is more rife amongst rural populations where there is less access to healthcare, clean water and sanitation.

Many of the diseases now commonly seen in developing countries were found in Europe in the recent past (and some, such as malaria, are threatening to return). Three factors led to the control of these diseases:

- improvements in nutrition and diet;
- improvements in hygiene – piped water supplies, sewage disposal;
- changes in reproductive behaviour – the falling birth rate.

All three factors were helped by improvements in education and literacy. These factors were more important than advances in curative medicine or even vaccination and immunization.

With colonialism, developing countries inherited healthcare based on costly Western-style hospitals with unreliable modern technology in cities. Doctors are trained for this system and often run lucrative practices for urban elites; there is no financial incentive to work in poor rural areas – or indeed in developing countries at all, hence the 'brain drain' of doctors, nurses and other health professionals to the North.

Developing countries face a choice between:

Selective biomedical intervention: in healthcare, interventions such as immunization campaigns to try to prevent the spread of disease.

1 **Selective biomedical intervention** such as mass vaccination programmes, distributing vitamin supplements or insecticide impregnated bed nets. This can lead to rapid reductions in child mortality, but these cannot always be sustained – reducing one disease may only mean that children die later from another disease.
2 Comprehensive, community-based primary healthcare with an emphasis on health education and prevention of disease – e.g. draining ponds so that mosquitoes can't breed, disposing of rubbish safely.

Modernization theory

Modernization theorists would expect health patterns of developing countries to follow those of the developed world in the past. Developing countries are still at the stage developed countries were at centuries ago, but are now entering the **epidemiologic transition**. Before the transition, infectious diseases are widespread and the major cause of death; life expectancy is low and infant and child mortality high. Improvements in nutrition, hygiene and sanitation lead to falling death rates from infectious diseases. After the transition, deaths from infectious diseases are negligible, infant and child mortality low and life expectancy much higher. Developing countries should draw on aid and expertise from the developed world, drop traditional medical practices and concentrate on centralized primary healthcare based on doctors and hospitals and on mass immunization against disease.

Epidemiologic transition: in health, the change from the main problem in a society being infectious diseases to it being 'diseases of affluence' such as cancer and heart disease.

Dependency theory

Dependency theorists argue that there is no reason to assume that today's developing countries can simply follow the path of the rich world. Colonialism changed health in the colonies, and neo-colonialism continues this trend. Health in developing countries is affected by a number of factors, including:

- the adoption of lifestyles of the rich world (for example, diets heavy in fats and sugars and refined and processed ingredients), leading to increases in cancers and heart disease;
- the power of TNCs to sell these products, to advertise them irresponsibly and to avoid attempts to restrict them;
- pollution and environmental damage caused by TNCs which can affect health;
- pharmaceutical TNCs being reluctant to make their medicines available at prices people can afford or to allow developing countries to manufacture their own generic versions;
- poor funding of medical research into medicines and treatments that would improve health in the South; research is geared more towards the lifestyle and pursuits of wealthy consumers in the North from whom more profits can be made (for example, weight loss and cosmetics);
- structural adjustment programmes which have imposed neo-liberal policies that give states little scope to effectively act to improve health. Charges often have to be made for medicines and treatment, so that the poor cannot afford them.

The health-related MDGS

MDG4

To reduce child mortality (by two-thirds, by 2015)
Child survival rates show some improvement, having fallen from 106 in 1990 to 83 in 2005. They are still worst in sub-Saharan Africa. In 2005, 10.1 million children died before their fifth birthday, mostly from preventable causes. Child deaths from measles fell by over 60 per cent between 2000 and 2005, as a result of improved immunization coverage.

MDG5

To improve maternal health; to reduce the maternal mortality ratio by two thirds from 1990 to 2015
Half a million women die each year in pregnancy and childbirth. A woman in sub-Saharan Africa has a 1 in 16 chance of dying from complications in pregnancy and childbirth in her lifetime; for women in the developed world, the chance is 1 in 3,800. The percentage of deliveries attended by skilled healthcare personnel has increased in developing countries from 43 in 1990 to 57 in 2005. Fewer than half of births in Africa are attended, but about two-thirds of women receive some antenatal attention.

MDG6

To combat HIV/AIDS, malaria and other diseases (halt by 2015 and begin to reverse)
HIV prevalence is levelling off, but the number of people dying of HIV/AIDS is continuing to rise, especially in Africa. Prevention measures are not keeping up with the spread of HIV. There are an estimated 15.2 million children who have lost one or both parents because of AIDS, 80 per cent of them in Africa; this is expected to grow to more than 20 million by 2010.
   Interventions to control malaria, notably insecticide treated bed nets, are beginning to pay off, but children under 5 and people in rural areas are unlikely to be using nets.

Demographic change

Demographers study population. The study of demographic change, both in world population and the populations of individual countries, is directly relevant to development. Amongst the terms demographers use are the following:

- *mortality rate*: the number of deaths per 1,000 in the population in one year;
- *infant mortality rate*: the number of deaths of infants under the age of 1 per 1,000 of the infant population in one year;
- *child mortality rate*: the number of deaths of children under the age of 5 per 1,000 of the child population in one year;
- *birth rate*: number of live births per 1,000 members of the population in one year;
- *total fertility rate*: the number of live births per woman over her lifetime.

World population growth

Demographic transition: in demography, the change from high birth and death rates to low birth and death rates.

Throughout most of recorded history there has been a slow rise in world population. The rise has accelerated over the past few centuries, with most of the increase in the past 100 years, from 2 billion people in 1925 to about 6.5 billion today. Most of this increase has been in the developing world; the population of the developed world is now stable. The world's population in 2050 is projected by the UN to be 9.3 billion, 90 per cent of whom will live in today's developing countries.

Today's developed countries went through a **demographic transition** during the period of industrialization and urbanization.

During the transition

High birth rate, high death rate
It made sense to have several children because children in pre-industrial societies were an economic asset – they would work from an early age, for example helping on the family farm. An extra mouth to feed became an extra pair of hands by about the age of 7. Also, without pensions or welfare, older people relied on their adult children to support them. Having more children meant a greater chance that at least one would survive to support you in your old age.

High birth rate still, death rate falling
Populations grew because the death rate fell. Fewer children died, and people began to live longer than had been the case. Life expectancy increased. This was partly due to improved systems of sewage and provision of clean piped water, which helped in the prevention of disease, and to advances in medicine, which reduced the numbers dying from disease.

Low birth rate, low death rate
Children are more of an economic burden in an industrial society. They have to be supported through formal education; they do not work, and their schooling can be expensive. Because infant and child mortality are low, children are much more likely to survive into adulthood – but with pensions and welfare adults are no longer dependent on them anyway. People therefore choose to have fewer children. The population of industrialized nations tends to stabilize, and may even begin to decline.

Figure 2.8
Demographic transition

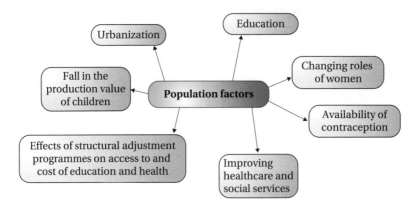

Figure 2.9
Factors involved in population in developing countries today

The shape of populations also changes. Today's developed countries before industrialization, and developing countries today, had large numbers of children and young people and few elderly people; this is conventionally represented as a pyramid. After the demographic transition, the pyramid is inverted, with growing numbers of elderly people and proportionately fewer young people.

The experience of the developed countries is important because many developing countries seem to be passing through the demographic transition; the death rate is falling, but the birth rate is still high, and so many developing countries still have high population growth.

Modernization theorists would expect there to be a transition, because the developing countries are expected to go through the same process of modernization as developed countries did. However, just because countries in the past went through the transition we should not assume that it is inevitable. Dependency theorists would argue that the situation today, as a result of colonialism and neo-colonialism, is fundamentally different. Demographic transition is a theory; it is not inevitable that it will happen, and some countries may get stuck in the transition phase – the 'demographic trap' (Hewitt and Smyth 2000: 128).

Population growth and consumption

The Malthusian view

At the end of the eighteenth century, an English clergyman, Thomas Malthus, put forward an influential argument about population growth. The population would inevitably grow faster than the food supply, because food supply would grow arithmetically (1, 2, 3, 4, etc.) whereas population would grow geometrically (1, 2, 4, 8, etc.). This, said Malthus, would bring about disaster: famines, and wars over food, which might end civilization. Malthus argued that it was essential to curb population growth. Today, followers of Malthus's basic idea – that the world cannot support a continually growing population – are referred to as neo-Malthusians.

For neo-Malthusians, population growth in developing countries is the main cause of their poverty, and also leads to economic stagnation, uncontrollable urbanization and environmental damage. Ultimately, it will also lead to disaster, in wars over resources such as food and water, because there will not be enough to go round. Controlling population growth is therefore the main objective of aid, because this is necessary for development to happen. This can be done by persuading people to have fewer children, by having family planning programmes and making contraception available. However, governments do not always see population control as a priority; they may even want to increase the population if they believe the country is under-populated.

Robert Kaplan (1994) drew on Malthus's ideas for his influential article, 'The Coming Anarchy'. Based on his travels in West Africa and elsewhere, Kaplan argued that parts of the poor world were collapsing into anarchy because of population growth, urbanization, resource depletion and tribalism. These factors undermined already weak states and led to instability that, he thought, could eventually threaten the developed world too. This argument is referred to as the **New Barbarism** thesis; Richards (1996, p xiv) describes it as 'Malthus-with-guns'. Richards's counter-argument is that what appears to be random and anarchic is in fact rational and can only be understood in the context of globalized modernity.

The doom foretold by Malthus and his successors has not yet happened, despite the fact that the world population has grown to a level many in the past would have thought impossible. Improvements in agriculture have averted a food crisis, and deaths from war and disease have also restrained population growth, but Neo-Malthusians would argue that these have simply postponed the inevitable.

> **New Barbarism:** Kaplan's theory, a variant of Malthusian theory, that overpopulation and exhaustion of resources were leading to civil wars in developing countries.

How can population be controlled?

1   Contraception: birth control pills need to be taken regularly, which is not always practical in the developing world. Women may find it hard to persuade men to use condoms, although they are fairly easy available in most places. Some religions (e.g. Roman Catholicism) disapprove of contraception. Attempts to increase the use of contraceptives have sometimes tended to assume that, if they are available, they will be used, but people who want children will of course not use them – and poor people often want more children because of the economic benefit they bring.

2   Abortion: this is not practical on a large scale because it requires trained medical staff and is therefore expensive. It is also very controversial in the USA, and so American NGOs and government aid bodies do not support it.

3   Sterilization: people tend to only want to be sterilized after having several children. Compulsory sterilization is an abuse of human rights, but in India in the late 1970s poorer people were bribed with goods or money to accept sterilization.

4   Financial incentives to limit family size: this is what China has practised with its one child per family policy. An unintended consequence of this has been female infanticide and a growing gender imbalance in the Chinese population, with many young men unable to find Chinese wives.

The social view

This approach turns Malthus's approach upside down. Rather than seeing poverty and lack of development as the consequences of high population growth, it sees them as the causes. Where children still have an economic value, because they can work and earn and relieve the parents of some work, it makes sense to have several children. Where infant and child mortality rates are high, the more children a couple have the more chance that at least one will survive to support them in old age; children may be not just the best, but the only, available insurance policy. Where traditional values are strong, having many children may also give the parents status. People have many children because they are poor, rather than being poor because they have many children.

From this point of view, aid that focuses directly on controlling population is misguided. The way forward is to focus on alleviating poverty, bringing infant and child mortality down and improving the situation of women. The parts of the developing world where fertility has declined, such as Sri Lanka, Thailand, Cuba and the Indian state of Kerala, are those where women have good access to resources such as health and education (Hewitt and Smyth 2000, p. 135).

There is now a widespread acceptance that women's status and fertility are closely linked. The education of girls is seen as very important for several reasons:

- educated women do not need to have children for status, because their education brings status;
- they are more likely to be able to work to support their children, rather than relying on their children for work and income;
- they are better able to look after the health of their children, reducing mortality;
- they are likely to have better access to and willingness to use contraception;
- they are more likely to take decisions about their own fertility, or negotiate with their husband, rather than accepting his authority.

Malthus's starting point was the relationship between population and food supply. Anti-Malthusians point out that a lot of land is used to grow fodder for animals to be consumed as meat in the developed world, by people and by pets. If this land was used to grow food for direct human consumption the planet could support an even larger population.

Famine and undernourishment

The media tend to treat famines as freak natural disasters, and often suggest that a major cause is that there are too many people. They also tend only to report the final stages of a famine, when normal survival strategies are exhausted and people have abandoned their homes and moved in search of food. If relief camps are established, infectious diseases often become a major cause of death. However, relief camps provide very good publicity and fundraising opportunities for INGOs. Famines can be precipitated by climate, for example a drought, but people in areas prone to drought will have survival strategies. Other factors will also be involved, and often these include war. Famine can even be used as a weapon of war; Keen (in Crow 2000, p. 62) argues that in Sudan, famines can be seen as a deepening of the exploitation of poor groups that already exists in 'normal' times.

Rather than famine, it is undernourishment that is a continual fact of everyday life for large numbers of people. About 854 million people were chronically undernourished in 2001–3, according to the Food and Agriculture Organization of the United Nations (FAO), nearly all of them in developing countries. The FAO estimates that 32 per cent of people in Africa are undernourished, although the total numbers are higher in Asia. In May 2006, 39 countries (24 of them in Africa) were experiencing serious food shortages. Since these statistics were published, the situation has worsened because of rising food prices. Long-term chronic hunger does not often attract media attention, but in the long run it costs more lives than spectacular famines. The problem is one of ownership and distribution, and poverty. Food is usually available but people cannot afford to buy it. Those most at risk are children, the elderly and women.

MDG1 (second part)

To halve the proportion of the world's population living in extreme poverty and hunger
This is operationalized as the proportion of children under the age of 5 who are underweight. The number of underweight children has been falling, from 33 per cent in developing countries in 1990, to 27 per cent in 2004, but not fast enough to achieve the goal.

Gender

MDG3

To promote gender equality and to empower women
The MDG Report in 2007 found that there had been slow progress towards gender equality in work, with growing numbers and proportions of women in non-agricultural paid employment. Women who work in agriculture, as contributing but unpaid family workers, lack job security and social protection. Women's participation in politics has continued to grow: women make up 17 per cent of MPs and equivalents, and 13 heads of state or government.

Women used to be invisible in the study of development. With the growth of feminism this changed. It is now not only feminists but also the UN, IGOs, NGOs and global social movements which take gender issues very seriously. For example, the Human Development Report includes a Gender Development Index. The Millennium Development Goals include the promotion of gender equality, the empowerment of women and improvement in maternal health. However, women are still a long way from parity with men. Other sections of this chapter have referred to women's disadvantages in education, employment and health. Underlying these is women's usually subordinate position within households and communities, owning far less land and property and having less control over their lives than men.

Issues that particularly affect women and can be used to gauge the extent of gender freedom include:

1   Can women decide whether and whom to marry, and can they terminate a marriage?
2   Do women have freedom of movement?
3   Do girls and women have access to education on the same terms as boys and men?
4   How much power do women have within families and households?
5   Are women able to control their fertility, deciding whether and when to have children, and how many children they have?

The continuing extent of gender inequality was vividly demonstrated in the 2005 tsunami. 'Four times as many women died in tsunami': it was under this headline that the *Guardian* reported on 26 March 2005 the far greater loss of life among women than men. Among the reasons put forward were:

- women were less likely to be able to swim;
- women were often trying to save their children as well as themselves;
- men were more likely to be away from home, for example working in cities, and were also more able to run and to cling to debris.

Oxfam reported that because of the shortage of women, young women would be more likely to have to marry earlier (abandoning their education) and to try to take on the roles of the missing women.

Applying the theories

Both modernization theory and dependency theory, arising before the impact of second-wave feminism in the 1960s and '70s on theory and research, had little to say about gender issues. Both can be seen as part of the 'malestream' of sociology and of academic sociology more widely at the time.

Modernization theory was closely associated with the sociological perspective of functionalism, and took from it the idea of the nuclear family as the family type suitable for modern society, with husbands and wives having complementary roles. The role of the man was to work outside the home for money, the role of the woman to work within the household. This was seen as fair and equal. As countries modernized, then, women would be restricted to work within the home. As Leonard (2003) comments, this was a very masculine view of what it is like to be modern. In dependency theory, the focus is on relationships between countries rather than social groups, and both here and in world systems theory there is little discussion of women.

One of the reasons that women were overlooked in these theories is that the work women tended to do, within the household and subsistence agriculture, including essential survival tasks such as grinding grain and preparing food, was overlooked in measures such as GNP and official statistics. In 1970, Boserup (in Leonard 2003, p. 79), working from modernization theory and adding a liberal feminist view, argued that such measures needed to be extended to include women, especially by bringing them into paid work, so that they also could benefit from modernization.

In the following 15 years, socialist feminist thinking began to have an influence. It was pointed out that Boserup was assuming that the modernization process was benign, and that attention needed to be paid to the ways in which women were exploited within the global capitalist system. Part of the problem was clearly male power, so discussion shifted from women to gender relations. Socialist feminism, looking at underdevelopment and neo-colonial exploitation, seemed more relevant to developing countries than radical feminism, which sees women's subordination to men as the most important issue. In the South, most women see a need to work with men with whom they share an unequal position compared to the developed world. Women in the developing world are united by their gender, but also divided by ethnicity, religion, class and culture. Recent work on gender and development acknowledges that gender relations vary around the world.

Socialist feminists and others draw attention in particular to a new form of exploitation, which they argue shows how the global spread of capitalism requires the exploitation of women. It is mainly young women who are employed in sweatshop factories in South-East Asia and elsewhere by TNCs. Companies pay little and treat female workers poorly, partly on the (false) grounds that the work is unskilled. This work can sometimes help young women achieve financial independence, but often the money goes straight to a man. The boss at work is invariably a man, and training and job security are rarely provided.

Gender issues today

One effect of globalization has been the nature of services traditionally offered by women. Ehrenreich and Hochschild (2002) describe how millions of women leave developing countries each year to work as nannies, maids and sex workers in the rich world. They suggest that the move into work for many women in developed countries has created a 'care deficit' because they are unable to spend the time that previous generations of women did on family and home. The use of cheap labour from developing countries eases this situation, but, at the same time, creates a 'care deficit' in developing countries because the women are working abroad. The sex industry employs many women from developing countries, both in the North and in sex tourist destinations. Bales (2002) estimates that in Thailand, with a total population of about 60 million, there are between half a million and a million sex workers and that about 1 in 20 of these is enslaved.

Ecofeminism: feminist theory based on the idea that women have a different relationship with nature and the environment to men.

Ecofeminists have argued that there is a special relationship between women and the environment, based either on innate nature or on social relationships which put women in a position of working with and understanding natural resources. Men are seen as responsible for most environmental damage, still treating the environment as something to be dominated and used rather than to be looked after. Women are therefore seen as vital to attempts to protect the environment.

Aid is not gender-neutral. It comes with Western values attached, and that usually means male-dominated values. For example, agricultural training programmes are offered more to men than to women, because it is assumed that men are more suited to technical and scientific training – but it is women who play a greater role in growing food. Aid often helps men rather than women with their work, again because women's work is still generally unrecognized or undervalued.

CHAPTER SUMMARY

After studying this chapter you should be able to:

- explain the different ways in which development can be defined and measured;

- explain and evaluate theoretical explanations of development and underdevelopment: modernization theory, dependency theory, neo-liberalism, traditional Marxism and world systems theory;

- apply the main theoretical explanations to topics within this chapter, such as aid, education and health;

- describe aspects of cultural, economic and political globalization, and explain and evaluate theoretical explanations of globalization;

- evaluate the role of aid, trade and debt in development;

- describe and evaluate the role of states, transnational corporations, non-government organizations and international governmental organizations in development;

- describe and evaluate the strategies for industrialization and development open to developing countries;

- describe and explain the process of urbanization;

- describe and evaluate the relationship between development and the environment;

- explain and evaluate the relationship between development and war and conflict;

- describe the main patterns of employment in developing countries;

- describe education in developing countries and evaluate the importance of education in development;

- describe health issues in developing countries and evaluate the importance of health in development;

- describe the main patterns of demographic change, and evaluate Malthusian and anti-Malthusian explanations of the relationship between population growth, food supply and the environment;

- discuss the significance of gender for development and for topics such as education, health and aid;

- know the Millennium Development Goals and describe and account for progress or lack of progress towards them.

KEY TERMS

aid	conditionality	ecofeminism	global decision-making
anti-globalization	cultural imperialism	economic growth	global warming
movement	debt boomerang	epidemiologic transition	globalists
bilateral aid	debt crisis	exhaustible resources	green revolution
biodiversity	deforestation	export-oriented	gross domestic product
bio-piracy	demographic	industrialization	(GDP)
bottom billion	transition	export processing zones	Highly Indebted Poor
Bretton Woods	dependency theory	(EPZs)	Countries Initiative
capitalism	desertification	fair trade	(HIPC)
cash crops	development	future generations	homogenization
colonialism	development state	global civil society (GCS)	human capital

human development
index
hybridization
imperialism
import substitution
informal sector
industrialization
industrialization
international
governmental
organizations (IGOs)
International Monetary
Fund (IMF)
McDonaldization
metropolis
micro-credit
millennium development
goals (MDGs)

modern world system
(MWS)
modernization theory
multilateral aid
multinational
corporations (MNCs)
neo-colonialism
neo-liberal economic
theory
neo-Malthusian
New Barbarism
new international
division of labour
(NIDL)
newly industrializing
countries (NICs)
non-governmental
organizations (NGOs)

Official Development
Assistance (ODA)
parastatals
predatory state
pull factors
push factors
satellite
selective biomedical
intervention
shared resources
South
stages of economic
growth
structural adjustment
programme (SAP)
structural violence
subsistence farming
sustainability

sustainable development
terrorism
Third World
trade liberalization
transformationalists
transnational capitalist
class
transnational
corporations (TNCs)
triangular trade
underdevelopment
urbanization
Washington Consensus
World Bank
World Economic Forum
World Social Forum

EXAM QUESTIONS

SECTION B: GLOBAL DEVELOPMENT

If you choose this Section, answer Question 4 and **either** Question 5 **or** Question 6.

Time allowed: 1 hour 30 minutes   **Total for this section: 60 marks**

4 Read **Item B** below and answer parts (a) and (b) that follow.

Item B
Rather than considering development as purely economic, the United Nations Development Programme's annual Human Development Report considers health and education as well as Gross National Product. The use of social indicators such as these reveals significant differences between countries. For example, health, as measured by life expectancy, is much lower in less developed countries than in wealthier countries; life expectancy in Malawi is only half   5 that in Japan. Many deaths in less developed countries are of infants and children, and are from preventable or treatable infectious diseases. Some of these diseases were once also big killers in developed countries, but were controlled as economies grew; today, interventions by governments, non-governmental organizations and others aim to improve healthcare without necessarily waiting for economic growth.   10

(a) Identify and briefly explain **three** ways in which governments of developed countries could improve health care in developing countries.   (*9 marks*)

(b) Using material from **Item B** and elsewhere, assess the view that social indicators such as those used in the Human Development Report (line 2) provide the best way of measuring development.   (*18 marks*)

EITHER

5 'Developing countries today cannot successfully follow the same path to development as that taken in the past by developed countries.' To what extent do sociological arguments and evidence support this view?   (*33 marks*)

OR

6 'By globalization, what is usually meant is the spread of Western culture and values.' To what extent do sociological arguments and evidence support this view?   (*33 marks*)

The Mass Media

KEN BROWNE

Contents

The Mass Media

KEY ISSUES

- The traditional and the 'new' media
- The significance of the new media in contemporary society
- The postmodernist view of the media
- Globalization, popular culture and high culture
- The power of the media: key questions
- Formal controls on the media
- Ownership of the mass media
- The mass media and ideology
- Control of the mass media
- The effects of the mass media
- Violence and the media
- The social construction of the news
- Media representations and stereotyping

The term 'mass media' is used in a number of ways, and may refer to:

1 The technology involved in communicating with large mass audiences without any personal contact, such as televisions, computers, DVD players/recorders, MP3 players, mobile phones, games consoles and satellites.
2 The institutions and organizations concerned with mass communication in which people work, such as the press, cinema, broadcasting, advertising and publishing industries.
3 The products of those institutions, such as the news, movies, television soaps, newspapers, magazines, websites, books, films, tapes, CDs and DVDs.

The main media of mass communication include terrestrial (earth-based), cable and satellite television, radio, newspapers and magazines, books, cinema, videos/DVDs, advertising, CDs, video games, the Internet, MP3 players and mobile phones.

The traditional and the 'new' media

The mass media is now often divided into the 'traditional' and the 'new'.

Traditional media

The traditional media refers to those media that communicated uniform messages in a one-way process to very large mass audiences, which were assumed to be homogeneous (all possessing much the same characteristics and interests). This is the type of communication associated with traditional broadcasting, like the terrestrial television channels (BBC 1 and 2, ITV 1, Channel 4 and 5), and BBC Radios 1 and 2, and mass circulation national and Sunday newspapers. There was little consumer choice, beyond a few TV channels, radio stations or newspapers.

New media

The new media refers to the screen-based, digital (computer) technology involving the integration of images, text and sound, and to the technology used for the distribution and consumption of the new digitized media content which has emerged

Examples of the new media – Apple's iPhone, BBC News website, satellite receivers, and the website of *Radio Times*. Identify as many ways as you can that these new media differ from traditional media like terrestrial television channels, magazines and newspapers.

in the late twentieth and early twenty-first centuries. These include computers and the Internet, digital cable and satellite TV, Sky boxes and DVD recorders enabling customized, individualized television viewing with a choice of hundreds of channels, digital media like CDs, DVDs and MP3, Internet downloads of films, videos and music onto mobile phones and MP3 players, user-generated media content through websites like MySpace, and interactive video/computer games through Play Stations and X-boxes.

Differences between the traditional and new media

Lister et al. (2003) suggest what distinguishes the 'new' from traditional forms of mass media are five main concepts: digitality, interactivity, hypertextuality, dispersal and virtuality:

1 *Digitality*. Essentially, this means 'using computers', where all data (text, sound and pictures) are converted into numbers (binary code), which can then be stored, distributed and picked up via screen-based products, like mobile phones, DVDs, digital TVs and computers.
2 *Interactivity*. Consumers have an opportunity to engage or interact with the media, creating their own material, customizing viewing to their own wishes, with much greater choice compared with the passive consumption and 'take it or leave it' features of the traditional media.
3 *Hypertextuality*. This refers to the links that form a web of connections to other bits of information, which give users a way of searching, interacting with and customizing the media for their own use.
4 *Dispersal*. This refers to the way the media have become less centralized and more adapted to individual choices, with a huge growth of media products of all kinds, which have become a part of everyday life. The routine use of the Internet for information, shopping and entertainment, email, laptop computers, interactive digital TV, social networking sites like Facebook, downloadable content onto mobile phones, and podcasts to MP3 players all show how the media have penetrated into the fabric of everyday life. The production of media content itself is now becoming more generally dispersed throughout the population, rather than restricted to media professionals. For example, people are now making their own videos and posting them on the Internet. According to Chad Hurley (*Guardian*: 3/12/07), Chief Executive of YouTube, there were eight hours of new consumer-generated video uploaded to YouTube every minute in 2007. Internet diaries – 'blogs' – are beginning to rival traditional journalism as sources of information and news, and in 2006 Technorati, a blog-tracking service, was claiming to be monitoring 47.6 million of them.
5 *Virtuality*. This refers to the various ways people can now immerse themselves in wholly unreal interactive experiences in virtual worlds created by new technology (as in computer games), and also create for themselves imaginary identities in online communication and networking sites, like MySpace, Bebo, YouTube and Facebook.

> **Activity**
>
> The best way to discover the features of the new media, if you're not already familiar with them, is to use them.
>
> 1 Go to www.en.wikipedia.org and look up digital media, interactivity, hypertext and virtual reality. Follow the hypertext links given in Wikipedia and give two examples of contemporary media that use each of these.
> 2 Use Wikipedia to find out what a wiki is, and explain in what senses Wikipedia is an example of a wiki, and what problems this might pose for the validity of the information given.
> 3 Using Wikipedia, find out who Jean Baudrillard was, what he meant by a 'media-saturated society' and what he said about the first Gulf War.
> 4 Go to http://uk.youtube.com/, do a search on sociology, and report your findings on any two sociology videos.
> 5 Go to http://news.bbc.co.uk/ and watch the UK news headlines online, making a note of the latest headline stories. Now do the same with www.sky.com. Compare the two sets of news stories, and whether they seem to be covering the same material. What might this suggest to you about how the media influences our views of the world?

The significance of the new media in contemporary society

There are very wide debates about the new media and their significance in contemporary society. Some have an optimistic view, seeing the new media as playing a positive role in society, while others are more pessimistic. The following sections summarize these two sides of the discussion, followed by postmodernist views of the role of the media.

Optimistic views of the new media

Widening consumer choice

There are now hundreds of digital cable and satellite TV channels, websites, and online newspapers for people to choose from.

More media user participation

Interactive digital TV, blogging and citizen journalism, video and photo-sharing websites like YouTube, and social networking sites like MySpace are all giving consumers more opportunities to participate in using and producing media content.

Greater democracy

There is now a far wider range of news sources, and a vast ocean of information available to all. More people, not just large media corporations, have the opportunity to communicate with vast numbers of people. New social movements and campaigns can now use the Internet, through blogging, email and websites, to spread their ideas and build support, like a kind of rolling conversation that can build up over time. Such campaigners can make it increasingly difficult for traditional media newspapers and news channels to ignore stories they might have dropped in the past.

More access to all kinds of information and 'high culture' entertainment

Everyone now has access to huge amounts of information and high culture which were formerly limited to educated elites. This is discussed later in this chapter.

The world becomes a global village

A **global village** refers to the way that the mass media and electronic communications now operate on a global scale so that the world has become like one village or community.

The **global village** is a term used by McLuhan (1962) to describe how the electronic mass media collapse space and time barriers in human communication. For example, satellite technology and the Internet globalize communication, and allow users from around the world to connect and interact with each other instantaneously. The way the electronic mass media enables people to interact on a global scale means the world has become like one village or community. In this global village, the new media promote cultural diversity, national barriers are reduced, the boundaries between the local and the global are blurred and different peoples and cultures are brought together, promoting greater understanding between different cultures.

Social life and social interaction is enhanced

The new media have opened up new channels for communication and interaction, enhancing or supplementing existing face-to-face interactions. Factors like gender, age, ethnicity and social class might once have meant that some conversations in the 'real world' would have been avoided, but alternative identities can be constructed in cyberspace or virtual worlds, and the media may become part of the means by which people express themselves. People can stay in touch via email when they are away, or meet anonymously in chat rooms or social networking sites, which may develop into face-to-face meetings. Social networking and sharing sites like MySpace, Bebo, YouTube, Facebook and Flickr, and 'Googling' friends, can enhance social networks, re-establish lost contacts between old friends, create online communities and bring people together. Figures from comScore (comscore.com), which do not include users under the age of 15, gave MySpace 109 million users each month worldwide in 2006, Facebook 86 million and Bebo 21 million. Boyle (2007) argues that for young people 'the media – in terms of music, fashion and popular culture more generally – have all been cultural and symbolic battlefields over image, identity, difference and being "cool"'. Boyle argues that the new media, particularly the Internet, have changed the patterns of media consumption among young people, with 16–24-year-olds making more mobile calls, sending more texts and spending more time online than ever before, and more than any other social group; the Internet is now an integral part of their entertainment and social networking through various user-generated sites and online communities. According to the marketing firm Alloy, 96 per cent of teens and tweens (8–12-year-olds), 70 per cent of 16–24-year-olds, and 40 per cent of adults with Internet access were using social networking sites like Bebo, Facebook and MySpace in 2007. Ofcom found that in 2007 one in four Britons logged onto such websites at least

23 times each month, making the UK the most 'digital' nation in Europe, and second only to Canada among world users of these websites.

Pessimistic views of the new media

Media imperialism

Media imperialism (or cultural imperialism) is the idea that the new media, particularly satellite television and global advertising, have led to the Westernization of other cultures, as Western, and especially American, cultural values are forced on non-Western cultures, leading to the undermining of local cultures (this is discussed later in this chapter).

A threat to democracy

Transnational corporations like Microsoft, Google, Yahoo, Vodafone and News Corporation control the Internet technology, the satellite channels and mobile networks. This poses a threat to democracy and enhances the power of the already powerful, as more and more of what we know is dominated and controlled by global corporations.

The lack of regulation

The global nature of the new media, such as the Internet and satellite broadcasting, means there is a lack of regulation by national bodies like Ofcom. This means that undesirable things like bias, Internet crime, paedophilia, pornography, violence and racism can thrive virtually unchecked.

There is no real increase in consumer choice

There is poorer quality media content, with 'dumbing down' to attract large audiences, much of the same content on different TV channels, and endless repeats. Celebrity culture will replace serious programming, and 'infotainment' (information wrapped up to entertain) will replace hard news reporting to encourage people to consume media.

The undermining of human relationships and communities

There will be an increase in social isolation, with people losing the ability to communicate in the real world as they spend less quality time with family and friends, and become more wrapped up in solitary electronic media. There will consequently be a loss of social capital or the useful social networks which people have, as they spend less time engaging with the communities and neighbourhoods in which they live.

The digital divide

Not everyone has access to the new media, and there is a digital divide between those who can and those who can't afford, or don't have the infrastructure to support, access to such media as pay-to-view satellite channels, computers and broadband Internet access. This creates national and global inequalities, and a new digital

Media imperialism (sometimes called cultural imperialism) is the suggestion that the new media, particularly satellite television and global advertising, have led to the Westernization of other cultures, as Western, and especially American, cultural values are forced on non-Western cultures, leading to the undermining of local cultures and cultural independence.

Social capital refers to the social networks of influence and support that people have.

The digital divide refers to the gap between those people with effective access to the digital and information technology making up the new media, and those who lack such access.

underclass, whose members are excluded from the alleged benefits of the new media. The box below illustrates this.

The digital divide

According to www.Internetworldstats.com, between 2000 and 2007, Internet usage grew by 244 per cent, and in 2007, there were 1,244,449,601 people using the Internet. This is only 18.9 per cent of the world's population. Europe and North America made up 46 per cent of the world's Internet users, even though these areas comprise just 17.4 per cent of the world's population. This contrasts with 3.5 per cent of the world's Internet users in Africa, which makes up 14.3 per cent of the world's population. This evidence suggests a clear global digital divide in terms of access to the new media.

Figure 3.1 shows the digital divide in Internet access in September 2007; even in Europe, there are divisions between the 75.6 per cent of people in Sweden having Internet access compared to 11.5 per cent in the Ukraine. In 2007, according to the Office for National Statistics, well over a third (39 per cent) of households in Great Britain did not have Internet access, and 70 per cent of households did not possess a mobile phone that could access the Internet.

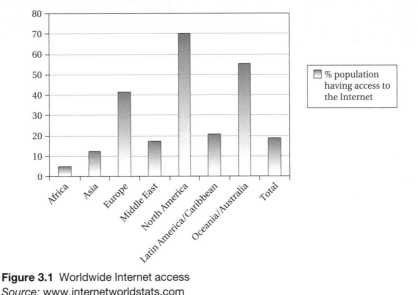

Figure 3.1 Worldwide Internet access
Source: www.internetworldstats.com

The postmodernist view of the media

The huge explosion of the new media is seen by some as part of the change to a post-modern society. Postmodernists argue that we inhabit a world shaped by the media. Media imagery and representations themselves become our reality, with computer technology creating virtual realities that potentially replace their real-life counterparts. Our view of reality is increasingly formed through media imagery and media interpretations rather than through personal experience.

Baudrillard argues that we now live in a media-saturated society, in which media images now dominate and distort the way we see the world. For example, media

Postmodernists suggest we are now living in a media-saturated society, in which our view of reality is formed through media imagery and interpretations, and we increasingly live media-led virtual lives rather than real ones. What arguments might you give to support or oppose this view?

images replace reality to such an extent that laser technology and video reportage have eliminated the blood, the suffering and the corpses from war, and the TV news presents a sanitized version of events, with battles shown as media-constructed spectacles, which have such an air of unreality about them that we are unable to distinguish them from Hollywood movies or video games. Baudrillard calls this distorted view of the world 'hyperreality', with the media presenting what he calls 'simulacra' – artificial images or reproductions/copies of real events viewed simultaneously across the globe.

The twenty-first century is likely to see an enormous increase in the power and influence of already powerful media companies. With global satellite, cable and digital television, and the huge growth of the Internet and other new media, postmodernists argue that the media no longer reflect reality but actively create it. Garrod (2004) suggests that Reality TV shows like *I'm a Celebrity . . . Get Me Out of Here*, *Wifeswap*, *Fear Factor* and *Big Brother* are blurring the distinction between 'reality' and 'hyperreality'.

Strinati (1995) emphasizes the importance and power of the mass media in shaping consumer choices. Popular culture – like the culture of celebrity – and media images and messages bombard us daily, through books, magazines, newspapers, TV, radio, advertising and computers, and form our sense of reality and increasingly dominate the way we define ourselves. In this media-saturated society, the mass media create desires and pressures to consume, and many of us actually define our identities – how we see and define ourselves and how we want others to see us – in terms of media imagery. Colour, form and media-induced trends become more important than the content of products: it is not the quality of the clothes, drink or mobile phones we buy that matters, but whether they conform to media-induced images, styles, brand names and trends. The media-promoted designer labels of popular culture become more important than the quality of the products. In films, it is not the story that matters so much as how good the special visual and sound effects are; not the script or the writing, more the icon and the big-name 'stars'. There are any number of people who are famous for no reason at all except for being made into 'celebrities' by the media.

We are now bombarded with so much information, imagery and ideas from the mass media that there is increasing uncertainty in the world: people no longer know what to believe as international media networks steadily loosen our grip on, and challenge our notions of, 'the truth'.

In this media-saturated postmodern world, we identify more with media images than we do with our own daily experiences, and we increasingly live media-led virtual lives rather than real ones. We are more likely to identify with the lives and communities of television soap characters than we are with our nextdoor neighbours and the communities we actually live in. An example of this hyperreality was found in the TV soap *Coronation Street* in 1998, when the character Deirdre Barlow was sent to prison *in the show* for a crime she did not commit. The British public started a big grassroots campaign, pleading with Granada Television to 'free the Weatherfield One'. Even more bizarrely, the real-world Home Secretary even involved the then Prime Minister Tony Blair, who, with only a touch of irony, attempted to intervene in this unreal world on Deirdre's behalf.

Such postmodernist views of the new media are controversial, and assume that people approach the media without any prior experiences of their own, and that they do not discuss, interpret, ignore or reject media imagery and messages. The mass media are only one element – albeit an important one – in shaping our lives. For many of us, our gender, ethnicity, sexuality, age and social class, whether we are able-bodied or disabled, our experiences of school, college, work, friends and family, our political or religious beliefs – all these are likely to influence how we select, interpret and respond to the mass media. These issues will be considered further as we go through this chapter.

Activity

1   Identify all the changes you can imagine might occur in the mass media over the next century. How do you think the relationship between the media and audiences might change?

2   How do you think the changes you imagine might affect our daily lives?

3   List all the ways you think the mass media influence you in your life, such as your knowledge about current affairs, your opinions, your tastes in music and fashion, and your views of different social groups, such as women and men, minority ethnic groups, the disabled and the elderly.

4   Do you think the media have a large effect on your beliefs and values, your sense of identity and your consumer choices? What other influences on your beliefs and values might also be important?

Globalization, popular culture and high culture

The speed of technological change is now so great that the world is rapidly becoming a 'global village', with many people exposed to the same information and messages through mass media which cut across all national frontiers. This is part of what is known as **globalization**, which refers to the way societies across the globe have become increasingly interdependent, and are exposed to the same cultural products across the world.

Popular culture

Popular culture, sometimes called **mass culture** and sometimes *low culture*, has also become increasingly globalized. It is highly commercialized, involving mass-produced, standardized and short-lived products, often of trivial content and seen by many as of no lasting 'artistic' value. These cultural products are designed to be sold on the global mass market to make profits for the large 'culture industry' corporations that produce them, especially the mass media.

Popular culture is everyday culture, aimed at popular tastes – simple, undemanding, easy-to-understand entertainment, rather than something 'set apart' and 'special'. Such products might include mass-circulation magazines, 'red-top' tabloid news-papers like the *Sun* or the *Mirror*; TV 'soaps' and reality shows; TV films, dramas and thrillers; rock and pop music; feature films for the mass market; thrillers bought for reading on the beach; and popular websites. Popular culture is largely linked to passive and unchallenging entertainment, designed to be sold to the largest number of people possible. Such products demand little critical thought, analysis or discussion, and rarely provide any challenge to the existing social structure or dominant cultural ideas.

High culture

Popular culture is generally contrasted with **'high culture'**. High culture is seen as something set apart from everyday life, something 'special' to be treated with respect and reverence, involving things of lasting value that are part of a heritage which is worth preserving. High culture products are often found in special places, like art galleries, museums, concert halls and theatres. High culture products, aimed at mainly middle-class and upper-class audiences with what might be viewed as 'good taste', might include 'serious' news programmes and documentaries, involving comprehensive detail, social and political analysis and discussion. Other products include classical music like that of Mozart or Beethoven, opera, jazz, foreign language or specialist 'art' films, and what has become established 'literature', such as the work of Dickens, the Brontës, Jane Austen or Shakespeare, and visual art like that of Monet, Gauguin, Picasso or Van Gogh.

The changing distinction between high culture and popular culture

Some argue that the distinction between high culture and popular culture is weakening. Postmodernist writers, particularly, argue that mass markets and consumption are making the distinction between high and popular culture meaningless. There has been a huge expansion of the media-based creative and cultural industries – such as advertising, television, film and music, and book, magazine and web publishing. This

Globalization refers to the growing interdependence of societies around the world, with the global spread of the same culture, consumer goods and economic interests.

Popular culture, sometimes called **mass culture** or *low culture*, refers to cultural products that are produced as entertainment for sale to the mass of ordinary people. These involve mass-produced, standardized, short-lived products of no lasting value, which are seen to demand little critical thought, analysis or discussion.

High culture refers to specialist cultural products, seen as of lasting artistic or literary value, which are particularly admired and approved of by intellectual **elites** and, predominantly, the upper and middle classes.

An **elite** is a small group holding great power and privilege in society.

means there is now a huge range of media and cultural products available to all.

Technology – for example, the Internet, music downloads, cable, satellite and digital television, film and radio, printing for both mass production and personal use in the home, the global reach of modern mass media technology, the advertising and mass production of goods on a world scale, and easier international transportation – make all forms of culture freely available to everyone. Such technology enables the mass of people to consume original music and art and other cultural products in their own homes, without visiting specialized institutions like theatres or art galleries. High culture is no longer simply the preserve of cultural elites.

Strinati (1995) argues that elements of high culture have now become a part of popular culture, and elements of popular culture have been incorporated into high culture, and that there is therefore no longer any real distinction between the two, and it is ever more difficult for any one set of ideas to dominate in society. High culture 'art forms' are themselves increasingly being turned into products for sale in the mass market for consumption by the mass of ordinary people, and there is no longer anything special about art, as it is incorporated into daily life. Technology has made it possible for mass audiences to see and study high culture products, such as paintings by artists like Van Gogh, on the Internet or TV, and to have their own framed print hanging on their sitting-room wall. The originals may still only be on show in art galleries and museums, but copies are available to everyone. High culture images are now reproduced on everything from socks and T-shirts to chocolates and can lids, mugs, mouse mats, tablemats, jigsaws and posters.

Mass marketing has broken down the distinction between 'high culture' and 'popular culture'. As seen here, Van Gogh's *Sunflowers* painting, an example of a high culture art form, is now available as popular culture, as a canvas reproduction, on playing cards, a shawl, greetings cards, a notebook, a book mark, a puzzle cube, jigsaw puzzles, a lunch box, a plate and a vase.

A global popular culture

Flew (2002) suggests that the evolution of new media technologies has played an important role in the development of a global popular culture. Globalization has undermined national and local cultures, with cultural products and ways of life in different countries of the world becoming more alike, and it may now be more appropriate to speak of a **global culture** than of national or local cultures.

Advances in multi-media technology, like satellite TV and the Internet, and the digitization of cultural products like music and visual art all mean that today's media operate in a global marketplace. As well as breaking down the distinction between high culture and popular culture, this new digital world also breaks down the cultural distance between countries, and popular culture is spread beyond the boundaries of particular nation-states, with the same cultural products sold across the globe. Inspired by a media-generated culture industry and global advertising and marketing, consumers around the world – from Los Angeles, USA, to Athens, Greece, to Rio de Janeiro, Brazil, to Singapore and to Bangkok, Thailand – increasingly have a shared popular culture, with similar TV programmes, music, movies, sports, consumer goods, designer clothes and labels, and video games.

Companies like McDonald's, Coca-Cola, Vodafone, Starbucks, Nescafé, Sony and Nike are symbols that can be recognised across the world, along with the consumer lifestyles and culture associated with them. As Ritzer (2008) shows, using the example of the American food industry, companies and brands now operate on a global scale. For example, McDonald's is a worldwide business with 26,500 restaurants in more than 119 countries (in 2007); Pizza Hut and Kentucky Fried Chicken operate in 100 countries and Subway in 72 countries, with Starbucks growing at a colossal speed. It is now possible to buy an identical food product practically anywhere in the world, promoting a global culture and also weakening local cultures, as local food outlets close in the face of competition and local diets change.

Television companies sell their programmes as well as their programme formats globally – *Big Brother* and *Who Wants to be a Millionaire?*, for example. By 2008, *Who Wants to be a Millionaire?* had been distributed to 106 countries, with a global audience of one billion people; *The Weakest Link* had been seen in 43 countries, *Pop Idol* in 42 countries and *Big Brother* in 64 countries. It is the media that have made some US and British film, music and sports stars known across the world, enabling huge success in marketing their merchandise in global markets; and it is the media that have contributed substantially to English becoming the internationally dominant and preferred second language of most of the world.

> **Global culture** refers to the way cultures in different countries of the world have become more alike, sharing increasingly similar consumer products and ways of life. This has arisen as globalization has undermined national and local cultures.

Activity

1 Explain, with examples, what is meant by popular culture.
2 Identify a series of consumer products that are available all over the world, and explain how they illustrate the idea of a global culture.
3 In what ways do you think the mass media might be responsible for imposing Western or American values and lifestyles on countries across the world? What effects do you think this might have on local cultures?

The pluralist view of the globalization of popular culture

Pluralists argue that there is no such thing as popular or mass culture. The Internet, cable, satellite and digital television, and the global reach of modern mass media technology, all offer a huge range of media products, giving consumers across the world a wide diversity of cultural choices and the opportunity to create and distribute their own media products. Rather than being doped into passivity, as Marxists argue (see below), consumers and audiences now have more choice and knowledge available to them than ever before in history. This, pluralists claim, makes it ever harder for any one set of ideas or culture to dominate in society, leading to a promotion of democracy and the blossoming of ideas that were never before possible.

A critical view of the media and the globalization of popular culture

Some Marxists argue that popular or mass culture maintains the ideological hegemony (or the dominance of a set of ideas) and the power of the dominant social class in society. This is because the consumers of popular culture are lulled into an uncritical, undemanding passivity, making them less likely to challenge the dominant ideas, groups and interests in society. The globalization of popular culture is of great advantage to the media owners, who gain colossal profits from exporting and advertising their products across the globe, along with promoting the identities and lifestyles that encourage people to consume them.

Media or cultural imperialism

As Fenton (1999) points out, the term 'global' rarely means 'universal', and normally disguises a process of media-led cultural imperialism. This is the suggestion that the new media, particularly satellite television and global advertising, and Western news agencies, films, music, programme formats and Internet companies have led to the Westernization of other cultures. Western, and especially American, media products and cultural values are being forced on non-Western cultures, with the consequent undermining of local cultures and cultural independence. Most media conglomerates are now based in the United States, and US transnational media and communications corporations, like Microsoft, Google, Yahoo, and AOL/CNN/Time-Warner, dominate global communications. In what has been called a process of cocacolonization (a derivative of the American soft drink Coca-Cola and colonization), most people around the world have, through advertising and marketing, become exposed to US movies and television, fast foods and soft drinks – like Coca-Cola, Pepsi and McDonald's – and consumer fashion goods – such as Levi's jeans and Nike trainers. American and, to a lesser extent, West European cultural commodities have overwhelmed a good part of the world. This global Western dominance is illustrated by the fact that the top-grossing international films of all time outside the United States are all primarily American films, as table 3.1 shows.

Table 3.1: Top-grossing films of all time at the international (non-USA) box office, December 2007

Rank	Film	Year	Country of origin	Total gross revenue (millions of US dollars) excluding USA
1	*Titanic*	1997	USA	1,235
2	*The Lord of the Rings: The Return of the King*	2003	USA/New Zealand	752
3	*Harry Potter and the Sorcerer's Stone*	2001	UK/USA	651
4	*Pirates of the Caribbean: At World's End*	2007	USA	649
5	*Harry Potter and the Order of the Phoenix*	2007	UK/USA	645
6	*Pirates of the Caribbean: Dead Man's Chest*	2006	USA	637
7	*Harry Potter and the Chamber of Secrets*	2002	UK/USA	604
8	*Harry Potter and the Goblet of Fire*	2005	UK/USA	602
9	*The Lord of the Rings: The Two Towers*	2002	USA/New Zealand	581
10	*Jurassic Park*	1993	USA	563
11	*Spider-Man 3*	2007	USA	549
12	*The Lord of the Rings: The Fellowship of the Ring*	2001	USA/New Zealand	547
13	*Harry Potter and the Prisoner of Azkaban*	2004	UK/USA	540
14	*The Da Vinci Code*	2006	USA	540
15	*Finding Nemo*	2003	USA	525
16	*Independence Day*	1996	USA	505
17	*Star Wars: Episode I – The Phantom Menace*	1999	USA	491
18	*Shrek the Third*	2007	USA	470
19	*Star Wars: Episode III – Revenge of the Sith*	2005	USA	468
20	*The Lion King*	1994	USA	455

Source: Internet Movie Database (www.imdb.com/boxoffice/alltimegross?region=non-us)

In light of the above, it might well be argued that the media-saturated global village is in fact a North American and Western one, with global audiences primarily consuming the same American music, fashion and media images found everywhere. In this sense, media imperialism has moved the world towards global **cultural homogenization** – making the world's cultures increasingly the same.

This globalization of popular culture has spawned a mass counterfeiting industry, producing fake designer clothes, perfumes, watches, CDs, computer programs and videos/DVDs, catering for those who aspire to the lifestyles and products portrayed in the global media, but who can't afford the 'real thing'.

Cultural homogenization refers to the idea that cultural differences are erased, with world cultures becoming increasingly the same. This is often linked to the ideas of globalization and media or cultural imperialism.

> ### Activity
>
> 1 Explain carefully what you understand by globalization, and the role of the mass media in creating a global popular culture.
> 2 To what extent do you think that the mass media might be creating a global popular culture of undemanding and uncritical consumers? Explain the reasons for your answer.

The power of the media: key questions

In the UK, viewers watch an average of 3.5 hours of television every day, seven days a week. More than 11 million national newspapers are sold every day. Digital broadcasting is leading to the creation of literally hundreds of cable and satellite television channels. Ofcom research showed that, at the end of 2006, there were 433 television channels available in the UK, 76 per cent of households had digital TV, over half of UK households had Internet broadband connections, 16 per cent of mobile phone users used them to connect to the Internet, and 10 per cent used them for email.

The media have become a gigantic international business, with instant news from every part of the globe. International marketing of TV programmes and films to international audiences is backed by huge investments. The Internet has millions more people going online every year, providing instant access to colossal amounts of information and entertainment from the entire globe. Bauman (2007) cites research that suggests 'during the last thirty years more information has been produced in the world than during the previous 5,000 years, while a single copy of the Sunday edition of the *New York Times* contains more information than a cultivated person in the eighteenth century would consume during a lifetime'.

Society has become media-saturated, with the media becoming important sources of information, entertainment and leisure activity for large numbers of people, and they have become key agencies of secondary socialization and informal education, often with an important formative influence on the individual's sense of identity and consumer spending choices. Most of our taken-for-granted knowledge and our opinions and attitudes are based, not on personal experience, but on evidence and knowledge provided by the mass media. Indeed, if the media didn't report an event, or distorted it, or totally made it up, the only people likely to know about it would be those who were actually involved. For most of us, the mass media are our only source of evidence, and they colour, shape and even construct our view of the world.

If most of our opinions are based on knowledge obtained second-hand through the mass media, then this raises important issues about the power of the media to mould and shape our lives and identities. Most people think and act in particular ways because of the opinions they hold and the knowledge they have. However, do the mass media inform us about everything, or do they 'filter' information, obscuring the truth and giving false, distorted or exaggerated impressions of what is happening in the world? Do they favour some points of view over others, spreading a dominant ideology that favours the more affluent over the poor, for example? Do they misrepresent or stereotype some social groups, like women, minority ethnic groups or the disabled? The main mass media are privately owned and controlled, and run to make a profit. What effects does this pattern of ownership have on the content of the media? Does it create bias in them, with subjects presented in one-sided, distorted or misleading ways? Do the mass media actually have any influence on people? These are the sort of questions which have interested sociologists and which will now be explored.

> **Bias** means that a subject is presented in a one-sided way, favouring one point of view over others, or ignoring, distorting or misrepresenting some issues, points of view or groups compared to others.

Formal controls on the media

Although the mass media in Britain are formally free to report whatever they like, and the government has no power in normal times to stop the spreading of any opinions by using censorship, there are some formal limits to this freedom.

The law

The law restricts the media's freedom to report anything they choose in any way they like. The principal legal limits to the media's freedom are shown in the box below.

Legal limits to the media's freedom

1 The *laws of libel* forbid the publication of an untrue statement about a person which might bring him or her into contempt, ridicule, dislike, or hostility in society;

2 The *Official Secrets Acts* make it a criminal offence to report without authorization any official government activity which the government defines as an 'official secret';

3 *Defence Advisory Notices* or 'DA-Notices' are issued by the government as requests to journalists not to report national security information which the government believes might be useful to an enemy – these usually concern military secrets and similar information;

4 The *Race Relations Acts* and the *Racial and Religious Hatred Act of 2006* forbid the expression of opinions which will encourage hatred or discrimination against people because of their ethnic group or religious beliefs;

5 The *Obscene Publications Act* forbids the publication of anything that the High Court considers to be obscene and indecent, and likely to 'deprave and corrupt' anyone who sees, reads or hears it;

6 *Contempt of Court* provision forbids the reporting and expression of opinions about cases which are in the process of being dealt with in a court of law or likely to prejudice a fair trial.

Ofcom

In 2003, Ofcom (the Office of Communications) was established as a powerful new regulator of the mass media, with responsibilities across television, radio, telecommunications and wireless communication services. This has responsibility for:

- furthering the interests of consumers;
- securing the best use of the radio spectrum;
- ensuring that a wide range of television, radio, electronic media and communications networks are available in the UK, with high-quality services having a broad appeal;
- protecting the public from any offensive or potentially harmful effects of broadcast media, and safeguarding people from being unfairly treated in television and radio programmes

---

Activity

Go to www.ofcom.org.uk , and identify and briefly describe four issues that Ofcom is currently dealing with.

The BBC

The BBC is a largely state-funded body, which operates under a Royal Charter. Under a new Charter established in 2007, the BBC is governed by the BBC Trust, whose members are appointed by the Queen on advice from government ministers. The Trust sets the strategic direction of the BBC and has a clear duty to represent the interests of licence-fee payers and to ensure that the BBC remains independent, and resists pressure and influence from any source. The day-to-day running of the BBC is carried out by an executive board which is answerable to the Trust.

The BBC is partly regulated by Ofcom, and partly by the Trust, which is meant to represent the public interest, particularly the interests of viewers and radio listeners. The BBC is financed by the state through the television licence fee, plus income from a series of private spin-off companies, which top up the licence-fee income with substantial profits. The state can therefore have some control over the BBC by refusing to raise the licence fee. Although the BBC is not a private business run solely to make a profit, like the independent commercial broadcasting services (independent TV and radio), and is not dependent on advertising for its income, it still has to compete with commercial broadcasting by attracting audiences large enough to justify the licence fee.

Independent broadcasting

Independent broadcasting includes all the non-BBC television and radio stations. These are regulated by Ofcom, which licenses the companies that can operate in the private sector, and is responsible for the amount, content, quality and standard of advertising and programmes on independent television and radio, and for dealing with any complaints.

The Press Complaints Commission

The Press Complaints Commission is a voluntary body appointed by the newspaper industry itself to maintain certain standards of newspaper journalism. It deals with public complaints against newspapers, but it has no real power to enforce effective sanctions as a result of these complaints.

Ownership of the mass media

The mass media are very big business. The ownership of the main mass media in modern Britain is concentrated in the hands of a few large companies, which are interested in making profits. This concentration of ownership is shown in table 3.2. Of the total circulation of national daily and Sunday newspapers, around 86 per cent is controlled by just four companies, and over half by just two companies (News International and Trinity Mirror). One individual, Rupert Murdoch, is the major force behind News International, which owns the *Sun* and *The Times*, newspapers that make up about 33 per cent of all national daily newspaper sales in the United Kingdom. Rupert Murdoch alone accounted for about 33 per cent of the total daily and Sunday newspaper sales in 2008. As table 3.2 shows, this concentration of ownership extends also to other areas of the media, such as TV and book and magazine publishing. The details of who owns what are continually changing, as concentration of ownership is an ongoing process with take-overs and mergers occurring, providing a stronger financial base for competition in the international market. Who owns what can be researched at www.mediauk.com.

The same few companies control a wide range of different media, and therefore a large proportion of what we see and hear in the media. In 2008 Rupert Murdoch, for example, also owned 40 per cent of BskyB, all of HarperCollins, the world's largest English-language book publisher, and MySpace, the Internet social networking site.

The concentration of media ownership has four distinct features:

1   There is concentration of ownership within a single medium; for example, one company owning several newspapers.
2   These owners also have interests in a range of media, such as newspapers, magazines, book publishing, television, the film industry, music, websites and as Internet service providers (ISPs).
3   This ownership is international – the owners have media interests in many different countries of the world.
4   Media companies are often part of huge conglomerates – companies that have a range of interests in a wide variety of products besides the media. Virgin, for example, has an airline, a train company, soft drinks, financial products and mobile phones, on top of its widespread media interests.

This is clearly illustrated by the media in the United States. Bagdikian (2004) says that five global-dimension firms (Time Warner, Walt Disney, News Corporation, Viacom and Bertelsmann) own most of the newspapers, magazines, book publishers,

Table 3.2: Who owns what: national newspaper group ownership and some of their interests in publishing, television and digital media, United Kingdom, 2008

Company	Share of UK national daily (excluding Sunday) newspaper circulation % (July 2008)	National Newspapers (all of which have related websites)	Also owns
News International (UK arm of News Corporation)	33	*Sun, The Times, News of the World, Sunday Times, Times Literary Supplement*	40% of BskyB – Sky television, broadband and telephony; HarperCollins book publishers; wide range of websites, including MySpace, and page3.com
Trinity Mirror	16	*Daily Mirror, Sunday Mirror, Daily Record, People, Sunday Mail*	More than 200 local and regional newspapers; more than 300 websites
Daily Mail and General Trust	21	*Daily Mail, Mail on Sunday*	Second-largest regional newspaper owners, with more than 100 papers; 90% of Teletext; 20% of ITN; various radio stations and large range of websites
Northern & Shell	13	*Daily Express, Sunday Express, Daily Star, Daily Star Sunday*	*OK!* magazine; various soft porn TV channels
Telegraph Media Group (part of Press Holdings Limited)	8	*Daily Telegraph, Sunday Telegraph, The Scotsman*	*Spectator*
Pearson	4	*Financial Times*	Longman, Pearson and Penguin book publishers; Ft.com
Guardian Media Group	3	*Guardian, Observer*	Guardian Weekly; more than 40 local newspapers; various local websites and TV channels; Guardian Unlimited network of websites; shares in various consumer magazines, including Sainsbury's magazine
Seven companies	98		

Source: Data compiled from Audit Bureau of Circulation and various corporate websites

motion picture studios, and radio and television stations in the United States. These firms have major holdings in all the media, from newspapers to movie studios. Each medium covers the entire country, and the owners prefer stories that can be used anywhere and everywhere. This concentration of ownership gives a lot of power to a small number of companies and individuals who control the media industry, and, as Bagdikian suggests, 'this gives each of the five corporations and their leaders more communications power than was exercised by any despot or dictatorship in history'.

This has given rise to three main and related concerns:

1   Are the media simply spreading a limited number of dominant ideas (the dominant ideology) through society, thereby protecting the interests of the dominant class in society?
2   Do the owners of the media control the content of the media?
3   What effects do the media have on the audiences they aim at?

Activity

1   Suggest reasons why the concentration of ownership of the mass media might be of some concern in a democracy.
2   Do you think there should be restrictions on the number of media that any one person or company should be allowed to own? Give reasons for your answer.

The mass media and ideology

Ideology refers to a set of ideas, values and beliefs that represent the outlook, and justify the interests, of a social group. Marxists see societies as having a **dominant ideology**, which is that of the dominant class in society. This dominant ideology is one that justifies the social advantages of wealthy, powerful and influential groups in society, and justifies the disadvantages of those who lack wealth, power and influence. It is spread through the rest of the population by what the Marxist Althusser called **ideological state apparatuses** – agencies like the mass media and the education system which seek to persuade people to accept the way things are presently organized, because persuading them and trying to obtain their consent is a far more effective means of controlling the population than using force.

Marxists like Miliband (1973) argue that the media play an important role in spreading this dominant ideology. He argues that the media control access to the knowledge which people have about what is happening in society, and encourage them to accept the unequal society in which they live. The media create a general consensus or agreement about what constitutes 'reasonable' and 'unreasonable' ways of thinking and behaving, which makes those who challenge the way things are presently organized seem unreasonable or extreme. This is because the media have the means to provide incomplete or distorted views of the world, and to ignore, attack, dismiss or present as 'unreasonable' any groups, events or ideas which challenge or threaten the dominant ideology. The media thereby create a climate of conformity among the mass of

Ideology refers to a set of ideas, values and beliefs that represent the outlook, and justify the interests, of a social group. The **dominant ideology** is one that justifies the social advantages of wealthy, powerful and influential groups in society, and justifies the disadvantages of those who lack wealth, power and influence.

Ideological state apparatuses are agencies which spread the dominant ideology and justify the power of the dominant social class.

the population which justifies the rule of the rich and powerful. The following section examines competing views on whether and to what extent the mass media are simply the tools of the dominant class.

Control of the mass media

Within sociology, there are three main approaches to the issue of ownership and control of the media. These are known as the manipulative or instrumentalist approach, the dominant ideology or hegemonic approach, and the pluralist approach.

The manipulative or instrumentalist approach

This is a traditional Marxist approach, adopted by writers like Miliband. It suggests that the concentration of ownership of the mass media in the hands of a few media corporations enables the owners to control media output, and serve ruling-class interests. The media are seen as an instrument through which the ruling class is able to manipulate media content and media audiences in its own interests.

According to this approach:

1   Owners of the media, like newspaper owners, have direct control of the content of the media, and they can and do interfere in media content.
2   The owners use the media to spread ideas (the dominant ideology) which justify the power of the dominant class.
3   Media managers have little choice other than to run the media within the boundaries set down by the owners.
4   Journalists depend for their jobs on supporting the interests of the owners – the reports of journalists are therefore biased (one-sided). Journalists censor their own reports to avoid criticism of the interests of the dominant class; ideas or groups that threaten the status quo (the existing arrangements in society) are attacked, ridiculed or ignored.
5   The audience is assumed to be passive – a mass of unthinking and uncritical 'robots'. This audience is exposed to only a limited range of opinions, and is manipulated through biased reports – it is 'fed' on a dumbed-down mass diet of undemanding, trivial and uncritical content. This stops people from focusing on serious issues, or encourages them to interpret serious issues in ways favourable to the dominant class.

Strengths of the manipulative or instrumentalist approach

1   There is evidence that, occasionally, media owners do interfere in the content of newspapers, and appoint managers and editors who conform to their views (and sack those who don't). For example, in February 2003, Rupert Murdoch was arguing strongly in interviews for a war with Iraq. It is unlikely to be coincidence that all his 175 newspapers around the world backed him. Murdoch admitted to the House of Lords Communication Committee in 2007 that he was 'hands on both economically and editorially' and exercised editorial control on major issues in

the *Sun* and the *News of the World*, such as which party to back in a general election or policy on Europe, though the law prevented him from instructing the editors of *The Times* or the *Sunday Times*.

2 Ownership of the media industry is highly concentrated, as are the news agencies which provide information.

3 Journalists do ultimately depend on the owners for their careers, and can't afford to upset their bosses.

Weaknesses of the manipulative or instrumentalist approach

1 Pluralists (see below) would argue there is a wide range of opinion in the media, and the media's owners and managers are primarily concerned with making profits. This means attracting large audiences to gain advertisers and the only means of doing this is to provide what the audiences – not the owners – want.

2 The state regulates media ownership so that no one person or company has too much influence. By law, TV and radio have to report news impartially, and can't therefore simply churn out biased, one-sided reports.

3 Audiences are not as gullible and easily manipulated as the manipulative approach suggests – people can accept, reject or interpret media messages, depending on their existing ideas and experiences.

The dominant ideology or hegemonic approach

This is a more recent, neo- (new) Marxist approach. This approach also suggests that the mass media spread a dominant ideology justifying or legitimizing the power of the ruling class. It differs from the manipulative approach by suggesting this is not carried out by the direct control of owners and direct manipulation of journalists, media content and the audience. It recognizes the power of owners, but suggests that they rarely interfere in media content, though they do have an influence upon it. Rather, this approach emphasizes the idea of **hegemony**. This is a term first developed by the Italian Marxist Gramsci, and refers to the idea that, through the spread of the dominant ideology of the ruling class, other social classes are persuaded to accept the values and beliefs in that ideology as reasonable and normal, and the values of the dominant class become part of everyday common sense. This approach suggests that the dominant ideology of the ruling class is shared by media managers and journalists, and so they spread the dominant ideology by choice and because it seems reasonable and sensible rather than because they are manipulated or told what to say by media owners.

According to this approach:

1 Owners of the media, like newspaper owners, rarely have direct control of the content of the media. Day-to-day control and media content are left in the hands of managers and journalists.

2 Media managers and journalists, while inevitably influenced by the desire not to upset the owners and to protect their careers, also need to attract audiences and

Hegemony means the dominance in society of the ruling class's set of ideas over others, and acceptance of and consent to them by the rest of society.

advertisers. Media content critical of the dominant ideology sometimes helps to attract audiences, and some occasional criticism maintains a pretence of objective, unbiased reporting most of the time.

3 Nevertheless, journalists do generally support the dominant ideology, not because the owners order them to, but because they share a similar view of the world to that of the dominant class. Most journalists tend to be white, middle class and male, and are socialized into a set of professional values which share a set of taken-for-granted assumptions in keeping with the dominant ideology. This makes groups, events or ideas threatening the status quo seem unreasonable, extremist, ridiculous, funny or trivial, to be attacked or not taken seriously. The dominant ideology generates a consensus (a wide agreement) about what is worthy, good and right for all.

4 These common-sense assumptions shared by journalists mean the audience is exposed to only a limited range of opinions, mostly within the framework of the dominant ideology. Audiences are therefore, over time, unconsciously persuaded to see the dominant ideology as the only reasonable and sensible view of the world. The hegemony of the ruling ideas is therefore maintained.

Strengths of the dominant ideology or hegemonic approach

1 This approach recognizes that owners are often not involved in the day-to-day running of their media businesses.

2 It recognizes that media managers, editors and journalists have some professional independence, and are not simply manipulated by media owners.

3 It recognizes that there can be a range of media content to attract audiences, some of it critical of the dominant ideology. Nevertheless, journalists are socialized into a culture where the dominant ideology suggests the most 'reasonable' explanation of events and the way they are reported.

Weaknesses of the dominant ideology or hegemonic approach

1 The approach underrates the power and influence of the owners. Owners do appoint and dismiss managers and editors who step too far out of line, and journalists' careers are dependent on gaining approval of their stories from editors.

2 **Agenda-setting** and **gate-keeping** (discussed later in this chapter) mean some items are deliberately excluded from being reported in the media, and audiences are encouraged to think about some events rather than others. Audiences have little real choice of media content, as newspapers and TV programmes are produced within a framework of the dominant ideology. This suggests a direct manipulation of audiences.

3 Journalists' **news values** (discussed later) mean that sometimes journalists do not simply trot out the dominant ideology, but can develop critical, anti-establishment views which strike a chord with their audiences. An example might be campaigns against government corruption or wrongdoing by large companies.

Agenda-setting refers to the media's influence over the issues that people think about because the agenda, or list of subjects, for public discussion is laid down by the mass media.

Gate-keeping is the power of some people, groups or organizations to limit access to something valuable or useful. For example, the mass media have the power to refuse to cover some issues and therefore not allow the public access to some information.

News values are the values and assumptions held by editors and journalists which guide them in choosing what is 'newsworthy' - what to report and what to leave out, and how what they choose to report should be presented.

The pluralist approach

Both the manipulative and the hegemonic approaches assume that those who own, control and work in the media shape their content, spreading the dominant ideology among media audiences and protecting the interests of powerful groups in society. The pluralist approach is very different from these. Pluralists suggest that there is no dominant ruling class, but many competing groups with different interests. All these different interests are represented in the media. The owners do not directly control the content of the media, but, rather, what appears in the media is driven by the wishes of consumers – audiences will simply not watch TV programmes or buy newspapers that do not reflect their views.

According to the pluralist approach:

1　Owners do not have direct control over the content of the media.
2　There is no single dominant class, but a wide range of competing groups in society with different interests. These differing interests are reflected in a wide range of media, covering all points of view.
3　Media content is driven not by a dominant ideology or the interests of owners, but by circulation and audience figures and the search for profits. This means the media will serve up whatever is necessary to satisfy audience tastes and wishes.
4　The mass media are generally free of any government or direct owner control and can present whatever point of view they want, and audiences are free to choose in a 'pick 'n' mix' approach to whatever interpretation suits them.
5　The media are controlled by media managers who allow journalists a great deal of freedom. They have to offer a wide selection of views to satisfy and maintain their audiences. Audiences are not manipulated by the media, but, rather, have some control over the media by the choices they make about the programmes they watch or the newspapers they buy. Audiences can select what they want from the wide range of media and media content available.
6　Journalists write stories using 'news values' (discussed later in this chapter) reflecting the wishes and interests most relevant to their audiences. There is no dominant ideology or ruling-class bias being pumped out and manipulating audiences, but journalists provide what the audiences want. Any bias simply reflects what the audiences want, and they have the freedom to accept, reject or ignore media content. The mass media don't manipulate or brainwash audiences, and indeed have little effect on them, as they already have views of their own.

Strengths of the pluralist approach

1　There is a wide range of newspapers, magazines, television channels and other media reflecting a huge range of interests and ideas, including those which challenge the dominant ideology.
2　The diversity of media enables investigative reporting to take place which can scrutinize and challenge the power and interests of the dominant class.
3　Journalists are not simply the pawns of their employers, but have some professional and editorial honesty and independence, and are often critical of the dominant ideology.

4   The fight for audiences in competition with other companies means that the mass media have to cater for audience tastes – newspapers and TV channels have to be responsive to their audiences, otherwise they'll go out of business.

Weaknesses of the pluralist approach

1   While managers, journalists and television producers have some independence, they work within constraints placed on them by the owners. Editors are controlled and appointed by owners. The main sources of information for journalists tend to be from those groups that consist of the most powerful and influential members of society, and their views are given greater weight than less powerful groups. News is collected by a few news companies and agencies, often paid for by the media owners themselves.

2   Media owners strongly influence who is appointed at senior levels of the media, and top managers, editors and owners often share a similar outlook on the world.

3   Not all groups in society have equal influence on editors and journalists to get their views across, and only very rich groups will have the resources required to launch major media companies to get their views across independently. It is the rich, powerful and influential who are more likely to be interviewed on TV, to appear on chat shows, to be quoted in newspapers, and so on.

4   The owners have on numerous occasions sacked uncooperative editors, and both governments and rich individuals have brought political or legal pressure to bear to stop programmes, newspaper stories and books which threaten their interests.

5   The pressure to attract audiences doesn't increase media choice but limits it – the media decline in quality, and news and information get squeezed out or sensationalized, as the media target large mass markets with unthreatening, unchallenging and bland content aimed at an undemanding mass audience.

6   Hegemonic theorists (see above) would argue that people have been socialized by the media themselves into the belief that they are being provided with what they want. The media themselves may have created their tastes, so that what audiences want is really what the media owners want.

Table 3.3 summarizes approaches to ownership of the media and media content.

Activity

1   Go through each of the following statements, identifying them as corresponding most closely to the manipulative or instrumentalist approach, or the dominant ideology or hegemonic approach, or the pluralist approach.

●   'I'm in the business of making money, and I'll use the media I own to provide whatever the audience wants.'

●   Generally the media supports the interests of the dominant groups in society, but a bit of criticism every now and then encourages people to believe the media are telling us the truth about society.

●   The concentration of media ownership means that the views expressed in the media reflect little more than the interests of the owners.

- There is such a wide variety of media to choose from that everyone's views are represented somewhere.
- The media are controlled and run mainly by white, middle-class males, so they generally spread the existing dominant ideas in society.
- Media audiences are exposed to only a limited range of opinions, and so over time people are persuaded to accept only a limited view of the world, mainly that of the most powerful groups in society.
- The media are owned by a few rich individuals, so the public are fed on a media diet of political propaganda protecting the owners' interests.
- Journalists are just the tools of the owners, and they can't criticize the interests of the powerful without losing their jobs.
- If readers aren't attracted, advertisers won't advertise and media companies will go out of business. Survival in the competitive world of the modern mass media means readers and audiences are the ones who decide in the end what they want to see in the media.
- The media cons people in subtle ways over a period of time that the only reasonable view of the world is that of the most powerful groups in society.

2 Answer the following essay question in about one and a half to two sides of A4: *'Critically assess the pluralist view of the mass media.'*

Table 3.3: Ownership of the media and media content: a summary

	Manipulative or instrumentalist approach	Dominant ideology or Hegemonic approach	Pluralist approach
Role of owners	Direct control and manipulation	Influence and persuasion	No direct control, and wide range of competing interests
Media content	Dominant ideology	Dominant ideology, but sometimes critical of it to attract audiences	Need for circulation and audience figures, and profits, means content is what audiences – not owners – want
Role of media managers and journalists	Told what to do by owners, or within framework set by them	Some independence from owners, but share dominant ideology, and so present most stories in that framework, but need to attract audiences and advertisers	Have high level of independence, so long as they attract audiences and therefore profits
View of audience	Passive – audiences manipulated by owners	Passive – audiences persuaded to accept dominant ideology	Active – audiences make choices between media and can accept, reject, reinterpret or ignore media content

The effects of the mass media

The debate above, particularly concerning the manipulative and dominant ideology approaches, suggests that the content of the media does have some effect on the audience. However, this cannot be taken for granted. People are conscious, thinking human beings, not mindless robots. They might not swallow everything they come across in the media, and they might respond in a variety of ways to what they read or watch on TV or see on the Internet. For example, they might dismiss, reject, ignore, criticize, forget or give a different meaning to a media message, and this is likely to be influenced by factors such as their own social experiences, their ethnic group, social class, gender and so on. For example, a black person is likely to reject a racist message in a TV broadcast or newspaper report.

We also need to be aware that the media comprise only one influence on the way people might think and behave, and there is a wide range of other agencies involved in people's socialization. Families, friends, schools, workplaces and workmates, churches, social class, ethnicity, gender, disability, age and so on may all influence individual and group behaviour and attitudes. It would be somewhat foolhardy to suggest that all behaviour can be explained by exposure to the media, so we must constantly situate media influences alongside these other factors.

This section examines the different approaches sociologists have adopted to the question of whether media content does actually have an influence or effect on audiences. There are competing views on this, mainly centred on the issue of whether audiences are passive 'dopes' mindlessly consuming media content, or active interpreters of that content, giving it different meanings and interpretations.

The hypodermic syringe model

The hypodermic syringe model, sometimes called the magic bullet theory, is a very simple model, and most commentators would now regard it as an old-fashioned and inadequate view of the relationship between media content and the audience – readers, listeners and viewers. This model suggests that the media act like a hypodermic syringe (or a bullet), injecting messages and content into the 'veins' of media audiences. Audiences are seen as unthinking, passive robots, who are unable to resist the 'drug' injected by the media. In this view, media messages fill audiences with the dominant ideology, sexist and racist images, scenes of violence or other content, and the audience then immediately acts on these messages. It is like seeing violence on television, and then going out and attacking someone. It is a simple view of the media as causing immediate changes in people's behaviour.

Strengths of the hypodermic syringe model

There are few strengths in the hypodermic syringe model, though there is some evidence that, on rare occasions, people do react quite directly to what they see in the media. For example, 'copycat' crimes or urban riots. Also, advertisers spend millions of pounds on advertising their products, and we might reasonably assume that these have some effect on consumers and the sale of the goods advertised.

Weaknesses of the hypodermic syringe model

1 The model assumes that the entire audience is passive and will react in the same way to media content. However, people may well have a range of responses to media content, depending on their own social situation and the experiences they have had. For example, violence in the media could have a variety of effects – people might be appalled and become determined to stamp it out; others might use it to work out their violent fantasies so it doesn't happen in real life; others might simply ignore it.

2 It assumes audiences are passive, gullible and easily manipulated – but people are active thinking human beings, who have their own ideas, and who interpret what they see and can give different meanings to it.

3 It assumes the media have enormous power and influence, overriding all other agencies of socialization and people's own experiences.

4 There is little evidence that media content has the immediate effects on audiences the model suggests.

The two-step flow model

The weaknesses of the hypodermic syringe model are tackled by what is known as the two-step flow model, developed by Katz and Lazarsfeld (1955). This model recognizes that audiences do not simply passively react to media content, and will respond in a variety of ways to it. These responses will be influenced by the beliefs and values they already hold, their own experiences and the opinions of those in their own family, at work, school or college, or in peer groups.

This model of media influence suggests that people are influenced by 'opinion leaders'. These are those respected members of any social group who get information and form views from the media, who lead opinion and discussion in their social groups, and whom others listen to and take notice of. It might, for example, be an assertive and popular student whose views others tend to take notice of. The two-step flow model suggests that it is these opinion leaders who are influenced by the media (the first step) and they then pass on these opinions, selectively and with their own interpretations, to others in their social groups (the second step). Members of these groups may then, in turn, pass on their opinions to others, in a kind of chain reaction leading from one person or group to another.

Strengths of the two-step flow model

1 This model recognizes that the effects of the mass media are not as direct, powerful and influential as the hypodermic syringe model suggests. It suggests that opinion leaders are the ones most subject to media influence, not the whole audience.

2 It recognizes that audiences are not completely passive and uncritically accepting of direct media messages, but that 'opinion leaders' select, interpret and filter media messages before they reach mass audiences, and it is this process that influences any effects the media might have.

3 It recognizes that media audiences are not a mass of isolated individuals, but that the social groups to which people belong influence the opinions they hold and how they respond to and interpret media content.

4 It recognizes that people form their own judgements on media content, although this is influenced by opinion leaders, and they can therefore give meanings other than those intended by the media. For example, a group of Labour Party supporters watching a Conservative Party election broadcast might critically discuss and mock the Conservative views expressed, and reconfirm their own support for Labour – presumably not the intention of those trying to persuade people to vote Conservative.

Weaknesses of the two-step flow model

1 There are probably more than two steps in the media's influence. Media content could be selected and interpreted by many different individuals in different groups. For example, parents (as opinion leaders) may have one view, an 'opinion-leading' workmate another view, and a sociology teacher still another. This might mean ideas and interpretations of media content get bounced around in discussions in a variety of groups, creating many steps in the flow of media influence.

2 It still rests on the basic assumption that the influence of the media flows from the media to the audience, and assumes that media audiences are more or less victims of media content, even if the mass audience is insulated by opinion leaders.

3 It suggests that people are very vulnerable to influence and manipulation by opinion leaders. It does not recognize that people may have views, opinions and experiences of their own on which to base their views of media content.

4 It suggests the audience is divided into 'active' viewers/readers (the 'opinion leaders') and 'passive' viewers/readers who are influenced by the opinion leaders. It doesn't explain why opinion leaders are directly influenced by media content when others in the audience are not.

The cultural effects model

Cultural effects theory recognizes that the media are owned and heavily influenced by the dominant and most powerful groups in society, and their interests strongly influence the content of the media. This content is mainly in keeping with the dominant ideology.

Like the hypodermic syringe and two-step flow models, the cultural effects model suggests that the media do have an effect on the audience. However, the media do not have the direct effects of the 'hypodermic' model, or the effects via opinion leaders of the two-step flow model. Rather, the cultural effects model suggests that the media gradually influence the audience over a period of time – a sort of slow, steady, subtle, ever-present process of brainwashing which gradually shapes people's taken-for-granted common-sense ideas and assumptions, and their everyday view of the world. For example, if we see minority ethnic groups nearly always portrayed in the context of trouble and crime, or women portrayed only as housewives, mothers, lovers and sex objects, over time this will come to form the stereotypes we hold of these groups, to the exclusion of other aspects of their lives.

However, cultural effects theory suggests the extent of these media effects will be affected by the social characteristics and experiences of audience members. For example, women might well resist gender stereotyping in the media, and black people (and many white people) may well reject racist stereotypes.

While the cultural effects model suggests that the media will generally spread the dominant ideology in society, it implies that audiences may respond in different ways depending on their own social situation and their own experiences and beliefs. They might support and agree with the content and 'slant' of TV and newspaper reporting, but they might also be critical of or even reject that content, in line with their own social experiences. For example, white people living in multicultural communities might well have different views of ethnic minorities from those who have no such experience of minority ethnic group life. This could mean that each group might respond differently to images of ethnic minorities presented in the media. The group with their own experiences of ethnic minorities might reject or modify media content because of their own first-hand experiences, while those without such experience may well take for granted the media content, as they have no experiences of their own to judge media content by.

The interpretivist selective filtering approach: selective exposure, selective perception and selective retention

Not everyone views the same media content in the same way.

Theories of the effects of the media on audiences often assume that people are like blank pieces of paper, with no choices or experiences of their own to interpret what they hear, see or read. However, Klapper (1960) suggested the mass media do not directly influence people, but that people filter what they read, see or hear in the media. This interpretivist selective filtering approach suggests people are selective in what media they consume and how they react to it according to their own viewpoint and experience. Klapper suggests there are three filters that people apply in their approaches to and interpretations of the media:

1 *Selective exposure.* This filter means people may only watch or read media that fit in with their existing views and interests

2 *Selective perception.* This filter means people will react differently to the same message depending on whether it fits in with their own views and interests

3 *Selective retention.* This filter means they will 'forget' material that is not in line with their views and interests.

An example of the application of these filters might be the way people respond to party political election broadcasts, depending on which political party they personally support, as suggested in the cartoon opposite. During the Iraq War of 2003, the *Daily Mirror* passionately opposed the war, yet half its readers were in favour. The *Daily Mail* was a strong supporter of the war – but one-quarter of its readers opposed it. People do seem to have their own views beyond what the media tell them.

Strengths of the cultural effects model

1 This model recognizes the power of the dominant class to influence the content of the media. The media transmit a dominant ideology as journalists generally share the worldview and assumptions of that dominant ideology.

2 It recognizes that media audiences are not passive absorbers of media messages, but that they can and do respond differently to media content. They actively interpret media content in the light of their own social circumstances and experiences, and their values and beliefs.

3 It recognizes that the media, although they generally present a biased, ideological view of the world favouring the dominant class, don't always have the same effect on media audiences.

4 It recognizes that the media are likely to be influential as a key shaper of people's view of the world, but these effects are likely to be over a long time period, rather than immediate and short-term. Over this long period, the media gradually persuade most people to accept that media content represents a mainstream, common-sense view of the world, though this in reality reflects the dominant ideology. Long-term media exposure will therefore ultimately influence and shape the way people think and behave.

Weaknesses of the cultural effects model

1 The model gives too much emphasis to the active role of media audiences. Those with power in society set the framework for media content, and over the long term socialization by the media limits the ability of audiences to resist media messages.

2 It assumes media personnel like journalists work within the framework and assumptions of the dominant ideology. This fails to recognize that journalists have some independence in their work, and can sometimes be very critical of the dominant ideology and the existing arrangements in society.

In general, the hypodermic, two-step flow and cultural effects models see the media, to a greater or lesser extent, as having an influence sooner or later over the way people think and behave. The final model of media effects – the uses and gratifications model – asks not so much what the media do to people as what people do with the media, and recognizes that audiences are not always or simply the unwitting 'victims' of media messages.

The uses and gratifications model

The uses and gratifications model starts with a view that media audiences are thinking, active and creative human beings. In this view, media audiences are active, and *use* the media in various ways for their own various pleasures and interests (*gratifications*). The emphasis changes from the various ways the media influence and manipulate people to an emphasis on the way that audiences use the media.

Media audiences are not simply passive robots who are easily manipulated, led by opinion leaders or have their ideas moulded over time by the routine process of constant exposure to the dominant ideology. They use the media in a whole variety of ways. For example, McQuail (1972) and Lull (1990) suggest a variety of uses and gratifications of the media. They may be used for:

- leisure, entertainment and relaxation, as an escape from daily routine;
- personal relationships and companionship, through identification with communities like those in *Coronation Street* or *EastEnders*, or situations and characters in reality TV shows like *Big Brother*, or as a conversation starter in group situations;
- personal identity, using the media to explore and confirm their own identities, interests and values, for example keeping up with contemporary trends in cooking, gardening or music, fashion changes and social attitudes;
- information, such as keeping up with the news and current affairs;
- background 'wallpaper' while doing other things.

This variety of uses of the media, providing a range of pleasures, means that people make conscious choices, select and interpret what they watch on TV or

People will use the media for different uses and gratifications.

read in newspapers and magazines, and use them for an array of needs which they themselves decide. These different uses mean the effects of the media are likely to be different in each case, depending on what people are using the media for. We therefore can't assume that the uses and effects even of the same media content will be the same in every case.

Strengths of the uses and gratifications model

1   This model recognizes the active role of media audiences. It recognizes that audiences make conscious choices about how they use the media, and media companies therefore have to provide a range of content to satisfy these choices.
2   It recognizes that audiences have the power to decide media content: a failure by media companies to satisfy audience pleasures will mean no viewers, listeners or readers – and therefore no advertisers – and so the companies or the particular channel, radio station or newspaper will risk going out of business.
3   It recognizes that the uses and gratifications of the media are likely to vary from one individual to the next, and these will be influenced by factors such as their age, gender, social class or ethnicity, and their previous experiences, attitudes and values. For example, a soft-porn cable TV channel or a programme about cars is likely to have rather different uses and gratifications for men and women. It therefore becomes very difficult to generalize about the effects of the media, as people will be selective in their exposure to, and perception and retention of, media content.

Weaknesses of the uses and gratifications model

1   The model overestimates the power of the audience to influence media content. It also underestimates the power and influence of the media and media companies to shape and influence the choices people make and the 'pleasures' they derive from the media. Media companies set the choices, and the media may create the different pleasures themselves, through devices like advertising.
2   It focuses too much on the use of the media by individuals. It doesn't allow for the group aspects of media audiences, unlike the two-step flow and cultural effects models, which recognize that people often relate to the media in social groups, and it is these group settings that will influence their uses and gratifications.
3   The focus on individual uses and gratifications ignores the wider social factors affecting the way audiences respond. Common experiences and common values may mean many people will respond in similar ways to media content.

Table 3.4 summarizes approaches to the media's effects on audiences.

Activity

1 Suppose you wanted to study the effects of a TV programme on an audience. Suggest how you might go about researching this.
2 Carry out a short survey finding out what use people make of the mass media in their daily lives (using ideas from the uses and gratifications approach outlined above). You might also ask them about how much and in what ways they think they are influenced by the content of what they see in the media.

Table 3.4: The effects of the media on audiences: a summary

	Hypodermic syringe model	Two-step flow model	Cultural effects model	Uses and gratifications and selective filtering models
Effect of media content on audiences	Direct and immediate effect on people's behaviour	Indirect effects, through role of 'opinion leaders' who make interpretations and pass them on to others	Long-term effects through continuous exposure and persuasion into acceptance of the dominant ideology	Effects vary from one individual to the next. Can't generalize about media effects – it depends what people use media for. People will demonstrate selective exposure, selective perception and selective retention
View of audience	Passive and easily manipulated	Not completely passive, as influenced only indirectly through 'opinion leaders' and through discussion in social groups	Not completely passive, as people will respond according to their own interpretations, social circumstances and beliefs.	Active, and make conscious choices, and select and use media for their own pleasures

Activity

1 Suggest three needs that people might satisfy by using the mass media.
2 Suggest three reasons why the media may not affect their audience.
3 Answer the following essay question, in about one and half or two sides of A4 paper:
   'Critically examine the "hypodermic syringe" approach to the effects of the mass media on audiences.'

Violence and the media

Violence, including pornography, on the Internet, in computer games, in TV news reports and dramas, and in films, videos and DVDs, is now part of popular culture, and more people are exposed to such violence than ever before. Estimates suggest that, by the time they are 18, American children will have seen on television around 16,000 real and fictional murders and 200,000 acts of violence.

Such media violence is often blamed for increasing crime and violence in society. A high-profile example of this was the murder in 1993 of 2-year-old James Bulger by two 10-year-old boys. The judge in the case commented: 'I suspect that exposure to violent video films may in part be an explanation.' This view was disputed by the police, who said they could find no evidence that videos viewed by the family could have encouraged the boys to batter a toddler to death.

Assertions, like that in the Bulger murder, that media violence generates real-life violence, are commonplace, and masses of research has been done to investigate whether such a link really exists, particularly in relation to children. Typical of this was the report by Newson (1994), which opened with a reference to the James Bulger murder the previous year, and asserted that violent videos could lead to violent actions. Newson's review gained enormous media attention, and was reported as conclusively establishing a link between video violence and real-world violence, a link that was allegedly even stronger than the one established between smoking and lung cancer. Similarly, a review by Anderson et al. (2003) claimed that research showed indisputably that media violence increased the likelihood of aggressive and violent behaviour, both immediately and in the long term. Although much of the experimental research claims to have established some links between violent TV viewing and violent behaviour, such claims have been very strongly disputed.

Cumberbatch (1994), for example, heavily criticized Newson's report, arguing that its findings were nothing more than speculation fuelled by the popular press. A review by Newburn and Hagell (1995) of more than 1,000 studies concluded that the link between media violence and violent behaviour was 'not proven', and children displaying tendencies to violence may have had such tendencies regardless of television viewing. A 2003 report by the Broadcasting Standards Commission found that children are fully aware that television production is a process and that they are not watching reality, with the report concluding: 'They are able to make judgements . . . they are not blank sheets of paper on whom messages can be imprinted.' A review of the research evidence by Cumberbatch (2004) for the Video Standards Council found the evidence for the view that media violence caused violence in society to be quite weak. Cumberbatch cites a review that claims there are only around 200 separate scientific studies that directly assess the effects of exposure to media violence, and that this evidence does not support the view that media violence causes aggression. It would therefore appear that, despite all the research, there is little reliable and undisputed evidence about whether violence in the media leads to an increase in aggressive behaviour.

Some competing claims about the effects of violence in the media

The mass of research that has been carried out on the effects of violence in the media on violence in real life has reached a range of different and contradictory conclusions, which are summarized below:

1 *Copycatting*. Like a hypodermic syringe injecting a drug, exposure to media violence causes children to copy what they see and behave more aggressively *in the real world* (as shown in Bandura et al.'s 'Bobo doll' experiments, discussed below)

2 *Catharsis*. Media violence does not make viewers more aggressive, but reduces violence as it allows people to live out their violent tendencies in the fantasy world of the media rather than in the real world.

3 *Desensitization*. Writers like Himmelweit et al. (1958) have suggested that repeated exposure of children to media violence has gradual 'drip-drip' long-term effects, with increased risk of aggressive behaviour as adults, as people tend to become less sensitive and disturbed when they witness real-world violence, have less sympathy for its victims, and become socialized into accepting violence as a normal part of life.

4 *Sensitization*. Exposure to violence in the media can make people more sensitive to and less tolerant of real-life violence, as Belson's 1978 study of more than 1,500 teenage boys found.

5 *Media violence causes psychological disturbance in some children*. Watching media violence frightens young children, causing nightmares, sleeplessness, anxiety and depression, and these effects may be long lasting.

6 *Media violence causes some people to have exaggerated fears about crime and the safety of their communities.*

Activity

1 Write an explanation of how each of the five effects models outlined earlier in the chapter – hypodermic syringe, two-step flow, cultural effects, selective filtering and uses and gratifications – might view the effects of media violence.

2 Suggest a range of different ways that people might interpret and respond to seeing violent content in the media – for example, switching off the television, walking out of a film, or going out and beating someone up.

3 Suggest reasons why children might be more vulnerable to media violence than adults.

4 The box above outlines a number of claims about the effects of violence in the mass media. Look at each of them, and try to criticize them in as many ways as you can, as in the following example:

Effect of violent media content	Criticism
Desensitization: repeated exposure to media violence increases the risk of aggressive behaviour, as people become less sensitive and disturbed when they witness real world violence, have less sympathy for its victims, and become socialized into accepting violence as a normal part of life.	Violent media content might so horrify and sensitize people to it that they become opposed to it in real life.

A lot of the research on the link between the media and violence has been carried out in laboratory conditions, and involves exposing people to violent media content to see if they then behave violently. The 'Bobo doll' experiment is typical of a lot of this experimental research (see box opposite).

The Bobo doll experiments

KenPyne

In one of a range of experiments conducted from the 1960s onwards, Bandura, Ross and Ross (1961) exposed three groups of children to violent scenes involving attacks with a mallet on a large, self-righting inflatable plastic doll. One group was shown the doll being attacked by an adult in real life, another group was shown the same adult attacking the doll in a film, and the third group was shown the same scene involving cartoon characters. A fourth group of children was not exposed to any violent scenes. When the first three groups were later placed in a room with a similar doll, they acted in the same violent ways they had observed earlier. The fourth group of children who had not been exposed to any violent scenes displayed no violent behaviour. The conclusion drawn was that exposure to scenes of violence causes violence among those who see it.

Methodological problems of researching media violence

Research into the area of whether violence in the media generates real-life violence is fraught with difficulty. There is a problem of how such violence is defined in the first place. Boxing and wrestling, fights in TV dramas, parents hitting children, police attacking protesters, shooting, and news film of warfare all depict violent scenes, but they may not be seen by researchers in the same way. There is a difference between scenes showing real-life violence, fictional violence and cartoon violence, and it is likely that people are able to distinguish between them, and react in different ways to them. Even if agreement is reached on what violence is, how can the effects be measured?

Much of the research has been conducted on small samples in artificial laboratory conditions. There are clearly ethical issues related to putting people in situations to test their reactions to violent imagery, but there are also several questions about the validity of findings obtained by such a research method. For example:

1   People may not react in the same way in real life as they do in the artificial conditions of a laboratory experiment.

2 People are aware that they are involved in an experiment, and it is almost impossible to avoid the **Hawthorne effect** – whereby people who are aware that they are the subjects of research change their behaviour. As Gauntlett (1998) points out, 'such studies (on media effects on children) rely on the idea that subjects will not alter their behaviour or stated attitudes as a response to being observed or questioned. This naive belief has been shown to be false by researchers who have demonstrated that the presence, appearance and gender of an observer can radically affect children's behaviour.'

3 It is difficult to separate out the media effects in the experiment from other possible causes of violent reactions to violent media imagery. Wider issues of socialization or peer group influences might mean that people react in different ways to the same violent images, even in experimental conditions.

4 A laboratory experiment lasts for only a short time, and therefore can only measure the immediate effects of media violence in the experimental situation. Even if there is violent behaviour in the long term, a laboratory experiment wouldn't prove it was the effects of violence in the media that caused this, rather than other social explanations like being brought up in a violent family or neighbourhood.

5 Laboratory experiments are necessarily small scale, using small samples. This raises questions over whether the results can be applied to, or generalized to, the whole population.

> The **Hawthorne effect** is when the presence of a researcher, or a group's knowledge that it has been specially selected for research, changes the behaviour of the group, raising problems of the validity of social research.

Giddens (2006) summarizes the problems of much of the research on media violence in the following way:

> The studies . . . differ widely in the methods used, the strength of the association [between violent media and behaviour] supposedly revealed, and the definition of 'aggressive behaviour'. In crime dramas featuring violence (and in many children's cartoons) there are underlying themes of justice and retribution. A far higher proportion of miscreants are brought to justice in crime dramas than happens with police investigations in real life, and in cartoons harmful or threatening characters usually tend to get their 'just deserts'. It does not necessarily follow that high levels of the portrayal of violence create directly imitative patterns among those watching. . . . In general, research on the 'effects' of television on audiences has tended to treat viewers – children and adults – as passive and undiscriminating in their reactions to what they see.

Much of the research has therefore been based on a hypodermic syringe model of media effects, and doesn't deal with how people interpret what they see, the context in which they view the violence (such as discussing with others or the uses they are making of the media), or with the wider range of influences on people's behaviour apart from the media. Gauntlett suggests that one conclusion to be drawn from the failure to identify the direct effects of media upon people's behaviour, despite detailed analysis of hundreds of research studies, is they are simply not there to be found.

Activity

On about two sides of A4 paper, answer the following essay question: 'Assess the extent to which exposure to the mass media makes people behave in a more violent manner.'

The social construction of the news

The mass media obviously cannot report all events and issues happening every day in the world, nor cover every interest in the world. This means that rather than simply being out there waiting to be collected, what counts as 'the news' is necessarily selected and processed, or *constructed* by a range of social influences. Of all the happenings that occur, how is the content of the news selected? Who decides which of these events or interests is worthy of media coverage? The content of the media, like any other product for sale, is manufactured. Journalists decide which issues to report or ignore, and how to present what they select. What factors affect the production and 'packaging' of this product? Is media content, and particularly the news, biased or does it present a balanced and truthful view? What decides the content of the mass media? This section will examine the process of news production in our society, and the way in which what counts as 'news' is socially constructed and created, through selection, interpretation, editing and processing on a daily basis.

The influence of the owners

Although the manipulative view discussed earlier in this chapter, with the owners controlling media content, is rather oversimplified, sometimes the private owners of the mass media will impose their own views on their editors. However, even when the owners don't directly impose their own views, it is unlikely that those who work for them will, if they want to keep their jobs, produce stories that actively oppose their owners' prejudices and interests. The political leanings of the owners and editors are overwhelmingly conservative.

Making a profit

The mass media are predominantly run by large business corporations with the aim of making money, and the source of much of this profit is advertising, particularly in newspapers and commercial broadcasting. It is this dependence on advertising that explains why so much concern is expressed about 'ratings' for television programmes, the circulation figures of newspapers, and the social class of their readers. Advertisers will usually advertise only if they know that there is a large audience for their advertisements, or, if the audience is small, that it is well off and likely to buy their products or services.

Advertising and media content

The importance of advertising affects the content of the media in the following ways:

1   Audiences or readers must be attracted. If they are not, then circulation figures, website 'hits' or TV ratings will fall, advertisers will not advertise, and the particular channel, website or newspaper may go out of business. The *Sunday Correspondent, Today, News on Sunday* and the *London Daily News* are all newspapers that have collapsed in the last 25 years for this reason. This means that

what becomes 'news' is partly a result of commercial pressures to attract audiences by selecting and presenting the more colourful and interesting events in society.

2   In order to attract the widest possible audience or readership, it becomes important to appeal to everyone and offend no one (unless offending a few helps to generate a larger audience). This leads to conservatism in the media, which tries to avoid too much criticism of the way society is organized in case it offends the readers or viewers. This often means that minority or unpopular points of view go unrepresented in the mass media, and this helps to maintain the hegemony of the dominant ideas in society.

3   It may lead to a distortion of the news by concentrating on sensational stories, conflict, gossip and scandal, which are more likely to attract a mass audience than more serious issues are. Alternatively, for those media which aim at a 'select' readership from the upper and upper-middle classes, it is important that the stories chosen should generally be treated in a conservative way, so as not to offend an audience which has little to gain (and everything to lose) by changes in the existing arrangements in society.

Globalization and new technology

The news market is now very competitive, and globalization means there are many news providers from across the globe to choose from. New technology like satellite phones and cameras, email, and digital TV and Internet websites means that news is instantly available from practically anywhere in the world 24 hours per day. News providers need to compete to survive. It is therefore crucial for media companies to

Electronic and digital media networks mean that news reporting is now almost instantaneous, and highly competitive in the need to attract audiences. How do you think this might affect the presentation of the news, and the type of stories that get reported?

be right up to date, and to tailor their media offering and the way in which news is presented to their market, if audiences and readers are to be attracted and retained. For example, short, simple, snappy news reports, using the latest gadgetry, for more youthful audiences, or celebrity gossip-type human-interest news stories for mass consumption.

Organizational constraints

Newspapers and TV news programmes tend to work within quite tight time schedules – this is often at most a 24-hour, or shorter, cycle, as news is reported on a daily or more frequent basis. Increasingly, digital news programmes run bulletins all day long – like BBC News 24 or the BBC website. This means that short cuts to news gathering may need to be taken, that inadequate evidence is collected to justify any conclusions drawn, and that stories aren't checked as carefully as they should be.

Agenda-setting

Agenda-setting refers to the media's influence in laying down the list of subjects, or agenda, for public discussion.

Obviously, people can only discuss and form opinions about things they have been informed about, and it is the mass media that provide this information in most cases. This gives those who own, control and work in the mass media a great deal of power in society, for what they choose to include or leave out of their newspapers, television programmes or websites will influence the main topics of public discussion and public concern. This may mean that the public never discuss some subjects because they are not informed about them.

Gate-keeping

The media's power to refuse to cover some issues and to let others through is called gate-keeping. The Glasgow Media Group, in a series of 'Bad News' studies, suggested that those who construct the news act as gate-keepers, influencing what the public gains knowledge of. The issues that are not aired are frequently those most damaging to the values and interests of the upper class. Sometimes the media do not cover issues either because journalists and editors think they lack interest to readers and viewers, or because they regard them as too offensive, controversial or threatening to existing society. For example, strikes are widely reported (nearly always unfavourably), while industrial injuries and diseases, which lead to a much greater loss of working hours (and life), hardly ever get reported. This means that there is more public concern with stopping strikes than there is with improving health and safety laws. Similarly, crime committed by black people gets widely reported in the media, but less attention is paid to attacks on black people by white racists. A final example of gate-keeping is the way welfare benefit 'fiddles' are widely reported, but not tax evasion, with the result that there are calls for tightening up benefit claim procedures, rather than strengthening those agencies concerned with chasing tax evaders.

Norm-setting

Norm-setting describes the way the mass media emphasize and reinforce conformity to social norms, and seek to isolate those who do not conform by making them the victims of unfavourable media reports. Norm-setting is achieved in two main ways:

1   Encouraging conformist behaviour, such as not going on strike, obeying the law, being brave, helping people and so on. Advertising, for example, often reinforces the gender role stereotypes of men and women.

2   Discouraging non-conformist behaviour. The mass media often give extensive and sensational treatment to stories about murder and other crimes of violence, riots, social security 'fiddles', football hooliganism, illegal immigrants and so on. Such stories, by emphasizing the serious consequences that follow for those who break social norms, are giving 'lessons' in how people are expected *not* to behave. For example, the early media treatment of AIDS nearly always suggested it was a disease only gay men could catch. This was presented as a warning to those who strayed from the paths of monogamy and heterosexuality – both core values within the dominant ideology.

> **Norm-setting** describes the way the mass media emphasize and reinforce conformity to social norms, and seek to isolate those who do not conform by making them the victims of unfavourable media reports.

Activity

1   Study the main newspaper headlines or major television, radio or Internet news stories for a week. Draw up a list of the key stories, perhaps under the headings of 'popular newspapers' (like the *Sun* and the *Mirror*), 'quality newspapers', (like the *Guardian*, the *Daily Telegraph* and *The Times*), 'ITN news', 'BBC TV news' and 'radio news' (this is easiest to do if a group of people divide up the work). You might also research these on the web, using the following sites:
  • www.bbc.co.uk
  • www.itn.co.uk
  • www.guardian.co.uk
  • www.timesonline.co.uk
  • www.thesun.co.uk
  • www.mirror.co.uk

2   Compare your lists, and see if there is any evidence of agreement on the 'agenda' of news items for that week. If there are differences between the lists, suggest reasons for them.

3   Try to find examples of norm-setting in the headlines and stories you have identified. Explain in each case what types of behaviour are being encouraged or discouraged.

These processes of agenda-setting, gate-keeping and norm-setting mean that some events are simply not reported and brought to public attention. Some of those that are reported may be singled out for particularly unfavourable treatment. In these ways, the mass media can define what the important issues are, what 'news' is, what the public should and should not be thinking about, and what should or should not be regarded as 'normal' behaviour in society.

Activity

1 Carry out a short survey asking people which of the mass media they use as their main source of news, and which they see as the most believable, truthful and reliable source of news, and why.
2 Analyse your results, and try to explain any differences you find.

The presentation of news

The way news items are presented may be important in influencing how people are encouraged to view stories. For example, the physical position of a news story in a newspaper (front page or small inside column), the order of importance given to stories in TV news bulletins, the choice of headlines and whether there is accompanying film or photographs, the camera angles used and so on, will all influence the attention given to particular issues.

Some issues may not be covered at all if journalists or camera crews are not available, especially in international news reporting, and the space available in a newspaper or TV programme will influence whether an event is reported or not. A story may be treated sensationally, and it may even be considered of such importance as to justify a TV or radio 'newsflash'. Where film is used, the pictures shown are always selected from the total footage shot, and may not accurately reflect the event. The actual images used in news films may themselves have a hidden bias. For example, the Glasgow University Media Group has shown how, in the reporting of industrial disputes, employers are often filmed in the peace and quiet of their offices, while workers are seen shouting on the picket lines or trying to be interviewed against a background of traffic noise. This gives the impression that employers are more calm and reasonable people and have a better case than the workers.

The media can also create false or biased impressions by the sort of language used in news reporting, such as words like 'troublemakers', 'rioters' or 'pointless'.

Inaccurate and false reporting

A **moral panic** is a wave of public concern about some exaggerated or imaginary threat to society, often created by media reporting.

Other sources of bias in news reporting lie in inaccurate reporting, because important details of a story may be incorrect. Politicians are always complaining that they have been inaccurately quoted in the press. False reporting, through either completely making up stories or inventing a few details, and the media's tendency to exaggerate and dramatize events out of all proportion to their actual significance in society, typical of much reporting of the royal family, are devices used to make a story 'more interesting' and to sell newspapers or attract viewers – this is particularly common in the mass circulation 'red-top' tabloid press. Such exaggerated and sensationalized reporting in the mass media can sometimes generate a **moral panic**. This is a wave of public concern about some exaggerated or imaginary threat to society. Such methods mean the media can be accused of manipulating their audiences (you can read more about moral panics on pages 407–9 in chapter 6).

News values and 'newsworthiness'

Events that are eventually reported in the news have been through some kind of gate-keeping process, with journalists, and particularly news editors, deciding what is newsworthy and what is not. Journalists therefore play an important role in deciding the content of the mass media, as it is they who basically select what 'the news' is and decide on its style of presentation. Research has shown that journalists operate with values and assumptions about which events they regard as 'newsworthy'. These assumptions are called news values, and they guide journalists in deciding what to report and what to leave out, and how what they choose to report should be presented. So news doesn't just happen, but is *made* by journalists. In this sense, it is socially constructed. Galtung and Ruge (1970) suggested that newsworthy items included some of the news values included in table 3.5.

The idea of news values means that journalists tend to include and play up those elements of a story that make it more newsworthy, and the stories that are most likely to be reported are those that include many newsworthy aspects.

The assumptions and activities of journalists

The Glasgow University Media Group, which generally supports a Marxist-oriented dominant ideology/hegemonic approach to the media, and a cultural effects approach to media effects, emphasizes the importance of the assumptions of journalists in forming media content and suggesting interpretations of issues to media audiences. The group emphasizes a number of features that affect the content of the media

First, journalists operate within what Becker called a **hierarchy of credibility**. This means they treat more seriously and attach the greatest importance to the views of powerful and influential individuals and groups. Hall et al. (1978) suggest such people are **primary definers** who regularly feature in the media and are in a position to set the news agenda and influence what journalists define as the news and how they present it. The views of primary definers appear more 'reasonable' to journalists than those of the least powerful or 'extremists' who present the greatest challenges to existing society. Manning (1999) suggests that journalists are under increasing pressure to use primary definers as their main source of news, as governments and large businesses try to manipulate the media and manage the news through their press and public relations departments.

Second, journalists tend to be somewhere in the moderate centre ground of politics, and so ignore or treat unfavourably what they regard as 'extremist' or 'radical' views.

Third, journalists tend to be mainly white, male and middle class, and they broadly share the interests and values of the dominant ideology. This influences whose opinions they seek for comment, what issues they see as important and how issues should be presented and explained to audiences (this is also linked to the news values discussed above). The Glasgow University Media Group has shown how the explanations given in the media often favour the views of dominant and powerful groups in society, such as managers over workers, or police over protesters.

A **hierarchy of credibility** means that greatest importance is attached by journalists to the views and opinions of those in positions of power, like government ministers, political leaders, senior police officers or wealthy and influential individuals.

Primary definers are powerful individuals or groups whose positions of power give them greater access to the media than others, and therefore puts them in a more privileged position to influence what and how journalists define the news.

Table 3.5: News values

News value	Features
Composition	Events that fit the style of a paper or TV channel, the balance of items (human interest stories, political news, domestic and foreign news, crime stories, etc.), its political slant and the values of the journalists.
Continuity	Events that are likely to have a continuing impact – the running story, which is also convenient as the news reporters and cameras will already be there.
Elite nations or people	Any story that involves what journalists and media customers perceive as important – powerful nations, people or organizations, are seen as more newsworthy than lesser ones. West European and American political leaders, celebrities and countries, for example, are seen as more newsworthy than ordinary people or more distant countries and cultures
Frequency	Events that fit into the routine schedules of a newspaper's or TV news programme's reporting and broadcasting or publishing cycles are more likely to be covered. Events that occur quickly or unexpectedly, and are of short duration, such as disasters and murders, are more likely to make it into the news as they fit the schedules better.
Meaningfulness	Events which, it is assumed, will have meaning and be of interest to the newspaper's readership or TV audience. This essentially involves giving the readers and viewers what journalists and producers think they want; this is of great importance if the audience or readership is to continue to be attracted and viewing figures kept up or papers sold.
Negativity	Bad news is nearly always rated above positive stories. A good news story is often bad news, as bad news involves many newsworthy aspects that encourage journalists to report the event, such as death, violence, disasters, floods and hurricanes.
Personalization	Events that can be personalized and linked to individuals in some way, and given a human interest angle, with some human drama attached to them, such as disputes between two political leaders or scandal involving the activities of famous personalities or celebrities.
Proximity	This generally involves items that will have some cultural meaning or proximity to news audiences. For example, what happens to British citizens is seen as more newsworthy than what happens to foreigners from remote cultures. Events in Britain are generally considered more meaningful than those happening in the rest of the world, and national events are generally considered more important than local ones.

Table 3.5 (continued)	
News value	Features
Threshold	Events that are considered large and significant enough to be in the news, and to have an impact – a single rape might make it into a local paper, but a serial rapist might become a national story.
Unambiguity	Events that are easily understood and not too complicated, without the need for lots of background explanation and detail.
Unexpectedness	Events that are in some way unexpected or out of the ordinary. Events that involve drama, conflict, excitement and action, such as natural disasters or terrorist attacks are more likely to be reported than predictable everyday events.

Fourth, journalists are doing a job of work, and they like to keep their work as simple as possible. This means they often obtain information from news agencies, government press releases, 'spin doctors', public relations consultants and so on. This means that powerful and influential groups, like businesses, the government, political parties and those with power and wealth (primary definers), are more likely to be able to influence journalists.

These features all suggest that the mass media generally present, at best, only a partial and biased view of the world, and the selection and presentation of the news is, in many ways, carried out within a framework of the dominant ideology in society. However, it must also be recognized that journalists do occasionally expose injustice and corruption in government and business, and therefore are not always or simply in the pockets of the powerful.

Activity

1 Refer to the three news stories here, or any other major news stories which are currently receiving wide coverage in the mass media. List the features which you think make these stories 'newsworthy'. To find more details on any story, try a Google search on the Internet.
2 Imagine you wanted to run a campaign to prevent a waste incinerator being built in your neighbourhood (or choose any topic of interest to you). In the light of the issues identified in this chapter relating to the social construction of news, suggest ways you might get the attention of journalists and activities so as to achieve media coverage of your campaign. Explain why you think the activities you identify might be considered newsworthy.

The terrorist attack on the twin towers of the World Trade Center in New York on 11 September 2001 was a massive international news story. Two passenger aircraft were hijacked and deliberately crashed into the towers, causing both to collapse and resulting

The twin towers of New York's World Trade Center before their destruction.

in the death of around 3,000 people. This dominated world news for weeks and months afterwards, and provoked a range of conspiracy theories on the Internet.

A town in Indonesia annihilated by the 2004 tsunami.

On 26 December 2004, the most powerful undersea earthquake in 40 years triggered tidal waves, or tsunami, that travelled thousands of miles to crash onto the coastlines of at least five Asian countries. More than 300,000 were killed, missing or unaccounted for, and millions of others were affected.

Three-year-old Madeleine McCann vanished from her holiday apartment in Praia da Luz, Portugal, on 3 May 2007. Thanks to a high-profile campaign run by the McCann family, Madeleine's face was rarely out of the public consciousness. At the time of writing, it was still not known what happened to Madeleine. The mystery of Madeleine's disappearance led to a feeding frenzy in the red-top tabloid press, with a mass of unsubstantiated theories and wild speculation about her disappearance. Both ITV's *Tonight with Trevor McDonald* and the BBC's

Panorama had documentaries on her disappearance, and six months after her disappearance the story was still dominating the headlines of the tabloid press, and theories abounded on the Internet.

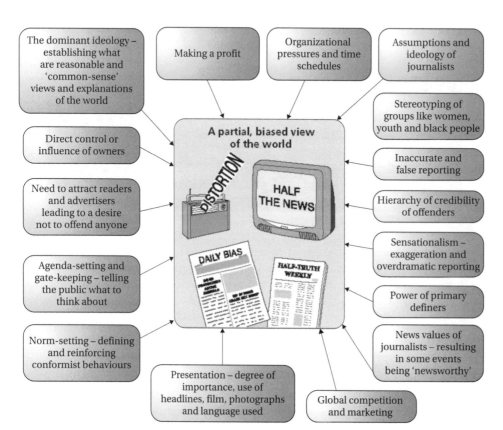

The dominant ideology – establishing what are reasonable and 'common-sense' views and explanations of the world

Making a profit

Organizational pressures and time schedules

Assumptions and ideology of journalists

Direct control or influence of owners

Stereotyping of groups like women, youth and black people

Need to attract readers and advertisers leading to a desire not to offend anyone

Inaccurate and false reporting

Agenda-setting and gate-keeping – telling the public what to think about

Hierarchy of credibility of offenders

Norm-setting – defining and reinforcing conformist behaviours

Sensationalism – exaggeration and overdramatic reporting

Power of primary definers

Presentation – degree of importance, use of headlines, film, photographs and language used

News values of journalists – resulting in some events being 'newsworthy'

Global competition and marketing

A partial, biased view of the world

DISTORTION

HALF THE NEWS

DAILY BIAS

HALF-TRUTH WEEKLY

Figure 3.2 What affects the content of the news?

Activity

1 Explain, with examples, what is meant by 'news values'.
2 Suggest three reasons why journalists might be reluctant to write articles critical of the most powerful groups in society.
3 With reference to figure 3.2, identify a range of reasons why both the selection and presentation of the media might be regarded as ideologically controlled.
4 Write an essay of about 2–3 sides of A4 answering the following question: *'Evaluate the view that the mass media may not tell us what to think, but they do tell us what to think about.'*

Media representations and stereotyping

The mass media are major sources of information, ideas, norms and values, as well as spreading images of, for example, fashion, music, role models and lifestyles that may influence people's values and behaviour.

Activity

Suggest two ways in each case that the mass media might be a source of identity and meaning for individuals.

> **Media representations** are the categories and images that are used to present groups and activities to media audiences, which may influence the way we think about these activities and groups.

One of the concerns of many media sociologists has been with the categories and images that are used to present groups and activities to media audiences, and therefore the way social groups and activities are portrayed in the mass media. These portrayals are known as **media representations**.

Media representations very often conform to and create stereotypes – generalized, oversimplified views of the features of a social group, allowing for few individual differences between members of the group. The following sections examine some of these representations in the media. As you read, it is important to remember that media representations and stereotypes do not necessarily mean that people will behave in accordance with those representations. The different interpretations of sociologists through the various media effects theories discussed earlier in this chapter (the hypodermic syringe, two-step flow, cultural effects, selective filtering and uses and gratifications theories) suggest that media audiences do not necessarily react to or interpret the same media content in the same way. People are *selective* in their exposure to, and perception and retention of, media content. People may therefore ignore, accept or reject media representations, or even, in the postmodern age, pick and mix media representations in a creative way to forge their own identities.

Age

Different age groups tend to be represented in different ways in the mass media. Children (up to the age of about 14) are often presented as consumers of toys and games, and are generally presented in a positive light.

Youth

Youth (from around the age of 15 to the early 20s) are often portrayed as a 'problem group' in society, and as a major source of anti-social behaviour, particularly young working-class, and especially African Caribbean, males. Exciting stories and sensational headlines help to sell newspapers and attract TV viewers. The mass media often generate this excitement by creating stereotypes of young people as troublemakers, layabouts and vandals, and by exaggerating the occasional deviant behaviour of a few young people out of proportion to its real significance in society. For many people, the mass media provide the only source of information about events, and therefore distort people's attitudes and give a misleading impression of young people as a whole. Old people, who tend to be more home-based, are particularly vulnerable to believing such stereotypes, as their impressions are likely to be formed strongly by the media.

Cohen (2002) argues that young people are relatively powerless, and an easily identifiable group to blame for all society's ills. Consequently, young people, particularly young African Caribbean males, have often been used as scapegoats by the media to create a sense of unity in society, by whipping up a moral panic against the folk devils who pose a threat to society, and uniting the public against a common 'enemy'. As a result of these media-generated moral panics, all young people may then get labelled and stereotyped as potentially troublesome or as an anti-social 'problem group'.

Older people

Older people, say in their late 50s onwards, are often presented in the media in quite negative ways, and elderly people suffer from negative stereotyping in the media perhaps more than any other identifiable social group. Old age is generally represented as an undesirable state; being poor, in ill-health, forgetful, anti-social, incapable of work and personally difficult and grumpy are typical stereotypes. Biggs (1993) found that UK TV sitcoms presented older people in largely negative ways, such as being forgetful and difficult. Cuddy and Fiske (2004) showed that, in the United States, TV portrayed just 1.5 per cent of its characters as elderly, with most of them in minor roles, and that older adults were more likely than any other age group to appear in television and film as figures of fun and comic relief, usually based on ineffective mental, physical or sexual capacities. There are sometimes different stereotypes for men and women. Older men are often presented in a positive light, for example as sexual partners of younger women in Hollywood movies; or as distinguished, experienced and informed 'wise old men', such as political and religious leaders, successful business people, experts of various kinds, and established and authoritative media journalists and commentators. By contrast, there are few positive images of older women, who are often rendered invisible, because women are, in media imagery, expected to be forever young and youthful, and there are not many positive roles for them as they get older.

In a study of the views of advertising executives in 19 London agencies about the types of products and services which they considered appropriate for representation by older people, Szmigin and Carrigan (2000) found they were wary of using models that they considered might alienate younger audiences for their advertisements. However, the growing numbers of older people in the population, and particularly the growing numbers of older women, with money to spend (the 'grey pound'), mean we might expect more positive images of ageing to emerge, and more positive roles for older women, as media conglomerates pursue the growing older people's market, as shown in the Dove Pro.Age campaign marketing beauty products to older people.

The Dove Pro.Age campaign sought to market a range of beauty products avoiding traditional media stereotypes of gender and age. Study the four images, and suggest ways they may, or may not, challenge media stereotypes of gender and/or age.

Social class

The representation of social class in the mass media has not been researched anything like as much as other issues, like ethnicity, gender and disability, and there is relatively little recent research. The following therefore represents a distillation of general media representations.

The working class

The working class is often presented in the stereotypical context of traditional working-class communities, such as those portrayed in soaps like *EastEnders* or *Coronation Street*. These community values are often praised, but they have little relation to reality, as such working-class communities have generally declined and disappeared with the collapse of traditional industries like coal-mining, shipbuilding, the steel industry and docking.

In a further stereotype, working-class people are often presented, like working-class youth, in the context of trouble, for example as strikers in industrial disputes – as shown in the Glasgow University Media Group's *Bad News* – as undesirable welfare scroungers, as lone parents or as inadequates unable to cope with their uncontrollable delinquent children and other difficulties. A similarly negative image is that of the 'couch potato', who sits around doing nothing but watching television all day. The working class is also linked to masculinity and physically hard work, and this is often the representation found in advertising, for products such as jeans and beer. The mass circulation tabloid press, like the *Daily Mirror*, the *Sun* and the *Daily Star*, which largely cater for working-class readers, give the impression that the sole interests of the working class are in sport, sex, celebrities and TV.

The middle class

In contrast to the representation of the working class, the middle class is generally presented as educated and successful, and coping with problems. The middle class is often over-represented in media content – there is more exposure of middle-class lifestyles than is justified by their proportion in the population as a whole. This fits in neatly with the dominant ideology/hegemonic and cultural effects models of media control and influence, as positive representations of the middle (and upper) class, and negative ones of the working class, help to reinforce the dominant ideology and the 'normality' of middle-class life. This helps to legitimize or justify the existing class structure and class inequalities, by suggesting that people become more competent, successful, able to cope and worthy of respect as they climb higher up the class structure.

The upper class

The most obvious and extensive representation of the upper class is through coverage of the monarchy. The upper class is generally seen as being 'well bred' and cultured, as cultivated, superior, with posh accents, country estates and a taste for shooting and hunting. It is often represented in the context of costume/period dramas.

Ethnicity

According to Hargrave (2002), the proportion of terrestrial television programmes in the UK containing people from minority ethnic groups had increased to 48 per cent by 2002, but these were far more likely to be African Caribbean than Asian. However, ethnic minority representation was found more in 'vox pop' interviews (interviews with people in the street) or in stereotypical programmes on minority group issues (like programmes dealing with issues of stereotyping, discrimination or prejudice, or religion), sport, music and sex. Malik (2002) found that African Caribbeans were more likely to be found in programmes consisting of social issues, music, light entertainment and comedy, rather than in heavyweight roles, such as political commentators or experts, or in subjects of a serious nature, such as politics, and were less often found in major roles in big-budget British films. She found Asians were often under-represented or missing altogether, and Asian audiences complain of an under-representation of Asian groups on terrestrial television, and a lack of Asian presenters or music on radio. There does then appear to be a form of **symbolic annihilation** of

Symbolic annihilation refers to the lack of visibility, under-representation and limited roles of certain groups in media representations, as they are omitted, condemned or trivialized in many roles.

the main Asian groups, let alone those from other ethnic groups, like the Chinese, Greeks or Poles.

There are improving levels of representation of minority ethnic groups in the media, and it seems likely that this improving trend will continue, as black and Asian people extend the range of programmes they can receive by moving to satellite and cable TV – something they are doing faster than any other ethnic groups. This is particularly true among younger people, who make up the fastest growing section of these minority ethnic groups. This change is one that terrestrial TV networks need to take account of if they are to retain viewers and therefore justify the licence fee (in the case of the BBC) or retain advertisers (in the case of commercial channels).

To improve diversity in British television and promote minority ethnic groups both among media company employees and among those portrayed in programmes, the Cultural Diversity Network was established by UK broadcasters in 2000. Nevertheless, it is still the case that only Channel 4 has a requirement under its licence to produce at least three hours a week, on average, of multicultural programming, with no other channel having such an obligation.

Although there is a high proportion of black and Asian TV presenters, ethnic minorities are under-represented in senior management of the media companies, including the BBC.

Media stereotyping of minority ethnic groups

Black and Asian people are frequently stereotyped and used as scapegoats in the media. Black and Asian people make up only about 8 per cent of the population of Britain, yet frequently this small minority is presented in quite negative ways in the media – as Hall (2002) suggests, as cheating, cunning and capable of turning nasty, and as the source of social problems that otherwise would not exist. These representations often reflect the news values and ideology of journalists.

As revealed by a range of research over time, such as Hall et al. (1978), Alvarado et al. (1987), van Dijk (1991) and Cottle (2000), black and Asian minority ethnic groups are often represented in the media in the context of violence and criminality, as scapegoats on which to blame a range of social problems, and are over-represented in a limited range of degrading, negative and unsympathetic stereotypes. These stereotypes, which are also becoming applied to other ethnic groups from the European Union, include:

- law-breakers, involved in drug-dealing, welfare fraud, 'mugging' (street robbery with violence) and gun culture – Hargrave (2002) found that black people were more than twice as likely as white people to be portrayed on terrestrial television as criminals involved in murder, drugs and criminal gang membership;
- low-paid workers;
- people with a culture which is seen as 'alien' and a threat to British culture – a kind of 'enemy within', with immigration seen as a threat to the British way of life and the jobs of white workers;
- people causing conflict and trouble, as in stories portraying racial problems or disruption caused by black students in schools;

- asylum-seekers, illegal immigrants, rioters, welfare scroungers, lone parents and so on – seen as people causing social problems rather than as people with social problems like persecution in the countries they have fled from, poverty, racial discrimination, poor housing, and racist attacks by white people;
- people who often do well in sport and music, but are rarely portrayed as academic or professional successes;
- people who have problems internationally – for example, who run their own countries chaotically, who live in famine conditions (images of starving babies), who are always having tribal conflicts, military coups and so on, who need the white Western populations to help solve their problems for them.

Activity

1 Go through the stereotypes listed above, and explore whether the different stereotypes are applied to particular minority ethnic groups.
2 Suggest examples of particular TV programmes, newspaper stories, advertisements and other media content that show these stereotypes. For example, examples of newspaper or TV news reports suggesting that immigrants from Eastern Europe might be posing a threat to or undermining the 'British way of life' (as in the third bullet point above).
3 Suggest criticisms of the media stereotypes you have identified, and the ways they may or may not give a misleading impression of the relevant ethnic groups.

Minority ethnic viewers, especially Asian viewers, rarely see the reality of their lives or the issues that concern them reflected on TV channels. Hargrave found ethnic minorities were themselves concerned about the content of such portrayals, as well as all Asians being stereotyped as the same, with the differences between Asians, for example Pakistani, Bangladeshi, and Indian Asian groups, not being recognized in the media. In particular, they complained about tokenism, negative stereotyping, unrealistic and simplistic portrayals of their community, and negative or non-existent images of their countries or areas of origin.

'Muslim' – a stigmatized identity?

The nature of media reporting of Muslims in the 2000s in Britain was such that the very word 'Muslim' was conjuring up images of terrorism and extremist preachers. Media coverage of the worldwide terrorist network of Al-Qaeda, which was behind the bombing of the twin towers in New York in 2001 and the London bombings in July 2005, and suicide bombings by Islamic fundamentalists across the world, meant the activities of a tiny minority of Muslims in Britain formed the basis for the stereotyping in the popular imagination of all Muslims. A 2007 report commissioned by the Mayor of London showed that, following research into one week's news coverage, 91 per cent of articles in national newspapers about Muslims were negative.

Because of media stereotyping, the identity 'Muslim' has practically become a stigmatized identity, which brings with it harassment and fear for many British Muslims who have little sympathy with Islamic fundamentalism, much less terrorism of any kind, and whom surveys repeatedly show are moderates who accept the norms of Western democracy. As Hargrave (2002) found, Muslims themselves are concerned about such negative media portrayals, and the way in which only certain aspects of the Islamic faith, such as the views of fundamentalists, are depicted.

Activity

The two stories depicted above both appeared in British newspapers in one week in November 2007. One concerned a British woman, Gillian Gibbons, who was teaching in the Sudan. Because she allowed a teddy bear in her classroom to be named by the children as Mohammad, she was jailed for 15 days, and there were angry protests in the Sudan against the alleged insult to the prophet Mohammad. In the same week, a teenager in Saudi Arabia was sentenced by the courts to 200 lashes after being gang-raped by seven men. Look at the reporting, pictures and wording of the stories. What kind of impression of Muslims do you think they give? Do you think such reporting might give a distorted impression of Islam, and increase anti-Muslim feeling in Britain?

The stereotypes considered above have in recent years also been applied to white people from Eastern Europe and countries close to Russia, like the Ukrainians, Poles, Latvians, Bulgarians, Lithuanians and Slovakians. These groups have been blamed for virtually every problem that has beset Britain, and frequently blamed for things that either aren't true or are not their fault. For example, as Dowling (2007) showed, in the late 2000s, immigrants from Eastern Europe were being attacked and blamed in the media for being benefit scroungers and lone parents, stealing unwanted clothes, causing a shortage of £50 notes, taking British jobs, having road signs put up in foreign languages, drunken driving, car crashes, driving down wages, groping women, cheaper heroin, counterfeit money, cheap guns, selling babies, overcrowding in churches, bad service in restaurants, and causing anglers to stop fishing as immigrants were stealing and devouring fish stocks, as well as swans, ducks and deer. These media stories were all either completely absurd and untrue or massively exaggerated, but they may well have had a negative influence on audiences, creating, confirming and reinforcing the public's racial prejudices, by blaming minority ethnic groups for problems that are not created by them at all.

As discussed earlier in this chapter, whether such media stereotyping has effects on audiences will depend on the experiences and perceptions of those audiences. Those who have no experience themselves of minority ethnic life to draw on to offset the impact of these stereotypes are vulnerable to being misled. However, those with experience, and those from the minority ethnic groups themselves, are more likely to ignore or reject such stereotyping.

Changing stereotypes

Media stereotypes of black and minority ethnic groups do appear to be changing. We are seeing black and Asian actors moving into more popular dramas and soaps, and they are now appearing more as 'ordinary', routine characters in soaps like *EastEnders* and *Coronation Street*, rather than in roles focused on their ethnic identity. This suggests growing acceptance in the media of ethnic minorities as a normal, mainstream part of British society. There are also more programmes, TV channels, websites, radio stations, videos and DVDs, and magazines being targeted at black and Asian audiences, such as terrestrial TV shows like *Goodness Gracious Me* and *The Kumars at Number 42*. There are some very successful media presenters and role models, like Sir Trevor McDonald, Hollywood stars like Denzel Washington, and models like Naomi Campbell. The Cultural Diversity Network aims to encourage more black and minority ethnic group people into senior positions in managing media companies and producing programmes, and to promote the writing of more roles for actors from minority ethnic groups. This may mean that there will be both more numerous and more positive representations of minority ethnic groups, with greater attention focused on their perspectives on the world.

Gender

Women are under-represented in positions of power and influence in the management of the media industry, and, among editors, journalists and TV producers. Women also appear on TV less than men, and in a narrower range of roles. Features like these mean that the mass media tend to be patriarchal (controlled mainly by men) and spread a patriarchal ideology – presenting a male view of women and 'femininity' in the interests of men.

The mass media are generally considered as an important influence on the social construction of gender differences between men and women, and Connell (2005) considers that gender identities are in part constructed by the media reproducing hegemonic or culturally dominant stereotypes of the roles and relations between men and women. The gender stereotype of men involves what Connell called a 'hegemonic masculinity', but we could also consider there to be a 'hegemonic femininity'. Some possible features of these are summarized in table 3.6.

Table 3.6: Hegemonic masculine and feminine characteristics

Hegemonic masculine characteristics	Hegemonic feminine characteristics
Heterosexuality	Heterosexuality
Sexual dominance	Sexual passivity (or a 'slapper' if sexually active)
Repression of emotions/emotional distance (except in sport, when males tend to get very emotional indeed)	Expression of emotions/emotional warmth, caring and sensitive
Physically strong/muscular/tall	Physically weak/fragile/small
Aggression	Gentleness and non-aggression
Independence and self-reliance	Dependence (on men)
Competitiveness and ambition	Lack of competitiveness
Lack of domesticity (housework and childcare) – only occasional practical DIY around the home	Concerned with and responsible for housework and practical and emotional aspects of childcare
Rational and practical	Emotional and unpredictable
Risk-taking	Avoidance of risk
Task-oriented – focus on 'doing things' like work success, playing sports, making things, DIY in the home or activities to escape from work	People-oriented – focus on forming and maintaining friendships, family, children, and 'customer care' (keeping customers happy)
Lack of concern with or interest in personal appearance, taste in dress or personal health and diet, and, sometimes, lack of personal hygiene	Major concern with physical appearance (being slim and pretty), health, diet, dress sense, and attractiveness to men

Activity

1 Discuss the suggested features of the hegemonic stereotypes of masculinity and femininity shown in table 3.6. To what extent do you think these stereotypes are shown in the mass media in Britain? Back up your view with evidence drawn from the media, such as magazines, advertising, TV programmes, films, music videos or the Internet. Refer to examples of both child and adult behaviour.

2 Are these stereotypes changing? Suggest ways, with examples, that these media stereotypes might be changing.

The mass media create and reinforce these hegemonic gender stereotypes in a number of ways. Comics, for example, present different images of men and women. Girls are usually presented as pretty, romantic, helpless, easily upset and emotional, and dependent on boys for support and guidance. Boys are presented as strong, independent, unemotional and assertive. Boys and girls are often presented in traditional stereotyped gender roles such as soldiers (boys) or nurses (girls). A similar pattern is shown on children's television, and much TV and other advertising show gender stereotypes. Around 80 per cent of TV advertising voice-overs are male voices – suggesting authority. Video games are predominantly a male preserve, and representations are often of men as powerful and women as the weaker sex. The media, and particularly advertising, often promote the 'beauty myth' – the idea that women should be assessed primarily in terms of their appearance. This occurs throughout the media, and women are often expected to be young and attractive, whether as actors, presenters or media personnel, no matter how successful or powerful they might be.

There are often very different types of story and magazine aimed at males and females. Romantic fiction is almost exclusively aimed at a female readership. A glance at the magazine shelves of any large newsagents will reveal 'Women's interests' and 'Men's interests' sections, reflecting the different hegemonic masculine and feminine identities which men and women are encouraged to adopt.

Female stereotypes

Women in the media have traditionally been shown as young, pretty and sexually attractive – whatever the role portrayed, television, film and popular magazines are full of images of women and girls who are typically white, extremely thin and heavily made up, even when playing in action roles. Women are more commonly shown indoors than outdoors – in the private sphere of the home rather than in the public world of the workplace and the street. They are frequently presented as emotional and unpredictable, and in their relationships to men, whether they be brothers, husbands, bosses, fathers or lovers, and in a limited number of stereotyped roles. These stereotypes include:

1. *The WAG* – the wives and girlfriends of men, or the *femmes fatales*, who are concerned with beauty, love, romance, being pretty and sexually attractive, being a good partner and getting and keeping their men.
2. *The Sex Object* – the slim, sexually seductive, scantily clad figure typically found on page three of the *Sun* newspaper, or in advertising aimed at men; or as objects of male fantasy in pornography.
3. *The Supermum* – the happy housewife or part-time worker, who is primarily concerned with childrearing, housework, cooking, and family relationships. She keeps the family together and is both source and manager of family emotions.
4. *The Angel* – who is 'good', displays little sexuality, and is sensitive and domesticated; she supports her man.
5. *The Ball Breaker* – who is sexually active, strong, selfish, independent, ambitious and career-minded, and not dependent on men.

6 *The Victim* – as in many horror and crime films and TV programmes, with men as both the cause of their problems and their 'saviours'.

The 'cult of femininity'

Ferguson (1983) argued that teenage girls' magazines prepared girls for feminized adult roles, and generated a 'cult of femininity'. This 'cult of femininity' included themes like getting and keeping a partner, being a good wife/partner, keeping a happy family, what to wear, how to be a good cook and so on. These themes socialized young girls into the stereotyped values and roles of femininity as established in our society, and are often reflected in adult women's magazines, with their concerns with personal and emotional relationships, family, beauty, health and fashion.

Tuchman et al. (1978) refer to the media stereotyping of women, where they are either invisible or represented in a limited range of identities, as the symbolic annihilation of women. This involves the three aspects of trivialization, omission and condemnation of women in the media.

Representations of men and patriarchy in the media

In contrast to women, men appear in a much wider range of roles, most often in the public sphere outside the home, and are generally portrayed both in a wider range of occupations and in those carrying higher status, for example as the 'boss' rather than the secretary. Male voices are more likely to be used in 'voice-overs' in TV and radio programmes and advertising, presenting and reinforcing the idea of men as authority figures, opinion-formers or experts. The stereotyped hegemonic masculine identity of the tough, assertive, dominant and rational male – what Gilmore (1991) described as 'the provider, the protector and the impregnator' – often appears, but not so exclusively as the stereotypes of women. Men are presented in a wider range of roles, and with interests that are seen as part of the hegemonic masculine identity. A look at men's magazines reveal these to be things like photography, stereos, computers, DIY and all manner of transport: cars, motor-bikes, aircraft, trains and boats. The 'top shelf' soft-porn magazines are aimed exclusively at men.

Various media analysts and researchers argue that media portrayals of male characters fall within a range of stereotypes. Three related American reports (see Children Now 1999), identified six media stereotypes of male characters which reinforce 'masks of masculinity'. These stereotypes are:

1 *The Joker* – who uses laughter to avoid displaying seriousness or emotion.
2 *The Jock* – who avoids being soft, and who shows aggression to demonstrate his power and strength to win the approval of other men and the admiration of women.
3 *The Strong Silent Type* – who is in control, acts decisively, avoids talking about his feelings or showing emotion, as this is a sign of weakness, and is successful with women.
4 *The Big Shot* – who is economically and socially successful and has high social status with possessions to match.
5 *The Action Hero* – who is strong but not necessarily silent, and who shows extreme aggression and often violence.

6 *The Buffoon* – who is well-intentioned and light-hearted, but is the bungling or inept figure found in TV ads and sitcoms who is completely hopeless when it comes to parenting or domestic matters (confirming that men shouldn't be doing these things).

Activity

1 Refer to the stereotypes of females and males referred to in the previous sections. While watching, reading or using your favourite media, make a note of examples of each of these stereotypes, explaining how they illustrate them in each case.
2 Identify any evidence of other stereotypes, or evidence that some of these stereotypes are changing or disappearing.

News values, discussed above, are often influenced by patriarchal ideology, with women facing symbolic annihilation as their interests are either ignored, given trivial treatment or removed into special women's TV or radio shows, or the women's pages of newspapers. Even the women's pages of newspapers are often filled with articles that 'speak to' the male media stereotype of what women are thought to be interested in.

While some or many women and men may reject these media stereotypes (in keeping with the uses and gratifications approach discussed earlier), these representations may have a long-term influence (as the cultural effects model suggests) on the way both men and women come to see their respective positions in society as inevitable and unchangeable. At present, these stereotypes are clearly to the benefit of men, with women presented as no threat to male dominance.

Harmful consequences of media stereotyping

Although the various 'effects' models will influence to what extent media gender stereotyping affects the behaviour of men and women, there is some evidence that these stereotypes have long-term harmful effects and consequences. For example, the reinforcement of gender roles, through socialization via the media, may encourage discrimination against women or limit the self-confidence, outlooks and ambitions of young women. There may be particularly harmful effects in those cases where the reality of women's lives does not conform to the media stereotypes. Stereotyping may succeed in inducing feelings of guilt, inadequacy and lack of self-confidence among the majority of women who do not match up to the 'sex object' or the 'supermum' images. Although things are beginning to change (as will be discussed below) women's magazines are much more concerned with changing bodily appearance, through diet, exercise and cosmetic surgery, for example, than men's magazines. The bodies of real women have, in effect, been rendered invisible and symbolically annihilated in the mass media, and replaced by airbrushed images of female beauty, like size zero models, that are unrealistic and unattainable for all but a very small number of women.

That these issues do matter was demonstrated by a 2000 report published by the British Medical Association on mental health and eating disorders, which concluded that 'the gap between the ideal body shape and the reality is wider than ever. There is a need for more realistic body shapes to be shown on television and in fashion magazines.' Research in 2001 from Glasgow University found women were up to 10 times more likely to be worried about their weight than men, even when they were not overweight. A 2005 survey for *Bliss* magazine, aimed at girls aged 13–18, found teenage girls were obsessed with body image and the desire to acquire a 'perfect' celebrity body, with just 8 per cent claiming to be happy with their body. Over half were unhappy with their face, teeth, skin, breasts, tummy, bottom, thighs and legs. Two 2007 reports by Girlguiding UK, *Girls Shout Out*, using both questionnaires and focus groups, found that over half of 16–25 year-olds resented media pressures that made them feel the most important thing for girls was to be pretty and thin. Girls under 10 linked appearance to happiness and self-esteem, and, even at the age of 7, they believed girls who were slim and pretty were more likely to be liked, happy, friendly and clever, with those being overweight or less attractive seen as unhappy and lonely (these reports can be viewed at www.girlguiding.org.uk/). The reports highlighted the way in which the media manipulate or doctor images of women's bodies, using techniques like air-brushing, to make them look thinner. Research indicates that exposure to images of thin, young, air-brushed female bodies is linked to depression, loss of self-esteem and the development of unhealthy eating habits in women and girls.

Media stereotyping and the growing exposure to images of 'perfection' in magazines, on TV, in films, music videos and advertisements may contribute to explaining why so many women are concerned with slimming and dieting, why anorexia and other eating disorders are illnesses affecting mainly teenage girls, and why many housewives in this country are on tranquillizers.

The growing concerns of men with such issues as their appearance and sexual attractiveness, their body size and shape, their diet, health and dress sense, and the growing use by men of cosmetics and cosmetic surgery – as well as the increase in eating disorders among men – all suggest that the factors that have traditionally affected women are now also beginning to have an effect on men.

Are media stereotypes changing?

McRobbie (1994) suggests that, in postmodern society, there is much more fluidity and flexibility in the representations of men and women in the media, in keeping with the changes in wider society. There is more emphasis now on independence and sexual freedom for women, and there is a growing diversity of imagery: women's position in society is changing rapidly, they are becoming more successful than men in education and they are doing better than ever before in the job market. As the pluralist model predicts, new magazines now cater for working women, reflecting a world in which advertising revenue and profits are driving forces of the media, and these forces may well lead to reduced gender stereotyping, as women demand more from the media than the increasingly outdated and patriarchal stereotypes. Gauntlett (2002) suggests that the ways in which the media present gender are changing all the time, and there is a growing social expectation that women and men should be treated equally. Magazines for women, like *More* and *Cosmopolitan*, are encouraging their readers to be more assertive (including sexually), self-aware, self-confident, ambitious and independent, and female roles in TV and film are becoming stronger, more assertive, more resourceful and complex characters, although women are still expected to be attractive and concerned with glamour, beauty and 'getting and keeping your man'.

Men's lifestyle magazines are also offering some new ways of thinking about what it is to be a man, and, as Gauntlett says, while 'sometimes going overboard with macho excess, encourage men to understand women, and face up to modern realities'. Male bodies are emerging in advertising as sex objects to sell things, in much the same way that women's bodies have always been used.

Although media portrayals of women and men in film, TV and magazines have been changing, and there has been a growth in the presence and influence of women in media management and production, female stereotypes continue to thrive in the media we consume every day, particularly in the red-top mass-circulation tabloid press, advertising and music videos. New media technology, such as the Internet, video-enabled mobile phones and MP3 players, have led to the exploitation of women as sex objects and as victims of sexual violence more extensively than ever. For example, the growth of the Internet has led to a huge expansion of porn sites, which overwhelmingly feature the commercial and sexual exploitation of women's, rather than men's, bodies.

Activity

1 Suggest two ways in each case that (a) men and (b) women might use gender representations in the mass media as a source of personal identity and meaning.
2 Try to identify three examples of how men are being represented more as sex objects in the contemporary mass media, including advertising.
3 Drawing on your own experiences of the mass media, discuss examples of the ways new masculine and feminine identities might be emerging in contemporary society.

Sexuality

Heterosexuality

In contemporary Britain, the dominant view of 'normal sexuality' is that of **heterosexuality**, which is a central aspect of both the hegemonic masculine and feminine stereotypes discussed in the previous section. **Sexuality** – people's sexual characteristics and behaviour – has always been a central part of the hegemonic feminine stereotype, as, in Britain and other Western countries, women have been defined largely by their physical attractiveness and sexual appeal to men. They have traditionally been regarded as sex objects, subjected to the 'male gaze', particularly in the mass media, advertising and through media pictures and stories of the exploits of female celebrities.

Heterosexuality involves a sexual orientation towards people of the opposite sex.

Sexuality refers to people's sexual characteristics and their sexual behaviour.

Increasingly, men are also becoming sexualized objects. This is reflected in the growing coverage in men's magazines of men's appearance and sexual attractiveness, their diet, health and dress sense, and their growing use of cosmetics. Men's bodies have also become much more sexualized in advertising: naked men's bodies appear in the media and advertising on a greater scale than ever before, and there is a growing importance attached to men's physical body image.

An example of this, almost paralleling men's traditional obsession with women's breasts, was the media obsession with 'moobies' (men's boobs) in the 2000s. This began when the *Sun* newspaper published a 'Hall of Shame' series of pictures in 2005 showing the different shapes and sizes of famous men's breasts, and making disparaging comments about them. Other tabloid newspapers soon followed with criticisms of flabby stomachs – 'holiday podges' – and love handles. This reflects what McRobbie (1994) was saying a decade earlier – that men are beginning to face the same sort of physical scrutiny, by both women and other men, as women have always had to put up with. As McRobbie put it: 'The beauty stakes have gone up for men, and women have taken up the position of active viewers.'

Nonetheless, women are still much more likely to be seen as sex objects than men, particularly in pornography, with even young boys and girls widely exposed to sexualized images of females. Porn now seems quite deeply embedded, through the Internet and mobile phone technology, in the culture of young men.

Homosexuality

The fear of loss of profits if investors, advertisers or media audiences are offended has meant that male homosexuality (gays) and female homosexuality (lesbians) have been traditionally treated by the media as deviant and perverse. The media has frequently stereotyped gay men as effeminate, and women as butch lesbians, and has portrayed gays and lesbians as marginal to society, as odd and colourful 'camp' characters, or as dangerous and violent psychopaths. Gross (1991) argues that the media has often symbolically annihilated gays and lesbians by excluding them altogether. This treatment of gays and lesbians has meant that the media has tended to present distorted views of homosexuality, portraying it as a social threat. This was particularly true during the early stages of the AIDS epidemic in the 1980s, when the disease was treated as the 'gay plague'.

Sexual orientation refers to the type of people that individuals are either physically or romantically attracted to, such as those of the same or opposite sex.

When gay and lesbian characters have appeared in the media, they are usually cast and defined in terms of their **sexual orientation**, rather than being other characters who also just happen to be gay or lesbian, as was the case even in a more recent sympathetic treatment of homosexuality – the 2006 film *Brokeback Mountain*.

In recent years, there has been evidence of some change in traditional representations of masculine and feminine and gay sexuality. Soap operas give us insights into lesbian and gay relationships, and other images of sexual identities with which we may not be very familiar. Media companies have woken up to the fact that the gay and lesbian market – the 'pink pound' – is large and affluent, and, as the pluralist approach would suggest, they are now beginning actively to court the gay and lesbian market through advertising campaigns and the provision of media products to attract gay and lesbian audiences, particularly in the new digital media and the plethora of gay and lesbians websites. The popularity and acceptance of gay media celebrities like Graham Norton, Elton John and George Michael would seem to confirm that media representations of homosexuality are beginning to change.

Activity

1 With examples, suggest ways that advertising, the mass media and shop displays show a sexual image of men today.
2 Do you think that men are as concerned with their physical appearance as women?
3 To what extent do you think that young people today have more freedom to express their sexuality?
4 To what extent have you been aware of gay and lesbian relationships in contemporary soap and reality TV shows?
5 In what ways do you think the media today might or might not help in attaching less stigma to homosexuality?

Gay and lesbian sexuality may traditionally have been treated unfavourably by the mainstream media, but there are thriving traditional and new media catering for the gay market, such as *AXM, Gay Times (GT)* and the *Pink Paper*. There are also a host of websites, such as www.pinkpaper.com, www.gayshopping.co.uk and www.stonewall.org.uk.

Disability

The social construction of disability

Disability refers to a physical or mental **impairment** which has a substantial and long-term adverse effect on a person's ability to carry out normal day-to-day activities. An impairment is some abnormal functioning of the body or mind, either that one is born with or that arises from injury or disease. An impairment is not the same as disability. Shakespeare (1998) suggests that disability should be seen as a social construction – a problem created by the attitudes of society and not by the state of our bodies.

Shakespeare argues that disability is created by societies that don't take into account the needs of those who do not meet with that society's ideas of what is 'normal'. The stereotype in any society of a 'normal' or acceptable body may generate a disabled identity among those with bodies that do not conform to this stereotype, particularly those with a physical impairment, even when the impairment does not cause mobility or other physical difficulties for that person. An example of this might be people of very small stature (dwarfs), or with facial disfigurements that cause an adverse reaction among others.

Whether someone is disabled or not is then a social product – it is social attitudes that turn an impairment into a disability, as society discriminates against them. As Shakespeare argues: 'People become disabled, not because they have physical or mental impairments, but because they have physical or mental differences from the majority, which challenge traditional ideas of what counts as "normal". Disability is about the relationship between people with impairment and a society which discriminates against them.'

Most of us learn about disability as part of the socialization process, rather than as a result of personal experience. Popular views of those with impairments, for those without direct experience, are often formed through media stereotyping, and people with impairments are frequently portrayed in quite negative ways or, more commonly, ignored altogether. White, middle-class and able-bodied men in control of the media industry are often those who form media representations of disability, and disability is nearly always represented as a problem for the individuals themselves who have impairments, rather than as something that is created by society.

The symbolic annihilation of disability in the media

There were about 10 million people (excluding children) in Britain covered by the 1995 Disability Discrimination Act (DDA) definition of disability in 2002/3. This defines disability as 'a long-term health problem or disability that substantially limits a person's ability to carry out normal day-to-day activities'. Estimates from the Department for Work and Pensions suggest that this definition means that about one in four people in the UK is either disabled or close to someone who is. Yet these disabled people are seriously under-represented on the radio, in advertising, in newspapers and magazines, on websites, on television and cinema screens, and among those who work in the media industry. People with impairments appear so infrequently in the media that they effectively face symbolic annihilation.

Wheelchairs are often used in the media as a means of representing disability. Why do you think this might be? How does it perpetuate stereotypes of disability? How might it contribute to the marginalization of those with other forms of disability?

Sancho (2003) reported on the representation and portrayal of disabled people in peak-time programmes (5.30 p.m. to midnight) on the five UK terrestrial television channels using content analysis, focus groups and questionnaires. Disabled people were identified in around 11 per cent of programmes in 2002, but contributed 0.8 per cent of the overall television population (people or characters appearing). A 2005 report by Ofcom found the representation of disabled people in sampled programmes had increased to 12 per cent by 2004, but was still less than one person/character in 100, and a quarter of these were repeat appearances by the same person/character. The Broadcasting Standards Commission (2003) found over three-quarters (80 per cent) of the disabilities portrayed were related to mobility, with visual impairments coming second. The wheelchair is often used as an 'icon' or index of disability by those wishing to represent disability in the media. Sancho noted the perception by disabled viewers themselves of the ongoing marginalization of other groups – for example, those with disfigurements.

Disabled people were seen most frequently in fiction and factual programming, followed by news and feature films, and had major (rather than minor or incidental) roles in almost a third of the roles portrayed. More than 4 in 10 appearances (42 per cent) were in the context of highlighting issues of prejudice, stereotyping and dis-crimination. The majority of appearances (60 per cent) portrayed the impairment as central to the participant's role – that is, they appear either as or playing disabled people, rather than as people or characters whose main role is doing something else, but who happen to have an impairment as well. Having a disability is rarely portrayed as an everyday, incidental phenomenon.

Analysing TV broadcasts

The representation of disability on television in the media research cited here was done using content analysis. All programmes broadcast during peak times (5.30 p.m. to midnight) on BBC1, BBC2, ITV, Channel 4 and Channel 5 were recorded for one week, twice a year. These recordings provided the sample programmes on which the research was based. The content of the sample programmes was then analysed, by coding each sampled programme for various characteristics, such as the presence of a participant with a disability, their disability, and their occupational role in the programme.

Media stereotypes of disability

Only rarely do the media treat disability as a perfectly normal part of everyday life. Barnes (1992) showed how the vast majority of information about disability in books, films, on television and in the press is extremely negative, consisting of 'disabling stereotypes which medicalise, patronise, criminalise and dehumanise disabled people'.

Cumberbatch and Negrine (1992) identified three broad categories of disability stereotype in the cinema: the criminal, the subhuman and the powerless or pathetic character, while Barnes identified 10 stereotypes that the media in general use to portray people with impairments:

1 *As pitiable or pathetic* – characters that stir emotions and encourage pity in audiences, and treat disabled people as objects of charity, as is played on by TV charity telethons such as *Children in Need.*
2 *As an object of atmosphere or curiosity* – disabled people are sometimes included in the storylines of films and TV dramas to enhance a certain atmosphere, such as menace, violence or mystery, or to add character to the visual impact of a production.
3 *As an object of violence* – as victims, such as being helpless and vulnerable to bullying at school.
4 *As sinister or evil* – this is one of the most persistent stereotypes, portrayed in characters like Dr Jekyll and Mr Hyde or the nasty criminals in James Bond films. Disability is often associated with evil and witchcraft in films and fairy stories, and with sexual menace, danger and violence.
5 *As the super cripple* – the disabled person is seen as brave and courageous, living with and overcoming their disability, or assigned superhuman, almost magical, abilities. For example, blind people are portrayed as visionaries with a sixth sense or extremely sensitive hearing.
6 *As laughable or an object of ridicule* – the disabled person as the fool, the 'village idiot' and so on.
7 *As his/her own worst enemy* – as individuals who could overcome their difficulties if only they weren't so full of self-pity or maladjusted, and started to think more positively.
8 *As a burden* – the view of disabled people as helpless and who must be cared for by others.
9 *As non-sexual* – disabled people are sexually dead and therefore their lives are not worth living. The exception to this, as Barnes notes, is the stereotype of the

mentally ill sex pervert, which features quite regularly in the mass circulation red-top tabloid press and horror movies.

10 *As unable to participate in daily life* – this stereotype is mainly one of omission, as disabled people are rarely shown as anything other than disabled people. They are rarely represented as a perfectly normal part of everyday life, as workers, parents and so on.

Activity

This activity could be divided up if working in a group, with people taking different media.

1 Drawing on media you use, such as websites, Internet advertising, video games, films, TV programmes, newspapers, magazines and so on, list the types of disability/impairments you come across in a one-week period.

2 Identify the response you think each example is designed to evoke in the audience, such as horror, pity or fear.

3 Identify from your survey a range of examples to illustrate the 10 stereotypes identified by Barnes.

4 Present your findings to the rest of the group, and discuss what conclusions might be drawn about the representation of disability in the contemporary media.

Sancho (2003) found that disabled television viewers objected to media stereotypes of disability, and sought more realism and attention to detail. Children especially were irritated by portrayals of, for example, miraculous cures, and the lack of attention to the day-to-day realities of life, like getting up stairs, and never seeing disabled people working.

These stereotypes are also reflected in, and reinforced by, the on-screen emotional responses to disability that are evoked, which Cumberbatch and Negrine (1992) found were generally fairly negative. They found that disabled characters were more likely to evoke sadness, pity and sympathy than able-bodied characters, and they were more likely to be patronized, feared, ridiculed, abused, mocked and avoided, and less likely to be seen as attractive or shown respect.

Disabled people – and those who have some personal experience of disability – may well apply selective filtering to these media representations, and ignore, resist, reject or reinterpret such general stereotypes. However, for the many who lack such experience, the media may have a role in forming distorted views and negative stereotypes of those with impairments. As with all media representations, it comes down once again to which effects theory most fully explains what the media do, or do not do, to their audiences.

Activity

1 Keep a diary for one week of your media viewing. While watching your favourite television programmes, advertising, films or websites, make a note of examples of some stereotypes of young and old people, men and women, gays and lesbians, different social classes, minority ethnic groups, and people with impairments. Explain what these stereotypes are.

2 Applying the media effects theories discussed earlier in this chapter, explain how each theory might view the effects of media representations on audience perceptions of the groups listed in question 1.

3 Write an essay on about 2–3 sides of A4 paper answering the following question: *'Explain what is meant by media representations, and examine the ways the media represents both gender and ethnicity.'*

CHAPTER SUMMARY

After studying this chapter you should be able to:

- explain what is meant by the mass media, and distinguish between the traditional and new media;

- identify and explain a range of arguments concerning the role of the new media in contemporary society;

- explain and evaluate the postmodernist approach to the media;

- consider the role of the mass media in relation to globalization and popular culture;

- identify formal controls on the mass media;

- critically discuss the issue of how media ownership influences the content of the media, including the strengths and weaknesses of the manipulative or instrumentalist approach, the dominant ideology or hegemonic approach and the pluralist approach;

- critically discuss the effects of the mass media, including the strengths and weaknesses of the hypodermic syringe, the two-step flow, the cultural effects and the uses and gratifications models, and how these are affected by the selective filtering approach;

- discuss and evaluate the effects of violence in the media, and the problems of researching it;

- identify and discuss the influences on the content of the mass media, and the issue of media bias;

- discuss the way 'the news' is socially constructed;

- identify the factors that make stories newsworthy;

- critically discuss a range of media representations and stereotypes, including age, social class, ethnicity, gender, sexuality and disability.

KEY TERMS

agenda-setting
bias
cultural homogenization
cultural imperialism
digital divide
disability
dominant ideology
elite
gate-keeping

global culture
global village
globalization
Hawthorne effect
hegemony
heterosexuality
hierarchy of credibility
high culture

ideological state apparatuses
ideology
impairment
media imperialism
media representations
moral panic
news values

norm-setting
popular culture/mass culture
primary definers
sexual orientation
sexuality
social capital
symbolic annihilation

EXAM QUESTIONS

SECTION C: MASS MEDIA

If you choose this Section, answer Question 7 and **either** Question 8 **or** Question 9.

Time allowed: 1 hour 30 minutes   **Total for this section: 60 marks**

7 Read **Item C** below and answer parts (a) and (b) that follow.

Item C

The manipulative/instrumentalist and the hegemonic/dominant ideology approaches to the mass media assume that the media are controlled by powerful groups in society, and protect their interests by spreading the dominant ideology among media audiences. In contrast, pluralists suggest society is composed of a great diversity of groups, none of which is able to dominate the media. The media reflect this diversity, and a wide range   5
of different interests are represented. What appears in the media is driven by the wishes and tastes of viewers, listeners and readers, rather than imposed on them by the powerful. Audiences will simply not engage with media that do not reflect their views. The 'new media', such as the Internet, digital broadcasting and social networking sites like Facebook, have increased the choices available, and make it increasingly difficult for   10
any one group to control the flow of information and ideas in contemporary society.

(a) Identify and briefly explain **three** ways that the mass media might protect the interests
     of powerful social groups 'by spreading the dominant ideology among media audiences'
     (**Item C**, line 3).   *(9 marks)*

(b) Using material from **Item C** and elsewhere, assess the pluralist view of the mass media.
                                                                       (18 marks)

EITHER

8 'The mass media have direct and immediate effects on the ideas and behaviour of audiences.'
   To what extent do sociological arguments and evidence support this view?   *(33 marks)*

OR

9 'The mass media, particularly the new media, have played a key role in producing a shared
   global popular culture.'
   To what extent do sociological arguments and evidence support this view?   *(33 marks)*

4 Power and Politics

MARGARET WHALLEY

Contents

CHAPTER 4

Power and Politics

> **KEY ISSUES**
>
> - What is power? What is politics?
> - The nature of power
> - The distribution of power in society
> - The role of the state
> - Voting behaviour
> - Political parties, pressure groups and new social movements
> - The role of the media
> - Globalization

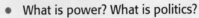

What is power? What is politics?

Power is the capacity of individuals or groups to get their own way in any given situation.

Politics involves the struggle for power and interaction between individuals and groups.

Power, in a sociological context, refers to the capacity of individuals or groups to get their own way in any given situation. **Politics** refers to a struggle for power, both within the institutions of government and parliament, but also in many other dimensions – for example, between men and women, between different religious organizations and between many other diverse groups and on every scale – from intimate relationships to global economic and social issues.

So that we can begin to understand what power is and how it is shared out in society, we need to try and define what is actually meant by 'power'. Max Weber (1864–1920) was one of the first sociologists to try to define the meaning of 'power' – a challenge, since there are many possible interpretations. Even Weber's own definition has been translated from its original German into English in eight different ways. Walliman et al. (1980) offer this version: 'Within a social relationship, power means any chance (no matter whereon this chance is based) to carry through one's [individual or collective] own will (even against resistance).'

Activity

Rank the following individuals/groups in order of power (using Weber's definition). Give a reason for your ranking in each instance.

- children under the age of 14
- Al-Qaeda
- prime minister
- the Queen
- suicide bombers
- men
- US President
- civil servant
- Roman Catholic Church
- David Beckham
- gay men

The nature of power

Sociologists are concerned not only with defining what power is in society, but also with the nature of power in society. In other words, they are concerned with what power is actually like and the ways it can be used in society. For example, Weber develops his definition from the notion of power being the capacity to achieve goals, and he suggests that it is not one single concept but that it can be broken down into several components:

1 Power – which is force, coercion, repression. It is using guns, fists, fines to gain compliance. For example, in Afghanistan under the rule of the Taliban, women were forced to wear the burqa in public, were not allowed to work outside the home or be educated after the age of 8. If these and many other rules were broken, they faced public flogging and even execution.

2 Authority – where power is used by superiors with the consent of the subordinates. Force is not necessary, although it is employed as the ultimate sanction if authority fails. For example, in 1989 there were large demonstrations across China broadly related to the ruling Communist government's economic policies and perceived authoritarianism. In a major protest in Beijing in Tiananmen Square, the soldiers and tanks were sent in with rifles, tear gas and tanks and many people were injured or killed.

3 Legitimacy – where power becomes authority. People see existing power structures as right and acceptable in a largely unquestioning way. This acceptance may be freely given or it may be actively generated by those who seek it. This is the case in many societies where the majority of people generally see those in power as rightfully there, and any major challenge to these power structures is infrequent – such as is the case in the UK.

Weber suggests that there are three types of legitimacy (ways in which a subtle acceptance of power structures is achieved):

Is the wearing of the burqa by women in Afghanistan a result of power, authority or legitimacy?

1 Traditional authority – which comes from customs and practice. Subordinates comply because things have always been this way. For example, in some pre-industrial, tribal societies, people submit to the authority of older members of the community because this is historically how things have been arranged.

2 Legal-rational authority – which is based on laws, rules and regulations. This is seen to be more sensible and logical than authority simply being based on tradition. Under legal authority, theoretically, if a regulation ceases to serve its purpose, it can be replaced. For example, in the late 1990s reforms took place in the House of Lords which led to the removal of many hereditary peers, perhaps based on the idea that, in a modern society, power should not simply be passed on unquestioningly from one generation to the next because of family position alone.

3 Charismatic authority – where a ruler is so personally liked that people will do what they say without question. This may extend also to anyone acting on the orders of, or in the name of, that individual. Charismatic leaders often arise in circumstances where one of the other types of authority has broken down but can generally be challenged by the death of that individual. For example, Fidel Castro, revolutionary leader of Cuba from 1959 to 2008 was known as 'The Giant'. Large throngs of people gathered to cheer at his fiery speeches, which typically lasted for hours. He retired only as a result of poor health, handing over the reigns of power to his brother Raul.

Weber, however, stresses that these three are **ideal types** and that, in reality, societies may experience a combination of types of authority at one given point in time.

Ideal types refers to a view of a phenomenon built up by identifying the essential characteristics of many factual examples of it. The purpose of an ideal type is not to produce a perfect category, but to provide a measure against which real examples can be compared.

Alternative views of power

Stephen Lukes (2005) presents a radical view of power, arguing that Weber concentrates too much on what he calls the 'first face of power':

1   The first face of power is based on decision-making – who has the power to influence decisions made? For example, in the foxhunting debate in the UK, several different groups presented views and arguments over many years before a ban was introduced.

2   The second face of power is based on non-decision-making, where many issues are not offered up to wider society to debate in the first place. In many **authoritarian** states – for example, Iraq under the leadership of Saddam Hussein – most political matters were not open for public debate. Even in democratic states, events may just happen without consultation and without people necessarily realizing that changes were to be made.

3   The third face of power is ideological, where people accept it, even when it is not necessarily in their interests. People are subtly controlled by having their thoughts and desires steered by, for example, the media and other forms of socialization.

> **Authoritarian** states are those in which there exists a system of rule which emphasizes the authority of a particular person, leading party or the state in general over the people.

Lukes contributes to the debate about the nature of power by suggesting that power can be exercised overtly, but covertly as well.

All these debates about definitions and the nature of power – in other words, what power is actually like and how it is used – pose difficult questions for sociologists. It is hard to assess how power is shared out, when power itself has many definitions and dimensions, and can be exercised in any number of ways in different societies and at different points in time.

Poststructuralism and power

Foucault (1926–84) took a different and sophisticated approach to the definition of the nature of power, suggesting that power was not necessarily something held by any specific group of people or particular institution such as the state. He suggested that power is present at all levels of human social interaction and in all social institutions, and that its execution is variable and transient; in other words, the way it is used can change and move with the times.

Foucault saw knowledge as a key aspect of power and used the concept of **discourses** – frameworks for thinking which exist in particular places at particular times – as mechanisms for the assertion of authority over others. For example, medical discourses often take precedence over alternative therapies such as aromatherapy, so doctors and other medical personnel are accorded higher levels of status and power. A discourse of heterosexuality in society exerts power and control over people's social and intimate relationships. Discourses can and do change over time, but the knowledge linked to them can be central in understanding the nature of power and how it is exercised in society. In other words, those who are seen as possessing the highest status of knowledge are seen as having the potential to exert power over others.

> **Discourses** are frameworks for thinking, bodies of ideas, which exist at particular times and in particular places. Discourses can be used as mechanisms for exerting power over people; they are often backed up by institutions.

A discourse of heterosexuality exists in UK society which portrays heterosexual relations as the norm.

Sociologists are interested in all aspects of power and have attempted to make sense of the nature and distribution of power in contemporary society.

The distribution of power in society

Key sociological questions concern the nature and distribution of power in society today. Where does power lie and what is it like? Is it distributed amongst a variety of competing groups in society, or is it more concentrated in the hands of specific groups? How is power used to achieve goals? Key concepts include those of **democracy** and the state.

Democracy

Democracy involves a system of rule based on the equal treatment of all citizens and offering them all an opportunity to be involved in their own governance.

A democracy is a political system in which, theoretically, the will of the people determines government policy. In other words, 'people power' or 'rule by the people' (the Greek *demos* means people and *kratos* means power). It is a system based on the idea that all citizens are treated equally and all are offered an opportunity to be involved in their own governance. Usually, in an indirect democracy this means that people have the right to vote to elect the representatives of their choice to act as rulers and decision-makers. Those elected individuals and groups will then use their own judgement to make decisions which they feel best reflect the interests of the electorate as a whole.

From a sociological perspective, the debate centres around whether or not the majority of individuals and/or groups are able to exercise any form of power in society beyond being able to vote. There are many competing sociological perspectives which act as frameworks to throw light on the nature and distribution of power in society today.

Functionalism

Parsons (1969) sees society in terms of value consensus, in the sense that he argues that there is widespread agreement within societies on the way things should generally be. It is suggested that everyone benefits from the exercise of power – it is a **variable sum view** (as opposed to a **constant sum view**, where some groups benefit to the detriment of others). Any authority is seen as acceptable and legitimate as it is for the benefit of society as a whole to maintain social order and social equilibrium.

Pluralism (or democratic elitism)

Pluralists too see power as shared out in society, but from a constant sum perspective (some groups gain, other groups lose) but they see this as a healthy process with no single group or groups remaining dominant at any one time. They argue that there is no single group that rules, but that there are multiple centres of power.

Pluralists disagree, however, with Parsons that there is value consensus in society. For example, although environmentalism has had a big impact on most people's lives, from domestic refuse recycling to environmental pollution controls and debates about global warming, there are still many different groups with varying ideas and agendas about future strategies and issues.

Pluralists, as their name suggests, argue that there is a plurality of power bases in society; in other words, that there is no single individual or group that holds power but that power is distributed throughout society. A pluralist society is one that contains a range of distinct social groups into which individuals might be integrated – these groups might be social classes, ethnic groups, occupational groups or groups based on gender, or more organized groups such as political parties and pressure groups or, more recently, groups that come together to form a social movement.

Variable sum view of power: a situation in which everyone generally benefits from the exercise of power.

Constant sum view of power: a situation in which some groups benefit to the detriment of others.

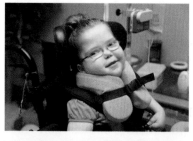

Pluralists see power in society shared among several groups each with their own interests, such as disabled people, people from working-class or minority ethnic backgrounds, and gay men.

These groups are seen as offering a richness to society and as useful in helping individuals to feel secure that their voices will be heard. It is argued that the leaders of these groups make up a series of **elites** who compete with each other for power and, in so doing, are serving and reflecting the interests of those individuals and groups.

An **elite** group consists of a small number of people at the top of an area of social life who are believed to dominate.

Pluralists generally attach a great deal of importance to the democratic political systems of Western nations – Europe and the USA, for example. In these systems, individuals acquire power through a competitive struggle to gain people's votes.

It is a partially revised theory of democracy in the sense that pluralists aren't suggesting that all individuals and groups have the power all the time to influence decisions and events, but that people vote every so often and, in the meantime, relinquish power to the elites who have offered themselves for election. These elites must compete with each other for popular support. Freedom is characterized not by individuals constantly 'having a say', but by the toleration of and election of these competing elites who, it is suggested, must to a degree take into consideration a broad range of viewpoints in order to stand any chance of remaining in power.

Two key institutions are crucial in support of pluralist arguments:

- political parties
- pressure groups

These groups are seen as representing a range of viewpoints and positions, allowing a diverse range of views to be heard and acted upon.

Three classic studies to support pluralist arguments

1   The American pluralist Robert Dahl (1961) carried out research in the town of New Haven, Connecticut, examining a series of concrete cases where key decisions were made about such issues as taxation, expenditure and welfare programmes. He maintained that there was clear evidence of a series of competing elites within the community who were all, in one way or another, having an impact on decisions made. He saw the entire process as reflecting multiple centres of power, where no one group necessarily had the upper hand. He suggested that in each case, different pressures were brought to bear by individuals and groups connected to that specific issue and that final decisions made reflected a balanced view.

2   In the UK, Hewitt (1974) looked at the period from 1944 to 1964 and identified 24 key policy issues which were being decided upon, and concluded that in every case the decisions made reflected the view within the general population, as generally evidenced by opinion poll data. However, the exception was the abolition of capital punishment in 1957 – opinion poll data was generally against the abolition, but the government proceeded nevertheless. The process of decision-making was seen to be fair and democratic, with a wide variety of views being consulted and compromises being reached in many cases as a result.

3   Grant and Marsh (1977) examined the role of the CBI (Confederation of British Industry) in the UK, which represents employers and their interests, on the basis that it might be expected that their interests would carry heavier weight than other groups related to their economic power. However, Grant and Marsh

identified numerous examples where relatively small pressure groups and other organizations had a fairly substantial influence on government policy and decision-making, at times to the detriment of employers.

Overall, these classic studies suggest that decisions made in political arenas are frequently the result of negotiation and compromise and that no one interest is predominant for a majority of the time. However, empirical research based on decision-making tends to be somewhat dated and it could be argued that in the twenty-first century decision-making is a much more complex process, frequently influenced by more global concerns. However, there are still some issues that are very specific to particular societies at particular times to which classical pluralist and other theoretical perspectives can be applied.

Foxhunting

For more than 100 years, many attempts were made to ban or at least restrict foxhunting, a pastime predominantly associated with the upper classes. During the 1940s, the Labour government set up the Scott Henderson Inquiry to investigate all forms of hunting and concluded that foxhunting was not cruel and no changes were needed to the legislation. Several members of this Inquiry were themselves involved in foxhunting.

During the 1960s and 1970s, three different private members bills on foxhunting were presented to Parliament. These are bills initiated by ordinary MPs rather than ministers, with the purpose of changing the law as it applies to the general population; they are frequently given less parliamentary time than those initiated by ministers and consequently stand a much reduced chance of being successful. All three failed to go on to become law.

In 1997 New Labour's manifesto promised a 'free vote in Parliament on whether hunting with hounds should be banned by legislation', and in 1999 they set up a Committee of Inquiry into hunting, chaired by Lord Burns. The Burns Inquiry resulted in votes in the House of Commons and the House of Lords on one of three options – a total ban, licensed hunting or self-regulation. The Commons voted for the total ban and the Lords for self-regulation.

In 2001, New Labour's election manifesto promised that a conclusion would be reached on this issue, and in 2003 a bill was issued that would have meant a system of licensing and regulation of foxhunting. This was debated as heatedly as all the other attempts had been to restrict foxhunting, by MPs, including groups such as the Middle Way Group, which was composed of MPs from all political parties who favoured licensing rather than a total ban, and by animal rights groups such as the League Against Cruel Sports, which all along had campaigned intensively for a total ban. Finally, in February 2005 the Hunting Act 2004 came into force, effecting a total ban on foxhunting.

Activity

1 How and why would pluralists suggest that the Hunting Act 2004 finally came into force?

2 Why do you think that there was a different result in response to the Burns Inquiry in the House of Commons compared to the House of Lords?

3 What strategies are used by groups such as the League against Cruel Sports in order to get their point of view across? www.league.org.uk/content.asp?CategoryID=1842

Criticisms of pluralism

Agenda-setting and non-decision making   Dahl has been criticized for focusing only on decisions that were actually being offered up for debate; it could be argued that the real power lies in **agenda-setting**. In other words, big issues may not even be offered up for discussion in the first place, as some individuals and/or groups may have the power to influence decisions by preventing them from getting as far as a public debate. This is referred to as 'non-decision-making'. Ruling elites, for example, might sideline the issue of social support for asylum-seekers and open up a debate on support for new small businesses. The illusion given ultimately is that people feel they are actively involved in decision-making but, in reality, they are only involved in very partial and possibly minor debates.

Bachrach and Baratz (1970) used the concept of **two faces of power** and argue that pluralism looks only at the first form of (visible) power – decision-making; the second face of power involves the 'mobilization of bias' against groups that are effectively excluded from the decision-making process, such as black people in many US cities. Consequently, decisions are made in stealth by a powerful minority. It could be argued that this second face is more powerful because it ensures that society is run in favour of the dominant group without opposition, since the policies that benefit that group are accepted without question as normal in the running of society.

Unheard voices   A further criticism of pluralism is that there is an assumption that all groups are able to compete equally in the public arena to get their voices heard. Many groups struggle to gain representation, for example because of racial and sex discrimination and white, middle-class males are often still predominant in centres of power.

Research issues   Polsby (1963) examined Dahl's research on New Haven and suggested that other local communities did have evidence of ruling elites and that New Haven was possibly not representative of all communities even in that locality and at that time. Polsby also suggested that the nature of the questions may have generated a particular response. For example, asking 'Does anybody rule?' may generate different findings from research that asks 'Who rules?'

Marxist perspectives on power

Marxists generally argue that power in society is held in the hands of the bourgeoisie or the owners and controllers of the means of production – for example, land and factories. Economic power is seen as shaping political power. The institutions of the superstructure such as the political system are seen as shaped by the underlying economic arrangements of society. In short, if the bourgeoisie or ruling class have economic power, they are able to use this to shape and influence, directly and/or indirectly, other key aspects of society.

In *Who runs Britain?* (2008) Robert Peston argues that senior business executives have had unprecedented access to top government departments and ministers since the election of New Labour in 1997. He sees this as a result of what he perceives to be New Labour's desire to disassociate itself from the anti-business image of 'old'

> **Agenda-setting** involves the power to manage which issues are to be presented for public discussion and debate and which issues are to be kept in the background.

> **Two faces of power**: the idea that power can be exercised not only by getting your own way against opposition (the first face) but also by preventing an issue from ever being raised as controversial in the first place (the second face of power).

Labour. He assesses their power and influence as significant enough to have had a major impact on taxation, such as the reduction of capital taxes from 40 per cent to 18 per cent in 2006.

Peston states that 54 billionaires paid just £15 million in tax on earnings of £126 billion in 2007. As a consequence, he sees the gap between the super-rich and the rest of the population as ever widening, and argues strongly against the 'trickle-down myth', which states that if business and enterprise are supported and sustained, this will result in a vibrant economy that will ultimately benefit everyone. Peston simply sees it as a case of increasing power for the business and financial sectors and incredibly high rewards for a small minority of individuals who are in a position to benefit personally. For example, in 2005 the retailer Philip Green, who awarded himself a £1.2 billion 'return' from his stores empire – most of which was paid to his wife who resides in Monte Carlo, thereby avoiding the tax owed on this sum – was given a knighthood by Prime Minister Tony Blair.

War against Iraq

In March 2003, the US invaded Iraq, having assembled 100,000 troops in neighbouring Kuwait. The decision was taken by the US government without the full support of the United Nations (UN) and with the wholehearted support of only a small number of governments, notably the British, worldwide. For example, both France and Germany strongly opposed the war throughout.

Iraq, and its leader Saddam Hussein, had for many years attracted the approbation of the US government and it has been argued that, after the 11 September 2001 terrorist attacks on the US, anti-Iraq opinion escalated within the US population. In 2001, George W. Bush declared the US government's so-called 'War on terror' which was to be characterized as pre-emptive military action, and became known as the 'Bush doctrine'. By 2002, the US campaign to overthrow Saddam Hussein had gained momentum and in 2003 UN authorization was sought for invasion. Opinion polls at the time in the US generally showed that more than 60 per cent of the population gave their full support to a US invasion of Iraq.

In February 2003, on the eve of the proposed invasion, massive worldwide protests broke out challenging the underpinning rationale for the action, and anti-war feelings were at an all-time high. Dominic Reynie, a French academic, estimated that at least 36 million people in 60 countries had been involved in at least 3,000 major demonstrations against the invasion. In London, on 15 February 2003 it is estimated that between one and two million people marched in London to demonstrate their opposition to the war. The US rationale for the invasion – that Saddam Hussein was a vicious tyrant, a threat to global peace and a sponsor of international terrorism and, in particular, that Iraq had invested heavily in WMDs (weapons of mass destruction) – was strongly questioned.

Nevertheless, Prime Minister Tony Blair and the Labour government were active supporters of the US plans to invade Iraq, and on 20 March 2003, the US declared war on Iraq. To date, around 250,000 British troops have seen active service in Iraq and 176 have died; there have been 4,000 US fatalities and between 100,000 and 150,000 Iraqi civilians (Iraqi health ministry).

The war officially ended with the defeat of Iraq declared on 1 May 2003. All subsequent investigations into the war have failed to find any substantive evidence of the presence of WMDs in Iraq.

Source: http://news.bbc.co.uk/1/hi/in_depth/629/629/7036068.stm

> **Activity**
>
> 1 How and why would pluralists argue that the decision to invade Iraq was made?
> 2 What criticism might be made of pluralist explanations of the decision-making processes in this instance?
> 3 How and why would Marxists argue that the decision to invade Iraq was made?

Table 4.1: Similarities and differences between Marxist and elitist theories

	Marxist theory	Elite theory
Is power concentrated in the hands of a minority?	Yes	Yes
Is power concentrated primarily in the hands of those who have economic power?	Yes – the 'owners of the means of production' – land and capital – are seen as central in any discussion concerning the distribution of power.	Not necessarily – while economic power may translate into social power, power may also be accessed via the holding of key roles within certain organizations such as the military and government.

Elite theory

Elite theorists basically argue that any system of government, indeed any organization, is dominated by elites, limited groups whose members possess 'superior' characteristics.

Classical elite theory

Classical elite theory was developed by Gaetano Mosca (1858–1941), who argued that power will always be distributed amongst a privileged few, leaving the masses relatively powerless in all societies, including democracies. Elites develop the three C's – group consciousness, coherence and conspiracy. In other words, they know who they are, they stick together and they work together to ensure the continuation of their power. The elite maintain their rule over the majority because they already control the apparatus of power. Elites may acquire their power in the first place in one of two ways:

- psychological – a view developed by Pareto
- organizational – a view developed by Michels

Pareto and the psychological basis of elites

The Italian sociologist Vilfredo Pareto (1848–1923) based his theory on the idea that 'governing elites' were simply people who occupied top jobs in any field such as politics, the media and large companies. He suggested that these governing elites were made up of two basic psychological types, which are constant throughout time:

1 Foxes – who rule through cunning and guile. Pareto referred to foxes as having an 'instinct of combinations' – they are able to theorise and hypothesise about what might happen and have an ability to bring ideas together to see in advance what the impact of one aspect might have even on seemingly unconnected other aspects. These characteristics link in well with innovation and change. They have the wisdom and skill to maintain their power through the exercise of such insight and planning.

2 Lions – who rule through the force of imposing their own will. Pareto referred to lions as having the 'persistence of aggregates' – they want to keep what they already have and will defend it at any cost. This resistance to change consequently escalates the conflict between lions and foxes.

Ultimately, Pareto sees history as a **circulation of elites** in which lions may hold power but be pushed out by the more scheming and innovative foxes, but then, as the solid determination of the consistent lions holds firm, the foxes wear themselves out and will be replaced once more.

There are three processes that can be identified in the way members of elites are replaced by others:

1 Circulation within the elite: older members retire and younger members take over.
2 Circulation between the elite and the rest: there is recruitment of talented individuals into elites.
3 Elite replacement: one elite is replaced by another, either through revolution or peacefully.

Pareto suggested that no matter how much circulation takes place, the overall situation remains the same with governing elites holding key powerful positions.

Michels and the organizational basis of elites

The German sociologist Robert Michels (1876–1936) suggests that organizational structures give rise to the dominance of those that run them. In his book *Political Parties*, he argues that for an organization to be effective its leaders need to be free to act quickly without being constrained by other members. This is why at party conferences there often seem to be tensions between the parliamentary leadership of the party at national government level and grassroots members, from local constituency parties and other groups.

Michels suggests that over time those who run organizations develop very high-level specific skills and become a professional elite separated from party members. For example, MPs, and now many local councillors, have no other occupation than their political role and once they have immersed themselves in those roles, they become very difficult to challenge and, as a result, further set apart from the electorate.

A key concept in Michels' work is that of **oligarchy**, which means control by a small elite. He is famously quoted as saying: 'Who says organization – says oligarchy'

A **circulation of elites** describes how social change may occur when there is a single unitary elite holding power, suggesting that the only possibility for change is the replacement of one elite for another. Also, a circulation of elites may be a gradual process, whereby younger members gradually replace older members within the exiting elite.

Oligarchy means control by a small elite.

Michels' **iron law of oligarchy** is the principle that all organizations eventually end up being ruled by a few individuals.

– the so-called '**iron law of oligarchy**'. In other words, an oligarchy is an inevitable consequence within any organization and power is vested in the hands of distinctly professional elites. Michels argues that, because they are smaller in number, those at the top of organizations are able to monopolize information and therefore hold power in their own hands, making true democracy very difficult.

The power elite

Some elite theorists see elites as inevitable and even desirable; however, there are others who see the presence of elites in society in a negative way, making true democratic processes difficult. The American sociologist C. Wright Mills (1916–62) was strongly influenced by Marxist perspectives; he suggested that not only did **power elites** exist, but that they were growing stronger in the America of the 1950s.

The **power elite** is the group that dominates society through its ability to control the important institutional positions in society. The elite is composed of those at the top of the great institutions of society, such as the government, the military, universities and industry.

Mills saw power as specifically linked to three main institutions in society:

- government;
- business corporations;
- the military.

He argued that top people in each of these power centres were able to make huge and far-reaching decisions and that they acted as a coherent and relatively unified group. The cohesiveness and unity of the power elite is strengthened by the similarity of social background of its members; they are drawn from the upper strata of society, they share similar educational backgrounds and they mix socially at certain specific events and places. As a result, they tend to share similar values and sympathies which provide the basis for mutual cooperation.

Mills argued that personnel are often interchangeable between the three power centres. For example, politicians often obtain positions as company directors, those with military backgrounds might become politicians, and, at any one time, some individuals might have a foothold in more than one elite. Mills argued that individuals who occupied these elite positions in society were not necessarily there as a result of meritocratic processes involving hard work, talent, intelligence and initiative; instead, they arrive in those positions via wealth and family connections, even via the mechanics of celebrity such as using the media. Because of the way in which power was concentrated in the hands of these interlocking elites, Mills argued, democracy was under threat. In addition, he portrayed the power elite as ruthless power-seekers and saw democracy as under attack from an uncultured and immoral elite.

Mills suggested that the rise of the power elite meant that politics was no longer a genuine debate about decisions to be made. He saw no differences between major political parties such as the Republicans and the Democrats in the United States, and people therefore had no real choice. However, the consequences of this were limited, since Mills portrayed the mass of the population as passive and manipulated.

Is there evidence of elite rule in Britain today?

A number of researchers have found that the majority of those who occupy elite positions in Britain are recruited from a minority of the population with highly privileged backgrounds. This appears to apply to a wide range of British elites, including politicians, judges and company directors, where there are high levels of elite self-recruitment. There is also evidence that there may be some degree of cohesion within and between various elites. Individuals may occupy positions within more than one elite and are also likely to have a common educational background. Many members of elites attended public schools and went to Oxford or Cambridge.

Hywell Williams (2006) uses Mills's ideas as a model in his research into power structures in Britain since the early 1980s. He identifies three elites:

- political elites;
- professional elites;
- financial /business elites.

Williams sees the financial/business elites as the most powerful, especially those working in the City of London, and he suggests that the political and professional elites often have to defer to the financial elites. These elites present themselves as working in the best interests of the nation and assume an air of unquestioned acceptance and legitimacy.

Political elites Like Mills, Williams sees little difference between the political parties, seeing ideological differences as having largely disappeared and leaders as interchangeable. He sees politicians and civil servants as having some power as they appoint agencies as regulators to public services, and recruit consultants and managers to work for the public and private organizations employed by the state – anything from the Office for Standards in Education, Children's Services and Skills (OFSTED) through to organizations such as the Water Services Regulatory Authority (OFWAT) and the Competition Commission (CC). Williams stresses the links between political and financial elites – many MPs still have significant business interests and many go on to become executive or non-executive directors of companies. He also stresses continued levels of elite self-recruitment: children of elite members are particularly likely to be themselves recruited to elite positions. Finally, he points out that those who are political radicals in their youth tend to lose their left-wing ideals as they progress to high government office.

Activity

Identify the members of the current Cabinet by looking at the UK Parliament or website:
- www.parliament.uk/directories/hciolists/hmg.cfm
- http://en.wikipedia.org/wiki/Cabinet_of_the_United_Kingdom#Current_cabinet

Divide the members of the Cabinet between your group or randomly select three members and identify the following points:
- their educational background – state or private? university? Oxford, Cambridge or other?
- family background – any parents or grandparents who occupied key 'command posts' in the past?
- political views – have they changed over time?

The professional elites Williams argues that this group has really only assumed greater importance since the late 1970s. Williams is referring not just to the traditional professionals such as lawyers and doctors, but also to what he calls the **new professions**, essentially management consultants who regulate, administer and monitor the work of other professionals. It is a world of targets, action plans and reviews. He suggests that the traditional professions, although they have maintained their status and high salaries, have lost power to the new professions and that they have lost autonomy and influence in relative terms.

> **New professions** are distinguishable from the traditional professionals such as lawyers and doctors, and usually refer to management consultants, who monitor and regulate the work of other professionals

The financial and business elites These elites have greatly increased their power in recent years. Here, Williams is talking about individuals and groups who work within banking, finance and money markets, often within the City of London. When crucial decisions are being made, it is suggested that the position of the City is paramount – for example, on decisions such as whether or not to adopt the Euro. Salaries for these individuals are often enormous and even bonuses can run into millions of pounds a year. Political parties often rely on significant donations from these companies for political campaigning and large companies benefit from the government as a major customer – for example, British Aerospace Engineering (BAE) and pharmaceutical companies for National Health Service (NHS) contracts. Many new government projects are sponsored by private capital, Private Finance Initiative (PFI), and present massive opportunities for those companies to make huge profits, not only now but indefinitely. For example, the government policy 'Building Schools for the Future' involves private companies as part of the biggest investment in new school buildings since the 1940s. Close relationships exist between the private sector of business and finance and governments departments at all levels and the potential for elite influence could be seen, in many ways, to have grown.

In summary, Williams argues that decisions overall strongly reflect the interests of the financial and business elites. He suggests that these groups have taken power in a very quiet and stealthy way, 'a very British coup'. In the past, the Labour Party may have tried to reflect the interests of workers and not just capital; the balance has now shifted and the financial and business elites have a major influence.

Elite backgrounds

Further evidence of the narrow range of backgrounds from which people are recruited into top positions comes from the Sutton Trust, an organization set up to increase the proportion of state-educated young people in high-status universities and professions.

Figure 4.1
Educational background of UK MPs (total numbers)

Source: Sutton Trust 2005; www.suttontrust.com

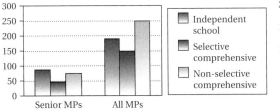
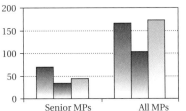
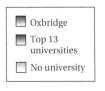

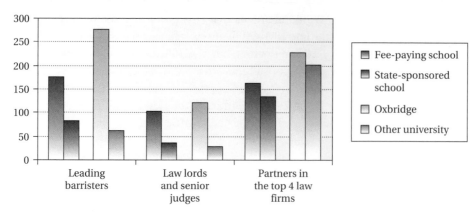

Figure 4.2
Educational background in the UK legal sector (total numbers

Source: Sutton Trust 2005; www. suttontrust.com

When Gordon Brown took over as Prime Minister in 2007, more than half the members of his first Cabinet were Oxbridge graduates (13) and 9 had been privately educated.

Information concerning the backgrounds of those in financial and business elites is more difficult to access because of the diversity of positions held and an overall lack of research. However, the London Chamber of Commerce (2006) found that a quarter of all managing directors of Britain's top 100 largest companies were Oxbridge educated and 33 per cent had been to one of the top 13 universities.

Overall, it would seem that those who hold the key 'command posts' are still drawn from a fairly narrow set of social backgrounds. It is also likely that there is a high degree of connectedness and shared perspectives within these social groups and a fairly high degree of social closure, despite the attempts of organizations like the Sutton Trust to break down those barriers.

Elite values

Edinger and Searing (1967) looked at elites in France and Germany and suggested that the attitudes of elite members could be predicted by their backgrounds. They argue that there is an elite who have a similar worldview or **Weltanschauung**.

Toynbee and Williams (2008) interviewed a small range of partners in top law firms and senior staff from merchant banks and found a high level of consistency in their *Weltanschauung*. For example, despite being involved in business and finance, their view of the distribution of income and wealth was fundamentally at odds with reality. For example, most thought that the top 10 per cent of earners were earning more than £162,000 a year. In fact, an income of £39,829 puts someone in the top 10 per cent, meaning that 90 per cent (of 32 million workers) earn less than that. The interviewees saw poverty wages as being less than £22,000, which, in reality, is closer to ordinary wages for most people.

Despite the high earners' lack of knowledge, they expressed strong views about the way social policy and taxation should be organized. Toynbee and Williams see their views as influential, because of their access to sources of power. These super-rich individuals, who earned anywhere between £150,000 to £10 million per year, saw themselves as 'economic benefactors' who were generating a booming economy which would benefit society more generally – the 'trickle-down' theory. However, it

Weltanschauung means the framework of ideas and beliefs through which an individual interprets the world and interacts with it.

Bankers, lawyers and financiers who were earning over £150,000 a year had little idea that 90 per cent of people earn less than £40,000 a year.

is argued that a greater contribution to GDP is made by the manufacturing and property services sectors of the economy and the wealth of lawyers and bankers basically benefits themselves more or less exclusively.

Very fixed views were expressed about the taxation system, which was seen as weighted against their interests – for example, in respect of capital gains tax and inheritance tax – even though they had been given information about the extent of low wages within the economy for the majority. Any suggestions that governments should do more to redistribute wealth were met with the response that benefits were too high anyway (even though estimates they gave of benefit levels were hugely over-inflated in comparison to reality) and that governments, if given more taxation revenue, would simply squander it. A similar view was expressed towards charities, which were seen as wasters of money. These high earners saw themselves as relatively poorly off, despite having been informed of the facts about the distribution of income and wealth. They complained of high school fees, the price of property in London and so on, and considered anything less than £100,000 a year as impossible to live on. They suggested that they worked harder than nurses and teachers and supported the view that mobility into jobs like their own was a simple matter of hard work and determination and that anyone could do it. This was despite the fact that they also generally agreed that recruitment into top law firms and merchant banks was increasingly dominated by those with private school backgrounds. The fact that these opinions were aired after the facts and realities had been presented to them by the researchers suggests the strength of their *Weltanschauung* as a result of their upbringing, socialization and relative social isolation.

In relation to debates about power, it is suggested that such individuals have increasingly gained access to governmental power structures and that, despite their lack of knowledge on such matters as the distribution of income and wealth and taxation, they can have a significant impact on government policy. For example, capital taxes have been reduced in recent years, while the 10 pence tax rate for low earners was abolished in 2008.

Evaluation of elite theories

Evidence for the existence of elites tends to be descriptive and speculative; empirically based research documenting the interlocking and coherent nature of elites and their impact on decision-making is scant, and such a position is virtually impossible to 'prove'.

The state is seen by pluralists as an 'honest broker', in existence to ensure that no one group gains overall power. Rules and legislation are theoretically designed to prevent any one group from gaining supreme power. For example, in 1994 the newly established Committee on Standards in Public Life laid down the seven principles of selflessness, integrity, objectivity, accountability, openness, honesty and leadership as requirements for those holding public office. The committee is also responsible for closely monitoring the behaviour of those in public office and acting upon any transgressions of the rules.

Pluralists would see pressure groups and new social movements (NSMs) as constantly seeking to defend the rights of individuals and challenge elite power (see below, pages 295–303, for more on pressure groups and NSMs).

In democratic societies, all people have access to power through the ballot box periodically and so are able to assert their views. Freedom House (2000) estimate that only 40.7 per cent of people live in a country where they have extensive civil liberties and political rights.

The role of the state

A further key concept in this debate about the nature and distribution of power in society is the **state**. Key questions include what the role of the state is in contemporary society and how it has changed over time, especially in more recent years under the influence of globalization. In short, the state is defined as a central authority which has legitimate control over a set territory. It encompasses a much wider meaning than government alone. The government is just one component of the state – Parliament, the Civil Service, local government, the police, the judiciary and the military are also key institutions included in what sociologists define as the state. Because the state carries a large amount of power, one focus of sociological investigation and analysis is to look at the structures that underpin the modern state. As in debates about the nature and distribution of power in society more generally, pluralists, Marxists and other theorists all have views about the role of the state in modern societies and how it has changed over time.

The **state** is a central authority, which has legitimate control over a set territory

The state generally has the following powers:

- to create and enforce laws, although it can be overruled on certain matters by the European Court;
- to own land;
- to raise money through both direct (usually income) taxes and indirect taxation;
- to control economic policy, for example, interest rates and exchange rates;
- to perform a major role as an employer in the UK – about 20 per cent of the workforce are in the state sector;
- to exert quality control over goods and services such as education, communications and health;
- to act as agent of social control, through controlling the police and other methods of surveillance, for example.

Table 4.2 An analysis of different theories of power and society

	Marxist theory	Elite theory	Pluralist theory
Nature of people How do they see people?	Rational, creative, unable to achieve full potential in a class society.	People are irrational and innately unequal in their abilities; individuals are self-seeking and competitive.	Unequal endowment. Some are more able than others and should be given more of a chance of leadership.
Society How do they see society?	Two basic classes being involved in inevitable conflict. Ruling class own the means of production, supremacy is based on wealth.	There is a distinct division of a cohesive elite and an amorphous mass.	A democratic framework exists in which different interests compete for consideration. There is no one elite in society, but many plus possibilities of social mobility. Society is necessarily stratified.
State What is their view on the role of the state?	Serves the interest of the ruling class, ultimately with force.	The state is a threat to society. It manipulates political power and threatens to encroach on the working of the economy – the market.	It should act as a mediator in clashes of interest to the best advantage of 'the nation'. It may need to intrude into economic life and should do so if necessary. It is impartial.
Power Who has power in society?	Those who own and control the means of production.	Those who form the political elite.	No one group has more power than can be checked by the others. Power is fragmented in society – between pressure groups and political parties for example. The political elite is the more powerful, and acts as mediator.
Social change How does social change take place?	Change basically takes place through class conflict. When economic development reaches a certain point, a classless society becomes a possibility.	Change can take place by recruitment to the elite by the middle class. Fundamental change takes place by elite circulation. One elite replaces another, often after a revolution or coup.	Change takes place slowly and gradually as improvements are seen to be necessary.

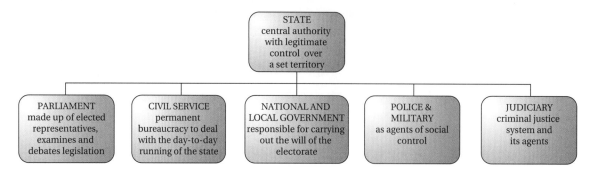

Figure 4.3 The structure of the state

Consequently, the questions of who has power through the state and what the nature of that power is are very important, and, at the same time, vast and complex. Sociological perspectives on power and the state offer a variety of contrasting theoretical frameworks for examining these crucial issues.

Brief history of the state

The power of the state has gradually increased as the power of the monarchy has declined and more democratic principles were established. In the nineteenth century, the power of the House of Commons grew, with the clear establishment of political parties to represent new sections of voters and elections to dictate which party should form the party of government. In the same period, the ideology of **laissez-faire** generally prevailed, meaning that the economy was free from overt government control, and economic intervention, for example, was minimal.

In the twentieth century, the state took on a greater sense of responsibility to manage the day-to-day affairs of citizens and state powers became more extensive, with the immediate post-war period characterized by significant changes in state operations.

In 1945 Labour won a landslide victory, which enabled a raft of policies centred around greater state control to be introduced. These included:

- setting up a national health service (NHS) in 1948;
- nationalization of key industries such as coal and steel;
- wide-scale social welfare reforms to address income inequalities and poverty;
- state education to include a formal system of secondary education – the 1944 Education Act.

Despite changes in the 1980s, largely implemented by Margaret Thatcher and her Conservative government in an attempt to reduce the power of the state, by the **privatization** or denationalization of key industries such as British Rail, British Steel and British Gas and by supporting the private sector in areas such as health and education, it can be argued that the state still plays a major role in society today.

In 1997, with the election of New Labour, a new ideology emerged – called **the third way** – which is a compromise between the principles of the market and the relative autonomy of the state, balanced by measures to ensure individual empowerment and responsibility (see below, page 281).

Laissez-faire is a philosophy of society in which government has only a minimal role; it suggests that the most efficient and free society is one in which the state provides only the most basic of society's needs.

Privatization refers to a government policy which is centred on reducing the public sector as much as possible through the transfer of industries and utilities from state ownership and control into the hands of private shareholders.

The third way is a political philosophy, pioneered by New Labour, which is committed to retaining the values of socialism, while supporting market policies for generating wealth and reducing inequalities.

> **The nation-state** has its own political apparatus over a specific territory, whose citizens are backed by their military and with a nationalistic identity.

In recent years, there have been many global challenges to the power of the **nation-state**. The increasing power of transnational corporations (TNCs), global financing and the growth of the Internet and communications technology, for example, mean that it is now virtually impossible to consider the role of the state without a global background.

Pluralist views of the state

Pluralists see the state as an 'honest broker', mediating between the interests and needs of the various groups to prevent a tyranny of the minority – in other words one group or a small number of groups always having power. The state may reflect and support the interests of different groups at different times – for example, there was strong government support for the tobacco industry in the 1960s but, as smoking bans became more widespread, anti-smoking organizations and research organizations have benefited from extensive government support. The state is seen as non-partisan and as acting in the national interest and is instrumental in ensuring that all competing interest groups are able to access power structures.

Marxist views of the state

In the *Communist Manifesto* (1848), Marx wrote: 'The executive of the modern State is but a committee for managing the common affairs of the whole bourgeoisie.' In other words, control of the state is in the hands of the ruling class and a key issue is the preservation and perpetuation of the capitalist system – a system based on private ownership of property and the accumulation of and concentration of wealth in the hands of the bourgeoisie.

Marxists argue that capitalism and democracy belong together. For capitalism to thrive, individuals must be free to act and make money for themselves without restraint. Democracy stresses freedom and individualism, in contrast to previous feudal systems which were very much about control, obligation and tradition. Although the capitalist system is based on inequality, the political system is, theoretically, based on equality. Marxists argue that all are free but some are freer than others. In other words, freedom is necessary for the capitalist class to defend and develop their position.

However, Marxists have different views about the way in which the state actually operates in such a way as to reflect the interests of the ruling class. Instrumentalist Marxists stress the direct impact of individuals and groups who form part of a privileged and powerful elite, holding key posts within state institutions and major private corporations which have a direct bearing on the structures of power. Structuralist Marxists stress that the inevitable structures of capitalism and the simple pattern of bourgeois ownership of the means of production mean that the system operates ultimately in the interests of the ruling class, without it being necessary for its members to be in key institutional positions. Classically, Ralph Miliband is seen as representing the instrumentalist Marxist position and Nicos Poulantzas as representing the structuralist Marxist position.

Miliband and the instrumentalist Marxist view

Miliband (1973) argued that the state largely carries out policies that benefit the bourgeoisie. In other words, the civil service, the armed forces and the judiciary, for example, are all seen as arms of the state that favour the bourgeoisie directly because the people within them are also part of the ruling class. He argued that most of those who occupy top positions in the state come from ruling-class backgrounds and are consequently more likely to support ruling-class interests. Even those from other backgrounds will generally have to accept ruling-class values to gain high office. The protection of private property is seen as a central role of the state and the state supports private enterprise which is further backed up by corporate advertising, stressing the benefits to the population of large capitalist concerns. However, an issue here is that there are policies which, on the surface at least, would seem to benefit the proletariat as much as the bourgeoisie, such as the introduction of the National Minimum Wage.

Poulantzas and the structuralist Marxist view

Poulantzas (1969) argued that the structure of capitalism is largely sufficient in itself automatically to serve the interests of the ruling class. It isn't actually necessary for members of the ruling class to occupy key positions within the state to ensure that it functions to benefit the ruling class; those who occupy positions in a state which inevitably functions to benefit the ruling class would automatically act in the interests of the ruling class, regardless of their own backgrounds. This happens because private ownership creates wealth which generates income for the state. For governments to get re-elected, they must keep private enterprise healthy – and keep the bourgeoisie happy – and then the wealth that is generated funds public policy.

Poulantzas also argued that ruling-class interests are best served if members of that class are themselves at a distance from the day-to-day operations of the state, for two key reasons:

1 This would mean an avoidance of internal struggles within the ruling class – for example, differences between owners of the means of production in different sectors. If the state is autonomous, such conflicts of interest can be avoided.
2 Concessions must be made to the working class to make the system seem fair and natural and if members of the ruling class were more directly involved, this could be more difficult to achieve. Also, if members of the ruling class are at a distance from the key 'command posts', the myth of egalitarianism is perpetuated and the view of democracy for the people is promoted.

In summary, the workings of the capitalist system are seen as automatically providing legitimacy and support for ruling-class interests, without the need for members of the ruling class to occupy key command posts.

Theories of the autonomy of states

Some sociologists are less concerned about the impact of external forces in society on the activities of the state and see the state as relatively independent or autonomous.

The police force is made up of people from all social classes and, in theory, the police work for everyone in society. However, the institution can work in favour of the ruling class by treating different groups unequally. For example, drug use in a deprived area is much more likely to be investigated and punished than drug use among rich city bankers or celebrities.

Nordlinger (1981) suggests that many theories are preoccupied with the notion that the state is, in one way or another, influenced by society. He presents an alternative picture, arguing that the state can act independently to change society. This can happen on one of three general levels, which Nordlinger classifies into types – from a more intense level of state autonomy through to a more partial independence.

Type 1 state autonomy – intense

This is where the state has quite a different agenda from the views of the mass of the population, but it nevertheless manages to dominate decision-making. Sweden and Norway are seen as examples of this type as they rely extensively on permanent career civil servants who adopt a range of well-rehearsed strategies to influence events. For example, they might cover up plans and issues, use honours to influence those who might resist, and seek to divide and rule opponents by causing mistrust between groups. The state is essentially seen as having a fairly clear mandate to make decisions and implement plans, regardless of the wishes and opinions of groups in society.

Type 2 state autonomy – middle way

This is where the state is largely autonomous but at times needs gently to persuade certain groups and opponents that events are being managed in their best interests. Key representatives of the state may be involved in processes to bring about the required change of opinion. For example, in Dahl's research in New Haven (see above, p. 263), the mayor was instrumental in ensuring that there was support within the community for policies linked to urban renewal, which had not previously been the case.

Type 3 state autonomy – partial

This is where the state follows policies that are supported by society generally, but where it can still act in an autonomous way in relation to the day-to-day management and organization of budgets and staffing because these operations are not subject to public scrutiny as a result of general apathy. The result is therefore that the state acts as an independent source of power.

In summary, Nordlinger is suggesting that the state is an autonomous entity that can generally have its own way in many respects, although the extent of this may vary to degrees from time to time and place to place.

Theda Skocpol (1985) also strongly supports the view that the state can be autonomous, and discusses 'bringing the state back in'. She is critical of neo-Marxist views that the state is exclusively influenced by the dominance of the ruling class in the economic infrastructure. She believes that states can have the autonomy to fulfil policy goals which reflect their own desires and that states in many circumstances constantly seek to increase their own power. She sees some states as more powerful than others: for example, those in more affluent countries where resources bolster power structures and where those involved in the day-to-day management of affairs are able and well educated.

New Right views of the role of the state

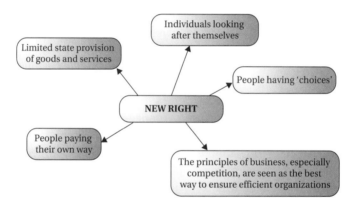

Figure 4.4 The values of the New Right

During the late 1970s and through the 1980s and '90s, the Conservative government, led mainly by Margaret Thatcher and then by John Major, was influenced by the views of US economists and sociologists whose ideas have been grouped together under the theoretical label of the 'New Right'. The views of the New Right, especially those of US writer Charles Murray, had a significant impact on government policy.

In short, there was a firmly held belief that the principles of the free market should prevail, and many of the policies pursued by Margaret Thatcher and her governments – such as the privatization of nationalized industries, the injection of competition into the public sector and the sale of council houses – were attempts to rein back the state and cut public spending, reflecting free market ideas. The state was seen as exercising too much power and control in many areas, although the ideology of Thatcherism is often seen as more of a blend of New Right ideology with elements of traditional conservatism, neo-liberalism and neo-conservatism, 'the free economy and the strong state'. In other words, despite policies that involved reducing state involvement, there was a deep commitment to strong government, leadership, law and order, and defence of Britain's national interests abroad. Overall though, New Right ideology is characterized by its stress on reducing state intervention, celebrating the benefits of the free market and focusing on individual responsibilities and choices.

The third way – an alternative view of the role of the state

Giddens (1998) is closely associated with 'third way' politics, which emerged during the 1980s as an alternative way of looking at and managing the role of the state and the distribution of power in society. It combines elements of more traditional left- and right-wing ideologies; for example, it follows the right in valuing enterprise and encouraging individual responsibility, while it generally follows the left in valuing social solidarity and promoting opportunities for the socially excluded. State involvement in many areas of social life is seen as positive and necessary, while private business, finance and entrepreneurialism, and free market forces are also seen as essential and desirable. It is a view most strongly linked to the advent of New Labour in British politics in the period after 1997.

Feminist views of the state

Feminist sociologists generally argue that the state is characterized by patriarchy. All key areas of the state are seen as dominated by male hierarchies – for example, the judiciary, the police, the army. State policy is also seen as largely reflecting male interests – the lack of pressure to bring about any fundamental change in the social position of women via family policy, education and employment law is still a major focus of concern.

The Equality and Human Rights Commission Report *Sex and Power* (2008) indicated that women still make up only 19.3 per cent of all MPs and 11 per cent of the FTSE 100 directorships (top companies in the UK), and that, at the current rate of growth, it will take 55 years for women to achieve equality within the judiciary. In summary, women are seen as making very slow progress, and in some areas no progress at all, in terms of gaining political representation.

Voting behaviour

A major focus for sociologists has always been the electoral process on a local, national and European basis. Debates about who votes and why they vote in the way they do are central to our understanding of how democracy works in practice. However, it has been suggested that the nature of political participation has been changing in recent years, and that while membership of mainstream political parties is decreasing, participation in the activities of pressure groups and new social movements has significantly increased.

Activity

Participation in political activity

Using your school or college as a resource, carry out the following survey with a small sample of respondents and assess the extent of political activism in your area.

Which of the following apply to you or your immediate family?	Yes/No
1. Follow general elections in the media or through personal conversations	
2. Pay attention to political campaigns	
3. Voted in the last general election	
4. Voted in the last local elections	
5. Member of a political party	
6. Member of a trade union	
7. Contacted a local councillor about any issue or problem at least once	
8. Contacted an MP about any issue or problem at least once	
9. Ever complained to a public or private company	
10. Ever formed a group to attempt to solve a community problem	
11. Ever given money to a political party, local or national	
12. Been a member of a political party	
13. Attended a campaign meeting during a general election	
14. Have a 'political attitude'	
15. Been a member of a pressure group	
16. Participated in a demonstration	
17. Used website forums to contribute to political debate	
18. Signed a petition for a political reason	

Although many sociologists suggest that voting is a long way, especially nowadays, from being the only way in which individuals seek to exercise power and influence, it is still a very important right, which a significant minority choose to exercise in local, general and European elections. The results of elections are closely scrutinised by **psephologists** – those who study trends and patterns in voting behaviour, both for the purposes of sociological research and for political purposes of strategy and persuasion.

It has been argued that post-war British politics manifests a number of clear patterns underpinning voting behaviour. However, in recent years the situation has

Psephology is the study of voting patterns. It comes from the Ancient Greek *psepho* meaning pebble; voting in Athens took place by the casting of pebbles to decide issues.

become more complex. A major debate concerns the extent to which social class is still a major influence on voting behaviour.

The continuing importance of class?

Left-wing is a description of a position on the political spectrum, and generally reflects those ideas and organizations that tend to be critical of existing social arrangements.

Research up to the 1970s suggested that social class was a major influence but since that time there has been a major debate, with some sociologists, such as Crewe (1986), arguing that it is no longer a key factor, but others such as Heath et al. (1985) suggesting that class position is still influential. The debate is further complicated by the fact that Labour party policies, certainly since 1997, have moved closer to the right, so although more working-class people may still be voting Labour, it is not the same Labour Party that the working classes of previous decades were voting for. There are also debates around the issue of how social class should be defined for the purposes of this psephological research.

1940s to 1970s

Right-wing is a description of a position on the political spectrum, and generally reflects the ideas and organizations that favour existing social arrangements and more traditional values.

During this period it has been suggested that social class was a major factor underlying voting behaviour. The identities of the two major political parties, Labour and Conservative, were clearly linked to different issues, which in turn reflected the preoccupations of the working class and middle class respectively.

Labour concerns were based on **left-wing** principles, such as redistribution of wealth through taxation from the affluent to the less well-off; the nationalization of key industries and state control of the economy; and a comprehensive welfare state, free at the point of access.

Conservative concerns were firmly based on **right-wing** principles, such as low levels of personal and business taxation, founded on the belief that this stimulated enterprise and a healthy economy; support for private sector investment, in health and housing, for example; and much more restraint in terms of government intervention and state-run provision.

Someone with a **partisan self-image** has a view of themselves as a supporter of a particular political party.

Butler and Stokes (1974) said that social class was crucially linked to voting behaviour: the concerns of the Labour Party best served the interests of the less well-off from working-class backgrounds, whereas Conservative Party concerns sought to advantage the more affluent middle class. Most voters had what Butler and Stokes described as a **partisan self-image** – in other words, they had a view of themselves that was closely linked to a particular party, it was very much part of their identity as an individual, and it was often a consequence of a strong political socialization, an immersion from an early age into the notion that to vote for a specific political party, linked to their community and upbringing, was 'normal'.

Floating voters are those who change the political party they vote for from election to election.

There were relatively few **floating voters** – that is, those who changed their allegiance from one election to another; in other words, there was a very low level of **voter volatility** – attitudes were developed early on and stay fixed, often for life. All this was compounded by the fact that there were really only two main parties: it was a two-party system, in which a vote for a minority party would never be likely to lead to any consequences. The class divide in voting behaviour was so entrenched that working-class Conservatives and middle-class Labour supporters were termed

Voter volatility describes voters who change the political party they vote for from one election to another.

deviant voters, as they were seen to be breaking with social norms in expressing such a preference.

Research was carried out to investigate the underlying causes of this 'deviant' behaviour and it was suggested that cross-class marriages (rare anyway in themselves) and having parents who voted for different parties (contradictory socializing influences) could possibly be linked. In addition, there were the concepts of deferential voting (working-class people who vote Conservative because of an internalized respect for middle-class leadership and a belief that they are more skilled and appropriate) and **embourgeoisement** (the idea that well-paid manual workers were adopting more middle-class norms and values in terms of lifestyle and that this might extend to political attitudes and voting behaviour). Finally, reference was made to secular voting, whereby individuals voted not on the basis of beliefs, but simply on the basis of which party at that time would serve their specific interests best – for example, in terms of living standards.

Frank Parkin (1968) examined middle-class deviant voters – in other words, middle-class Labour voters – and found that common factors included public sector employment, often in a 'caring' field such as the NHS, teaching and social work, and that this connected with Labour's more sustained support for public services.

1970s to 1990s

During this period, it has been argued, the relationship between social class and voting began to break up. British Election Studies after every general election, using a positivist approach to identify trends and patterns, have identified a range of underlying reasons to explain the apparent changes in this phase:

1 A decline in manual employment: the nature of the economy shifted from being based on manufacturing industries towards more of an emphasis on service sector jobs. Consequently, there were fewer workers whose occupations linked them to a culture of Labour voting.
2 The rise of the third party in British politics – namely the Liberal Party, especially as part of a newly formed centre party, the SDP, which later became the Liberal Democrats – led to a blurring of the class divide in voting; it has recruited from both Labour and Conservative voters.

Overall, there was a significant rise in this period in volatility and the number of deviant voters increased.

Sarlvick and Crewe (1983) strongly supported the view that major changes were taking place both within society and within the electorate, including the following:

1 **Partisan dealignment**: voters did not present identities that were strongly party political anymore.
2 Class dealignment: voters were identifying less with the political party that would seem most naturally to reflect their class position. Sarlvick and Crewe suggested that the decline in trade union membership in the workplace and an increase in home ownership led to a different perception of political expediency for many voters. In other words, voters felt they had more to gain by voting for a

Deviant voters are those who vote for a political party which does not, on the face of it, seem best to reflect their class interest – such as a working-class Tory.

Embourgeoisement is the notion that working-class manual workers were adopting more middle-class norms and values.

Partisan dealignment – the idea that fewer and fewer individuals are strongly identifying with a particular party and remaining loyal to that party over long periods of time.

party which reflected the interests of home owners and the more affluent middle classes.

3 Policies: it was suggested that voters were taking more notice of particular issues, especially at election times, and that votes would be cast related to specific strategies being highlighted by the parties, rather than according to overall ideological standpoints.

However, an alternative view was put forward by Heath et al. (1985), who argued that class still had a major influence on voting. They identified five social class groupings and this subtlety revealed that the link between occupation and voting was still strong; it was suggested that a more two-class conception could exaggerate the picture of deviant voting. They were also the first researchers to ensure that women were correctly categorized in line with their own occupations rather than simply their husband's position.

Heath et al. also developed a complex form of measurement called the 'odds ratio', which calculated the relative likelihood of someone voting in line with their class position, using data going back to the 1960s. They concluded there was no long-term dealignment. Indeed, class voting seemed to be stronger in the 1980s than in the 1970s. They did suggest that, to a degree, changes in the social structure along the lines of a decreasing proportion of manual jobs had some impact on Labour support.

The rise of the Liberal Democrats further complicated the picture, but overall Heath et al. found no evidence to support the view that changes in the class structure were a major influence on voting.

It was also suggested that it was still the case that the overall ideological image of a party was more important than specific policy issues. Few voters delve into the minutiae of party manifestos, and a growing free market approach to economic issues (and a more supportive strategy in relation to public services) was beginning to attract more support, suggesting that the Labour Party was perceived as too left wing by many and that structural changes in society maybe had less of a role to play.

Indeed, by the early 1990s it seemed that the Conservatives were insurmountable. However, although Labour lost the 1992 election, there were nevertheless signs that a change was on the horizon, signalled by a number of crucial factors:

1 Labour was presenting a united front as a party. There had been many divisions within the party up to this point over key ideological matters, but these issues had to a certain extent been addressed and there was a growing confidence in the party as a force in itself.

2 Economic problems, including rising rates of unemployment and rising interest rates for all the homeowners, were negative forces against the Conservative government.

3 After an initial revival of interest with the establishment of the Social Democratic Party (SDP) and the subsequent creation of the Liberal Democrats, support for a third party seemed to be diminishing, especially as Labour began to reflect more centre-ground policies itself – for example, downplaying support for nationalized industries and any need for rises in taxation.

Table 4.3: UK governments, 1979–2005

Year of election	Winning party	Prime minister
1979	Conservative	Margaret Thatcher
1983	Conservative	Margaret Thatcher
1987	Conservative	Margaret Thatcher (John Major from 1990)
1992	Conservative	John Major
1997	New Labour	Tony Blair
2001	New Labour	Tony Blair
2005	New Labour	Tony Blair (Gordon Brown from 2007)

Despite these developments in Labour's favour, the result in 1992 was a resounding defeat. It was argued that the declining proportion of traditional working-class manual workers in the economy, Labour's 'natural' supporters, and the fact that incomes and qualification levels were rising meant that Labour would find it difficult, if not impossible, ever to win an election again.

The 1997 election and beyond

The 1997 election was a landslide victory for what was termed 'New Labour'. The British Election Study of the 1997 election and other supporting research has indicated a range of key reasons underpinning this change in the political landscape after 18 years of Conservative government.

1 Ideological convergence: huge changes had taken place within the Labour Party to distance Labour politics from its traditional standpoint of association with the trade union movement, high taxation for higher earners and opposition to the principles of the free market. The Labour Party had moved more to the centre, occupying the ground held more recently by the Liberal Democrats, while retaining its traditional support. Evans et al. (1999) suggest that this helped to attract increasing numbers of middle-class voters to Labour.
2 Volatility: more floating voters meant more potential support for Labour and the possibility of a large number of the electorate switching their vote from Conservative.
3 Issues: the Conservative Party had experienced many difficulties of a single issue status. For example, there were instances of 'sleaze', where key individuals within the party had their reputations tarnished by allegations of underhand dealings of a financial and sexual nature. There were also issues around competency – for example, Britain was forced out of the European Exchange Rate Mechanism (ERM) – and this was seen across Europe as incompetence and a lack of ability to govern.

4 Ethnic diversity: according to Saggar and Heath (1999), strong support for New Labour came from those from ethnic minority backgrounds.

5 Gender: Norris (1999) identified the fact that the longstanding tradition of women being inherently more Conservative than men was overturned in the 1997 election; in particular, younger women were far more likely to vote Labour, and this was seen by Norris as a statement of refusal in the post-feminist generations to accept the politics of a party which, despite being led by a woman for the first time, had actually done far less than the Labour governments of the 1960s to break down the structural disadvantages still faced by women in key areas of social life in the 1990s.

Activity

Clause 1V(4) of the Labour Party constitution sets out the aims and values of the party. It was the focus of a major debate in the run-up to the party's landslide victory in 1997. In 1995, the original version adopted by the party in 1917 was changed.

Make a list of (a) the similarities and (b) the differences between the two statements:

Original version

To secure for the workers by hand or by brain the full fruits of their industry and the most equitable distribution thereof that may be possible upon the basis of the common ownership of the means of production, distribution and exchange, and the best obtainable system of popular administration and control of each industry or service

New Labour version

The Labour Party is a democratic socialist party. It believes that by the strength of our common endeavour we achieve more than we achieve alone, so as to create for each of us the means to realize our true potential and for all of us a community in which power, wealth and opportunity are in the hands of the many, not the few, where the rights we enjoy reflect the duties we owe, and where we live together, freely, in a spirit of solidarity, tolerance and respect.

The 2001 and 2005 elections

Labour continued its reign of success in 2001 and again in 2005 (although Labour's share of the vote dipped to less than 40 per cent for the first time since 1997).

How far has dealignment gone?

Crewe and Thompson (1999), using the British Election Survey (based on exit polls after each general election), suggested that the 1997 result had seen significant class realignment; however, there was also evidence of a significant increase in partisan dealignment – in other words, far fewer individuals strongly and permanently identifying with a particular political party. By 2005, just 49 per cent of people identified fairly strongly with one political party (down from 84 per cent in 1964).

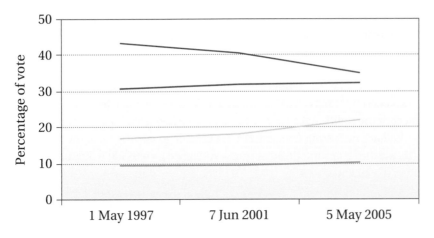
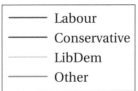

Figure 4.5 UK election results since Labour's 1997 win

Is class still a major influence?

Evans et al. (1999) found that the relationship between class and voting was less significant than in the past and attributed it largely to Labour's taking over the centre ground in terms of policies, rather than anything else. If ideological convergence is occurring, then future election results are hard to predict.

How important are policies?

Norris (2001) used opinion poll evidence from the 2001 election to conclude that Labour lost support among the unskilled working class, but increased in popularity with the lower middle class. She cited as the reason for this the Labour Party's pledge to improve public services, including health and education, but without raising taxes and otherwise managing the economy well.

In contemporary society, politics is much more issue-based. People are more likely to vote for the party whose policies will offer them the best deal on petrol prices, for example, rather than identifying with a particular party.

Social characteristics and voting

Age

Many sociologists have pointed towards the implications of Britain's ageing population on future election results. In 2003 there were 9.5 million people aged 65+, nearly as many as those aged under 16 (11.7 million). It is estimated that by 2013 the number of over-65s will exceed the number of those under 16, and there is a view that the elderly will carry increasing political weight, the so-called 'grey power'.

It is broadly the case that the older a person is, the more likely he or she is to vote – the over-55s generally manifest around a 75 per cent turnout compared to a 37 per cent turnout amongst the 18–24 age group. Amongst the over-65s there is generally more support for the Conservative Party, reflecting a more restrained view on issues of personal morality and freedom such as drugs, race relations, crime and sexual orientation, attitudes which sociologists such as Butler and Stokes (1974) suggest may be linked to a political socialization formed by age-generational experiences during their formative political years. They also suggest that the dominant political concerns of earlier years can leave a significant impression – for example, those reaching early adulthood during the Labour government's period of office in the 1950s may end up with a much more pro-Labour view than those reaching early adulthood during the Conservative-led 1980s. Additionally, amongst the young there have been tendencies among the white majority and within ethnic minority groups for involvement in more extremist political involvement, for example in racist politics such as the British National Party (BNP).

Amongst both the young and the old, though, there are significant differences which can have an influence on political orientations. For example, among the young there are divides between graduates and non-graduates, those in full-time employment, those more casually employed and the unemployed. Among the elderly, there are those on poverty state pensions all the way through to those who have taken early retirement on very comfortable occupational pensions. In other words, care must be taken when generalizing about the young and the old, and there are dangers in seeing either group as homogeneous or necessarily drawn together in terms of their political outlook. It is also the case that these groups are likely to be affected by the more general movement towards greater volatility in the electorate. It cannot necessarily be assumed that the increase in older voters and the decline in younger voters will equate with right-wing success in the future.

Gender

The view that women are inherently more conservative than men disappeared when Margaret Thatcher became Prime Minister in 1979. Women swung marginally back towards the Conservatives during John Major's leadership, but have been more pro-Labour than men ever since that time. On balance, it is suggested that women have been behind New Labour's successive election victories and that they are now remarkably similar to men in terms of their overall level of interest and involvement in politics, although they are still significantly under-represented at elite levels within political organizations and in parliament (Norris 1991).

Class

The issue of social class has been a major focus of research in voting behaviour especially throughout the post-war period. At the beginning of the twenty-first century, there are still many contentious and unresolved debates about both the nature of social class and its impact on politics. It is recognized that significant social inequalities exist in modern British society, with the poorest 50 per cent owning just 6 per cent of total marketable wealth (Social Trends 2005); the gulf between the rich and the poor remains and is more marked in Britain than in many other advanced industrial countries. Social class – traditionally linked to occupation and then subsequently to income, norms and values, and lifestyle – is still seen by many sociologists as crucial.

The concept of '**cleavages**' has also been developed, meaning that there is a distinction between different groups in society based, for example, on consumption. Those who rely almost exclusively on public services – for example, health, education and housing – are seen as more supportive of policies which link to higher public spending and better public services, while those who can pay for private health and education are more likely to opt for parties that seek to keep taxation to minimal levels. Changes in patterns of home ownership have been examined to see if there has been any related impact on patterns of voting and political involvement. This seems not to be the case, despite a 50 per cent decrease in council house occupation and a large increase in owner occupation. Initially, it led to increased support for the Conservatives, but this effect has now disappeared.

Cleavages occur when groups in society are distinguishable from each other by their different patterns of consumption.

Additionally, attempts to increase and broaden those who have a stake not just in property but also in stocks and shares were successful, for example, as a result of people buying shares in privatizing previously nationalized companies like British Gas, but in the longer term most individuals have very small, if any, share portfolios and any impact on political processes seems to have been minimal. Overall, it would seem that there is still some linkage of class position to voting potential, but the relationship no longer has any clear polarities and consequences.

Region

Region continues to play a degree of significance in the shaping of political issues and identities. Although the UK is made up of four distinctive countries – England, Scotland, Wales and Northern Ireland – even within these countries there are marked differences in life chances and lifestyles which may suggest an impact on political allegiances and political issues. For example, levels of income per head in Wales and Northern Ireland are generally lower than average income levels overall, and in England, the south remains far more affluent than the north – leading to the so-called north–south divide. However, in the north there are pockets of great affluence and in the south areas of significant social deprivation. Issues of gender, ethnicity and age all make the picture more complex still. Overall, it is still the case that the majority of Labour's support comes from the industrial north of England, central Scotland and South Wales, while the Conservatives dominate the south of England, and especially the south-east. Constituencies in the industrial Midlands are particularly hotly contested and marginal.

Politics and voting habits vary greatly amongst different communities. For example, the voice of Britain's Muslim communities is growing, as seen, for example, in the widespread protests against the publication of cartoons of the Prophet Mohammad which were offensive to many Muslims. People living in rural areas are often very supportive of foxhunting, which is a traditional activity and provides a large income for the countryside. National identity is on the rise in Scotland and Wales, and certain measures for self-government have already been brought in.

The underpinning rationale for these patterns has traditionally been linked with the greater preponderance of social and economic deprivation in the areas of Labour support. However, in Northern Ireland, Scotland and Wales, the politics of identity and cultural factors have always been the dominant influence. This is particularly the case in Northern Ireland, where the majority are Protestants (72 per cent in 1999) who see themselves as British and only 2 per cent see themselves as Irish, whereas among the minority Catholic population only 9 per cent think of themselves as British. This translates into direct support for specific parties, clearly pro- or anti-republican. Similarly in Scotland, some 30 per cent see themselves as Scottish more than as British, which broadly reflects the proportion of the population voting for the pro-independence Scottish National Party in Scottish Parliament elections.

Finally, it is argued that there are still perceived differences between 'town' and 'country', with especially those identifying themselves as 'country' ascribing great importance to a small but significant range of political issues, such as those represented by the Countryside Alliance and the Council for the Protection of Rural England and consequently linked with more conservative ideologies.

Ethnicity

It is estimated that four to five million people in Britain belong to ethnic minority groups; those from Asian and African Caribbean backgrounds form the most significant ethnic minority groups, and reflect the period of immigration from the late 1950s to the early 1960s when there was free entry to citizens of the British Commonwealth until the tightening of restrictions from 1962 onwards.

Since that time, issues of racism and racial discrimination have affected the life chances of many groups and there are still widespread inequalities between ethnic groups. Although it is impossible to generalize about the structural position of ethnic minority groups overall, it would seem that the relative disadvantages faced have historically led to a greater sense of allegiance with the Labour Party.

However, as with other groupings within the electorate, more recent developments have led to a much greater degree of volatility. For example, after 11 September 2001 and even more significantly after 7 July 2005, prejudice and discrimination against some ethnic minorities were further complicated by Islamophobia. It is likely that ethnic divisions and tensions will have an increasing rather than a diminishing significance for British politics, both in terms of mainstream politics such as voting, representation and pressure group activity, and more seriously possibly in terms of riots and more violent protests.

Generally, older Muslims still maintain a more active involvement with the Labour Party. In 2005, five Muslim MPs were elected, doubling their level of representation in the House of Commons. Conversely though, amongst many younger Muslims there has been a growing sense of disenchantment with parliamentary politics, and opposition within Muslim communities about the decision to support the US invasion of Iraq in 2003 has introduced a new dimension into the political sphere, especially in areas where there are high numbers of Muslim voters.

For example, in 2005 Labour MP Ann Cryer was safely re-elected, having made her own anti-war sentiments clear, but Oona King, despite being a black daughter of an American civil rights leader, was defeated in Bethnal Green, having supported government policy in the war against Iraq. In Birmingham Ladywood, Clare Short had a huge swing against her even though she resigned from the Cabinet over the Iraq War. Overall, the changing patterns of ethnic minority voting could have a growing significance and their volatility makes prediction difficult.

Who participates and why?

Social class

Participation in political processes tends to be more predominant amongst the higher social classes. Individuals from more middle-class professional and managerial backgrounds are far more likely to have contacted their local councillors or MPs than those from more manual working-class backgrounds. This is seen as linked to higher levels of education, giving individuals the confidence to know who to contact and what to say to get their point across

Gender

There are still issues around the 'invisibility' of women in politics at both a local and national level. Legislation in France now requires political parties to put up equal numbers of male and female candidates in local, regional and European elections, and the proportion of women in local councils in France in 2001 increased hugely from 22 per cent to 48 per cent as a result. In the UK, employment law currently prevents positive action of this nature in politics. Some positive action in Wales and Scotland has led to greater proportions of female representatives in the Welsh Assembly and the Scottish Parliament. The Fawcett Society estimate that it will take until 2033 before women reach parity with men in the parliamentary Labour Party.

Futility/lack of impact

The 2005 Electoral Commission survey asked people if they felt that by participating in politics they could have an impact: 41 per cent disagreed, while only 36 per cent thought they could and the rest expressed no opinion. Also, although 67 per cent of people wanted to have a say in how the country was run, only 27 per cent really felt their views would be listened to.

Age

Henn et al. (2005) examined reasons why young people seem to be less involved in politics than older generations: they have less knowledge of politics and are less likely to vote. Only 37 per cent of 18–24-year-olds voted in the 2005 election, a fairly typical percentage. This seems to be the case despite major governmental attempts to engage young people in politics – through the compulsory introduction of the teaching of citizenship in schools, and politics being a key part of the government's strategy 'Every Child Matters'. A range of reasons has been suggested by Henn et al. for this apparent political apathy, including the following:

1 Single issues: young people are more concerned about single issues such as global warming and environmental pollution, so are more likely to join pressure groups and be part of new social movements rather than join mainstream political parties.
2 Lack of impact: young people feel that they had a very limited ability to influence political parties and government policies
3 Political alienation: young people feel cut off from the world of politics.

Politicians are seen as out of touch with young people, despite the fact that their concerns are very similar to those of adults – public services, the economy, law and order, war and so on. Somehow politicians are seen as not providing the right stimuli for young people to get engaged and involved in the issues they see as important; it is not simply a case of apathy.

Future elections

It is clear that structural changes in the economy and occupational structures did not result in Labour being unelectable, as was thought by some sociologists at the end of the 1980s. However, it does seem to be the case that there is much greater voter volatility and that issue politics are more prevalent, which makes the outcome of future elections much harder to predict. In addition, support for nationalist parties contributes to further diversity and unpredictability overall.

Political parties, pressure groups and new social movements

When examining issues concerning the nature and distribution of power in society, it is important to consider the role and functions of political parties and pressure groups. Additionally, sociologists have become interested in the apparent growth of new social movements (NSMs) on a wider scale and the ways in which the media impacts on political processes.

Political parties

Pluralists generally see political parties as functional and representative organizations because:

1   They need to get elected and to do so they must reflect the wishes and interests of the electorate.
2   If they don't reflect the wishes and interests of the electorate, new parties may emerge to take their place – such as 'Respect', the party formed by MP George Galloway to represent anti-war feelings in relation to the 2003 invasion of Iraq.
3   Parties are accountable to the electorate because they won't regain power if they disregard the opinions and interests of the public.
4   Parties cannot simply represent a sectional interest, they must have broader support within the electorate to survive longer-term e.g. Respect was a short-lived phenomenon.

In summary, pluralists are saying that political parties are important because they have to reflect the views of large groups of people; they are seen as the cornerstone of a democratic society.

Party ideologies

Politics is a fluid process, subject to constant change over time. The Conservative Party and the Labour Party represent the two main alternatives in Britain today as parties of government, due, in part, to the nature of the electoral system. However, the centre ground as represented by the Liberal Democrats and the significance of nationalist parties should also be taken into consideration.

The Conservative Party   Traditionally, the Conservative Party, as a right-wing party, has been closely linked to the middle class and to more affluent groups in society. Key ideologies include individualism, the free market, entrepreneurialism and a more paternalistic approach (in some cases) to social welfare. However, it is important to remember that conservative thinking has shifted over time. Conservative governments in the more immediate post-war period were committed to major social welfare reforms and state policies to bring about full employment, whereas in the 1980s the New Right ideology was influential in stressing a withdrawal of state intervention and the implementation of free market principles in many areas of social life. In more recent years, it has been suggested that there has been an ideological convergence between the Conservatives and Labour, made more apparent with the election of David Cameron as party leader in 2005.

The Labour Party   The Labour Party has its origins in the struggle for improved pay and conditions for the working class at the end of the Industrial Revolution. It has a left-wing ideology, very much connected with the history and origins of the trade union movement. Like the Conservatives, Labour ideology has shifted and changed over time. Post-war Labour governments keenly followed a socialist agenda, nationalizing a substantial number of key industries and focusing very much on centralized state controls. Social welfare has always been a major focus of concern, and issues of inequality and egalitarianism have been central to Labour policies overall. The biggest changes to the Labour Party were brought about during the 1990s, as the party modernized, calling itself New Labour, in order to occupy a more centre ground position.

Pressure groups

Pluralists also see pressure groups (also known as interest groups) as central in representing a broad cross-section of views and ensuring that power is distributed. Pressure groups do not aim to take power in the sense of forming a government; rather, they seek to influence political parties and various departments of state. They do not represent a wide range of interests; instead, they aim to represent a very specific interest in society.

Traditionally, it was thought that there were TWO main types of pressure group:

1   Promotional pressure groups: these support a particular cause, such as the RSPCA, Greenpeace and Fathers-4-Justice.
2   Protectional pressure groups: these aim to protect the interests of a particular social group such as trade unions and employers' associations.

Membership of promotional groups is generally larger and more varied and requires only a commitment to the particular cause as a reason for joining. Protectional membership is limited to individuals of a particular status, such as the Royal Society of Authors and Equity (for actors).

However, Wyn Grant (2000) made a further distinction between insider and outsider groups, which has a bearing on their potential impact. **Insider groups** are, in a sense, inside government – they are consulted by governments on a regular basis, with representatives often being called upon to sit on government committees and working groups. Examples include the National Farmers' Union, the RSPCA and the NSPCC. **Outsider groups** are those that generally operate outside the day-to-day machinery of governments. Examples include Fathers-4-Justice and OutRage!

It has also been traditionally thought that insider groups stood more of a chance of being successful in getting their point of view across, as they were closely connected to government. They are seen as credible, with political skills, able to participate in formal consultations with well-researched evidence. However, in more recent years it has been suggested that the more dramatic tactics of some outsider groups has led to enhanced power and influence. Additionally, some groups have both insider and outsider status, such as the Howard League for Penal Reform, which is frequently asked to participate in government-led discussions, but also campaigns on its own issues such as prison suicides and self-harm, which then sometimes leads back into government initiatives. Finally, some groups are outsiders by necessity; they have no choice but to be outside parliamentary processes because they are too small, for example, or because their strategies are seen as too radical (for example, Fathers-4-Justice). Other groups are outsiders by choice; they see themselves as too radical to be fettered by parliamentary constraints and value their autonomy too highly (for example, the gay rights group OutRage!, of which six members invaded the Archbishop of Canterbury's pulpit on Easter Sunday 1998, accusing him of discriminating against homosexuals).

Insider groups are pressure groups which have an active relationship with governments, offering representatives opportunities to sit on government committees or act as consultants for government policy.

Outsider groups are pressure groups which, for whatever reason, do not have everyday operational links with governments.

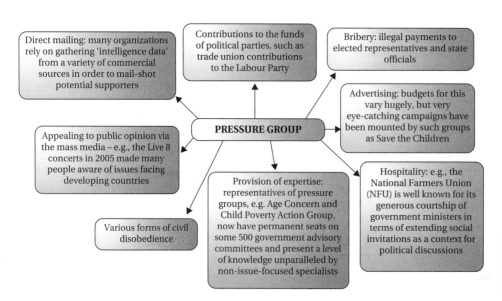

Figure 4.6 How do pressure groups bring pressure to bear?

How can pressure groups mobilize public opinion?

Pressure groups provide the means through which the public can make their own views known to a governing party. They generally support individuals and groups in terms of strategies for increased publicity for their particular issues. Typically, pressure groups present comprehensive website information on their aims and intentions and access to further information to substantiate the reason for their campaigning. Various lobbying strategies, such as email campaigns to MPs, are frequently facilitated through these websites. Links to further sources of information are presented and also to other related pressure groups. Funds are raised as individuals subscribe to pressure groups, allowing the organizations to develop further campaigning strategies.

> ### Activity
>
> Using the Internet, search for and identify THREE pressure groups: two promotional and one protectional.
>
> In each case, identify the aims of the group and list the strategies they have used/are using to promote their issue(s).

In summary, pressure groups are seen as central to pluralist arguments as their very existence indicates the representation of a wide range of viewpoints in society; their campaigns illustrate the political process as being dynamic and changeable, with opportunities for diverse concerns to be debated and pursued. Indeed, it has been suggested that pressure group activity has been broadened into the activities of new social movements which represent an even wider range of issues and positions for public consumption.

New social movements

New social movements (NSMs) are much looser informal and less organized coalitions of groups or individuals pushing a cause or broad interest than the more traditional pressure groups, which are generally more focused and structured. They are often global in scope and scale. Examples include the women's movement, the green movement and the anti-war movement

Some sociologists have suggested that the forms of political participation have changed and that the decline in party political activity has been replaced by increased involvement in issue-based politics via the membership and activism associated with **new social movements** (NSMs). These are essentially groups that have emerged since the 1960s, and which have generally sought to challenge the status quo in some way or another, usually by focusing on one particular issue or broad range of connected issues. Examples include the environmental movement, feminism, gay rights, anti-war movements, etc. It is suggested that there has been a move away from more formally organized pressure groups to loosely linked campaigns, where a variety of individuals/groupings may be involved at any one time, and that these movements frequently transcend national boundaries in the sense that they frequently have a global context.

Giddens (1994) argues that there have been some changes in the nature and frequency of political participation as a result of the development of these NSMs; other sociologists such as Callinicos (2003) and Klein (2000) suggest that more powerful changes are at work and that there has been much more of a transformation in the

New social movements, which are concerned with campaigning for issues such as the environment and human rights, are a very popular form of political involvement amongst young people.

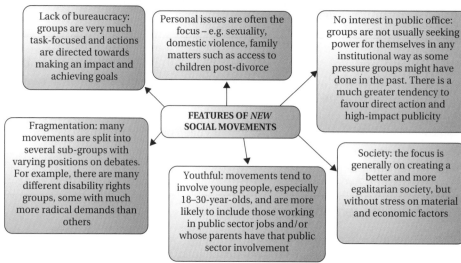

Figure 4.7 Unique features of new social movements as opposed to established pressure groups

Lack of bureaucracy: groups are very much task-focused and actions are directed towards making an impact and achieving goals

Personal issues are often the focus – e.g. sexuality, domestic violence, family matters such as access to children post-divorce

No interest in public office: groups are not usually seeking power for themselves in any institutional way as some pressure groups might have done in the past. There is a much greater tendency to favour direct action and high-impact publicity

FEATURES OF *NEW* SOCIAL MOVEMENTS

Fragmentation: many movements are split into several sub-groups with varying positions on debates. For example, there are many different disability rights groups, some with much more radical demands than others

Youthful: movements tend to involve young people, especially 18–30-year-olds, and are more likely to include those working in public sector jobs and/or whose parents have that public sector involvement

Society: the focus is generally on creating a better and more egalitarian society, but without stress on material and economic factors

way citizens participate and seek to activate change. There is also a major debate about the effectiveness of the ways in which these movements seek influence and the extent to which these groups have impacted on political processes.

Many NSMs are based around two types of campaign:

1 Defending the natural and/or social environment – for example, animal rights and environmental campaigning.
2 Improving the social position of marginal groups – for example, gays and lesbians, and disabled people.

Hallsworth (1994) suggests that an underpinning principle seems to be an anti-materialist stance – involving **post-materialist** values – and links this to the idea that fundamental issues such as widespread poverty have already been tackled and it is more specific issues that are now attracting societal concern.

Post-materialism is the theory that the need to acquire material goods is declining in importance as people give higher priority to non-material values, such as freedom, justice and personal improvement.

Cohen and Rai (2000), however, argue that there is no real difference between old-style pressure groups and so-called new social movements, apart from the way they use technology such as websites, text-messaging and advertising to get their message across, and that they are more global in nature

High modernity

Giddens argues that social movements have developed in line with certain key characteristics of society which he identifies as existing in high modernity; he describes this as a late state of **modernity** rather than as a new and separate stage of societal development. Giddens links these key characteristics with specific types of NSMs.

Giddens adopts an interesting and measured approach, stressing the way in which some aspects of NSMs are in response to societal changes, while others are simply a development and modification of movements that had their origins in the earlier

Modernity describes the condition of society from the Enlightenment of the seventeenth century to the middle of the twentieth century. It includes a rational outlook on social issues and highlights the role of science as a basis for understanding.

Table 4.4: Links between late modern values and NSMs

Key characteristic of late modernity	Linked social movement
CAPITALISM – private ownership of the means of production and concentration of wealth in the hands of a minority.	LABOUR MOVEMENTS – these still exist to try and control the workplace and defend workers' interests collectively, although their power has declined relative to their role in early modernity, and other movements have emerged.
INDUSTRIALISM – concerned with the mass production of material goods and consumption.	ECOLOGICAL/GREEN MOVEMENTS – concerned with the impact of uncontrolled industrialism; they existed in early modernity but their prominence has rapidly developed in response to major environmental concerns such as damage to the ozone layer and the severe implications of global warming.
SURVEILLANCE – the monitoring of populations in multidimensional ways from CCTV to ID cards.	HUMAN RIGHTS/FREEDOM MOVEMENTS – linked with safeguarding existing rights to freedom of speech, freedom of movement, political participation and also campaigning for greater transparency in terms of state activities where technology has given governments a hugely enhanced repertoire of strategies.
MILITARY POWER – the use of the police, the army and other forces.	PEACE MOVEMENTS – concerned with the development of the potentially hugely high consequences of war in a late modern society where technological warfare including nuclear weapons remain an ever-present threat.

phase of modernity. In other words, there is continuity underpinning change and a steady evolution of social movements linked to changing circumstances.

The anti-capitalist movement

Callinicos argues that significant changes have taken place in the way in which people are actively involved in political processes. In particular, he charts the development of what he refers to as the **anti-capitalist movement**, which is defined not as one single group, but as the collectivity of a wide range of groups, united overall in their stand against the capitalist system and its related exploitative and inequality-generating activities, and within the context of global economic structures. It is concerned with issues that affect workers throughout the world and the way in which those issues are often linked. Major examples of the activities of the anti-capitalist movement include the demonstrations in Seattle in 1999, when 40,000 protestors focused on a meeting of the World Trade Organization (WTO), and in Genoa in 2001 at the G8 Summit (a meeting of the eight leading capitalist countries).

> The **anti-capitalist movement** consists of a collectivity of a wide range of groups, united in their stand against the social inequality and exploitation fostered by capitalism.

Reasons for the emergence of the anti-capitalist movement

1   *The spread of capitalism.* During the 1990s, communism in the Soviet Union and Eastern Europe largely collapsed and social scientists such as Fukuyama (1992) talked about the 'end of history', suggesting that there were no ideological debates anymore and that there was an unquestioning acceptance that there was only one economic system – capitalism. Even attempts by sociologists and politicians to suggest that there was a 'third way', a compromise between the structures of planned economies and the freedom of market economies, hadn't really gathered support or led to any diminution of inequalities. The anti-capitalist movement is seen by Callinicos as, in part, a reaction to this ideological cul-de-sac, and he cites events such as the Seattle Protests of 1999 as a turning point, when many thousands of mainly young people took to the streets to protest about poverty, inequality and social justice.

2   *Globalization.* Many anti-capitalist groups have gained strength from the coming together of organizations on a global scale. For example, Amnesty International and Greenpeace have operated across international borders and have drawn support from individuals and groups across many countries. This sense of global connectedness and power, Callinicos argues, has sustained and engendered further political activity. Many of the campaigns link one country's anti-capitalist fight with another – for example, campaigns to cancel third world debt.

3   *Expansion of East Asian economies.* There was a growing awareness that countries such as China were developing their industrial bases with a rapidity that threatened to dominate world markets in a very much less regulated way.

Overall, it is suggested that significant numbers of individuals and groups have no longer been content to stand to one side and let the free market take an unchallenged and unfettered role in global domination. This has been paralleled by a degree of grassroots protest directed at the power of transnational corporations.

Branding

Klein (2000) has been very critical of the ways in which transnational corporations such as Nike and Coca-Cola operate, and her writings have further inspired people to join the various anti-capitalist groups and participate in campaigns. Her basic argument is that, since the 1940s, companies began to recognize that they could sell more of their products via branding – in other words, establishing their own recognizable brand, rather than any specific product itself. Consequently, companies like Coca-Cola began to invest heavily in marketing and promoting Coca-Cola as a globally desirable brand, even though there is little difference between the taste of one cola and the next.

In the 1980s, this was further expanded upon with the concept of logos, in the sense that, once the logo had been established, it could go on any product and give that product desirability in terms of quality and saleability. For example, in the 1980s Burberry as a brand was a little-known label, mainly used for expensive raincoats for the upper-middle classes. By the 1990s, its distinctive logo and patterns were on everything from prams to baby carriers to the baseball caps and belts of mass consumers. The Nike label is now widespread – a 'superbrand' with the potential for mass market saturation.

Companies establish their brand in a variety of ways:

1 Advertising: companies are willing to spend unlimited sums on marketing and advertising. For example, Nike's advertising bill grew from $50 million in 1987 to $500 million in 1997.
2 Sponsorship: when advertising in conventional ways has been used to excess, sponsorship often takes over, such as the Reebok stadium in Manchester and the Ricoh stadium in Coventry.
3 Incorporating and neutralizing challenges: when street styles show any sign of taking over, these changes are taken on and sold back – for example, Gap selling jeans that fit low on the hips; and when alternative ideologies begin to appeal – for example, via music, when that music is used in TV ads.
4 Obliterating the opposition: when people still express support for the individual rather than mass corporate products, aggressive policies of expansion have been undertaken.
5 Censorship: companies take a very aggressive view, Klein maintains, when their authority is challenged. For example, McDonald's have prosecuted even very small groups that use their name, or even a variation on it.

Culture jamming – subverting the messages transmitted by large corporations about the desirability of their brand.

Klein identifies the phenomenon of **culture jamming**, meaning that the messages pumped out by these large corporations have been subverted by direct action. For example, the Nike tick has been renamed by some as the 'swooshtika' – a negative connotation with the swastika that links it with excessive power and control and exploitation of labour in developing countries. Campaigns have been mounted to make people aware of the way in which logos are used relentlessly in the pursuit of profit by large corporations and that the presence of a logo says little about quality and a lot a more about successful marketing and money-making.

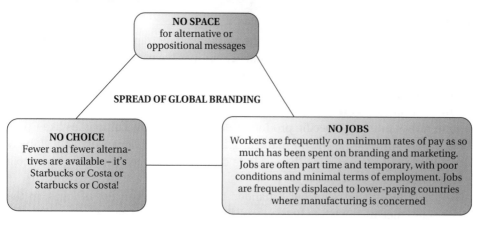

Figure 4.8
The three consequences of global branding

Evaluation

1 Limited impact of culture jamming: although this might alert some individuals and groups to the power of transnational corporations (TNCs) linked to branding, it is unlikely to impact significantly on their profits or behaviour.
2 Other companies benefit from culture jamming: although one company may lose business as a result of negative publicity, another expanding company may simply benefit. For example, don't buy Nike, just buy Adidas instead.
3 Other non-branding companies are free: manufacturing companies that may be equally exploitative in their use of labour and business activities are no longer in the public eye.
4 Subjectivity: Klein is actively involved in the 'No Logo' movement and adopts an anti-capitalist stance. She has therefore been accused of exaggerating the potential power and impact of the movement.

Klein argues that there is now a much higher awareness of the activities of TNCs and of the impact of branding, and a considerable following of individuals and groups whose consumer behaviour has been enlightened. Large companies know that, even if they don't change their behaviour, they are under scrutiny and that bad publicity on an organized global scale could result if ethical working practices are not pursued.

Michael Hardt and Antonio Negri (2004) suggest that a 'plurality of resistance' (citing Foucault) is the only practical way for people to get their voices heard. They argue that it is no longer possible for there to be organized groups and movements with established leaders and that there has been the spontaneous emergence of self-organized networks of resistance. The complex and diverse nature of societies and their location within a global context generates a multitude of issues that stimulate the growth of broad networks of political activism, which frequently span international boundaries. Oxfam International believes that a global citizens' movement, rooted in social and economic justice, is emerging and is necessary for ending global poverty.

In *The Shock Doctrine: The Rise of Disaster Capitalism*, Klein sees corporatist states as having enormous powers to bring significant benefits to global capitalism. She suggests that a key role of governments in any given country is 'to act as a conveyor belt for getting public money into private hands'. She argues that major private corporations profiteer from 'shocks', or the aftermath of catastrophic events, to embed the capitalist system and the principles of the free market still further. As examples, Klein quotes the aftermath of Hurricane Katrina in New Orleans in 2005, when the Bush administration refused to use emergency funds to pay public sector workers, and instead awarded contracts to private companies; and the post-war situation in Iraq, which became an immediate magnet for Western investment with the opening up of large new markets and the opportunities generated by Iraq's rich oilfields. In short, Klein is suggesting that major private corporations have huge global powers and frequently benefit massively from what would seem to be more random catastrophic events.

In summary, individuals and groups can use political parties and pressure groups as vehicles through which to push and express their concerns. Increasingly, it is NSMs that coordinate these issues on a global scale, and protest is rarely confined to one particular locality. The extent to which such organizations and groups can be used to impact on the distribution of power in society varies significantly from time to time and issue to issue.

The role of the media

Many sociologists stress the significance of the media and its impact on public opinion and power structures. However, the relationship between politics and the media is increasingly diverse and complex. The study of the links between politics and the media obviously includes far more than simply radio, newspapers and television, and the issues and debates go a long way beyond simply studying media coverage of elections; the broadest of day-to-day political issues and events are under minute and constant scrutiny by cable, satellite and digital television – and especially via the Internet (the 'new media').

Increasingly, this communication is interactive and multi-directional, enabling a much wider expression of views and positions in a global context. While many sociologists stress the power and influence of the media on their audiences, others have pointed to the fact that messages are often received by different individuals and groups in a variety of ways. For example, postmodernists generally see media messages as **polysemic**, meaning that they can be interpreted in different ways by different individuals.

Polysemic – used to describe a sign (such as a media message, picture or headline) which can be interpreted in different ways by different people.

Pluralist views on politics and the media

Pluralists generally argue that events are presented in the media in a way that fairly reflects reality on the whole. Society is seen as consisting of many different groups with diverse interests and it is suggested that:

- a plurality of interests is reflected in the media – for example, Labour, Conservative, Liberal-Democrat, Welsh Nationalists and new political movements;

Interpretations of media output varies greatly depending upon where in the world the media message is received.

- the media operate in the public interest and the general public expect and demand that a variety of viewpoints are covered;
- the media reflect what people think in equal measure and follow rather than create public opinion.

The role of the media in the political process is thus seen as reflecting a range of different points of view, in proportion to the support those viewpoints generally have within the community. For example, concerns are routinely expressed in the media about Britain's relationship with the European Union (EU), with issues raised concerning immigration and asylum-seekers and law and order. Pluralists would suggest that reporting on these matters reflects a widely held consensus that these are key issues. Additionally, in Britain, the BBC has a statutory obligation to report political matters in a broad and balanced way. The expectation is that radio and television are neutral in their presentation of events; no such restrictions apply to the press.

Media and politics since 1997

In the run-up to the 1997 general election it was argued that the Labour Party capitalized on the disenchantment of the British press with the Conservative Party. Relationships between John Major's government and the media were seen to have deteriorated as a result of negative reporting of his government's ability to manage economic affairs – for example the coverage of Black Wednesday in 1992, when the pound was forced out of the European Exchange Rate Mechanism by intense financial speculation. New Labour, under the leadership of Tony Blair, saw management of the media as crucial in securing an election victory and he worked tirelessly to build relationships with the press and other media outlets, to the extent that, by the 1997 election, six out of ten of the national daily newspapers were pro-Labour, compared to three out of eleven in 1991 (Harrop and Scammell 1997)

Curran (2005) suggests four main reasons for this transformation in support:

1   Ideological convergence: as Labour Party policies moved more to the centre ground, this more closely reflected the views of newspaper proprietors and editors. Pluralists could also argue that the shift in ideology reflected the views of the electorate more closely, so the newspapers fell in line with the changing mood.
2   Courtship: New Labour was keen to win the support of Rupert Murdoch's News International, which owns the *Sun*, *The Times* and newspapers in many other Western countries, and has interests in radio, cinema, books and satellite and digital television. Until the 1997 election, the *Sun*, with a circulation of around 3.5 million (the best-selling British daily newspaper), was pro-Conservative. Blair himself spoke to senior executives during the election campaign. There was speculation that no tough cross-media ownership laws would be introduced should Labour win the 1997 election. In 1997, the *Sun* firmly switched allegiance from Conservative to Labour and its very direct support has been seen as a critical factor in the success of New Labour.
3   Construction: the Labour Party devoted time, resources and the skills of highly qualified and experienced media personnel throughout the 1997 election campaign to present carefully constructed items for easy media consumption, presenting positive images of themselves and 'newsworthy' personalized criticism of the Conservatives.
4   Reflection: as support for New Labour grew, newspapers and other media, in line with the pluralist model, increasingly reflected the party's ideology as a way of ensuring maximum consumption. Newspapers, for example, could be seen to be giving people what they wanted, circulations were maintained and profits were secured.

Marxist views on politics and the media

Marxists see patterns of ownership and control as linked to media content. From a traditional Marxist point of view, because the ruling class own the means of production and have economic power, this translates into power within the institutions of the superstructure of which the media is an important part. In particular, the ruling class owners and controllers of the media are seen as having tangible power in key political processes.

For example, it is generally agreed that Rupert Murdoch himself was instrumental in changing the political direction of the *Sun* to become pro-Labour, and while pluralists might argue that this simply reflected changing public opinion and a huge groundswell of support for Tony Blair and New Labour, for Marxists it could be seen as an example of how the power of individual newspaper proprietors can have a major impact on political events.

Neo-Marxist views on politics and the media

Neo-Marxists put less emphasis on the direct impact of newspaper proprietors and more focus on the almost automatic way in which the media in a capitalist society reflect the interest of the ruling class. It is argued that the dominance of ruling-class culture or cultural hegemony has a powerful influence on the media. For example, during the 1970s and 1980s, the Glasgow University Media Group (GUMG) documented the way in which industrial disputes were generally portrayed very negatively and how there was an underlying assumption that such behaviour was unacceptable and not in the public interest.

The GUMG subsequently examined the coverage of foreign affairs in television news in *News from Israel* (2004), using both content analysis of coverage and panel discussions with an 800-person sample audience. The group concluded that there was a definite bias towards Israeli perspectives, especially on BBC 1, where Israeli leaders were twice as likely to be interviewed as Palestinians; that there was more stress on Israeli casualties (although more Palestinians were killed); and that the language used was partisan – for example, Palestinians planting bombs were 'terrorists', whereas Israelis were simply 'vigilantes' or 'extremists'. It could be suggested that this bias in reporting arises from ruling-class views being automatically reflected and represented, thus reinforcing the existing social order.

Role and influence of the media: audience responses

Many sociologists have stressed that it is important to look not only at media output but also at possible audience responses to media coverage of political issues.

The hypodermic model

The hypodermic model suggests that media messages are almost intravenously injected into audiences, almost to the extent that they can have a narcotic and hypnotic effect on audiences.

Ivor Crewe (1986) suggested that the media has become increasingly important because changes in the employment base have led to geographical and social mobility, the development of new social classes, embourgeoisement and the growth of instrumentalism. Consequently, natural identifiers with political parties are now few, partisan dealignment has occurred, and elections are more likely to be decided by issues presented by the media.

All the major political parties are very conscious of the impact of the media and, in particular, after the 1997 election, the Labour Party made some key changes to the relationship between politics and the media because of the perceived high impact of the media on political attitudes within the electorate:

1   *Centralization*: central control was exercised by the Prime Minister's press secretary (for many years, the very powerful Alastair Campbell) who had to agree all interviews and events.

2 *Professionalization*: – many ex-journalists were employed, from *The Times* and the *Daily Mirror*, for example, to ensure the media got what they wanted and in the format they needed it.

3 *Politicization*: the power of long-standing civil servants to present news was reduced and special advisers who were much more partisan – pro-Labour at this time – were located in a number of government departments to deal with the media.

These changes all indicate that the media is seen by politicians as instrumental in the maintenance of public support for government actions. It is seen as a powerful tool.

The normative/two step flow model

Katz and Lazarsfeld (1955) suggested that the media did not generally have a hypnotic effect but, rather, that after the 'first step', after the message had reached a member of the audience, there is a 'second step' involving social interaction, when the views of respected opinion leaders are sought. In other words, people want further insights from others concerning what they have read/heard/seen and that, as a consequence, political messages may be accepted or rejected as a result of this dialogue.

For example, in recent years politicians have increasingly appeared on various audience-participation programmes, which serve not only as the first step, but also as the second step, when the views of others, often respected opinion leaders, are also heard. In early 2003, Tony Blair appeared on a number of such programmes to argue the case for military intervention in Iraq; he was often subject to very hostile questioning from the public and at times seemed visibly shaken by the experience. Clearly, with such complex and important issues, audiences would be unlikely simply to accept one view. Opinions are shaped and formed by more complex processes of social interaction.

The uses and gratifications model

McQuail (1972) suggested that people use media for different purposes and that, consequently, media messages or intentions do not always have the resonance intended. He suggests four likely uses:

- diversion or escape;
- developing personal relationships, e.g. with characters in programmes;
- identity: developing a sense of self drawing on specific media output;
- surveillance: finding out what is happening in a wider context.

These uses may vary according to class, gender, age and ethnicity. It would suggest that the role of the media in the political process would need to address at least one or more of these needs in order to be successful. For example, politicians have increasingly participated in chat show programmes, which people often watch as diversion or entertainment; they are anticipating a more personal and intimate relationship with the individual on the couch and are maybe looking for points of connection with that individual and their own lives, while finally keeping on top of current affairs and issues. Such programmes have increasingly become part of the role of the media in the political process.

The mediatization of Blair's leadership, 1997–2007   The media image of the party leader is seen by many to be of crucial importance in determining party fortunes, and this personalizing of issues to satisfy people's needs for diversion and to generate notions of more personal relationships has become widespread. Tony Blair, as Prime Minister, was generally considered to be well aware of all of these issues. He was regarded as having polished telegenic and rhetorical skills, and took seriously the need to satisfy the media. The resulting image that was generated by the media had many dimensions, perhaps the two most important of which were 'decisive political leader' and 'everyday family man'. Blair was keen to be regarded as 'tough', on law and order, for example, but also 'caring' on issues such as education and health. A big stress was placed on his personal integrity and, consequently, in the aftermath of the invasion of Iraq, when serious questions were being asked about the evidence for going to war in the first place, his public image became seriously under attack. The invasion of Iraq was possibly the single most controversial issue of Blair's leadership.

The interpretive model

In *The Effects of Television* (1970), Halloran suggests that we should not ask 'what the media do to people' but 'what people do with the media'. Different levels of media literacy will influence the extent to which individuals can filter media messages – but to greater or lesser degrees. It is argued that people receive media messages in a selective way, ignoring, reacting to, forgetting or reinterpreting them according to their own viewpoints. For example, a divorced father, struggling to reach a contact agreement to see his children, will take note of a Fathers-4-Justice protest on the television and possibly view the actions of the group as legitimate and appropriate. Conversely, individuals who have never had to deal with such issues may only be aware of the news item as a protest and an unnecessary outburst which undermines the social order. In essence, news output may be one issue, but news receivership is another; it cannot always be guaranteed that dramatic tactics will have dramatic results. The relationship between media output and influence is a complex and uncertain one.

The postmodernist model

Baudrillard (1988) points out that, rather than being interpreted in one way by a passive audience, media messages are read in very different ways by different portions of the audience or by the same people at different times. Individuals are seen as creating their own set of values and understandings within a condition of **hyperreality** as they are bombarded with such a weight of information that it becomes open to multiple, shifting interpretations.

For example, the general public was not present at the US-led invasion of Iraq in 2003, so they were not able at any tangible level to assess the nature of the conflict. However, it is likely that the majority of individuals would have a view on whether the invasion was a success, and if the troops were acting in an acceptable way in relation to the treatment of civilians. This is an entirely constructed view, a consequence of a barrage of media coverage of this theme (often at the expense of accurate detail) over

Hyperreality is the idea that, as a result of the spread of electronic communication, there is no longer a separate 'reality' to which news coverage, for example, refers. Instead, what we take to be 'reality' is created for us by such communication itself.

many months in the press and on television. Baudrillard would say that the public had no opinions on or knowledge of the war itself; all they knew about the war was being shown on television and written about in newspapers.

Lloyd (2004) suggests that there has been a 'dumbing down' of political coverage in the last decade or so, which has led to raised levels of disenchantment with politicians and a greater reluctance within the population to engage with political processes. The quality and quantity of serious political coverage has been seen to have been reduced, to be replaced by gossip and scandal about politicians and their personal lives, and 'sound bites' – memorable sentences or phrases plucked out of context. Coverage is seen as partial and fragmented and it is left to individuals to make sense of the barrage of mini-messages that surround them.

Political advertising

In the US it is possible for political parties and pressure groups to buy airtime for political advertising and 35–60-second adverts are frequently shown across all channels. In the UK, direct political advertising is constrained to party political broadcasts, which mainly appear in the run-up to general elections. How much time individual parties get depends on the number of candidates they have standing for election and the number of votes secured in previous elections. This means that party political broadcasts are tools that only the main parties have access to, although the British National Party (BNP) qualified for the first time in 2005. In the past, party political broadcasts would be presented on all channels simultaneously and form a focus for a degree of public debate; increasingly, with the plethora of channels available via digital and satellite TV and the power of the remote control, the potential of such a strategy remains questionable.

Too professional?

In recent years, the increasing attention paid to the media by politicians has become a focus of scrutiny and criticism. In particular, the public gradually became aware of the growing number of media professionals involved in day-to-day news management on behalf of New Labour, and the term **spin doctor** became widely used to mean someone who tries to forestall negative publicity by publicizing a favourable interpretation of events.

In the early days of the 1990s, New Labour was relatively successful in deflecting criticism despite difficult issues – for example, MPs' financial misdeeds and extra-marital relationships. As time went by, however, the competitive striving for 'newsworthiness' by the media linked to personalities challenged even experienced spin doctors. A significant point was reached in the aftermath of the events of 11 September 2001, when it transpired that a press officer, Jo Moore, had sent an email to her superior describing it as 'a very good day to get out anything we want to bury'. She later issued a public apology, but the incident was seen by many as characterizing the cynical and manipulative approach to the use of the media. Overall, a high level of public awareness had developed concerning the mechanisms by which control over the news media had been sought.

'Spin doctor' is the label given to those who are seen as manipulating news coverage in such a way as to emphasize positive events, for the government, for example, and sideline negative news.

Invasion of Iraq

Conflict emerged between the government and the BBC in 2003 in the run-up to the invasion of Iraq. A BBC journalist accused the government of 'sexing up' the claim for war based on intelligence reports. The government strongly denied this and demanded resignations, but BBC bosses initially stood firm in support of their position. The subsequent suicide of a key adviser to the government and weapons inspector, David Kelly, led to further controversy, resulting in the setting up of an official inquiry. Ultimately, the Hutton Report backed the government and top BBC bosses resigned.

However, the focus on the government's relationship with the media stimulated further attempts to restore public confidence in the reporting of news and eventually the 2004 Phillis Report made recommendations – such as that there should be more direct communication by ministers rather than via government spokespersons – which were largely adopted, with the government's communications staff playing a less obtrusive role compared to the time when the Prime Minister's press secretary was a well-known public figure.

However, overall, the media were clearly seen as central to the continued success for the government.

New technology enables soldiers in war zones to have access to media coverage and to communicate with the rest of the world. How might this change the way in which war is reported and mediated?

Activity

For each war, identify the key characteristics of media coverage and consider the consequences of such coverage.

The Falklands War

In April 1982, Margaret Thatcher's Conservative government entered into a conflict with Argentina as a result of their invasion of the Falkland Islands, a small set of islands in the South Atlantic which had been under British rule and occupation since 1833. Throughout the war, media coverage was very carefully controlled and the absence of media technology meant that the public were dependent on government information. The remote location of the Falkland Islands meant that the news media were out of range of the satellite communications which existed at the time. Consequently, there were no television images of the war immediately available, and the small number of journalists and reporters who were allowed to go with the troops were only able to make use of controlled military communication systems.

The war itself came at a critical moment for Thatcher, as there had been a downturn in support for the Conservatives at that time and a general election was just around the corner. The war ended with an Argentinian defeat in June 1982.

The First Iraq War

During the first Iraq War (1990–1), the media were allowed into Iraq, but were mostly 'embedded' – in other words, they resided with the troops and were largely under the control of the military in terms of where they could go and what they could see and comment on. At first, formal briefings provided most of the information and journalists could only conduct interviews with military personnel in the presence of officers, and they were subject to censorship afterwards. About half way through the war, Iraq's government decided to allow live satellite transmissions and it became a heavily televised war. For the first time, people all over the world were able to watch live pictures of missiles hitting targets and fighters taking off from aircraft carriers. The American news channel CNN had 24-hour coverage of events as they happened, including the beginning of dramatic air strikes on Baghdad.

The Second Iraq War

Reporters in the war zone were once again embedded with the troops. New technologies facilitated much greater freedom of transmission of information. In particular, the extensive use of the Internet and websites on a global scale ensured that information was comprehensive and from all angles. Also, the troops themselves were sending out emails telling what things were like.

There were many anti-war protests in Western Europe prior to the invasion of Iraq in 2003, and although a majority of Americans had supported the action initially, as time wore on and no evidence of weapons of mass destruction was found, increasing numbers of them began to question the validity and success of the war.

Although the US and UK governments may have wished to exert maximum control over such a volatile event, they became increasingly unable to do this, as new technology facilitates the spread of information in a way that is very hard to control.

The future

The media clearly have a very important role in the political process. While pluralists inevitably see the media as reflecting fairly a multiplicity of viewpoints, Marxists stress the impact of patterns of ownership and control on media output, both directly and indirectly. However, other sociologists recognize that the relationship between politics and the media is a complex one, not least because of the diversity of the audience and the complexity of audience reactions.

Globalization

Many sociologists have argued that it no longer makes any sense to look at issues of the distribution of power in any one society without locating such issues within a global context. It is suggested that major changes have taken place which have effectively made the world into one huge interlinked economy, encompassing developed and developing nations, which has had a profound effect on power structures.

However, some sociologists have suggested that, despite the trend towards the internationalization of capital, an individual nation-state still exerts a major influence on the distribution of power within it own society.

Globalization is seen as having had several key effects; it has

- shifted the borders of economic transactions;
- expanded communications into global networks;
- fostered a new, widespread 'global culture';
- developed new forms of international governance;
- created a growing awareness of shared common world problems such as 'cyber-crimes', which are often spread across continents;
- created a growing sense of risk – related to new technologies and manufactured risks such as genetic engineering, terrorism and cloning;
- led to the emergence of 'transnational global actors', which network – groups that make the global their local: for example, Greenpeace.

The changing role and power of the state

Ohmae (1994) argues that the world increasingly consists of one huge economic system, linking developed and developing countries. He stresses the declining influence of the nation-state as a result, and points to certain key characteristics of the global economy:

1 Transnational corporations (TNCs) dominate the economic landscape, and, given the fast pace of economic growth in many parts of the world, are able to operate in many countries simultaneously.
2 Movement of trade: TNCs can easily move production and services to cheaper countries, which makes them very powerful.

3 Purchasing power: people are able to buy things from wherever they want because of improved communication – for example, using the Internet.

4 Corporate and consumer power: the ability to go beyond the nation-state can reduce the power of governments to completely control economies in the ways they may have done in the past.

In this state-centred theory, Ohmae is seeing the power of the nation-state as seriously in decline as a consequence of globalization. However, he has been criticized for overstating the way in which states have lost power. For example, governments still have control over imports from immediate economic neighbours and states still wield the more ultimate form of power – that is, control of their armed forces.

In contrast to Ohmae, Bonnett (1994) suggests a less exaggerated view of the impact of globalization. He does not see the nation-state as totally weakened by globalization, but identifies a range of changes and consequences:

1 Power is no longer held simply within nation-states. Bonnett sees power as extended across groups of nation-states, such as the European Union.

2 The extension of power across nation-states has weakened the power of the state within specific countries.

3 The weakening of power within countries has led to independence movements being able to gain momentum – for example, in the former Soviet Union.

4 States are under pressure both from outside their boundaries by internationalism and from within by nationalism.

In summary, Bonnett is saying that the distribution of power has changed; that nation-states are less powerful, which is related to globalization, and that nationalistic factions within countries have gained in power. For example, we now have a Scottish and a Welsh Assembly in the UK. It is almost as if the threat of a global merging of identity has meant that states have had to step back to recognize nationalistic identities in order to maintain control overall.

An individual's association with a national identity is clearly visible in worldwide sporting events. What consequences does this have for the power of nation-states in a global world?

The global and the local: is globalization really leading to major changes?

Hirst and Thompson (1999) suggest that most companies are still based in a specific home location with a largely domestic market; that states may have lost some power as a result of global factors, but they still retain key control over territory and people in the main; and that most individuals subscribe to a national identity which gives that nation-state some power over them.

Giddens (1990) concludes that although globalization might have led to some changes in the nature and distribution of power in society, not all state power has been lost.

Arguments for the loss of state power

1 *Global and local.* Giddens argues that there are global social relationships – for example, in terms of economic relationships – between countries that shape local events. For example, American ownership of Jaguar cars by Ford led to a decision to cease production in the UK (Coventry) in 2004, with the loss of more than 1,000 jobs, which was in turn linked to the weakness of the dollar against the pound, with most of the production being sold in the United States.

2 *Time–space distanciation.* Giddens suggest that as people no longer need to be physically with other people in order to interact with them, this very much opens up the global arena via the Internet, webcams and all forms of communication.

3 *Competition.* The better the communication with companies, the more competitors there are. Competition in business and financial markets has created a global economy.

4 *Nation-state power reduced.* Governments are forced to compete to gain inward investment, which ties their hands and reduces their power in certain contexts; for example, they cannot tax companies significantly higher than other similar countries would.

Arguments for the continued existence of state power

1 *Nationalism.* Governments can encourage people to retain and develop a cultural identity which may help them to retain some economic power. For example, the massive campaign to encourage people to defend and keep what they have and stave off competition, the development of strong regional government, the demand to consume local produce and the engendering of a desire to reduce their carbon footprint to the extent of holidaying 'at home'.

2 *Unity.* Governments can work together to stave off the power of TNCs. For example, ethical concerns have been raised many times about Nike's use of child labour in Vietnam – as exposed by *Panorama* in 2001.

The spread of liberal democracy and human rights

Many key political issues have now taken on a truly global focus. In particular, the issue of human rights is seen as central to a democratic world order. Klug (2001) outlines three main waves of human rights activity:

1   *Wave One* is seen as emanating from the late eighteenth century against a background of struggle for basic religious freedoms and restrains on state power. In both France and the United States, in particular, significant progress was made, which was ultimately encapsulated in the French 1789 Declaration of the Rights of Man and the 1776 US Declaration of Independence, both of which talked of 'inalienable rights' and focused on life and liberty.

2   *Wave Two* is seen as incorporating the development of the United Nations in the aftermath of the Second World War in the 1940s. International human rights treaties, enforced by international courts and monitoring bodies, are seen as central in safeguarding equality and dignity of citizens in a global context. The Universal Declaration for Human Rights (UDHR) remains a key focus, and 140 out of 190 states have so far officially subscribed to its main covenants.

3   *Wave Three* is the period from the end of the Cold War in the 1990s and towards the approach of the new millennium, when human rights issues on a global scale gathered further momentum, with a high degree of mutuality and collaborative working between countries in the development of their own 'human rights regimes'.

The Human Rights Act, 1998

This came into force in the UK on 2 October 2000 and was the first actually enforceable human rights law. It had its origins in the European Convention of Human Rights. All new legislation must fit in with these rights. The main rights include:

- right to life;
- freedom from torture, inhuman and degrading treatment;
- freedom from slavery;
- freedom from arbitrary arrest and detention;
- the right to a fair trial;
- freedom from retrospective penalties;
- right to privacy and family life;
- freedom of religion;
- freedom of expression;
- freedom of assembly and association;
- the right to marry and establish a family;
- prohibition of discrimination;
- restrictions on political activity of aliens;
- prohibition of abuse of rights.

The Act also stresses:

- the right to peaceful enjoyment of property;
- the right to education;
- the right to free elections;
- abolition of the death penalty;
- preservation of the death penalty in times of war.

Activity

Answer the following questions using the Amnesty and Liberty websites to help you:
- www.amnesty.org.uk
- www.liberty-human-rights.org.uk/

China

'By allowing Beijing to host the Games you will help the development of human rights.' – Liu Jingmin, Vice-President, Beijing 2008 Olympic Games Bid Committee, April 2001. Identify which of the articles of the UK's Human Rights Act do not seem to be being upheld in China.

United Kingdom

Identify and describe TWO cases where the Human Rights Act has not been complied with and what happened in each instance.

A graphic representation of a pro-Tibet protester's opinions on China's policy in Tibet. What human rights does this protest suggest are being denied Tibetans in China?

Global citizens

Albrow (1996) suggests that there is now a notion of 'global citizens' who are entitled to have a basic measure of control and freedom over their own lives, whatever the global context. In a sense, debates about power over individuals and groups have transcended national boundaries and human rights are seen as a global concern to be dealt with on an international basis.

Global problems

The international drugs trade

In a global context, it is much more difficult for governments to control trade and this especially includes largely illegal drug-trafficking. Drugs are big business. The UN estimates that there are more than 50 million regular users of heroin, cocaine and synthetic drugs like Ecstasy worldwide. It is thought that the global illegal trade could be worth as much as $400 billion per year, almost as much as the international tourist trade, creating employment for tens of thousands of people both legally and illegally. It is possibly the world's largest 'industry'. Predominantly, the US and Europe provide the demand and the market, and the poorest countries supply.

The illegal drug trade is found all over the world – cocaine in Colombia and the Andes, opium and heroin from the South-East Asian Golden Triangle and all along the Mexican border, Turkey, the Balkans and Afghanistan and Central Asia. Drugs are produced, trafficked and consumed in most countries of the world – by many different nationalities and via many different places.

The end of the Cold War and consequent greater global economic freedom has facilitated the traffic. It is generally accepted that it is easier than ever before to move legal or illegal goods around the world. Heroin and opium produced in Afghanistan flows west through Iran or Central Asia into Turkey and Eastern Europe and on to markets in Britain, Holland and Germany. Cocaine produced in Peru moves east into Brazil, across the Atlantic to Nigeria, down to South Africa and northwards towards Europe. Even laboratory-produced synthetic drugs like Ecstasy are being trafficked out of Europe to parts of Africa and the Middle East.

Do governments have the power to curtail the international drugs trade? For years, governments and international organizations have sought to disrupt the movement of drugs between developing countries like Colombia and the lucrative markets in the West. These attempts have been relatively unsuccessful for a number of reasons:

1 Poverty: those who produce drugs are often located in some of the poorest countries in the world and producers frequently earn 20 times more than they would from poverty wages in a legitimate occupation. Consequently, individuals will take huge risks, even when governments clamp down on such activities, to maintain production. In Colombia, it is estimated that 20 per cent of the population depends on the production of cocaine for their livelihood and it outsells all other exports, including coffee.

2 War: countries like Afghanistan (which produces around 80 per cent of all opium on world markets) have been war-torn for many years, and so the focus has not been on the production of illegal drugs. Interestingly, under Taliban rule more effort was made to clamp down on opium production than after the US invasion. Since that time, Afghanistan's share of world opium production has risen from 76 per cent in 2003 to 86 per cent in 2004 (UN Office on Drugs and Crime 2005).

3 Lack of financial aid and personnel to police the marketing of drugs, especially since production generally takes place in countries with struggling economies: in the 1980s George Bush Senior provided Colombia with financial aid and military personnel to tackle the power of the well-known Medellin drugs cartel, which had acted more or less as a state within a state. After a year on the run, Pablo Escobar, the world's biggest cocaine boss, was arrested, but was still able to dictate the terms of his own imprisonment in luxury surroundings with his own personal bodyguards to protect him from those who were out to get him.

4 Culture: in many countries, such as Somalia, Jamaica and Colombia, it is suggested that there is no overt and firm boundary between legal and illegal business activity. Individuals and groups move between the worlds of politics, crime and business almost seamlessly, and this sustains and extends the illegitimate activity.

5 Global markets: if producers and traffickers find themselves under scrutiny in any one particular country, business simply moves elsewhere – as happened, for example, when the US moved into Colombia, and neighbouring Bolivia became the new focus of activity.

6 Impact of laws in other countries: again in a global context, laws in one country impact upon another. For example, the Netherlands has a very relaxed policy towards cannabis, but other countries argue that this simply encourages drug tourism and does not drive out the organized criminal networks which embrace international boundaries.

7 Marketing techniques: it has been known for illegal drug cartels to use sophisticated and carefully planned marketing techniques to develop consumer tastes. For example, in Puerto Rico in the 1990s, Colombian gangs tested out a new form of higher-quality heroin for the US market by giving out 'free' samples of it whenever they sold any cocaine. The product was successfully launched, but at the expense of many Puerto Ricans who had just been using cocaine and who then became heroin addicts. Colombian cartels are now the largest single supplier of heroin to the North American market.

The power of transnational corporations (TNCs)

Transnational corporations are dominant players in global affairs. Dicken (1992) argues that the TNC is the single most important force in the creation of a global economic system. He sees the era of nationally competing and separate economies as past history.

Hirst and Thompson (1999), however, argue that TNCs are not major threats to nation-states. They studied data on more than 500 TNCs from five countries in 1987 and compared activity with similar information on more than 5,000 TNCs in six countries for 1991–2. They were interested in the extent to which these companies were

Figure 4.9
Characteristics of TNCs

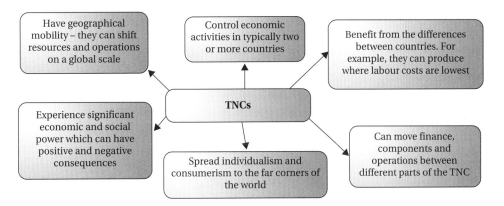

operating at an international and global level, while moving away from their home and host government. They ultimately concluded that TNCs still relied upon their home base as the hub of all their economic activities and that, although international links were clearly crucial, the activities of these TNCs had not moved beyond the parameters of the nation-state into a totally global economy.

Hirst and Thompson also identified constraining factors in the operation of TNCs:

● a preference for locations where they felt secure, with a good rapport with local culture and markets;
● plant and equipment and infrastructure are not always easily portable;
● employees face major disruption in permanent relocations and vital skill sets may be lost if they are unwilling and there may also be legal restrictions on citizenship.

However, there are two main criticisms of this view that TNCs are still located firmly within the parameters of nation-states and do not wield an inordinate amount of power over and above national governments:

1 Dunning (1993) argued that the largest TNCs (those with annual sales over $1,000 million) in 1989 produced one-third of their output outside their home countries. Whereas Hirst and Thompson would see this as evidence only for the existence of an international economy, Dunning sees it as growing evidence of a global system.
2 Lash and Urry (1994) argue that a distinction needs to be made between more knowledge-based industries and those with more of a manufacturing base. The former are pre-eminently more portable than the latter and can consequently possibly wield more power in relation to nation-states.

Overall, though, Hirst and Thomson are keen to stress that notions of TNCs being beyond the control of the nation-state need to be treated with care, as such arguments could be seen as a mandate for governments relinquishing attempts to control economic activity and just letting the principles of the free market take over. They stress that states should still deploy their existing power responsibly in the broadest context.

While there are many advantages for individual countries either to be the major base for a TNC or to be involved in the operations of a TNC, there are also many possible implications for national power structures.

1   Competition: local companies may have difficulty competing, as TNCs simply require labour and are likely to be in a position to pay more

2   Marketing power: TNCs are able to sustain initial losses in order to establish a brand in a particular locality which can then ultimately wipe out local products and livelihoods.

3   Bribery and corruption: local politicians may be bribed to cooperate with company plans and this can result in limited taxation revenue being collected and profits being exported.

4   Consumption patterns: TNCs have the power to change consumption patterns to generate profit, often with negative consequences for individual consumers. For example, the Inuit, indigenous Canadian people, had survived on a very healthy diet of fresh meat and berries for many thousands of years, roaming over an area the size of France in the process, but pressures for integration into mainstream society led to the extensive marketing of processed foods and alcohol within Inuit communities, leading to many related health and social problems.

Activity

Using the website www.tobaccofreekids.org, make a list of campaigns around the world that are working to reduce the use of tobacco.

The case of tobacco

From 1900 to 1975, the smoking of cigarettes increased in Western countries. However, from the mid-1970s a growing recognition of the link between cigarettes and diseases such as lung cancer and heart disease led to a marked decline. Gradually, Western governments, faced with pressure both from the general public and economic pressures related to dealing with the effects of smoking on health, progressively restricted tobacco advertising and increased the severity of warnings on cigarette packets, and many Western countries now outlaw smoking in all public places.

However, faced with such a marked decline, large cigarette TNCs simply turned their attention to alternative markets, especially South-East Asia and China. Around 70 per cent of Chinese males now smoke, compared to around 35 per cent in the West. From the mid-1980s, US manufacturers, led by Philip Morris, manufacturers of the famous Marlborough brand, put pressure on China and other Asian countries to remove trade restrictions on the importation of Western tobacco products or face import duties on their products (Godrej 2004). Indeed, faced with barriers to legitimate trade, British American Tobacco, the second biggest tobacco TNC, avoided this stand-off by establishing a secret factory in partnership with the government in communist North Korea. All this economic pressure is paralleled by intensive marketing campaigns stressing tobacco as a passport to a more exciting lifestyle, presented in similar ways to the successful campaigns in Western countries many decades earlier.

Consequently, the decisions of governments in the West to exert their power and curtail the actions of TNCs means that activities with very negative consequences are simply displaced and set to rise again in other circumstances. In summary, it could be argued that, in this context, the activities of TNCs are beyond the control of individual nation-states or even wider groups which may seek to exert authority over their activities.

However, pressure is now mounting in many developing countries for them to sign up to the tobacco treaty, the Framework Convention on Tobacco Control (FCTC), and, increasingly, restrictions are being brought to bear which will reduce the spread of the use of tobacco in developing countries including China.

1 Highlight the various ways governments interact with TNCs (e.g. instances of cooperation and of opposition).
2 What factors might lead to TNCs having success in markets in the developing world?
3 To what extent are TNCs independent of nation-states?

It is suggested that while the state has a measure of accountability – through regular elections and people being able to exercise their democratic rights to protest and challenge government actions – there are no similar constraints on the activities of TNCs, which have power without responsibility.

Shareholders in such companies are often pension funds and banks, rather than individuals with consciences that can be alerted when TNCs act in ways that are detrimental to individuals and the environment. Examples of this detrimental activity are fairly widespread.

Exxon Valdeez   In 1989 this oil tanker, owned by the then largest petroleum company in the world, caused the largest oil spill in history when 42 million litres of crude oil went into the sea causing widespread pollution and damage to wildlife.

Bhopal   In 1984, in Bhopal in India, poisonous gas escaped from a plant owned by US company Union Carbide. More than 2,800 workers died and more than 20,000 were injured. Compensation has been very difficult for those affected because the company claimed that it was a subsidiary company which was actually responsible.

The Indian directors of the local company were arrested, but the corporate bosses based in the US were not made to be accountable, which is frequently an issue when TNCs operate across international boundaries. Governments of individual countries are rendered relatively powerless, with the subdivision and diffusion of responsibility and the complexity of dealing with legal systems in many different countries simultaneously.

Shell in Nigeria   In the 1990s, Shell continued its policies of aggressively exploiting oil reserves in Nigeria. Despite having the backing of the government, little consideration was taken of local communities and environmental damage – oil and waste from the plant had been polluting local villages and fishing grounds, for example. Ken Saro-Wiwa, who took part in organising resistance to Shell's plans, was arrested, and after a complex trial, which was heavily criticized by human rights activists around the world, was executed by hanging in November 1995. In December 1995, Shell announced the building of a £2.5 million plant in Nigeria.

Resistance to TNCs

Despite the power of TNCs, there have been many instances where the activities of such companies have been successfully challenged. For example, Shell's dismantling of an oil-rig at sea, which was a pollution threat, was prevented as a result of the activities of Greenpeace and other organizations, linked to a boycott of Shell petrol. McDonald's and Coca-Cola have also been the focus of many campaigns to improve their business practices and level of ethical awareness; such campaigns are more usually the prerogative of non-governmental groups, although the backing of governments can be crucial in ultimately gaining action in the face of TNCs.

Terrorism

Terrorism is generally defined as violence used by a group or individual as a political strategy. Thiel (2008) sees terrorism as a tactic and a process used by political groups to increase their power, involving violence directed largely at a non-combatant public. He sees the logic underpinning terrorism as its relative ease for its perpetrators and its high impact. It is seen as a theatrical process where highly symbolic actions are amplified through global media. It is suggested that, increasingly, societies are faced by groups and individuals who would seek to exert their power through violent means and that the global scale of such networks and activities make containment a major challenge for governments, frequently working in partnership, worldwide.

Johnson (1981) makes some key observations about terrorism:

1 Legitimate political tactic: terrorists portray violence as a legitimate weapon, despite its generally universal social condemnation.
2 Bypassing of established methods of negotiation: being excluded from existing political structures leads to groups in the subordinate position using dramatic tactics to make statements which can instantly draw global focus to the issue.
3 State terrorism: governments and their agents can also use violence, frequently beyond existing laws, against groups and individuals. Intimidation and violence have been used around the world to exert power – for example, by the government in North Korea and in Iraq under Saddam Hussein.
4 Democracies are more at risk: because citizens can move more freely and there is less surveillance, planning of terrorist attacks could be facilitated. Responses to terrorism are difficult to formulate – the shadowy nature of such groups frequently means that specific reprisals are not possible and more generic responses could have the impact of unsettling intergovernmental relationships on a global scale. Frequently, the suspension of civil liberties in the short term within specific countries is the only option available, and may be more about reducing public anxiety and demonstrating that action has taken place, rather than a high impact strategy to really reduce further threats.
5 Definitions: 'terrorism' is just one interpretation of a tactic or process; governments may label violence used by their opposition as 'terrorism' when others may perceive such terrorists as 'freedom fighters' resisting repression and exploitation.

11 September 2001 is seen by many as a day that changed the world. The suicide bombings of the World Trade Center and the Pentagon were seen as symbolizing the extremities of the struggle for power in the twenty-first century on a global scale.

Martin (2004) argues that there are four key ways in which terrorism has developed in recent years:

1   Organizational decentralization: hierarchies and chains of command are far less frequent. Clusters of activity around chains, hub and spoke networks are a predominant pattern.
2   Operational asymmetry: attacks are very unpredictable and frequently involve unanticipated objects.
3   Religious centrality: underpinning events is frequently a belief that that battle is about good versus evil and religious fundamentalism has a high profile as a key influence.
4   Weapons of mass destruction: increasing concern is being directed towards the methods within reach of terrorist groups – the bombs of the past are giving way to biological, chemical and even nuclear processes with a much higher potential for human destruction on a mass scale.

So although terrorism has been a characteristic of late modernity, it is certain that the growth of high-impact terrorist activity, and strategies to combat it located within a global context, will remain central in discussions concerning the nature and distribution of power in the first half of the twenty-first century.

Economic migration

Many political issues facing nation-states seem, at face value, to be very difficult, if not impossible, for individual countries to deal with. While most migration is internal, international migration has been the focus of much discussion and debate, especially the extent to which countries are able to control the movement of populations at specific times and in specific places.

International migration is seen as a characteristic of globalization; people are taking advantage of the increased interdependency of the world's economies and identifying alternative locations within the global labour market for a wide variety of reasons.

Movement largely relates to:

- economic well-being: with people moving to improve their material circumstances;
- forced emigration: where war, other violent political conflicts, dangers or persecution mean people have limited choices and where work and residential rights in another country are a necessity for survival.

Cohen (2006) highlights the significant sensitivities, both political and sociological, around the issue of migrants. Despite arguments which suggest that globalization has led to a blurring of cultures and identities and an erosion of boundaries, many people perceive the movement of people as threatening and disturbing to their own sense of economic well-being and way of life. Cohen suggests that the media contributes significantly to these views, exaggerating the number of undocumented migrants, for example, compared to the number who come legitimately because of family links or who have permits or visas. Expected increases in workers from the newly joined countries of Bulgaria and Romania did not occur and the number of asylum applications in the UK usually stands at around 23,000 annually (Home Office UK Border Agency). Nevertheless, images abound of migrant workers aggressively taking jobs, housing and benefits, and bringing terrorism, alien cultures and illnesses.

Activity

Carry out a content analysis of a week's coverage in a quality newspaper or use the website of one of these newspapers (*Guardian*: www.guardian.co.uk; *The Times*: www.times.co.uk; *Independent*: www.independent.co.uk, etc.) of migration and population issues. What are they key themes in the stories presented?

However, the unpredictability of illegal migrant flows and the sense that authorities are losing control of national borders fuels the fears of local populations and this, in turn, has led to a plethora of strategies to 'manage' these circumstances.

Population movement on a mass scale is not a new phenomenon. In the twentieth century approximately 9.5 million people were displaced by the First World War, a further 11 million by the Second World War and more have been displaced by the creation of new states – for example, Pakistan and Israel. However, it is the case that from the late 1970s onwards there have been significant increases in the movement of people; the number of refugees alone increased from 10 million to 27 million in the 1990s (UNHCR), without including purely economic migrants. This is linked to:

- the opening up of borders in the former Communist countries of the Eastern bloc;
- war, famine and ethnic conflict in African and Asian countries;
- tensions within previously Communist countries – for example, Yugoslavia, where, in early 1999, half a million refugees fled from Kosovo as a result of the 'ethnic cleansing' by Serbian forces.

Undocumented workers

Concern is frequently expressed about what are perceived as large numbers of undocumented (or 'illegal') workers and their movement within the global labour market. There are two main forms of undocumented labour – those who overstay on legitimate visas and work permits, and those who deliberately enter illegally, with forged documents, etc. London Heathrow is the biggest airport hub in the world, with 60 million people passing through annually, and it is clearly impossible to control and monitor the movements of all those who enter the UK. The pressures on people to migrate can be intense; border controls can be expensive and impossible to police and complicit employers all combine to make the situation prohibitively difficult to manage. Governments are forced to rely on international cooperation and strategies. Political issues extend beyond the scope of individual nation-states.

In December 2003, UN Secretary General Kofi Annan set up the Global Commission of International Migration (GCIM) to present policy suggestions to deal, on a global scale, with matters of migration. Six key recommendations were made:

1 Migrating out of choice: people should be migrating out of choice not out of necessity. It was seen as the responsibility of individual countries to develop economies and freedoms which allow populations to thrive and fulfil their aspirations in their country of origin and any migration should be based upon the sharing and deployment of skills where needed.
2 Promoting development: migration should help countries of origin and receiving countries to develop and foster economic growth.
3 Irregular migration: in other words, all labour should be documented and there should be no 'illegal' migration, but the UN recognized that such scenarios needed careful handling to avoid human rights issues where individuals may have claims as asylum-seekers.
4 Social cohesion and integration: destination countries should engage in a mutual programme of integration and support and media discourses should be objective and fair.
5 Migrant rights: human rights and labour standards should be rigorously implemented and controlled.
6 Intergovernmental cooperation: governments should work together to arrive at mutually beneficial solutions and strategies concerning the distribution of migrant labour.

It has been recognized that these principles are all sensitive and commendable; however, in a global context, the concerns of resident populations have encouraged more and more nation-states to maintain a strong grip on immigration. The nature of a developing world market for labour may well place governments under significant pressure to work much more collaboratively to address the issues they face.

Transnational politics

A global economy, in which finance, products and services all now flow daily across the globe, and where transnational corporations play a dominant role supported by instant worldwide communication, is a feature of society today. However, there is still some debate as to the extent to which globalization has had an impact on the power structures in individual nation-states.

There are some obvious ways in which political structures and decision-making are now far more interconnected, and institutions that are involved:

- the European Union (EU) which now comprises 27 states;
- the Association of South-East Asian Nations (ASEAN), which draws together countries such as Malaysia, Singapore and Thailand for economic and political reason;
- the United Nations (UN) has provided a layer of global government since its establishment in 1945.

> **Activity**
>
> Use the Internet to identify the full name of the following organizations, and briefly describe the role and function of each:
> - UNICEF
> - UNESCO
> - WHO
> - UNHCR
>
> Identify a decision that each has been involved in and consider to what extent this has impacted upon the structures of power in the UK.

TNCs frequently have more economic power than countries and the Information Revolution means that individual nation-states are no longer able to control and confine their activities and manage political events within their borders. NSMs draw together individuals and groups on a global scale to respond to political situations, with the potential for high-level impact in many areas.

In summary, the study of politics and the exercise of power has shifted from within national boundaries to include global issues and the exercise of power in a much wider context. While differences between countries in terms of the nature and distribution of power are still apparent, and systems and institutions may differ in many ways, such matters cannot be considered without the context of a fully global perspective.

CHAPTER SUMMARY

After studying this chapter you should be able to:

- explain what sociologists mean by the concepts of power and politics;
- explain the different ways in which sociologists have examined the nature of power – in other words, what power is like in society;
- recognize the importance of political parties and pressure groups in the pluralist view of the distribution of power;
- evaluate pluralist views, using such concepts as agenda-setting and non-decision-making;
- discuss Marxist views of the distribution of power and provide some evidence for and against the view that there is a ruling class in society today;
- discuss classical and contemporary elite theories, and present evidence for and against the view that elites exist in society today;
- explain what is meant by the state and identify its key functions;
- provide a brief history of the role of the state in contemporary societies;
- explain pluralist, Marxist, New Right and feminist views of the role of the state and related evidence for and against these views;
- describe the importance of social class as an influence on voting behaviour, especially in the post-war period;

- analyse the breakdown of the relationship between class and voting using such concepts as deviant voting and partisan dealignment;
- analyse voting patterns, particularly since the election of New Labour in 1997, using such concepts as instrumentalism and volatility;
- describe the impact of key characteristics other than class on voting behaviour such as age, gender, ethnicity and locality;
- understand the historical and ideological differences between the main political parties and key policy differences;
- explain the different types and roles and functions of pressure groups in contemporary society, and their possible impact;
- explain the different types and activities of new social movements (NSMs) in contemporary society, often in a global context;
- understand the relationship between politics and the media and different theoretical models concerning how media and politics interact;
- understand the significance of globalization and its possible impact on the nation-state;
- describe examples of the breakdown of international barriers and the interconnectedness of issues of power and politics on a global scale.

KEY TERMS

agenda-setting	constant sum view	elite	insider groups
anti-capitalist movement	culture jamming	embourgeoisement	iron law of oligarchy
authoritarian	democracy	floating voters	laissez-faire
circulation of elites	deviant voters	hyperreality	left wing
cleavages	discourse	ideal types	modernity

nation-state
new professions
new social movements
oligarchy
outsider groups
partisan dealignment

partisan self-image
politics
polysemic
post-materialist
power
power elite

pressure groups
privatization
psephology
right wing
spin doctor
state

third way
two faces of power
variable sum view
voter volatility
Weltanschauung

EXAM QUESTIONS

SECTION D: POWER AND POLITICS

If you choose this Section, answer Question 10 and **either** Question 11 **or** Question 12.

Time allowed: 1 hour 30 minutes   **Total for this section: 60 marks**

10   Read **Item D** below and answer parts (a) and (b) that follow.

Item D

Traditionally, much psephological research indicated that there was a strong relationship between social class background, as defined by occupational status, and voting behaviour. The pattern of the working-class Labour voter and the middle-class Conservative voter was established to the extent that working-class Conservative voters were defined as 'deviant voters'. However, this relationship has appeared to become far less clear as increasing num-   5 bers of voters focus on specific issues within politics which reflect their personal views at any given moment in time. Indeed, it has been suggested that many look outside conventional party politics to express 'political' opinions. The widespread coverage by the media of a whole variety of groups campaigning to bring about change in many areas of society, region- ally, nationally and globally, has led to a huge level of interest and participation in these New   10 Social Movements (NSMs), which lie outside established parliamentary processes.

(a)   Identify and briefly explain some of the sociological evidence, **apart from** that referred to in **Item D**, that might be used to support the view that social class is no longer a major influence on voting behaviour.   *(9 marks)*

(b)   Using material from **Item D** and elsewhere, assess the view that conventional political parties and party politics are being replaced by participation in new social movements.   *(18 marks)*

EITHER

11   'Power in Britain today is distributed evenly amongst multiple centres of power, each competing in an open and democratic way to achieve their goals.'

     To what extent do sociological evidence and arguments support this view of the nature and distribution of power in contemporary society?   *(33 marks)*

OR

12   'The media play a crucial role in political processes in society today.'

     To what extent do sociological arguments and evidence support this view?   *(33 marks)*

Theory and Methods

KEN BROWNE

Contents

Theory and Methods

KEY ISSUES

- What you should know from AS
- Sociological theory
- Structuralism
- Social action or interpretivist theories
- Integrated approaches – combining structure and action
- Modernism and postmodernism
- The scientific method
- Positivism
- Interpretivism
- Positivism, interpretivism and research methods
- Science and the study of society
- The social construction of scientific knowledge
- Is a value-free sociology possible?
- Is a value-free sociology desirable?
- Postmodernism, science, values and methodology
- Social policy and social problems

Note to students

It is very likely that you will have come across a number of the theories in this chapter during your AS course, and in the topics you study in this book. In answering any question on theory and methods, it is important that you illustrate your answers with examples drawn from the topic areas you've studied at both AS and A2. It is also worth noting that when you critically discuss a theory or a method, you can often do so using other theories or methods. For example, the weaknesses and limitations of structural theories are often the strengths of action theories.

This chapter will examine a range of sociological theories, and a number of important debates regarding methodology, the scientific status of sociology, the role of values in sociology and the links between sociology and social policy. It assumes that you are familiar with the research methods you learned during the AS course. You will be expected to extend your knowledge and understanding of these research methods through the use of examples drawn from either chapter 6 ('Crime and Deviance') or chapter 7 ('Stratification and Differentiation'), and you will be tested on them in the exam. These chapters include sections on methodological and theoretical issues to help with this.

The first section of this chapter is designed to highlight the key issues you should already know and understand from AS. If you don't, you need to revise them further – you ignore them at your peril! Some definitions of key terms from AS are included to help you, and there are summaries on a number of methods and issues referred to here downloadable from www.politybooks.com/browne, drawn from Ken Browne's *Sociology for AS AQA*, the companion volume to this book, to help your revision. These are indicated in brackets with a 5W prefix to indicate chapter 5 on the website.

What you should know from AS

- the difference between **quantitative** and **qualitative data**, the advantages and limitations of each, and the type of methods used to obtain them;
- the difference between **primary** and **secondary sources**, and the strengths and limitations of the data obtained from each;
- the problems of **reliability** and **validity** of research evidence;
- the considerations over **ethics** that sociologists must consider when carrying out social research;
- the advantages, uses and limitations of official statistics;
- the uses and problems of the experimental method in sociology, including issues of validity and the **Hawthorne effect**;
- how the comparative method might be used as an alternative to the experimental one;
- the main features and stages of the social survey, including pilot surveys;
- the various sampling methods sociologists use to gain representative samples;
- the uses, strengths and weaknesses of different types of questionnaire and interview, including the problems of imposition and the validity and reliability of these methods (see tables 5W.1 and 5W.2);
- the problem of **interviewer bias**;
- the uses, strengths and weaknesses of participant and non-participant observation, including the issues of getting in, staying in and getting out, and overt and covert roles (see table 5W.3);
- the strengths and weaknesses of longitudinal studies, case studies and life histories (see table 5W.4);
- what is meant by **methodological pluralism** and **triangulation**, and why sociologists might want to use a range of methods in sociological research (see figure 5W.1);

Quantitative data is information that can be expressed in statistical or number form or can be 'measured' in some way. **Qualitative data** is information concerned with descriptions of the meanings and interpretations people have about some issue or event.

Primary sources are where researchers themselves gather information. **Secondary sources** contain data which already exists and which researchers haven't collected themselves.

Reliability concerns whether another researcher, if repeating or replicating the research using the same method for the same research on the same group, would achieve the same results. **Validity** is concerned with notions of truth – how far the findings of research actually provide a true, genuine or authentic picture of what is being studied.

Interviewer bias occurs when the answers given in an interview are influenced or distorted in some way by the presence or behaviour of the interviewer.

- a range of theoretical, practical and ethical considerations that influence choice of topic, choice of method(s) and the conduct of research (see figure 5W.2);
- the difference between positivism and interpretivism, and how these two approaches use different research methods. You should already have some familiarity with this from AS, but there is a more in-depth review of the positivist and interpretivist approaches underpinning different research methodologies later in this chapter.

The **Hawthorne effect** occurs when the presence of the researcher, or the group's (or individual's) knowledge that it has been specially selected for research, changes the behaviour of the group or individual, raising problems of the validity of the research.

Sociological theory

There are various dimensions to sociological theory, but there are, broadly, two main themes:

1   *The extent of consensus and conflict in society:* how is social order maintained, and how do people manage to live together with some degree of relative harmony and stability despite any differences they may have?
2   *The problem of* **determinism** *and choice:* how much freedom and choice do people have to influence society? Is the individual's identity and life moulded or determined by social forces outside her or his control, or does the individual have control over these social forces?

The theme of the degree of consensus or conflict in society runs through much of sociology, so it worth beginning with an introduction to this.

Methodological pluralism is the use of a variety of methods in a single piece of research. **Triangulation** is the use of two or more research methods in a single piece of research to check the reliability and validity of research evidence.

Consensus and conflict theories

Consensus theory assumes that society is primarily harmonious, and social order is maintained through a consensus or widespread agreement between people on the important goals, values and norms of society. Consensus theory is primarily associated with functionalist theory, which is discussed below.

Conflict theory has its origins in the work of Marx (1818–83) and Weber (1864–1920). Conflict theory takes the opposite view to that of the consensus theorists. Rather than seeing society as mainly harmonious and stable, it sees it as primarily conflict-ridden and unstable, emphasizing social differences and conflicts between groups. It is concerned with issues such as social inequality and the conflicts it produces, the power and control of dominant groups and classes, the role of the education system in reproducing and legitimating inequality, and elite rule and the dominant ideology. This is illustrated below in the discussion of Marxist theory, but it is also worth mentioning the conflict approaches of Weber and of feminist writers.

Ethics in research involve the morality and standards of behaviour when carrying out research. These include the informed consent of those being studied, avoiding physical, social and mental harm to those helping with research, respecting confidentiality, and giving accurate and honest reports of findings.

Determinism is the idea that people's behaviour is moulded by their social surroundings, and that they have little free will, control or choice over how they behave.

Weber: class, status and party

Weber was concerned, like Marx, with the unequal distribution of power in society. He saw conflicts in society arising between social classes pursuing economic interests, between status groups pursuing social honour, prestige and respect (shown in lifestyles and consumption), and between parties, which are specifically concerned with influencing policies and making decisions in the interests of their membership. Society was therefore fundamentally unstable, as individuals and groups struggled with one another as they pursued their competing interests (see page 519 for a discussion of Weber's ideas of class, status and party).

Feminism

The feminist approach in sociology is also a form of conflict theory. Feminists view society as fundamentally patriarchal, with men in positions of power and dominance over women in many areas of social life. This generates conflict between men and women, an issue that has been explored in various aspects of both the AS course and in this book, and is particularly explored here in chapter 7 ('Stratification and Differentiation'). Feminists' main focus of research is to expose these gender inequalities, often using interpretivist methods to understand the feelings and experiences of women. Feminism challenges much of mainstream sociological research, which it labels 'malestream', for overlooking the gender dimensions of inequality and rendering women invisible in much sociological research in the past. Different strands of feminist thought (see pages 520–25) propose different solutions to tackling the problems of gender inequality. For example, liberal feminists look to improve opportunities in existing society, Marxist socialist feminists challenge both patriarchy and capitalism as causes of women's inequality, and radical feminists focus on the removal of patriarchy, which it regards as simply turning women into sex objects. They are all nonetheless united in recognizing the essential conflicts between men and women that gender inequalities create in society. These themes of consensus and conflict are further explored in the sections below.

Determinism and choice

The second theme in sociological theory is concerned with the problem of determinism and choice – the extent to which the individual has control over, or is a passive victim of, social forces.

There are three main sociological approaches in this debate:

* *structuralism* – the sociology of system or structure;
* *social action* or *interpretivist approaches* – the sociology of action;
* *integrated approaches*, combining the structure and action approaches – this includes Weber's sociology and Giddens's theory of structuration.

Structuralism

Structuralism is concerned with the overall social structure of society, and the way social institutions, like the family, the education system, the mass media and the economy, act as a constraint on, or limit and control, individual behaviour.

Structuralism is a perspective that is concerned with the overall structure of society, and sees individual behaviour moulded by social institutions like the family, the education system, the mass media and work.

Structural approaches see individuals formed by the wider social forces making up the social structure of society.

Structuralist approaches have the following features:

1   The behaviour and values of individual human beings, and the formation of their identities, are seen as being a result of social forces which are external to the individual. Individuals are determined, or moulded, shaped and constrained, by social forces acting upon them – like socialization, positive and negative sanctions – and material resources – like income and jobs. They have little control or choice in how they behave. According to the structuralist approach, the individual is like a puppet, whose strings are pulled by social institutions such as the family, the education system, the mass media and the workplace.

2   The main purpose of sociology is to study the overall structure of society, the social institutions that make up this structure, and the relationships between these social institutions – such as the links between the workplace and the economy, the economy and the political system, the family and the education system, and so on. The focus of sociology is on the study of social institutions and the social structure as a whole, not on the individual. This focus on large-scale social structure is sometimes referred to as a *macro-approach*.

3   The main methodological approach is **positivist**, using quantitative research methods, as individual behaviour is seen as a response to measurable social forces outside individuals acting upon them to control their behaviour. The focus of sociological research should then be on these social forces. The individual states of mind and meanings of individuals are seen as a reflection of these external forces, and so are not seen as worth studying in their own right.

Positivism is the view that the logic, methods and procedures of the natural sciences, as used in subjects like physics, chemistry and biology, can be applied to the study of society with little modification.

There are two main varieties of structuralism:

●   functionalism (consensus structuralism);
●   Marxism (conflict structuralism).

Functionalism (consensus structuralism)

Functionalism is a consensus theory rooted in the work of Durkheim (1858–1917), and refined by Parsons (1902–79) and Merton (1910–2004). Functionalism regards society as a stable, harmonious integrated social system, with social order and cohesion maintained by a fundamental value consensus.

Society as a system

Functionalism views society as a system – a structure of interconnected parts which fit together to form an integrated whole. The basic unit of analysis is the social system as a whole, and social institutions such as the family, religion and education are analysed in relation to the contribution they make to the maintenance of this system.

Functionalists often draw an analogy between the workings of society and the human body. For example, understanding the workings and importance of the heart, lungs and brain involves understanding what function or purpose each carries out and how they work together to satisfy and maintain the needs of the human body as a whole, such as the role of the heart and lungs in refreshing and pumping blood around our bodies. Similarly, functionalists argue that, just like the human body, any society has what Parsons (1951) called **functional prerequisites** – basic needs or requirements that must be met if society is to survive. These include the production of food, the care of the young and the socialization of new generations into the culture of society. Social institutions like the family, education and the workplace exist to satisfy these basic needs, and, as in the human body, the various social institutions are connected and work together to meet functional prerequisites for the benefit of society as a whole.

> **Functional prerequisites** are the basic needs that must be met if society is to survive.

All social phenomena are regarded by functionalists as having some function in society, just as all parts of the human body do. For example, pain in the human body is very unpleasant but serves a valuable function in alerting us to something wrong. Similarly, parts of society also sometimes malfunction. Deviance (rule-breaking) is a sign of disorder, but can act as a useful warning that something is wrong in society,

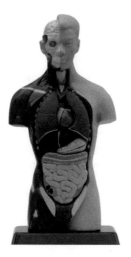

Functionalists view society as working much like the human body, with all the parts having a function and working together harmoniously to maintain the system as a whole.

and people's reaction of disapproval encourages action to prevent further rule-breaking and also helps to strengthen the rule. For example, the occasional incident of child abuse reminds us all how we should *not* treat children, reinforces our values around the protection of children, and strengthens sanctions against potential future offenders.

Functional prerequisites: Parsons' GAIL model

Parsons suggests that to survive in a healthy state all societies have to resolve two sets of problems, instrumental and expressive, and satisfy four functional prerequisites which are met by four related sub-systems. This has come to be known as the GAIL model, and is shown in table 5.1

The establishment and maintenance of social order: value consensus and social integration

Durkheim (1982 [1895]) suggested that people are basically selfish, and that society would soon fall into chaos and disorder unless they learned to share some common values and show commitment to cooperation in society. Durkheim therefore placed great importance on socializing people into what he called a value consensus or **collective conscience**. This means a widespread agreement on values, norms and moral beliefs, which binds people together, builds social solidarity or social cohesion, and regulates individual behaviour.

A **collective conscience** means shared beliefs and values, which form moral ties binding communities together and which regulate individual behaviour

Table 5.1: Parson's GAIL model

Instrumental problems	Setting and achieving social goals; adapting to and achieving basic needs for survival	
Prerequisite or system need	Description/explanation	Sub-system
Goal attainment	The selection and definition of a society's priorities and aims/goals, and providing the means of achieving them. For example, parliament and the government set the goals by making and carrying out policy decisions, and provide the means of achieving them by allocating resources raised through taxation.	*Political system* For example, political parties, pressure groups, government, parliament, and state agencies.
Adaptation	Adapting to the environment and providing the basic material necessities for continued human existence, and sufficient resources to achieve valued social goals.	*Economy* For example, organizations like factories, financial institutions and shops concerned with economic production.

Table 5.1 (continued)

Expressive problems	Maintaining efficient cooperation and social solidarity; managing conflicts and tensions between individuals	
Prerequisite or system need	Description/explanation	Sub-system
Integration	Coordinating all parts of the system to achieve shared goals, with people having a sense of belonging to society. Socialization into shared values, beliefs and goals promotes social harmony and solidarity, with social control to prevent deviance.	*Cultural/community organizations* For example, mass media, education and religion socialize individuals into conformity to social norms and values, and the criminal justice system and other social control agencies restrict any threats to social order.
Latency (or pattern maintenance)	Minimizing social tensions and interpersonal conflicts which might prevent individuals and society working efficiently, and preserving/maintaining commitment to culture and pattern of values.	*Family and kinship* For example, family is key agency of socialization and social control. Place to recharge batteries, let off steam and escape and recover from stresses and destabilizing influences of daily life outside the family.

Functionalists see the role of agencies of socialization as integrating individuals within society by means of shared values and goals, enabling social life to become stable, orderly, predictable and harmonious, without much conflict between people or groups. Parsons (1951) shared Durkheim's view on the importance of agencies of socialization in building a value consensus and maintaining social order; in addition, he particularly emphasized the importance of primary socialization in the family, as a way of passing on norms and values from generation to generation, so that they would become internalized as part of a person's personality.

Social change and social evolution

Functionalists regard social change as occurring when new functions emerge or society needs to adapt. They view change as a slow process of social evolution, as gradual shifts occur in social values and people adapt to changes and reaffirm their commitment to them. As all the parts of society link together, a change in one part will result in changes elsewhere, but the system will remain balanced and stable. Parsons explains this in terms of **structural differentiation**. This means that as societies evolve and new needs arise for both society and individuals, institutions become more specialized, and functions they once performed are lost to new institutions. For example, the family used to be responsible for work-training and education, but these

Structural differentiation refers to the way in which new, more specialized social institutions emerge to take over functions that were once performed by a single institution.

functions gradually transferred to a specialized education system and work-based training, as the family (and as individuals within it came to realize) was no longer able to provide the skills and training necessary for a more complex industrial society.

Manifest and latent functions and the concept of dysfunction

Merton (1968 [1957]) criticized Parsons for his assumption that all social institutions performed beneficial, positive functions for society and individuals. Merton recognized that in a highly complex interdependent social system, there is plenty of scope for things to go wrong, and there may be unforeseen consequences when some apparently beneficial functions are performed. Merton introduced the idea of **dysfunction** to describe the situation whereby some parts of the social structure don't work as intended, and there can sometimes be negative consequences, with harmful effects for society, or for some individuals.

> **Dysfunction** refers to a part of the social structure which does not contribute to the maintenance and well-being of society, but creates tensions and other problems.

For example, the growth of new technology may have been functional in so far as it made possible huge leaps in scientific progress and the production of cheaper and better-quality products, but at the same time it had dysfunctional effects, such as the generation of environmental pollution, climate change and industrial diseases among workforces. To this extent, Merton recognizes that there were, potentially, conflicts within the functionalist view of all parts of society working for the benefit of everyone. As part of an integrated system, these dysfunctions can affect all other parts of the system. For example, just as a diseased heart can weaken the whole human body, so dysfunctional families can have consequences beyond the family, such as on mental health, educational attainment, crime and anti-social behaviour.

Merton suggested there were **manifest functions** of an institution, with intended and recognized consequences, but that there were also **latent functions** alongside them, with unintended or unrecognized consequences. For example, a hospital has the manifest function of dispensing healthcare, but a latent function is that it provides a means for those who work there to meet their potential marriage partners. Similarly, a manifest function like a hospital providing healthcare can also have a dysfunctional side, providing a locus for the spread of infection through antibiotic resistant 'superbugs' – such as MRSA and *C. difficile*.

> A **manifest function** is the recognized and intended outcome of the action of an individual or institution.

> A **latent function** is the unrecognized or unintended outcome of the action of an individual or institution.

Evaluation of functionalism

Strengths

1 It recognizes the importance of social structure in understanding society, how it constrains individual behaviour, and how the major social institutions, like the family, education and the economy, often have links between them.
2 It provides an explanation for social stability, and why most people generally conform to the rules of social life.

Weaknesses

1 It is too deterministic, and sees individuals as simply passive products of the social system, which socializes them into conformity and controls their behaviour. It doesn't allow for individual choice, as the social action theorists do.

2   It is a metanarrative or grand theory, which tries to explain everything from a single perspective. Postmodernists emphasize that such metanarratives can no longer explain contemporary societies, where social life is essentially chaotic, values are diverse and social structures are fragmented. The functionalist metanarrative has no more validity in explaining social life than any other.

3   It does not explain social change very effectively, as socialization, value consensus and social control contributing to social stability and conformity should limit social change. Functionalists can't explain periods of very rapid social change.

4   It over-emphasizes the beneficial aspects of functions performed by social institutions, and (with the exception of Merton) ignores harmful dysfunctions. For example, Davis and Moore's (1945) functionalist theory of stratification (see chapter 7, pages 514–15) sees only the benefits of inequality, while ignoring the resentments, divisions and conflicts it can generate.

5   It takes for granted that there is a value consensus in society, and that this will provide social stability. However, value consensus in itself does not provide stability – it depends what those values are. For example, a consensus on aggressive individualism in which dog-eats-dog, the winner takes all and losers are cast aside, is more likely to generate conflicts and resentment than social stability and harmony. Conflict theorists would argue that the value consensus functionalists assume is not a consensus at all, but just the ideas of the dominant social class imposed on the rest of society through institutions like the education system, religion and the media. Postmodernists would argue that there is a wide diversity of values in society, and no consensus at all.

6   It over-emphasizes harmony and consensus and ignores or downplays the extent of conflict and the unequal distribution of power in society, with which Marxist and feminist conflict theorists are concerned.

7   It tends to be very conservative, supporting the way society is presently organized. It sees society as working more or less harmoniously for the benefit of all, and therefore there is no fundamental need to change it. It has no sense of inequalities in life chances and power, and how these might generate social conflict and social problems needing fundamental social change.

Activity

1   Suggest how functionalists might explain how (a) social inequality and (b) crime perform necessary functions for the benefit of society.

2   Using Parsons' GAIL model (see table 5.1, on pages 339–40), explain in your own words what is meant by society's:
   - expressive problems
   - need for integration
   - instrumental problems
   - need for adaptation

3   Explain in each case above which sub-system(s) deal with these problems and needs, and, taking one example of your own, explain carefully how it does this.

4   In 45 minutes, answer the following essay question: *'Critically assess the contribution of the functionalist perspective to a sociological understanding of society.'*

Marxism (conflict structuralism)

Classical Marxism comes from the work of Karl Marx, who founded the political creed known as communism.

Base and superstructure

Marx believed that the economy was the driving force in society, and it was this that determined the nature of social institutions, and people's values and beliefs. Marxism sees the structure of society divided into two main parts, illustrated in figure 5.1:

Karl Marx, 1818–83

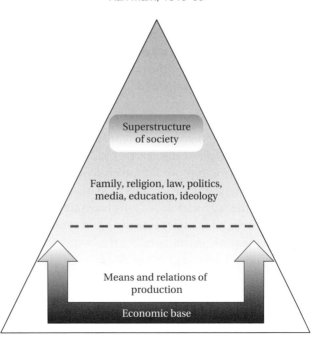

Figure 5.1 The base and superstructure in classical Marxist theory

1   The economic *base, or infrastructure*, which underpinned and determined everything else in society; this consisted of:
    - the **means of production**, like the land, factories, raw materials, technology and labour necessary to produce society's goods;
    - the **relations of production**: the relations between those involved in production, such as shared ownership or private ownership, who controls production, and the relationship between owners and non-owners e.g. whether people are forced to work, like slaves, or paid for their work.
2   *The superstructure*, which includes society's social institutions, such as the family, education, the mass media, religion and the political system, and beliefs and values (ideology), which Marx saw as primarily determined (or influenced) by the economic system.

Private ownership and social classes

Marx argued that work (labour) is the sole source of wealth. In primitive societies, when society produced only enough for its own essential needs, everyone had to work in order to survive. As a result, all people were producers on the same economic level. However, as soon as society began to produce more than was necessary for mere survival, it became possible for a section of society not to work, and to be supported by the labour of others. It was at this stage that Marx saw private ownership of the means of production emerging, and he argued that the means of production have been privately owned ever since the existence of the simplest societies, with most people dependent on the owners for employment. Society is then divided into two fundamental social classes: the owners and the non-owners of the means of production. For example, slave-owners and slaves in Ancient Rome, landowners and serfs in medieval feudal society, and capitalists and workers in contemporary societies. Marx argued that as the means of production developed – for example, as production became more sophisticated and technologically based – so new relations of production would emerge, and society would evolve through revolutionary changes arising from conflicts between the owners and the non-owners, from slavery, to feudalism, to capitalism and eventually to communism.

Exploitation

Marx argued that the workers (non-owners) produce more than is needed for employers to pay them their wages – this 'extra' produced by workers is what Marx called **surplus value**, and provides profit for the employer. For example, in a burger chain in contemporary society, it is the workers who make, cook, package and serve the burgers, but only half the burgers they sell are necessary to cover production costs and pay their wages. The rest of the sales provide profit for the owners of the burger chain. This means that the workers who produce the burgers do not get the full value of their work, and they are therefore being exploited.

Capitalists and workers

Marx argued that there were two basic social classes in capitalist industrial society: a small wealthy and powerful class of owners of the means of production (which he

The **means of production** are the key resources necessary for producing society's goods, such as land, factories and machinery.

The **relations of production** are the forms of relationship between those people involved in production, such as cooperation or private ownership and control.

Surplus value is the extra value added by workers to the products they produce, after allowing for production costs and the payment of their wages, and which goes to the employer in the form of profit.

The **bourgeoisie**, or **capitalists**, are the class of owners of the means of production in industrial societies, whose primary purpose is to make profits.

The **proletariat** is the social class of workers who have to work for wages, as they do not own the means of production.

Labour power refers to people's capacity to work. In capitalist societies people sell their labour power to the employer in return for a wage, and the employer buys only their labour power, but not the whole person, as they did, for example, under slavery.

False consciousness is a failure by members of a social class to recognize their real interests.

called the **bourgeoisie** or **capitalists**) and a much larger, poorer class of non-owners (which he called the **proletariat** or working class). Because they owned no means of production of their own, the proletariat had no means of living other than to sell their labour – or **labour power** as Marx called it – to the bourgeoisie, in exchange for a wage or salary. The capitalists exploited the working class by making profits out of them by keeping wages as low as possible instead of giving the workers the full payment for the goods they'd produced.

Class conflict

Marx asserted that exploitation of the non-owners by the owners created major differences in interest between the two classes, and this created conflict. For example, the workers' interests lay in higher wages to achieve a better lifestyle, but these would be at the expense of the bosses' profits. The bosses wanted higher profits to expand their businesses and wealth, and to be able to compete with one another and beat their opponents, but this could only be achieved by keeping wages as low as possible and/or by making the workers produce more by working harder. The interests of these two classes are therefore totally opposed, and this generates conflict between the two social classes (class conflict). Marx believed this class conflict would affect all areas of life.

The ruling class

Marx argued that the owning class was also a ruling class. For example, because they owned the means of production, members of the bourgeoisie could decide where factories should be located, and whether they should be opened or closed down, and they could control the workforce through hiring or firing. Democratically elected governments could not afford to ignore this power of the ruling class: if the bourgeoisie were to decide not to invest their money in the production process, it could lead to rising unemployment or other social problems.

Dominant ideology

Marx believed that the ruling or dominant ideas in any society – what he called the dominant ideology – were those of the owning class (hence it is sometimes also called 'ruling class ideology') and the major institutions in the superstructure of society reflected those ideas and the interests of the bourgeoisie. For example, the law protected the interests of the owning class more than it did those of the workers; religion acted as the 'opium of the people', persuading the working class to accept their position as just and natural (rather than rebelling against it) and 'drugging' them with promises of future rewards in heaven for putting up with their present suffering; and the mass media was owned by those in the ruling class, so only their ideas were put forward. In this way, the workers were almost brainwashed into accepting their position. They failed to recognize that they were being exploited and therefore did not rebel against the bourgeoisie. Marx called this lack of awareness of their own interests **false consciousness**.

Revolution and communism

However, Marx thought that one day the circumstances would arise in which the workers did become aware of the exploitation. Wealth and power would become ever

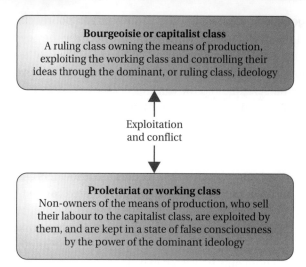

Figure 5.2 A summary of the Marxist view of capitalist society

more concentrated in the hands of the few, and, on a global scale, the workers would become poorer and remain relatively poor. This contrast between wealth and poverty would lead the working class to develop **class-consciousness** – an awareness of their real interests and their exploitation – and the population would become polarized into two opposing and hostile camps of capitalists and workers, with the battle lines clearly drawn between them. The working class would join together to act against the bourgeoisie through strikes, demonstrations and other forms of protest. This would eventually lead to a revolution against, and overthrow of, the bourgeoisie. The means of production would then be put in the hands of the state and run in the interests of everyone, not just of the bourgeoisie. A new type of society – **communism** – would be created, which would be without exploitation, without classes and without class conflict.

> **Class-consciousness** is an awareness in members of a social class of their real interests.

> **Communism** is an equal society, without social classes or class conflict, in which the means of production are the common property of all.

Evaluation of classical Marxism

Strengths

1 It recognizes the importance of the economy and how economic changes can influence a wide range of other social institutions.
2 Its focus on private ownership of the means of production provides an explanation for the extreme social inequalities in wealth, income and power that persist in contemporary societies, and for the conflicts and upheavals that periodically surface, many of which are rooted in social class inequalities.
3 It recognizes the importance of society's social structure, and links this to the ideas, consciousness and behaviour of individuals and groups.
4 It remains a highly influential theory, which has had a significant influence on a range of other sociological theories, such as those of Weber and of Marxist feminists.

Weaknesses

1 Marx's predictions have not come true. Far from society becoming polarized and the working class becoming poorer, almost everyone in Western societies enjoys a far higher standard of living than ever before. The collapse of the so-

called 'communist' regimes of the Soviet Union (now Russia and the surrounding countries) and Eastern Europe, and growing private ownership and continuing extreme inequality in communist countries like China, cast some doubt on the viability of the practical implementation of Marx's ideas.

2   Classical Marxism over-emphasizes the extent of conflict in society. Functionalists would argue that society is primarily stable, and there must be some shared values for social life to be possible. That Marx's predicted revolution has not succeeded in any Western society reflects this.

3   Marx's two-class model of inequality is inadequate. A new middle class has emerged, consisting of managerial, professional and clerical workers, which falls between the bourgeoisie and the proletariat; Marx's theory cannot account for all the differences in power, rewards, consciousness and status within the mass of the population who are not capitalists, such as between manual and non-manual workers.

4   It over-emphasizes social class as a source of inequality and conflict, and pays little attention to other sources such as ethnicity, age and gender.

5   The economic base and superstructure model is too deterministic, giving too much importance to the economy. Classical Marxism doesn't allow for the possibility that the ideas and institutions of the superstructure may themselves influence behaviour and cause social change independently of the economy, as Weber (2001 [1904]) saw in the ideas of the Protestant work ethic influencing change in early capitalism (see pages 26–7, 355 for a discussion of Weber's Protestant ethic).

6   Classical Marxism is too deterministic, and sees individuals as simply passive products of the social system, which socializes them into conformity and controls their behaviour. It doesn't allow for individual choice, as the social action theorists do.

7   It is a metanarrative or grand theory, which tries to explain everything from a single perspective. Postmodernists emphasize such metanarratives can no longer explain contemporary societies, where social life is essentially chaotic, values are diverse and social structures are fragmented. The Marxist metanarrative has no more validity in explaining social life than any other.

8   Postmodernists suggest that the economy is not the key factor influencing people's ideas; instead, in what is regarded as a media-saturated society, it is the mass media that forms and dominates people's consciousness and view of the world.

9   Postmodernists argue that the metanarrative of class is no longer important, and the main social divisions now arise around individual choices in consumption patterns and lifestyle.

Neo-Marxism

Neo-Marxists are those who have further developed and modified the ideas of classical Marxism, partly arising from some of the criticisms made above.

Gramsci's concept of hegemony

The Italian Marxist Antonio Gramsci (1891–1937) thought Marx was mistaken in giving such overriding importance to the economy; he saw ideology as having **relative autonomy** from the economic base.

Gramsci's concept of **hegemony** placed much more emphasis than Marx did on the role of ideas (ideology), rather than just the economy, in maintaining the power of the ruling class and in influencing people's behaviour. By hegemony, Gramsci was referring to the dominance in society of the ruling class's set of ideas over others, and acceptance of and consent to them by the rest of society. He saw this control of people's minds by the dominant ideology as one of the main reasons why the working class had never rebelled against the bourgeoisie. The concept of hegemony meant that Gramsci was leaning more towards a social action approach to society, focusing more on people's ideas and meanings, and less on the structuralist approach and economic determinism of classical Marxism.

Althusser and the economic, political and ideological levels

Althusser (1969, 1971) argued that the structure of capitalist society consists of not just the economic base and superstructure, but of three levels:

1   *The economic level*, consisting of the economy and the production of material goods.
2   *The political level*, consisting of the government and organizations involved in the political organization and control of society, including what he called the **repressive state apparatus** (RSA). The RSA refers to those parts of the state that are concerned with mainly repressive, physical means of keeping a population in line, such as the army, police, courts and prisons.
3   *The ideological level*, concerned with ideas, beliefs and values. This consists of the **ideological state apparatuses**, which are a series of institutions that spread the dominant ideology and justify the power of the dominant class. These include the mass media, the education system and religion.

While the economy remains of overall importance, and all three levels ultimately preserve and justify the power of the dominant class, the political and ideological levels can affect society independently of the economy. Each level has relative autonomy and *some* independence from the economic base, distinguishing this from classical Marxist theory, while still retaining some link to it. Figure 5.3 tries to illustrate this idea of relative autonomy.

Evaluation of neo-Marxism

Neo-Marxists have tried to overcome some of the weaknesses of classical Marxism, and particularly its economic determinism, whereby everything is explained by the operation of the economic base. The concept of relative autonomy recognizes that people's ideas and institutions in the superstructure can impact on the economy, and not simply the other way round. However, some classical Marxists would argue that Marx himself did recognize the importance of ideas and meanings, with his

Relative autonomy is the idea in neo-Marxist theory that the superstructure of society has some independence from the economy, rather than being directly determined by it.

Hegemony refers to the dominance in society of the ruling class's set of ideas over others, and acceptance of and consent to them by the rest of society.

The **repressive state apparatus** refers to those parts of the state that are concerned with mainly repressive, physical means of keeping a population in line, such as the army, police, courts, and prisons.

Ideological state apparatuses are agencies that spread the dominant ideology and justify the power of the dominant social class.

Figure 5.3 The relative autonomy of the superstructure in neo-Marxist theories

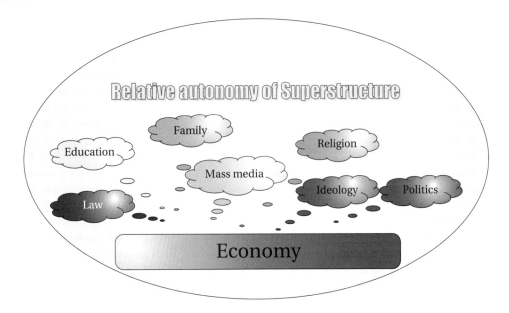

discussions of class-consciousness, and they also suggest that neo-Marxists can underplay the importance of the economy in shaping social reality.

> **Activity**
>
> 1 To what extent do you agree with Marx's view that the dominant ideas in Britain today are those of a wealthy and powerful ruling class?
> 2 Do you think an analysis of Britain today fits more closely the consensus perspective of functionalism or the conflict perspective of Marx? Explain your view, with examples.
> 3 What evidence might you use from contemporary Britain to suggest that Marx's ideas are (a) still relevant today or (b) out of date?
> 4 Explain in your own words what you understand by the following concepts, giving examples to illustrate them: relative autonomy; base and superstructure; hegemony; class-consciousness; exploitation; class conflict.
> 5 In 45 minutes, answer the following essay question: 'Marxism and other conflict theories have little to contribute to an understanding of contemporary society.' Examine the extent to which sociological arguments and evidence support this view.

Social action or interpretivist theories

Interpretivism is an approach emphasizing that people have consciousness involving personal beliefs, values and interpretations, and these influence the way they act. People have choices and do not simply respond to forces outside them. To understand society, it is therefore necessary to understand the meanings people give to their behaviour, and how this is influenced by the behaviour and interpretations of others.

The main focus of social action or **interpretivist** theories is on individual behaviour in everyday social situations. These theories are concerned with discovering, and thereby understanding, the processes by which interactions between individuals or small groups take place, how people come to interpret and see things as they do, how they define their identities, and how the reactions of others can affect their view of things and the sense of their own identity.

Social action or interpretivist theories include the following features:

Social action or interpretivist theories emphasize the free will and choice of individuals, and their role in creating the social structure.

1   Society and social structures/institutions are seen as socially constructed creations of individuals, not something separate from and above them.

2   An emphasis is placed on the voluntarism, or free will and choice, of people to do things and form their own identities, rather than them being formed by external social forces as suggested in the determinist approach of structuralism.

3   The focus of sociological research is placed on the individual or small groups of individuals rather than the overall structure of society. Instead of studying general trends and the wider causes of crime, for example, interpretivists are more likely to study a juvenile gang, to see how they came to be seen and labelled as deviant, and how they themselves see the world. This is sometimes referred to as a *micro approach*.

4   People's behaviour is viewed as being driven by the beliefs, meanings, feelings and emotions they give to situations: their definitions of a situation, or the way they see things and therefore behave, become very important. For example, a parent might interpret a baby crying as a sign of tiredness, hunger, fear or illness. The action the parent takes – putting the baby to bed, feeding her, comforting her or taking her to the doctor – will depend on how the parent defines the situation, and to understand the parent's behaviour we have to understand the meaning he or she gives to the baby's crying. In turn, how the parent acts in response to the meaning given to the baby's behaviour is likely to affect the baby's behaviour – whether it stops crying because it is no longer tired, hungry, afraid or ill.

5   The main methodological approach is *interpretivist*, using qualitative research methods, as the purpose of sociology is to study, uncover and interpret the meanings and definitions individuals give to their behaviour.

There are two main branches of social action theory – symbolic interactionism and ethnomethodology. Weber is often regarded as the first sociologist to place an emphasis on social action, but he will be considered later, as he really combines both structure and action approaches.

Symbolic interactionism

Mead (1863–1931) was the founder of symbolic interactionism, though it was Blumer (1969), a follower of Mead, who actually first used the term. Symbolic interactionism sees society as built up by interactions between people that take place on the basis of meanings held by individuals. Blumer suggests that interactionism has three basic features:

> A **symbol** is something, like an object, word, expression or gesture, that stands for something else and to which individuals have attached some meaning.

1 People act in terms of **symbols**, which are things, like objects, words, expressions or gestures, that stand for something else and to which individuals have attached meanings; they act towards people and things in accordance with these meanings

2 These meanings develop out of the interaction of an individual with others, and can change during the course of interaction

3 Meanings arise from an interpretive process, as people try to interpret the meanings others give to their actions by imagining themselves in their position and taking on their role. Individuals can only develop a conception of themselves by understanding how others see them, and they will be unable to interact successfully with others unless they can do this. For example, successful interaction involves correctly interpreting what sort of person you're dealing with, how they see you, what they expect from you and what you expect from them.

Smiling is a useful way of illustrating this process. A smile is just a physical contortion of the face, but people have learnt through interaction with others to attach to smiling the symbolic meaning of warmth and friendliness. When interacting with someone who is smiling, individuals may, because of this meaning, be encouraged to smile back, particularly if they interpret this as a gesture of warmth and friendliness by the other person. If someone smiles and the individual doesn't respond to this symbol by smiling back, this is likely to influence how the other person sees that individual (as perhaps cold, rude or unfriendly), and if the non-smiling individual doesn't realize this by putting himself in the other person's position, then interaction is likely to end or become fraught. Language is one of the main ways by which humans negotiate meanings, and language – words – are symbols that carry meaning: 'little honey', for example, carries a rather different meaning from 'cheating bastard'.

Symbolic interactionism therefore sees society made possible by, and based on, meanings that are developed, learned and shared through the process of interaction. The task of sociology is to understand how:

- the meanings individuals give to situations are constructed in face-to-face interaction;
- how individuals and situations come to be defined or classified and labelled in particular ways;
- the consequences for individual behaviour of such definitions, as people will behave according to the way they and others see situations.

These pictures show some common symbols that are used in everyday social interaction. What do these symbols stand for, and what consequences might follow if someone misinterpreted or did not understand their meanings?

For example, the sociologist's task might be to understand the point of view and experience of the disillusioned black youth who is very hostile to the police, and feels 'picked on' because of misleading stereotypes and racist assumptions held by the police about black people. Sociologists should try to understand how and why the police classify some black youth as deviant, and what happens to the behaviour of those young people once they have been classified in that way, and whether it amplifies deviance and generates deviant careers (these issues are discussed in chapter 6). Interactionists might also study the way teacher attitudes, streaming and labelling can influence educational achievement and lead to self-fulfilling prophecies.

Ethnomethodology

Ethnomethodology is associated with the work of US sociologist Harold Garfinkel (1984, [1967]). Ethnomethodology refers to the description of the methods or interpretive procedures which people use to make sense of and construct order in their everyday social world.

Ethnomethodology differs from most other social theories, including interactionism, in that it rejects the view that society has any kind of social structure, social order or patterned interaction that exists outside the consciousness of individuals. Social order is an illusion, and only appears to exist because members of society create it in their own minds and impose a sense of order using their own common-sense procedures and culturally embedded rules and assumptions; society only retains some semblance of stability and order because people share these assumptions. Social reality is simply a social construction. For example, Maxwell Atkinson's (1971) study of suicide (see pages 449–500) suggested that classifying a sudden death as a suicide was simply a social construction of meaning – a corpse is nothing more than a lifeless body, and remains so until people decide to construct it as, for example, a 'murder', an 'accident' or a 'suicide'. Suicide therefore doesn't exist 'out there' as something to go and find the causes of; all that can be done is to find out why some unexpected sudden deaths get classified as suicides. This involves looking at the methods or procedures used by coroners to make sense of and impose their classifications of suicide.

Corpses are simply non-functioning biological beings. It is people who give meaning to them, by labelling them as relatives, partners or friends. When people die suddenly in unexpected circumstances, their death only becomes a suicide, an accident, a murder or a natural death when someone decides to give it that label. Ethno-methodologists are interested in how such meanings are constructed.

Garfinkel was interested in discovering how individuals make sense of the social world and create some sense of order in their daily lives. He sought to expose their taken-for-granted assumptions and the rules they impose on the world by experimental techniques aimed at disrupting people's taken-for-granted everyday assumptions. For example, one of Garfinkel's experiments involved asking students to behave as visitors or lodgers in their own homes, and to record how their parents reacted to the sudden change in the taken-for-granted relationship they had with their children. Their reactions of concern, bewilderment, anger and confusion revealed not only the assumptions and rules that people held, but also how fragile the social order people create really is.

Activity

1 The way ethnomethodology tries to explore the rules and assumptions which people use to make sense of the world can be illustrated by language. Understanding language involves a whole host of taken-for-granted rules, which is why learning a new language can be quite difficult, and why we can't make sense of it until we do learn the rules. In the following passage, the accepted rules of the English language have been removed, and the text therefore appears meaningless. Try to reapply the rules of the English language to rediscover its meaning (the answer to this activity is at the end of the chapter):

Ethn omet hod olo gyis asoci olog icaldis cipl inew hich stud iest heways inw hich peo plem akes enseof the irwor lddisp layt hisun derst an dingtoo the rs a ndp roduce themu tuallys har edso cia lor derinw hichth eylive thete rmw asin iti ally co ined byh ar old gar fink elin 1954

2 Try a bit of Garfinkel's experimentation yourself. Think of an everyday encounter in a familiar situation, and how you might alter it in some way to disrupt taken-for-granted rules, such as behaving or speaking in unexpected ways. For example, if someone asks 'How are you today?', give them a full, blow-by-blow detailed and lengthy report on the state of your health, or ask them what they mean by 'How are you?' In what sense? Your health? Your financial situation? and so on. Be careful not to cause too much offence. Describe what happens, and analyse the rules you have exposed, and explain how this shows the way social order and reality are socially constructed.

Evaluation of social action or interpretivist theory

Strengths

1 It shows that human beings create and negotiate meanings, and make sense of the world either through interaction with others (symbolic interactionism) or by drawing on their own common-sense understandings (ethnomethodology). By recognizing that people have reasons and motives for what they do, and by focusing on their particular role in creating meanings, it can be seen that they are not simply puppets moulded by the social system, and this therefore overcomes the determinism of structuralism.

2 Social action theory provides real insights into how the social construction of meanings through interaction has consequences for individuals. For example, in the processes of streaming, labelling and the self-fulfilling prophecy in education; and the labelling of primary and secondary deviance and deviant careers in the study of deviance (see pages 421–5).

3 The interpretivist approach and the use of qualitative methods means that research findings often have high levels of validity. For example, Maxwell Atkinson's qualitative research on suicide, through detailed interviews with coroners and observations of them at work, gained a highly valid in-depth understanding of how coroners came to classify some sudden deaths as suicides.

Weaknesses

1 Social action theory doesn't pay enough attention to the structures of society, and the constraints on individual behaviour that come from these with which structural theorists are concerned. People do not have free choices, and structures and differences in life chances are real, not simply social constructions in the consciousness of individuals. For example, poverty is a real phenomenon, affecting people's health and life expectancy, and their opportunities for choice.

2 It does not really explain people's motivations – the reasons for what they do, and what they hope to achieve by them. Where do people get their goals from?

3 It tends to under-estimate or ignore the distribution of power in society. Not everyone has the same chance of getting their definition or classification of others to 'stick'. For example, the interaction between young people and a police officer who seeks to define their behaviour as deviant does not take place on equal terms.

4   Postmodernists would suggest that action theory is as much a metanarrative as any other theory that claims to provide a full explanation of social life. Action theory is just one of many competing points of view, all of which provide equally valid insights into society.

Integrated approaches – combining structure and action

A third or middle way between structuralism and action theories recognizes the importance of both the constraints of social structure and of the possibilities for choice. In real life, society is probably best understood as using a mixture of both structural *and* action approaches. In other words, constraints from social structures, like the family, work (and the income it does or doesn't produce), the law and education, limit and control the behaviour of individuals or groups, and have important influences on the formation of individual and group identities. However, individuals can, within limits, make choices within those structures and thereby change them. Two theorists operating within this integrated approach are Max Weber and Anthony Giddens.

Weber's sociology

Weber's sociology does not fit neatly into either structuralist or action approaches. He is often regarded as the original social action theorist, and he was the first sociologist to emphasize the importance of understanding the subjective meanings people held and how they viewed the world, reflected in his concept of **Verstehen** – which literally means 'understanding', and involves seeing the world through the eyes of others. Weber rejected what he regarded as the crude determinism of structuralist theories, and particularly Marx's economic determinism, and recognized that people had choice and could act to change structures, and were not simply puppets controlled by them. At the same time, Weber did not dismiss the importance of social structures, particularly the structures of inequality, with his concepts of class, status and party, and how these influenced people's ideas, shaped their lives and life chances, and limited the choices available to them. In many ways, therefore, Weberian sociology combines both structure and action approaches.

> **Verstehen** is the idea of understanding human behaviour by putting yourself in the position of those being studied, and trying to see things from their point of view.

This was illustrated in Weber's study of the emergence of capitalism in Western Europe, *The Protestant Ethic and the Spirit of Capitalism* (2001 [1904]). In this, he identified the significance of the religious ideas (the Protestant ethic in the Calvinist religion) that people held in generating changes in the social structure. He saw these ideas as a major reason why capitalist industrialization developed first in Western Europe, even when other societies had similar levels of technological and economic development. This illustrated well Weber's view that explaining society involves understanding the meanings and motives for people's actions, such as the meaning of Protestantism to Protestants, by the process of *Verstehen*, as well as the influence of social structures such as the level of development of the economy.

Giddens's theory of structuration

Giddens's (1986) theory of **structuration** is an attempt to combine both structure and action, which he regards as two parts of the same process. Structuration refers to the two-way process by which people are constrained or shaped by society and social institutions, but they can at the same time take action to support, shape and change them. The theory suggests that the existence of the social structure, including social institutions, beliefs, values and traditions, provides people with a framework of rules and established ways of doing things that enable them to live in society, and by doing so they are at the same time reproducing that structure. At the same time, individuals can change this structure by ignoring, modifying or replacing rules or conventional ways of doing things. So people are shaped by society, but at the same time can act to shape society. Structuration theory can be illustrated by the legal system.

The legal system is part of the social structure, and the law has an existence separate from and above the individuals living in society at any one time. People are constrained (forced) by the law to behave in particular ways, and this allows them to go about their daily lives in some orderly fashion; because their actions conform to the law, the law is able to continue from one generation to the next. However, the law can continue only so long as people continue to support it. For example, laws might prohibit the use of cannabis, and those who disobey this law risk punishment by the criminal justice system. But if there is very widespread use of cannabis and disregard for the law, the law would either have to be enforced despite the wishes of the majority of the population, risking it becoming treated with widespread contempt, or it would have to be abandoned or changed. This shows human beings can create and reinforce, or change or destroy, structures. The cannabis laws are a good example of this, as attitudes to the law and the use of cannabis have changed dramatically over the years as people acted in defiance of the law and campaigned to change it, and it

> **Structuration** refers to the two-way process by which people are constrained or shaped by society and social institutions, but they can at the same time take action to support, shape and change them.

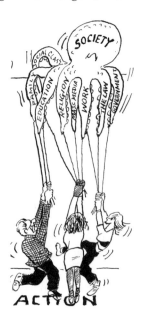

Structuration theory refers to the two-way process by which the actions of individuals shape their social world, but they are themselves shaped by society.

became clear that the social structure (the law and punishments) needed to change to reflect changing attitudes.

This shows that social structures, like the law, while constraining human action, also enable human action to take place in an orderly way, and people constantly reproduce these structures by their actions in supporting them. The social structure has to be supported by people, and constantly recreated by their active involvement and support of social institutions. At the same time, people can also act in ways to change that social structure. This doesn't mean that they can act in any way they like, as the reactions and expectations of others will limit their possibilities of doing so, and often even minor infringements of social rules can shock people, as you may have found in the earlier Garfinkel activity of responding to the question 'How are you today?'.

Evaluation of integrated approaches

Integrated approaches which combine structural and action theories have been criticized by structuralists for overstating the capacity of individuals to change society, and under-estimating the constraints on individual choices of action. Action theorists tend to regard them as perhaps understating the capacity of individuals to change society, and over-estimating the constraints of the social structure on individual choices of action. This probably means that integrated approaches have got it about right.

Structure, action and integration: a conclusion

It is easy to get the impression that sociological theory and research is divided into two opposing camps, with structuralists focusing on macro social structural forces, using research methods generating quantitative data, and action theorists focusing on micro group or individual action, using interpretivist research methods generating qualitative data. In the real world of practical research, most sociologists will combine structural and action theoretical approaches – a kind of real world Weberian or structuration approach. There is often a similar process of theoretical pluralism and triangulation as the methodological pluralism and triangulation found in combining quantitative and qualitative research methods. Sociologists are in most cases interested in explaining the social world, and they will use whatever theories and methods seem most suited to achieving this.

Modernism and postmodernism

The terms 'modernism' and 'postmodernism' refer to the beliefs and theories which are associated with two periods in human society known as modernity and, following it, postmodernity. The features of modernity and postmodernity are contrasted in table 5.2 on pages 361–2, which you should study carefully, as it covers a lot of important material.

What is modernism?

The main features of modernity and modernist views are shown in table 5.2 below; they include:

- industrialization and the manufacture of standardized goods for a mass market;
- work and social class as the main forms of social division and social identity, and both culture and politics are social class-related;
- independent nation-states, national economies and national identities;
- one-way mass media more or less reflecting social reality;
- a belief in rational thought and science as a means of improving the world;
- a view that sociological theory and research can provide insight into and explanations of the social world, and could be used to improve it.

What is postmodernism?

Chaos, uncertainty and the collapse of social structures

Unlike modernism, postmodernism stresses the chaos and uncertainty in society, and argues that social structures like the nation-state, the family and social class are breaking down. Postmodernists argue that it is nonsense to talk of an institution called the family, for example, as people now live in such a wide range of ever-changing personal relationships. Gay and lesbian couples, cohabiting heterosexual couples who do not marry, multiple partners, high rates of divorce and remarriage, lone parents, step-parents and stepchildren, dual income families with both partners working, people living alone, people living in shared households with friends, couples who have differing arrangements for organizing household tasks: all mean that any notion of the 'typical family' or 'the family as an institution' is absurd.

Postmodernists see national cultures and identities dissolving, as globalization means the same product brands and designer labels are found in many countries of the world.

Globalization

Supra-national bodies, like the European Union and the United Nations, interconnected economies, multinational and transnational corporations and global cultures are displacing national states and national identities.

Metanarratives and the 'myth of truth'

Lyotard (1984) described postmodernism as 'an incredulity towards metanarratives', and argued that people no longer believed in the 'myth of truth'. Because society is now changing so constantly and so rapidly, societies can no longer be understood through the application of general theories or metanarratives. Metanarratives are 'big' theories like Marxism or functionalism, which seek to explain society as a whole, but these no longer apply, according to postmodernists, because society has become fragmented into so many different groups, interests and lifestyles that are constantly changing that society is essentially chaotic. There has been a loss of faith in the superiority of rational thought and science, and the idea of progress. All knowledge of any kind is now equally valid.

Choice, identity and consumption

Postmodernists believe there are few of the social constraints on people that structuralist approaches identify, and society and social structures cease to exist – there is only a mass of individuals making individual choices about their lifestyles. In postmodern societies, the emphasis is on individuals as consumers, making their own choices in education, health, their personal relationships and lifestyle. People can now form their own identities – how they see and define themselves and how others see and define them – and they can be whatever they want to be. Postmodern society involves a media-saturated consumer culture in which individuals are free to 'pick 'n' mix' and change identities and lifestyles chosen from a limitless range of constantly changing consumer goods and leisure activities, which are available from across the globe.

A media-saturated society

Baudrillard (2001) sees life in the postmodern era as being so dominated by media imagery that it has become what he calls 'media-saturated'. The mass media used more or less to reflect some basic reality, but media images now dominate and distort the way we see the world. Baudrillard suggests that the media present what he calls

To what extent do you think contemporary society is media-saturated and both distorts reality and creates the way people see the world?

simulacra – images that appear to reflect events in the real world but that have no basis in reality, and which are viewed simultaneously across the globe. Even images of real events are so distorted and distanced from reality that they actually replace reality. For example, the reality of a missile hitting its target is not shown to a viewer, but is a simulacrum of the real event. Laser technology and video reportage have eliminated the blood, the suffering and the corpses from war, and the TV news presents a sanitized version of conflicts. As a result, wars become media-constructed spectacles, which have such an air of unreality about them that we are unable to distinguish them from Hollywood movies or video games.

Baudrillard calls this distorted view of the world **hyperreality**. The view is actually created and defined by the media, and the image becomes more real than reality as it tries to make viewers feel they are experiencing an 'event'. Some 'celebrities', for example, are well know not for actually doing something, but just because they have been made famous by the media. All this means, as Giddens (2006) puts it, that 'much of our world has become a sort of make-believe universe in which we are responding to media images rather than to real persons or places', as is shown by people who write to characters in television soaps, imagining that they are real. For example, in *Coronation Street* in 1998, the character Deirdre Barlow was sent to prison *in the show* for a crime she did not commit. A media-fuelled grassroots campaign began, pleading with Granada Television to 'free the Weatherfield One'. The real-world home secretary even involved the prime minister, who, with only a touch of irony, attempted to intervene in this unreal world on Deirdre's behalf.

> **Simulacra** are images or reproductions and copies which appear to reflect things in the real world but have no basis in reality.

> **Hyperreality** is a view of the world which is actually created and defined by the media.

'Pick 'n' mix' identities

Baudrillard (2001) sees postmodernism involving the consumption of media-created desires, and pressures to consume, with individual identity no longer formed predominantly by factors such as class, ethnicity or gender, but by information, images and signs like designer labels gained from the media. In a globalized popular culture, the mass media present to us a massive choice of lifestyles, images and identities drawn from across the world. Bradley (1996) argues that new identities are created by globalization, bringing different cultural groups into contact. People now adopt different identities to meet the diversity in their lives – they no longer identify with class alone, but with ethnicity, gender, sexuality, disability, race, religion, nationality, music, fashion designer labels, dress, sport and other leisure activities – they can 'pick and mix' to create whatever identities they wish.

You are what you buy

Bauman (1996) argues that life in postmodern society resembles a shopping mall, where people can stroll around consuming whatever they like, trying out and constructing whatever identities they choose, and changing them whenever they want. In this postmodern 'pick 'n' mix' consumer society, the influences of class, gender and ethnicity are no longer so relevant, and people can become whatever they want to be, adopting lifestyles and identities built around the almost unlimited choice of leisure activities and consumer goods available in what has become a globalized consumer market.

Table 5.2: Modernity and postmodernity

Modern society or modernity	Postmodern society or postmodernity
Industrialization and the use of technology for the manufacture of standardized goods for a mass market, usually produced by full-time (5-day) manual workers in lifetime jobs.	Rapid and continuous introduction of new goods and services, with much wider consumer choice. Manual work and mass manufacturing replaced by service economy, like finance, telecommunications, various kinds of information processing and customer service. Jobs for life disappear, with more job changes, job-sharing, more flexible, 24/7 and part-time working.
Central importance of work and social class as the main form of social division and source of identity. Bradley (1996) saw identity as fairly predictable, unchanging and stable, formed by social structural factors, like family life, work, social class, gender, ethnicity and community.	Consumption, media images and lifestyle become the major sources of identity. Bradley suggests identities become less predictable, more fluid and fragmented, and based more on choice than constraints of social structural factors. People can now have 'pick 'n' mix' multiple identities and change them at will. There is a fragmentation of identities even among people in the same social groups, reflecting the fragmentation of classes and other social structures. Bauman (1996) suggested that lives now gain meaning through consumption choices, influenced by designer labels, lifestyles and images gained from the global media in a media-saturated society.
Culture reflects the class structure, with clear distinctions between high and mass or popular culture.	Culture becomes more diverse and fragmented, and people 'pick 'n' mix' elements from an increasingly diverse global culture, which becomes just another product to consume. The distinctions between high and low/popular/mass culture dissolve.
Politics centre around social structural class interests, focused around political parties and government.	Politics become more personalized and linked to the diversity of consumer, lifestyle and identity choices. Party politics are displaced by identity politics, such as gay, lesbian, feminist, ethnic and religious (e.g. Islam) politics. New social movements emerge based on personal concerns rather than structural influences, such as the peace movement and environmental campaigns. The macro politics of political parties and government decline, and are replaced by micro politics of single issue more localized campaigns and locally based transnational, global campaigns.
Nation-states, national economies and national identities predominate.	Nation-states and national identities are displaced by globalization. Supra-national bodies, like the European Union and the United Nations, and multinational and transnational companies making global products, like Starbucks, McDonald's, Ford, Sony and Samsung, eclipse national and local identities. Global media and global marketing in a media-saturated society turn the world into a global supermarket.
Mass media concerned with one-way communication, more or less reflecting or mirroring a basic social reality, through media like terrestrial TV, newspapers and magazines.	Society becomes dominated by the new global interactive digital media, like social networking websites and electronic communication, including the Internet. Media become more removed from reality. Strinati (1995) suggests that media imagery becomes a source of individual identity, and the mass media now dominate and create our sense of reality, generating what Baudrillard called hyperreality in a media-saturated society.

Table 5.2 (continued)

Modern society or modernity	Postmodern society or postmodernity
Tradition, religion, magic and superstition are displaced by rational thought and scientific theories, which are seen as superior forms of knowledge for discovering the truth about and understanding the world, and therefore improving it.	Objective truth is undiscoverable. Lyotard (1984) argues that individuals have lost faith in progress and in metanarratives – the all-embracing 'big stories' like the natural and social sciences which try to produce all-inclusive explanations of the world. Metanarratives are just myths, and there are no certain or absolute truths about the world. Every question has an infinite number of answers, and all forms of knowledge are equally valid. For example, scientific theory is no more valid than knowledge provided by New Age beliefs and religions. There is a loss of faith in the certainty, rational thought and scientific and technological progress of modernism. These are replaced by risk, doubt, uncertainty and anxiety.
Scientific knowledge and scientific and technological progress are forces for good, providing the means to understand and solve the world's problems and make the world a better place.	Science and technology often cause rather than solve problems, such as climate change, pollution and antibiotic resistant superbugs. There is growing scepticism about the idea of progress, and science as a force for good and its ability to explain and improve the world.
Sociology developed to try to understand and explain society in a scientific way, with rationality and scientific methods providing the tools to understand the workings of society in order to improve it. The development of positivist structural theories like functionalism and Marxism reflected the modernist concern with using the same scientific methods used in the natural sciences to explain society.	Everything is in a permanent state of flux. Society is changing so constantly and rapidly, with social structures breaking down, that there is chaos and uncertainty. Societies can no longer be understood through the application of metanarratives like Marxism or functionalism which seek to explain society as a whole, because society has become fragmented into so many different groups, interests and lifestyles that are constantly changing that society is essentially chaotic. There are few of the social constraints on people that structuralist approaches identify, and society and social structures cease to exist – there is only a mass of individuals making individual choices about their lifestyles. Sociological theories are just one set of ideas competing against other equally valid ideas, and provide no basis for improving society.

Activity

Refer to table 5.2 and answer the following questions:
1 Identify the following statements about postmodernism as true or false
   a) the mass media reflect reality
   b) individual identity is formed by the social structure
   c) scientific knowledge is superior to common sense
   d) politics is based around social class interests
   e) science can solve the world's problems
   f) the social structure has become fragmented
   g) you can be whatever you want to be

2 Suggest whether each of the following statements is more likely to be regarded as true by a modernist or postmodernist, and explain your reasons in each case:
   a) There is no such thing as society, only individuals.
   b) Philosophers have merely interpreted the world; the point is to change it.
   c) If there is one thing we should have learned by now, it is the total obsolescence of any idea that it is possible to distinguish truth from falsehood, or science from ideology.
   d) People trip on pavements because they walk under ladders.
   e) Industrialization and urbanization, the growth of science and the abandonment of religious beliefs in order to understand the world gave way to the need for new ways of understanding and explaining society.
   f) A rational understanding is an understanding of reality which is valid because it starts from valid premises.

Strengths of postmodernism

1 It has highlighted some important cultural changes, particularly in the areas of the media, culture and identity.
2 It emphasizes that the construction of identity has become a more fluid and complex process, and cannot be reduced to simply a response to social structural factors.
3 It provides insight into most contemporary social changes, such as growing risk and uncertainty, globalization, and the growing power of the media.
4 In challenging sociological metanarratives, it has perhaps encouraged sociologists to reflect more on some of their assumptions, how they set about their research, and the meaning of some contemporary social changes.

Critical views of postmodernism

Giddens: late modernity and reflexivity   Giddens (1991, 2006) doesn't dispute that the changes in society that postmodernists identify have occurred, such as globalization, the declining power of nation-states and the growing diversity of identities, social movements, cultures and ways of life. He accepts that we live in what he calls a 'runaway world' marked by new risks and uncertainties, and that neither people nor institutions can any longer take for granted established ways of doing things. However, he says that these changes have not brought us into a new era of postmodernity, but into what he calls late modernity or high modernity. Giddens sees late modernity as characterized by what he calls social **reflexivity**. This means that the knowledge we gain from society can affect the way we act in it (much as the interpretivists say). In late modernity, reflexivity grows in importance, as the speed of social change and growing uncertainty mean that social institutions are constantly having to reflect on what they do and how they do things, and people are having to think about and reflect on the circumstances in which they live their lives. In late modernity, reflexivity for individuals focuses on personal freedom and fulfilment as people

Reflexivity refers to the way the knowledge people gain about society can affect the way they behave in it, as people (and institutions) reflect on what they do and how they do it.

establish goals for what Giddens calls their 'life projects'. This social reflexivity means that people and institutions can act to change and improve the world, which is part of the modernist era.

Beck: 'risk society' and reflexive modernity   Beck (1992) suggests that there is a new phase of modernity – 'reflexive modernity' – in which there are high levels of uncertainty and risk in what he calls the 'risk society'. These risks occur in rapidly changing everyday life in social institutions like the family, as seen in things like rising divorce rates and the growing diversity of personal relationships; they can also be seen in the failings or abuse of so-called scientific and technological progress in modernity, such as environmental pollution, climate change, nuclear accidents, genetically modified crops, avian flu, *E. Coli*, MRSA, *C. difficile* and other antibiotic resistant superbugs. These risks from science are different from the natural disasters and plagues of the past, which were beyond human control, as many are generated by progress itself. While Beck recognizes that science still carries risks of making things worse, it also has the capacity to make things better – and that is a feature of modernity. Beck shares with Giddens the idea of reflexivity, and suggests that we are living in a period of reflexive modernity, as people and institutions need to think and reflect more about risks today, work out how to resolve problems, and therefore change society.

Harvey and Marxism   Harvey (1990) suggests that many of the changes claimed by postmodernists to be evidence of postmodernity can be explained by modernist theories such as Marxism. Harvey suggests, for example, that changes like globalization, rapid cultural change, the growth of consumerism and the individualization of identity reflect capitalism opening up new markets and new sources of profits in a global economy.

The work of Giddens, Beck and Harvey suggests that, though there has been a lot of very rapid social change, and that everyday life is breaking free from tradition and custom and is more fluid and chaotic today, the distinction between modernity and postmodernity is exaggerated. What is called 'postmodernity' is little other than the latest developments within modernity, and the changes can be explained by adapting existing sociological theories like Marxism, and developing more sophisticated new ones, as in Giddens's theory of structuration, or Beck's and Giddens's ideas of reflexivity. These changes do not mean that knowledge is always relative as the postmodernists contend, and that rational thought and research cannot explain society and find solutions to its problems. It is still possible to develop general theories of the social world, and such theories can help to shape society in a positive way, and governments still have the power to intervene to improve society.

Other criticisms of postmodernism

1   It is all criticism, and since it sees no knowledge or vision as any better than any other, it lacks any values, vision of society or progress. It undermines any idea of progress and improvement, and, in a world with widespread poverty, inequality and injustice, this is, in effect, ignoring widespread social problems.

2 It overemphasizes the influence of the mass media, and tends to assume that people are passive, and easily duped and manipulated by the media. People are perfectly able to make judgements about what is real and what is not, and are aware that the media do not always, or even often, provide the truth about the world.

3 It exaggerates the scale of social change, such as that cultural distinctions are blurred, and that there is a global culture. Cultural tastes are still strongly influenced by class, gender and ethnicity, and national cultures and identities are still strong.

4 It is too voluntaristic, in that it assumes that all individuals are free to act as they wish and can create, pick and choose and change identities at will. Social structural factors still exert major influences. For example, people are still constrained by economic factors, which influence their consumption. Class, gender and ethnicity are still major defining characteristics in contemporary societies.

5 Postmodernism is itself a metanarrative, and if metanarratives and absolute truths are dismissed by postmodernists, then it has, in effect, dismissed itself as having anything to say that is any more valid than anything else

6 Ollocks (2008) suggests that postmodernism is simply an exhausting intellectual game using obscure ideas and complicated and flowery language to disguise what are, in effect, nonsensical ideas, with one critic dismissing much postmodernist writing as 'verbose stretches of important sounding but ultimately meaningless rhetorical gymnastics'.

This was shown by the *Social Text* affair in 1996. Alan Sokal, a physicist and critic of postmodernism, wrote an article that appeared to be about interpreting physics and mathematics in terms of postmodern theory. It was in fact nonsense, and an experimental hoax designed to test whether a postmodernist journal would publish any nonsensical article with elaborate words that flattered the editors' political views. *Social Text*, a postmodernist journal, published the article as a serious work, which subsequently triggered an academic scandal.

Activity (and a bit of fun)

Go to www.physics.nyu.edu/faculty/sokal/ (the site of Alan Sokal), and have a glance at the material that is there (it contains the original *Social Text* article, but you are only advised to read it if you have masochistic tendencies).

1 Suggest reasons why you think there was an academic scandal after Sokal's article was published in *Social Text*.

2 Do you think such an experimental method has any ethical problems?

3 Go to www.elsewhere.org/pomo/. This is the postmodernist essay generator. This produces a random and ultimately meaningless essay in postmodernist style. Each time you click the Refresh button, a new essay is generated. Spend a few minutes reading one of the essays and comment on the style. To what extent do you think such writing, whether meaningless or not, helps to develop our understanding of the world?

The scientific method

Popper (2002) suggests that science involves the hypothetico-deductive method. This involves drawing up a specific question or idea for research (a hypothesis), which is based on previous research, observation and hunches. For example, a researcher looking at official crime statistics might deduce that young people have a greater involvement in crime, leading to the formation of a hypothesis for investigation and testing that this might be due to status frustration. Popper's features of the scientific method include:

1 *Hypothesis formation*: forming ideas or informed guesses about the possible causes of some phenomena. For a hypothesis to be scientific, it must be capable of being tested against evidence derived from systematic observation and/or experimentation
2 *Falsification*: the aim of testing hypotheses against the evidence is to try to prove them wrong, as just one exception can prove a hypothesis false.
3 *Prediction*: through establishing cause-and-effect relationships rooted in evidence, precise predictions of what will happen in the same circumstances in future can be established.
4 *Theory formation*: if the hypothesis is capable of being tested against evidence and cannot be shown to be false, and predictions appear sound, then there can be some confidence that the hypothesis is probably true. This may then become part of a scientific theory.
5 *Scrutiny*: a scientific theory will be scrutinized by other scientists, and will stand only until some new evidence comes along to show the existing theory is false.

Underpinning this approach to science is the testing of hypotheses against **empirical evidence**, which is observable data collected in the real physical or social world. **Objectivity** is an important part of the scientific process, and the data collected are seen as objective facts, not distorted by the value judgements and personal beliefs of the scientist. Objectivity involves three main aspects:

● open-mindedness on the part of the researcher, and a willingness to consider all possibilities and evidence, to demonstrate 'fair play' and act in good faith;
● **value-freedom** – keeping personal prejudices, opinions and values out of the research process;
● findings should be open to inspection and criticism by other researchers: the 'community of scientists' should have the opportunity to scrutinize and check findings, and criticize them.

Empirical evidence is observable evidence collected in the physical or social world.

Objectivity means approaching topics with an open mind, avoiding bias, and being prepared to submit research evidence to scrutiny by other researchers.

Value-freedom is the idea that the beliefs and prejudices of a researcher should not influence the way research is carried out and evidence interpreted.

Positivism

Positivism is the view that the logic, methods and procedures of the natural sciences, as used in subjects like physics, chemistry and biology, can be applied to the study of society with little modification. Such claims were made by many of the founders of

How does studying society differ from the procedures used in the natural sciences?

sociology. Comte, for example, argued that the application of natural science methodology to the study of society would produce a 'positive science of society', showing that behaviour in the social world is governed by laws in the same way as behaviour in the natural world.

Durkheim, in *The Rules of Sociological Method* (1895), argued clearly for a positivist approach in sociology, with his fundamental rule: 'Consider social facts as things' (see below). Sociology rarely produces results that are as precise and repeatable as those produced by natural scientists (although this is not seen as a major problem by positivists). This is partly because sociologists are unable to control all the variables in the situations they study, as natural scientists are able to do under laboratory conditions. Nonetheless, positivists argue that applying the procedures of the natural sciences to the study of society enables an objective and value-free science of society.

Social facts

Social facts are phenomena that exist outside individuals and independently of their minds, but which act upon them in ways that constrain or mould their behaviour.

Positivists believe that just as there are causes of things in the natural world, so there are **social facts** that cause events in the social world. Durkheim said the aim of sociology should be the study of these social facts, which should be considered as things, like objects in the natural world, and could in most cases be observed and measured quantitatively – in number/statistical form. By social facts, Durkheim meant social phenomena that exist outside individuals but act upon them in ways that constrain their behaviour. These include customs, belief systems and social institutions, such as the family, law and the education system. For example, social classes are social facts, with clear measurable differences between them, such as in income, crime rates, housing, health and educational achievement; although social classes exist independently of individuals, they shape the way they act. For positivists, society has a reality that is external to individuals, and social facts – for example, customs and norms – although independent of the individual, exercise constraint on and limit the options of individuals. Simply put, individuals cannot do exactly as they wish without coming up against a whole range of social sanctions which curb the opportunities for anti-social behaviour.

The main features of positivism in sociology

Positivists argue that the scientific approach in sociology should follow the hypothetico-deductive method and consists of the following features:

1. First is a view that human behaviour is a response to observable social facts, and can be explained in terms of cause and effect relationships
2. Direct observation and the use of quantitative, statistical methods of data collection should be used to study society. Only those factors that are directly observable and can be statistically measured form acceptable data: the feelings, motives and mental states of individuals cannot be observed, and are therefore inadmissible evidence. Without quantification, sociology will remain at the level of insight, lacking evidence, and it will be impossible to replicate (or repeat) studies to check findings, establish the causes of social events or make generalizations.
3. Research should focus on the search for the social causes of events in society. Examples might be to establish hypotheses about why people in some social classes suffer poorer health, are more likely to commit suicide or get involved in crime than those in other classes, and look for causes by studying official statistics or carrying out surveys. This is what Durkheim tried to do in his 1897 study *Suicide*, in which he suggested that the causes of suicide were imbalances in the degrees of social integration and moral regulation in society (see pages 493–6 for a discussion of Durkheim's study of suicide).
4. The focus of sociology is on the study of social institutions and the social structure as a whole, not on the individual.

Interpretivism

Interpretivism emphasizes the difference between studying society and studying the natural and physical world. Interpretivists argue that people do not simply respond to external forces, as positivists claim; they interpret and give meaning to a situation before responding to it. It is therefore impossible to predict human behaviour or to establish simple cause-and-effect relationships by simple observation, experimentation and the collection of empirical, quantitative data obtained through surveys or

How might positivists and interpretivists differently explain the fact that (most) people conform to the norm of stopping at a red traffic light?

official statistics. In order to understand and explain human society, it is necessary to discover and interpret the meanings given to situations. This is achieved by allowing people to 'speak for themselves'. Weber argued that this is a process of 'understanding', which he termed, in German, *Verstehen* (pronounced *ver-stay-en*). *Verstehen* involves recognizing the meanings that people give to their actions, and researchers try to put themselves in the position of the people whose actions they are trying to understand.

Interpretivists emphasize that meanings do not exist independently of people. For example, social phenomena such as suicide, crime and social class are social constructions that have no reality outside the meaning given to them by people. A tree or mountain exists whether people are there or not. A sudden unnatural death only becomes a 'murder', a 'manslaughter', an 'accident' or a 'suicide' because people define it as such, and these definitions can change from place to place and from person to person. There can be no laws of human society, and no possibility of prediction as human behaviour is variable and changeable. Sociologists cannot hope to explain anything without moving from quantitative, empirical data towards a more qualitative understanding of peoples' own subjective views of the world.

Positivism, interpretivism and research methods

Positivists and interpretivists have differing conceptions of the nature of society. For positivists, society has a reality external to individuals – there are social facts independent of the individual which exercise constraint over her or him. For interpretivists, society is a socially created set of meanings shared by a social group. As a result, there are conflicting views and a basic disagreement about what counts as proper sociological research evidence, and different explanations and understandings of human behaviour.

Since they begin with different assumptions about the nature of society, positivist and interpretivist perspectives employ different research methodologies to gain knowledge about society.

Positivism and quantitative data

Positivists prefer observable (empirical), measurable data to test their ideas. Positivist research is therefore more likely to involve large-scale or macro research on large numbers of people, and is generally associated with structural theories of society, like those of Marxism and functionalism (discussed above). This means they tend to record 'social facts', using *quantitative*, statistical techniques, including:

- the use of official statistics, like those on suicide, crime, or social class;
- the experiment;
- the comparative method;
- social surveys;
- structured questionnaires;
- formal/structured interviews;
- non-participant observation.

Interpretivism and qualitative data

Interpretivists are more concerned with understanding the meanings that individuals give to situations – how they see things and how these perceptions direct social action. They therefore see a need to get personally involved with people, through deep conversations with them in unstructured interviews, by close observation and by participation in their activities, in order to understand how they see the world and the motives and meanings behind their actions. For example, interpretivist research on crime is less likely to use the positivist approach of looking for the *causes* of crime, but is more likely to study, as Becker did, how and why some behaviour becomes defined as deviant while other similar behaviour does not, and how people respond to being labelled as deviant or criminal. Interpretivists are therefore more likely to use *qualitative* research methods, giving in-depth description and insight into the attitudes, values, meanings, interpretations and feelings of individuals and groups, which they see as the only way to produce a valid (or truthful) understanding of society. Such methods involve small-scale or micro research on small numbers of people, associated with social action theories such as interactionism, and include:

- participant and (sometimes) non-participant observation;
- informal (unstructured/in-depth) interviews;
- open-ended questionnaires;
- use of personal accounts like diaries and letters.

Figure 5.4 shows the broad links that exist between the two different theoretical approaches of positivism and interpretivism, other wider theories of society identified with them and the research methods most likely to be used.

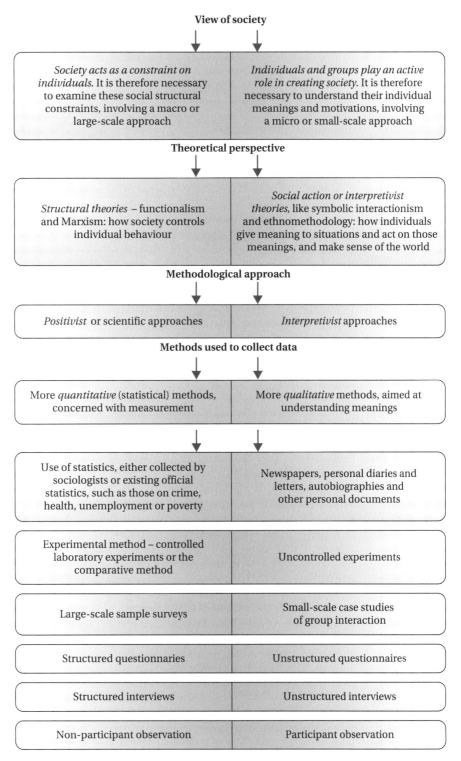

Figure 5.4 A summary of the link between sociological theories and research methods

> **Activity**
>
> Take one or both of the following topic areas:
> - a study of cannabis smoking among white youth in an inner city
> - a study of what social class people are in
> 1 Suggest in each case a question that interpretivists might wish to explore, and a hypothesis that positivists might wish to test.
> 2 Outline the different method or methods that might be used by interpretivists and positivists to do this, and explain your reasons.
> 3 Explain how valid and reliable the research by these different methods might be, giving your reasons

Science and the study of society

As outlined earlier, there are disagreements within sociology as to how far the logic, methods and procedures of the natural sciences can be applied to the study of society. Many sociologists argue that the methods of the natural sciences (such as the laboratory experiment and the use of observable, quantitative data) are inappropriate or insufficient for the study of society. This is because there are fundamental differences between the social world and the natural or physical world, and sociology therefore cannot simply copy the approach and methodology of natural science, as the following points suggest:

1 *The problem of prediction*. In natural science, experiments can be carried out to test ideas and it is possible to isolate causes in laboratory conditions; therefore, natural scientists can accurately predict what will happen in the same circumstances in the future. Human beings, however, might behave differently in an experiment knowing they are being observed. Human behaviour cannot be predicted with certainty: people might react differently to the same circumstances on different occasions – for example, not everyone facing the same set of circumstances will commit suicide

2 *Artificiality*. Sociology wants to study society in its *normal* state, not in the artificial conditions of a laboratory experiment.

3 *Ethical issues*. Human beings might well object to being boiled, weighed, wired, prodded with sticks, interrogated or observed in laboratories

4 *The Hawthorne effect*. In the natural sciences, the presence of the scientist does not usually affect the behaviour of chemicals or objects. However, sociologists studying people may themselves change the behaviour of those being studied. When people are being interviewed or observed, they may become embarrassed, be more defensive and careful about what they say, or act differently because they have been selected for study (this is known as the 'Hawthorne effect'). If this happens, then the results obtained will not give a true picture of how people behave in society.

5 *Validity*. The natural scientist does not have to persuade objects, chemicals or, usually, animals to cooperate in research, but people may distort and conceal

the truth, refuse to answer questions or otherwise cooperate, making sociological research difficult or impossible. Those who have attempted, but failed, to commit suicide may, for example, later invent reasons for their suicidal behaviour which might be quite different from their real motives at the time. This raises the possibility of obtaining invalid or untruthful evidence.

6   *Empirical observation.* Popper suggests that scientific hypotheses must be capable of being tested against evidence derived from systematic observation and/or experimentation. However, not all social phenomena are observable or quantifiable, such as the meanings and motives people have for their behaviour. However, the realist view of science suggests that this is also true in the natural sciences (see below).

The earlier discussion of positivism and interpretivism highlighted different approaches to the study of society, with the positivists seeing 'good sociology' modelled on the natural sciences. Nonetheless, sociology as a whole (including positivist research) is often seen as inferior to the natural sciences, and made out to be sloppy and less scientific than natural science research. This is because sociology rarely produces results or is able to make predictions with the same kind of precision as those of natural scientists, and sociological research is often difficult to replicate to check findings. However, this comparison rests on assumptions that natural scientists are wholly objective and value-free, remorselessly engaged in the pursuit of scientific truth as they attempt to falsify their hypotheses through the scrupulous and detached collection of observable empirical data, and able to make accurate predictions based on scientific laws. There are two general reasons to doubt this view of natural science:

1   It is based on mistaken assumptions about what natural science and scientific method are really like, as the realists suggest.
2   It ignores the way scientific knowledge is socially constructed.

The realist view of science

Bhaskar (1998) adopts a realist view of science. He suggests that not all phenomena are material objects or (for positivists) social facts capable of observation and measurement, but there can be underlying, unobservable structures that cause events. Part of 'doing science' is the discovery and explanation of what these structures are. Bhaskar argues that these underlying structures are a feature of both the natural and the social worlds, and the positivist view is based on an incorrect assumption that the natural scientific method, as Popper suggests, is based only on that which can be observed. For example, many of the greatest scientific discoveries have not been directly observed, but are inferred or worked out from their effects. These include things like sub-atomic particles, viruses, germs, energy and solar fusion. The view that the earth is round has been an accepted view of science for hundreds of years, yet it was only physically observed in the 1960s, with the start of space exploration.

That the earth is round has been an accepted scientific fact for hundreds of years, yet it was only physically observed last century with the start of space exploration. Studying the social world also includes many things that aren't observable, but does this make it any more 'unscientific' than natural science?

Even Durkheim, who as a positivist claimed to use natural science methodology, used the twin social forces of social integration and moral regulation to explain suicide, though neither was observable or quantifiable. So natural science is not simply limited to the observable, as Popper suggests. Sayer (1992), another realist, points out that prediction is often not as precise a process in natural science as Popper claims. Natural science has an advantage over social science in predictive powers when it can study events in what Sayer calls *closed systems*, when all the potential causal factors are under the control of the researcher, as in the closed environment of the laboratory experiment. However, much natural scientific research, like most sociological research, takes place in much more *open systems*, where these factors can't be controlled, and prediction is much more difficult and imprecise. An example might be weather forecasting, where, despite a huge range of sophisticated technology and scientific knowledge, natural science still often fails to give accurate predictions of whether or not it will rain tomorrow. In short, the claim that sociology is unscientific because it is unable to predict human behaviour, and shouldn't aim to copy natural scientific methods because all the factors necessary to explain human behaviour are not observable, as the interpretivists suggest, is based on a mistaken view of what real natural scientific research is like. Researching the social world and the natural world therefore may have more in common than might first appear.

The social construction of scientific knowledge

Popper's principle of falsification

Popper suggests that no hypothesis can ever finally be proven true, as there is always the possibility of some future exception. However, a hypothesis can easily be proven false, as just one observation to the contrary can disprove it. Popper used the famous case of the 'white swan' to make his point. He argues that the hypothesis that 'all swans are white' can never be finally proven true because there is always the possibility of finding an exception; but it can easily be proven wrong or falsified by finding just one example of a non-white swan. So Popper argues that the aim of researchers should not be to prove that their hypotheses are true, but to falsify them, or prove them wrong. The more a hypothesis stands up to such attempts, the more likely it is to be a 'scientific truth' – though it will remain only a probability and not a proven fact, as an exception may always come along.

Kuhn, the influence of paradigms and 'scientific revolutions'

Kuhn's book *The Structure of Scientific Revolutions* (1962) challenges whether scientists really do in practice set out to collect evidence with the specific aim of trying to falsify their hypotheses, as Popper suggests they should. Kuhn argues that, on the contrary, scientists work within a **paradigm** – a set of values, ideas, beliefs and assumptions about what they are investigating which is not called into question until the evidence against them is overwhelming.

> A **paradigm** is a set of values, ideas, beliefs and assumptions within which scientists operate, and which provide guidelines for the conduct of research and what counts as proper evidence.

A paradigm, a set of values, can be compared to a pair of coloured lenses through which scientists look at the world. The paradigm colours their views of the nature of the problem or problems to be investigated, the 'approved' methods that should be followed to tackle these problems, and what should count as proper and relevant scientific evidence. Paradigms are learnt by scientists in their training, during which they are socialized into the accepted view of 'normal science', based on the values of the scientific community at the time. This is just like sociologists learning different methodological approaches such as positivism or interpretivism, and what counts as 'good sociology'.

Popper argues that a proposition like 'all swans are white' is a scientific hypothesis because it can be tested by empirical research; but it can never be finally proven true because there is always the possibility of finding an exception. So scientists should hunt for the exception, or the non-white swan, to falsify their hypotheses, rather than for evidence to prove them true.

Kuhn argues that most scientists in their experimental work try to fit observations into the paradigm rather than actually attempting to falsify their hypotheses, as Popper suggests. The more an idea challenges the dominant paradigm, the more experimental work is scrutinized for error; the more findings do not fit into the existing paradigm, the more likely they are to be dismissed and the blame laid on experimental errors or freak conditions. Only when there are many anomalies, or things that the existing paradigm can't explain, will the established paradigm change, as scientists begin to question their basic assumptions and produce a new paradigm that explains the new evidence that cannot be fitted into the old paradigm.

In other words, scientific paradigms change radically only when a series of discoveries cannot be fitted into the dominant paradigm. Kuhn therefore argues that science changes in dramatic leaps: that there are 'scientific revolutions', when one scientific paradigm breaks down and another comes along to take its place.

Because hypotheses and experiments to test them are fitted into the existing paradigm, it can be argued that scientific method and scientific knowledge are therefore socially constructed products, produced by the community of scientists in terms of agreed, taken-for-granted assumptions and methods.

> ### Activity
> Try to think of times in your own science lessons at school when you got the 'wrong' result. Did you immediately question the validity of the theory or just assume that you had, for example, a dirty test-tube or did something wrong? Did you investigate the new finding – or stick with the paradigm, and keep trying until you got the 'right' result?

Do scientists cheat?

Much of the 'science debate' concerns the methods and procedures that scientists should use and, indeed, claim to use. However, there may be a large gap between the methods scientists claim they use, and those they really do use. Kaplan (1964) suggested that scientists write up research using what he called *reconstructed logic* – the formal scientific methods they are meant to use as scientists, and which are essential for the scientific community to accept their results as 'proper science'. However, in practice, scientists depart from these procedures, and the research process is much more haphazard, unsystematic and ad hoc (made up as they go along) than the ideal suggests. Kaplan calls this *logics in use*. There is, then, no guarantee that scientists will actually follow the rules of the good scientific practice that they might publicly claim to support. This is, in effect, a form of scientific cheating. Surveys show that only about one in four scientists is prepared to provide original data for checking by others, which suggests that there may be something to hide and that cheating is common in natural science.

One form of cheating is to keep re-running an experiment until the desired result is obtained, and then publish it, ignoring the failed experiments. Evidence suggests that only experiments that confirm hypotheses get written up, while the negative results are ignored. In 1998, the editor of the *British Medical Journal* said that only 5 per cent of published articles reached minimum standards of scientific soundness. Many clinical trials were too small to be relevant, and most of the published studies were the positive ones; a lot of negative evidence is being concealed.

There is little prestige or career progress to be gained by replicating (repeating) other scientists' work to check their findings, so scientific research is not really scrutinized as carefully as it should be. Acceptance of findings by the scientific community may therefore all too often be more an act of faith in scientific values than of scientific rigour.

Scientists may get things wrong simply because the power of the paradigm may mean that they focus on what they are looking for, and overlook or fail to see evidence which doesn't fit the paradigm. Sociologists may well face similar problems when they are trying to decide on the significance of observations and their interpretations of them.

Social influences on the nature and direction of scientific research

There is a range of other factors that undermine objectivity and introduce values into scientific research. The values and beliefs of researchers will inevitably influence whether they think issues are important or unimportant and therefore worthy of study or not. Scientists are professionals with careers and promotion prospects ahead of them, and they face a constant struggle to get money to fund their research. There is therefore an understandable desire to prove their own hypotheses right, and for experiments to succeed. The desire for promotion may influence what topics are seen as useful to research, as will the current state of knowledge and what constitutes a cool or lucrative research area. The search for funding may determine which research is carried out and how it is approached. For example, research for military or defence purposes might attract funding more readily than research into help for disabled people. Government-backed research is likely to open more doors to researchers and produce more sponsorship than private individuals or small research departments are able to achieve by themselves. Objectivity may be limited by the institution or funding constraints within which the scientist is working; for example, medical research on the effects of smoking funded by the tobacco industry, or research on genetically modified crops funded by the biotechnology industry. Publication of scientific papers is an important aspect of a scientific career, particularly in academic circles. Publishers' deadlines or the pressure to publish findings may mean that data are misrepresented, or that exhaustive experiments to attempt to falsify a hypothesis are not carried out. The availability of existing data on a topic, the practicality of and resources available for collecting data, and whether the subject matter is open to the use of certain methods or not will all influence what is researched.

All such influences on scientific research, summarized in figure 5.5, raise important questions about whether natural science, or indeed any research, lives up to its own supposed 'objective' scientific procedures. Science is itself a social product, produced within a set of agreed, taken-for-granted assumptions and methods (a

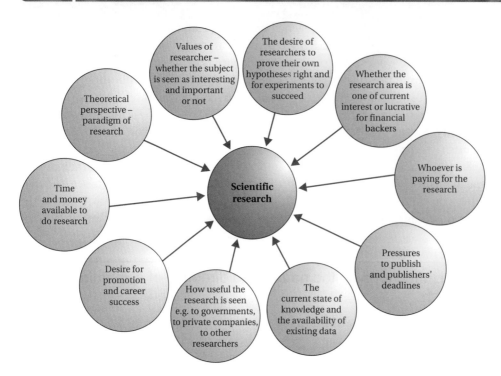

Figure 5.5
Influences on
scientific research

paradigm). Evidence that doesn't 'fit' the dominant paradigm may be dismissed or downgraded. This suggests that natural science, far from being the detached, objective and rigorous process we are led to believe, is very much a social product created by the interpretations and values of the scientists themselves.

The discussion above suggests that positivists are perhaps exaggerating how objective and value-free the natural science model really is. The answer to those critics who accuse sociologists of sloppiness and question whether sociology is scientific might well be: 'Does natural science live up to its own criteria of objectivity and lack of bias?' In short, people in glasshouses shouldn't throw stones, as natural science and social research are equally vulnerable to the influences and biases summarized in figure 5.5.

Activity

Drawing on the material in the previous sections and figure 5.5:

1 Go through each of the points in figure 5.5 and explain briefly in each case how the factors identified might distort the objectivity and value-freedom that is meant to be a feature of science, drawing on examples from both sociology and the natural sciences.
2 Identify and explain three reasons why scientific knowledge might be regarded as socially constructed.

Is a value-free sociology possible?

As seen above, the early positivists like Comte and Durkheim thought it possible for sociology to be value-free, so long as it followed similar procedures to those used in the natural sciences. This rests on an assumption that the natural sciences use procedures that are objective and free from the researcher's own values, and that conclusions are based on factual evidence collected in an unbiased way, unaffected by the subjective views and opinions of researchers.

The previous section has questioned this view, and pointed to a range of social factors that influence and threaten objectivity and value-freedom in natural science. These social influences on research are bound to affect sociology for the same sort of reasons. However, sociologists are criticized even more forcefully for lacking value-freedom because they are themselves a part of the society that they are investigating. This means it is almost impossible for them to avoid being influenced to some degree by the dominant values of their society that they have absorbed through socialization.

The myth of value-freedom

It is impossible for any natural or social scientist to avoid the influence of values completely. For example, their academic training, the paradigm or perspective they have learnt to interpret and evaluate evidence, their assumptions about society, and their beliefs about what are important or unimportant areas to study are all sources of values. Sociological facts – like those in the natural sciences – never 'speak for themselves'. 'Facts' are not meaningful in themselves. For example, untrained observers looking at an X-ray picture will see only meaningless blotches and shadows, and

Is the wine bottle half-full or half-empty? Such difficulties in interpretation affect both natural and social science.

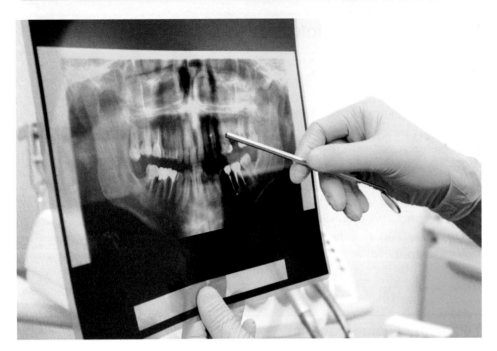

The facts never speak for themselves, and only become meaningful because people apply their understandings and interpretations to them, and make judgements about what they see. Everyone will see the same X-ray picture, but only some people will be able to understand and interpret what they see.

will have difficulty in making sense of what they see because they lack the theoretical background and training. Radiologists, however, can make sense of the X-ray as they have the theoretical training to do so. In sociology, participant observers must have some framework for identifying what they should look at and interpreting the significance of what they see. Without a theoretical framework, it is impossible to know what to observe, what research methods to use, or how to make sense of what is observed. These depend on the theoretical assumptions and interpretations of the researcher. Sociological investigation is ultimately based on researchers' assumptions about the nature of people in society, such as the differing assumptions of positivists, concerned with the causes of social behaviour, and of interpretivists, concerned with the meanings and motivations of behaviour, or of Marxist and feminist writers. These assumptions guide the selection of the problem for investigation, the research methods employed, and what data are selected as 'significant' and 'important' (and what aren't).

Consider, for example, the differing assumptions underlying the analysis of suicide. Positivists look at the social facts which constrain individuals and make some more vulnerable to suicide than others, while interpretivists are more likely to examine the process by which some sudden, unnatural deaths come to be labelled as suicide, while others do not (see pages 493–502 for a discussion of different approaches to suicide).

The personal prejudices and political views of the researcher may influence the selection of the subjects studied. For example, feminist sociologists, who are concerned with the male dominance of sociology ('malestream' sociology) and the unequal position of women in a patriarchal society, are likely to study subjects that highlight these inequalities. Marxist sociologists will begin with a conception that society is fundamentally class-divided and in social conflict, and will investigate issues with a view to highlighting evidence of exploitation and the need for social change. Functionalists, too, like Durkheim, thought that sociological research was worth doing because it could provide a means for improving society and resolving social problems. All these involve values to some extent, and they are unavoidable.

Dealing with values in social research

Even though sociologists can't be completely value-free, they do need to *strive for* objectivity and reliable data (like natural scientists do) if they are not to be ignored. Most sociologists have political views about society, such as about the extent of inequality, the need for social change and how it should be achieved. Clearly, research data that was selectively collected and manipulated to justify and promote the political beliefs of the researcher is not likely to be taken very seriously, and would be regarded as little better than poorly-researched, value-laden tabloid journalism. However, the fact that sociology can't escape the influence of values does not mean that it is completely value-laden and worthless. There are three ways of thinking about this:

1   *Values and personal prejudices should never be allowed to enter the research process itself.* Evidence must be collected and analysed as objectively, systematically and rigorously as possible, with conclusions based on this evidence, not on personal values.
2   *Values and personal prejudices should be considered* when examining the ethics of research. For example, what should researchers do if they come across serious crime like murder or armed robbery in their research, or offences like child abuse or paedophilia? Should they shop the respondents to whom they have promised confidentiality? Should they publish data likely to harm those researched? These ethical considerations ultimately rest on the moral values of researchers, but they should properly be considered as part of sociological research.
3   *Values can't be avoided when choosing the topic to research.* The topic of research is bound to reflect what the sociologist thinks important and relevant, and also the values of those funding the research.

Is a value-free sociology desirable?

The section above suggested that sociological research cannot avoid some influence from values. However, other sociologists have posed the question differently: even if a value-free sociology were possible, would it actually be desirable?

Some sociologists have argued that value-freedom and objectivity are themselves value-laden concepts. Gouldner (1971), for example, argues that the idea of value-freedom is not value-freedom at all but simply a refusal to criticize society as it is. For example, if you were observing a fight between a large bully and a small victim, would you really be 'neutral' if you stood aside and let the victim get beaten up? Or would your supposed neutrality really be supporting the bully and more concerned with self-preservation than neutrality? Not taking sides supports the powerful in an unequal society. Can you and should you be neutral when you are studying the poorest and most disadvantaged people in society? Or should you be applying your research skills to help them to escape their poverty and to tackle social exclusion? Can you avoid taking moral responsibility for your work?

Becker (1967) posed this question more forcefully, when he asked: 'Whose side are we on?' All knowledge must favour somebody, he argues, and therefore we have to choose whom to favour. Sociologists should be committed to social change for human improvement and take responsibility for the moral implications of their work. In other words, they should abandon any idea of value-freedom. This does not mean that such sociological work is any less scientific, but that the choice of research area is committed to a particular value position. Becker's own research reflected this, as it was clearly aimed at understanding how some people became labelled as 'outsiders' by those with power (see pages 421–6 for a discussion of labelling theory). Such a view of sociology involves siding with the underdogs in society, seeing what life is like from their points of view, and giving society's deprived and other outsiders a voice through such research, and thereby hopefully leading to social change.

Postmodernism, science, values and methodology

The debate in sociology between positivism and interpretivism, and over scientific method and values, is largely dismissed by postmodernists as a pointless waste of time. Postmodernists take the view that:

1   Science is simply a metanarrative, another 'big' theory alongside theories like Marxism and functionalism seeking to explain everything. There is a loss of faith in science as it has created problems such as genetically modified foods, climate change, environmental pollution and antibiotic resistant superbugs, leaving uncertainty instead of solutions. Rational thinking has failed, and social science has nothing to learn from copying from the natural sciences.
2   Sociological research does not provide a factual description of social life, but is a social construction created by sociological researchers. Concepts like social structure, social class, gender and ethnicity are simply frameworks imposed on the world by sociologists, and have no meaning separate from them.
3   It is pointless trying to find the social causes of behaviour. Social structures like class, ethnicity and gender have diminished in importance, and society has become fragmented into so many different groups, interests and lifestyles, all of which are constantly changing, that society is essentially chaotic. There is no longer anything called society or a social structure; there is only a mass of individuals making separate choices about their lifestyles. It is pointless to try to find the wider causes of their behaviour or even the construction of their meanings, as these will be specific to each individual.

4　The attempt at objectivity and value-freedom by sociologists is simply a pretence aimed at presenting their views as somehow superior to others, when all are equally valid, because all are just social constructions.

Is sociology a science?

The debate over sociology, science and values raises a range of issues, which have been seen as important in sociology, even if postmodernists are rather dismissive of them. The question is whether the choice of approach in sociology is purely arbitrary, a kind of methodological lottery, or whether it can be regarded as a science, to the extent that its findings should be taken at least as seriously as those in the natural sciences.

It is most unlikely that sociological theory will ever be as 'accurate' as a theory in physics, and those formed in the closed systems of laboratory experiments. We are not dealing with emotionless electrons, but with people with consciousness, emotions, free will and values. Like perfect cleanliness, a completely objective, value-free sociology may be impossible to achieve, but this does not mean we should stop washing or adopting a rigorous approach to the study of society as suggested below. So long as sociologists *strive* to achieve objectivity and detachment, and keep their personal values out of the research process, then sociologists of any perspective can justly claim that their work is no less objective or more value-laden than research which is carried out in the natural sciences. Sociology can then be regarded as scientific, regardless of the perspective used, as long as it strives to achieve the following five objectives:

1　Value-freedom: the personal beliefs and prejudices of the researcher, while obviously affecting the topic chosen for study, are kept out of the research process itself.
2　Objectivity: the sociologist approaches topics with an open mind, considering all the evidence in a detached and fair-minded way.
3　The use of systematic research methods to collect evidence, whatever perspective is used: for example, the use of careful sampling techniques and skilfully designed questionnaires in positivist survey research, or the careful recording of observations and interpretations in unstructured interviews or participant observation in interpretivist research
4　The careful analysis and evaluation of data and hypotheses in the light of evidence and logical argument, and the use of evidence to support research and the conclusions drawn from it, rather than personal opinion or hearsay.

Activity

1　Imagine you are an adviser to a researcher about to start a study of child poverty. You know this researcher holds very strong beliefs that child poverty is due to inadequate parents. What advice would you give the researcher to ensure that the research findings are not simply seen as a reflection of her or his values?

2 Answer the following essay question in 45 minutes: *'Sociologists are members of the society they are studying, and it is therefore impossible for them to conduct value-free research.'* To what extent do sociological arguments and evidence support this view?

5 Findings should be open to inspection, criticism, debate and testing by other researchers, if necessary by replicating the research (carrying out the same or similar research again to check the findings of earlier research). This may be difficult with interpretivist research (such as participant observation), but even here the published findings and research notes should be open for other researchers to assess.

Social policy and social problems

Social policy refers to the packages of plans and actions adopted by national and local government or various voluntary agencies to solve social problems or achieve other goals that are seen as important. A **social problem** is something that is seen as being in some way harmful to society, causing, as Worsley (1978) puts it, public friction and/or private misery, and which needs some collective action to solve it. This 'collective action' to reduce social problems involves a raft of social policies implemented through the services provided by governments and the measures they take to achieve goals that have an impact on the life chances and welfare of citizens, such as those concerned with health, housing, employment, social care, education, crime and transport.

> **Social policy** refers to the packages of plans and actions adopted by national and local government or various voluntary agencies to solve social problems or achieve other goals that are seen as important.

Social problems and sociological problems

Sometimes, social problems are confused with sociological problems, but they are not the same things. A **sociological problem** is any social or theoretical issue that needs explaining, whether it is a social problem or not. For example, the huge improvement in the achievement of girls in education might need explaining, but it is not a social problem. However, all social problems are sociological problems, and very often sociologists have been able to show by research that many social problems – such as crime, poverty or ill-health – are not simply a result of the behaviour of individuals, but are created by wider social factors. A useful example is that of accidents.

> A **social problem** is something that is seen as being harmful to society in some way, and needs something doing to sort it out.

Accidents as a social and a sociological problem

Accidents are a social problem, and the accident statistics show a clear social pattern in terms of age, class and gender. For example, young people and older people, the poor and males are more likely to die or be seriously injured as the result of an accident. Accidents may happen to us individually, and sometimes randomly, but the causes are often socially influenced, by factors such as poor-quality housing,

> A **sociological problem** is any social or theoretical issue that needs explaining.

inadequate home care for the elderly, low income, dangerous working conditions and a dangerous environment, with busy roads and no safe play areas for children. Accidents provide an often dramatic and tragic, but nevertheless excellent, example of how seemingly random or individual experiences and events are in fact socially patterned and socially influenced. The study of accidents illustrates Mills's (1970) distinction between 'the personal troubles of milieu' (immediate social surroundings) and 'the public issues of social structure'. Every single accident is a personal experience, but the pattern of these experiences in Britain every year is a social problem – not least because of the harm and widespread suffering that accidents cause and the millions of pounds spent treating them by the National Health Service. This social problem is also a sociological problem – something that needs explaining by sociologists. To paraphrase Mills: when, in a nation of 60 million, only one person has an accident, then that is his or her personal trouble, and its solution can be found in the circumstances of that person. But when, in a nation of 60 million, eight million have an accident, with a clear social pattern, that is a public issue and a social problem, and a solution cannot be found within the personal situations and characteristics of the individuals.

It is research into issues like accidents, ill-health, obesity, crime, poverty or educational failure – and drawing attention to the fact they are social problems with social explanations rather than individual ones, and need social policy solutions to tackle them – that has enabled sociology to make major contributions to the formation of social policies adopted by national and local government or various voluntary agencies.

The contribution of sociology to social policy

Governments are more likely to produce social policies that are effective and work as intended if they base them on proper evidence gained through research. The work of sociologists in areas such as education, health, poverty and crime has had quite important effects on the social policies of governments, and government will often commission research from academics in universities to assist policy-making. There are also a number of bodies that are specifically concerned with social policy research within which sociologists work. For example, the Institute of Public Policy Research (www.ippr.org/) and the Joseph Rowntree Foundation (www.jrf.org.uk) are both concerned with research to feed into the formation of social policy.

Activity

Go to www.jrf.org.uk:
1 Identify three pieces of social policy research with which the Joseph Rowntree Foundation is currently involved.
2 Explore one of these pieces of research. Identify the aims, the sociological research methods used, the conclusions reached and how you think the research might influence government policy.

Giddens (2006) suggests a number of ways that 'sociology can help us in our lives', and his ideas are incorporated into the following discussion of the contribution that sociology can make to the formulation of social policy.

Nine ways sociology contributes to social policy

- providing an awareness of cultural differences and of others;
- providing self-awareness and understanding;
- changing assumptions;
- providing a theoretical framework;
- providing practical professional knowledge;
- identifying social problems;
- providing the evidence;
- identifying the unintended consequences of policies;
- assessing the results.

Providing an awareness of cultural differences   Seeing society from different perspectives, and developing an 'informed awareness' of and sensitivity to the ways of life, needs and problems of others, helps policy-makers to tailor policies more effectively, such as research on ethnicity or disability

Providing self-awareness and understanding   Sociology develops a knowledge and understanding of ourselves, why we behave as we do, and our position within society. There is a growing reflexivity in late modernity, which was discussed in terms of Giddens and Beck earlier in this chapter; sociological research can enable individuals and groups to develop self-awareness and understanding of their positions in society by reflecting on it. Reflecting on experiences like racism, domestic violence, sex discrimination, and prejudice and discrimination arising from disability can have the effect of empowering people to change their lives. This can encourage people to form support and pressure groups with those facing similar experiences. Such groups are often concerned with criticizing the inadequacies of existing social policies, forming new ones to address their needs with evidence to support them, and exerting pressure on government to implement them. Late modernity has seen the development of a wide range of new social movements and self-help groups which demand new policies from governments to meet their needs, such as disability and gay rights, environmental changes, and equal opportunity, anti-racist, anti-ageist, and anti-sexist policies.

Changing assumptions   McNeill (1986) suggests that social research can indirectly influence social policy by being absorbed into the taken-for-granted common-sense assumptions involved in society's dominant culture. This can make government social policies seem either reasonable and acceptable, or subjects of ridicule. For example, a social policy aimed at tackling the problem of crime by locking up everyone with a specific body type, on the grounds they were more prone to criminality, would face ridicule, while one based on the provision of social facilities for young people to divert them from crime might be seen as more reasonable and sensible.

Providing a theoretical framework Sociology can often provide a theoretical framework for social policies adopted by governments. Between 1979 and 1992, the Conservative governments were strongly influenced by the New Right ideas of the American Charles Murray (1984), whose views about poverty and the undeserving work-shy welfare-dependent underclass provided a basis for savage cuts in welfare benefits and welfare state funding and attacks on the poor throughout the 1980s. This was combined with a prime minister, Margaret Thatcher, who had a contempt for most sociology and sociological research, reflecting her almost postmodern view 'that there is no such thing as society, only individual men and women and families'.

By contrast, the New Labour government of 1997 was led by a prime minister who was a fan of sociologist Anthony Giddens. In his book *The Third Way* (1998), Giddens provided the theoretical basis for new social policies based around building social cohesion and social solidarity, and reducing social problems posing threats to social order. These were implemented by the Labour government in the late 1990s and the early years of the twenty-first century, and included a more supportive welfare, health and education agenda, and policies to tackle social exclusion, including the establishment of the social exclusion unit (now taskforce – www.cabinetoffice.gov.uk/social_exclusion_task_force) and the national minimum wage to reduce poverty. Similar theoretical frameworks have been provided by Townsend's (1979) work on poverty, which helped to establish the concept of relative poverty, and Left and Right Realism which both had important influences on crime policy (see pages 488–92 in chapter 6).

Providing practical professional knowledge Sociologists are not just academics working in universities, or sociology teachers. They work in a wide range of other occupations, such as town planning, social work, journalism, human resource management, and in the civil service. All of these can provide professional inputs as social policy is formed in a range of areas. Journalism, for example, has an important role in setting the agenda for publicly acceptable social policies. Sociologists are also employed as civil servants in government departments like the Department for Work and Pensions and the Home Office, where they play a direct role in shaping and evaluating policy. For example, it was researchers in the Home Office who helped to improve the validity of crime statistics by the development of the British Crime Survey. Such researchers are constantly involved in both commissioning and carrying out research, and briefing the media, MPs and government ministers about the effectiveness of social policies.

Identifying social problems Sociologists, particularly academics who are not locked into applied research for very specific already-identified policy purposes, can do some 'blue sky' thinking, peering into the future, and can ask questions and identify social problems that arise from more open sociological thinking. Sociological ideas can also help shape policy by showing that social problems have wider causes than simply individual behaviour, and that wider social structural factors are important too, as shown by sociological research on poverty and crime.

Many social problems have been identified by the work of sociologists. Feminist sociologists have carried out a great deal of theoretical and practical research revealing the extent of inequalities and discrimination against women in areas such as pay and employment, and suggesting solutions to it. This fed into legal changes such as the Sex Discrimination and Equal Pay Acts. Poverty research by Townsend (1979), as well as that carried out by the Joseph Rowntree Foundation, have exposed the extent of poverty in the UK, and the Black Report of 1980 revealed the huge inequalities in health in the UK. Similar examples include research highlighting the continuing problems of racism, and attacks and harassment of gays.

Providing the evidence   This is the most obvious form of input, as sociologists are frequently those who do the surveys, collect the statistics, analyse the problems, suggest explanations and so on, which policy-makers can then draw on to form evidence-based policies. The use of research evidence can guide practice and decision-making, and often provide some assurance that policies will work as intended.

Identifying the unintended consequences of policies   Sociological research can evaluate existing policies, to see if there are any unintended consequences of policies, such as Merton's latent functions or dysfunctions. For example, have policies aimed at reducing crime in a community simply displaced it to other areas or onto more vulnerable targets?

Assessing the results   Sociological research can help to establish whether policies have worked, whether they achieved what they set out to, and whether they need changing or scrapping.

Influences on social policy-making

The previous section suggests a range of ways sociology might influence social policies. However, it would be naive to think that social policies were formed purely on the basis of evidence, with sociologists producing clear research reports, documenting the evidence of social problems, identifying explanations for them and making policy recommendations to governments which were then accepted and implemented. This rarely happens. Part of the explanation for this lies in the nature of sociology and the multidimensional, changing and slippery causes of social phenomena which have been discussed throughout this chapter. Sociological research therefore rarely produces clear-cut explanations and solutions in the way that natural scientists generally can when they identify the causes of disease and means of preventing it. Crime, for example, has been a social problem from time immemorial, and has probably been the subject of more social research than any other social area. Every new government rehearses old arguments, commissions more research and draws up new or recycled policies to defeat crime, but still it continues. It is this complex nature of social explanation that makes it relatively easy for governments to choose to ignore research, or elements of it that do not conform to their preconceptions.

Social policies on prostitution and cannabis are both examples of where expert advice has been ignored by government.

Davies (2008) points out that debates about social policy do not take place in a vacuum, but have an ideological basis to them, and depend on current public and other perceptions of the problem or issue. For example, if governments or others with power consider something to be morally offensive in some way, like prostitution, or politically sensitive, like cannabis use, they may, when formulating policy, ignore evidence that doesn't fit their preconceptions.

Davies cites the findings of the Parliamentary Science and Technology Select Committee (*Guardian*, 8 November 2006), showing that the government often misused or distorted scientific research to justify policy decisions that were really based on ideological or social and political grounds. The findings suggested that the government hid behind a fig-leaf of scientific respectability to make controversial policies more acceptable to voters. The investigation highlighted several examples of misuse of research, including evidence from a criminologist at Keele University, who told the committee that his work on crime statistics had been given a different interpretation by the Home Office for political reasons. Two examples illustrating this are policies on prostitution and cannabis.

Prostitution

Davies found the government's Coordinated Prostitution Strategy of 2006 was highly selective in its use of social research in order to bolster support for its own hostile view of prostitution. Davies argued that, while the government didn't ignore social research in formulating its prostitution policy, it did ignore, dismiss or misrepresent research that might undermine its policy. In particular, the government ignored:

- research on prostitutes' clients, which showed they were fairly typical men, and not the violent and abusive stereotypes assumed in the strategy;
- evidence from Sweden that undermined their own strategy;
- the effectiveness of alternative approaches adopted in other countries.

Cannabis

The government decided in May 2008 to reclassify the legal status of cannabis from a Class C (less harmful) to a Class B (more harmful) drug, reversing its own policy

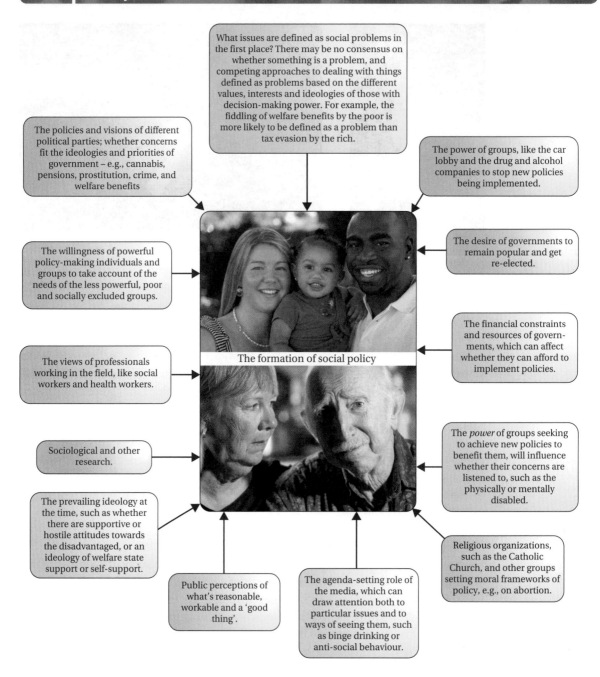

What issues are defined as social problems in the first place? There may be no consensus on whether something is a problem, and competing approaches to dealing with things defined as problems based on the different values, interests and ideologies of those with decision-making power. For example, the fiddling of welfare benefits by the poor is more likely to be defined as a problem than tax evasion by the rich.

The policies and visions of different political parties; whether concerns fit the ideologies and priorities of government – e.g., cannabis, pensions, prostitution, crime, and welfare benefits

The power of groups, like the car lobby and the drug and alcohol companies to stop new policies being implemented.

The willingness of powerful policy-making individuals and groups to take account of the needs of the less powerful, poor and socially excluded groups.

The desire of governments to remain popular and get re-elected.

The views of professionals working in the field, like social workers and health workers.

The formation of social policy

The financial constraints and resources of govern-ments, which can affect whether they can afford to implement policies.

Sociological and other research.

The *power* of groups seeking to achieve new policies to benefit them, will influence whether their concerns are listened to, such as the physically or mentally disabled.

The prevailing ideology at the time, such as whether there are supportive or hostile attitudes towards the disadvantaged, or an ideology of welfare state support or self-support.

Public perceptions of what's reasonable, workable and a 'good thing'.

The agenda-setting role of the media, which can draw attention both to particular issues and to ways of seeing them, such as binge drinking or anti-social behaviour.

Religious organizations, such as the Catholic Church, and other groups setting moral frameworks of policy, e.g., on abortion.

of downgrading the drug from Class B to Class C in January 2004. It did this despite advice from its own scientific and professional advisers, the Advisory Council on the Misuse of Drugs, that such a reclassification was not necessary and would not have the desired effect in curbing cannabis use. The reasons given were that the gov-ernment had to take into consideration public perceptions, the health of children and the pressures on policing. This was despite evidence that cannabis use among

Figure 5.6
Influences on the formation of social policy

Activity

1 Refer to figure 5.6 and identify and explain one example of a social policy to illustrate each of the points in the boxes.
2 Suggest three ways that the unequal distribution of power in society influences whether a social activity is defined as a social problem or not, illustrating your answer with examples.

young people had fallen from 13.4 per cent to 9.4 per cent since downgrading to category C, so there were declining risks to health and less demands on policing. This policy of reclassification was based, then, not on any kind of research evidence, but was about giving a message to young people that this was not a 'safe' drug to take.

The process of social policy formation involves something much more complex than simply looking at the evidence produced by sociologists and acting on it, given that governments may, and frequently do, choose to ignore evidence when they form policy. Figure 5.6 shows a range of the factors that influence social policy.

Should sociologists be involved in social policy research?

Figure 5.6 shows that the formation of social policy is shaped by a range of social, political and economic circumstances, and, in this context, the work of sociologists is a relatively small one. The final decisions on what constitutes social problems and what measures should be taken are ultimately political decisions; in an unequal society, it is those who have the most power who will ultimately decide what policies are adopted and implemented, no matter how good sociological research may be. For example, the Black Report in 1980 on inequalities in health was buried by the Conservative government of the time, yet in the 1990s similar research had a direct influence on health policy under a Labour government.

McNeill (1986) points out that what becomes defined as a social problem will depend on individuals or groups being able to whip up enough support among those with power to make their concerns or interests an issue for public debate and public action. This is the real world of power and politics, and not the sheltered world of the sociology classroom.

McNeill points out much sociological work is ignored by governments and others with power. He suggests this is because sociology often concerns itself with social inequalities and related social problems, like those to do with income and wealth, inequalities, educational underachievement, poverty and ill-health. In addition, sociologists have not been slow in questioning the effects of government policies and highlighting uncomfortable truths about society – for example, the 1980 Black Report, which exposed deep social class inequalities in health. Those with power therefore often prefer to see sociology as a biased and value-laden subject, rather than confront the uncomfortable information it places before them.

Throughout this chapter, there have been discussions about objectivity, value-freedom and detachment in sociological research, and such discussions are often

The Economic and Social Research Council (ESRC) is an important source of funding for social research.

particularly heated when it comes to the link between sociology and social policy. So far, an emphasis has been placed on the factors influencing whether policy-makers choose to use sociological research, but there is another issue of how sociologists themselves see the role of sociology in relation to social policy. There are two broad positions in this discussion – those who argue that sociologists should get involved in applied research for policy ends, and those who believe they shouldn't.

The view that sociology should be involved in applied social policy research

The founders of sociology, such as Comte, Durkheim and Marx, all saw the study of the social world as a means of improving society, reflecting the modernist concern with scientific study and a belief in progress. Since that time, many sociologists have taken the view that their work in identifying and explaining social problems should lead them to make specific social policy recommendations for the implementation of practical measures to solve the problems they've identified. Not to do so is simply to refuse to take any responsibility for the findings of their work.

Another very practical reason to get involved in applied research is the issue of funding. In order to carry out research, grants are needed, and the largest funding agencies for research are the government and other public bodies. For example, the Departments of Health, Work and Pensions, Children, Schools and Families and the Home Office all have large research budgets, and commission research from universities to develop their policies.

The Economic and Social Research Council (ESRC) is an independent government-funded body for the promotion of social science research, with research spending of more than £100 million in 2007–8, providing substantial grants to social science researchers, often linked to social policy issues. Other funding bodies are charitable trusts like the Joseph Rowntree Foundation, which is specifically concerned with applied research on poverty, and provides over £5 million a year for these purposes, much of it to university researchers. These research funds are so substantial that those who choose not to get involved in applied social research are likely to find themselves short of funds for any research.

Marsland (1994) argues for a 'fully engaged' sociology that is committed to social policy and that 'systematic empirical sociological research has a necessary, important, and constructive role to play in relation to policy formulation, implementation and evaluation'. He suggests that much policy work doesn't take proper account of sociological research, but that most sociologists themselves lack commitment to applied policy research, and would rather 'shout or hiss from the sidelines' than risk getting their hands dirty by becoming involved in policy-making. Marsland argues that sociologists should be fully and actively involved in the policy process, and this would produce positive benefits for the community through evidence-based policy-making, and assessment of policy objectives and achievements. He argues that if sociologists don't involve themselves in applied research, this won't stop the research being carried out, but sociology will become marginalized, and policy areas will be less well informed. He also suggests that either 'social policies will take account of relevant sociological knowledge or they are bound to fail'.

As seen earlier, social policy-making is a complex process with a diversity of influences, but if sociologists do not involve themselves in social policy research, then social policy will be even more vulnerable to manipulation by powerful groups with particular interests of their own to follow.

The view that sociology should not be involved in applied social policy research

The arguments in favour of sociologists not involving themselves in applied social policy research relate to the issues of detachment, objectivity and non-involvement discussed earlier in this chapter, and how funding issues can constrain the nature of research.

Funding for research comes from government and other agencies, which, understandably enough, will only fund research that meets with their approval. Sometimes, as for ESRC funding, these approval criteria regarding the value of research may be quite broad, but for government-funded research and some charitable foundations, like the Joseph Rowntree Foundation, research for particular purposes is funded. Such funding sources can have theoretical and methodological implications for the way in which research is conducted. For example, government agencies generally prefer more positivist research methods, producing easily digestible quantitative data, rather than in-depth qualitative research. Funding sources can also limit the parameters of research. The Department of Work and Pensions website specifically states that 'all the research which is carried out flows directly from the policy agenda, and there is no "blue skies" research'. In other words, there is no scope for open-ended free thinking outside the policy framework.

There are also potential ethical difficulties. As seen earlier, sociological research is only one of many influences on the formation of social policy. Radical sociologists, like Marxists, may well regard detachment and non-involvement in policy research as preferable to inadvertently contributing to social policies that might eventually be used against the interests of the poorest and least powerful groups in society on which they carried out research, thereby bolstering and legitimizing the power of the dominant social class.

Sociological research may well produce findings that are opposed to the interests of the government or that actively challenge existing policies by throwing up dysfunctional aspects, creating social problems, as was the case with the Black Report. There is also a risk that too close an involvement in applied research can mean that policy-making – a political process – becomes the driving force of sociology, with sociology being reduced to an extension of the political arm of government and serving its needs. What happens then to objectivity in research? Governments may be able to pick and choose which research evidence they accept or ignore, but sociologists who wish to retain some professional integrity and scientific objectivity cannot do the same thing.

Sociologists may have different conceptions from those in power of what the social problems are, and what measures are necessary to solve them. In such circumstances, applied social research in which sociologists have no control over the use to which their research is put may involve them in unreasonable compromises and unwittingly contribute to policies dealing with the symptoms of a problem rather than the problem itself. For example, the view of many Marxist sociologists is that most social problems are rooted in social inequality, which only radical change, rather than a few new policy initiatives, will resolve.

There is no simple or obvious answer to these two contrasting points of view, and, as long as sociological research, whether applied to social policy or not, follows the five principles identified on page 383. then it should retain high research value.

Ultimately, perhaps, the issue is a political one, and sociologists may decide how to proceed once they answer the question posed by Becker: Whose side are we on?

Activity

1 Suggest two areas where sociological research may have influenced social policy.
2 Suggest and explain two factors that will influence whether or not the findings of sociological research are used by governments to form or change social policies.
3 Suggest, with examples, two possible dysfunctions or unintended consequences of government social policies.
4 Suggest reasons why postmodernists might see sociology as having no useful contribution to make to social policy formation.
5 Answer the following essay question in 45 minutes: *'Assess the view that sociological research has little effect on the social policies of governments.'*

CHAPTER SUMMARY

After reading this chapter, including the revision of research methods from your AS course, you should be able to:

- discuss a range of theoretical and practical issues that sociologists consider in conducting research;

- distinguish between quantitative and qualitative data, and the advantages and limitations of each;

- identify the difference between primary and secondary sources, and the strengths and limitations of the data obtained from each;

- explain the problems of reliability and validity of research evidence

- identify the ethical considerations sociologists must consider when carrying out social research;

- explain the advantages, uses and limitations of official statistics, with examples;

- explain the uses and problems of the experimental method in sociology;

- explain how the comparative method might be used as an alternative to the experimental one;

- explain the main features and stages of the social survey, and the various sampling methods sociologists use to gain representative samples, and their strengths and weaknesses;

- explain the uses, strengths and weaknesses of different types of questionnaires and interviews, including the problems of imposition and the validity and reliability of these methods;

- explain fully the problem of interviewer bias;

- explain the uses, strengths and weaknesses of participant observation as a research method, including theoretical and practical problems, and the issues of validity and reliability;

- discuss the strengths and weaknesses of longitudinal studies, case studies and life histories;

- explain what is meant by methodological pluralism and triangulation, and why sociologists might want to use a range of methods in sociological research;

- describe and explain consensus and conflict theories in sociology;

- describe and evaluate structural and action theories in sociology, including functionalism, classical Marxism and neo-Marxism, symbolic interactionism and ethnomethodology;

- describe and evaluate integrated approaches, including Weberian sociology and Giddens's theory of structuration;

- describe the features of modernity and postmodernity, the differences between them, and evaluate the contribution of postmodernism to sociological theory and an understanding of society;

- explain what is meant by the scientific method, and assess the extent to which it can be used in the study of society;

- describe and evaluate the features of, and difference between, positivism and interpretivism, and how these two approaches use different research methods;

- explain the realist view of science;

- explain how scientific knowledge is socially constructed and the social influences on scientific research;

- discuss whether sociology can be or should be value-free;

- discuss whether sociology can be or should be a science;

- explain the links between sociology and social policy, including the various ways sociology can influence the formation of social policy, and the arguments over whether sociology should involve itself in applied research for social policy purposes.

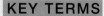

KEY TERMS

bourgeoisie	ideological state	proletariat	social problem
capitalists	apparatus	qualitative data	sociological problem
class-consciousness	interpretivism	quantitive data	structural differentiation
collective conscience	interviewer bias	reflexivity	structuralism
communism	labour power	relations of production	structuration
determinism	latent function	relative autonomy	surplus value
dysfunction	manifest function	reliability	symbol
empirical evidence	means of production	repressive state	triangulation
ethics	methodological pluralism	apparatus	validity
false consciousness	objectivity	secondary sources	value-freedom
functional prerequisites	paradigm	simulacra	*Verstehen*
hegemony	positivism	social facts	
hyperreality	primary sources	social policy	

Answer to activity on page 353

Ethnomethodology is a sociological discipline which studies the ways in which people make sense of their world, display this understanding to others, and produce the mutually shared social order in which they live. The term was initially coined by Harold Garfinkel in 1954.

6 Crime and Deviance

KEN BROWNE

Contents

6

Crime and Deviance

Social control, deviance and crime

In order for people to know how to behave in society, to be able to predict how others will behave, and therefore to live together in some orderly way, some shared values and norms are necessary. Without some measure of agreement on beliefs on what is important in society and on general guidelines for behaviour (values) and the basic social rules (norms), social life would soon fall into confusion and disorder. Norms and values are learnt through socialization, but knowing what the values and norms are does not necessarily mean people will follow them. **Social control** refers to the various methods used to persuade or force individuals to conform to the dominant social norms and values of a society or group, which have been learnt through socialization, and to prevent deviance. **Deviance** is rule-breaking behaviour of some kind, which fails to conform to the norms and expectations of a particular society or social group.

Processes of social control may be formal, through institutions like the law or school rules, or they may be informal, through peer-group pressure, personal embarrassment at doing something wrong, or the pressure of public opinion. **Sanctions** are the rewards and punishments by which social control is achieved and conformity to norms and values enforced. These may be either positive sanctions, rewards of various kinds, or negative sanctions, various types of punishment. The type of sanction will depend on the seriousness of the norm: positive sanctions may range from gifts of sweets or money from parents to children, to merits and prizes at school, to knighthoods and medals; negative sanctions may range from a feeling of embarrassment, to being ridiculed or gossiped about or regarded as a bit eccentric or 'a bit odd', to being fined or imprisoned.

Social control refers to the various methods used to persuade or force individuals to conform to the dominant social norms and values of a society or group.

Deviance refers to rule-breaking behaviour of some kind, which fails to conform to the norms and expectations of a particular society or social group.

Sanctions are the rewards and punishments by which social control is achieved and conformity to norms and values enforced. Positive sanctions are rewards of various kinds; negative sanctions are various types of punishment.

Agencies of social control

Social control is carried out by agencies of social control.

Formal social control

Formal social control is carried out by agencies specifically set up to ensure that people conform to a particular set of norms – specifically, the law. The police, courts and prisons force people to obey the law by means of formal sanctions such as arrest, fines or imprisonment of those who break the formal laws of society.

Informal social control

Informal social control is carried out by institutions whose primary purpose is not social control, but they play an important role in it nonetheless. These include the family, the education system, religion, the workplace, the mass media and peer groups.

Activity

1 Give examples of three norms in each case to which you are generally expected to conform in *two* of the following:
   a) at your school or college
   b) in your peer group
   c) at work

Explain in each case how these norms are enforced, and outline the sanctions applied
if you fail to conform to them.
2 Suggest and explain two ways in each case that religion and the mass media might
carry out social control.

The family is an important
agency of informal social
control.

The social construction of crime and deviance

The social construction of crime

Crime is the term
used to describe
behaviour that is
against the criminal
law – law-breaking.

Crime refers to acts that contravene criminal law. Many crimes, but not all, as will be
seen shortly, are often regarded as deviant as well.

Newburn (2007) suggests that crime is basically a label attached to certain forms
of behaviour which are prohibited by the state, and have some legal penalty against
them. While crime therefore seems to be easy to define, as the law states what a criminal act is, there is no act that is in itself criminal. An act only becomes a crime when
a particular label of 'crime' has been applied to it, and even quite similar acts can
be treated very differently depending on the interpretations of the law-enforcement
agencies, and the context in which the act takes place. For example, killing someone is
not in itself a criminal act: if it happens during a knife fight outside a pub in Britain, it
is likely to be defined as criminal, but not if that knife fight is with an enemy soldier in
wartime. As Newburn points out, even if crime is defined as whatever the criminal law
says it is, the fact that the criminal law varies from country to country, and changes
over time, reinforces the idea that there is nothing that is in itself criminal. Even with

an act that appears to be against the law, the police and other criminal justice agencies have to interpret – or make a judgement – about whether it was prohibited. If the police do decide to define the act as a criminal one, that does not necessarily mean they will do anything about it, in terms of recording the offence or prosecuting the offender. Crime is therefore socially constructed, because there is no act that is, in itself, criminal or deviant – it largely depends on how other members of society see and define it.

Crime covers a very wide range of behaviour, from relatively trivial acts like pilfering from work to very serious acts like rape and murder. This means that it is extremely difficult to develop explanations that account for the vast diversity of acts that are labelled as criminal, since it is not difficult to see that the reasons for shoplifting are likely to have different motivations from premeditated murder.

The social construction of deviance

While defining crime is not without difficulties, the wider concept of deviance is even more complex. Deviance consists of rule-breaking or non-conformist acts that don't follow the norms and expectations of a particular society or social group. This conception of deviance includes both criminal and non-criminal acts. However, it is in fact quite difficult to pin down what members of any society or group actually regard as deviant behaviour. Downes and Rock (2007) suggest that *ambiguity* is a key feature of rule-breaking, as people are frequently unsure whether a particular episode is truly deviant, or what deviance is. Their judgement will depend on the context in which the act occurs, who the person is, what is known about them, and what their motives might be. What is defined as deviance will depend on the social expectations about what constitutes 'normal' behaviour, and therefore whether something is defined as deviant or not will depend on how others react to it. For example, swearing at your mates in your peer group is unlikely to be defined as deviant, but swearing at your teacher in a school is likely to be viewed quite differently.

Societal and situational deviance

Plummer (1979) discusses two aspects of defining deviance, using the concepts of **societal deviance** and **situational deviance**.

Societal deviance refers to forms of deviance that are seen by most members of a society as being deviant, as they share similar ideas about approved and unapproved behaviour: murder, child abuse, drunk-driving in the UK and rape are all likely to fall into this category. Situational deviance refers to the context, such as the location, in which an act takes place, and how this affects whether or not an act is seen as deviant. These two conceptions of deviance suggest that while there may be some acts that many people agree on as being deviant in a particular society, this view may not be shared across a range of different societies. Similarly, those acts defined as deviant may vary between groups within the same society, and they change over time. Whether or not an act is defined as deviant will therefore depend on the time, the place, the society and the attitudes of those who view the act. The following examples illustrate how definitions of deviance can vary according to a range of circumstances,

Societal deviance refers to acts that are seen by most members of a society as deviant.

Situational deviance refers to acts that are only defined as deviant in particular contexts.

In 1948, 85 per cent of men smoked some form of tobacco, and 65 per cent smoked cigarettes (41 per cent of women). Today, cigarette smoking is a minority activity, restricted to around 24 per cent of the population, and falling. What was once a common, normal practice, is now increasingly a deviant one, and in many circumstances also an illegal one.

and therefore show quite clearly that deviance, like crime, is very much a social construction, rather than something that is a characteristic of the act itself.

1   *Non-deviant crime?* Most people commit deviant and even illegal acts at some stage in their lives, and there are many illegal acts that most people don't regard as particularly deviant. For example, parking and speeding offences, under-age drinking, use of soft drugs like cannabis, or pinching office stationery are all extremely common, so it is difficult to see them as being deviant.

2   *The time.* Definitions of deviance change over time in the same society, as standards of normal behaviour change. For example, cigarette smoking used to be a very popular and socially acceptable activity, but is increasingly becoming branded as deviant. Since July 2007, it has been illegal in the UK to smoke indoors in workplaces and buildings open to the public, and smokers are now unwelcome in many places. Attitudes to homosexuality have also changed dramatically. Homosexuality was illegal in the UK before 1967, but since then has become legal and widely accepted; it is now possible to have an officially approved gay marriage in the form of a civil partnership.

3   *The society or culture.* Deviance is culturally relative – what is regarded as deviance in one society or group is not necessarily so in another. For example, consumption of alcohol is often seen as deviant and illegal in many Islamic countries, but is seen as normal in Britain.

4   *The social group.* What may be acceptable in a particular group may be regarded as deviant in the wider society. For example, smoking cannabis is perfectly acceptable behaviour among Rastafarians in Britain, and among many young people who are not Rastafarians, although it is regarded as deviant by many adults, and it is illegal.

5   *The place or context.* For example, it is seen as deviant if people have sex in the street, but not if it takes place between couples in a bedroom. Killing someone

may be interpreted as heroic, manslaughter, self-defence, murder, a 'crime of passion', justifiable homicide or euthanasia (mercy killing).

Activity

Apart from the examples given above:

1 Identify and explain two examples of acts that are against the law but are not usually regarded as deviant by most people.

2 Give three examples of deviant acts that are not against the law.

3 Identify and explain two examples of situational deviance, acts that are generally accepted by the majority of people in Britain, but which might be regarded as deviant in some social groups in Britain, for example minority ethnic or religious groups.

The mass media and the social construction of crime and deviance

The media and agenda-setting

Both fictional and non-fictional stories about crime and deviance are staple parts of the mass media diet, and the media provide knowledge about crime for most people in society, including politicians, the police, social workers and the public at large. The media play a key role in agenda-setting in relation to crime and deviance. Agenda-setting refers to the media's influence over the issues that people think about, because the agenda, or list of subjects, for public discussion is laid down by the mass media. The mass media clearly can't report every single criminal or deviant act that occurs, and media personnel are necessarily very selective in the incidents they choose either to report on or to ignore. People are only able to discuss and form opinions about the crime and deviance they have been informed about, and this information is provided in most cases by the agenda-setting media. This means that people's perceptions of crime and deviance in society are influenced by what media personnel choose to include or leave out of their newspapers, television programmes, films or websites. Media representations may therefore influence what people believe about crime and deviance, regardless of whether these impressions are true or not.

News values and 'newsworthiness'

Reiner (2007) points out that media coverage of crime and deviance is filtered through journalists' (and one could add fiction and script writers') sense of what makes an event 'newsworthy' – a good story that media audiences want to know about. The idea of newsworthiness is driven by what are known as *news values*. These are the values and assumptions held by editors and journalists which guide them in choosing what is newsworthy, and therefore what to report on and what to leave out, and how what they choose to report should be presented. The idea of news values means that journalists tend to include and play up those elements of a story that make it more newsworthy, and the stories that are most likely to be reported are those that include many newsworthy aspects. In relation to crime, Jewkes (2004) suggests these news values include those shown in table 6.1.

Table 6.1: News values and crime and deviance

News value	Meaning
Threshold	Events have to be considered significant or dramatic enough to be in the news – a single rape might make it into a local paper, but a serial rapist might become a national story.
Proximity	Proximity involves items that will have some cultural meaning or geographical closeness to media audiences. For example, British criminals or victims are more newsworthy than foreigners, significant national crimes are generally considered more important than local ones, and the murder of a 'respectable' woman is more likely to be reported than that of a prostitute.
Predictability	Stories that are predictable (known in advance) are more likely to be covered, like the publication of the latest crime statistics, as media can plan ahead.
Individualism	Focus on the actions of, or conflict between, individuals, avoiding complex explanations.
Simplification	Events that are easily understood and not too complicated, without the need for lots of background explanation and detail.
Risk	Crime becomes newsworthy when it can be presented (or misrepresented) as serious, random and unpredictable enough so that we're all at risk of becoming victims, and we all have something to fear.
Spectacle and graphic images	Events, particularly violent ones, accompanied by film, video, CCTV or mobile phone footage are more newsworthy, as they enable the media to provide a visual and dramatic impact for audiences.
Celebrity or high-status people	Crime and deviance, even if quite trivial, involving celebrities or important or powerful people, whether they are victims or offenders, is seen as more newsworthy than that involving ordinary people.
Children	Children as offenders or victims of crime have the potential to be newsworthy (e.g. the Madeleine McCann story: see pages 231–2 in chapter 3).
Sex	Sex crimes, crimes with a sexual dimension, women as victims and non-criminal sexual deviance like BDSM (bondage domination sado-masochism) – especially involving celebrities or other famous people – are more newsworthy.
Violence	Violent events enable media to report using the drama, excitement and action which appeals to audiences.
Conservatism	Events are made newsworthy by calls for more punishment and deterrence – e.g. more police, higher fines, jailing young people, more prisons and longer sentences.

Source: Devised from Jewkes 2004

> **Activity**
>
> 1 Study national newspapers and TV news reports for a few days, and think about TV dramas and films you've seen. What impressions do they give about the levels and seriousness of crime in society?
> 2 On the basis of what you found above, draw up a profile of the media stereotype of a 'typical criminal', explaining where you got your ideas from.
> 3 With reference to table 6.1, choose any two current big media news stories, fiction or non-fiction TV dramas or films, and try to identify the news values that have given them 'audience appeal'.
> 4 To what extent do you think media reporting tends to exaggerate the risks of individuals becoming victims of crime? Give reasons for your answer.

The distortion and exaggeration of crime

Greer (2005) found that *all* media tend to exaggerate the extent of violent crime, and the news values identified in table 6.1 help to explain this, and why practically any form of deviance by celebrities receives massive media coverage. The tabloid 'red-top' newspapers are always seeking out newsworthy stories of crime and deviance, and they seek to exploit the possibilities for a 'good story' by dramatizing, exaggerating, over-reporting and sensationalizing some crimes out of all proportion to their actual extent in society, in order to generate audience interest and attract readers or viewers. Despite the fact that most crime is fairly routine, trivial and non-dramatic, TV programmes like *Crimewatch* often pick up on the more serious and violent offences – like sexual assault, murder or armed robbery – with reconstructions giving quite frightening, dramatized insights into the crimes committed.

This focus on the exceptional and the dramatic is a routine feature of crime dramas on TV or film, as well as of news reports, and gives a false and misleading impression of the real extent of such crimes. Reiner points out that crime fiction presents property crime less frequently than is shown in crime statistics, but the property crimes it does portray are far more serious than most recorded offences. He concludes that the picture of crime shown by the media is the opposite of that shown by statistics on crime. Such media representations tend to create distorted perceptions of crime among the majority of the public, exaggerate the threat of crime, and unnecessarily increase the public's fear of crime.

Greer (2003) found that news reporting tended to exaggerate the risk of people becoming victims of crime, particularly among adults who were of higher social class, female and white. The media's emphasis on sexual and violent crime not only gives a distorted impression of the real pattern of crime, and the risk of becoming a victim, but it also attaches less importance to some very large and serious **white-collar crimes** and **corporate crimes**, such as widespread tax frauds, false claims in advertising, environmental pollution, and the manufacture of harmful drugs, which rarely get reported.

The process of exaggerating, distorting and sensationalizing crime also applies to the media treatment of deviant (non-conformist) behaviour in general. The media

Corporate crime refers to offences committed by groups or individuals on behalf of large companies, which directly profit the company rather than individuals.

White-collar crime refers to offences committed by middle-class individuals who abuse their work positions for personal gain at the expense of the organization or its clients.

have the power to label and stereotype certain groups and activities as deviant, and present them as acting irrationally, outside the boundaries of 'normal' behaviour, and as a threat to society which should be condemned, even when such behaviour is not illegal. Those they define as deviants are frequently used as scapegoats for social problems, and this is seen by some sociologists as part of the process of strengthening the status quo and marginalizing those who challenge or threaten it. Some examples of such groups are shown in figure 6.2 on page 407.

Deviancy amplification, moral panics and folk devils

A **moral panic** is a wave of public concern about some exaggerated or imaginary threat to society, stirred up by exaggerated and sensationalized reporting in the mass media.

Even if much of what is reported is untrue or exaggerated, as Cohen (2002 [1972]) showed (see below) it may be enough to whip up a **moral panic** – a wave of public concern about some exaggerated or imaginary threat to society, generating growing public anxiety and concern about the alleged deviance. The deviants themselves, who are seen as presenting this threat to society, may become labelled as **folk devils** – individuals or groups posing an imagined or exaggerated threat to society, providing visible reminders of what we should *not* be. In this view, some deviant groups play much the same role as witches in the past – an easy scapegoat to blame for all of society's problems.

Folk devils are individuals or groups posing an imagined or exaggerated threat to society.

This process can sensitize the police, courts and other agencies of social control to the group or problem, and lead to demands by the media and public for action by them to stop the alleged deviance. Often, these agencies, such as newspaper editors, the churches, politicians, schools, social services, the police and magistrates, will respond to the exaggerated threat presented in the media by 'pulling together' to overcome this imagined or exaggerated threat to society by taking harsher measures against the apparent troublemakers. Such action, particularly by the police, can turn what was a minor issue into something much worse, for example by causing more arrests, and amplify (or make worse) the original deviance. It's possible that such action, combined with media coverage and pre-publicity over the possible trouble looming, might even create deviance where there was none before, as people get swept away by the excitement of events, and the presence and attention of reporters and TV cameras might encourage people to act up for the cameras and misbehave when they might not otherwise have done so. The way the media may actually create or make worse the very problems they condemn is known as **deviancy amplification**.

Deviancy amplification is the way the media may actually make worse or create the very deviance they condemn by their exaggerated, sensationalized and distorted reporting of events and their presence at them.

Figure 6.1 illustrates the way in which the media can amplify deviance and generate a moral panic, and figure 6.2 shows a range of moral panics that have arisen in Britain since the 1950s.

An example of deviancy amplification: Stan Cohen's ' Folk Devils and Moral Panics'

In *Folk Devils and Moral Panics* (2002 [1972]), Stan Cohen showed how the media helped to create two opposing youth groups in the 1960s – the mods (who drove scooters and wore parkas) and the rockers (who drove motorbikes and wore leather gear).

On an Easter bank holiday weekend in 1964, at Clacton and other seaside resorts, there were some minor acts of vandalism and a few scuffles between some mods and rockers, though the level of violence was little different from that occurring anywhere else in the country. However, the media carried hugely exaggerated reports of what happened, and front-page headlines gave the misleading impression that Clacton had been terrorized and torn apart by pitched battles between rival gangs.

This generated a moral panic, with widespread public fear of, and hostility towards, the mods and rockers, who came to be seen in the period after this as folk devils posing major threats to public order. The police were forced to stamp down hard on these groups in response to the alleged deviant behaviour, which had been so exaggerated by the media. This resulted in a growing number of arrests.

Before these events, the mods and rockers had not seen themselves as rival groups, and most young people did not identify with either of them. However, the publicity created by the media's exaggerated, distorted and sensationalized reporting encouraged more young people to identify with the two groups, and to adopt their styles as fashionable and exciting lifestyle choices. This raised public fears to even greater heights. The example of the mods and rockers shows how the media's reporting of deviance can actually create the very problems they are allegedly concerned about, and generate public concerns about a problem that only existed because the media created it.

How relevant is the concept of moral panic today?

McRobbie and Thornton (1995) suggest that the concept of 'moral panic', as used by Cohen in the case of the mods and rockers in the 1960s, is now outdated, and is no longer a useful concept in the contemporary world. This is because new media technology, the growing sophistication of media audiences in a media-saturated society, and intense competition both between different types of media – such as the Internet, cable, print, broadcast and satellite – and media companies have changed the reporting of and reaction to events that might once have caused a moral panic. There is now such a huge diversity of media reports and interpretations of events, and of opinions and reactions to these events by the public, that people are now much more sceptical of media interpretations and less likely to believe them. This means that it has become more difficult for the media to define issues or events in such a way that can develop into a moral panic. This is also made more difficult by the way news reporting now involves 24/7 rolling news, which is constantly broadcast and instantly updated. As a result, most events have short shelf-lives in sustaining audience interest, and are unlikely to be newsworthy for long enough to become a moral panic.

Activity

1 Suggest and explain three reasons why the mass media might distort, exaggerate and sensationalize the extent of deviance and crime in society. Try to illustrate your answer with examples drawn from current TV or newspaper or other media reports.
2 Refer to figures 6.1 and 6.2 opposite and try to fill in each of the stages of any current moral panic in society.
3 To what extent do you agree with the view that the nature of the mass media in the contemporary world has made the concept of moral panic largely redundant? Give reasons for your answer.
4 Suggest reasons why the lifestyles and activities of young people are often the focus of media amplification of deviance and why they are most often portrayed as folk devils.

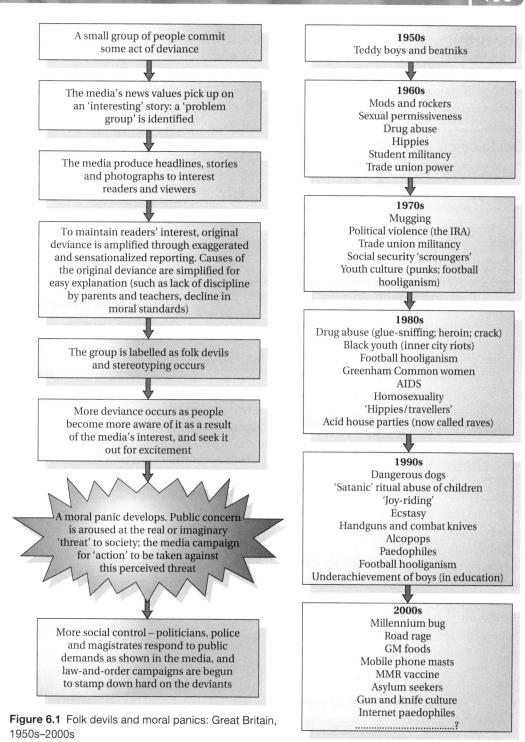

Figure 6.1 Folk devils and moral panics: Great Britain, 1950s–2000s

Figure 6.2 Deviancy amplification, moral panics and the media

Theories of crime and deviance

This section will examine a range of sociological theories of crime and deviance, a number of which are applied in explaining patterns of crime and policies to reduce crime in later sections.

Sociological and non-sociological theories

Deviance and crime have always existed in some form, and have been regarded as social problems to be tackled. There have consequently been a huge number of attempts to explain the causes of deviance, and particularly crime, and why some people commit crime while the majority appear not to. Many explanations have come from biology and psychology, but sociologists generally regard such explanations as, at best, inadequate, and in many cases as simply wrong.

Biological and psychological theories

These theories suggest that deviant/criminal behaviour is determined by physiological and/or psychological conditions which prevent some individuals from conforming to conventional norms and legal rules. Crime is put down to there being 'something wrong' with criminals, rather than with society.

Biological theories suggest that there is something in the genetic make-up of criminals that make them turn to crime – the idea of the 'born criminal'. For example, Cesare Lombroso in the nineteenth century suggested that criminals had abnormal physical features that distinguished them from the rest of the population, such as having large jaws and cheekbones, and other features more associated with humans from an earlier stage of evolution. Phrenology, which was very popular in Victorian times, believed that people's personality could be explained by the shape of their skulls, and criminals could be identified in this way.

Psychologists have linked criminal behaviour to genetically based personality characteristics, such as the presence of an extra Y-chromosome creating neurotic extroverts, who are less rational, less cautious and more impulsive and excitement-seeking than normal people. Current technology, such as PET scans, have shown that known psychopaths often have brain abnormalities which suggest organic reasons for their deviant behaviour. Others have suggested that psychological factors like poor relationships with a mother or father in childhood can create maladjusted personalities and adult criminals.

Sociologists generally reject these explanations, as they fail to recognize that the very meanings attached to crime and deviance are created by social and cultural factors, and there is no act that in itself is ever always regarded as criminal or deviant. It is very difficult to see how some people can have a biological or psychological predisposition to crime and deviance when such behaviour involves breaking socially defined rules that are subject to change over time and vary between cultures and sub-groups in the same society. To suggest that criminals are different from normal people fails to recognize that many people will commit acts of deviance and crime, albeit trivial

Early attempts to explain crime were derived from the physical features of criminals, such as their facial features and the shapes of their skulls.

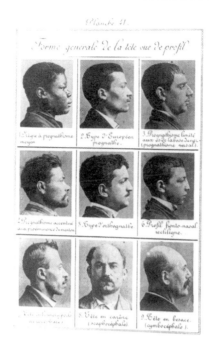

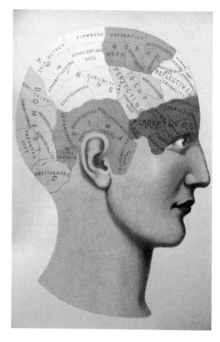

offences, at some time in their lives, and many criminals are never detected. Many biological and psychological theories are based on an unrepresentative sample of criminals who have been caught, and publicly labelled as criminals. Finally, crime is not randomly distributed by genes or personality, but follows a social pattern, linked to features such as age, class, gender and ethnicity. Most young people engage in deviant or criminal acts, but most eventually give it up – something they could not easily do if they were driven by their biological or psychological make-up.

Functionalism and subcultural theories

Functionalism is a consensus structuralist theory, which sees the source of crime and deviance located in the structure of society. Social order and cohesion are based on a value consensus, and the agencies of social control seek to protect this by controlling the threat posed by crime and deviance. Despite this, Durkheim saw some benefits of deviance.

The benefits of crime and deviance

Durkheim (1982) argued that crime is an inevitable feature of social life, because individuals are exposed to different influences and circumstances, and so not everyone can be equally committed to the shared values and moral beliefs of society. Despite the potential threats to social order, he saw some deviance and crime as necessary and beneficial, as it could perform positive functions in contributing to the well-being of society in the following ways:

1 *By strengthening collective values.* Values can 'atrophy' (waste away) unless people are reminded of the boundaries between right and wrong behaviour. For

example, outrage about incidents of child abuse have the effect of reinforcing social control against child-abusers and improving the protection of vulnerable children. Such events give society the opportunity to condemn deviant behaviour and, by punishing criminals, reassert the boundaries of acceptable behaviour, and strengthen collective values.

2   *By enabling social change.* Some deviance is necessary to allow new ideas to develop, and enable society to change and progress.

3   *By acting as a 'safety valve'.* Deviance can act as a 'safety valve' releasing stresses in society. For example, mass violent protest demonstrations might be seen as an outlet for expressions of discontent avoiding wider and more serious challenges to social order.

4   *By acting as a warning device* that society is not working properly. For example, high rates of suicide, truancy from school, drug addiction, divorce and crime point to underlying social problems that need solving before serious threats to social order develop.

Strain theory and anomie

Merton (1968 [1957]) develops functionalist theory by attempting to explain why deviance arises in the first place. He suggests that social order is based on a consensus around social goals and approved means of achieving them. Most people share goals – for example, financial success, having their own home and possessing consumer goods – and most conform to the approved means of achieving them, like working in paid employment. However, in an unequal society, Merton argues that not all individuals have the same opportunity of realizing these goals by approved means. This means they face a sense of strain and anomie (normlessness), as the dominant rules about how to achieve success don't meet their needs. He argues that there are different 'modes of adaptation', or responses to this situation, ranging from the conformity most people display, to one of four forms of deviance, which he calls innovation, ritualism, retreatism and rebellion. These are illustrated in table 6.2.

Activity

1   Explain, with examples, how deviance and crime might be important as a source of social change.

2   Classify each of the following as one of Merton's five modes of adaptation, and explain your reasons:
   - a successful banker
   - a drug-dealer
   - a monk living in a monastery
   - a person cheating in exams
   - a shoplifter
   - a drug addict
   - an indifferent job centre clerk

Table 6.2: Merton's strain theory

Mode of adaptation	Accept means?	Accept goals?	Example
Conformity	✓	✓	The non-deviant, non-criminal conformist citizen.
Innovation	✗	✓	Factors like poor educational qualifications or unemployment mean that some people can't achieve goals by approved means, so they turn to crime as an alternative.
Ritualism	✓	✗	Give up on achieving goals, but stick to means – e.g. teachers who have given up caring about student success, or office workers who have abandoned hopes of promotion and are just marking time until they retire.
Retreatism	✗	✗	Drop outs, like drug addicts or tramps, who give up altogether.
Rebellion	✗ (✓)	✗ (✓)	Reject existing social goals and means, but substitute new ones to create a new society, like revolutionaries or members of some religious sects.

✓ = accept ✗ = reject

Evaluation of Merton's strain theory While Merton's strength is that he clearly explains deviance as arising from the structure of society, there are some criticisms:

1 He takes a consensus around means and goals for granted, assuming that most people accept them. But some people do not accept goals like financial success, and, for example, may value job satisfaction and helping others more than a high income.
2 He focuses on individual responses, and doesn't recognize that there is a social pattern of crime and deviance affecting whole groups of people, linked to social class, age, gender, ethnicity and locality.
3 He doesn't explain why most people who face strain do not turn to crime or other deviance.

4   He doesn't recognize that there may be many outwardly respectable, apparently conforming successful people who are 'innovators' engaged in illegal activities, as in white-collar and corporate crime (which are discussed in later sections – see pages 454–6 and 475–8).

Subcultural theories

Subcultural theories of Cohen (1971) and Cloward and Ohlin (1960) build on Merton's work, but they focus on the position of groups in the social structure rather than just on individuals, and how these groups adapt in different ways to the strain facing them in achieving social goals. They deal with working-class juvenile **delinquency**, as these young people constitute the largest group of criminals and deviants.

Cohen: status frustration and the reactive delinquent subculture

Cohen argues that working-class youth believe in the success goals of mainstream culture, but their experiences of failure in education, living in deprived areas and having the worst chances in the job market all mean that they have little opportunity to attain these goals by approved means. They feel they are denied status in mainstream society, and experience **status frustration**. They react to this situation by developing an alternative distinctive set of values – a *delinquent subculture*. This subculture is based on a reaction to, and deliberate reversal of, accepted forms of behaviour. For example, stealing replaces hard work, vandalism replaces respect for property, and intimidation and threats replace respect for others. This gives working-class youth an opportunity to achieve some status in their peer group which they are denied in the wider society. Cohen identifies elements of revenge in this subculture, to get back at the society that has denied them status. This element of revenge helps to explain why a lot of juvenile crime is not motivated by financial gain. Offences like vandalism, joy-riding, fighting and general anti-social behaviour offer little financial gain, and seem to be motivated more by a desire to achieve peer-group status by being malicious, intimidating, having a laugh at the expense of others and generally causing trouble.

Evaluation of Cohen   A strength of Cohen's theory is that it helps to explain working-class delinquency as a group response rather than being a focus on individuals, as is the case with Merton's theory. However, Cohen makes an assumption that young working-class delinquents accept the mainstream values as superior and desirable, and develop delinquent values only as a reaction to what they can't achieve. Miller (1962) cast doubt on this. He argues that it is false to suggest that lower-working-class delinquents reject mainstream values, as the lower working class has always had its own independent culture. This means that young people couldn't generate delinquent subcultures seeking revenge and rejecting and reacting against mainstream goals, as they never held them. Matza's (1964) studies of delinquency found that most young delinquents were not committed to delinquent values. Many showed a commitment to mainstream values and merely drifted in and out of occasional delinquency rather than showing any serious commitment to it. Miller's and Matza's theories are outlined below.

Delinquency is crime committed by those under age 17, though the term 'delinquency' is often used to describe any anti-social or deviant activity by young people, even if it isn't criminal.

Status frustration is a sense of frustration arising in individuals or groups because they are denied status in society.

Cloward and Ohlin: three working-class delinquent subcultures

Cloward and Ohlin (1960) argue that Cohen's theory doesn't allow for the diversity of responses found among working-class youth who find the approved means for achieving society's goals blocked. They suggest that the varied social circumstances in which working-class youth live give rise to three types of delinquent subculture:

1. *Criminal subcultures* are characterized by utilitarian (useful) crimes, such as theft. They develop in more stable working-class areas where there is an established pattern of adult crime. This provides a learning opportunity and career structure for aspiring young criminals, and an alternative to the legitimate job market as a means of achieving financial rewards. Adult criminals exercise social control over the young to stop them carrying out non-utilitarian delinquent acts – such as vandalism – which might attract the attention of the police.

2. *Conflict subcultures* emerge in socially disorganized areas where there is a high rate of population turnover and a consequent lack of social cohesion. These prevent the formation of a stable adult criminal subculture. Conflict subcultures are characterized by violence, gang warfare, 'mugging' and other street crime. Both approved and illegal means of achieving mainstream goals are blocked or limited, and young people express their frustration at this situation through violence or street crime, and at least obtain status through success in subcultural peer-group values. This is a possible explanation for the gang culture which is increasingly appearing in the run-down estates and inner-city areas of Britain's largest cities, and which has been a common feature of some American cities for a long time.

3. *Retreatist subcultures* emerge among those lower-class youth who are 'double failures' – they have failed to succeed both in mainstream society and in the crime and gang cultures of the criminal and conflict subcultures. The response is a retreat into drug addiction and alcoholism, paid for by petty theft, shoplifting and prostitution.

Evaluation of Cloward and Ohlin   Cloward and Ohlin's research is helpful, as it gives insights into why working-class delinquency may take different forms in different social circumstances. However, they exaggerate the differences between the three types of subculture, as there is overlap between them. For example, utilitarian crime features in all three subcultures, criminal subcultures may involve drug-dealing for sale in the retreatist subculture, and many drug addicts in the retreatist subculture are also money-making drug-dealers. Goods stolen in the retreatist subculture areas to pay for drugs may be disposed of in the more stable criminal areas where there is more of a market for stolen goods.

Miller: the independent subculture and the focal concerns of working-class life

Miller explains deviance and crime in terms of a distinctive working-class subculture which he suggests has existed for centuries. This subculture, which mainly relates to males, revolves around central issues that Miller calls focal concerns. These emphasize things like being tough and masculine, a resentment of authority and being pushed around, and a search for excitement and thrills. Such values carry with them the risk of law-breaking. These values become exaggerated in the lives of young people, as the search for peer-group status – for example, through being the toughest – leads them into delinquency. It is therefore over-conformity to lower-working-class subculture, rather than the rejection of dominant values, that explains working-class delinquency.

Criticisms of functionalist-based explanations of deviance

1 They generally assume there is some initial value consensus, from which people deviate in some way. Taylor et al. (1973) say it is wrong to assume this, pointing out that not everyone is committed to mainstream goals. For example, some religious sects reject the struggle for material success in favour of alternative spiritual goals, and job satisfaction may be more important than career progression, financial success and lots of consumer goods.

2 Subcultural explanations only explain working-class delinquency, and do not explain white-collar (middle-class) crime and corporate crimes. These are discussed later in this chapter.

3 They rely on the pattern of crime shown in the official crime statistics. However, a lot of crime is never reported, and a lot of offenders are never caught. This makes it difficult to know who the real offenders are, so subcultural explanations are inadequate as they are based on an unrepresentative sample of offenders.

4 The idea of a delinquent subculture implies that working-class youth are socialized into and committed to central values of delinquency. If true, this should lead to delinquent behaviour being widespread and persistent, but, as Matza found, most working-class youth don't engage regularly in illegal acts, and most of those who do give it up in early adulthood.

5 Matza criticises subcultural theories for making the delinquent out to be different from other people. Matza stresses the similarity between the values held by delinquents and those of mainstream society, and shows how *ordinary* delinquents actually are. He points out, for example, that they show similar feelings of outrage about crime in general as most people do. When they are caught offending, most delinquents express feelings of remorse, guilt and shame, and use what Matza calls 'techniques of neutralization' rooted in mainstream values to explain their offending as exceptions to the rule. For example, they were only shoplifting because they wanted to get their Mum a birthday present and didn't have any money. This shows a commitment to mainstream values, not a rejection of them. Matza also suggests that many young people commit only occasional delinquent activities as a means of achieving identity, excitement and peer-group status for a short period of 'drift' in their lives before reaching full independent adult status. They have little serious commitment to delinquent values or a delinquent way of life, as many give it up as they grow older. Matza's ideas are discussed further in the later section on crime and age.

> **Activity**
>
> Answer the following essay question in 30 minutes:
> 'Assess the strengths and limitations of subcultural theories in explaining deviance.'

Control theory: Hirschi's social bonds theory

Hirschi (1969) is the most well-known figure in control theory, and he shares a similar view to Durkheim that social order is based on shared values and socialization through institutions integrating individuals into society. However, control theory takes the opposite approach from other theories in criminology. Instead of asking what drives people to commit crime, Hirschi asks why most people do *not* commit crime. Control theorists argue that all human beings suffer from weaknesses which make them potentially unable to resist temptation and turn to crime, but that there are social bonds with other people that encourage them to exercise self-control, tie them to conformity and restrain them from committing crime. If these social bonds with other people are weakened or broken, their self-control is weakened, and they will turn to crime.

Four social bonds

Hirschi identifies four social bonds which pull people away from crime and persuade them to conform: belief, attachment, commitment and involvement. These are illustrated in figure 6.3. Gottfredson and Hirschi (1990) later added that inadequate self-control arising from weakened social bonds is not in itself enough to explain crime; opportunities for offending must also be present for a crime to be committed. This opportunity theory is explored later in Right Realism and the crime prevention sections.

Evaluation of control theory

1. It recognizes the importance of socialization and social control in maintaining a cohesive society, and the idea of social integration through social bonds is well established in functionalist theory.
2. It assumes that those who commit crime and deviance have broken away from the bonds tying them into mainstream values, but Merton's theory and Matza's work suggest that criminals are committed to those values.
3. It doesn't explain why some have weaker bonds than others, or, for that matter, why all those with weaker bonds don't turn to crime.
4. It doesn't explain the variety of forms of deviance and crime.
5. It doesn't recognize, as labelling theory does, that it is possible to be deviant and have tight social bonds, as for example among well-integrated middle-class drug users with successful careers.
6. It suggests that everyone is a potential criminal, and therefore our behaviour should be closely controlled and monitored. Those who conform may well resent the constant surveillance this implies, and some groups may be stereotyped and

subject to unwarranted harassment, as labelling theory suggests. This may in itself undermine respect for belief in the law and justice, and weaken social bonds.

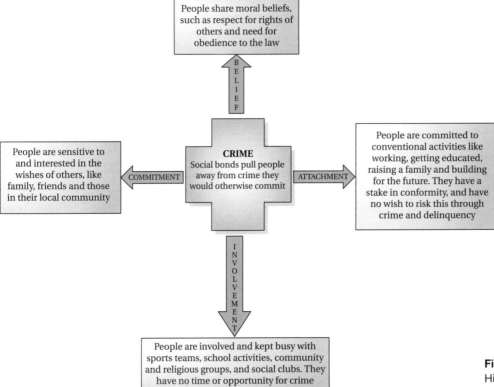

People share moral beliefs, such as respect for rights of others and need for obedience to the law

BELIEF

People are sensitive to and interested in the wishes of others, like family, friends and those in their local community

COMMITMENT

CRIME
Social bonds pull people away from crime they would otherwise commit

ATTACHMENT

People are committed to conventional activities like working, getting educated, raising a family and building for the future. They have a stake in conformity, and have no wish to risk this through crime and delinquency

INVOLVEMENT

People are involved and kept busy with sports teams, school activities, community and religious groups, and social clubs. They have no time or opportunity for crime

Figure 6.3
Hirschi's control theory

Radical criminology: Marxist and neo-Marxist theories of crime

Marxist theories of crime, including more recent neo-Marxist theories, are conflict approaches, as opposed to the consensus approaches of the functionalist-based theories of Merton and the subcultural theorists. They see society based on conflict between social classes, and social inequality as the driving force behind crime. There are a number of Marxist-inspired theories that are often lumped together under the heading of radical criminology, and this section will summarize the key features of such approaches. Later sections will discuss the theories in the context of specific social groups and crime.

Traditional Marxist theories

These theories have the following features:

1 Laws are *not* an expression of value consensus as functionalists contend, but a reflection of ruling-class ideology (the values and beliefs of the ruling class).

2 At the heart of the capitalist system is the protection of private property, and criminal laws reflect this basic concern.

3 The law, the definition of crime and deviance, and the agencies of social control reflect and protect ruling-class interests and power, and are used to control the workforce, and criminalize those who oppose ruling-class interests.

4 Crime is a 'natural' outgrowth of capitalist society, with its emphasis on economic self-interest, greed and personal gain. Crime is a rational response to the competitiveness and inequality of life in capitalist societies.

5 The impression in official statistics that crime is mainly a working-class phenomenon is largely due to the selective application of the law, with crime control focused on the working class. There's one law for the rich and another for the poor – the working class are those most likely to get prosecuted for crime, while the rich get away with their offences. This diverts attention away from the biggest crimes of all – those committed by the ruling class in the form of white-collar and corporate crime (these are discussed later).

6 Selective law-enforcement ensures that individuals, not the system of inequality, are blamed for crime.

7 Working-class crime is a form of resistance to the ruling class – a challenge to its property and power.

Neo-Marxist theories

The New Criminology emerged as a theory in the 1970s, and was developed by Taylor et al. (1973). It was based on a Marxist approach, but also drew on interactionism. This was an attempt to develop a more sophisticated approach to crime than the rather crude traditional Marxist view that the law and law-enforcement were simply aspects of ruling-class power and control of the working class. The New Criminologists recognized that working-class crime may have a political motive, but it needed to be established by finding out what crime meant to the criminal. They also recognized that no one was forced to commit a crime, and that offending therefore involved a choice made by the criminal. To understand crime and deviance fully, and how it was socially constructed, and develop what they called 'a fully social theory of deviance', Taylor et al. suggested that it was necessary to draw on both structural and interactionist approaches to explore the six dimensions shown in table 6.3, which together could explain crime and deviance. Hall et al. (1978) applied this approach, looking at the various dimensions involved in their study of black crime, particularly 'mugging', in the 1970s (see below).

Other neo-Marxist approaches, largely developed in the 1970s, took the view, first, that working-class crime is a form of political action and resistance to ruling-class oppression, in the form of police racism and harassment, such as that adopted by Gilroy (1982) in his discussion of black crime in the 1970s. Second, crime is used to

Table 6.3: The New Criminology and a 'fully social theory of deviance'

Dimension to be explored	Explanation
The wider social origins of the deviant act	The wider context of crime, like the unequal distribution of wealth and power.
The immediate origins of the deviant act	The specific situation leading criminals to choose to commit a deviant act.
The actual act and what it means to the deviant	Is it a political act against the ruling class? Is it a Robin Hood act, robbing the rich to help the poor? Is it just an alternative to a job in paid employment? Is it to support a drug habit?
The immediate origins of societal reaction	How do other people react to the act – such as the family and neighbours of the deviant or victim?
The wider origins of societal reaction	How does wider society react to the act – such as those with the power to define acts as deviant, like the mass media or the police?
The outcomes of the societal reaction on the deviants' further action	What happens to deviants once they've been labelled as a deviant? Does it stop them from re-offending, or does it just lead to acceptance of the label and further deviance?

reassert the dominance of ruling-class **hegemony** at times when it is under threat. To reassert hegemony, the ruling class-owned media exaggerate the problem of the working class, and particularly black crime, to stir up the public, create moral panics and, thereby, demand that something is done to stamp out the exaggerated crime problems. In the 1970s, Hall et al. argued that media exaggeration created a moral panic and growing public concern about a black crime wave at a time of crisis, which helped to justify more repressive and aggressive policing. This became a means of re-establishing ruling-class hegemony in society generally, and cracking down on all opposition to the ruling class. Neo-Marxist theories of crime are discussed more in the section on crime and ethnicity.

> **Hegemony** is a term used by the Italian Marxist Gramsci, to describe the dominance in society of the ruling class's set of ideas over others, and acceptance of and consent to them by the rest of society.

Evaluation of Marxist and neo-Marxist theories of crime

These theories help to locate crime in the wider context of inequalities of wealth and power in society, and certainly the official statistics on crime conceal the extent of white-collar and corporate crime, as will be seen later in this chapter. However, such theories have a number of limitations:

- they over-emphasize class inequality in relation to crime, and neglect other inequalities like those relating to ethnicity and gender;
- they over-emphasize property crime, and don't have much to say about non-property offences like rape, domestic violence and murder;

- they have little to say about non-criminal deviance;
- they fail to develop any possible solutions to crime, apart from destroying the capitalist system and reducing social inequality;
- they pay little attention to the victims of crime – in particular, they fail to recognize that the crimes that matter most to people in their daily lives are the everyday ones like burglary, vehicle crime, street violence and anti-social behaviour; these offences are mainly committed by working-class people against other working-class people – the poor don't generally commit crimes against the rich, but against others like themselves;
- they fail to recognize (traditional Marxism particularly) that the law does not simply protect ruling-class interests – there is a wide range of laws that are in everyone's interests, such as those on health and safety, consumer protection, traffic laws, and those against household and vehicle theft and violence of all kinds; the police try to protect the public from victimization, and are not simply ruling-class agents who repress the working class.

Later theories came to regard traditional Marxism, the New Criminology and some neo-Marxist theories of crime as idealistic. They were regarded as a sort of Left Idealism, producing theoretical ideas that did not take the problem of crime seriously, did nothing to explain the reality of crime, in contemporary societies, or produce realistic policies to protect the victims of crime who were overwhelmingly working class. It was disillusionment with these approaches among some conflict theorists that led Lea and Young (1984) to reconsider and develop a more realistic theory of crime called Left Realism, which is considered later in this section.

Interactionist theories of crime: labelling theory

Interactionist views of crime and deviance are most commonly referred to as labelling theory. Labelling theory suggests that many people involve themselves in some deviant or illegal behaviour, so it is hard to sustain a distinction between deviants and non-deviants; attempts to find the *causes* of crime (as in many of the theories examined so far) are therefore pointless. Official crime statistics are regarded as *social constructions*, as these simply represent offenders who have been caught and publicly labelled as 'criminal'. These statistics do not on the whole reveal the real pattern of crime, but the stereotypes and explanations that the police and other social control agencies themselves believe give rise to crime.

Labelling theory seeks to explain why only *some* people and *some* acts are defined as deviant or criminal, while others carrying out similar acts are not. Labelling theory therefore takes as its focus:

1 *The interaction between deviants and those who define them as deviant*, and why particular individuals and groups are defined as deviant, and the circumstances in which this occurs.
2 *The process whereby rules are selectively enforced*, and why the response to rule-breaking is not always the same. What assumptions are used by the police when they choose whether or not to take action? For example, why might the police

respond differently to groups of black male youths compared to white youths engaged in similar activities?

3   *The consequences of being labelled deviant.* How do others respond to those labelled as deviant, and what effect does the attachment of a deviant label have on the self-concept, or the way they see themselves, of those labelled? For example, does it prevent further deviance? Is it a self-fulfilling prophecy? Does it make deviance worse (deviancy amplification)?

4   *The circumstances in which a person becomes set apart and defined as deviant.*

5   *An analysis of who has the power to attach deviant labels and make them 'stick'.*

Howard Becker (1997 [1963]) (www.home.earthlink.net/~hsbecker/index.html) is the key figure in labelling theory. He suggests that an act only becomes deviant when others perceive and define it as such, and whether or not the deviant label is applied will depend on societal reaction (how an act is interpreted by those whose attention is drawn to it). The following quotation from Becker's *Outsiders* is a classic, and sums up the problematic nature of deviance well:

> Social groups create deviance by making the rules whose infraction constitutes deviance, and by applying those rules to particular people and labelling them as outsiders. From this point of view, deviance is not a quality of the act the person commits, but rather a consequence of the application by others of the rules and sanctions to an 'offender'. The deviant is one to whom the label has successfully been applied. Deviant behaviour is behaviour that people so label.

Becker calls groups, such as the mass media and the police, who have the power and resources to create or enforce rules and impose their definitions of deviance, **moral entrepreneurs.**

A **moral entrepreneur** is a person, group or organization with the power to create or enforce rules and impose their definitions of deviance.

Howard Becker's book *Outsiders* is the defining text in labelling theory, in which, as he says on his website, 'I said everything I have to say about labelling theory'.

Selective law-enforcement

Agencies of social control use considerable discretion and selective judgement in deciding whether and how to deal with illegal or deviant behaviour. The police, for example, can't prosecute all crime: it would require very heavy policing which would not enjoy much public support, and would be a massive drain on resources. So 'criminal' labels are not attached to every breach of the law, and the same courses of action are not always taken in response to the same offence. Labelling theorists therefore suggest that it is necessary to study how, and to whom, deviant labels are attached.

Becker suggests that the police operate with pre-existing conceptions and stereotypical categories of what constitutes 'trouble', criminal types, criminal areas and so on, and these influence their response to behaviour they come across. What action is taken will depend not so much on actual offences or behaviour, but on the stereotypes of groups and offences they hold.

Cicourel

Cicourel (1976) uses a phenomenological approach to understand how law-enforcers make sense of and interpret what they see. He suggests their subjective perceptions and stereotypes can affect whether criminal labels are attached, and how these lead to the social construction of crime statistics. In his study of juvenile delinquency in two US cities, he found juvenile crime rates to be consistently higher in working-class areas than in middle-class areas. He found that this was because the police viewed the behaviour of middle-class and working-class juveniles differently even when they were engaged in the same actions. Cicourel argued that this was because the police had a perception that middle-class youth came from 'good backgrounds' with lots of family support, and so their behaviour was interpreted as temporary lapses, and charges weren't brought. They held the opposite perception of working-class youth, and so more formal police action was taken against them. Cicourel's research suggests that we need to look at the choices made by police over where they patrol, who they regard with suspicion and, therefore, who they choose to stop and search, arrest and charge.

Primary deviance is deviance that has not been publicly labelled as such.

Secondary deviance is deviance that follows once a person has been publicly labelled as deviant.

A **master status** is one that displaces all other features of a person's social standing, and a person is judged solely in terms of one defining characteristic

The labelling process – primary and secondary deviance

Lemert (1972) distinguishes between **primary deviance** and **secondary deviance**. Primary deviance is deviance that has not been publicly labelled as such. For example, people might break traffic laws, use illegal drugs, pinch stationery from work, or even download child pornography to their computers. This has few consequences for the person, so long as no one knows about it. However, once an offender is discovered and publicly exposed and the label of 'deviant' attached, then secondary deviance may occur. The stigma attached to people caught downloading child pornography is a good example.

Becker points out that the attachment of the label may have major consequences for the individual's view of themselves – their self-concept – and their future actions. This is because the deviant label can become a **master status** – a status that overrides all other characteristics which the individual may possess. For example, if caught downloading child porn, other identities like manager, worker, husband, father,

A fictional deviant career

A young man is caught by the police carrying a knife, and is charged with an offence.

Gets sent to a young offenders institution Label of 'young offender' attached.

Gets immersed in a criminal subculture.

On release, former friends and family regard him with suspicion and distrust.

Criminal record makes work difficult to find, and it is harder to live a conformist life.

Opportunities for normality are reduced because of labelling.

Mixes with other former offenders who share his problems. Develops deviant self-concept.

Further deviance results, and a deviant career begins.

Adapted from Young's participant observation of hippie drug-users

The police have a media-derived stereotype of hippie drug-users as junkies and layabouts. The marijuana users feel persecuted, as dope smoking is a fairly peripheral activity.

Police action unites marijuana smokers and makes them feel 'different' - outsiders.

In self-defence, hippies retreat into small closed groups united around marijuana smoking. Deviant norms and values develop.

Defined and treated as outsiders, hippies express this difference, through bizarre clothes and longer hair. Drugs become more central to users' identity – drug subculture develops.

The original police stereotype is created and confirmed. Moral panics over drug-taking develop, and media put pressure on police to 'solve the drug problem'. The self-fulfilling prophecy is confirmed.

Opportunities for normality reduced because of labelling and police persecution and arrests, the drug problem is amplified, and publicity gets more drug-users involved.

Drug charges may close off opportunities in normal life, such as paid employment, possibly leading to a deviant career.

Figure 6.4 Deviant self-concepts, deviant careers and the self-fulfilling prophecy

sportsman or vicar become displaced by the label of 'child pornographer and sex offender', which becomes seen by others as that person's defining status. Others see and respond to the individual in light of this master status, and assume that he or she has all the negative attributes of the label. This is where secondary deviance begins, arising from the attachment of the label, and societal reaction to the deviant. Sustaining an alternative image in the deviant's own eyes and in those of others becomes difficult once the master status is applied.

Deviant careers and the self-fulfilling prophecy

A **deviant career** is where people who have been labelled as deviant find conventional opportunities blocked to them, and so are pushed into committing further deviant acts.

Becker suggests that the labelling process and societal reaction can lead to a self-fulfilling prophecy and a **deviant career** similar to an occupational career, as those labelled face rejection from many social groups, are placed outside conventional society and become 'outsiders', and continue to act even more in the way they have been labelled. Institutions like prisons for the punishment of offenders help to make the label stick, and even after leaving prison, labels like 'ex-con' are still applied. Such labelling may lead to further deviance because of the closing off of alternative legitimate opportunities and a lack of means by which to live their lives and shake off the label. A deviant career begins when the individual eventually joins an organized deviant group facing similar problems, which provides support and understanding for the deviant identity. This too may generate further deviance. Becker therefore suggests that societal reaction and the application of the deviant label produces more deviance than it prevents. Cohen's work on moral panics, discussed earlier in this chapter, also illustrated this process, with labelling by the media generating more of the deviance it apparently condemned. Young's (1971) participant observation study of hippie marijuana-users in Notting Hill carried out between 1967 and 1969 also demonstrated this process. The two examples shown in figure 6.4, one fictional and one based on Young's research, illustrate the labelling process and its possible consequences.

Evaluation of labelling theory

Strengths

- it provides insights into the nature of deviance not provided by structural theories;
- it challenges the idea that deviants are different from 'normal' people;
- it shows the importance of the reactions of others in defining and creating deviance;
- it reveals the importance of stereotyping in understanding deviance;
- it reveals the way official crime statistics are a product of bias in law-enforcement;
- it reveals the importance of those with power in defining acts and people as deviant;
- it highlights the role of moral entrepreneurs, like the media, in defining and creating deviance and generating moral panics;
- it shows how labelling can lead to a self-fulfilling prophecy and to deviant careers;
- it shows how the deviant label can affect the self-concept of the deviant.

Weaknesses

- it tends to remove the blame for deviance away from the deviant and onto those who define him or her as deviant: the deviant becomes a victim too;
- it assumes an act isn't deviant until it is labelled as such, yet many know perfectly well that what they are doing is deviant;
- it doesn't explain the causes of deviant behaviour which precede the labelling process (primary deviance), nor the different kinds of acts that people commit – for example, taking drugs is a different act from murder;
- it is too deterministic:
  - it doesn't allow that some people *choose* deviance and the attachment of a deviant label or of a deviant identity, like adopting a gay identity; it is not simply or always imposed on them by societal reaction
  - labelling doesn't always lead to a self-fulfilling prophecy and more deviance: the attachment of a deviant label and the stigma attached by societal reaction may reduce deviance rather than increase it, like a shoplifter so mortified by being caught they never want to do it again; Becker himself recognizes that individuals can choose to avoid a deviant career by seeking to rehabilitate themselves
- it doesn't explain why there are different reactions to deviance, nor where stereotypes come from in the first place;
- it ignores the importance of wider structural factors in creating deviance, and assumes it is all down to societal reaction;
- it has little to say about the victims of crime;
- it has no real policy solutions to crime, beyond making fewer rules and not 'naming and shaming' offenders – this isn't much consolation for the victims of crime;
- it does not explain why some people should be labelled rather than others, and why some activities are against the law while others aren't; it points to the issue of power in the labelling process, but not, as the Marxists have done, at the structures of power in society which create the wider framework for the labelling process.

Activity

1 Explain, with examples, how the definition of deviance does not depend on the act itself but on societal reaction to it.

2 List some deviant labels you know of. Explain how and why these labels are applied, and what groups and circumstances are important in making the labels stick.

3 Referring back to earlier work on the mass media, explain how the mass media can act as moral entrepreneurs and how this might affect the crime statistics.

4 Outline, with examples, what assumptions you think the police operate with when they go about their work, such as their stereotypes of typical criminals and criminal areas.

5 Suggest ways how, in the process of interaction, a delinquent may avoid being labelled as such.

6 Drawing on Cicourel's research, explain how phenomenologists might explain the pattern in official crime statistics that most criminals are young, male and working class, with an over-representation of black youth.

7 Answer the following essay question in 30 minutes:
  'Assess the contribution of labelling theory to a sociological understanding of deviance.'

Left Realism

Left Realism developed in the 1980s and is particularly identified with Lea and Young (1984). It developed as a response to traditional Marxist and neo-Marxist approaches, which it accused of:

- not taking crime seriously, and reducing it to simple moral panics induced by the capitalist state;
- romanticizing working-class criminals as 'Robin Hood' characters, fighting against social inequality and injustice;
- failing to take victimization seriously.

Like Marxists, Left Realists accept that structural inequalities and perceptions of injustice are the major causes of crime. Through victim surveys, they found that the sort of crime that worries people most is primarily street crime like 'mugging', violence, car crime and burglary, which is mainly performed by young working-class males, both black and white. The main victims of these offences, and those who have the highest fears about crime, are the poor, the deprived, the ethnic minorities and inner-city residents. They recognize that most people don't care much about white-collar or corporate crime, as it has little impact on their lives.

Left Realists develop practical policies to tackle crime. For example, they see better and more democratic policing as central to reducing crime, and protecting its main victims – working-class people. Kinsey et al. (1986) suggest that the police need to improve clear-up rates (crimes solved and offenders caught), to deter offenders from committing crime, improve relations with the community on whom they depend to report crime and provide leads on offenders, and spend more time investigating crime to reassure people and restore confidence in the police.

Left Realist policies to reduce crime are explored in the section on crime prevention (see pages 488–9).

Explaining crime

Lea and Young attempt to explain why people turn to crime using three key concepts:

1 *Relative deprivation.* It is not deprivation as such that causes people to commit crime, but whether they see themselves as deprived in comparison with others.
2 *Subculture.* Working-class deviant subcultures emerge as group solutions to problems arising from social inequality, though they take different forms over time and in different contexts. These can act as motivators for crime, as some working-class subcultures see offending as acceptable behaviour.
3 *Marginalization.* Some groups find themselves politically and economically 'on the edge' of society, through factors like poor educational achievement, unemployment, and lack of involvement in community organizations.

These three concepts are all explored more in the section on crime and ethnicity (see pages 460–1).

Understanding and tackling crime

In order to understand and tackle crime, Lea and Young suggest it is necessary to examine the inter-relationships between four elements, and how they influence or interact with one another in influencing crime levels in any community:

1 *Social structural factors and formal social control.* These influence the context of crime, such as how crime is defined and its social causes, how law-enforcement is carried out and decisions over whether or not an act is labelled as criminal, styles of policing and the ability of the police to influence crime levels by deterring and catching offenders.

2 *The public and informal social control.* How do people react to crime in their communities? Are offenders condemned by family, peer groups and neighbours? Does the public report offences? Do they trust the police? Do they buy stolen goods? Is the offence just seen as part of normal life in their community?

3 *The role of victims.* Why do people become victims and what do they do about it? Victims are often of the same ethnic group, class and community as the offenders, or partners in a relationship with them. How do victims view offenders? Will they report them? Could or would the police do anything?

4 *The offenders.* What meaning does the act have to the offender? Why do they choose to offend? Is it because they feel marginalized? Or because they belong to a deviant subculture? Or because they feel relatively deprived? Offenders choose to commit crimes – to what extent are they driven to it by outside forces and how is this choice influenced by the other three factors?

Activity

1 Look at the four elements above, and suggest and explain how:
  a) the attitudes of the public might affect whether or not an act is defined as a crime;
  b) the attitudes of the public towards the police might affect the police's ability to reduce crime levels in a community;
  c) the attitudes of a community towards offenders might influence whether or not they commit offences in the future;
  d) the attitudes of victims and their relationship with offenders might affect crime reporting in a community;
  e) the attitudes of the police towards offending and their clear-up rates might influence crime levels in community;
2 On the basis of this activity and your understanding of Left Realism, suggest four practical policies that Left Realists might adopt for reducing crime in a deprived community.

Evaluation of Left Realism

Strengths

- it explains the social causes of crime, and recognizes that tackling crime means tackling inequalities;
- it recognizes that most victims of crime are poor and working class, and the importance of tackling crime and the fear of crime;

- it recognizes the importance of community solutions to crime; the police, public, victims and offenders are all involved in generating crime levels, and all need to be involved in reducing crime.

Weaknesses

- it neglects other responses to relative deprivation and marginality apart from crime, such as Merton's *retreatism, ritualism* or *rebellion*;
- it doesn't pay much attention to white-collar and corporate crime (perhaps not unreasonably given its concern with everyday victimization);
- it relies on victim surveys to measure the extent and fear of crime, but these have some difficulties, as they tend to over-report some crimes and under-report others (see the section below on researching crime and deviance – pages 503–4 for more on victim surveys).

Right Realism and rational choice theory

Right Realism is now, arguably, the greatest influence on current Home Office policy of all theories of crime, because of the practical policies for crime prevention which derive from it. The origins of Right Realism are found in the work of Wilson (1985 [1975]), who was concerned that sociology had not explained and solved the problem of crime. Wilson argues that attempts to tackle the causes of crime are pointless, and the best solution is to reduce its impact upon people's lives. Heavier punishment for those convicted to deter future crime will not succeed, because potential criminals often have little chance of being caught. The most important thing is that the risk to criminals is increased by greater chances of detection.

Right Realism has the following key features:

1   *Value consensus and shared morality underpin society.* This is reflected in the law, and criminals are immoral because they breach this consensus. Social order is crucial, and individuals should be able to live their lives without fear of crime.
2   *People are naturally selfish.* Like control theory, it suggests that people are essentially self-seeking, and need to have their natural tendency to take short cuts by committing crime regulated by the agencies of socialization and social control, including the law. This links to the next point on community control.
3   *Community control.* The most effective form of crime control is through strengthening the bonds of community – the types of bond suggested by Hirschi's control theory. Stricter socialization through the family and education and community pressure, and re-establishing social cohesion and a sense of individual responsibility are all likely to be more effective in preventing crime than police action. It is poor socialization and lack of community controls that lie behind crime and anti-social behaviour.
4   *Rational choice and opportunity.* People are rational, and make choices over any course of action they take after weighing up the costs of doing so against the benefits gained. Cornish and Clarke (1986) applied this to crime using rational choice theory, suggesting that people choose to commit crime because they

Rational choice theory suggests that people weigh up the costs and benefits before choosing whether or not to commit a crime.

decide that the benefits gained are greater than the potential costs, the opportunities for crime are available, and the risk is worth it. The solution is, then, to increase the costs, such as heavier policing to increase the risks of being caught, and to reduce the opportunities for crime.

5   *Crime will always exist.* There will always be some people whose natural selfishness and greed will slip through other controls. It's a waste of time trying to find out what the social causes of crime are, as the Left Realists and Marxists seek to do, because, for example, most deprived people don't commit crime. The most that can be achieved is to reduce the impact of crime on victims, particularly crimes like violence and burglary, which are of major concern to the public. White-collar and corporate crimes are largely victimless, in the sense that they don't directly impact on individuals in their daily lives, so they shouldn't be a major focus for policing.

The broken windows thesis and zero tolerance

Wilson and Kelling (1982) developed what has become known as the 'broken windows' thesis. This suggests that unless what the authors call 'incivilities' – for example, anti-social behaviour of all kinds – are kept to a minimum, then there will be a gradual deterioration of neighbourhoods, with growing anti-social behaviour like noise, litter, graffiti and vandalism and growing crime rates as a sense of 'anything goes' develops (see broken windows picture). They saw such growing disorder weakening the bonds of community, and the police should therefore have a policy of zero tolerance of all crimes, anti-social behaviour and any potential threats to social disorder, even if not strictly illegal. This would prevent a deterioration of social cohesion and the sense of community, and keep neighbourhoods safe.

Wilson's broken window thesis suggests that if a few broken windows are left unrepaired, further damage and anti-social behaviour will occur, more serious crime will follow, and whole neighbourhoods will deteriorate into high crime areas. The solution? Zero tolerance of all anti-social and criminal behaviour, no matter how trivial.

The 'broken windows' thesis has been criticised on the grounds that it is lack of investment, not 'incivilities', that causes neighbourhoods to decline, and that there is little evidence that tolerance of incivilities leads to crime. Zero tolerance policing of very trivial offences can also generate widespread resentments and make disorder problems worse.

Right Realism and social policy

The social policies arising from Right Realism involve more strict socialization of young people into the differences between right and wrong, stricter control in communities and heavier policing to increase the risk of offenders being detected. However, Right Realists particularly emphasize the importance of reducing opportunities for crime to be committed in particular settings, through situational crime prevention and 'target hardening'. These are discussed in a later section on crime prevention (see pages 489–92).

Evaluation of Right Realism

Strengths

- it addresses the immediate causes of crime, and provides policies for reducing the opportunities for crime;
- it recognizes that if minor problems like anti-social behaviour aren't nipped in the bud, they may grow into more serious crime, and destroy a sense of community;
- it recognizes, like Left Realism, the importance of community control and community responses to crime in affecting crime levels.

Weaknesses

- it doesn't address the wider structural causes of crime that other theories do;

- it suggests a strong police presence in local communities to increase the detection of offenders and zero tolerance will prevent crime; it is also possible, as labelling theorists suggest, that this might create resentment and hostility in those communities – a self-fulfilling prophecy creating problems rather than solving them; this is especially likely if stereotypes of 'typical offenders' are held by social control agencies;
- zero tolerance policing, based on the 'broken windows' thesis, can involve an over-emphasis on minor and trivial offences, diverting resources away from more serious offences which cause greater harm to people and property; there is also the possibility of crime simply being displaced to other areas – moving crime around rather than actually reducing it;
- it doesn't pay any attention to white-collar and corporate crime, and other 'hidden crimes' like domestic violence and child abuse;
- it assumes that offenders act rationally, weighing up costs and benefits, but some crimes are impulsive or irrational and do not have any obvious gain, like vandalism or violence; Lyng's conception of 'edgework' or Katz's on the seductions of crime, both discussed later in this chapter, with the risk-taking, thrill and buzz making crime attractive, are not explained by rational choice theory.

Feminist theories of crime and deviance

Feminist theories and research are applied in the crime and gender and victimization sections later in this chapter (pages 444–50 and 482–4). This section will focus on the main features underlying feminist contributions.

Feminism views society as patriarchal, and, in this male-dominated society, the control of women by men discourages female deviance, but also generates crimes by men against women, particularly in the form of domestic violence and sexual offences like rape.

'Malestream' sociology and the invisibility of women

Gender issues and female offending have been ignored, until fairly recently, in most sociological theories of crime; studies have generally been about male offenders and deviants. There has therefore been little attempt to explain female offending, the gender gap between male and female offending, and other forms of female deviance. For example, studies of working-class crime pay scant attention to the fact that working-class women in the same social class position as men commit far less crime. Feminists also point out that female victimization was ignored, and particularly female victimization by men in the form of domestic and sexual violence. Newburn (2007) identifies this problem of the invisibility of women in criminology when he refers to Heidensohn's (1996) example drawn from Cohen's study of delinquency, where Cohen begins with '. . . the delinquent is the rogue male'. The feminist view was, in a nutshell, that male dominance in society was reflected in a male dominance of mainstream theories of crime, which was seen as 'malestream' sociology.

Heidensohn suggests various reasons for this invisibility of females:

- academics and researchers in the sociology of crime and deviance were predominantly men;
- 'malestream' middle-class sociologists had a kind of romanticized male preoccupation with macho working-class deviance – by studying rogue males, male academics might attach to themselves some of the alleged glamour, and increase their 'street cred';
- there is actually less to study, due to the relatively low level of female crime and the often invisible nature of the offences committed by women, which are more likely to be *less detectable offences*, like prostitution and shoplifting.

The growth of feminist criminology

Like other areas in sociology, since the women's movement of the 1960s and 1970s there has been a growing interest in female crime and deviance, led by feminist researchers, and this is now one of the key areas of sociological research. Much feminist criminology focuses on female offending, women's treatment by the criminal justice system, the study of female victimization and the gender gap in offending. This involves both applying existing theories of male deviance to explain female deviance, and also criticizing their shortcomings and developing new theories to explain female offending. Feminists bring the issue of gender and male power into the sociological study of crime and deviance. A major theme has been the importance of gender identity in understanding crime and deviance, rather than simply focusing on offending and structural features like strain, subcultures, social class or power. Smart (1976), for example, pointed out that women offenders are often seen as double deviants, because they break not just the law, but breach traditional gender roles too, which means that their offences are more highly stigmatized than those committed by men, even if they are less serious.

This focus on gender and identity is also developed to explore how conceptions of femininity and female gender roles might lead women to be less deviant than men. Messerschmidt's (1993) research into how crime and violence, including domestic violence, can be a means of 'accomplishing masculinity' (achieving a masculine image) for men who have failed to achieve this in other areas of their lives, owes much to the impact of feminist ideas in sociology (this is discussed later in the crime and gender section).

The feminist perspective has contributed a number of points to the study of crime and deviance, including the following:

- a new focus on female offending and the experiences of women in the criminal justice system;
- the application of existing theories, criticisms of them, and the development of new theories, to explain female deviance;
- a new focus on the various types of victimization suffered by women, particularly from male physical and sexual violence, including rape and domestic violence;
- a challenge to the popular misconception that women enjoy 'chivalry' from the criminal justice system, and are treated more leniently than men;

- an important new focus on gender and gender identity issues in explaining deviance, and the adaptation of existing theories to refocus them on gender rather than simply offending – feminists have raised questions in control theory, for example, concerning how men and women experience different levels of control, and in labelling theory concerning why female offending carries higher levels of stigmatization than male offending.

Postmodernist theories of crime

Postmodernist theories stress that society is changing so rapidly and constantly that it is marked by chaos and uncertainty, with society fragmented into a huge diversity of groups with different interests and lifestyles. Social structures have collapsed, and have been replaced by growing individualism expressed through a consumer culture in which individual consumers assert choices about their lifestyles, values and the identities they wish to adopt. Lea (1998) suggests that this is reflected in postmodernist views about the nature of crime, the causes of crime and the control of crime.

The nature of crime

Postmodernists view the category 'crime' as simply a social construction, based on a narrow legal definition, reflecting an outdated metanarrative of the law which does not reflect the diversity of postmodern society. In postmodern society, people are increasingly freed from the constraints arising from social norms and social bonds to others, yet crime as presently defined is simply an expression of a particular view of those with power of how people should conduct themselves, and denies people's freedom, self-identity and difference. It is necessary to go beyond narrow legal definitions of crime, and develop a wider conception of crime based on justice and respect for people's chosen identities and lifestyles. Henry and Milovanovic (1996) suggest that crime should be taken beyond the narrow legal definitions to a wider conception of social harm, embracing all threats and risks to people pursuing increasingly diverse lifestyles and identities.

Crime as social harm

Henry and Milovanovic suggest that crime should be reconceptualized not simply as breaking laws, but as people using power to show disrespect for others by causing them harm of some sort. They identify two forms of harm:

1 *Harms of reduction.* Power is used to cause a victim to experience some *immediate* loss or injury.
2 *Harms of repression.* Power is used to restrict *future* human development. This conception of harm brings a wider range of actions into the criminal net, which are either not illegal or not traditionally taken very seriously or perceived as part of the current crime 'problem'. These include harms threatening human dignity and respect, such as sexual harassment, racist abuse and hate crime (crimes motivated by prejudice or hate of a group or individual).

The causes of crime

Most sociological theories of crime and deviance explain crime in relation to a social structure and core values from which the criminal deviates for some reason, such as through marginalization, relative deprivation, strain, inadequate socialization, sub-cultural values or weakened social bonds. Postmodern society is characterized by a fragmentation of this social structure. The metanarratives of social class, work and family, which formed people's identity and gave them their social roles and values, and integrated them into society, have been replaced by uncertainty and individual choice of identity. Individuals increasingly focus on themselves, often with little regard and respect for others.

The individualism of identity in postmodern society means that the social causes of crime are undiscoverable. Each crime becomes a one-off event expressing whatever identity an individual chooses, and is motivated by an infinite number of individual causes, including intangible emotional reasons. For example, low individual self-esteem may be overcome by criminal activities designed to earn respect from others by harming them, perhaps by humiliating, bullying or intimidating victims – as in anti-social behaviour or bullying at school – or hate crimes directed at others simply because of such characteristics as ethnicity, religion, gender, sexual orientation, disability or nationality. The previous section mentioned Messerschmidt's work on crime as an expression of masculinity for some men. Katz (1988) examines the pleasures and seductions of crime for individuals, and Lyng (1990) examines crime as 'edgework', committed for the risk-taking, excitement and thrills those involved get from living 'on the edge'. For postmodernists, crime may be committed simply for the kicks derived from doing so, and the causes of crime lie in the individual, not in society.

The control of crime

In the postmodernist view, the fragmentation of society is reflected in a similar frag-mentation of more formally organized crime prevention through a publicly controlled and accountable centralized criminal justice system, like the police and the courts. A growing emphasis is placed on private crime prevention and more informal localized arrangements for controlling crime. There is increasing use of informal control agen-cies, like private security firms that control private 'public' places such as shopping complexes. Contemporary societies use surveillance techniques to control everyone, not just offenders. Foucault (1991) pointed out that surveillance is penetrating more and more into private aspects of our lives, aided by new surveillance technology like CCTV, which monitors the movements of people in every sphere of life. Widespread surveillance of all public and mass private spaces (like shopping malls), is now endemic throughout the UK, which has more surveillance cameras than any country in Europe. This is accompanied by growing control of entry to streets and housing complexes in 'gated communities'. In addition, vast amounts of data are collected on individuals through things like consumer tracking. The Tesco Clubcard, for example, collects information about every product a customer purchases in their stores, pro-viding a profile of the lifestyle of that person.

People are regarded less as citizens with rights, and more as consumers and customers. They are seduced and co-opted into avoidance of social harm by participation in the consumer society. Those who aren't so seduced, or can't afford to participate, face stricter control, for example through heavier and more repressive policing.

Postmodern approaches draw attention to the growing detachment of the criminal justice system from centralized control to more informal localized arrangements, as it starts to take account of people's different lifestyles and needs. For example, policing policies become very localized and community-based, reflecting the fragmentation of society into a diverse range of smaller groupings of localised identities, such as those around ethnic and gender identities. The voluntary use of Sharia courts, based on Islamic rather than British law, among some sections of the Muslim community to deal with disputes might be seen as an example of the growing informality and localism of criminal justice, as it becomes responsive to local identities.

Evaluation of the postmodernist approach

Strengths

- it can explain contemporary developments like widespread surveillance, for example using CCTV, and consumer tracking;
- it recognizes that there are other dimensions to the causes of crime beyond the more structural theories which have dominated in the sociology of crime and deviance;
- it explains the growing localism attached to policing strategies;
- it offers explanations for non-utilitarian crime, with no material benefit, like hate crimes and anti-social behaviour;
- it provides a fuller picture of the pattern of crime than traditionally provided, as the conception of crime as 'harm' encompasses a range of behaviour that has been largely neglected in the law and in sociological theories.

Weaknesses

- it doesn't explain why most people don't use their power to harm others, and why particular individuals or groups find it necessary to actively engage in acts of harm as a means of asserting their identity – Lea suggests that traditional theories like marginality, relative deprivation and subculture still provide a useful starting point for explaining why certain groups have been denied access to less harm-causing sources of identity;
- it ignores the issues of justice and citizen rights for all, and not just for those who are significant consumers and customers;
- it doesn't recognize that decentralized and more informal arrangements for crime control, like the use of private security firms and localized policing, to respond to local identities are likely to benefit the most well organized and articulate groups – these are most likely to be middle-class groups, who have the power to get their needs attended to; the poorest in society, who cannot afford to establish identities by consuming goods, nor are seen as significant customers, are likely to be neglected;

- it fails to recognize that the consumer society, where personal identity and fulfilment are tied up with the purchase of consumer goods, can lead to resentment by those who can't afford to participate – this may generate the wish to cause harm to those who they might see harming them through social exclusion;
- it fails to recognize that many people still have strong conceptions of right and wrong behaviour, which underpins the law and much sociological theory of crime;
- Lea points out that postmodernist theories are not much more than a rediscovery of labelling theory or radical criminology, which concluded long ago that crime was simply a social construction, and that power was a crucial element in that construction.

The pattern of crime

The use of crime statistics

The picture of crime that is generally presented to the public is the one derived from official statistics. These statistics are used for a variety of purposes:

- for comparison with previous years to discover trends in crime;
- to look at the police clear-up rate to measure police efficiency;
- to show where the police should concentrate resources to reduce crime;
- to provide the public (often via the media) with information on crime patterns;
- to provide a basis for sociologists to explain crime, including what is and what is not shown in the statistics;
- to reveal police assumptions and stereotyping, as the statistics are in part generated by the activities of the police themselves and the offenders they choose to pursue and the offences they choose to record.

The source of crime statistics

Crime statistics are compiled from several main sources:

1 *Police-recorded crime.* These are offences either detected by or reported to the police, and recorded by them.
2 *Victim surveys.* These include, for example, the British Crime Survey (BCS). They survey the victims of crime and include unreported and unrecorded crime. They give a more accurate picture than police-recorded crime, and are not affected by the recording/counting rules that police statistics are bound by.
3 *Self-report studies.* These include the Home Office's *Offending, Crime and Justice Survey.* They consist of anonymous questionnaires in which people are asked to own up to committing crimes, whether or not they have been discovered.
4 *Court and prison records, and records on police cautions.* These reveal the characteristics of offenders who have been caught.

Victim surveys and self-report studies are discussed in the section below on researching crime and deviance – see pages 503–5.

Trends in crime

Official statistics show that from the 1930s to the early 1950s, there was a gradual rise in recorded crime, with a steeper rise between the 1950s and the early 1980s. There was a rapid increase in crime from the 1980s. Figure 6.5 shows trends in crime between 1981 and 2007/8, for both the British Crime Survey (BCS) and for police-recorded crime. As can be seen, crime in England and Wales peaked in 1995, since when it has fallen by 48 per cent according to the BCS. Both sets of figures show similar trends, with crime falling. The apparent increase in police recorded crime after 1999/2000 is due to changes in the methods the Home Office used to record and count crimes in 1998 and 2002, and the introduction of the National Crime Recording Standard (NCRS) in 2002/3, rather than representing a real increase in the number of crimes compared to pre-1999. Although crime remains at a much higher level than in the 1960s and earlier, the crime level now seems to have stabilized, and although there are changes between one year and the next, which always receive intense media scrutiny, these are not generally significant.

Figure 6.6 shows a breakdown of the main types of offence recorded by the police in 2007/8, and those revealed by the BCS victim survey.

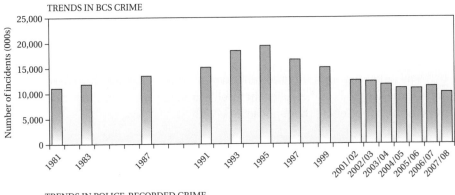

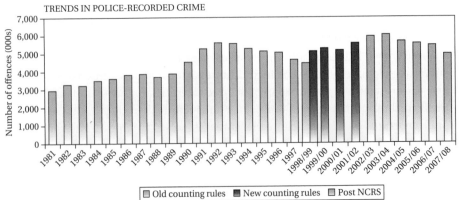

Figure 6.5 Trends in crime, 1981 to 2007/8

Source: Crime in England and Wales, 2007/8, Home Office 2008

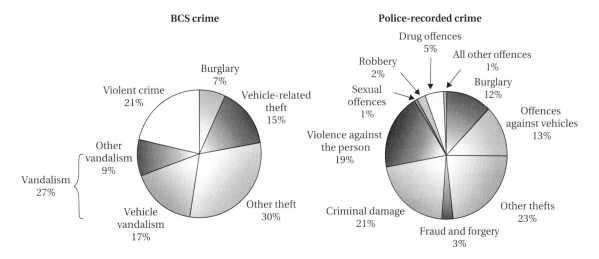

BCS crime

Burglary 7%

Violent crime 21%

Vehicle-related theft 15%

Other vandalism 9%

Vandalism 27%

Vehicle vandalism 17%

Other theft 30%

Police-recorded crime

Drug offences 5%

Robbery 2%

All other offences 1%

Sexual offences 1%

Burglary 12%

Offences against vehicles 13%

Violence against the person 19%

Criminal damage 21%

Other thefts 23%

Fraud and forgery 3%

Figure 6.6 The pattern of crime in official statistics: police-recorded crime and British Crime Survey crime, England Wales, 2007/8

Source: Crime in England and Wales, 2007/8, Home Office 2008

The pattern of offending

The pattern of crime revealed by the various statistical sources mentioned above shows that most crime is committed:

- in urban areas;
- against property (80 per cent of all crime);
- by young people (half of all those convicted are 21 or under, with the peak age for crime being 18 for males, and 14 for females), particularly working-class males.

For some offences, such as street crime and some drug offences, there is – according to official statistics – an over-representation of some minority ethnic groups, particularly black minority ethnic groups.

Age and crime

The peak age for offending is between 15 and 18, with young males much more likely to offend than females.

Deviant activity and juvenile delinquency have always been features in the lives of young people, and young people have always been over-represented in the crime statistics, and in deviant activity in general. Each generation seems to discover young people anew as major problems, with each adult generation insisting that it was 'never like that when we were young'. In fact, it has always been the case that young people form the largest group of criminals and deviants, from, for example, rioting apprentice boys in medieval times, to 'hooligans' in the 1890s, razor gangs in the 1920s, the Teds and the Beatniks in the 1950s, the Mods, the Rockers and the hippies in the 1960s, black muggers in the 1970s, and, in the 2000s, anti-social behaviour, vandalism, street gangs, illegal drug-use and a knife and gun culture. Official statistics show that roughly half of all those convicted are aged 21 or under, and a 2002 self-report survey found that almost half of Britain's secondary school students admitted

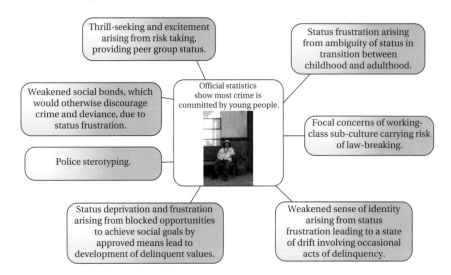

Figure 6.7 Young people and crime

Thrill-seeking and excitement arising from risk taking, providing peer group status.

Status frustration arising from ambiguity of status in transition between childhood and adulthood.

Weakened social bonds, which would otherwise discourage crime and deviance, due to status frustration.

Official statistics show most crime is committed by young people.

Focal concerns of working-class sub-culture carrying risk of law-breaking.

Police sterotyping.

Status deprivation and frustration arising from blocked opportunities to achieve social goals by approved means lead to development of delinquent values.

Weakened sense of identity arising from status frustration leading to a state of drift involving occasional acts of delinquency.

to having broken the law. Roe and Ashe (2008), based on findings from the 2006 *Offending, Crime and Justice* self-report survey, found that 22 per cent of 10–25-year-olds admitted to having committed at least one out of 20 core offences in the previous 12 months, with assault and theft making up the main offences. The reasons most often given for law-breaking by young people are to impress others, and boredom. The Edinburgh Study of Youth Transitions and Crime (www.law.ed.ac.uk/cls/esytc/) is a continuous longitudinal study of events in the lives of 4,300 young people in the city of Edinburgh who were aged 11–12 in autumn 1998. This found that about half the offences committed by 11–15-year-olds involved rowdiness and fighting in the street, with the rest consisting mainly of shoplifting (usually sweets) and vandalism (usually graffiti). While most young people will break the law at some time, the kinds of offence they commit are usually fairly trivial, opportunistic, short-lived and isolated incidents, and peer-group related, such as under-age drinking, vandalism and shoplifting.

Explanations for links between age and crime

There are several explanations for the link between age and offending. Most prevalent are status frustration and the influence of the peer group

Status frustration

Cohen (1971) argues that most delinquents are motivated by status frustration (see also the discussion of this in the section above on theories of crime – page 414). Young people are frustrated at their lack of an independent status in society, and are caught in the transition between child and adult status. The peer group provides some support for an identity and status that is independent of school or family, and therefore takes on a greater importance among young people than at any other age. The lack of responsibilities and status, and the search for excitement and peer-group status, mean that many young people drift into minor acts of delinquency and clashes with the law. Peer-group pressure may also give young people the confidence and encouragement to involve themselves in minor acts of delinquency, which they would not engage in on their own.

This problem of status frustration affects all young people, and explains why many of them, from all social classes, occasionally get involved in delinquent and deviant activity. However, Cohen argues that young people from the lower working class – the largest group of criminal offenders – experience status deprivation and frustration particularly acutely, and they consequently develop a subculture which provides them with alternative ways of gaining status, particularly in their peer group, which carries with it the risk of delinquency.

Peer-group status and the focal concerns of lower-working-class subculture

Miller (1962) also suggests that lower-working-class young males are more likely to engage in delinquency than females or middle-class males, because their subculture has a number of focal concerns, or characteristics, which carry with them the risk of law-breaking. These concerns include:

- toughness and masculinity;
- smartness – having street cred by looking cool, being shrewd, quick-witted, clever and amusing;
- excitement and thrills;
- fatalism – a sense that they can do little about their lives, so they need to make the best of it while they can;
- autonomy and freedom – they won't be pushed around by anybody, including their peers, but especially by authority figures like the police or teachers;
- trouble – an acceptance that life involves violence and fights.

Miller suggests that these focal concerns are shared by many lower-working-class males of all ages, but they are likely to become exaggerated in the lives of young people as they seek to achieve peer-group status by, for example, constantly demonstrating just how much tougher, more masculine, smarter and willing they are to get into fights than their mates.

Edgework and the peer group

The pursuit of excitement and thrills may apply to all young men, and increasingly to young women as well, not just those from the lower working class. Writers like Katz (1988) and Lyng (1990) suggest that much youthful criminal activity is motivated by what is called 'edgework', rather than material gain. The pleasures of thrill-seeking and risk-taking, and the 'buzz' generated by the excitement and adrenalin flows involved in living on the edge in acts like shoplifting, vandalism, doing drugs, fighting and other fairly petty offences is a gratifying seductive adventure, and more important than any worry about the risk of being caught or need for items stolen. Peer-group status can be achieved through such activities, which take on a symbolic value as a trophy of the risk-taking game. The peer-group offers support and encouragement for such activities, and group involvement increases the chances of getting away with it.

The 'thrills and spills' of edgework as a motivation for crime may appeal to all people at various times, but are likely to appeal particularly to lower-working-class young men, as a way of expressing the masculinity Miller suggested was a focal concern in lower-working-class subculture.

The peer group and weakened social bonds

Control theory suggests that criminal and deviant activity become more likely when individuals' bonds to society and the controls that help to prevent crime and deviance, such as social integration through the family, school, workplace and community, are weakened. The period of status frustration can weaken these bonds, as they are temporarily displaced by the peer group, where deviance may become a means of achieving status and respect from peers. This may well apply to all young people, but is most pronounced in the case of the working-class young, for the reasons identified by Cohen and Miller.

Delinquency, drift and techniques of neutralization

Matza (1964) suggests that the period of status frustration weakens young people's sense of identity – of who they are. This, in combination with the weakened bonds of control discussed above, means that young people lack a sense of identity and direction, and they are therefore in what Matza calls a state of drift.

In this period of drift, the peer group can provide a sense of identity, excitement and status, and, combined with the other factors discussed earlier, this makes young people vulnerable to occasional acts of delinquency. However, Matza suggests they have no commitment to criminal or deviant values, as he suggests these occasional acts of delinquency are accompanied by what he calls **techniques of neutralization**. These are justifications used to excuse or neutralize any blame or disapproval associated with deviance. Matza suggests that young people recognize wrongdoing and

Techniques of neutralization are justifications used to excuse acts of crime and deviance.

How does this picture help to explain why young people are in a state of drift? Using the explanations in this section, suggest how the peer group might help to overcome the types of problem identified in the picture, and how this might be linked to delinquency.

condemn it in others because when they do commit delinquent acts and are caught, they seek to justify or excuse their particular offences in terms of mainstream social values. For example, that their behaviour on this occasion was an exception to the rules, and that there were special exceptional circumstances to explain their behaviour which meant it wasn't really as wrong as it normally might be.

Matza identifies five techniques of neutralization used by delinquents when they try to neutralize their guilt:

1 *Denial of responsibility.* Denying responsibility for the deviant act, claiming that the circumstances were unusual – for example, having had a row with a girl/boy-friend, or being drunk or on drugs at the time the offence was committed.
2 *Denial of injury to the victim.* Denying that the victim had suffered any injury or loss – for example, in cases of vandalism of rich people's property, for which insurance will pay.
3 *Denial of victim.* Denying that the victim was a victim at all – for example, after beating up a bully in order that she or he will stop bullying others.
4 *Condemnation of condemners.* Condemning those who condemn them – for example, claiming that the people who condemn their behaviour had no right to do so, as they were being unfair or unjust, or were just as bad or corrupt themselves.
5 *Appeal to higher loyalties.* Appealing to higher loyalties or moral justifications – for example saying that they were only fighting because they had to stop their brother being bullied.

The period of status frustration generally disappears as people get older, as young people begin to establish clearly defined and independent adult status and are integrated into society as they take on responsibilities like a home, marriage or cohabitation, children, and paid employment. The peer group subsequently diminishes in significance as a source of status, and most young people consequently give up delinquency in early adulthood.

Police stereotyping

All the reasons above mean that the police are likely to see young people as the source of problems, and this stereotype involves them in spending more time observing and checking youths. As a result, more get caught, become defined as offenders and appear in the statistics.

Activity

1 Suggest reasons why the 'focal concerns' identified by Miller might be more likely to lead younger working-class people than older people into trouble with the law.
2 Explain, with examples, how the lifestyles of the young might
   a) give them greater opportunity to commit crime; and
   b) expose them to greater risk of being victims of crime, than those in other age groups.

3 Have you ever been involved in any delinquent activity? Which, if any, of the various explanations suggested above do you think explain your delinquency? Explain your answer.

4 Explain how, with examples of your own, the ways the techniques of neutralization identified by Matza might show some commitment by offenders to mainstream values.

5 Outline the techniques of neutralization you have adopted in your life to justify or explain any deviant or delinquent behaviour you have been involved in, whether criminal or not.

6 Identify how the concept of status frustration might explain both why many young people occasionally get involved in illegal or deviant behaviour, and why many also eventually give it up.

7 Answer the following essay question in 30 minutes:
'Examine sociological explanations for the high proportion of young people shown in official statistics on crime.'

Gender and crime

Official statistics show that males in most countries of the world commit far more crime than females. By their 40th birthday, about one in three males have a conviction of some kind, compared to fewer than one in ten females. Men are responsible for about four *known* offences for every one committed by women, they are more likely to be repeat offenders, and in general they commit more serious offences. Men are many times more likely to be found guilty or cautioned for offending than women (as shown in figure 6.8), for example:

Figure 6.8
Offenders found guilty at all courts or cautioned by type of offence and sex, England and Wales, 2006 ('000s)

Source: Data from *Criminal Statistics, 2006*, Ministry of Justice 2007.

- about 50 times more likely for sex offences;
- about 14 times more likely for burglaries;
- about 8 times more likely for robbery and drug offences;
- about 7 times more likely for criminal damage;
- about 5 times more likely for violence against the person, though this is much greater for violence which results in serious injury.

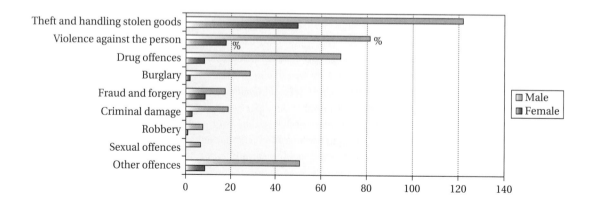

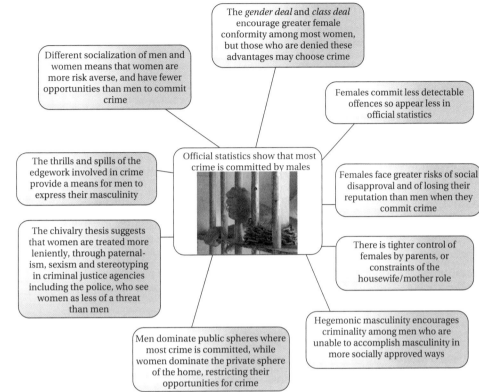

Figure 6.9 Gender and crime

Why do females appear to commit less crime than men?

Sex-role theory and gender socialization

Sex-role theory is concerned with gender socialization and the different roles of men and women in society. Women's traditional roles involve caring for partners, children and dependent elderly relatives, and these are combined with responsibilities for housework and family management, and often paid employment. Gender socialization encourages women to adopt feminine characteristics such as being more emotional, less competitive, less tough and aggressive, and more averse to taking risks than men. These combine to make many women both more afraid of the risk-taking involved in crime, as well as giving them fewer opportunities than men to commit crime.

Control theory and rational choice

Carlen (1988) and Heidensohn (1996) build on control and rational choice theories to explain why women generally commit less crime than men. Heidensohn suggests that the differences between male and female crime arise from their different social circumstances, opportunity, the socialization process and the different impacts of informal and formal social control.

The gender deal and the class deal   Following a study of a small number of working-class women who had a criminal conviction, Carlen suggested that women are encouraged to conform by what she calls the *class deal* and the *gender deal*.

- the *class deal* refers to the material rewards that arise from working in paid employment, enabling women to purchase things like consumer goods and enjoy a respectable life and home;
- the *gender deal* refers to the rewards that arise from fulfilling their roles in the family and home, with material and emotional support from a male breadwinner.

Most women accept and achieve these deals and the rewards and security arising from them, and therefore conform. However, the rewards arising from the class or gender deals are not available to some women, because of things like poverty, unemployment, lack of a family through being brought up in care, or abusive partners. Such women may then make a rational decision to choose crime: such a choice has few costs, as they have little to lose (for example, a job, family or status), but at least crime, such as shoplifting or fraud, offers the possibilities of benefits like money, food and consumer goods which are not otherwise available by the approved or legitimate class and gender deals.

The constraints of socialization   Heidensohn suggests that women have more to lose than men if they get involved in crime and deviance, because they face a greater risk of stigma or shame. Carlen argues that women are socialized into performing a central role as 'guardians of domestic morality', and they risk social disapproval when they fail to do so. Women who take the risk of involving themselves in crime therefore face the double jeopardy of being condemned both for committing a crime and behaving in an unfeminine way – unlike a 'proper woman'.

Social control   Agencies of social control work to discourage people from choosing crime over conformity. Heidensohn suggests that there is an ideology of different spheres, with men dominating the public spheres, like work, pubs and clubs, and the streets at night, in which most crime is committed, and women the private sphere of the home.

The different agencies of social control include the following:

1   In the *private domestic sphere* of the home, responsibilities for domestic labour and childcare provide less time and opportunity for crime, and women face more serious consequences if they do become involved. Teenage girls are likely to be more closely supervised by their parents than boys, reducing their chances of getting into trouble.
2   In the *public sphere* outside the home, women are faced with controls arising from fear of physical or sexual violence if they go out alone at night, and at work they are often subject to sexual harassment and supervision by male bosses which restricts their opportunities to deviate.
3   Women face the threat of losing their reputation of being 'respectable' if they engage in deviance, for example through gossip, the application of labels like

'slag' or 'slapper' by men, and the threat to their reputation that comes from being caught, as men will condemn them for a lack of femininity.

All these put greater pressure on women than men to conform, because of their greater risks of losing more than they might gain by law breaking.

The chivalry thesis

The chivalry thesis suggests that more paternalism or sexism on the part of the criminal justice system, such as the male-dominated police and courts, means that women are treated more leniently than men.

Evidence for the chivalry thesis

1   According to the Home Office, women are consistently treated more leniently by the law, with first offenders about half as likely to be given a sentence of immediate imprisonment as their male counterparts.
2   Female offenders are generally regarded by the police as a less serious threat than men, and are therefore more likely to benefit from more informal approaches to their offences, particularly for minor offences, such as cautions or warnings rather than being charged. Women do receive more cautions than men, but this is partly because they commit relatively more minor offences like shoplifting, and they are more likely than men to admit their offences, which is necessary before the police can issue a caution.

Evidence against the chivalry thesis

1   Although women are far less likely to commit serious offences than men, those who do are likely to face more severe punishment than men, particularly for violent crime, as it violates socially acceptable patterns of feminine behaviour. Women are often defined in terms of relationships with others, in which they are expected to act with warmth, emotion and caring – for example as mothers, daughters or partners. Carlen (1997) suggests that the sentences handed out to women by the criminal justice system are partly influenced by the court's assessment of their characters and performance in relation to their traditional roles as wife and mother, rather than simply by the severity of the offence. Consequently, violent women are perceived by the criminal justice system in far worse terms than men – they are seen as 'really bad' because they violate the norms of traditional feminine behaviour. Men are in general far more violent than women, but are given comparatively lighter sentences for similar levels of violence because they are perceived as just overstepping the mark of what men are expected to be like anyway.
2   Women offenders are more likely to be remanded in custody (put in prison) than men while awaiting trial for serious offences, but in three-quarters of cases, women do not actually receive a prison sentence when they come to trial.
3   Women are about twice as likely as men to be denied bail when charged with drug offences, and three times as likely for serious offences involving dishonesty.

4   Many women in prison appear to have been sentenced more severely than men in similar circumstances – for example, they have been imprisoned rather than given community punishment.

In general, then, women might commit less crime, and less serious offences, than men, but they appear to suffer more severe consequences than men when they do commit serious offences. This may well be because in our society women are expected to be 'good' – feminine and conformist – and they are punished when they're not, while men are expected to be a bit tough and aggressive and periodically go off the rails, and so are punished less severely when they do so.

Police stereotyping

Police stereotyping means that women who commit crimes may benefit from the police view that they are less likely than men to be criminals, and so are less likely to have their behaviour watched and get caught.

Growing female criminality

Although men still commit a lot more crime than women, that pattern is slowly changing in the UK and other European countries, and there is a growing increase in the proportion of crime committed by females, most noticeably by young women. In 1957, for example, men were responsible for 11 times as many offences as women, but by 2008 that ratio had narrowed to 4:1. The number of crimes committed by girls (aged 10–17) in England and Wales went up by 25 per cent between 2004 and 2007, with significant increases in minor assaults, robberies, public order offences and criminal damage.

Changing gender roles and 'laddette' culture

Adler (1975) suggests that growing female crime may be due to changing gender roles. Women in contemporary Britain have more independence than in the past, and they are becoming more successful than men in both education and the labour market. At the same time, some of the traditional forms of control on women discussed above are weakening, particularly among younger women. As Denscombe (2001) found, there is much more of a masculinized 'laddette' culture, where young women are adopting behaviour traditionally associated with young men, as they assert their identity through binge drinking, gang culture, risk-taking, being hard and in control, and peer-related violence. There is some evidence that the police are now reacting in a more serious way, taking more action and prosecuting girls involved in such behaviour rather than dealing with it informally by other means, which would increase the statistics for such offences.

Why do males commit more crime than women?

Sex-role theory and gender socialization

Men's traditional role has been that of family provider/breadwinner, and the adoption of the independent, self-confident, tough, competitive, aggressive, dominant and risk-taking behaviour associated with their image in the world. The male peer group reinforces these tendencies, particularly among younger men, and this can lead to higher risks of crime and delinquency. Men's traditional roles in employment, their lack of responsibility for housework and childcare, and the lack of the various constraints encouraging women's conformity that were identified above, all give men more independence than women, and more opportunities to commit crime. A development of this kind of explanation centres on the features of masculinity and male gender identity, rather than simply the different roles performed by men and women in the family and society.

The assertion of masculinity

A **hegemonic masculinity** is a male gender identity that defines what is involved in being a 'real man', and is so dominant that those who don't conform to it are seen as odd or abnormal in some way.

Connell (1987, 1995) suggests there is what she calls a **hegemonic masculinity**. This is a male gender identity that defines what it means to be a 'real man'; men who don't want to be regarded as 'wimps', abnormal or odd are meant to accomplish this masculinity. It features such things as toughness, aggression, competitiveness, control, success and power over – and subordination of – women. It is the masculinity that was identified earlier by Miller as a focal concern of lower-working-class subculture.

Messerschmidt (1993) suggests that men sometimes turn to crime and violence as a means of asserting their masculinity when legitimate and traditional means of demonstrating masculinity and being 'real men' are blocked. Legitimate means include things like success at school, having a steady, reliable, well-paid job, a stable family life and secure status as a family breadwinner. When these are missing, Messerschmidt suggests, men seek out alternative, 'masculine-validating resources', such as the threatened or actual use of violence, through fights and self-defence, violence against women as an assertion of power, and crime. Those lacking legitimate masculine-validating resources are most likely to be those from more deprived backgrounds (the most common criminals).

As discussed earlier under the section on age and crime, the 'thrills and spills' involved in what Lyng called 'edgework' may also be a motivating factor among some men to get involved in crime as a means of expressing their masculinity. This is more likely to occur among those for whom legitimate means of asserting masculinity are blocked or missing, but the nature of hegemonic masculinity might also explain why middle-class men try to assert masculinity through ruthlessness, ambition and thrill-seeking in business, leading to white-collar and corporate crimes (discussed later), such as computer hacking, embezzlement, fraud, illegal stock market or money market trading. The nature of hegemonic masculinity might also explain why men from all social classes commit domestic violence and rape.

Problems of the masculinity thesis

The difficulty with Messerschmidt's analysis is that, while it provides a plausible explanation for why men might commit more crime than women, it doesn't have explanations for why all men who don't have access to legitimate means of asserting masculinity don't turn to crime – and most don't – or for the different types of crime that are committed. Not all male crime can be interpreted as an expression of masculinity.

Police stereotyping

Because of the pattern shown by official statistics, the police are more likely to see men than women as potential criminals, and they are more likely to press charges in the case of men.

Control theory and rational choice

The discussion above on control theory and rational choice in relation to why women commit less crime than men can be reversed to explain why men commit more crime. Men dominate the public sphere where most crime is committed, and they face fewer constraints than women, such as responsibility for housework and childcare; also, they have less to lose in terms of reputation. Indeed, crime and deviance may actually enhance their reputation, particularly among young men. The demands of hegemonic masculinity may mean that some men who lack legitimate means of accomplishing masculinity may have more to gain than lose by choosing to commit crime or other forms of deviance, and have more independence and opportunities to do so than women.

Activity

Read the previous section on gender and crime, then answer the following questions:

1 Outline the ways that the differences between male and female crime rates might be explained by sex role theory and gender socialization, linking them to examples of offences that men and women are most likely and least likely to commit.
2 Explain, with examples, the ways hegemonic masculinity is linked to male criminality, and why most men don't turn to crime.
3 Suggest ways that the changing role of women might explain the fact that the female crime rate is rising faster than that of males.
4 Explain what is meant by each of the following concepts and theories, and identify how they might be used to explain why, among offenders who have been caught, it is mainly working-class men and women who seem to turn to crime.
  ● sex role theory
  ● masculinity and femininity
  ● rational choice
  ● control theory
  ● personal reputation
  ● police stereotyping
5 Given that women commit far less crime than men, identify and explain *three* reasons why those women who do turn to crime might choose to do so.

Social class and crime

Official statistics show that working-class people, particularly those from the lower working class, are more highly represented among offenders than those from other social classes. Taken together, the following explanations combine to explain this pattern.

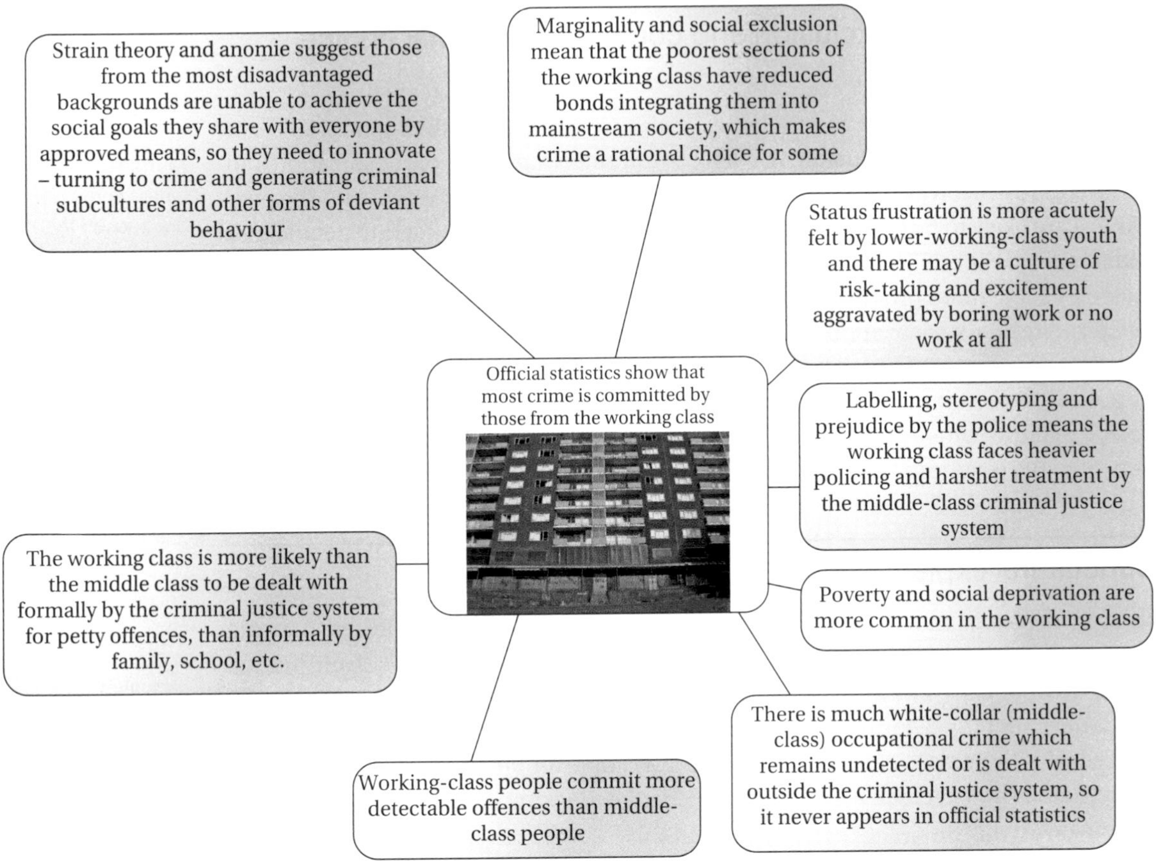
Strain theory and anomie suggest those from the most disadvantaged backgrounds are unable to achieve the social goals they share with everyone by approved means, so they need to innovate – turning to crime and generating criminal subcultures and other forms of deviant behaviour
Marginality and social exclusion mean that the poorest sections of the working class have reduced bonds integrating them into mainstream society, which makes crime a rational choice for some
Status frustration is more acutely felt by lower-working-class youth and there may be a culture of risk-taking and excitement aggravated by boring work or no work at all
Official statistics show that most crime is committed by those from the working class
Labelling, stereotyping and prejudice by the police means the working class faces heavier policing and harsher treatment by the middle-class criminal justice system
The working class is more likely than the middle class to be dealt with formally by the criminal justice system for petty offences, than informally by family, school, etc.
Poverty and social deprivation are more common in the working class
There is much white-collar (middle-class) occupational crime which remains undetected or is dealt with outside the criminal justice system, so it never appears in official statistics
Working-class people commit more detectable offences than middle-class people

Figure 6.10 Social class and crime

Social deprivation

There is a link between the level of crime and the state of the economy. Property crime in particular seems to rise when people are hard up, when poverty is on the increase and people need to provide for their families. Such hardship provides an obvious explanation for the most common offences of property crime, and would account for the high proportion of criminals coming from deprived backgrounds.

Strain theory and anomie

Merton's (1968) strain theory provides a further possible explanation linked to social deprivation. Those living in deprived communities have poorer life chances as a result of ill-health, poor housing, educational underachievement and unemployment. This means they lack the same opportunities as others to achieve the goals they aspire to. These circumstances push people to 'innovate' and find alternative means of reaching these goals, and one form of innovation involves turning to crime.

Marginality, social exclusion and control and rational choice theories

In the most disadvantaged communities, there are likely to be the highest levels of **marginality** and **social exclusion**. In such communities, agencies of socialization and social control – such as the family, the workplace, the education system and the peer group – are likely to be less effective in providing the bonds that integrate people into wider mainstream society. Control theory points to the weakening of these factors as making people more prone to offending, and, in the most disadvantaged communities, less effective socialization and control may generate either indifferent or positive attitudes towards law-breaking. In such communities, when pondering whether or not to choose crime, as rational choice theory suggests, potential offenders may decide that the benefits of crime, giving them access to money and consumer goods, outweigh the costs and risks of being caught.

Marginality is where some people are pushed to the margins or edges of society by poverty, lack of education, disability, racism and so on, and face social exclusion.

Subcultural explanations

As seen earlier in the section above on age and crime, Cohen suggested that the circumstances of lower-working-class life mean that the status frustration that all young people experience is particularly accentuated among working-class youth, and Miller identified focal concerns in lower-working-class subculture that often carried with them risks of brushes with the law. For example, there may be a culture of risk-taking and a search for excitement otherwise lacking in work life, or as a result of being without work.

Cloward and Ohlin (1960) suggest that in some working-class neighbourhoods, where social deprivation is high and the legitimate opportunities for achieving success are blocked (as Merton suggested), criminal subcultures may develop, characterized by property crime and a thriving market for stolen goods as an alternative means of achieving financial success.

Social exclusion is where people are excluded from full participation in education, work, community life and access to services and other aspects of life seen as part of being a full and participating member of mainstream society. Those who lack the necessary resources are excluded from the opportunity to participate fully in society, and are denied the opportunities most people take for granted.

Labelling, stereotyping and prejudice

The poorest sections of the working class make up what has been described as the 'underclass' – a group in which poverty, long-term unemployment and dependency on welfare benefits are the highest. This group, and the areas in which they live, fit more closely the stereotypes held in police culture of the 'typical criminal' and criminal neighbourhoods. This arises in part because official statistics show these are not only the most likely offenders, but also that they live in the areas where the risk of being a victim of crime is highest. There is therefore a greater police presence in poorer working-class areas than in middle-class areas. As a result, there is a greater likelihood of offenders being regarded as acting suspiciously, being stopped and searched, or being arrested by the police when involved in offending. Crime rates will therefore be higher in working-class areas simply because there are more police to notice or respond quickly to criminal acts, as well as there being more victims.

Labelling theory suggests that the activities of the working class, and particularly working-class youth, are more likely to be labelled by the police as criminal than the same behaviour in the middle class. The prejudices of middle-class judges and magistrates may mean that, when working-class people appear in court, they are more likely to be seen as fitting the stereotype of typical criminals, and they will therefore face a higher risk of being found guilty.

Informal social control

Working-class youth are more likely to be prosecuted if they are caught than those in the middle class. This is perhaps because they are less likely to benefit from informal processes of social control. For petty offences, middle-class youth are more likely to be dealt with by parents and teachers than by the law, or by informal cautions such as the police visiting the parents to give them a warning.

More detectable offences

Those in the working class tend to commit more detectable offences than those in the middle class, and so are more likely to get caught and become a criminal statistic. The issue of white-collar and other types of crime associated with the middle class is discussed later, but the main offences committed by working-class people – for example, acquisitive crime like burglaries and theft, and vehicle crime – are far more likely to be reported to the police and result in the prosecution of offenders than the types of crime committed by those from other social class backgrounds.

Criticisms of these explanations

There are three major criticisms of the explanations above:

1   They don't explain why all those in the same circumstances in the poorest sections of the working class do not turn to crime (and most don't).
2   There is a vast amount of crime that remains undetected and unrecorded, or offenders haven't been caught, so we don't actually know who the offenders are. Official statistics therefore may not provide a representative view of offenders.
3   There is widespread evidence of crime committed by members of other social classes which may be undetected and unrecorded, or dealt with outside the criminal law even though criminal offences have been committed. The suggestion that most criminals are working class may therefore be exaggerated. These 'hidden' crimes of the middle and upper classes are discussed below.

Activity

Refer to the section above on social class and crime.
1   Suggest three reasons why agencies of socialization and social control might be less effective in integrating people into society in deprived communities than in more affluent ones.

> 2 Identify and briefly explain all the reasons you can for why those living in deprived communities might decide that choosing crime is a rational way to behave. Be sure to consider both the costs and the benefits.
> 3 Suggest reasons why middle-class offenders might be treated less harshly by the criminal justice system than working-class offenders.

White-collar or occupational crime

Much of what has been said so far suggests that crime is predominantly committed by the working class, and, as Newburn (2007) notes, the sociology of crime and deviance has tended to focus on the crimes of the powerless rather than the powerful, or, as Timner and Eitzen (1989) put it, the crimes of the streets rather than the crimes of the suites.

It was Sutherland (1949) who first sought to show that crime was not simply a working-class phenomenon, but was widespread throughout all sections of society. He introduced the idea of white-collar crime, which he described as crime committed by the more affluent in society, who abused their positions within their middle-class occupations for criminal activity for personal benefit.

What is white-collar crime?

White-collar crime includes offences such as bribery and corruption in government and business, fiddling expenses, professional misconduct, fraud and embezzlement. Croall (2001) cites examples of crimes against the NHS by doctors, pharmacists and dentists, who falsify prescriptions and patient records to claim more from the NHS than that to which they are entitled, including one GP who made £700,000 over five years by writing fake prescriptions. In 2007, the millionaire press baron Conrad Black, former owner of the *Daily* and *Sunday Telegraph*, was convicted and jailed for six and a half years in the United States for abusing his position as chair of Hollinger International to defraud shareholders of millions of dollars for private gain.

> '*Bank robbers are masked and they use guns. Burglars wear dark clothes and use crowbars. These men dressed in ties and wore suits. They did it with memos and documents and a few lies.*'
> Quoted from the opening statement of the US prosecutor in the trial of Conrad Black, the millionaire fraudster and racketeer.

The under-representation of white-collar crime

White-collar crimes are substantially under-represented in official statistics, including both police-recorded crime and victim surveys like the British Crime Survey, giving the misleading impression that most crime is committed by the working class, and that the middle class commit fewer offences. However, there may be many white-collar criminals who simply don't get caught or ever have their crimes detected.

There are several reasons why white-collar crimes are under-represented in official statistics:

1 *They are hard to detect.* Croall (2001) points out that white-collar offences are relatively invisible, as they take place in the workplace and offenders simply appear to be doing their normal jobs and are quite justified in being present at the scene. The offences often involve some form of technical or insider knowledge, making many offences complex, and the extent and duration of offending, and the offenders themselves, hard to discover.

2 *They are often without personal or individual victims.* Often the victim is impersonal, like a company or the public at large, rather than an individual, so there is no individual victim to report an offence.

3 *The crime may benefit both the parties concerned.* For example, in cases of bribery and corruption, both parties stand to gain something, and therefore both parties will be in trouble if discovered so they seek to conceal the offence, making it hard to detect.

4 *They are hard to investigate.* Even if crimes like business or computer fraud are suspected, they can be very hard to detect or investigate, as they require a lot of skill and expert knowledge, which local police forces often lack.

5 *There is often a lack of awareness that a crime has been committed* and therefore it is not reported. For example, stealing very small amounts of money from a large number of customers' accounts leads to barely perceptible small losses to individual victims. Members of the public may lack the expertise to know if they are being misled or defrauded.

6 *Institutional protection means they are often not reported and prosecuted*, even if these crimes are detected. For example, crimes involving computer fraud, such as Internet banking fraud, are rarely reported, to protect the interests or reputation of the profession or institution, and avoid the loss of public confidence which the surrounding scandal might cause. It is more likely that a private security firm will lead any investigation rather than it being reported to the police, with suspected offenders dealt with by internal systems of control, such as being sacked or forced to retire rather than being prosecuted.

7 *Even if reported, offenders have a better chance of being found not guilty.* Most juries, like the public at large, hold the stereotype that crime is a mainly working-class phenomena, rather than committed by affluent, well-educated, so-called respectable middle-class people. Defendants are often of the same background as the judge, and may appear more plausible, honest and respectable to juries, and so may be less likely to be found guilty, or to have their offences seen as temporary lapses in otherwise good behaviour, and receive more lenient sentences than working-class offenders.

In general, the higher up you are in the social class hierarchy:

- the less likely are your crimes to be detected;
- the less likely are your crimes, if detected, to result in your arrest;
- the less likely you are, if arrested, to be prosecuted;
- the less likely you are, if prosecuted, to be found guilty;
- the less likely you are, if found guilty, to be given a prison sentence.

Activity

1 Identify and explain three reasons why white-collar crime may not result in a criminal conviction.
2 What are the implications of the under-representation of white-collar crimes in official statistics for the view that most criminals are working class?

Explaining white-collar crime

White-collar crime covers a wide range of offences, so it is not easy to identify explanations that cover them all. Some white-collar offenders are ordinary people who have got into financial difficulty, and who use their jobs to find a way out of it through fraud and similar offences. Such low-level white-collar crime can probably be explained in much the same way as much working-class crime. However, this is more difficult when offences are committed by people who are often quite affluent, and even very rich, and who are very successful in terms of society's values and goals. How then can we explain their turning to crime?

Strain theory, anomie and relative deprivation

While it is hard to see successful middle-class people as having the means to achieving social goals blocked – and many are already successful in terms of these goals – it may be that, despite their success, they still have a sense of relative deprivation, of still lacking things they see others having, and want even more than they can achieve by legitimate, approved means, so they innovate, and turn to crime. This may be fuelled by personal economic difficulties, like large debts generated by living a lifestyle above their means, or quite simply greed – they have a lot, but want more.

Control theory

The moral controls on offending may be weakened as there is often no personal, individual victim of white-collar crime, and this may weaken the perception that offenders are doing anything very wrong or harmful. Socialization into self-seeking company business practices encouraging aggressive and ruthless competition with other companies may encourage this, and this may be adapted to bring some personal rewards to employees as well.

Edgework

As Katz (1988) and Lyng (1990) suggest, pleasure, thrill-seeking and risk-taking may be motivations for crime rather than simply material gain. This is a plausible explanation for some white-collar crime, especially for those who are already rich.

Ethnicity and crime

The links between ethnicity and crime are complex, as it is quite difficult to discover whether differences between ethnic groups are a result of their ethnic identity, or because of differences in age, social class and the areas in which they live. For example, compared to white people, minority ethnic groups tend to have higher proportions of young people, those suffering social deprivation and those living in deprived urban communities. Higher crime rates therefore might reflect these factors rather than greater criminality arising from ethnicity itself.

The evidence on ethnicity and crime

Table 6.4 on page 458 shows the proportions of different ethnic groups involved at various stages of the criminal justice system.

In 2008, the Ministry of Justice reported that, compared to white people, black people (African Caribbeans) were:

- more likely to be arrested for robbery;
- three times more likely to be cautioned by the police;
- three and a half times more likely to be arrested;
- if arrested, more likely to be charged and face court proceedings than to receive a caution;
- more likely, if found guilty, to receive a custodial (prison) sentence;
- five times more likely to be in prison.

Asians compared to white people were:

- twice as likely to be stopped and searched (mainly for drugs);
- more likely to be charged and face court proceedings than to receive a caution;
- more likely to receive a custodial sentence if found guilty;
- more likely to be arrested for fraud and forgery.

In 2007, 26 per cent of male prisoners and 29 per cent of females were from black and minority ethnic groups, even though they make up only about 9 per cent of the general population.

These patterns, shown in contemporary official statistics, reflect a pattern that first emerged in the 1970s, suggesting what appear to be higher levels of criminality among some minority ethnic groups, particularly the black population. Sociologists have developed a number of explanations to try to explain this.

Sociological explanations of black criminality

Neo-Marxist approaches

Gilroy (1982) argues that crime by black people, particularly in the 1970s, was a form of political action, representing a culture of resistance to oppressors in the form of police racism and harassment. He denies that there was greater criminality among

Table 6.4: Proportion (%) of ethnic groups at different stages of the criminal justice process, England and Wales, 2006/7

| | Ethnicity | | | | | |
	White	Black	Asian	Other	Unknown/ not recorded	Total
General population (aged 10 & over) @ 2001 Census	91.3	2.8	4.7	1.2	0.0	100
Stops and searches	72.3	15.9	8.1	1.5	2.1	100
Arrests	83.1	9.6	5.3	1.3	0.7	100
Cautions	81.3	6.4	4.4	1.2	6.6	100
Youth offences	87.6	6.2	3.2	0.3	2.7	100
Tried at Crown Court	75.2	13.2	7.7	3.9	*	100
Prison population	81.5	11.0	6.0	1.1	0.4	100

Note: Figures may not add to 100% due to rounding.
Source: *Statistics on Race and the Criminal Justice System, 2006/7*, Ministry of Justice 2008

Activity

Refering to table 6.4, analyse the data and describe what conclusions you might draw about the links between ethnicity and crime. Give figures to back up your conclusions.

black people than whites, suggesting this was a myth created by negative stereotyping by the police, who saw minority ethnic groups as untrustworthy, with African Caribbean youth labelled as potential 'muggers' and Asians as potential illegal immigrants, and this helped to generate official statistics on crime as these groups were treated unfairly by the police. However, this explanation does not explain the fact that black crime, including mugging, is often committed against other black or poor people, so it is difficult to see it as resistance or a political act against oppressors. Lea and Young (1984) pointed out that most crimes are reported by the public, not uncovered by the police, so it is hard to explain black crime in terms of police

Figure 6.11
Ethnicity and crime

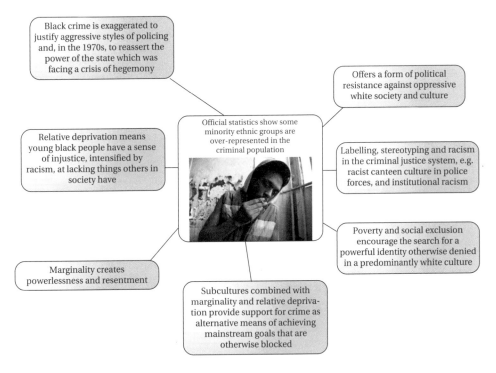

Black crime is exaggerated to justify aggressive styles of policing and, in the 1970s, to reassert the power of the state which was facing a crisis of hegemony

Offers a form of political resistance against oppressive white society and culture

Relative deprivation means young black people have a sense of injustice, intensified by racism, at lacking things others in society have

Official statistics show some minority ethnic groups are over-represented in the criminal population

Labelling, stereotyping and racism in the criminal justice system, e.g. racist canteen culture in police forces, and institutional racism

Poverty and social exclusion encourage the search for a powerful identity otherwise denied in a predominantly white culture

Marginality creates powerlessness and resentment

Subcultures combined with marginality and relative deprivation provide support for crime as alternative means of achieving mainstream goals that are otherwise blocked

racism. The fact that Asian crime rates are, in general, similar to those of whites suggests that police racism is rather inconsistent, which is unlikely. However, recent self-report studies, which will be considered shortly, suggest that Lea and Young's view of racism in the police as being unable to explain the black crime figures in the 1970s is not the case today, and there is now much evidence of racism in the criminal justice system.

The crisis of hegemony and the creation of the 'black mugger' In another Marxist analysis based on the 1970s, Hall et al. (1978) argue that Britain was facing a crisis at the time. Unemployment was very high, there was war in Northern Ireland, students were constantly protesting about a wide range of social and political issues, and there were very high numbers of strikes. Hall et al. argued that this led to a crisis of hegemony, or a threat to the dominance of ruling-class ideology in society. At the same time, there was growing conflict between the police and the African Caribbean community. This was fuelled by selective publication of crime statistics showing black youth involvement in particular offences, including street robbery (theft with actual or threatened use of force, now commonly called 'mugging'). The media picked up on this, as making good headlines, and promoted the idea that black people were more prone to criminality than whites, and the media image of the black 'mugger' was born. A moral panic developed – a media-fuelled exaggeration of the problem of black crime – with growing demands by the public that something should be done to stamp out the problem. The 'black mugger' came to be a folk devil symbol for all society's problems, and helped to justify more repressive and aggressive policing in some inner-city areas.

In the 1970s, the 'black mugger' emerged during a crisis of hegemony of the British state, and came to symbolize all of society's problems, also helping to justify more repressive and aggressive policing in some inner-city areas. Britain's police riot squads, using paramilitary equipment such as shields and riot sticks, first emerged in 1970s Britain.

Hall et al. argued that there had not been a real increase in street robbery (mugging), but the moral panic was used to justify the use of force by the state, such as a more aggressive style of policing, which was then also used against a range of other groups, like trade unionists fighting unemployment. This was required because the economic and political crisis of the state meant that the dominant class could no longer rely on people's consent to maintain their power. The tactics of the police against the black community – including repeated stop and search – actually made things worse. All black youth were seen as a threat, even when they weren't doing anything wrong, and police hostility provoked them into violence as a means of defending themselves. The exaggerated extent of black crime therefore became a way of reasserting the dominance of ruling-class ideas, and re-establishing their hegemony in society generally, as the public shared their concerns over black criminality.

The difficulty of this theory is that, while it might have been a plausible explanation in the late 1970s, the conflicts between minority ethnic groups, the criminal justice agencies and negative media stereotypes still exist, but the 'crisis of hegemony' does not, suggesting that the explanation is inadequate.

Left Realism

Lea and Young's (1984) Left Realist approach accepts that black crime, for some offences, is higher than for the white population. Lea and Young argue that we need to consider three elements in order to understand crime in relation to ethnic minorities:

1 *Marginality.* Some minority ethnic groups are pushed to the edges of mainstream society by underachievement in education, lack of employment or low pay, and lack of legitimate opportunities to influence events. These create resentments and a sense of powerlessness, further fuelled by the experience of racism.

2 *Relative deprivation.* This refers to a sense of lacking things compared to others, such as not being able to possess the sorts of consumer goods that others have. While it is possible for everyone to experience this, depending on their aspirations, it is most likely to be felt by those facing more deprived social situations, as many of those in minority ethnic groups do.

3 *Subculture.* Marginality and relative deprivation can combine to develop subcultures in deprived communities, which provide a form of support for those, particularly young black males, who aspire to the same things as the rest of society, but find legitimate or approved means of achieving them blocked. This subculture may involve greater levels of violence and street crime in order to meet these aspirations and as a reaction against the resentments and status frustration they feel.

Poverty, social exclusion and the search for identity

Bowling and Phillips (2002) suggest that higher levels of robbery by black people could be linked to poverty and social exclusion, which black communities are more likely to suffer from, and such activities can generate both peer-group status and a sense of a powerful black identity otherwise denied. Poverty and social exclusion clearly affect Asians as well, particularly Pakistani and Bangladeshis who are among the poorest groups in British society. However, their lower crime rate may be because Asian cultures offer a much clearer identity, and there are generally stronger controls within Asian families and communities, limiting the opportunities and perhaps the desire to commit crime.

Labelling, stereotyping and racism in the criminal justice system

The official statistics quoted earlier show higher rates of offending among some minority ethnic groups, and particularly blacks, and the explanations so far offer some suggestions of why this might be the case. However, many sociologists have argued that the criminal statistics in general, and on ethnicity in particular, are socially constructed. They are not a valid (or true) record of ethnicity and offending, but are created as a result of discrimination towards blacks and Asians by the police and other criminal justice agencies. It is this that creates the misleading impression that blacks and Asians are more likely to be offenders than whites.

How the police go about their work – what they look out for – is guided by their ideas over who the 'troublemakers' or criminals are. Black and Asian people (especially youths) fit the police stereotype of 'troublemakers'; they are therefore subject to heavier policing and are more likely to be stopped and searched than white people. Racism and racist stereotypes in police culture might account for the higher arrest rates of blacks than whites, as their behaviour may be more likely to be labelled as criminal, and the law selectively enforced to target blacks more than whites. This would have the effect of over-representing them in crime figures.

In support of this view, Reiner (2000) points to a racist 'canteen culture' among the police, which includes suspicion, macho values and racism, and this encourages racist stereotypes and a mistrust of those from non-white backgrounds. Bowling and Phillips (2002) suggest that higher levels of robbery among blacks could be a product of labelling that arises from the use of regular stop-and-search procedures by the police which in turn leads to a self-fulfilling prophecy, as young black males act in accordance with the labels and stereotypes the police have of them. Black and Asian people are therefore more likely to get caught, arrested and charged, and the original police stereotype is confirmed by the activities of the police themselves.

The Macpherson Report of 1999 into the murder of Stephen Lawrence (see box) suggests that labelling, stereotyping and racism as an explanation for the links between ethnicity and crime in official statistics is a persuasive one, as Macpherson identified institutional racism in the police and the criminal justice system. The persistence of such racism led the Metropolitan Black Police Association, in 2008, to warn people from minority ethnic groups not to join the force, because of 'a hostile atmosphere where racism is allowed to spread'. In addition, self-report studies, like the *Offending, Crime and Justice Survey*, suggest that official statistics do not merely exaggerate the extent of offending among ethnic minorities to an alarming degree, but present a wholly incorrect picture of who the main offenders really are.

The Stephen Lawrence Inquiry and the Macpherson Report (1999)

The investigation into the police handling of the murder of 18-year-old Stephen Lawrence by five white youths in 1993 led to the Macpherson Report in 1999. This was highly critical of the Metropolitan Police, pointing to a series of mistakes and a 'lack of urgency' and mishandling of the police investigation, including their assumption that Stephen Lawrence was involved in a street brawl rather than being the victim of an unprovoked racist attack. It pointed to the existence of *institutional racism* in the police force, and recommended a series of improvements. These included race-awareness training, more minority ethnic police officers and stronger disciplinary action to get rid of racist police officers. The Macpherson Report established an official view of the widespread existence of institutional racism in many areas, including policing, the health services and education, and led to a campaign to stamp out racism in a wide range of public and private organizations.

Activity

1 Explain how each of the following concepts or theories might be applied to explain apparently higher levels of criminality among some minority ethnic groups:
- strain theory and anomie
- marginality and social exclusion
- control and rational choice theories

2 Drawing on the various explanations you have identified above, as well as the other explanations in this section, suggest reasons why:
- some minority ethnic groups, like the Chinese, have lower levels of crime than any ethnic group;
- Asians generally have lower levels of offending than black people.

Ethnicity and the pattern of crime shown in self-report studies

Self-report studies, in which people report their own offences with assured confidentiality, will be considered later in the section on researching crime and deviance (pages 504–5). It is generally accepted that self-report studies provide far greater insights into the real pattern of offending in society than official statistics do, as they cover offences regardless of whether or not they have been reported to, or recorded by, the police, or indeed whether they have come to the attention of anyone at all.

The *2003 Offending, Crime and Justice Survey* is a self-report survey that found considerable variation between ethnic groups in lifetime offending, as shown in figure 6.12:

- white people had the highest rate of offending;
- black people were significantly less likely to offend than white respondents;
- robbery ('mugging') was higher in the black group, but was rare across *all* groups;
- for offences committed in the previous 12 months, white males aged 10–25 were far more likely to have committed an offence – and more likely to be classed as serious or frequent offenders – than the same category in other ethnic groups;
- for violent offending and drug-selling, the rate for white respondents was higher than the average, and that for Asians lower than the average.

Discrimination in the criminal justice system

Sharp and Budd (2005) point out that of all ethnic groups, black offenders were most likely to have contact with the criminal justice system in their lifetime, and significantly

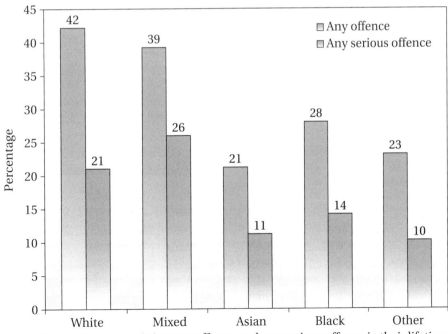

Figure 6.12 Self-reported lifetime offending (%)

Source: Sharp and Budd 2005

Percentage committing any offence and any serious offence in their lifetime

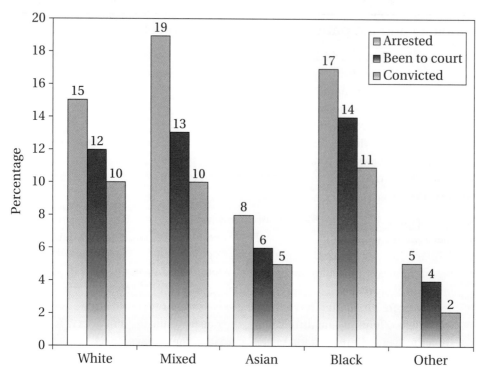

Figure 6.13 Percentage of respondents aged 10–65 who have ever been arrested, been to court or been convicted (2003 OCJS)
Source: Sharp and Budd 2005

more likely to have been arrested, been to court and convicted (see figure 6.13). This is despite their lower levels of offending compared to white people generally, and particularly white youth, and this suggests that ethnic minority groups are treated unfairly in the criminal justice system in relation to the extent of their offending.

Other evidence on discrimination in the criminal justice system shows that, compared to white offenders:

- black and Asian offenders are more likely to be charged where white offenders are cautioned for similar offences;
- black and Asian people are more likely to be remanded than released on bail;
- black and Asian people are more likely to be given prison sentences rather than probation or community punishment.

The pattern whereby official statistics suggest that the highest levels of criminality are found among black people, while self-report studies show white people to be the highest group of offenders, points to racism in the criminal justice system. It is perhaps, then, not surprising that many of those from minority ethnic groups see the criminal justice system as discriminatory, causing them to lack confidence and trust in the police, and creating the sense of grievance that Gilroy and Hall et al. first identified in the 1970s, and which the Macpherson Report suggested remains justified in contemporary Britain.

Locality and crime

Official crime statistics show that *recorded* crime is not evenly distributed between geographical areas. It is higher in urban areas than in rural areas, and is also higher in particular areas/neighbourhoods of towns and cities. The environment of the city has often been blamed for the deviant behaviour of its population, and the environment of rural areas for the lower rates of offending.

The patterns of crime in urban and rural areas

It is important to note that the following figures cannot just be explained by the fact that there are more people in urban areas. They are based on rates, such as per person or per household, so the total number of people or households will not make a difference to the rate, or the risks per person/household.

The British Crime Survey and police recorded crime show that rural areas, compared to urban areas:

- have lower rates of all types of crime (see, for example, figure 6.14);
- have a lower proportion of people with high levels of worry about crime;
- have lower levels of perceptions by people of high levels of anti-social behaviour in their area (including behaviour like noisy neighbours, teenagers hanging about, rubbish or litter lying about, vandalism, graffiti, and using drink or drugs in public places).

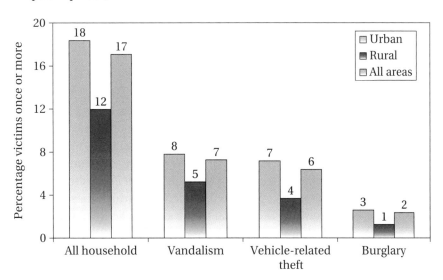

Figure 6.14 Risk of crime in urban and rural areas (2007/8 BCS)

Source: Crime in England and Wales, 2007/8, Home Office 2008

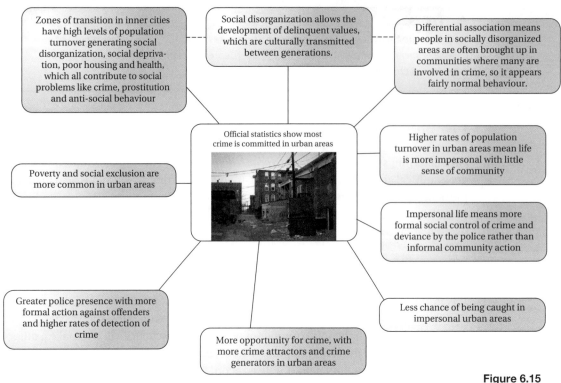

Figure 6.15
Locality and crime

Marshall and Johnson (2005) cite evidence showing that anxiety and worry about all crime types is less in rural areas compared to urban and inner-city areas, and that rural residents see themselves as less likely to become a victim of crime than those in urban areas. Marshall and Johnson also show that rural areas have a higher risk of burglaries among high-income households than among lower-income ones. This is a reversal of the pattern found in urban areas, where low-income households are more at risk of burglaries. Put crudely, in urban areas the poor rob the poor; in rural areas, it seems, the poor rob the rich.

There are a number of explanations for the differences in the crime rate between urban and rural areas, some of which are outlined below.

The ecology of crime – the Chicago School and the zone of transition

The ecological or environmental approach to crime was first developed at Chicago University in the United States, in what became known as the Chicago School of sociological thought. Shaw and McKay (1931, 1942) argued that cities like Chicago were divided into a series of concentric circles or zones radiating outwards from the centre (see figure 6.16), with each zone having particular social and cultural neighbourhood characteristics. There was one zone they identified which they called the *zone of transition*; it lay just outside the central business zone, and had the highest levels of crime.

The zone of transition was a run-down area, with poor and deteriorating housing, where the poorest people lived, and there was a high turnover of population. There

Figure 6.16 The zone of transition is characterized by high levels of social disorganization, cultural transmission of crime and delinquency between generations, and association with others who favour law-breaking.

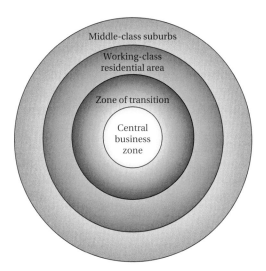

was therefore little social stability, and a concentration of social problems like crime, prostitution, poor health and poverty. This 'zonal hypothesis' gave rise to three related concepts, which were used to explain crime and deviance:

1   *Social disorganization.* The high rates of population turnover prevented the formation of stable communities, and weakened the hold of established values and informal social controls over individuals, such as pressure and supervision from the community, neighbours and family, which in more stable and established communities discourage deviance and crime.

2   *Cultural transmission.* In areas of social disorganization, different delinquent values develop – a subculture of delinquency – to which children living in such communities are exposed, and which young boys (and it *is* mainly boys) learn from older ones of the criminal traditions that are established and accepted in the area. Criminal behaviour like shoplifting, theft from cars, and joyriding become a normal part of everyday life, and these delinquent values are passed on (transmitted) from one generation to the next.

3   *Differential association.* This idea was developed by Sutherland (1948) and suggests that people's behaviour is conditioned by reference to the behaviour of others around them. If people associate with others who more commonly support crime over conformity, and live in a situation where it seems that 'everyone' is involved in deviant or criminal behaviour, then they are more likely to commit crime themselves. It is more probable that this will occur in zones of transition because of the social disorganization and cultural transmission.

Ecological theory has been criticized on several grounds:

A **tautology** is something that is explained by the same thing that it seeks to explain.

1   *It is tautological.* A **tautology** is something that is explained by the same thing that it seeks to explain. It is not always very clear what social disorganization actually is. It appears to be another phrase for 'areas with high crime and disorder', and if this is what it is, it is a tautology, because the phenomenon (crime) that the theory seeks to explain is explained by the same phenomenon (an area

of high crime and disorder). In other words, crime develops because crime exists, which doesn't actually explain why crime exists in the first place.

2   *Cultural transmission and differential association ignore choice.* If cultural transmission is so significant in zones of transition, and associating with criminals increases the likelihood of becoming a criminal, then why don't all those in similar positions turn to crime? It doesn't explain why some choose to commit crime while others do not.

3   *It is unclear how subcultures form and cultural transmission is possible.* If zones of transition are so socially disorganized, with a constantly changing population, then it is hard to see how a delinquent subculture develops, and is able to pass its ideas on between generations, as there must be at least some continuity and stability for this to be possible.

It is not difficult to identify areas similar to Shaw and McKay's zones of transition (even if not in the concentric circle pattern they found in Chicago) in many contemporary inner-city areas of British cities, and on 'sink estates', where there are high turnovers of population and 'problem families' grouped together, and where there is a concentration of poverty, anti-social behaviour, crime, prostitution, drug and alcohol abuse, poor health, and where crime confronts those who live there as almost a normal part of their everyday lives.

The contrast with rural areas Rural communities generally lack the social disorganization found in zones of transition. Inhabitants change addresses much less frequently than urban-dwellers, and Marshall and Johnson (2005) point out that rural areas are more 'close knit', with higher levels of social interaction between people in the area, including kin relations. People are likely to know other members of the community through informal knowledge of their family and community history, rather than through their formal positions, like their job. The opposite is often the case in urban areas, where many people will hardly even know their next-door neighbours, or the ones in surrounding flats, let alone those living in the wider area. Community bonds are therefore stronger in rural areas, which may contribute to lower crime rates.

More opportunity for crime

Felson and Clarke (1998) argue that no crime can occur without the physical opportunities to carry it out and therefore opportunity should be considered as a 'root cause'. Brantingham and Brantingham (1995) suggest that urban areas have more crime generating and crime attracting areas than rural areas, such as shopping precincts, warehouses, businesses, leisure facilities, transport hubs, large insecure car parks and areas like red-light districts that offer more opportunities for crime, and attract offenders who go there in search of crime.

Policing styles

There is a greater police presence in urban areas, so more crime is likely to be detected. Police in urban areas are less likely to have roots in the community and to know who the offenders are, so they adopt more formal procedures for dealing with offenders, such as arresting and charging them. In rural areas, they may be less likely to arrest offenders, especially in the case of more trivial offences, preferring merely to issue informal warnings, or, in the case of young people, perhaps visiting the offenders' parents or their school.

Less chance of being caught

In the large cities, life is more impersonal and people do not know each other so well. Strangers are more likely to go unrecognized, and are therefore more able to get away with offences. In rural communities, there is a higher level of natural surveillance as people recognize each other and strangers are more likely to be noticed, which can discourage offending because of the higher risks of being caught.

Social deprivation

Social deprivation and social problems, such as poor housing, unemployment and poverty, are at their worst in the inner cities. As has been seen earlier, these have been linked to crime, as people try to achieve success by illegal means that others can achieve by approved and legal means.

Activity

1 Drawing on the work of the Chicago School, identify and explain three differences between living in a large city compared to living in a small village or town that might explain why the crime rate is lower in rural areas than in urban areas.
2 Suggest ways that the changing nature of rural life might affect the crime rate. Identify specific changes and explain carefully how you think each one might affect crime.
3 Are there any distinctive areas or zones of towns and cities that you know which are seen as having greater or lesser problems of crime and disorder than others? Discuss this as a group and attempt to explain the differences using ecological and any other possible sociological explanations.
4 Answer the following essay question in 30 minutes:
   'Examine sociological explanations for the lower rates of recorded crime in rural compared to urban areas.'

The limitations of official crime statistics

Sociologists are very critical of official crime statistics, arguing that they are highly unreliable in terms both of the amount of crime and of the characteristics of offenders. Many sociologists would argue that the crime statistics are *socially constructed* – a manufactured product that tells us more about the process of reporting (by the public) and the stereotypes and activities of the police and other agencies of social control than it does about the real number of crimes and the characteristics of criminals.

The previous sections outlined some explanations of the pattern of crime as revealed in official crime statistics. However, sociologists know from self-report studies and victim surveys that the number of crimes is far higher than official statistics suggest, and the high proportion of young, urban, working-class males in official statistics may give a misleading impression of the criminal population as a whole.

Official statistics only show crimes that are known to the police and recorded, or that are reported in victim surveys like the British Crime Survey. Many offences go unreported and undiscovered. Figure 6.17, taken from the 2007/8 British Crime Survey, shows a large gap for many offences between the amount of crime committed and that reported to the police. This survey suggests around 58 per cent of crimes covered by the BCS are never reported to the police, and this rises to nearly 70 per cent for some crimes. This is known as the 'dark figure' of unrecorded and unreported crime.

Only about 30 per cent of recorded crimes were detected or 'cleared up' in 2007–8, with an offender identified and action taken against them. Maguire (2002) estimates that only about 3 per cent of all crime in England and Wales ends with a conviction. This means we don't really have very reliable evidence about who is committing the majority of offences, leaving open the possibility that much crime may be committed by very different criminal types from those who come before the courts.

This all means that official statistics are unreliable and inadequate as sources of evidence about the nature and extent of crime and the social characteristics of criminals, as those appearing in official statistics are an unrepresentative sample of officially classified criminals who happen to have been caught. Official statistics may be telling us less about the real pattern of crime than about the activities of the agencies of the criminal justice system, such as the operating assumptions of the police and the courts, and the way they go about their work, and the way in which 'crime', the 'delinquent' and the 'criminal' are socially constructed phenomena. Because the statistics can't be taken at face value, theories of crime and delinquency based on them need to be treated, at best, with considerable caution. Why are official crime statistics so inaccurate?

Like an iceberg, where most of the ice is hidden beneath the surface, so it is with crime, with a hidden 'dark figure' of undiscovered, unreported or unrecorded crime. Only about 3 per cent of all crimes are estimated to result in an offender being convicted.

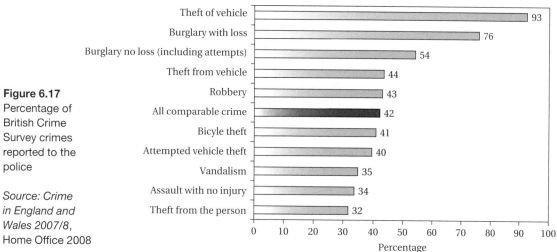

Figure 6.17
Percentage of British Crime Survey crimes reported to the police

Source: Crime in England and Wales 2007/8, Home Office 2008

Activity

Study figure 6.17 and answer the following questions:

1 What percentage of crimes of vandalism were reported to the police in 2007/8?
2 What percentage of thefts from vehicles were reported in 2007/8?
3 Which offence was most likely to be reported in 2007/8?
4 Suggest reasons, with examples, why some offences are reported to the police much more than others.
5 Suggest reasons, with examples, why the police may decide not to record a crime (a) which has been reported to them, and (b) which the police themselves have detected.
6 Explain how the information given in figure 6.17 might be used to show that official crime statistics give a misleading impression of the extent of crime in society. Is there any evidence for the opposite view for particular types of crime? (Be sure to give statistical evidence from figure 6.17.)

The failure to report crimes to the police

Figure 6.17 suggests that a large number of people who are victims of crime don't bother to report it to the police, and table 6.5 shows a range of reasons victims give for this in the British Crime Survey.

Activity

Refer to table 6.5:

1 Which offence did 85 per cent of people say they didn't report because it was too trivial, involved no loss or the police wouldn't or couldn't do anything?
2 Which offence was most likely not to be reported because people dealt with the matter themselves?
3 For all offences, what were the three most common reasons given for not reporting crime to the police?

4 Suggest examples of offences and/or the circumstances for victims not reporting crimes to the police in each of the following cases:
   a) dislike, distrust, or have little faith in the police;
   b) sympathize with the offender;
   c) do not wish to harm the offender;
   d) fear of public shame, embarrassment or humiliation;
   e) fear of self-incrimination – that they will themselves be in trouble;
   f) fear of reprisals;
   g) wish to protect the institution in which the offence occurs.
5 How do you think the evidence in table 6.5 and your answers to question 4 might be used to challenge the view in official crime statistics that most criminals are young, male and working-class?

Table 6.5: Reasons for not reporting crimes to the police: by type of offence (%) (2007/8 BCS)

	Vandalism	Burglary	Thefts from vehicles & attempts	Other household theft	Other personal theft	BCS violence	All BCS crime
Trivial/no loss/ police would not/ could not do anything	85	68	88	84	71	52	76
Private/dealt with ourselves	9	22	7	10	10	35	15
Inconvenient to report	4	3	5	5	6	6	5
Reported to other authorities	2	1	2	1	12	6	4
Common occurrence	2	0	2	1	2	3	2
Fear of reprisal	2	5	0	2	0	5	2
Dislike or fear of the police/ previous bad experience with the police or courts	2	3	2	1	0	2	2
Other[1]	3	5	3	4	6	10	6

[1]Includes: partly person's own fault; offender not responsible for actions; thought someone else had reported incident; tried to report but not able to make contact with police/police not interested.
Source: Adapted from *Crime in England and Wales 2007/8*, Home Office/Office for National Statistics 2008

The failure of the police to record a crime

The police may decide not to record an offence that has been reported to or observed by them because:

- they may regard the matter as too trivial to waste their time on, such as the theft of a very small sum of money;
- it has already been satisfactorily resolved, or because the victim does not wish to proceed with the complaint;
- they may regard the person complaining as too unreliable to take his or her account of the incident seriously, as in the case of complaints made by a tramp, a drug addict, or someone who is drunk;
- they may think that a report of an incident is mistaken, or that there is simply insufficient evidence to show that a crime has been committed;
- they may interpret the law in such a way that what is reported is not regarded as an offence;
- they may regard an incident as nothing to do with them, even though an offence has been committed – this has traditionally been true in cases of domestic violence, such as rape and other violence within marriage or cohabiting relationships;
- they may use their discretion to decide, when they see an offence being committed, to ignore it or not to investigate it, or to bring charges.

Activity

The police often have a great deal of work to do, and every arrest they make involves considerable paperwork. The police also have discretion over whether to arrest and charge someone for some offences.

1 Suggest three examples of crimes which the police might turn a blind eye to. Give reasons for your answer.

2 Suggest three crimes the police would be forced to record and investigate. Give reasons for your answer.

3 In some circumstances, the police have the power and discretion to decide whether an offence has been committed or not, such as drunkenness, obstruction or fighting in the street. Suggest ways in which the interaction between the police and the potential offender might influence the course of action the police choose to follow. What does this suggest about the social construction of the crime statistics?

4 Sometimes the police seem to take some offences more seriously than at other times, and this results in increasing numbers of arrests and prosecutions for these offences – for example, drink-driving over the Christmas period. List, with examples, all the factors you can think of that might make the police occasionally increase their levels of activity against some offences.

Is the crime rate increasing?

The public and media always express great concern at any increase in recorded crime, but such increases need not necessarily mean there are more crimes being committed, or that people are at greater risk of being victims of crime. The increases could be explained by a wide range of factors, which suggest that more offences are being discovered, reported and recorded by the police, but not necessarily that more offences are actually being committed. These factors include:

1   *The mass media.* The role of the mass media through stereotyping and deviancy amplification, and the exaggeration and distortion of events, may make problems seem worse than they are. This sensitizes people and groups to particular offences or groups of people, and therefore raises demands for police action against the perceived (often imaginary) threats to law and order.

2   *Changing counting rules.* Changing rules for counting crimes can lead to higher numbers of offences being recorded, but not necessarily more crime. For example, before April 2002, theft of a cheque-book and using these cheques in shops would have counted as one offence. Changes to the counting rules meant that, after April 2002, there would now be one crime recorded for each cheque that was used. Similarly, a person who vandalizes six cars in a street now faces being accused of six separate offences, whereas before this would have counted as one.

3   *More sophisticated police training, communications and equipment.* For example, the use of computers, CCTV, forensic science, DNA testing and higher policing levels all lead to increasing detection rates. Neighbourhood Watch schemes may also lead to more crimes being reported and detected.

4   *Changing police attitudes, priorities and policies.* A stronger desire by the police to prosecute certain offenders due to changing attitudes and policies towards some offences, such as a crack-down on prostitution, drug-dealing and drink-driving. This may give the impression of an increase in crimes of that type, when it is simply that the police are making extra efforts and allocating more officers to tackle such crimes, and therefore catching more offenders.

5   *Changes in the law.* These can lead to more things becoming illegal, such as rape in marriage.

6   *Easier communications.* Mobile phones, email and police community websites, for example, all make reporting of crime easier.

7   *Changing social norms and public attitudes.* For example, changing attitudes to rape among the police and the public may have resulted in more rapes being reported, even though no more have been committed. The same might apply to crimes like domestic violence and child abuse, which are also statistically on the increase.

8   *People have more to lose today.* In addition, more people have household contents insurance cover. Insurance claims for crimes such as theft or criminal damage to property need a police crime number, as a result of which, more crime is reported. For example, nearly all thefts of cars and burglaries with loss tend now to be reported so people can claim the insurance money.

9   *Higher policing levels.* This means that more crimes may be detected and offenders caught.

10 *People may be bringing to the attention of the police less serious incidents which they may not have reported in the past.* For example, they may have become less tolerant of vandalism and anti-social behaviour, and expect the police to stop it.

11 *The growing privatization of life.* Maguire (2007) suggests that growing privatization and the break-up of close-knit community life means that people may now be reporting to the police incidents that they would once have dealt with by taking action themselves.

It is an irony of the official statistics that attempts to defeat crime by increased levels of policing, more police pay and resources, and a determination to crack down on offences can actually increase the levels of recorded crime. The more you search for crime, the more you find; and the official crime rate rises.

Activity

Go to the Home Office Research Development and Statistics website (www.homeoffice.gov.uk/rds/) or the National Statistics website (www.statistics.gov.uk) and, searching for 'crime statistics':

1 Identify the three most common crimes recorded by the police in England and Wales, or Scotland or Northern Ireland, in the latest year for which statistics are available.
2 Identify what percentage of all crimes in England and Wales were not solved (or 'cleared up') by the police. Try to find the latest clear-up rate for your local police force.
3 Find the latest British Crime Survey, and identify the two offences that are least likely to be reported to the police.
4 On the Home Office site, find out two measures that the Home Office is taking to try and reduce crime.

Corporate crime

Many of the crimes in this section, rather like the discussion of white-collar and occupational crime earlier, are concerned with the crimes of the powerful, emphasizing once again that crime is not simply a working-class phenomenon. Often, the amounts of money involved in the crimes discussed below are so colossal, and the human consequences so serious, that they dwarf the everyday patterns of crime discussed so far in this chapter.

What is corporate crime?

Corporate crimes are offences committed by or on behalf of large companies and directly profit the company rather than individuals. Slapper and Tombs (1999) suggest both that there is a diverse range of corporate crime and that it is very widespread. They identify six types of corporate offence, which are considered below.

Paperwork and non-compliance

These are offences such as where correct permits or licences are not obtained, or companies fail to comply with health and safety and other legal regulations. An example is the *Herald of Free Enterprise* disaster in 1989, when this cross-channel ferry capsized in a calm sea just outside Zeebrugge harbour. Because the rules governing the closing of the bow doors of the ship had not been complied with, 197 people died.

Do you regard destroying the Amazon rainforest as an environmental crime, even if the companies involved aren't technically breaking the law? Do you think environmental damage and destruction of the environment for business interests and profit should be outlawed and officially classified as crimes?

Environmental (or 'green') crimes

Environmental crime is damage to the environment caused either deliberately or through negligence, and can cover a wide range of offences. While some of these may be committed by individuals, and some are not technically illegal, the most serious offences are likely to be those committed by businesses. Environmental crimes include:

- illegal dumping or disposal of toxic/hazardous waste, and waste in general;
- discharge or emission of dangerous or toxic substances into the air, soil or water – the 1984 disaster in Bhopal in India is an example of an environmental crime, when the Union Carbide chemical company leaked poisonous gas, which affected half a million people: by 2007, there had been 22,000 deaths, with at least a further 120,000 suffering severe symptoms like blindness and birth defects in children;
- the destruction of wide areas, such as through oil spills or unchecked exploration or development – examples might include the destruction of the Amazon rainforest by logging companies, increasing CO_2 emissions and contributing to global warming and climate change.

Manufacturing offences

These involve offences such as the incorrect labelling or misrepresentation of products and false advertising, producing unsafe or dangerous articles, or producing counterfeit goods. These are mainly offences against consumers, and include offences like ignoring or failing to correct or recall unsafe or dangerous products, like the Ford Pinto in the 1970s (see box). The rigging of test results on the fertility drug Thalidomide in the 1970s led to birth defects in thousands of babies.

> **Profits versus safety**
>
> The Ford Pinto car, advertised in the 1970s as the car that gave you a warm feeling, was found to have a fault that meant the car tended to erupt in flames in rear-end collisions. The car – which became known as 'the barbecue that seats four' – continued in production for eight years before the safety faults were corrected, in which period between 500 and 900 people were thought to have died in burn deaths after accidents. The failure to rectify the fault followed the notorious 'Ford Pinto memo', which showed that it was cheaper to pay out to victims ($50 million) than to rectify the safety problems ($121 million).

Labour law violations

These include offences such as failing to pay legally required minimum wages, ignoring dangerous working practices, or causing or concealing industrial diseases. Such offences, including health and safety violations, are likely to hit the lowest paid workers the hardest.

Unfair trade practices

These include things like false advertising and anti-competitive practices, such as price fixing and illegally obtaining information on rival businesses. For example, in 2007 UK supermarkets and dairy companies were fined £116 million for fixing the price of milk and cheese, costing consumers £270 million more than they would have paid without price fixing.

Financial offences

These include offences such as tax evasion and concealment of losses and debts. In the USA in 2001, Enron concealed large debts of around $50 billion, eventually causing the company to collapse, many people to lose large amounts of their investments, and thousands of employees to lose their jobs.

Explanations for corporate crime

Marxists like Box (1983) argue that the push to corporate crime is driven by the need to maintain profits in an increasingly global market, which leads to offences like:

- concealment of profits to avoid taxation;
- lying about losses to avoid hitting share prices and upsetting investors (as in Enron);
- illegal dumping of waste to avoid costs, or shipping it to other countries where disposal costs and safety regulations are lower, especially for toxic waste;
- concealment of dangerous or unsafe products to avoid legal action, or continuing to sell products in other countries that fail safety tests in their own – this happens with many drug companies that continue to sell to developing countries drugs that are either banned or out of date at home.

Control theory would suggest that the individuals who carry out offences to benefit companies are driven by aggressive management cultures, which see business success in global markets as a key focus. This might well involve taking illegal short cuts which they regard as not really doing wrong, but simply as an extension of acceptable business practice, and so there are reduced moral controls about doing wrong.

Why corporate crimes are under-represented in official statistics

Corporate crimes tend not to appear in official statistics, and they are certainly unrepresented compared to typical working-class offences like household burglary, vehicle crime and street violence. This is mainly because:

- *they often involve powerful people*, who can persuade the government, the police and the public that their actions are not very serious or even illegal;
- *they are often hard to detect*, as corporate cover-ups and networks of influence by powerful businesses mean that offences may never actually be discovered, or discovered only much later when the damage might already have been done, as in the example of the Thalidomide drug mentioned earlier;
- *even if these crimes are detected, they are often not prosecuted and dealt with as criminal acts* – for example, corporate offences like violations of health and safety legislation, price-fixing and environmental offences often lead only to a reprimand, a fine or enforcement notices from regulatory bodies and government agencies like the Health and Safety Executive, the Office of Fair Trading or the Environment Agency, rather than to police action and prosecution through the criminal justice system.

Crime and globalization

Globalization is the growing interdependence of societies across the world, with the spread of the same culture, consumer goods and economic interests across the globe. Corporate crimes are increasingly global and transnational, with corporations moving money and staff around the world to avoid prosecution, and shifting resources, waste, manufacturing and products to countries where health and safety regulations, labour controls and environmental pollution regulations are less demanding than in Western countries, or where they are less likely to be enforced or officials more easily bribed to look the other way. Growing globalization and global communications offer new opportunities for crime and new means of carrying out crimes. Local and national crime is increasingly interlinked with crime happening in other countries through global criminal networks. These networks, combined with modern global communications like the Internet, mean, for example, that credit cards 'skimmed' (copied) one day in the UK can be used in Australia the next. This globalization of crime means that a crime committed in one country may have its perpetrators located in another country; without the cooperation of other states, it may be impossible for a police investigation in any one country to track down and convict the offenders. The prevention, detection and prosecution of global crime therefore requires policing and other criminal justice agencies to operate internationally if they are to tackle the problem effectively, through agencies like the United Nations, Interpol (The International Police Organization) and Europol (the European Police Office).

Activity

Go to the websites of Interpol (www.interpol.int) and Europol (www.europol.europa.eu).
1 Identify three types of transnational crime (which spans more than one country) which these agencies are currently tackling.
2 Identify two ways that cooperation between different countries is being used to combat the crimes you identify.
3 Suggest reasons why the crimes you have identified might be difficult for the criminal justice agencies of a single country to tackle.

Karofi and Mwanza (2006) suggest that global crimes include, among others, the international trade in illegal drugs, weapons and human beings; money-laundering; terrorism; and cybercrime. Some of these are examined below.

The international illegal drug trade

Gross Domestic Product (GDP)
refers to the total value of goods and services produced by a country in a particular year.

The global illegal drug market was estimated by the United Nations *2003 World Drug Report* at $321 billion, which was higher than the **Gross Domestic Product (GDP)** – the total value of goods and services produced each year – in 88 per cent of the countries in the world.

The international drugs trade provides the drugs that are available in local communities in the UK, and drug addiction is responsible for a high proportion of acquisitive crime (theft) as people steal to support their drug habits. A report by the Audit Commission in 2002 suggested that half of all recorded crime in England and Wales was drug-related.

Human-trafficking

The international trade in illegal drugs begins with the growth of crops, like poppies in Afghanistan (shown here) or coca in Colombia, and eventually appears on the streets of Western cities as heroin and crack cocaine, where they become the generators of more crime, as people turn to theft to support their addiction.

Human-trafficking is the illegal movement and smuggling of people, for a variety of purposes ranging from the exploitation of women and children for prostitution and other forms of sexual exploitation, to forced labour and practices similar to slavery,

and the illegal removal of organs for transplants. There is also a related global criminal network dealing with the trade in illegal immigrants – smuggling into countries at high costs those people who are unable to legally enter.

Money-laundering

Money-laundering is concerned with making money that has been obtained illegally look like it came from legal sources. This is necessary because criminals, like drug-dealers and human-traffickers, deal with large amounts of cash, which they need to 'launder' to prevent their criminal activities from coming to the attention of law-enforcement agencies. Money-laundering uses modern communications technology to launder 'dirty money' by moving it around the world electronically through complex financial transactions. This makes it very difficult for law-enforcement agencies to track the sources of money, and hard to identify which country is responsible for law-enforcement.

Cybercrime

Cybercrime refers to a wide range of criminal acts committed with the help of communication and information technology, predominantly the Internet. Cybercrime is one of the fastest-growing criminal activities in the world, and web-based crimes and the use of the web to build global criminal and terrorist networks are huge global problems in contemporary society. Cybercrimes are global, in the sense that many online frauds, illegal pornography, hacking, identity theft offences and so on in the UK often have their offenders outside the country. Examples of cybercrimes include:

- Internet-based fraud, such as various financial scams, credit card fraud and the money-laundering discussed above;
- child pornography and paedophilia;
- terrorist websites and networking, involving recruitment, illegal acquisition of weaponry and planning of attacks;
- hacking – gaining illegal or unauthorized access to computers to steal data or other forms of disruptive activity;
- phishing, where emails that claim to be from a bank are actually sent by fraudsters seeking personal banking details;
- identity theft, where criminals trawl the web or other public databases, as well as discarded documents, for people's personal details, which they then use to take on another person's identity and apply for credit cards and loans, running up large bills that are then sent to the person whose identity they have stolen.

State crimes

It is ironic that the state that is responsible for enforcing the law also sometimes breaks the law itself. Crimes that are carried out by the agents of the state are known as state crimes. Some examples of these offences include:

- the torture and illegal treatment or punishment of citizens;
- corrupt or criminal policing;
- war crimes, involving illegal acts committed during wars, like the murder, ill-treatment, torture or enslavement of civilian populations or prisoners of war, and the plundering of property;
- genocide, involving the mass murder of people belonging to a particular ethnic group with the aim of eliminating that group, normally carried out by state action or with its support;
- state-sponsored terrorism, like secret British army units working with terror gangs to murder at least 14 Catholics opposed to British rule during the war in Northern Ireland between 1969 and the early 1990s;
- violations of human rights.

Activity

Go to www.yourrights.org.uk or www.liberty-human-rights.org.uk and answer the following questions:
1 Identify four human rights that are contained in the UK Human Rights Act.
2 Identify three breaches of the Human Rights Act which the British government has recently been found guilty of.

One of the worst state crimes of the twentieth century was the systematic attempted genocide of European Jews by Hitler's Nazi regime between 1933 and 1945. In Auschwitz concentration camp, shown here, an estimated one million Jews were murdered in gas chambers, out of a total of about six million murdered across Europe.

The victims of crime

Victimology

Since the 1980s, there has been a rapid growth in victim surveys and studies of the impact of crime on victims and their needs and rights. **Victimology** is the term used for the study of victims and patterns of victimization.

All sections of the criminal justice system, such as the police and the courts, are increasingly paying attention to the interests of victims and the impact of crime on local communities. For example, the police are making greater efforts to engage with the community and keep victims informed about progress on catching offenders, and victims of sexual assault are getting more specialist help and more sympathetic and specially trained police to deal with them. Victim Support schemes are now an integral part of the criminal justice system.

It has been increasingly recognized that if the victims of crime do not have confidence in the criminal justice system to support them and catch and punish offenders, then most crime will remain unreported, victims will be unwilling to give evidence and offenders will go unpunished.

> **Victimology** is the term used for the study of victims of crime and patterns of victimization.

Gender and victimization

British Crime Survey research shows that women are more likely than men to have high levels of worry about being victims of burglary and violent crime. Young men (aged 16–24) have about twice the risk of young women of being the victim of violent crime, while older men and women are the least likely to be victims of violent crime

There are certain types of crime of which women are far more likely than men to be the victims. These are 'intimate crimes', like sexual assault and rape, and non-sexual physical violence committed in the home: domestic violence. These crimes are also the least likely to be reported to the police, recorded in official statistics, or to result in offenders being convicted.

Domestic violence

There is widespread evidence of violence by men and women against their partners. It is estimated that one in four women, and one in six men, will suffer some form of domestic violence at some point in their relationships. Most of the assaults and physically most violent incidents resulting in injury – 89 per cent – are committed by men against their female partners, and those men who experience domestic violence suffer less serious attacks and do so less frequently than women. Each year, about 150 people are killed by a current or former partner, 80 per cent of whom are women. An estimated two-thirds of victims of domestic violence do not report it or seek help from any source, because they are afraid the violence will get worse, are ashamed, or see it as a private matter.

In the past, domestic violence was not taken very seriously by the police or courts: they did not see it as their responsibility but, rather, as a private family or personal

Every week 2 women die due to domestic violence. Don't let your friend be 1 of them.

matter. Walklate (2004) points out, though, that the police are now beginning to treat it more seriously, with domestic violence units and rape suites in many police stations. Nevertheless, only about a quarter of all incidents are reported to the police and, as Hester and Westmarland (2006) found, only around 5 per cent of those that are reported result in a conviction.

Rape

Women make up 92 per cent of all rape victims, but the Rape Crisis Line estimates that two out of three rape victims do not report the offence. This may be because, as Walklate suggests, in rape trials it is often female victims rather than male suspects who seem to be on trial, with their reputation and respectability being scrutinized before the evidence is taken seriously or regarded as believable. Another reason may be that the rapes that *are* reported have a very low conviction rate: only 5 per cent of all reported rapes in 2006 led to a conviction.

A common conception is that rapists are strangers unknown to the victim and that they suffer from social or psychological problems which make them different from normal men. The reality is that a high proportion of rape victims are likely to be attacked by men they know in some way, with a considerable proportion experiencing repeated attacks by the same man. As figure 6.18 shows, 57 per cent of rapes are committed by partners or acquaintances, with only 8 per cent perpetrated by strangers. Only about a quarter of rapes, according to the BCS, take place in public or other places; 75 per cent occur in the home of the victim or offender.

The misleading stereotype of the rapist as an abnormal stranger means that when the police and courts are faced with a person accused of rape, the fact that he is often

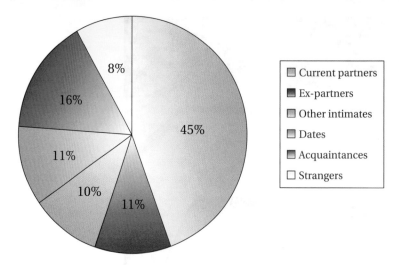

Figure 6.18
Relationship
to perpetrator,
victims of rape

Source: Myhill and
Allen 2002

acquainted with the victim and appears to be no different from other men leads to doubts about whether what occurred was really rape at all, and that the victim may in some ways have been partly to blame for what occurred. This may partly explain the low conviction rates.

Explaining rape and domestic violence

Feminist writers generally explain 'intimate crimes' like rape and domestic violence of which women are the main victims as an aspect of male power in a patriarchal society. Men are socialized into a sense of superiority over women, and sexual and physical violence are aspects of the network of male control of women. Marxist social-ist feminists see these unequal relations intensified by class inequality and poverty.

Activity

1 Women are more likely to be victims of some crimes than men. Suggest, with reasons, examples of some of these crimes.
2 Describe the types of male criminality which occur within the family unit, and suggest explanations for it.
3 Suggest reasons why male victims of rape (by other males) – an estimated 8 per cent of all rapes – might be even less likely to report it to the police than female victims of rape by men.

Age and victimization

The lifestyles of the young, as well as giving them greater opportunity to commit crime, also expose them to greater risk of being victims of crime. While young people are more likely to be the perpetrators of violent crime, they are also most likely to be the victims of it. Wilson et al. (2006) found young people to be the group most likely to be victims of crime, with 27 per cent of 10–25-year-olds reporting being victims of personal crimes like assault without injury and theft.

Ethnicity and victimization

With the exception of racial attacks and homicide, those from minority ethnic groups do not appear to face a higher risk of becoming a victim of most crimes than the white population. Any differences can be explained by the younger age profile of minority ethnic groups, their social class and the fact that they live in areas of social deprivation – it is these that explain victimization, rather than that they are part of a minority ethnic group. Nonetheless, even allowing for age, social class and locality differences, all minority ethnic groups report a higher fear of crime than the white population.

In terms of homicide, 21 per cent in 2005/6 were of people from minority ethnic groups – more than twice the risk facing the white population, and this risk rises to six times higher for black people. The BCS estimates that there were around 139,000 racially motivated incidents in 2005/6, including harassment, abuse, threats, intimidation and violence – more than 380 incidents every day of the year. Both black people (African Caribbeans) and Asians were up to 14 times more likely to be the victim of a racially motivated incident than white people.

Social class and victimization

The poorest sections of the working class are the most likely victims of crime. The highest rates of victimization are found:

- *among the 'hard pressed'* – the unemployed, the long-term sick, low-income families and those living in rented accommodation;
- *in areas of high physical disorder* – with widespread vandalism, graffiti and deliberate damage to property, rubbish and litter, and homes in poor condition;
- *in areas with high levels of deprivation.*

The 2007/8 BCS showed that, compared to the 20 per cent most affluent households, those in the 20 per cent of poorest areas face around twice the risk of being a victim of burglary, and nearly double the risk of vehicle-related thefts, as well as higher risks of vandalism and overall household crime (see figure 6.19).

The double whammy and the inverse victimization law

A great irony of crime and victimization is what we might call the 'inverse victimization law'. This is that those who have the fewest and least valuable material possessions are those most likely to have them stolen or vandalized, while those who have the most, and the most valuable, material possessions are the least likely to have them stolen or vandalized. The second irony is that those who steal from the poor are mainly other poor people.

Explaining victimization

The section above suggests that much crime is not random, and that some social groups are more likely to be the victims of crime than others. There are two major approaches in victimology to explain this: positivist victimology and radical victimology.

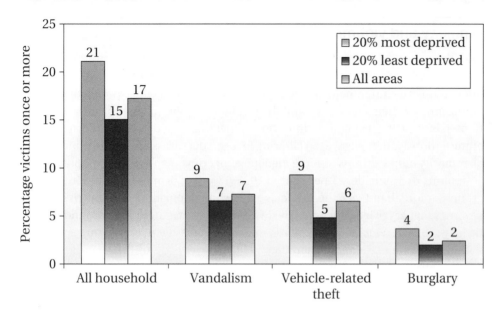

Figure 6.19 Risk of crime by level of deprivation in England (2007/8 BCS)

Source: Crime in England and Wales 2007/8, Home Office 2008

Positivist victimology

Tierney (1996) suggests that the positivist approach to victimology involves identifying something in the characteristics or circumstances of victims which makes them different from non-victims. The focus is on *victim precipitation* and *victim proneness*. Victim proneness identifies the characteristics of individuals or groups that make them more vulnerable to victimization. Victim precipitation suggests that victims are actively involved, or to blame, for their victimization. For example, women who make themselves vulnerable by dressing 'provocatively' or 'leading men on' in rape offences, or victims who fail to lock doors or conceal valuables in cars, or who carry large amounts of cash around.

Positivist victimology has been criticized in a number of ways:

1 It tends to blame the victims of crime rather than the offenders, in effect making the victims more responsible than the criminals themselves. Feminist writers, for example, have been particularly critical of suggestions arising from positivist victimology that victims of rape and sexual offences or domestic violence are somehow to blame for making themselves vulnerable.
2 It downplays the role of the law, the police and other criminal justice agencies in not tackling crime effectively and thereby contributing to victimization.
3 It focuses too much on the characteristics of individual victims, and does not pay enough attention to the wider structural factors, like poverty and unemployment, that often make some groups and communities more vulnerable to crime than others.

Radical victimology

Radical victimology focuses much less on blaming the victims for their victimization and much more on the role of the law and the criminal justice system in producing victimization. They see victimization arising from wider social issues and circumstances than from the individual characteristics or behaviour of the victims. Social deprivation means it is the weakest and most deprived members of society who are most likely to be victims, and patriarchal ideology generates the victimization of women.

Activity

Explore the Home Office website on victims of crime (www.homeoffice.gov.uk/crime-victims/victims/ and www.homeoffice.gov.uk/crime-victims/how-you-can-prevent-crime/). There are further links here on particular crimes and various crime reduction strategies you might wish to explore further.

1 Identify three current government policies in relation to crime victims which might suggest a positivist approach, focusing on the characteristics that make individuals vulnerable to and responsible for their own victimization. Explain your reasons for choosing those particular policies.

2 Suggest alternative policies to these issues which might remove the focus away from the victim and onto the offender.

3 Go to www.homeoffice.gov.uk/crime-victims/reducing-crime/ and explore policies for reducing the number of victims of crime which suggest an approach more in keeping with radical victimology, focusing on offenders and issues and circumstances in wider society rather than the individual victims, such as community safety or youth crime strategies. Explain your reasons for choosing those particular policies, and how they remove the focus away from victim-blaming.

Crime control, prevention and punishment

The criminal justice system

The criminal justice system consists of agencies like the police, Crown Prosecution Service, courts, prisons and the probation service. These are overseen by the government departments of the Home Office and the Ministry of Justice. The Youth Justice Board oversees youth justice, and advises the Ministry of Justice on youth offending. These agencies are the main means of identifying, controlling and punishing known offenders.

Does imprisonment prevent crime?

The prison system is meant to be the ultimate deterrent, both controlling crime and punishing offenders, but it doesn't actually seem to work very well as a crime-prevention measure.

Research by the Downing Street Strategy Unit in 2003 showed that a 22 per cent increase in the prison population since 1997 was estimated to have reduced crime by only around 5 per cent, at a time when overall crime had fallen by 30 per cent, and suggested that there was no convincing evidence that putting more people in prison would significantly reduce crime. Nonetheless, the prison population continued to grow, and England and Wales now have the highest imprisonment rate in the European Union. Home Office research shows that about 65 per cent of former prisoners released in 2004 were reconvicted within two years of being released, and for young men (18–20) it was 75 per cent. This means that imprisonment isn't stopping people from reoffending, nor are high levels of imprisonment making much impact on reducing crime.

Realist theories and social policies for crime prevention

Realist theories regard themselves as 'real' because they primarily concern themselves with explaining the crimes that really matter to people and impact on their daily lives. These theories also concern themselves with practical crime prevention through social policy measures, although Left and Right Realism have different emphases.

Left Realism tends to emphasize the social causes of crime, which might be characterized as *tough on the causes of crime*, while Right Realism lays more stress on situational crime prevention (discussed below) and being *tough on the criminals*.

Left Realism: social crime prevention and being tough on the causes of crime

Left Realist approaches to crime prevention recognize that both the offenders and the victims of the crimes that worry people most are found in the more disadvantaged communities – those with the highest levels of marginality and social exclusion. They therefore emphasize the need to tackle the material and cultural deprivation – such as poverty, unemployment, poor housing and education, poor parental supervision, and broken families and family conflict – that are the risk factors for crime, particularly among young people. Preventing crime involves addressing these social issues through policies such as:

- building strong communities to work out local solutions to local problems, and create community cohesion;
- multi-agency working, involving everyone in the fight against crime, not just the criminal justice agencies;
- creation of Safer Neighbourhood or Police and Community Together (PACT) groups, where local people can identify the issues that worry them, and get the police and other agencies to deal with them;
- more democratic and community control of policing to win public confidence to tackle the causes of crime, and encourage victims to report crime;
- more time spent by the police in investigating crime;
- tackling social deprivation and the other risk factors for crime by improving community facilities to divert potential offenders from choosing crime – for example, youth leisure activities – and reducing unemployment and improving housing;
- intensive parenting support that gets parents and young offenders together to work out solutions, and early intervention through strategies like Sure Start to help get children in the poorest communities, where the risk factors for crime are

greatest, off to a better start in life by bringing together early education, child-care, health and family support (see www.surestart.gov.uk/ for more information).

Criticism of social crime prevention approaches

Policies derived from Left Realism face three major criticisms:

1 They are 'soft' on crime, as they focus too much on the social causes of crime, downplaying the role of the offender in choosing to commit crime. The offender almost becomes a victim him- or herself.
2 The explanations are inadequate, as the majority of those in deprived communities do not turn to crime. Social deprivation and other risk factors do not apply equally to all those in similar circumstances.
3 They deflect attention away from more practical crime-prevention measures, like the tighter social control and situational crime prevention measures advocated by Right Realists.

Right Realism: situational crime prevention and being tough on the criminals

Right Realist approaches to crime prevention tend to focus on individuals rather than on the wider social issues. They argue that individuals choose crime and must be dissuaded from doing so, and, if they can't, must be punished for it. Such an approach leads to two main policies:

Left Realists focus on social crime prevention by tackling the causes of crime. How might a deprived neighbourhood contribute to crime?

- situational crime prevention (SCP);
- increased social control.

Situational crime prevention (SCP)

Situational crime prevention derives from opportunity theories of crime, like routine activity theory (see Felson and Clarke 1998), and rational choice theory (see Cornish and Clarke 1986).

Routine activity theory suggests that a crime occurs as part of everyday routines, when there are three conditions present:

- there is a suitable target for the potential offender, which could be a person, a place or an object;
- there is no 'capable guardian', like a neighbour, police, or CCTV surveillance to protect the target; and
- there is a potential offender present, who thinks the first two conditions are met (suitable target and no guardian), and then chooses whether or not to commit the crime.

Rational choice theory focuses on the decision-making process of the potential offender, relating to the last bullet point above. This theory sees offenders as acting rationally, weighing up the benefits and risks when they see an opportunity for crime before choosing whether or not to commit an offence. SCP aims to make potential targets of crime more difficult and risky for potential offenders by 'designing out crime' in particular locations by 'target-hardening' measures, like post-coding goods, use of anti-climb paint, CCTV, locks, premises and car alarms. This both reduces the opportunities for crime in particular locations and poses greater risks for offenders and encourages them not to commit an offence. SCP is therefore concerned with preventing crime in particular locations rather than with catching offenders.

Increased social control

The policy of increased social control is linked to Hirschi's (1969) control theory, which suggests that strong social bonds integrating people into communities encourage

Right Realists focus on reducing the opportunities for crime through situational crime prevention, like the use of surveillance cameras to deter potential offenders

individuals to choose conformity over deviance and crime. The focus is then on tighter control and socialization, by strengthening social institutions like the traditional family, religion and community, and constraining and isolating deviant individuals through community pressure. Policies flowing from this might include the following:

1. Making parents take more responsibility for the supervision of their children, and socializing them more effectively into conformist behaviour. Those who don't may be issued with Parenting Orders. These are court orders issued to the parents of persistent truants or young offenders who fail properly to supervise their children. They compel a parent to attend parenting classes, counselling or other requirements to improve their child's behaviour.
2. Schemes like Neighbourhood Watch, which involve informal surveillance and 'good neighbourliness' (by keeping an eye on each other's houses), helping to build community controls over crime.
3. Cracking down on anti-social behaviour like graffiti, hoax calls, verbal abuse, noisy neighbours, drug and alcohol abuse in public places, and intimidating behaviour by groups of youths through 'naming and shaming' measures like Anti-Social Behaviour Orders (ASBOs)
4. Supervision of offenders – for example, electronic tagging to restrict and monitor their movements.
5. Adopting zero tolerance policing, which involves taking steps against all crimes, even low-level offences like graffiti and vandalism, to prevent community breakdown and a climate where 'anything goes' and individuals come to believe they can get away with offending, and crime subsequently escalates.
6. More policing and more arrests, particularly in high crime areas, to deter potential criminals by increasing their risks of being caught.
7. Fast-track punishment of offenders, with more imprisonment and harsher sentences.

Criticism of policies derived from Right Realism

Policies derived from Right Realism face several criticisms:

1. They don't address the wider social causes of crime that the Left Realists do.
2. They don't allow that some people may be targeted unfairly by police – for example, through stereotyping, labelling and racism, generating resentment and making problems worse.
3. They assume that offenders act rationally in choosing crime and derive some benefits from it, but some crimes are impulsive or irrational and do not have any obvious gain, like vandalism or violence. Lyng's conception of 'edgework', and Katz's work on the seduction of crime discussed earlier in this chapter, with the risk-taking involved in crime being attractive because of the thrill and buzz, is not addressed by opportunity theories for those who want to take the risk.
4. SCP, particularly, has been criticized for a number of reasons:
   - it tends to be geographically limited and only prevents crime in particular locations;

- it removes the focus from other forms of crime prevention, such as looking at wider economic and social policies which cause crime;
- it doesn't pay enough attention to catching criminals or punishments to deter offenders;
- it doesn't prevent crime overall, but simply *displaces* crime to softer targets in other areas. This is perhaps the major criticism of SCP, and is discussed further below.

Displacement theory

Displacement theory argues that situational crime prevention does not prevent crime but merely shifts it around – displaces it. For example, Felson and Clarke suggest SCP may divert potential offenders to committing crime somewhere else, at some other time, or to other more vulnerable targets where the risks of being caught are lower.

While there is some evidence of these things occurring, Felson and Clarke point out that SCP can still have positive effects in preventing crime. Potential offenders may believe that measures, like CCTV, that are in place in one location may also be in place in others, even if they aren't, and therefore SCP measures may have an impact beyond the immediate location. SCP may result in less serious or less damaging crimes being committed, to property, people and communities. For example, potential offenders may be diverted away from burglary of houses at night, theft from cars or crimes like mugging in streets with CCTV surveillance, with harmful consequences to individuals and the community, towards shoplifting at busy times, where the crime is more impersonal and less harmful to individuals. This means that, even if some displacement does occur, the consequences of crime may be less serious for both individuals and the wider community than if no SCP measures were taken.

Activity

The Home Office crime reduction website is excellent for sociologists, and if you wish to read a bit more about any of these theoretical and practical approaches to reducing crime, including criticisms, you should take a look, particularly at www.crimereduction. homeoffice.gov.uk/learningzone/lz_learning.htm.

1 Go to www.crimereduction.homeoffice.gov.uk/learningzone/scptechniques.htm and study the 'Twenty-five techniques of situational crime prevention' developed by Cornish and Clarke. Write a brief paragraph on each of the following five groups of techniques, explaining how each puts into practice routine activity theory and rational choice theory, and illustrating it with explanations of the examples given. If you are in a group, you could divide these up between you.
   - increase the effort
   - increase the risks
   - reduce the rewards
   - reduce provocations
   - remove the excuses

2 Go to www.crimereduction.homeoffice.gov.uk/cpindex.htm and identify two current social policies for preventing crime which might be regarded as in keeping with Left Realist approaches, and two with Right Realist approaches.

3 What do you think are the major causes of crime and deviance in society, and what social policies do you think are most likely to reduce crime? Explain your reasons, linked to sociological theories of crime.

Suicide

Suicide might in many ways be regarded as the ultimate act of deviance. In a society where the protection of human life is an important social value, and most people do all they can to cling onto it, taking one's own life becomes a highly deviant act; in England and Wales until 1961, suicide was actually a criminal offence. Nonetheless, in 2006, there were 5,554 suicides in adults aged 15 and over in the UK, which represented almost 1 per cent of the total of all deaths in this age range; three-quarters of these suicides were men.

The sociological study of suicide has become a classic case study in two main methodological approaches in sociology – positivism and interpretivism – and the extent to which quantitative (statistical) methods can be used to produce valid analyses of society.

The positivist approach to suicide

Durkheim's (2002) 1897 study *Suicide: A Study in Sociology* is often taken as a model of positivist research methodology in sociology. Positivism is an approach that suggests the same quantitative methods derived from observable and measurable data that scientists use to study the natural world to discover the causes of phenomena can also be used to study the social world. Positivists see human behaviour formed by social forces external to the individual consciousness and meanings of individuals. Durkheim aimed to show that even an apparently highly individual, personal and private act like suicide is a product of social forces, and that explaining the suicide rate in any society did not depend on understanding the consciousness, intention or mental/psychological state of suicide victims.

Durkheim's work used quantitative data in the form of suicide statistics from a number of European countries to compare suicide rates in different nations and between different sub-groupings within each society. From his analysis of these statistics, Durkheim found that, although the individuals making up that society or group changed over time:

● in each society and sub-group, the suicide rate was fairly constant and stable over a period of years;

● there were significant differences in the suicide rate between societies – for example, between Protestant and Catholic countries;

- there were significant differences between social groups in the same society – for example between married and single people, and between those living in urban and rural communities.

Durkheim believed it was impossible to explain the stability and consistency of these patterns over substantial periods of time if suicide was simply a personal, private act, as the statistics would then be expected to show a random pattern. He concluded therefore that the causes of suicide must lie outside the individual and in forces at work in society itself. He then tried to identify and isolate the most important factors that appeared to be linked to the suicide rate, such as religion, family ties and political upheaval. From this, he suggested that suicide was linked to two social forces: **social integration** and **moral regulation**.

Social integration and moral regulation

Social integration refers to the extent to which individuals are integrated into social groups and experience a sense of belonging to society. This is achieved by building social cohesion through institutions like the family and religious organizations. Moral regulation refers to the social processes, like social control and socialization, that keep the actions and desires of individuals in check and regulated by social values, so, for example, they don't develop unrealistic or unachievable ambitions.

Durkheim believed social stability depended on social integration and moral regulation being balanced, with neither too much nor too little of either. In situations where this state of balance was weakened or disrupted, there would be an increase in social disorder, including the number of suicides. Table 6.6 summarizes Durkheim's main findings derived from official statistics, and his explanations.

Social integration refers to the integration of individuals into social groups, binding them into society and building social cohesion.

Moral regulation refers to the regulation or control by social values of the actions and desires of individuals.

Table 6.6: Durkheim and the social factors linked to the suicide rate			
	High suicide rate	Low suicide rate	Explanation
Location	Urban areas	Rural areas	Urban areas are more impersonal, with fewer social bonds integrating people into society, compared with close-knit rural communities
Family status	No family or children	Children and relatives	The family and its responsibilities integrates individuals into society and avoids social isolation, and helps regulate behaviour
Marital status	Single/ divorced	Married	Partners and responsibilities to them act as integrating and regulating forces
Religion	Protestant	Catholic	Protestantism is individualistic, leaving people to make their own decisions and choices. Catholicism integrates individuals into the church and wider community, and regulates individuals by providing clear guidelines on behaviour and values

Four types of suicide

Durkheim identified four major types of suicide arising from his research, summarized in Figure 6.20:

1 *Egoistic suicide*: This is where there is insufficient integration or 'excessive individualism'. Individuals are not well integrated into society through social institutions like the family, marriage or tight-knit religious organizations or communities, and have weakened ties with others.

2 *Altruistic suicide*: This is where there is excessive integration, and the individual has little value compared to the needs of the group. For example, traditional Hinduism involved widows throwing themselves on the funeral pyres of their dead husbands. A contemporary example might be suicide bombers, who value a cause even more than their own lives.

3 *Anomic suicide*. This is where there is insufficient regulation or anomie (normlessness). It arises when social guidelines and a clear framework for behaviour are unclear, absent or confused. For example, during periods of rapid social change, existing norms and customs are undermined and subject to constant change. People feel 'lost' over how to behave and what to believe, and lose a sense of purpose and meaning. The higher suicide rate amongst young men in contemporary society, for example, might be explained by a 'crisis of masculinity' and the uncertainly about quite what the male role is in contemporary society.

4 *Fatalistic suicide*. This is where there is excessive or oppressive regulation of individuals, with suicide providing an escape from a future of unending despair and hopelessness. Durkheim suggested this might have been found amongst slaves, but this may also explain the high suicide rate among prisoners in contemporary society, which for male prisoners is around five times greater than that for men in general.

Through his research into suicide, Durkheim believed he had established the social causes of suicide without studying the consciousness or intentions of suicidal

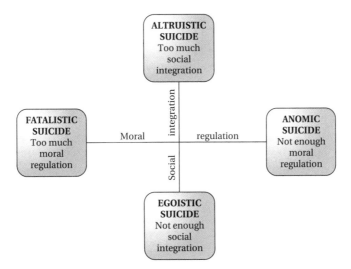

Figure 6.20 Four types of suicide

individuals. He did this, as in the natural sciences, using observable quantitative data (suicide statistics) and he established a law of human behaviour: that the suicide rate rose during periods when there was either too little or too much social integration or moral regulation.

Criticisms of Durkheim's study of suicide

Positivist criticisms

Positivists admire Durkheim's work, and confine themselves to criticisms within the same approach. For example, Halbachs, writing in 1930, suggested that Durkheim gave too much emphasis to the significance of religion at the expense of the features of rural and urban life, and that he is too vague in defining social integration and ways of measuring it. Halbachs also argues that Durkheim's explanations of suicide are based on assumptions about what group membership means to the people concerned (see below). Others are critical of the validity of the statistics he used. For example, there was no systematic medical examination of the dead until the late nineteenth century, particularly in rural areas, which meant the causes of death weren't always properly established.

Durkheim's own failings

Durkheim argued that only external social forces should be considered in explaining suicide rates, but his own work makes reference to the need to understand individual consciousness and meaning.

Durkheim's definition of suicide is: 'All cases of death resulting directly or indirectly from a positive or negative act of the victim himself which he knows will produce this result.' This creates the problem of how we establish, after the event, the intentions of suicide victims and that their actions would lead to their deaths. Reference to the individual's consciousness and intention therefore becomes essential even in Durkheim's terms.

The four main categories of suicide (egoistic, altruistic, anomic and fatalistic) are based on assumptions about what group membership means to the individuals concerned. For example, Durkheim *assumes* that the Catholic religion is a more integrating religion than Protestantism, but individual Catholics may not see it that way. Many people may practise religion out of custom, habit or social pressure, and may not experience them as integrating or individualistic, as Durkheim suggests. Similarly, marriage may be a destructive and stressful institution, as contemporary divorce rates might suggest, and be neither integrating nor regulating for those involved. Durkheim again defeats his own objective of explaining suicide without regard to the consciousness or meanings of individuals, as he simply takes for granted a meaning that individuals may not have.

Durkheim's work rests on official suicide statistics, which he regards as a true record of the number of suicides. These are, however, problematic, and Durkheim disregards the way these might themselves be social constructions.

The social construction of suicide: the interpretivist (anti-positivist) approach

Interpretivist sociologists reject many of the basic principles underpinning the positivist approach to the study of suicide adopted by Durkheim, and particularly his reliance on suicide statistics. Interpretivists argue that suicide statistics are neither valid, in the sense of giving a true picture of the extent of suicide, nor reliable, as different coroners (who are responsible in law for deciding whether a death is a suicide) may reach different verdicts even on similar evidence.

To describe a death as a 'suicide' involves knowing what the person in question was intending to do when he or she died. Suicide can only occur where an individual actively intends to kill her- or himself. Since we cannot ask dead people what they actually intended, the classification of a death as suicide can only be arrived at through the interpretations of others, and there are likely to be differences of opinion as to how such an intention to die may be established. Suicide then becomes simply that which is so defined and interpreted by, for example, coroners, doctors, relatives and friends who try to make sense of the death.

Interpretivists suggest that defining a death as a suicide involves social constructions of meaning placed on the event by others, and to understand suicide it is necessary to understand the meanings and interpretations that people attach to it. From this point of view, suicide statistics are simply social constructions – a record of the interpretations made by officials of what are seen to be unnatural sudden deaths. It is therefore pointless trying to discover the causes of suicide as Durkheim did, since it is impossible to be certain whether an act is really a suicide or not. Such approaches suggest that it is necessary to move away from quantitative analysis using suicide statistics, and to use more qualitative methods, like studying diaries and suicide notes, and interviews with coroners, relatives and attempted suicides.

Douglas and the social meanings of suicide

In his *The Social Meanings of Suicide* (1967), Douglas is particularly critical of Durkheim's use of official suicide statistics, and points out that whether a sudden death is *classified* as a suicide or not depends on the very factors that Durkheim claimed caused suicide, and that these vary between countries and between social groups within the same society.

Douglas suggests the degree of social integration influences whether a death gets classified as suicide. The family and friends of socially integrated victims may try to cover up a suicide, for example by destroying evidence (for example, suicide notes) or by trying to persuade the coroner it wasn't suicide, because of their own sense of shame, guilt and failure. Those who are less integrated – those who are single, or without relatives or friends – may have no one to cover up their suicide or argue on their behalf that it wasn't in fact suicide.

Douglas also points out that the social meaning given to suicide can affect the statistics. Among Catholics, for example, suicide is regarded as a sin, and in Catholic countries coroners may be more willing to bring in a verdict of accidental death or

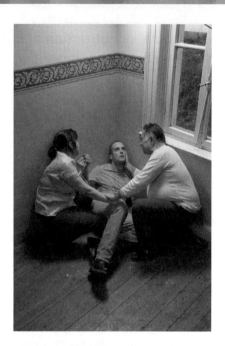

How might the level of social integration influence whether or not a sudden unexpected death is classified as a suicide?

Table 6.7: Douglas and the different meanings of suicide

Meaning of suicide	Explanation
Transformation of the self – repentance suicide	Suicide as self-punishment to show repentance for wrongdoing.
Transformation of the soul – escape suicide	Suicide as a means of escaping from the misery of this life.
Revenge suicide	Suicide to attach guilt and blame to those who have wronged them.
Sympathy suicide	Suicide as 'cry for help' and sympathy, often found among attempted suicides, who hope they may be found in time.

misadventure to spare the relatives the social stigma attached to suicide. By contrast, in some societies like Japan, suicide is seen as an honourable death, so there is less stigma attached to coroners bringing in a suicide verdict.

These provide quite different explanations to Durkheim's, as the differences in suicide rates between societies and groups are explained by different social attitudes to suicide and levels of social integration leading to different chances of a sudden death getting *classified* as a suicide.

Douglas also argues that suicide is not always the same act. The victim can construct how others interpret their deaths. Some may construct the death, by a suicide note for example, as a form of revenge on those who have harmed them in some way, and seek to inflict maximum blame and guilt on them. Others may go to considerable lengths to disguise their suicide as an accident, perhaps to spare relatives from guilt and anguish. Understanding suicide therefore involves examining the meanings that individuals give to their suicide, as summarized in table 6.7.

Douglas's approach to suicide provides an alternative explanation to Durkheim's in explaining the different suicide rates between societies. In Japan, which has one of the highest suicide rates among rich countries, the transformation of self through repentance suicide, arising from a sense of shame, failure or bankruptcy for example, is seen as an honourable death, and there may therefore be less reluctance to bring in a verdict of suicide. However, in Western societies suicide is often seen as a desperate last resort, a transformation of the soul through escape, which may leave relatives or friends shamed, guilty and bewildered, and coroners reluctant to bring in a verdict of suicide if it can be avoided. Such factors may explain variations in suicide statistics between groups and societies, rather than the social forces identified by Durkheim.

Activity

1 With reference to table 6.7, suggest and explain a range of circumstances and clues which might be used to identify the meanings behind the action of a suicide or attempted suicide. Do this for each of Douglas's four types of suicide.
2 Suggest ways in which the circumstances and clues you use may influence whether or not coroners bring in a suicide verdict.

Atkinson and the role of coroners' definitions

Atkinson (1971, 1983) is concerned with the process whereby some deaths get categorized as suicide, and completely rejects the quantitative methods of Durkheim and other positivists. He argues that whether or not a death is classified as a suicide is simply a product of the interpretations of others, and that the real number of suicides is unknowable.

Atkinson studied coroners' decision-making, using interviews with coroners and their staff, the study of case records, and attendance at inquests. While suicide is, by definition, the death of a person who intended to kill him or herself, the problem for coroners is that they can't ask dead people if they meant to kill themselves, so they can only guess at the truth by looking for clues in the circumstances surrounding the death. Based on his research, Atkinson suggested that coroners, like the rest of us, hold common-sense theories about the causes of suicide, and if information about the deceased fits their theory, they are likely to categorize the death as a suicide. Atkinson has suggested there are four main types of evidence which coroners take into account when deciding whether people intended to take their own lives:

1 *Suicide notes*. These are important clues, as they may show a person's intention to die (but it is possible they might be faked, disguising a murder for example, or intended to be found before the person died, as a way of appealing for help).
2 *Modes of death*. The way the person died, for example by hanging, drowning or a drug overdose. Death by hanging is more likely than death in a car crash to result in a suicide verdict, even if the hanging was an accident, or the car crash really a suicide.

3   *Location and circumstances of death.* This concerns the place the death occurred and the circumstances surrounding it; for example, a drug overdose in a remote wood would be more likely to be seen as a suicide than if it occurred at home in bed. A coroner might also consider circumstances such as whether the person had been drinking before taking the drugs, and whether the drugs had been hoarded or not.

4   *Life history and mental condition of the victim.* The life history and mental state of the victim, such as whether or not he or she was a socially isolated 'loner', the state of mental and physical health, and whether the victim was in debt, had just failed exams, lost a job, got divorced or suffered a bereavement.

Atkinson found that coroners are not consistent in the ways they interpret these clues and the significance they attach to evidence. For example, one coroner believed a death by drowning was likely to be a suicide if the clothes were left neatly folded on the beach, but another coroner might attach little importance to this. Such differing interpretations of evidence exist not only in the same society but also between different societies, arising from different cultural attitudes to suicide. These varied interpretations may mean that some sudden deaths can be wrongly classified as suicides – for example, death by hanging may have been an accident during the course of bizarre sexual practices. Similarly, some deaths in what appear to be road 'accidents' may be successfully disguised suicides. As seen earlier with Douglas's research, those with relatives may well intervene with coroners to influence the way they interpret evidence.

Atkinson argues that this means that all suicide statistics are really showing is a highly selective, socially constructed set of classifications of sudden deaths as suicides reflecting coroners' decision-making, and they tell us nothing about the real causes or extent of suicide.

Activity

1   On the basis of Atkinson's four types of evidence used by coroners, and the different meanings that Douglas attaches to suicide, discuss how the features of the scenario below might be interpreted differently by a coroner to reach a verdict of (a) suicide or (b) an accident (misadventure). Explain your reasons in each case.

  A 57-year-old married woman with children was found dead in her kitchen one evening by her husband, having taken an overdose. She had a long history of depression, for which she was prescribed anti-depressant tablets. There was evidence she had been drinking alcohol, and she'd had a row with her husband before he left for work. Her husband was unusually late home that day because of traffic congestion. She had recently heard that her eldest son had contracted cancer, and her 14-year-old daughter had the previous day announced she was pregnant.

2   In the above situation, suggest ways in which the intervention of relatives might influence whether or not a coroner brought in a suicide verdict.

3   What are the implications for official suicide statistics of this activity?

Realist approaches to suicide: 'persons under trains'*

Taylor (1982, 1988, 1990) is a realist, steering something of a middle way between positivism and interpretivism. Realism differs from positivism in that it does not suggest that all social causes of phenomena need to be observable and quantifiable; events can also be caused by underlying, unobservable structures. Taylor suggests that Durkheim wasn't really a positivist at all, as the social forces of social integration and moral regulation that he identified were neither observable nor quantifiable.

Taylor studied suicides and attempted suicides (para-suicides) on London's Underground and found, like Atkinson, that coroners constructed biographies of suicide victims by looking at their life history and mental condition, and that, if this fitted with the coroners' conceptions, then a suicide verdict was likely. Taylor agrees that suicide statistics are highly unreliable and socially constructed, and agrees with Atkinson that specific factors and common-sense theories influence the verdicts reached by coroners and distort suicide figures. Despite this, he thought it was still possible to identify the causes of suicide.

Certainty and attachment

Taylor's two central concepts are certainty and the degree of attachment to others. He suggests that it is the degree of certainty or uncertainty of individuals about themselves or their relationships with others that makes people commit, or attempt to commit, suicide. He suggests that suicides and para-suicides fall into two main categories (table 6.8 summarizes Taylor's theory of suicide arising from his research):

Table 6.8: Taylor's theory of suicide

	Inner-directed suicide (about self and identity)	Other-directed suicide (about communicating something to others)
Certainty	*Submissive suicide* Life is over and others cannot help – e.g. arising from a terminal illness or death of a partner.	*Sacrifice suicide* Others made life intolerable and they are left with no choice but to kill themselves, because they have harmed, or been harmed, by someone they relate to – e.g. partner goes off with another lover, or they have been exposed as a paedophile.
Uncertainty	*Thanatation suicide* Unsure whether to live or die, and others aren't helping to find a solution. Risk-taking and gambling with death, and perhaps surviving it, might provide a remedy and a re-evaluation of life's meaning.	*Appeal suicide* Others have made the potential victim's life difficult, and this is a cry for help to save them from death – e.g. an attempt to win back a partner who has gone off with another lover.

* ('Persons under trains' is how rail companies record deaths of people killed in trains.)

1   *Inner-directed suicides.* These are private acts that are concerned with an individual's identity and what they think about themselves. The individual is concerned with him- or herself, and is detached from others. Certainty is more likely to lead to a successful suicide. Uncertainty is more about risk-taking and gambling with death than a determined suicide attempt, and is often found among attempted suicides, though uncertainty may still lead to death.
2   *Other-directed suicides.* These are about individuals' relationships with others and communicating some message to them.

Taylor's research is useful, as it helps us to explain both suicides and attempted suicides, and how the degree of certainty that individuals feel about themselves and their relationships to others can influence suicide attempts, whether successful or not. What Taylor doesn't explain is what the wider social factors are that influence the unobservable structures of certainty and uncertainty, and people's attachment or detachment from others. In this sense, Taylor may be indebted to Durkheim, whose concept of anomie and the unobservable structures of social integration and moral regulation might be precisely the forces that govern certainty and uncertainty in individuals, and the extent of their relationships with others.

Activity

1   Drawing on Taylor's work, suggest what circumstances might indicate certainty or uncertainty on the part of a suicide or attempted suicide.
2   Identify and explain two ways that differing interpretations between coroners might lead to the *same* sudden death being classified by some coroners as a suicide, while not by others.
3   Suggest two reasons why the presence or absence of a suicide note might be an unreliable 'clue' to a dead person's intention to die.
4   Suggest reasons why (a) some deaths classified as suicides may have been accidental, and (b) some deaths classified as accidents may in fact have been suicides.
5   Identify and explain three ways that Atkinson's research challenges the statistical foundations of Durkheim's research.
6   Identify and explain four reasons why sociologists should be very careful about using official statistics on suicide as a record of the real number of suicides in society.
7   Write an essay in 30 minutes answering the following question:
    'Examine the view that Durkheim did not produce an adequate account of suicide.'

Researching crime and deviance

Note to students

This section assumes that chapter 5 has already been studied, and that you have a good grasp of the sociological methods studied at AS. If you haven't yet studied chapter 5, or need to brush up on your AS methods, you are advised to return to this section once you have done so.

The aim of this section is to get you to apply your knowledge and understanding of sociological theory and research methods to the study of particular issues in crime and deviance. Many of the research methods and types of data discussed in chapter 5 and during your AS course have been used in researching the areas of crime and deviance, and this chapter has shown how theories of crime are used not only to explain patterns of offending, but also for the formation of social policies to reduce crime. The discussion of suicide identified key debates between positivist and interpretivist approaches, and the limitations of using quantitative methods to study the social world. What follows aims to get you thinking a bit more about some of these issues, and some of the theoretical, practical and ethical difficulties in using different research methods to study crime and deviance.

Quantitative data

Research on crime involves huge amounts of quantitative data, mostly drawn from government-sponsored large-scale surveys and other official statistics. Police-recorded crime statistics, collected by the Home Office from local police forces, are a major quantitative source, but most crime is not reported to the police. To overcome this, further information is obtained by victim surveys, like the annual British Crime Survey, and self-report studies, like the *Offending, Crime and Justice Survey*. These all combine to give a fuller statistical pattern of the extent of recorded crime, offending and victimization in society, and might be regarded as a form of *triangulation*, as police-recorded crime can be checked against figures obtained from victims and offenders.

As many of these statistics are collected on a regular basis, they are effectively *longitudinal* surveys, and help to build up a picture of trends over time. The limitations of official crime statistics were discussed earlier in this chapter, but victim surveys and self-report studies also have problems.

The British Crime Survey (BCS)

The BCS is an annual victimization survey, using a representative sample of around (in 2007–8) 47,000 adults living in private households. It uses face-to-face interviews, and has a response rate of around 75 per cent. Respondents are asked about their experiences of crime and crime-related incidents in the previous 12 months, and about other issues like their perceptions of the police, the criminal justice system, crime and anti-social behaviour. The survey includes property crimes such as vehicle-related thefts and burglary, and personal crimes such as assaults. Along with police recorded crime statistics, the BCS is a major source of evidence used by the Home Office and other policy-makers to track trends in crime and tackle crime prevention.

Victim surveys

Victim surveys ask the public whether they have been victims of crime, whether or not they reported it to the police. They help to overcome the problem of offences not reported to or recorded by the police, and they provide insights into the victims of crime. They do have a number of weaknesses or limitations:

1   People may exaggerate, or lie, perhaps because of a desire to impress researchers or be dramatic.

2   People may forget they were victimized, particularly the more trivial incidents, or forget *when* they were victimized. In an annual survey like the BCS, errors may arise if victims think incidents occurred outside the time period (the previous 12 months) covered by the survey, even if they were in it, or report incidents outside the time period.

3   People may not realize they have been the victims of a crime, nor that what happened to them was actually a criminal act. For example, in the case of white-collar and corporate crimes, they may not realize that have been duped, 'conned' or sold dangerous products.

4   They often don't include all crimes. The BCS, for example, surveys households and excludes commercial premises and, therefore, business crime, shops and fraud.

5   As with all surveys, there is the issue of whether the survey is representative, and therefore whether the findings can be generalized to the whole population. The BCS, for example, excludes commercial premises and the under-16s (though younger age groups were being considered for inclusion in 2009).

6   Victims may feel embarrassment or guilt at admitting to being a victim, such as in the case of sexual offences or domestic violence. Sexual offences are under-reported in the BCS for this reason.

7   Crimes without victims, like drug offences or white-collar crimes like bribery and corruption and fraud, where both parties have something to lose, are not likely to be recorded.

Self-report studies

Self-report studies are surveys that ask people to 'own up' to their offending and tell researchers what offences they have committed, whether or not they were caught. An example is the Home Office's *Offending Crime, and Justice Survey,* of which more details are given in an activity below. They have both strengths and weaknesses or limitations.

Strengths

- they provide information on the characteristics of offenders not reported to or caught by the police, and offences not recorded by them;
- they help to find out about victimless crimes like fraud, bribery and corruption or illegal drug use;
- they enable the study of patterns of offending and the factors associated with them;
- they enable the identification of changes in the pattern of offending, if they are repeated over time.

Weaknesses and limitations

- offenders may exaggerate, understate or lie about the number of crimes they've committed, perhaps because of a desire to impress researchers or be dramatic – the truthfulness and accuracy of responses is a major issue in any self-report survey;

- offenders may not own up to some offences, particularly more serious ones, and especially those with a strong social stigma, like child abuse or paedophilia – this means such surveys tend to over-emphasize more minor or trivial offences, like vandalism/criminal damage;
- those who live more chaotic lifestyles, probably like many young offenders, and those who are persistent, prolific and serious offenders are the least likely to participate in such surveys.

The points considered above all raise questions about the *reliability, validity* and *representativeness* of quantitative data in providing a true picture of the extent of crime and deviance.

Qualitative data

While quantitative data is widely used in crime research, a wide range of other research methods are also used, particularly for non-criminal deviance, a number of which try to provide more qualitative data. These are often used to explore what lies beneath statistics, to check whether the statistics are providing a valid or true picture of what they claim to show – another form of triangulation to check findings. Interpretivists also use them to gain insights and understanding of the world of those defined as deviant or criminal. As seen with Atkinson's suicide research, those adopting a more interpretivist approach use methods like in-depth unstructured interviews, participant and non-participant observation, and the study of personal documents and diaries to gain insights into what criminal and deviant behaviour means to those involved, and to show how statistics like those on suicide are not 'facts' but social constructions. Interpretivists have undertaken various participant observation studies, using covert and overt methods, to explore forms of deviance. The insights gained through classic participant observation research, such as Humphreys' (1970) study of the gay subculture at a time when homosexuality was a stigmatized and illegal activity and Patrick's (1973) study of a Glasgow gang, may have been very difficult to achieve by other methods. Those being studied may have refused to cooperate or may have changed their behaviour, undermining the validity of the information gained.

Participant observation is rarely used in government-funded research, but even 'official' research increasingly draws on a range of more qualitative methods, including unstructured face-to-face or telephone interviews, group interviews and focus groups to gain more insight.

Ethical issues

Ethical issues, regarding the morality of research, are always of great concern in any research, but crime and deviance, in particular, carry personal risks for both researcher and those being researched. For example, researchers may find themselves torn between a responsibility to protect an offender with whom they have developed a relationship of trust, and their responsibilities as a citizen to uphold the law, protect victims or report serious offences. Similarly, victims of crime may be depressed or angry at their victimization, and are often quite vulnerable, with heightened fears of crime. Sociological researchers may risk causing anxiety by opening old wounds that victims prefer to forget. Offenders may find researchers intrusive or personally threatening. Sociological research in the area of deviance will face great difficulties if those assisting in research find themselves 'outed' by sociologists in the local press as gay, perpetrators or victims of domestic violence, burglars, drug-users and so on. So care and sensitivity is needed in such research.

Activity

Either working alone, or sharing them out between your class, for each group listed below:

1 Identify a research hypothesis or aim you wish to find answers to.
2 Suggest how you might go about selecting a representative group to study – what sampling method might you use, if this is necessary for your hypothesis or aim?
3 Suggest *two* methods you might use to collect quantitative data, explain *how* you might collect it and what information you might expect to find.
4 Suggest *two* methods you might use to collect qualitative data, and explain *how* you might collect it and what information you might expect to find.
5 For each of the four methods you have identified, identify two strengths and two weaknesses or problems, and how you might overcome them.
6 Explain for each method how valid or reliable or both the findings might be, giving reasons for your answer.
7 Identify any ethical difficulties you might encounter, and suggest ways of overcoming them.

The groups

- serving prisoners
- victims of domestic violence
- illegal drug-users
- coroners

Two examples of research

The Offending, Crime and Justice Survey (OCJS)

The OCJS is a Home Office longitudinal, self-report survey of young people aged from 10 to 25 in England and Wales. It aims to discover the attitudes of young people to the criminal justice system and the extent of their victimization, but especially the extent of their offending, anti-social behaviour and illegal drug-use. The survey uses computer-based interviews and self-completion questionnaires. The interviews on less sensitive issues, such as the characteristics of the interviewee, their attitudes to the criminal justice system and the extent of their victimization, are conducted by the interviewer reading questions from a laptop and entering the respondent's answers.

For sensitive questions, such as those concerning anti-social behaviour, drug-use and other criminal offending behaviour, the interviewer gives the respondent the laptop. The questions are either read by the young person on the computer screen, or pre-recorded and listened to through headphones (to help overcome problems of illiteracy). The young person then enters his or her own answers, unaided by the interviewer.

Activity

With reference to the OCJS described above:

1 Identify two methods that were used.
2 Give three reasons why these methods might have been used.
3 Identify two possible difficulties with using each method.
4 Identify and explain the advantages and disadvantages of two other methods that might have been used to gather information about offending by young people.
5 Suggest *two* reasons why questions on offending by young people might not produce valid answers.
6 Suggest *two* reasons why sensitive questions about young people's offending were recorded via a self-completion questionnaire on a laptop, unaided by the interviewer.
7 Identify *two* steps that the researchers should take in investigating offending by young people to show they were aware of ethical issues in conducting such research.
8 The Home Office notes, in the OCJS survey: 'The accuracy of information obtained … depends on respondents' ability to understand questions, their ability to recall events accurately, and their willingness to provide complete, honest and accurate responses.' What steps would you take to try to overcome such problems, particularly given the survey covers respondents as young as age 10?

Bouncers: Violence and Governance in the Night-Time Economy

This research was a case study carried out by Hobbs et al. (2003), who explored the world of doormen (commonly called 'bouncers') at clubs, bars and pubs in venues around the UK. It examined how the leisure industry had taken over after-dark city spaces in a rapidly developing and changing night-time economy. It used observations and interviews in an ethnographic study of the changing world of the bouncers, and the strategies of violence they developed and employed to police the night-time economy.

The research involved a nine-month-long covert participant observation study, with one of the team working as a bouncer. Three of the team trained as bouncers to build up background knowledge and understanding. Interviews were carried out with bouncers, police, local authority personnel, trainers, venue managers, licensees and other key personnel. Thirty interviews were formal and transcribed (written down word for word), a questionnaire was sent out to bouncers, and a large number of informal interviews were carried out. The researchers accompanied police officers on various late night patrols, and they also examined police records and documents.

Activity

With reference to the research described above:

1 Identify and briefly explain two advantages and two disadvantages of using covert participant observation in studying bouncers.
2 Suggest reasons why participant observation might produce more valid information about the world of bouncers than non-participant observation or structured interviews.
3 What methods were used in this research?
4 Which methods do you think added reliability to the research and which added validity?
5 Suggest reasons why a variety of methods were used.

CHAPTER SUMMARY

After studying this chapter you should be able to:

- identify a range of agencies of social control, and how they seek to ensure social conformity;

- identify and explain how crime and deviance are socially constructed;

- explain the role of the mass media in constructing perceptions of crime and deviance, generating moral panics and amplifying deviance;

- outline and criticize non-sociological theories of crime and deviance, and explain how sociological approaches differ from them;

- explain and evaluate the following theories of crime and deviance: functionalist, strain, subcultural, control, Marxist and neo-Marxist, including the New Criminology, interactionist (labelling), Left Realism, Right Realism and rational choice, feminist and postmodernist;

- describe the pattern and trends in crime shown in official statistics, and provide and evaluate a range of explanations for patterns of offending in relation to age, gender, social class, ethnicity and locality;

- describe and explain the nature of white-collar and corporate crime, and why they are under-represented in crime statistics;

- explain how crime statistics are socially constructed, and why apparent increases in recorded crime might be deceptive;

- examine, with examples, how globalization affects crime;

- explain, with examples, what is meant by state crime, environmental crime and human rights crime;

- identify and explain patterns of victimization by gender, age, ethnicity and social class;

- identify and evaluate strategies for controlling and preventing crime, including the theories behind them: Left and Right Realism, rational choice and situational crime prevention, and displacement theory;

- describe and evaluate the different theoretical and methodological approaches to the study of suicide;

- identify and discuss the links between sociological theories and methods in the study of crime and deviance, including the limitations of quantitative methods like the use of official statistics, victim surveys and self-report studies.

KEY TERMS

corporate crime	hegemonic masculinity	secondary deviance	techniques of
crime	marginality	situational deviance	neutralization
delinquency	master status	social control	victimology
deviance	moral entrepreneur	social exclusion	white-collar crime
deviancy amplification	moral panic	social integration	
deviant career	moral regulation	societal deviance	
folk devils	primary deviance	status frustration	
Gross Domestic Product	sanctions	tautology	

EXAM QUESTIONS

SECTION A: CRIME AND DEVIANCE

Answer **all** the questions from this section
You are advised to spend approximately 45 minutes on Question 1
You are advised to spend approximately 30 minutes on Question 2
You are advised to spend approximately 45 minutes on Question 3

Time allowed: 2 hours   **Total for this section: 90 marks**

1 Read **Item A** below and answer parts (a) and (b) that follow.

Item A

White-collar crimes are offences committed by people in the course of their middle-
class occupations. These include offences such as bribery and corruption in government
and business, fiddling expenses, professional misconduct, fraud and embezzlement.
Such crimes are substantially under-represented in official statistics. Many white-collar
offences are seen as victimless, or victims may not be aware of any harm. Victims' lack   5
of awareness and the invisibility and complexity of white-collar offences means they
have a relatively low rate of detection and prosecution. Obtaining evidence means that
offences are difficult to prosecute, and white-collar criminals, if caught, generally get
more lenient treatment in the criminal justice process than working-class offenders.
Some suggest this is related to the class and status of offenders. The impression gained   10
from the official statistics, that most crime is committed by the working class, may
therefore be quite misleading.

(a) Examine the reasons why white-collar crimes are under-represented in official crime statistics.   *(12 marks)*
(b) Assess the usefulness of realist theories for an understanding of crime and deviance in contemporary society.   *(21 marks)*

2   This question requires you to **apply** your knowledge and understanding of sociological
research methods to the study of this **particular** issue in crime and deviance.
Read **Item B** below and answer parts (a) and (b) that follow.

Item B

The British Crime Survey is a large annual victim survey of a representative sample
of people aged 16 and over living in private households in England and Wales. It asks
questions about people's experiences and perceptions of crime, and includes questions
on people's attitudes towards crime-related topics, such as anti-social behaviour, the
police and the criminal justice system. Some suggest that this provides the most reli-   5
able measure of the extent of victimization and of national trends over time, as it is not
affected by whether the public report crime or by changes to the way in which the police
record crime.

(TURN OVER)

Police-recorded crime statistics are those supplied by the police to the Home Office. They cover crimes that are reported to and recorded by the police. They provide a meas-   10 ure of trends in well-reported crimes and also the less common but more serious crimes, and provide data on small areas.

Source: Adapted from *Crime in England and Wales, 2007–8*, Home Office

(a) Identify and briefly explain:
  (i) **one** problem of using self-report studies to study the extent of crime.   *(3 marks)*
  (ii) **two** problems of studying crime by interviewing police officers about their perceptions of criminals.   *(6 marks)*

(b) Using material from **Item B** and elsewhere, assess the strengths and limitations of official statistics as a means of investigating the extent of crime in society.   *(15 marks)*

3   'Sociology can and should be value-free.' To what extent do sociological arguments and evidence support this view ?   *(33 marks)*

Stratification and Differentiation

PAMELA LAW

Contents

7 Stratification and Differentiation

- The concept of power
- Theories of stratification
- The bases for differentiation
- Defining and measuring class
- UK social classes
- Changes in the stratification system
- Social mobility
- The persistence of inequality in contemporary society
- Research methods and social stratification and differentiation

The concept of power

Underlying all known systems of stratification and differentiation is the concept of power: who has it and who does not? What kind of power is it – physical, economic or social? Is it seen as legitimate or not? Physical power may involve violence or the threat of violence; economic power will involve control over scarce resources; and social power will involve some degree of acceptance of power. When power becomes accepted or legitimated, it becomes authority.

Power is found in any relationship, whether two people are involved or many. Power within the family tends to rest with parents rather than children, and often with men rather than women. Power in the wider world is held by governments and large corporations rather than individuals.

Differentiation is the way in which people perceive each other as different, whereas stratification means using those perceived differences as a basis for power or authority. The concepts of stratification and differentiation have been crucial since sociologists began the study of society. In recent decades, it has been fashionable in the UK to deny that stratification or social difference are important. However, research undertaken by the Department of Transport in 2008 showed that children under the age of 16 in the poorest areas of the UK are 4.5 times more likely to be killed and injured on the roads than those living in the richest areas. It would seem that income differences and poverty, at least, are still vitally important.

Theories of stratification

Many theories of stratification were written a long time ago, but that does not detract from their relevance to today's society – many of the arguments described here are currently being reiterated by politicians.

Functionalism

Nearly all sociological theories accept that stratification exists in society. However, they do not agree about the basis of that stratification. Functionalists see stratification as being based on a **meritocracy**, meaning those who are at each level in the system deserve to be there because of innate abilities. Those at the top are superior in some way to those below them. This leads functionalists to see stratification as inevitable and necessary for the smooth running of society.

> **Meritocracy** is a social system in which rewards are allocated on the basis of merit or ability.

Functional necessity of stratification

Davis and Moore (1945) suggest that society needs to ensure that the right people are motivated to fill certain positions. They argue:

* that certain jobs are more important for society;
* that these jobs will require great talent or training;
* that not everybody has these talents or is prepared to undergo the necessary training.

Therefore, in order for these functionally important jobs to be done, those people who are prepared to do them must be rewarded by:

* material goods/access to scarce resources;
* extra leisure and pleasure;
* increased self-respect or status.

A position or job does not have great power and prestige just because it has a great income; rather, it has a high income because it is functionally important and the skilled people to fill it are very scarce. This argument is currently used by highly paid managers to justify their pay. If a job is functionally important but easy to fill (e.g. dustmen are important for public health but require little training), then high rewards are not needed. However, if a position is important and needs training (e.g. a doctor) then the rewards must be great to persuade the right people to undergo the training.

Criticisms of Davis and Moore

From within the functionalist school of thought, Tumin (1953) suggests that Davis and Moore are wrong for a number of reasons:

1   Some positions are functionally more important than they may appear to be in Davis and Moore's system. For example, in the 1900s, mathematicians were not highly regarded, yet, without their work, space exploration would not have occurred, and the Internet would not exist.

2   It is wrong to suggest that only a limited number of people have the necessary talent for important jobs. No society has ever known how great a pool of talent it has. Education systems are unequal, with children from higher classes doing disproportionately better than anyone else. The system of stratification itself prevents the pool of talent being larger

3   Training is not a 'sacrifice' that needs rewarding. The costs are usually paid by parents or the state, and being a student can be pleasurable.

4   People do not need to be promised financial rewards in order to be persuaded to undertake training: money is not the only motivator. Not enough is known about the human psyche to assume that money and status are the only ways to reward people.

5   Far from being functional, Tumin argues that stratification may be dysfunctional because:

   - it limits the possibility of developing the full range of talent in a society;
   - it limits the expansion of a society that might occur if there was equality of opportunity;
   - it provides the elite group with enough power to dominate the ideology of their society and stifle change;
   - it limits the creative potential of many individuals;
   - it makes people feel less important to society thus giving them less motivation to participate in society.

Tumin therefore concludes that stratification is not uniformly functional in guaranteeing that the most important jobs are filled by the most competent people.

Functionalist writings, on the whole, suggest that stratification systems like those of industrialized nations are essentially meritocratic and open societies. Functionalism is not concerned with explaining differentiation on the basis of ethnicity or disability, although stratification by sex is seen as inevitable, as will be discussed on page 530.

Activity

1   In your own words, describe the main points of Davis and Moore's argument.
2   From your own experience do you think that Tumin's criticisms are valid? Give reasons for your answer, or examples from your experience.
3   Can you think of other criticisms of Davis and Moore? Explain your answers/criticisms.
4   Can you think of any criticisms of Tumin? Again, explain your answer/criticisms.

Can training be considered a sacrifice? What positive aspects of professional training might Davis and Moore have overlooked in claiming that high salaries and status are rewards necessary to persuade people to undertake professional qualifications?

Marxism

Marx saw the basis of all stratification systems as being linked to the ownership and control of the means of production. In the past, this meant control of land, water or other scarce resources. Since the Industrial Revolution, it has meant ownership and control of manufacturing and the production of essential supplies. Society is divided into two groups: the bourgeoisie and the proletariat. The **bourgeoisie**, a minority group, own all primary production (such as mines, land, forests, etc.), the factories, and the banks and financial institutions. They employ the **proletariat** to work for them and they pay the minimum needed to survive, selling the goods produced by the proletariat for a profit, thus growing richer and richer. (For more on the Marxist theory of stratification, see pages 344–6.)

> In Marxist theory, the **bourgeoisie** is the class of owners of the means of production.

Neo-Marxism

Empirical evidence shows that there are different levels of pay within the proletariat, so Marxist ideas have been modified, but the basic premise still remains. Neo-Marxists talk of different groups such as the 'petit bourgeoisie', the intellectual classes and the underclass, but, at heart, the distinction still remains: a few individuals own the means of production; the rest, the majority, do not. Classical Marxists regard the division of the non-bourgeoisie into separate groups as an example of false **class-consciousness**, because emphasizing the differences between, say, skilled workers and teachers hides the fact that, essentially, they are all members of the proletariat and, as such, powerless compared to the bourgeoisie.

> **Proletariat** is the social class of workers who have to work for wages, as they do not own the means of production.

> **Class-consciousness** is an awareness in members of a social class of their real interests.

Exploitation

Wright (1978) suggested that a better distinction between the classes might be exploitation: one class exploits the other. This allows distinctions to be made between different types of bourgeoisie, from the owner who does not work at all but employs many people, to the one-man business. The important point about exploitation is that the class *doing* the exploiting would be harmed if those *being* exploited were to stop working. Wright envisages a situation where there is a gradation of classes dependent upon the skills and negotiating powers of different groups in the acquisition of scarce or desirable resources.

However such distinctions are difficult to apply in practice, since the owner and the small businessman cited above may in reality have little in common. Edgell (1993) claims that mere skill in negotiating for scarce resources is not, in itself, an exploitative relationship.

Activity

Read the following extract from *The Communist Manifesto*, by Karl Marx and Friedrich Engels:

> Modern industry has established a world market . . . [and] the bourgeoisie cannot exist without constantly revolutionising production, and the relations of society. Constant . . . disturbance of all social conditions, everlasting uncertainty and agitation distinguish the bourgeois epoch from all earlier ones. All old prejudices and opinions are swept away; all new-formed ideas are outdated before they become fixed . . . All that is solid melts into air . . . and man is, at last, compelled to face with sober senses his real conditions of life and his relations with his kind.
>
> The need of a constantly expanding market for his products chases the bourgeoisie over the whole surface of the globe. He must nestle everywhere, settle everywhere, establish connections everywhere. Through this exploitation of the world market the bourgeoisie has given a cosmopolitan character to production and consumption in every country. . . . All old-established national industries have been destroyed or are being destroyed . . . in place of the old wants, satisfied by the production of the country, we find new wants, requiring for their satisfaction the products of distant lands and climes . . . we have the universal interdependence of nations. And as in material, so also in intellectual production. The intellectual creations of individual nations become common property . . . and from the numerous national and local literatures there arises world literature.

Slightly adapted from *The Communist Manifesto* of 1848.

Now answer the following questions:

1 Is there any evidence to support the view expressed here about the growth and effect of monopoly capitalism? Write a short essay giving evidence for and against. (It might help to consider the growth and power of transnational companies, such as Coca-Cola, the Disney Corporation, CNN, HSBC, the Volkswagen Group and Toyota Cars when looking for evidence which might support the view. Evidence against might be provided by finding a growth of small independent companies.)

2 This kind of evidence is referred to by sociologists as 'empirical evidence'. List the advantages and disadvantages of such data for sociologists.

Classic Marxist theories tend to ignore differentiation on the basis of sex/gender, ethnicity, disability and age, which has led to sub-groups such as Marxist feminists to explain some of these aspects of stratification. These will be discussed on page 552.

Marxism suggests that, by human action, it is possible to end stratification and create equality for all. Because Marx believed that all stratification systems are based on the economy, until there is a change in the nature of the economy, stratification into classes is inevitable. But the economic base could be altered if the subordinate class, the proletariat, became aware of their position and acted together to change society. This could only happen if they became class-conscious, that is, totally aware of their own position. But this is unlikely to happen, as all the institutions of society serve the interests of the bourgeoisie – directly, through laws on property ownership, or indirectly through ideology. Because the dominant ideology states that capitalism is best, class-consciousness is more likely to be found among the bourgeoisie than among the proletariat. The bourgeoisie will realize that their best interests lie in acting together to keep wages down and increase profits. Although the proletariat forms a single class, they are blinded by the divisions within the group and cannot see their true position. As a result the proletariat never acts in a concerted way as a class for itself – it suffers from **false consciousness**.

Marx thought that the unity of the bourgeoisie would eventually be destroyed as each individual strove to be bigger and better than the rest. Competition leads to a monopoly, the monopolist would become over-powerful and the inequalities of the system would become so obvious that members of the proletariat class would realize their true position and revolution would occur. Thus, from a Marxist perspective, stratification may not be totally inevitable, but it will take a great struggle and requires action to remove it. In more recent years, neo-Marxists such as Althusser (1971) have concentrated on explaining why revolution has not occurred, examining the role of the state and other institutions in maintaining false consciousness through both **ideological** and **repressive state apparatuses**.

> **False consciousness** is the failure by members of a social class to recognize their real interests.

> **Ideological state apparatuses** are agencies that spread the dominant ideology and justify the power of the dominant social class.

> The **repressive state apparatus** refers to those parts of the state concerned with mainly repressive, physical means of keeping a population in line, such as the army, police, courts and prisons.

Schools and nurseries are examples of agencies within the educational ideological state apparatus, a method by which states maintain control over the population by teaching children certain values. If a child fails to learn accepted social codes at school, then later in life agencies of a repressive state apparatus, such as the justice system, might be needed to control their deviant behaviour.

Weberian theory

Max Weber suggests that stratification is somewhat more complicated than Marx indicated. Weber suggests that there is a need to distinguish between class, which has an economic base; status, which is based on esteem; and party, which is based on access to and use of power.

All three aspects of stratification are related to aspects of power. By power, Weber meant the chance of one person, or a group of people, realizing their own will in a communal action, even when the rest of the population might not want the same thing. He distinguished between political power, which is realized through party; prestige power, which is realized through status; and economic power which is realized through class.

Class is the market situation of a person. If someone has a rare skill or one that is in much demand, then that person's worth to society will be greater than that of an unskilled person. For example, a highly trained doctor will command more money in the marketplace than an unskilled labourer unless there is a surplus of doctors, and few unskilled workers. If that situation were to arise, then the laws of supply and demand would mean that doctors would be paid less and unskilled workers more. Different classes have different **life chances**, which are described by Weber (1947) as access to certain necessary or desirable goods and services, such as food, healthcare, police protection and status.

Status is honour accorded to certain individuals or groups. A person may have a low economic value but high social status. For example, a postman may be a Justice of the Peace (magistrate), and thus have status; religious leaders often earn relatively little money, but are accorded prestige by the general public.

A political **party**, or organization for the pursuit of power, exists in any and every group. Wherever there are two or more people, then there will be a struggle for power. The amount of political power exercised by individuals is often linked to both their class and their status.

In many ways, the Weberian view of class underlies the model of class used by British governments since 1901 to classify the population. The Registrar General devised a schedule of class based on a mixture of occupation, education and social status, as well as income. This will be discussed in detail later when looking at how to measure class (see page 543).

Life chances are chances to obtain those things defined as desirable and to avoid those things defined as undesirable in a society.

Status is the amount of prestige or social importance a person has in the eyes of other members of a group or society.

Party is a term used by Weber to describe any group of individuals who organize for the pursuit of power based on their shared backgrounds, aims or intersts.

Activity

1 Identify and explain two ways in which Weber's view of class differs from that of Marx.
2 Explain in your own words what is meant by both 'status' and 'party' as used by Weber.
3 From your own experience, give two examples where people's class position and their status position are widely different – for example, high status/low income or vice versa.
4 Assess the usefulness of the Weberian distinction between class, status and party in describing the stratification system in modern Britain. Write your answer as a short essay of two or three pages.

Feminism

Feminism developed as a response to what were seen as **malestream** tendencies in sociology pre-1970. It was suggested that studies concentrated on men and assumed that what was true for men was true for everybody. Feminists said that women's social experience was different from that of men, that women were treated as inferior and therefore saw life differently from men. Some feminists (radical feminists) subscribed to the view that 'all men are bad', while others (marxist/socialist feminists) suggested that class elements might be involved and that only 'some men are bad'; yet another group (liberal feminists) suggested that men are merely misguided and that society could be changed.

Feminism is sometimes described as falling into four main types: radical, Marxist/ socialist, liberal and black. This distinction is not always helpful and many feminists cross boundaries, but all consider the concept of patriarchy.

> **Malestream** is a word coined by feminists to describe the type of sociology that concentrates on men, is mostly carried out by men and then assumes that the findings can be applied to women as well.

Patriarchy

Patriarchy is the belief that society is dominated by men and that all institutions work for the benefit of men, rather than for the benefit of all. Patriarchy is based on the belief that men are superior to women. In order for this idea to survive, it needs to be widely held as 'what men believe to be real, is real in its consequences'. Most people would now agree that patriarchy/male superiority is merely a belief and not a biological fact. Millett (1970) and Walby (1990) have written in detail about patriarchy and the dimensions of patriarchy

In *Sexual Politics* (1970), Millett explored the idea that politics occurs in every aspect of life and that patriarchy is the politics of the relationships between men and women. Men may be biologically stronger, but the strength of patriarchy lies in ideological control. Both sexes are socialized into their superior/inferior roles and the family is a key institution in this respect. As the main socialisers, women are responsible for the continuance of patriarchal ideas. They are born to be inferior in this system and even class cannot completely cut across it. Women of all classes are subordinate to the men in their class (though they may be superior to men from a lower class). Other agents of socialization help to maintain this situation. Education is especially important because girls were treated differently from boys and were thus fitted for different parts of the workforce, which were, and still are, low paid. Millett's book was written before the Equal Pay Act (1970) had fully come into force, and there has been some change since then. Millett suggested that men's patriarchal power over women is psychological, and ultimately physical. Few women commit sexual offences, and male violence against women (and other men) is much greater than female violence.

For Walby, the key elements of patriarchy are pay inequality, unequal household roles, sexuality, male violence and the state itself. Despite legislation, women's wages still lag behind men's, even in the same occupation, and women are still less likely to be found in positions of power and influence. However, the position is gradually improving: the Welsh Assembly has more women than men, and women are now reaching high-level posts in medicine and surgery.

> **Patriarchy** refers to power and authority held by males.

How might patriarchy be experienced differently by women of different ages and ethnic groups?

Work within the household remains largely gendered, although there is slow change. Male violence is still much in evidence. Walby argues that legislation like the Sex Discrimination Act (1975) has tried to reduce patriarchy, but that many state policies still suggest that women and men have different roles – for example, between maternity and paternity rights after the birth or adoption of a child. Statutory maternity pay for women far outweighs the ten days of statutory paternity pay allowed to men. This would suggest that it is the role of the woman to be the main carer for a child.

Walby points out that patriarchy is experienced differently by different groups of women. Usually, younger women experience it less than their mothers and grandmothers, though there are class variations here; some ethnic groups experience it more than others. So patriarchy should now be seen as non-universal in its dimensions.

Radical feminism

This strand of feminism is seen as being most 'anti-men', though this is not necessarily true. Firestone (1972) argues that women's biology is the basis for their inequality and domination by men in all societies. Because women menstruate, give birth and breastfeed, they are sometimes physically dependent on others. This dependency allows men to develop physical and psychological power and control, and men thus dominate the social world. Equality between the sexes can only occur when this psychological dominance is destroyed and the physical dependency of women is ended. Therefore, until human babies can be conceived outside the womb (now already possible) and brought to full gestation outside the mother's body, the inequality between the sexes will remain.

This theory has been criticized by other sociologists, both feminists and non-feminists, because it ignores other forms of inequality such as class and ethnicity, and fails to acknowledge that the dependency described by Firestone is both time- and society-dependent.

Ortner (1974) suggests that **culture** is the basis of differentiation between the sexes, because it is always valued more highly than biology and is controlled by men, whereas women are seen as being closer to nature because they give birth. However, Ortner fails to consider wide differences between societies and over time. There is little clear evidence that culture is always more highly prized than nature, or that women are not involved in the creation of culture. As mothers are the first point of socialization, women, it can be argued, have great control over the transmission of a society's culture and how it is shaped.

Culture is the languages, beliefs, values and norms, customs, roles, knowledge and skills which combine to make up the way of life of any society.

The connection between biology and inequality also occurs in the work of Rosaldo (1974), although she is more concerned with how biology places women within the domestic rather than the public sphere. Since most power lies in the public sphere, women are less likely to join in this aspect of social life because of being confined to the house looking after children. Again, the criticism is mostly that this is not true in all societies and that conditions change over time.

Radical feminists tend to view men and the family as 'the problem' and suggest that women cannot be free until the family structure, as it now exists, is either abolished or greatly changed.

Marxist/socialist feminism

This strand of feminism suggests that although men may sometimes be 'the problem', the class dimension is more important. Engels (1972 [1891]) suggested that in the past people lived in 'promiscuous hordes', where sexual relationships were not fixed and property passed from mother to child. As men became more determined to pass their property on to their own offspring, they began to demand fidelity from their womenfolk, thus leading to monogamous marriage and the power of men over women. Engels's theory has very little basis in known civilizations. In some societies, childless men who want to pass their property on to blood relatives give it to the children of their sisters, since, as long as a man and his sister share the same mother, the genetic link is certain, even if there is doubt about the father.

Patrilocal describes family systems in which the wife is expected to live near the husband's parents.

Coontz and Henderson (1986) attempted to link Engels's theory with other anthropological material, suggesting that patriarchy was more likely to occur in societies that were **patrilocal** rather than **matrilocal**. When a woman moved to live with her husband's family (patrilocality), she was more likely to lose control over the goods produced; as a result, men became more powerful. Most societies appear to have been patrilocal.

Matrilocal describes family systems in which the husband is expected to live near the wife's parents.

Marxist feminists see the family as playing an important part in the maintenance of capitalism because:

- the family reproduces the next generation of workers for the owners, at no cost;
- the women and children act as a brake on revolutionary ideas – the men cannot afford to strike to improve their working conditions because their families would starve while the strike lasted;
- men come home from work stressed out and angry, and the wives and children calm them down, give them a reason for continuing to work and send them back the next morning, ready for another day's labour;

- women form a reserve army of labour which can be called away from the home into paid employment when circumstances demand – for example, in times of war, or when there is a labour shortage.

Marxist feminists, however, feel that, given the right conditions and a higher level of class-consciousness, this situation can be changed to one of equality.

Liberal feminism

This strand of feminism is more optimistic about change and sees that progress has already been made, at least in the USA, the UK and Europe. Oakley's (1974a, 1974b, 1981) work falls most easily into this tradition, though elements of her work come from other traditions.

Oakley points out that the position of women varies greatly between societies and over time. Women have always worked; with the **Industrial Revolution**, married women and mothers were taken out of the paid workforce. Before this time, both men and women worked inside and outside the home producing agricultural goods or cloth. During the 1800s, more and more people – men, women and children – began to work in factories, moving to towns from the countryside. But the Factory Act of 1819 banned children under the age of 9 from being employed, which meant that women were more likely to have to stay at home to care for them, leading to their primary role becoming that of 'housewife'. Thus the family became reliant on the wages of the husband alone. Historically, this transfer of financial power to the husband was relatively short-lived, lasting only three or four generations, but the psychological effects are still being felt, as today's women are still socialized into the role of housewife as practised by their mothers and grandmothers. Whether their own daughters and granddaughters will take up this role is less certain.

Since the end of the Second World War in 1945, the position of women has been ambiguous. Oakley suggests that government policy and social norms imply that married women's primary role is to care for her children, but that, at the same time, such women should work and help to support the family financially. Women in the UK therefore have a dual burden.

Liberal feminists suggest that the differences between men and women have lessened as a result of legislation such as the Equal Pay Act (1970) and the Sex Discrimination Act (1975) and may improve further as more laws come into force. Obviously, these Acts are now 40 years old, and critics have pointed out that women are still paid less than men and treated as of lesser value. The 'glass ceiling' prevents women from reaching top jobs. Issues such as the equalization of the age of retirement will also have a profound effect. This, at least, will treat men and women as the same, although for women this has meant that their age of retirement has been raised.

There is optimism that gender stratification could be eradicated. But legislation does not change attitudes quickly. In defence of liberal feminists, it must be said that the life of most women in the UK has improved since the 1950s; this may not be true worldwide. This universal dimension has been addressed by Oakley in her book *Gender on Planet Earth* (2002), which suggests that patriarchy has far-reaching

---

The **Industrial Revolution** describes the process by which the UK developed in the 1800s from an agricultural society into a society based on manufacturing.

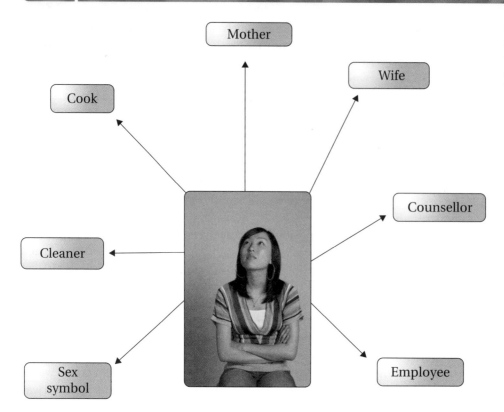

Figure 7.1 The multiple roles that patriarchy attaches to women

consequences for the planet as a whole. She maintains that patriarchal ways of thinking and the desire to maintain patriarchal power lie behind most of the violence in the world and underpin most of the ideologies which she describes as delusional, such as postmodernism, psychoanalysis and even economics. Economics is especially delusional since it concentrates on such aspects as Gross Domestic Product (GDP) and ignores all the unpaid labour, mostly undertaken by women, that allows the workforce to be able to work at all and thus produce the very thing economists measure.

Black feminism

Black feminism developed first in the USA as a response to what it saw as the **ethnocentrism** of feminism as a whole. Others have criticized feminism for being a middle-class concern, and black feminists also accuse it of ignoring the problems faced by ethnic minorities in the US and elsewhere. Black feminists argue that many of their problems have stemmed first and foremost from having to fight against racism, which blinded them to the problems they were facing as women in a patriarchal world. It was, therefore, essential to unpick these strands and understand in detail the forces that contributed to black women being at the very end of the queue when the good things in life are handed out.

Mirza (1992) has argued that although black British women suffer many of the same problems as white British women, they have the added dimension of racism to contend with and thus their experience of life is different.

Ethnocentrism is a view of the world in which other cultures are seen through the eyes of one's own culture, with a devaluing of the others.

Black feminism is criticized for emphasizing the differences rather than concentrating on the shared problems of all women. It is a similar argument to that levelled against those who distinguish between the different classes in feminist analysis. These criticisms ignore the perceived, if not real, differences between the experiences of different ethnic groups and different classes.

Activity

1 Explain in your own words what is meant by 'patriarchy'.
2 From your own experience, describe three occasions/events/situations that might suggest that patriarchy still exists.
3 From your own experience, describe three occasions/events/situations that might suggest patriarchy does *not* still exist.
4 From your own experience, describe the ways in which men and women are treated differently in the home, at school, at work and in the media.
5 In an essay of two or three pages, assess the extent to which sex/gender is a greater source of differentiation than class in modern Britain.

Postmodernism

Postmodernists tend to regard class and, to some extent, gender and ethnicity as concepts that are no longer relevant in modern society. These dimensions, they argue, have been replaced by an individualistic society in which consumerism and choice are the key elements. What are now important are the choices that each individual consumer makes and which give them their identity. Allegedly, this is a pick 'n' mix society, in which each person can choose their own identity by what goods they decide to buy. At the same time, with choice also comes risk.

Consumerism as a form of differentiation

Pakulski and Waters (1996) discuss the decline of group solidarity, and the way in which individualism is now paramount and stratification is based on lifestyles. Individuals now belong to many different groups at different times, and hence have a multifaceted identity and are able to redefine themselves by changing consumption patterns. One of the reasons Pakulski and Waters give for this shift from class identity to a consumer identity is that wealth has become progressively more equally distributed and, because of the growth of education, there is now what they call a 'market meritocracy', based on an ability to buy a consumer identity.

However, it is actually not true that wealth has been redistributed. In the UK between 1988 and 2006, wealth remained in the hands of the same small proportion of the population and may even have become more concentrated within that group. Pakulski and Waters's argument concerning the growth of education and professional skills leading to a 'market meritocratic' relationship is somewhat more plausible, but is still a major generalization; it might apply to Western, developed societies, but is not true across the globe.

One feature of postmodernism is that individuals are freer than ever to construct their own identities based on their consumer choices, rather than solely on features such as age, gender, ethnicity or social class.

Grusky (1996) noted that the postmodern focus on consumption is based on the idea that there has been a decline in class-based identities as conflict in the workplace has diminished, and that cultural globalization has allowed people to sample different cultures and ideas. There is now a difference between the old Weberian idea of the life chance and what is termed 'life choice'. A life chance is usually beyond the control of the individual, whereas life choice suggests individual control and the right to take risks, either unconscious or conscious. Life choice in the field of education, for example, might involve choosing to stay on at school; the risks, both positive and negative, may not be fully known to the individual, but the choice is a risk to be taken in relation to future lifestyle, earning capacity, etc.

Objective and subjective differentiation

Postmodernists have explored consumerism in depth, and their writings concentrate on the subjective aspects of differentiation, especially class, rather than the objective aspects. Writers such as Strinati (1995) are concerned with the image people project through the choices they make as consumers. Someone who wears designer labels and drives an Audi Coupé is projecting an image of their worth which is different from someone who travels on the bus wearing clothes from the market stall. It would seem that the first is of higher status than the second and is also more likely to have more wealth or income. Postmodernists suggest that consumer choice has now overridden the old divisions based on gender, ethnicity and class, and the image an individual projects is accepted by the rest of the society in which he or she lives.

Do individuals really have such power? Does the rest of society accept the self-image that individuals choose to portray? The concrete reality of class, income and wealth cannot be so easily overcome. That is to say, although consumer choice says a lot about the subjective aspects of social differentiation, it cannot completely overshadow the objective dimensions of class, gender and ethnicity. The image that one chooses to project should at least be plausible to the audience – that is, society at large. The old-age pensioner is not only probably unlikely to be able to support the lifestyle associated with driving a Porsche, but such a projected image would not be plausible to the onlookers. Society reflects back not only the actors' view of themselves but also the perceptions of those surrounding them.

A plausible image, or a mismatch of stereotypes?

Activity

1 Describe in your own words what is meant by consumer choice.
2 From your own experience, how far do you think it is true that consumer choice is a basis for differentiating between people? Give reasons for your answer.
3 Decide what methods sociologists might use to test the theory that consumer choice has replaced class in differentiating between groups.
4 How might this be done using one qualitative method and one quantitative method?
5 List the advantages and disadvantages of the methods chosen.

The bases for differentiation

People have always distinguished themselves from others in a variety of ways. When meeting someone for the first time, people tend to classify them at once as either taller/shorter, more beautiful/ugly, or as having some other characteristic that makes them either like or different from themselves. Physical attributes are the most common way of differentiating people, though other characteristics might be used too. In this way subjective judgements are made and often this subjective view becomes an objective inequality, or, as W. I. Thomas put it in 1928: 'What men believe to be real is real in its consequences.' When two people, A and B, meet, A will begin to act in ways that match what B instinctively feels about them, or A will begin to act out his or her beliefs about B. This might mean treating B with respect if A thinks of B as superior, or with disdain if A thinks of B as inferior. Person B will then respond in an appropriate way. In a short time, both A and B will be convinced that their original assessment of each other was correct.

In many ways, it is irrelevant whether the differences are real or not. It is the perception of the differences that is important, and the way in which people respond to these ideas. If women, for example, are constantly told they are inferior, they may begin to believe themselves to be inferior and teach their children that sons are more important than daughters. As the children believe this, it becomes the truth that boys are more important than girls and hence the differentiation becomes reality. The same can be said of any group perceived of as inferior or superior. Over time the group itself may come to believe that its status is objective and justified.

The bases for differentiation may be physical attributes, such as:

- sex
- age
- ethnicity
- health and disability

Or they might be non-physical attributes, such as:

- education
- sexuality and sexual orientation
- religion
- economic bases – access to wealth/power/class

Stratification is the systematic ordering of differentiations such as those listed above, so that some groups are seen as more important or as having more power than others. Members of each particular layer or stratum will have a common identity and culture, and similar interests, lifestyles and, usually, life chances. Some stratification systems are said to be open and others closed. An **open system** is one in which it is possible to move from one social level to another (for example, in the UK it is possible for the child of a shop-worker to end up becoming a Member of Parliament). A **closed system** is one in which social position is fixed at birth, and nothing can alter it – such as the Indian caste system (see below, page 540).

Sex

This basis for differentiation appears in nearly all societies: men are seen as more powerful and important than women. Evolutionary biologists Tiger and Fox (1972) suggest that equality between the sexes is impossible, because men's genetics make them physically dominant, and they have a natural propensity to hunt, while women are predisposed to a nurturing role. However, others say that all differences between the sexes are, in fact, a product of society and can be eliminated. Cameron (2007) argues that the differences *between* men and women are much smaller than the differences *within* each of the two groups, and, therefore, it is incorrect to say that men are inherently superior. Employing a technique of **meta-analysis**, it can be shown that previous studies on differences between the sexes are unreliable. It may not be coincidental that the vast majority of the studies that argue in favour of men's natural superiority are written by men. Statistics from the United Nations estimate that 53 per cent of the total world population is female, with women doing three-quarters of the world's work but only earning 25 per cent of all earnings and holding 10 per cent of the world's wealth. In the UK, women in every economic group occupy a position below the men of that same group. Despite Equal Pay Acts, the situation remains the same.

An **open system** is a society in which it is possible for an individual to move from the social group in which he or she was born into a different social group.

A **closed system** is a society in which there is very little social mobility. Usually, members of such a society are likely to spend their whole lives in the class or group into which they were born. Status is therefore ascribed rather than achieved.

Meta-analysis a statistical technique of collating many different research findings and testing the reliability of the results by controlling the variables within each individual study.

Activity

Read the following passage taken from the UN Development Fund for Women publication, *Progress of the World's Women 2005: Women, Work and Poverty* (UNIFEM 2006):

In the last decade, the number of people living on less than $1 a day has fallen; the gender gap in primary and (to a lesser extent) secondary education has been reduced; and women enjoy greater participation in elected assemblies and state institutions. In addition, women are a growing presence in the labour market. However, the decline in overall poverty masks significant differences not only between but also within regions. Asia experienced the greatest decline in extreme poverty, followed by Latin America, but sub-Saharan Africa experienced an increase. Even where the numbers of extremely poor people have declined, notably China and India, poverty persists in different areas and social groups, reflected in rising inequalities (UN 2005). For women, progress, while steady, has been painfully slow.

Despite increased parity in primary education, disparities are still wide in secondary and tertiary education – both increasingly key to new employment opportunities. And while women's share of seats in parliament have inched up in all regions, women still hold only 16 per cent of parliamentary seats worldwide. Finally, although women have entered the paid labour force in great numbers, the result in terms of economic security is not clear. Women's access to paid employment is lower than men's in most of the developing world. Women are less likely than men to hold paid and regular jobs and more often work in the informal economy, which provides little financial security.

Today's global world is one of widening income inequality and increasing economic insecurity. Informal employment, far from disappearing, is persistent and widespread. In many places, economic growth has depended on capital-intensive production in a few sectors rather than on increasing employment opportunities, pushing more and more people into the informal economy. In others, many of the jobs generated by economic growth are not covered by legal or social protection, as labour markets are deregulated, labour standards are relaxed and employers cut costs.

Strengthening women's economic security is critical to efforts to reduce poverty and promote gender equality, and decent work is basic to economic security. Data shows that:

- the proportion of women workers engaged in informal employment is generally greater than the proportion of men workers;
- women are concentrated in the more precarious types of informal employment;
- the average earnings from these types of informal employment are too low, in the absence of other sources of income, to raise households out of poverty.

Unless efforts are made to create decent work for the global informal workforce, the world will not be able to eliminate poverty or achieve gender equality.

Now answer the following questions:

1 Name *three* things the authors see as possible solutions to the inequalities currently suffered by women.
2 What do the authors see as the main causes of the inequality suffered by women?
3 What methods might have been used to collect this data?
4 What difficulties might have been faced by researchers using the methods you have identified in question 3?

Early sociology textbooks tended to assume that the differences between the sexes were innate and biologically based, referring to differences between the **instrumental role** of male and the **expressive role** of the female as if this was unchangeable. The assumption was that men are more fitted to go out to work, and physically or mentally more able to supply economic support for the women and children in their family; women are best fitted to remain in the domestic sphere, providing emotional comfort and physical support to the man, the worker, and the children. These roles were considered to be 'natural', though proper **socialization** was needed to ensure that all boys learned to be 'men', and all girls learned to be 'women'.

However, it is now argued that socialization leads to **gender** differences, and this is the explanation for the perceived differences between men and women in today's society. Indeed, in Britain, normal gender behaviour is learned from a very early age, starting at birth.

Other societies have different gender roles for men and women from those found traditionally in Britian. In the 1930s, the anthropologist Margaret Mead (1935) examined differences among tribes in New Guinea. She discovered gender differences to be entirely social, rather than based on sex. In one tribe, women were the traders, leaving home to work, while the men stayed in the domestic sphere and reared the children. Different tribes reared their offspring to have gender expectations that were distinct from those in neighbouring tribes, and were markedly different from the norms then prevalent in the USA and Europe. Thus, Mead concluded, gender is a learned response, not an innate difference.

Instrumental role: The provider/breadwinner role in the family, often associated by functionalists with men's role in family life.

Expressive role: The nurturing, caring and emotional role, often linked by functionalists to women's biology and seen as women's 'natural' role in the family.

Socialization is the process by which people learn the accepted ways of behaving in their society.

Gender refers to the culturally created differences between men and women which are learnt through socialization.

Activity

1 Explore the ways in which girls and boys are socialized through their early childhood and how this differs between groups or over time. There may be different ways to do this:
   - short interviews with two or three parents of today's 5-year-olds, and compare their answers to the way in which you were brought up;
   - interview your parents about how they were raised and compare it to how you were raised;
   - interview parents from different classes about their childrearing practices;
   - interview parents of all-boy families and compare with the childrearing practices of parents of all-girl families;
   - interview different ethnic groups about their childrearing practices.
2 Consider the advantages and disadvantages of interviews in collecting such information.

Gender differences are complicated by the issues of both class and ethnicity. Studies on masculinity and on the rise of girl gangs and 'laddette'-type behaviour show that within each gender there are many subcultures. Swain (2007) discovered different attitudes to masculinity, sports and peer groups in three different schools which all had widely different social class intakes. Thus gender and gender expectations need to be considered alongside class when seeking to explain behaviour. The effect of gender differentiation has specific consequences for women in many fields, as can be seen from the excerpt in the box on equal rights

---

Equal rights: prejudice contributes to women earning less, says ONS

Two-thirds of the earnings divide between men and women is due to 'unobservable factors', including discrimination, and has nothing to do with lower skills or productivity, according to a government study released yesterday.

More than 30 years after the passing of the Equal Pay Act, a report from Andrew Barnard of the Office for National Statistics concluded that prejudice still meant women were taking home smaller pay packets than men doing the same job.

Barnard said that according to his model 'almost two-thirds of the wage gap is because of reasons unexplained and one-third is for reasons explained'. Discrimination was only one of the 'unexplained' factors resulting in women earning less than men. Other influences might include educational qualifications and motivation.

The report found that the gender pay gap was wider outside London. Wages in the capital tend to be higher, but the effect of not working in London is greater for women. In the south-east, for example, men earn 4% less than in London whereas women earn 7% less.

The ONS study also found a larger wage premium for men in manufacturing. 'This could be a result of women working in less skilled manufacturing positions, or could be evidence of discrimination in that sector.'

Barnard said the argument that men were benefiting in industry from being in the better paid jobs was supported by the fact that women made up 25% of those reading manufacturing-related degrees, 3% of modern apprentices in manufacturing and engineering, and 6% of professional engineers. There was also a larger wage premium for males in finance, mining and quarrying, energy and water, and agriculture and fishing.

The one area where there was a female wage premium was in the public sector.

Source: Larry Elliott, *Guardian*, 12 August 2008
Copyright: Guardian Newspapers Limited 2008

Activity

Read the excerpt presented in the box above, then answer the following questions:
1 Go to the website of the Office for National Statistics (www.ons.gov.uk) and find more recent data on comparative earnings of men and women, by class and ethnic group.
2 Are things different from the picture presented in the box?
3 How might these differences/lack of differences be explained by different feminist sociologists.

Age

Most societies distinguish between the rights of the very young, adults and the elderly. In Britain, children acquire more rights as they grow older, but as this happens they may lose some control over portions of their lives. For example, from the age of 70, motorists have to declare their medical conditions and renew their driving licence every three years. Discrimination on the basis of age, in employment and other areas, is now illegal under the Age Discrimination Regulations, which came into force in October 2006.

Age-sets

In some other societies – one example is the Zulu of South Africa – boys are assigned to an **age-set** and in this group they pass through various stages in their life. The groups all have rights and duties, and as they pass each milestone, the men within the age-set act together and look after the interests of their group. The stages include puberty, warrior-hood, the right to marry and have children, and, finally, elder statesman status. Within their age-set, men support each other, marrying the sisters of fellow members and striving to maintain the unity of the group. Such systems are dying out, but where they exist they have powerful political dimensions.

In the UK, different ages are marked by semi-ritualized responsibilities or rights, such as being allowed to smoke tobacco, drive cars, borrow money and vote.

The social construction of age

If other forms of stratification and differentiation partly rely on people's perceptions, this is certainly true of childhood, the teenage years and old age. It is said that childhood is not a biological time span, but a **social construction**. This means that what is thought of as childhood changes through time and between societies.

Childhood   Ariès (1973), writing of pre-industrial European societies, suggested that childhood consisted of a very short period of time when a child was dependent on his or her parents. After the age of 4 or 5, children were treated as small adults and took part in all aspects of life. Postman (1994) dated the emergence of childhood to the invention of the printing press and the spread of literacy among the general population. Once knowledge could be written down, rather than spread only orally, it became possible to keep information secret from certain groups, most notably from those who could not read. Postman maintains that this contributed to an idea of childhood as a time of innocence. However, the growth of the mass media, especially the Internet, is now allowing children access to knowledge far greater than that experienced by their parents at a similar age and so this notion of childhood is disappearing. Lee (2005) suggests that there has been a marketization and sexualization of children, which has made the difference between childhood and adulthood less distinct.

Teenagers   The term **teenager** to describe a separate group did not really appear until the late 1940s/early 1950s. In other societies, where age-sets exist, the transition from child to adult is mapped out with specific staging posts. This is not generally true of

An **age-set** is a group of people of a similar age, who have shared status and roles. Often, the transition from one stage of life to the next is accompanied by a rite of passage.

Social construction means the way something is created through the individual, social and cultural interpretations, perceptions and actions of people. Official statistics, notions of health and illness, deviance and suicide are all examples of social phenomena that only exist because people have constructed them and given these phenomena particular labels.

Teenagers are young people at a time of life between childhood and adulthood – in their 'teen' years. The teenager's status is often ambiguous and changes from one situation to another, which reflects the confusion felt by teenagers themselves as to their exact status.

Table 7.1: Two experiences of being a 'teenager'

19th Century	21st Century
Legal aspects	
I can work	I am still at school
Work involves a 12-hour day	If I have a job, it's only part-time
I can have sex	I can't have sex until I'm 16
I can smoke	I can't smoke until I'm 18
I can drink alcohol	I can't drink alcohol until I'm 18
I have a 50:50 chance of dying before I'm 50	I am likely to live to 80
I won't ever be able to vote	I can vote when I am 18
Social aspects	
The money I earn will never be my own	I can have my own bank account
I cannot associate with men outside of my family, and very soon it is likely my parents will choose a husband for me	I am freer to express my sexuality as I wish
If my parents are poor, I would only have had a few years of education and would have had to work from a young age	I have the right to a free education until I am 18 and I am protected from exploitative child labour by law

Western societies, where there is a grey area during which time childhood ends and adulthood begins. This period of time is not a fixed number of years, and changes in society have added to the blurring of the edges between one stage and the next. For example, the age at which sexual activity, tobacco-smoking, marriage (with parental consent) and work are permitted have all changed radically over the years, often arbitrarily. In the early nineteenth century, there was no age bar to any of these activities, except marriage; today, there are regulations concerning, for example, the age for buying cigarettes, and in many societies there is an official 'age of consent', although this varies from one country to another. Clearly, being a teenager is a changing condition.

Hobbs et al. (2003) suggested that, even as late as the 1950s, specifically teenage problems, such as binge drinking, did not occur, because drinking took place in the local pub or club, where the young, usually boys, learned to drink in a responsible fashion surrounded by relatives and workmates who had some control over their behaviour. Girls learned to drink responsibly in a similarly closed environment. However, as family sizes have declined, and local communities have been dispersed, these social constraints have disappeared and young people now learn to drink alcohol within their peer group. This, it is argued, has led to the greater incidence of binge drinking.

Old age British society tends to think of the elderly as somehow different – as less capable, likely to be frail and in need of help and support. However, it is unclear what constitutes being elderly; old age is a social construct. Consider the feisty 90-year-old who refers to 70-year-olds as 'those poor old things', but would be mortified to be included in the group him- or herself.

As the chance of long life increases, social perceptions of old age change. Novels of the 1930s refer to 60-year-olds as 'old', but most of today's 60-year-olds do not think of themselves as elderly. Questionnaires concerning social attitudes to age have found that most of those under 60 think of old age as beginning at about 65, although, by the time they actually reach 65, most people tend to place the onset of old age as later than this. In addition, the experience of old age can vary widely, depending on a person's class, ethnicity and gender.

These women are all of a very similar age. However, their levels of physical activity, independence and knowledge of the latest technology are very likely to determine which one you consider to be the 'oldest'.

> **Activity**
>
> 1 Find the latest figures for the proportion of the population over retirement age.
> 2 Write a short essay on the implications for government policy-makers of this elderly population (think of health, housing, social care, tax, income).

Whatever the arguments as to how long childhood or the teenage years last, and whether these are changing, it does seem to be the case that the lines between the various stages of life are now blurring – that is, between the stages of childhood, the teenage years, adulthood and old age – which supports the suggestion that such distinctions are socially constructed.

Today, approximately 50 per cent of the world population is under the age of 16. But in Britain, there are now more people over the age of retirement than there are under the age of 16. The implications of this for the future are profound, and probably under-estimated. The potential of the over-50s to live to their 100th birthday is increasing every decade and has important ramifications in terms of healthcare, housing and the funding of pensions.

> **Activity**
>
> Look at table 7.2 on page 536 and answer the following questions:
> 1 What percentage of the population was aged under 25 for each of the years listed? (Add columns 3 and 4 and subtract from 100 to get the answer.)
> 2 Assuming that more than 40 per cent of that number were under the age of 10, what percentage of the population was under 10 for each of these periods? (For example, for 1811, 56.6 per cent were under 25; therefore 22.6 per cent would be under 10 with this assumption.)
> 3 What implications might this have for government spending/income if such a large proportion of the population was/is under 10 and unlikely to be economically active? (Bear in mind that this is not unlike the situation found in much of the world today.) What areas would need increased spending? What areas might not need so much money? Where would the money come from?
>
> *Source*: Adapted from Laslett 1983

Ethnicity

Theories concerning **ethnicity** and differentiation based on perceived racial differences have, mostly, a genetic or a biological base. Following Darwin's theory of evolution, social scientists such as Spencer (1996 [1885]) suggested that different human groups developed in isolation and were distinct from one another, and also that white races were inherently superior to others. These theories reflected the underlying beliefs of the British Empire, then at the height of its powers, and have since been discredited.

Twentieth-century understanding of genetics, particularly the work of Jones (1994), has dispelled this idea. All human groups are capable of interbreeding, and the

Ethnicity refers to the shared culture of a social group which gives its members a common identity in some ways different from other social groups.

Table 7.2: Proportions of the English population in various age groups for selected five-year periods

Five-year period centring on	Proportion aged 0–4 (%)	Proportion aged 25–59 (%)	Proportion aged 60 and over (%)
1571	13.3	40.1	7.3
1661	10.9	42.6	9.7
1751	12.6	41.4	8.2
1811	15.0	36.5	6.9
1841	13.9	37.9	6.6
1871	14.0	38.3	7.0

Source: Adapted from Laslett 1983

genetic differences that exist *between* so-called 'racial groups' are no greater than the range of genetic differences found *within* each of these groups.

In global terms, white European groups are an ethnic minority, or group of minorities, whereas in the UK they form the majority. In modern Britain, it would be difficult to deny that ethnicity still plays a part in stratification given that ethnic minorities make up 8 per cent of the total population but are markedly absent from positions of power; they are also disproportionately represented in prison, among the unemployed, the under-educated and the low paid.

There are also great differences in the residences of such groups. Many towns of the UK could truly be referred to as 'white ghettoes', being 99.9 per cent white. Others contain 20–30 per cent non-white people, but such areas are comparatively small (several streets, or a ward within a local authority area), and very few places have a majority non-white population. Leicester was the first city for which this was true, and this was not apparent until after the 2001 Census.

Ethnic minorities, in any society, are not necessarily among the downtrodden. The British Empire was a classic example of a minority group dominating large populations of different ethnic origins. However, in the UK today, membership of an ethnic minority tends, on the whole, to be linked to social exclusion and disadvantage, though the dimensions of class and gender can alter the situation.

Activity

Read the following extract from a report by the Joseph Rowntree Foundation:

Poverty and ethnicity in the UK

This wide-ranging review of the literature, by Lucinda Platt at the University of Essex, summarizes the findings on poverty and ethnicity research since 1991. It describes differences in poverty rates and experiences by ethnic group. The study found that:
- There are stark differences in poverty rates according to ethnic group. Risks of poverty are highest for Bangladeshis, Pakistanis and Black Africans, but are also above average

for Caribbean, Indian and Chinese people. Muslims face much higher poverty risks than other religious groups.

- The differences in poverty rates are found across poverty measures (income poverty, material deprivation) and across sub-populations (older people, children). The high rates of child poverty in some groups are of particular concern, both for their present welfare and their future opportunities. Over half of Pakistani, Bangladeshi and black African children are growing up in poverty.
- Evidence suggests that there is variation between ethnic groups in both the reasons for lower sources of income (for example, lower and less regular earnings, lower use of particular benefits) and in the numbers of people likely to need supporting from low income.
- Educational qualifications, employment sector, labour market experience, discrimination, location, disability, ill health and family form and structure all play a role in different poverty rates.
- When the contribution of individual characteristics (such as fewer qualifications) to employment disadvantage is analysed, there are some unexplained outcomes. For example, black Africans have very high rates of higher education qualifications, but also suffer from high rates of unemployment and poor occupational outcomes. This 'ethnic penalty' includes the effects of discrimination.
- There also appear to be 'ethnic penalties' in access to social security benefits and other financial support.

Source: Adapted from Platt 2007; further details can be found on www.jrf.org.uk

Now answer the following questions:
1 Describe *three* difficulties that the original researchers may have encountered when collecting this data.
2 How might such difficulties be overcome?
3 Briefly describe what this data tells us about social exclusion in the UK.

An **apartheid** system is where society is divided on the basis of ethnic grouping, more especially, skin colour. Found in South Africa until the mid-1990s.

One example of stratification based on ethnicity occurred in South Africa during the period of **apartheid**, when access to land, jobs and political power depended on having white skin. In various forms, this type of stratification is still found in many societies. In the West Indies, in particular Jamaica, and in Brazil, the possession of light skin colour is highly prized and most of the ruling elites in such countries are drawn from this group. This is also true of India, where darker skin in any caste can lead to being seen as not quite belonging to the group. A current example of ethnicity being the basis of access to political power can also be seen in Israel/Palestine.

Perceived ethnicity was the basis for much of the 'purification' of the fatherland that took place in Hitler's Germany, where large numbers of non-Aryans, such as Gypsies and Jews, were sent to the gas chambers. Ethnicity was also given as a reason for the genocides and conflicts in the former Yugoslavia in the 1990s, and in the genocide in Rwanda in 1994.

Racism

Differentiating people on the basis of perceived ethnic differences can lead to both personal and institutional racism.

Racism occurs when people act in a way that discriminates against others on the basis of their ethnic origin and/or skin color. **Institutional racism** occurs when aspects of society, especially the state or large institutions, have rules or procedures that directly or indirectly treat people differently. Direct racism would be, for example, not allowing non-whites to enter certain jobs. Indirect racism might occur if only qualifications gained in the UK were acceptable for a certain post, which would automatically disbar those who were educated outside the UK.

> **Racism** happens when people are treated differently on the basis of their ethnic origin.

> **Institutional racism** is when patterns of discrimination based on ethnicity have become structured into existing social institutions.

Activity

1 Use the Office of National Statistics website (www.ons.gov.uk) to find figures relating to ethnicity and employment.
2 Write a short essay of two or three pages assessing the extent to which these figures might be affected by racism in UK society.

Health and disability

While there are no existing stratification systems which openly use physical attributes other than age, gender and ethnicity as a basis for stratifying populations, in the past, notably in Hitler's Germany, physical and/or mental disability were used as a reason not to grant full citizen rights to certain sectors of society, or to send them to closed asylums or the gas-chambers.

Most commentators tend to think of disability as a physical condition, which prevents an individual from leading what is seen as a 'normal' life. However, Oliver (1990) suggests that physical impairment (or an inability to carry out certain physical activities) only becomes a disability when society fails to make provision for the individual concerned to live a normal life. In theory, almost any physical difference could be made into a disability if society were to act in certain ways. For example, left-handed people sometimes argue that, in many ways, the UK is a right-handed society; and shorter people have difficulty reaching high shelves in supermarkets. With a little bit of social engineering, both these conditions could be transformed into full-scale disabilities. For example, if all food were to be placed on shelves above five feet high in supermarkets, then shorter people would become disabled, needing help from able-bodied tall people before they could do their shopping.

Finkelstein (1980) has dated the perception of the physically impaired as a distinct disabled group with the arrival of industrialization and the need for factory hands to work. It is argued that until that point they were merely one of several marginal groups in society, but not seen as distinctly different. Shakespeare (1994) has argued that prejudice against the physically impaired has a long history and existed before industrialization. Degrees of prejudice and discrimination may well be linked to the level of disability and how far it affects day-to-day living and working. People who are deaf say they are frequently treated as if they are also stupid, since it is, mostly, an invisible impairment and therefore frequently not recognized as existing, whereas those in wheelchairs report being ignored by people standing around them who see them only as disabled or impaired.

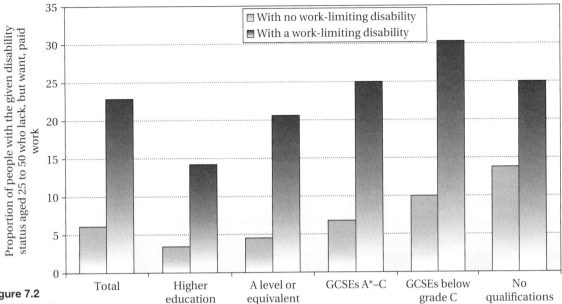

Figure 7.2
Disability and
the ability to get
employment

Source: Labour
Force Survey,
ONS; the data
is the average
for 2005–7, UK;
updated April
2008

Disability, therefore, is a concept that is hard to define, since it is relative. It implies a level of exclusion and is widely used to suggest that the individual is precluded in some way from leading life in the same way as the majority of the population. Since estimates of the number of disabled people vary widely – some suggesting that up to half the population is disabled in one way or another – it might be said that the usefulness of the concept is limited. In official statistics, it is often left to respondents to define themselves as disabled or as suffering from 'a limiting condition'. Thus, such statistics are often less useful than they might at first appear.

In theory, disability is not a bar to access to the highest levels of power in the UK. In reality, there are very few politicians or controllers of large businesses and financial institutions who have noticeable disabilities, though it is suggested that the incidence of bipolar disorder may be higher in this group than in the general population. However, since the stigma of mental illness is still great in British society, many people keep this aspect of their lives completely hidden, making it difficult to investigate this point. It is known that various types of disability are more likely to be found among the unemployed or those on exceptionally low wages than in the general population. The 'social selection' explanation suggests that certain forms of ill health lead to a lower-class position rather than the reverse. Figure 7.2 shows how disability affects working life.

Sexuality and sexual orientation

Differentiation on the basis of sexuality is widespread and pervasive. Gay men and women are still likely to be physically attacked and, despite anti-discrimination legislation, to be treated unequally in the workplace. Because of these dangers, homosexuals are not always open about their sexuality and their exact numbers are therefore not known. In some countries, for example Saudi Arabia, homosexuality is illegal and a capital offence. In the UK, the public perception of homosexuality can also be affected by the media portrayal.

Activity

1 Suggest *two* reasons why physical differences might be used as a base for stratification.
2 Explain, with reasons, how differentiation on the basis of skin colour might create problems within families.
3 Give *three* examples from your own experience of occasions when you feel age discrimination has occurred either to you or to others.
4 It is suggested that the differences between children and adults are disappearing. Give *three* pieces of evidence for this theory, and *three* pieces of evidence against it.
5 Using the information given above, assess the truthfulness of the assertion that childhood and adulthood are merging. Write your answer as a short essay of two or three pages.
6 From your own experience, think of at least *four* occasions when either men or women have been treated differently from others because of their sex/gender/sexuality.
7 Do you think women suffer more discrimination than men? Give reasons for your answer.
8 Assess the extent to which disability might be a source of more differentiation and discrimination than gender, ethnicity, sexuality or age. Write your answer as an essay of about two pages.

Religion

A powerful example of a society with a stratification system based on religion is modern-day India. Other examples exist, but are not always recognized as based on religion.

The caste system

India still has a system based on castes, despite several Acts of the Indian Parliament to abolish it. Technically, it does not exist but, in reality, it still shapes the lives of hundreds of millions of people. Although the caste system is based on Hindu beliefs, the influence of caste affects not only Hindus but other groups too – such as Sikhs, Muslims, Jains and Parsees. It is centred on a belief in reincarnation, that one life is followed by another until a state of perfect knowledge and harmony is reached and the individual dies for the last time to become part of the universe – the state of Nirvana. Birth into a high or low caste is dependent on the purity of one's previous life. Caste is fixed at birth and one lives throughout life within that caste, working at the same job as one's father, and marrying within the caste. It is essentially a closed stratification system. The only mobility that can take place is when someone is excluded from the caste – becomes an outcast – for breaking the rules that govern it. In other words, the only possible mobility is downward. Since complete purity and Nirvana can only be attained after seven lifetimes as a Brahmin, Brahmins are deemed to be the most

A Dalit in India, a member of the lowest caste. The caste system would have made it impossible for this man, or his child, to escape poverty. Even though the caste system is now officially outlawed, there are still great obstacles to social mobility for those traditionally from the Dalit caste.

holy, have the highest esteem and, traditionally, have controlled the state and had great wealth.

Modern society and religious differences

In the UK, religion still is a factor in the stratification system, especially in Northern Ireland. In the 1970s one of the main complaints of the Catholic population was that certain jobs were closed to them and they were thus denied a chance of higher standards of living. In addition, religion is an intervening variable in the study of ethnic minority groups in the UK. It is sometimes argued that Islam acts as a unifying force between different ethnic groups, such as Arabs, Palestinians, Bangladeshis and Pakistanis. Religious differences between Sikhs, Muslims and Hindus divide those coming from the Punjab or Gujarat, who might be thought to have a geographic link, into different groups. The same is possibly true also of those coming to Britain from Ulster, where whether they are Catholic or Protestant seems to be of greater importance in linking people than the town where they were born.

In the UK there is a connection between Islam and poverty, but it is not currently known if there is a causal connection; it is possible that the link is coincidental. But it is possible there is discrimination on the basis of religion, just as much as on the basis of race and ethnicity. For some commentators, the two are intertwined, and discrimination must be considered when looking at religion as a form of stratification.

Economics

The economic bases for differentiation are to do with the control of essential resources, usually water and land, or the means of producing desired goods.

Hydraulic societies

Where control of water is the basis for power, and the way of distinguishing between groups, the society is known as a **hydraulic society.** Wittfogel (1957) described how complex irrigation works in Asia needed an organizational structure in order to maintain them. The state had to attract labour from the population at large, and this required a large **bureaucracy** staffed by competent and literate officials. These bureaucrats controlled all the wealth and power of the country, and themselves became rich and powerful. China, and much of Asian society, as well as the early empires of the Middle East, were – and to some extent still are – hydraulic societies.

> A **hydraulic society** is one in which power is related to the control over access to water.

Water is both a powerful destroyer as well as a giver of life, and controlling the supply is therefore essential for all societies, even where it is no longer the sole basis for power. The future of the Middle East may depend as much on who controls the water as on who controls the oil. Some commentators suggest that Israeli incursions into neighbouring countries are as much about water as about security.

> **Bureaucracy** is a term derived from the works of Weber and means a system of organization in which there is a hierarchy of officials, each with different levels of authority.

Feudal/estate system

Control of land has been, and is, at the heart of many systems of stratification. In medieval Europe, the **feudal (or estate) system** depended on ownership of land, which was the basis of all power. The king owned all the land, often acquired by the right of conquest. The nobility held and administered large areas of the country, but owed allegiance to the king, providing an army when required. The nobles, in turn, granted land to lesser nobles who provided the actual fighting men. Each piece of land was worked by the peasants and serfs, who were owned by the lords. Peasants and serfs had no, or only very few, freedoms and were called upon not only to farm the land held by their lord, but to go to fight when required.

> A **feudal system** is one in which the hierarchy of power and prestige is closely tied to the ownership of land.

Society was therefore broadly divided into what was called Estates of the realm: the First Estate was the Church or Spiritual Estate, the Second Estate was the nobility and the Third Estate were the commoners, who made up over 90 per cent of the population.

The First Estate had gradations: the Pope, cardinals, archbishops, bishops, priests, curates, etc., alongside a monastic tradition. The monasteries were often large land-owners. Everyone paid taxes to the Church – the tithe, or one-tenth of one's income – and the Third Estate also owed tax or labour to the Second Estate. The idea of tithes still exists in some religions today, though the legal obligation to give it to the Church of England finally died out completely in the 1930s. Groups such as the Unification Church (the Moonies) and Jehovah's Witnesses still expect such payment from their followers.

The estate system survived, largely, in Russia until the emancipation of the serfs in 1861, and it could be argued that it still persists in some parts of Europe today.

> **Activity**
>
> 1 Use the Internet to discover the landholding of several members of the aristocracy. Good starting points are the Dukes of Westminster, Devonshire, Buccleuch, Norfolk and Cornwall. Also discover the landholding of the Church of England and discover how many Bishops sit in the House of Lords.
> 2 In a short essay, examine what this might indicate about the openness of the UK system.
> 3 What difficulties did you encounter in uncovering this information? What single database might help overcome this problem?

Industrial capitalist societies

Since the Industrial Revolution, which started in Britain around 1750 and has now spread to most of the planet, control of land and land ownership are considered less important. Instead, control of industry and commodity production is, in much of the world, a basis for stratification systems, although remnants of previous systems still remain in place. In the UK, the aristocracy still hold some power and the Church still has a voice in Parliament in the House of Lords. But people are now more likely to talk of class rather than caste or estate, the notion of peasants and nobles no longer exists. Class was considered by both Marx and Weber to be a defining characteristic of society and central to an understanding of society. Class is a concept that will be discussed in more detail throughout the remaining sections of this chapter.

> **Activity**
>
> 1 Suggest *three* reasons why the control of water might be of importance to any society.
> 2 From your own experience, how important is religion in distinguishing between people in the UK today. Give reasons for your answer.

Defining and measuring class

Most British studies of class that look at either its inevitability or its changing nature have tended to measure class in a very specific way, using occupation, education and social status as well as income to categorize occupations.

The Registrar General's scale

The categories that are still widely used in all government statistics were first devised by the Registrar General in 1901 (see table 7.3). There have been changes in some categories as society has changed, but the basis has remained relatively constant, which allows comparisons to be made between various eras of the twentieth century and today.

Activity

In small groups, study table 7.3 and list the advantages/disadvantages of the categorization of occupations as listed in official statistics. Take five minutes and then share each group's answers with the whole class.

Table 7.3: The Registrar General's classification of class

Class	Typical occupations
Class I Professional	Accountants, dentists, doctors, lawyers, university teachers, vets, vicars
Class II Intermediate	Actors, airline pilots, chiropodists, diplomats, MPs, teachers, journalists
Class III Skilled N = non-manual M = manual	Bank clerks, police officers, secretaries Bus-drivers, miners, plumbers, printers
Class IV Semi-skilled	Farm labourers, gardeners, postal workers, bar staff
Class V Unskilled	Builder's labourers, ticket collectors, chimney sweeps, porters, office cleaners

Criticisms of the Registrar General's scale

One of the great problems with the Registrar General's scheme was that it became inaccurate as certain occupations changed their social status over time, some became deskilled, and others disappeared altogether. It also classified whole families by the occupation of the male head of household, and it ignored people who did not work, whether it was because they had enough wealth to live on or because they were unemployed or retired.

Feminists, in particular, objected to the false picture this produced, especially in those households where the woman's job was of a higher status or more highly paid than that of the man.

The National Statistics Socio-economic Classification

For government purposes, the National Statistics Socio-economic Classification (NS-SEC) scale has been used since 2001 (see table 7.4). This scale recognizes women as a distinct group of wage earners and categorizes them according to their own occupation rather than that of their father or husband. It considers occupation, security of income, prospects of advancement and how much authority or control the occupation in question has over other people/employees. In order to assign an occupation to a particular rank, certain questions are asked, such as:

- What education or training is required?
- Does the post involve supervising others?

- How much autonomy or control over their own actions do post-holders have?
- How much security of tenure is attached to the post?
- How much job advancement exists in the post?
- How much money is paid, and is it a pensionable post?

It is hoped through this mechanism to have a more specific and accurate ranking of occupations so that those found in the same level could be said to have much in common with each other.

Table 7.4: The National Statistics Socio-economic Classification

Occupational classification	Percentage of working population	Common name	Examples
Higher managerial and professional	11	Upper-middle class	Company directors, doctors, clergy, barristers, solicitors, accountants, dentists, university lecturers
Lower managerial and professional	23	Middle class	Teachers, nurses, police inspectors and above, physiotherapists, journalists, authors, sportspersons, musicians
Intermediate	14	Lower-middle class	Secretaries, clerks, computer operators, travel agents, nursery nurses, ambulance staff, fire officers, lower police officers
Small employers and self-accountable workers	10	Lower-middle class	Taxi drivers, publicans, self-employed one-person businesses, child-minders, plasterers
Lower supervisory, craft and related	10	Skilled manual/upper-working class	Train-drivers, printers, plumbers, motor mechanics, electricians, TV engineers
Semi-routine	18	Semi-skilled manual/working class	Traffic wardens, shop assistants, call-centre workers, scaffolders, forklift-truck drivers, farm workers, shelf-fillers, security guards
Routine	13	Unskilled manual/lower-working class	Cleaners, road-sweepers, carpark attendants, labourers, van-drivers, bar staff
Long-term unemployed or the never-worked		The poor/underclass	

Four professions that fall into the same class, according to the NS-SEC scheme. How helpful is it to place teachers, musicians, pharmacists and sports people in the same class group? Would these people necessarily share the same leisure pursuits, social backgrounds, political attitudes and tastes just because they fall into the same NS-SEC class?

Problems with using occupation to measure class

All systems based on occupation have problems for sociologists, for the following reasons:

1   They always exclude the very wealthy who do not need to work, and thus hide some very real differences that exist in society.
2   Unpaid workers, such as houseworkers/housewives, voluntary workers and those never employed and the long-term unemployed, are also excluded.
3   They tend to be based on the occupation of the highest earner in a household, ignoring households with two incomes, whose class position may well be different from a single-earner household.
4   Occupational scales can be very broad and include within them people whose interests might be seen as very different – for example, a headteacher and a classroom teacher fall in the same category, though their responsibilities and powers are very different.

5 They assume a similarity of tastes and attitudes amongst people in the same occupation or ranking. This may be untrue, given that personal interests are formed in many ways. Also those who are born into and remain in the same class may well have different attitudes from those who have entered the class through **social mobility.**

Social mobility: the movement of individuals or groups from one social class to another, both upwardly and downwardly.

> **Activity**
>
> 1 Consider how occupation might affect other aspects of life. Take two people from different occupations, such as a solicitor and a shop-assistant, and compare aspects of their lives such as income, health, housing, life chances for their children and any others you can think of.
> 2 Do the two jobs you have chosen have any aspects in common. If so, list them.
> 3 How many of the differences/similarities can be linked to their respective occupations? Give reasons for your answers.
> 4 Write a short essay of two or three pages assessing the importance of occupation in people's lives.

Objective and subjective views of class

Whatever scale is used, they consist of objective views of people's social class. An individual's own view of his or her social class may well be different. Few people are likely to say 'I belong to social class seven', but they may well say, 'I am working class'. Subjective classifications need to be considered especially when attitudes to and relations between classes are examined. Giddens (1991), considering the subjective aspects of class, suggested that employment/occupation is being replaced by patterns of consumption as an indicator of the group one sees oneself as belonging to, an idea much espoused by postmodernists, as we saw above. In 'Class, Mobility and Identification in a New Town' (2002), Southerton showed that **consumption patterns** were important in people's minds when describing other inhabitants of the new town as 'them' or 'us'. Thus, class identification has been replaced by consumption patterns as a way of identifying others' as well as one's own social position.

Consumption patterns describe the ways in which people spend their money – some sociologists, such as Giddens, suggest this is as important as class in demonstrating identity.

> **Activity**
>
> 1 As a group, devise a questionnaire to discover how people define their own social class. Do not forget to include questions that can help you identify people's objective class as well as questions asking them how they would describe themselves and why.
> 2 Administer the questionnaire to a range of relatives/friends.
> 3 Compare people's subjective class with their objective class.
> 4 Write a short report outlining your major findings.
> 5 From your evidence, do you think that consumption patterns have replaced occupation as a way of defining one's own class position? Give reasons for your answer based on your findings.

UK social classes

Although it has become fashionable to assume that class is becoming of little importance in the UK today, studies show that great differences between social classes do still persist.

There have been more studies of the poor and powerless than there have been of the wealthy and powerful. More is known about life in the slums of Salford than it is about life in the leafy gardens of Kensington and Chelsea, or in the country estates of the gentry. This is partly due to the fact that the wealthy have an ability to remain hidden, which is denied to the poor.

The upper class

One aspect of the upper class is the amount of wealth and income its members possess. There are different sources of wealth and income. Some people inherit their wealth and the income that derives from it; others earn both their wealth and their income.

Wealth

Attitudes to **wealth** will differ between those who inherit it and those who earn it. There are different forms of wealth:

- land and property, including mining rights;
- industrial ownership;
- finance and banking;
- stocks and shares ownership.

> **Wealth** refers to the total value of the possessions held by an individual or society.

All these forms of wealth can be passed from one generation to another. There is no official register of ownership in the UK. At present, it is impossible to know who owns what. Thus the exact wealth of the upper classes is unknown. All that can be easily seen are the figures for death duties (inheritance tax) and the income tax paid on the income derived from their wealth. Some wealth, such as paintings and furniture, and property, creates no income until it is sold, and is uncountable until then. When the Hesketh family sold Easton Neston House in 2006, for example, the sale of the house contents raised a sum of money equivalent to the wages of more than 500 teachers for a year.

According to the Office of National Statistics, Social Trends 2005: '1 per cent of the population owns 21 per cent of wealth of the UK. In contrast, half the population shared only 7 per cent of total wealth. The results are even more skewed if housing is excluded from the estimates, suggesting this form of wealth is more evenly distributed. Wealth is considerably less evenly distributed than income, and life cycle effects mean that this will almost always be so. People build up assets during the course of their working lives and then draw them down during the years of retirement, with the residue passing to others at their death' (see figure 7.3).

In 2003, half the population of the UK owned between them 7 per cent of the wealth of the country, which included all the houses they might own (or just 1 per cent if the

Figure 7.3
Distribution of
wealth in the UK,
1976–2003

Sources:
Compiled from
ONS data, Social
Trends 2005

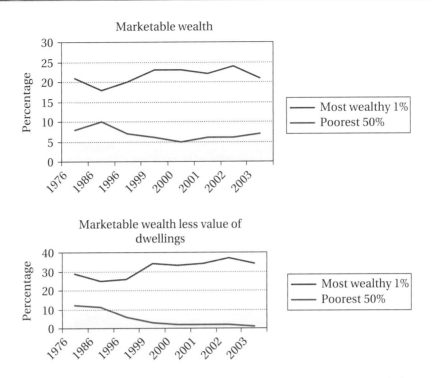

Marketable wealth

Marketable wealth less value of dwellings

houses were excluded). It is self-evident that Britain is a very divided country, with the top 1 per cent owning more than the bottom 75 per cent put together. The situation worldwide is similar. In 2006, the World Institute for Development Economics Research found that the richest 1 per cent in the world owned 40 per cent of the planet's wealth. The richest 10 per cent owned 85 per cent, while the poorest 50 per cent owned just 1 per cent of this wealth. Even within this bottom half, there will be vast discrepancies between the wealth of individuals.

Income

Income refers to an inward flow of money over time. For most people this consists of wages/salary, but other sources are benefits, pensions, interest on savings and dividends from shares

Income, both in the UK and worldwide, shows similar disparities. In the UK in 2006, the median wage (the wage at which half the wage-earners are above and half are below) was approximately £17,000 per year. Certain Premier League footballers were earning several times that amount per week. Dorling et al. (2007) showed how wealth and poverty have polarised in the UK in the latter part of the twentieth century. Not only is wealth (and poverty) increasingly concentrated; but it clusters geographically as well. Dorling et al. point, in particular, to the fact that poverty is clustered in urban areas, while wealth is more concentrated in the south-east of the country.

Activity

Use the Internet to visit www.statistics.gov.uk/socialtrends.
1 Discover the differences in income between the top 10 per cent of earners and the median wage. Take note of how the gap has widened or narrowed.
2 Write a short essay to describe what these figures show about the divisions in UK society.

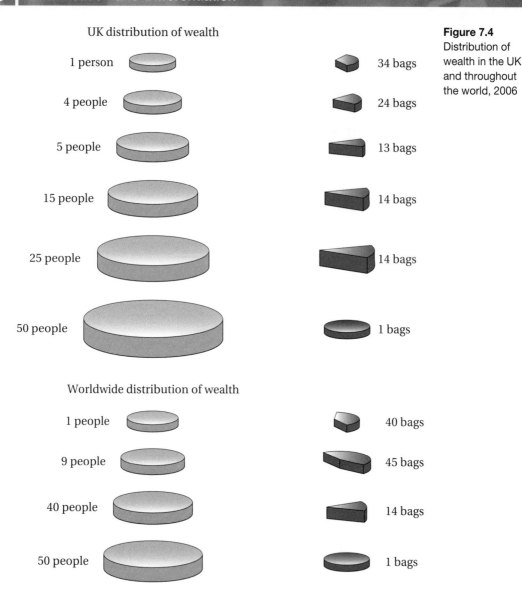

Figure 7.4
Distribution of wealth in the UK and throughout the world, 2006

UK distribution of wealth

1 person	34 bags
4 people	24 bags
5 people	13 bags
15 people	14 bags
25 people	14 bags
50 people	1 bags

Worldwide distribution of wealth

1 people	40 bags
9 people	45 bags
40 people	14 bags
50 people	1 bags

Ruling elites

It has been suggested that the upper classes in the UK have maintained their position from generation to generation through their control of the political life of the country, and indeed, until the extension of voting rights to all people over 21 in 1929, this may have been true. Now it is suggested that their power is somewhat more diffuse.

Writing from a Marxist perspective, Westergaard and Resler (1975) have suggested that the private ownership of capital provides the key to understanding class divisions in the UK. Since the whole ideology of the UK is a capitalist one, the system will work in favour of those who own the means of production or who control the financial institutions that make the major decisions concerning life in the UK. However, Saunders (1990), writing from a New Right perspective, has disputed this notion of

The **elite** consists of a small group that holds great power and privilege in society.

a wealthy ruling **elite**. He maintains that much wealth is now bound up in pension funds: anyone with a private or work pension is bound to have an interest in the workings of capitalism since their hard-earned pensions are invested in the stock market. Therefore, he argues, the capitalist class has 'fragmented into millions of tiny pieces' spread across society. Nevertheless, this ignores the role played by financial institutions in controlling these pension funds, and the large incomes of the employees of such institutions.

Chapter 4 referred to the Sutton Trust (see pages 271–2), which reveals that political and economic power is, on the whole, maintained across generations through the class system (also see below, pags 568–9).

> ### Activity
>
> 1 Working in pairs, and using the Internet and a source such as *Who's Who?*, see how much you can find out about the directors of the major pension funds. (Start with the directors of groups such as Clerical and Medical, Equitable Life, the Prudential, Standard Life, Norwich Union – all of which provide personal pension plans.)
> 2 Do your findings lend credibility to Saunders's theory, or do the directors still tend to come from the privileged social groups which make up the majority of top earners in financial institutions?
> 3 Write a short essay to assess the extent to which elites in the UK can be said to be self-recruiting.

The middle class

Normally the distinction between the middle and the working class is based on the kind of work done by members of these groups. In the past, non-manual jobs were considered to be middle class and manual jobs were considered working class. However, how are jobs defined? Is typing or inputting data at a computer manual or non-manual? In so far as hands are needed, it is manual.

Weber suggested that it is probably more useful to consider life chances in distinguishing between the two groups. On the whole, non-manual work tends to take place indoors, in pleasant working conditions, with shorter hours, more job security, more fringe benefits and better promotion prospects. Non-manual workers also enjoy better health and better standards of healthcare, live longer, are less likely to be convicted of a crime, own their own home and retire earlier than manual workers. There has also been a consistent gap between the earnings of manual and non-manual workers throughout the twentieth century.

Proletarianization is the process whereby other groups take on the attributes and characteristics of the proletariat.

The **professions** are those types of occupation which are self-governing and generally of relatively high status.

However, during the course of the twentieth century this very diverse group of non-manual workers, whose occupations range from university professors to routine call-centre workers, have become divided into different groups with different interests. Many of these jobs have lost skills which they once had and, it could be argued, have become **proletarianized**. It now makes more sense to talk of the **professions** and the lower middle class as two quite distinct groups.

The professions

Professional groups grew in numbers throughout the twentieth century. They went from comprising about 4 per cent of the working population in 1901 to more that 20 per cent by 2001. Most commentators divide professionals into two groups: higher professions, such as judges, barristers, solicitors, architects, doctors, dentists, accountants, university lecturers, scientists and some engineers; and lower profession, which include schoolteachers, nurses, social workers and librarians.

Professionals have mostly been rewarded with relatively high levels of pay. Explanations for this depend on the theoretical perspective of the commentator. Functionalists such as Parsons (1967) and Barber (1963) contend that professionals have four attributes that distinguish them from other workers:

1 They hold a body of knowledge about their field of work which can be applied to any situation that arises.
2 They have a concern for the interests of the community rather than self-interest. The primary motivation of all professionals is to serve the public, not to get rich.
3 Professionals' conduct is always guided by a code of ethics, which is maintained and upheld by a professional body to which they must belong if they wish to continue to practice. Should they break the code of ethics, they may be barred from practising their skill.
4 The high rewards are a result of their prestige and the high regard they are held in by the community they serve.

Critics of the functionalist view argue it makes huge assumptions about professionals – for example, in the claim that they serve the whole community rather than just a section of it, and that they are public-spirited rather than in it for the money. Weberians would suggest that professions are occupational groups that have succeeded in controlling the labour market to their own advantage. Parry and Parry (1976) argue that professionals and professionalism have the following attributes:

1 By controlling the training and entry requirements necessary for membership, professionals control the supply of qualified practitioners at a level that will guarantee high fees. Scarcity of professional skills means they can charge more.
2 By forcing all members to belong to the professional association, the group can claim to be maintaining the highest public standards; by demanding the right to investigate and punish their own members, they make it difficult for outside scrutiny to take place.
3 Professionals have, on the whole, managed successfully to claim that only their members are qualified to carry out this work. The monopoly enjoyed by lawyers and doctors, for example, is backed by law; it is a criminal offence to impersonate a doctor and only solicitors have the right to carry out certain legal procedures.

Because of this market strategy – that is, closing access to the group and restricting their numbers – professionals have become wealthy and secure. Lower professionals, such as teachers, are, in the eyes of Parry & Parry, not really professionals at all since they do not have the market control such as that enjoyed by doctors.

Activity

1 From the list of occupations below, pick out the ones that Barber would regard as professionals, and the ones that Parry and Parry would regard as professionals:
- university lecturers
- nursery nurses
- general medical practitioners
- surgeons
- solicitors
- primary school teachers
- bank clerks
- nurses
- airline pilots
- army officers

2 From your own experience, which of the above groups would consider themselves to be professionals?

3 What does the difference in the three lists you have compiled tell us about different views of the status of professionals in the UK today? Give reasons for your answer.

The lower middle class

The lower middle class is often described as consisting of routine white-collar workers, such as clerical staff, secretaries and call-centre workers. Their jobs have changed so much, however, that some sociologists speak of proletarianization, others claim they are still part of a distinctive middle class, while a few suggest they are now a distinct group somewhere between the middle and the working class.

The theory of proletarianization is most associated with Marxists such as Braverman (1974), who suggested that although the number of white-collar jobs has grown enormously, the skill needed to do the job has declined. Early clerical workers were able to run all aspects of the small company that employed them. As companies grew larger, each clerk took over one part of the operation and specialized in it. However workers were only able to carry out that one specialism and, if the need for it disappeared, they became effectively redundant. Also, new technology was developed which removed many of the skills required in clerical work, and this is what Braverman called **deskilling**. Automation and computerization have both continued the process of deskilling. Braverman says that in an age of mass literacy and numeracy, the work of white-collar workers can be done by almost anyone, and they are no better off, in bargaining terms, than manual workers.

Stewart et al. (1980) found that there is a high rate of turnover and promotion amongst male clerical workers. By the age of 30, 51 per cent of men who started out as clerical workers have been promoted into management, and 30 per cent leave clerical work altogether before they are 30. For men, clerical work is merely a stage in a career path. However, Crompton and Jones (1984) show that, although this may be true for

Deskilling is a situation in which the skills and knowledge previously needed to do a job are no longer required.

Here for life?

 →

A male clerical worker has only a 25 per cent chance of staying in that position for life. For most men, it has historically been the starting point of an upward career.

men, the vast majority of clerical workers are now women. In their study of three workplaces, they concluded that for the women employed there, the work was lacking in skill, they had no control over their work and that, therefore, the female clerical workers could be labelled a white-collar proletariat.

The middle class or the middle classes?

Sociologists disagree about whether it is accurate to talk about a single middle class or several different groups – the middle classes. Giddens (1973) argues that there is one middle class whose members are distinguished from those in the upper class because they do not own 'property in the means of production'. They are also distinguished from the working class by the fact that they can sell their mental labour power rather than just their manual labour power because they possess educational or technical qualifications. However, groups such as electricians and plumbers also increasingly have technical qualifications, but are still considered by most to be manual workers.

Savage et al. (1992) argued that the middle class consists of three distinct groups:

- those with property assets, which includes the self-employed and small employers;
- those with organizational assets, who hold important positions in large organizations;
- those with cultural assets deriving mainly from educational qualifications.

In the twentieth century, the fates of these three groups began to vary. Those with property assets still have the ability to pass these on to their children. However, those with organizational assets gradually declined in importance as industry entered more

Lifestyle describes the way in which people live, usually indicating something about their disposable income.

Norms are social rules that define what is expected behaviour for an individual in a given society or situation.

Values are ideas or beliefs that govern the way individuals behave. There is often an ethical dimension to this concept

Ideal type refers to a view of a phenomenon built up by identifying the essential characteristics of many factual examples of it. The purpose of an ideal type is not to produce a perfect category, but to provide a measure against which real examples can be compared.

Social solidarity refers to the integration of people into society through shared values, a common culture, shared understandings, and social ties that bind them together.

Activity

1 List *three* reasons why clerical workers could be considered to be part of the middle class.
2 List *three* reasons why clerical workers might not be considered to be part of the middle class.
3 From your own experience, list *three* jobs that could be said to have been deskilled in the past 20 years. Give reasons for your answers.
4 Suggest *three* reasons why women are less likely than men to be promoted from routine clerical work to higher positions.
5 Assess the importance of education in allowing access to the middle class in contemporary Britain. Write your answer as a short essay of two or three pages.

---

specialized areas demanding greater flexibility. In this situation, those with educational qualifications and potential flexibility have become more valuable to owners of industry. However, a major flaw with this theory is that it ignores a great part of the traditional middle class – it fails to consider at all the routine white-collar workers.

The working class

Again, the question has to be asked: is there a single working class, as classical Marxism would suggest, or is it more accurate to speak of the working classes?

Marxist sociologists argue that, in order to be considered part of a social class, people must at least recognize themselves as having similarities. It has been found that most manual workers will define themselves as working class. It is assumed that there will be a similarity of **lifestyle**, **norms** and **values** – that is, a common culture – amongst the members of this group, and that they will show a tendency to mix socially with members of the same group rather than with members of other groups/classes.

Proletarian traditionalists

While there may be differences within the working class, and therefore a number of working-class subcultures, David Lockwood has drawn up what could be described as an **ideal type** working-class subculture, found among those he labelled 'proletarian traditionalists'. This group was based on a range of studies of working-class life and is frequently used as a basis for comparison when considering other working-class groups.

Among other traits, proletarian traditionalists display the following characteristics:

- living in close-knit working-class communities often based on long-established industries such as mining, dockwork, steel, etc.;
- have a strong sense of **social solidarity**;
- workmates are often neighbours and friends, and leisure time will be spent in each other's company

- little geographical or social mobility;
- tendency to seek collective goals rather than individual ones, often linked to **trade union** membership;
- **fatalism and** a fatalistic attitude to life, emphasis on **present-time orientation** and **immediate gratification**;
- tendency to see the world divided into 'us' and 'them'.

Is this an accurate picture of working-class life in the early twenty-first century? There has been a marked decline in the industries that formerly employed the proletarian traditionalist. Mining as a way of life has all but disappeared, as deep mines have been replaced by open-cast mining; steel is now a minority industry; dock work has been replaced by containerization. The change has been so great that Beynon (1992) estimated that more people now work in the hotel and catering industries than were employed in steelworks, shipyards, car manufacturing, mechanical engineering and coal-mining combined. He also points out, however, that the jobs in hotel and catering are often themselves essentially manual, boring and repetitive. Nevertheless, the overall figures of those who could be considered working class from their occupations has declined.

McKenzie et al. (2006) found that even when the steelworks of South Wales closed and the steelworkers were dispersed to other jobs or were made unemployed, they still took their identity from being steelworkers, and felt a strong sense of solidarity with their former work-mates. They concluded that the decline of the traditional working-class occupations, mostly undertaken by men and generally attached to a trade union, did not necessarily lead to a difference in the way the were identified, or identified themselves.

The new working class

At the same time as the number of working-class jobs was falling, the average living standards for those manual workers in regular employment improved. Their increased affluence led many political commentators to suggest that the attitudes of the working class would wither away and that most people would form a single homogenised mass. These ideas started from as early as the election slogan of 1959 – 'You've never had it so good' – through to 1992 and the claim of then Prime Minister John Major that 'We are all middle class now'. It was argued that, rather than middle-class employees becoming deskilled and proletarianized, the opposite was occurring, and the working class was becoming more like the middle class, through a process of **embourgeoisement**.

In 1962, Goldthorpe et al. began work on what was later published as *The Affluent Worker in the Class Structure* (1969). They set out to test the theory that the working classes were becoming more middle class. They chose to focus on the town of Luton, where they felt such a transformation was most likely to occur, arguing that if they failed to find the tendency there, it would be reasonable to assume that it was not happening anywhere. Their choice of Luton was based on the absence of long-established industries, the decline of a closely-knit community, higher than average home-ownership and, above all, higher wages. The study looked at four aspects of class:

A **trade union** is an organization of workers whose aim is to protect the interests of its members and improve their life chances

Fatalism and a fatalistic attitude is a state of mind in which someone believes there is nothing they can do to alter their situation or circumstances.

Present-time orientation involves a concentration on today without much consideration for the future or the past.

Immediate gratification is a desire to have rewards now rather than waiting to acquire them in the future, which is known as deferred gratification.

Embourgeoisement refers to the idea that working-class manual workers were adopting more middle class norms and values.

1 Attitudes to work: such as whether affluent workers would enjoy their work and have an instrumental relationship to work (i.e. work for money) rather than to make friends and build a sense of community.

2 Political views: whether embourgeoisement would mean more people voting for the Conservative Party.

3 Aspirations and perspectives of society: how affluent workers viewed the various social classes.

4 Social interaction between groups within the community and those from different classes.

They argued that if embourgeoisement was occurring, there would be few discernable differences between the various groups of workers. However, they concluded that embourgeoisement was *not* taking place, but, rather, that a new working class was being formed with a privatized family lifestyle and an **instrumental attitude** to work and politics.

Later studies by Hill (1976) on the London dockers suggested that this new working class was more widespread than originally thought. In the 1980s, Devine (1992) returned to Luton to see if there had been further changes. Her findings suggest that the employment insecurities of the 1970s and 1980s had effected some attitudes, but, in the main, the affluent workers remained instrumental in their attitudes to work, concerned about their consumption patterns but also keen to see a more egalitarian society.

A study that has brought the picture of one working-class community more up to date is by Dench et al. (2006), which looks in detail at how the close-knit networks of the old docklands of East London have gradually disappeared as work was transferred elsewhere and no other obvious employment took its place. The reliance on neighbours has all but disappeared, extended families have been priced out of the neighbourhood and new housing in Essex took the younger generation away, leaving the older members to cope in an increasingly unrecognizable world. The role of the working-class family as a source of status, solidarity and support has gone, and with it the traditionalist solidaristic community that was so important in the lives of the dockworkers. Here, the traditional proletarian lifestyle described by Lockwood no longer exists.

> **Activity**
>
> Write a short essay of two or three pages to assess the extent to which it is true to speak of the working classes rather than the working class.

An **instrumental attitude** is one in which wages/money are the most important aspect of work.

The **underclass** is a concept developed by Murray to describe a group considered to be outside the mainstream of society, below the working class.

Lumpenproletariat is a term used by Marx to describe the group of unorganized working class people. It is now seen by many commentators as being synonymous with the underclass.

The underclass/the poor

Many argue that there is a stratum below the working class. It has been given many names. At present, the one most in vogue is the term **underclass**. Marx referred to this group as the **lumpenproletariat**. The underclass is described either in *economic* terms: those within its ranks are unemployed, dependent on benefits and poor; or in *normative* terms: they have a different culture and subculture from the rest of the population. Some commentators, most notably Murray (1984), would suggest that both economic and normative differences exist.

According to Marx, the main problem facing the lumpenproletariat was the diverse nature of the group – its fluctuating population, which would prevent it from becoming class-conscious. Its very presence might also hinder the formation of class-consciousness within the proletariat, since the fear would always exist that employers can recruit a new labour force from within the lumpenproletariat. This led Marx to describe this group as the '**reserve army of labour**', a concept that has been widely used by feminists to describe the role of women in the twentieth century.

A study by Coates and Silburn (1970) showed that the poor live life very much as others do: they have the same hopes and aspirations, the same coping strategies and do not consider themselves different in any great way. The study group referred to others, worse off than themselves, as 'poor' and did not regard their own position as poverty stricken at all. Later pan-European studies have come to similar conclusions – poverty is a relative concept, even to those whom others would regard as poor.

Writing originally about the USA, Murray (1984) argued that the poor have traits and characteristics that distinguish them from the rest of society and suggested there was a growing underclass which was a threat to the stability of society. Government policies are increasing the numbers of people who no longer work and who rely on government welfare for their subsistence; this discourages self-sufficiency and this group then turns to crime, delinquency and other forms of anti-social behaviour. In 1989, Murray visited the UK and declared that here too an underclass flourished.

Murray's definition emphasizes the normative or cultural features of the underclass, distinguishing features like:

- high levels of illegitimacy;
- absent fathers or fathers who are incapable of keeping a job;
- an unwillingness to work, particularly among the young;
- drunkenness;
- poor education;
- delinquency.

Murray says that, in certain neighbourhoods, traditional values such as honesty, belief in family life and the virtue of hard work have been so seriously undermined that generations are being born with no such ideas or access to them. He blames the underclass for the situation they are in, paying no attention to any structural causes and making no attempt to see any coherent solutions other than to cancel all benefits.

Dahrendorf (1959) explains how such an underclass has been formed through changes in the economic structure of society. Technology now allows for more production with fewer workers, thus creating unemployment. In the USA, moreover, wages are kept so low in some industries that the workers concerned cannot rise out of poverty. Even better-paid workers are increasingly employed on short-term or

> The **reserve army of labour** consists of a group of people not normally in the paid workforce who can be called on in times of need. Marx saw them as members of the lumpenproletariat; feminists see them as married women and mothers.

Mechanization has led to widespread deskilling and the loss of many jobs. In such a situation, who stands to lose and who stands to gain?

part-time contracts. Education is the key to a successful job, but the education system fails members of the underclass; thus, argues Dahrendorf, 'those who are in, by and large, stay in, but those who are not, stay outside'.

There is clearly an economic base to the underclass, but fragmentation will prevent class-consciousness. Members of the underclass have little security and do not feel like full citizens of their societies. The group includes newly arrived immigrants and those who either have not gained a job at all, or who have lost their job. As they have no real stake in society, they feel no need to conform to mainstream values and this lack of conformity will be passed on to their children. Their frustrations often come to the surface through rioting and violent crime, which affects the lives of other citizens, but because of the different strands in this group, Dahrendorf does not regard them as a class in itself, but rather as a group of people who are not needed by society and whose presence is a challenge to dominant values.

Gallie (1988, 1994) argues that certain groups within the so-called underclass are really members of the working class. Among these, most particularly, are the unemployed or those on very low wages. Groups drift in and out of employment and thus have similar class interests. The only people for whom this might not be true, according to Gallie, are the very long-term unemployed, but most of these were formerly manual workers or came from such a background. Whether this is also true of people who have never been able to find a job is left unconsidered.

The term 'ghetto poor' has been used by some US commentators to describe the group that exists as the lowest strata of capitalist societies. They are considerably worse off than manual workers in regular employment. Whether they form a separate class is still undecided.

Non-legal citizens

With the constant movement of people across borders in search of work and a better life for themselves and their families, there is a growing number of residents who are not legally citizens of the country where they are currently living. This group has a very unusual position in the class structure. Some, who have false documents, manage to rise to positions in the semi-professional classes and routine clerical class, but do not, on the whole, appear in official statistics, as they are reluctant to draw attention to themselves. Others find themselves working in the black economy, paying no tax or national insurance, prey to unscrupulous employers and landlords, with no chance of escaping from this semi-slavery. The exact numbers cannot be known, but raids by various branches of the police routinely uncover cases every week. Their position in the class structure is impossible to determine.

Activity

1 Describe in your own words what is meant by 'the underclass'.
2 Give three examples of evidence or theories that might suggest that an underclass exists in the UK today. Give reasons for your answer.
3 Give examples of evidence or theories that might suggest that there is no such thing as an underclass.
4 From your own experience assess how far the mass media might be responsible for the view that there is an underclass.

Changes in the stratification system

In this section, most of the emphasis will be on the UK, but many of the causes of change will apply to other societies. The major causes could be said to be the result of:

- changes in the economy;
- changes in patterns of education;
- changes in fertility and death rates;
- global changes;
- migration and immigration.

The economy

It was thought that, historically, the stratification system was relatively rigid, with people being born into one class and staying there for life. But social mobility has always existed. When servants were much more commonplace amongst the wealthy, employment in a rich man's house often led to social advancement. For those who had learned to read and write, the future was promising. The chances altered with the Industrial Revolution, as the economy shifted from an agricultural to an industrial base. People moved from countryside to town. Similar changes are occurring in the developing world today, with urbanization occurring everywhere.

Social closure means a system whereby members of a group can act to prevent others from joining them.

In the twentieth century, the pace of change increased, though it will be seen later that upward social mobility is slowing down in the UK as **social closure** becomes more rigid in the higher social groups.

Employment has changed in many ways. There is now a more service-based economy, dependent on international trade and transnational employers. This inevitably alters the power of the state to control events within its own borders. Even employment law is now international. The growth of women's rights has led to a feminization of the workforce. Although it is the case that women have always done the bulk of the world's work, now they are being paid for some of it. This has led to a major shift in power within family relationships, as women bring in income in terms of cash and the power of the men to dictate to the family is severely diminished.

Activity

1 Pick an older member of your family and ask questions about their family history to discover what class movement there has been in the last two or three generations (or as far back as the respondent can remember).
2 Report your findings to the whole class, to compare just how much class fluidity there has been.
3 List the advantages and difficulties of this kind of in-depth interviewing and empathetic research.

Education

Universal education means that occupations that were previously open only to those who could afford education can now be open to all. In the UK, this began towards the end of the nineteenth century. However, the changes to the education of women, on an equal footing, did not really occur until the 1970s, with the Sex Discrimination Act. This had a major impact on the ability of women to compete with men for higher positions. The full effect is now being felt, as women enter the higher professions in larger numbers.

Worldwide, the importance of education is widely recognized by many governments. One of the United Nation's Millennium Development Goals is free universal education for all – girls as well as boys. This is likely to change the position of women greatly: as they achieve more equality with men in one field, they are unlikely to accept lower positions in terms of power in the home or in the public sphere. Patriarchy may become a thing of the past.

Fertility and death rates

Changes in women's fertility rates have had major impacts on class throughout the world. As the number of children a woman has falls, populations grow smaller, thereby leading to labour shortages. When women are allowed schooling and achieve educational success, one of the first effects is a reduction in the number of children they have, partly because the age at which they get married is delayed in many societies, but also as women learn about the medical dangers of too many pregnancies. Their aspirations for their children also rise and having fewer children makes it easier to achieve those aspirations.

Until the mid-twentieth century, high death rates in the UK before the age of 20 meant that in certain groups there was a shortage of labour. This resulted in a fairly fluid workforce as people moved from one social class to another. Historically, one of the greatest shifts in stratification in Europe followed the Black Death in the mid-fourteenth century. Currently, in sub-Saharan Africa and elsewhere, HIV/AIDS is having a similar effect, as whole generations are often halved in size.

Global changes

One major global change, particularly in the past 50 years, has been the rise of the transnational corporation (TNC); the owners of an industry may be resident in another country and have the factories that produce the goods and services spread throughout the world. One consequence of this has been the decreasing power of national governments over the economic structure of their own society. For example, if the Ford Motor Company decides to move production of cars from the UK to India, because wages are cheaper there, the UK government will be unable to prevent this from happening, and a proportion of skilled and semi-skilled jobs will be lost to the UK economy. As this happens more frequently, the whole structure of the economy and employment changes. A country could easily go from having a highly trained workforce, earning good wages, to one where there is mass unemployment, as the jobs move.

Migration and immigration

Labour shortages in the UK have already led to migration within the country, and immigration from outside the country. Internal migration from north to south, in particular into London, has been a feature of British society for centuries. In the past, the British Isles, and in particular Wales, Scotland and Ireland, have been exporters of people. That situation has now been reversed, and immigration into the UK, particularly of certain sections of the workforce, is commonplace.

Many of the migrants are here on a temporary basis and return home after only a brief spell. If economic situations in their home country improve, or if the scarcity of labour that their emigration has created pushes up wages in the mother country, they are more likely to return home. This has certainly been the case with migrants from Poland, since that country joined the European Union in 2004. Other immigrants return to their motherland as they retire – something that is particularly common among West Indians.

At present, the UK economy needs more people of working age, and in the future, with a growing elderly population unable to work and requiring support, this need could become even greater. This will have an effect on the stratification system. As workers become more scarce, their status will increase, and this, in turn, will have great consequences for all kinds of government planning and policies, such as health, education and housing.

There are both benefits and problems involved in the migration of labour. Maybe the greatest problem – and one that Britain has yet, as a society, to consider in detail – is that migrants can leave as well as arrive. They owe no particular loyalty to their new home and, if conditions are better elsewhere, they are likely to leave.

This is also true of people born in the UK. Many countries, notably Australia, New Zealand, Canada and South Africa have all experienced, and are still experiencing, immigration from the UK, while Spain is home to a large English expatriate community, amongst them many retired people.

Activity

1 List and explain in your own words *five* possible causes of change in the stratification system.
2 Identify *two* pieces of evidence that would suggest that each of these causes might be occurring.

Social mobility

Social mobility, or the movement of people from one class to another, has long fascinated sociologists, and raises a number of interesting questions, for example:

- Why is it important?
- Are there different types of mobility?
- How is social mobility measured?

How much social mobility exists within a society, and who is mobile, can be affected by several variables:

1 The occupational structure of a society at a given time: are all jobs open to all members of society? How easy is it to gain the qualifications necessary for a professional position, such as being a doctor?
2 Fertility differences between groups within society: if women from higher social classes have fewer children, then not all professional jobs can be 'inherited' and some positions will need to be filled from people lower down the class scale.
3 The structure and availability of education: is education freely available to all, or do hidden barriers exist, such as expensive uniforms, or the need to belong to a certain faith? Will universities favour those from private schools, or will government policies mean that universities are more likely to encourage working-class students to apply?
4 The distribution of opportunities: in London, for example, there is a wider array of job types than in rural areas, making upward and downward mobility much easier. Children of professionals may also be more aware of what opportunities exist in society, as opposed to children who have grown up in a working-class community.
5 The distribution of motivation: in some working-class communities, there may be pressure on boys to resist upward mobility and to link working-class jobs to their masculine identity.

Why is social mobility important?

Many sociologists have argued that a study of social mobility tells us a great deal about a society, for example:

1   High rates of mobility, both up and down, would suggest a society in which status might be awarded on merit.
2   High upward rates with little downward mobility would suggest an economy that is expanding.
3   A society with a low rate of mobility is likely to lead to higher levels of class-consciousness, solidarity and class cohesion, as people are born into and stay in one class which they then pass on to their children, creating a distinctive culture.
4   A fluid system that allows people to move easily from class to class will lead to a free exchange of ideas and be more open to change, while a closed system, such as the caste system, will be less likely to experience great social change.

It is important to understand what effect mobility has on those who are mobile: do they hold on to the norms and values of their original class, or do they adopt those of their new class? What effect does this have on their children? Maintenance of class attitudes from a previous class might explain certain voting patterns – for example, middle-class Labour voters who came from a working-class background, and working-class Conservatives who may have been born into the middle class and been downwardly mobile.

High levels of social mobility can lead to dissatisfaction in society. In their study of the geographical dimensions of wealth and poverty Dorling et al. (2007) examined the tenfold increase in the number of university graduates between 1968 and 2002. They suggest that those who have been educated to a level undreamt of by their parents will have aspirations that society may be unable to meet if, in reality, there are only a few jobs that require a university education. This failure to attain greater status and income within a new class may lead to resentment.

> **Activity**
>
> 1   In your own words, give *four* reasons why sociologists consider mobility to be worth studying.
> 2   Assess the importance of mobility in maintaining social order. Write your answer as a short essay.

Different types of social mobility

Social mobility can be considered in many forms. An important distinction is that between individual and group mobility. Group mobility occurs when a specific occupation alters its status, such as farm work. As agriculture has become more mechanized, farm workers have acquired other skills, whereas computerization has deskilled the printing industry and printers have, as a group, been downwardly mobile.

Perfect social mobility is a situation in which every position in a society is filled on merit and the society is constantly changing. This is perhaps what Davis and Moore (1945) claimed to be describing – as discussed earlier in this chapter (see page 514). It is also necessary to distinguish between intragenerational social mobility and intergenerational social mobility. Intragenerational social mobility is that which occurs within an individual's own lifetime – for example, when someone starts by working in a factory, then goes to teacher training college and finally becomes a teacher, thus moving from manual work to professional work.

Intergenerational social mobility is when there has been movement between the occupation of a child and the parents – for example, if the father is a white-collar clerical worker and the son becomes a dustman, he is downwardly mobile; if, instead, he becomes a teacher, he is upwardly mobile. It is worth noting that, until now, all studies of social mobility have considered fathers and sons rather than mothers and sons, fathers and daughters or mothers and daughters.

Activity

1 Describe, in your own words, the main difference between intra- and intergenerational social mobility.
2 How might you measure each form of social mobility using interviews? What questions would you need to ask?
3 What are the difficulties of using questionnaires to measure intergenerational social mobility?
4 If measuring the social mobility of women what advantages might there be in comparing them to their mothers rather than their fathers?

How is social mobility measured?

Studies of social mobility, until now, have been based on occupation in employment, as this is easily measurable. Out of a current population in the UK of about 60 million, those in employment number about 30 million. So how can the other 30 million be classified? The retired could be assigned a social position on the basis of previous employment, and children on the basis of their parents' occupation. Mothers raising children were traditionally assigned a class based on the occupation of their partner. But what if they have no partner, and have never worked themselves? In the past, they have been assigned a class based on their father's occupation. Feminists, among others, have suggested that this is not a very satisfactory or accurate measure. This dilemma has led to three main positions on how to measure class and thus how to measure whether social mobility has occurred:

1 Goldthorpe (1980) suggests staying with convention and counting the person in the family with the most direct link to the labour market.
2 Heath and Britten (1984) suggest still using the family, but taking the labour position of both the adult male and the adult female to give a class position for the whole family.

3   Stanworth (1984) suggests that the family is left out of the equation, and that individuals should be the unit of stratification.

However, the class system of the UK remains very heavily gendered and there is an uneven distribution of men and women in the different classes. For example, following the Registrar General's classification of class (see above, pages 543–4), Goldthorpe found that Class I consisted mostly of men, while Class IV contained more women than men. In addition, there are different mobility chances for men and women, and within any one class men are advantaged. At any specific skill level, men with that skill are often higher placed than women with the same skill; for example, with a teaching qualification, men are more likely to be found in education management than women.

> **Activity**
>
> Working in small groups, list the advantages and disadvantages of each of the three possible models described above for assigning people to a social class. The ideas of each group should be shared with the whole class at the end.

Studies of social mobility

There have been many studies of mobility since the 1930s, both in the UK and worldwide. Here, studies concerning the UK will be considered.

The Glass Study

Using what is known as the Hall–Jones scale of social class, which graded occupations according to their prestige, Glass (1954) compared the occupations of men over 21 with those of their fathers. Two-thirds of the men interviewed were in a different social class from their fathers (one third went down, one-third moved up). Most movement was to a class adjacent to that of the father. Long-range mobility from top to bottom or bottom to top was very rare. The figures, however, disguised the high degree of self-recruitment. In general, Glass discovered a high degree of social closure.

Criticisms of the Glass Study   Critics have suggested that much of Glass's evidence was based on people's recollections of their father's occupations, which may have been faulty. Also, that many of the fathers had been working, or perhaps not working, through the great depression of the 1930s, which may have also given false data as to their actual occupation. Another problem is that this was a snapshot in time, and it is possible that the men interviewed in 1949 went on, through the expansion of the 1950s, to higher and better positions – that they were intragenerationally socially mobile. However, other studies done at a similar time, in the UK, USA and other societies, suggested that intragenerational social mobility, too, was relatively short range, from manual to routine clerical rather than from manual to managerial.

The Oxford Mobility Study

The next major British study was started in 1972 by Goldthorpe (1980) at Nuffield College, Oxford. It is sometimes referred to as the Nuffield study and sometimes as the Oxford Mobility Study. It is almost impossible to compare this study with the one by Glass, since different criteria were used for the various strata. Glass had used groups based on occupational prestige; Goldthorpe used his own classification based mainly on market rewards. However, this study seemed to show higher rates of long-range mobility (and more upward and downward), and fewer than half of the people surveyed were still in the social class into which they were born. Goldthorpe therefore concluded that the chances of upward movement, particularly from the manual classes, had improved during the twentieth century.

Criticisms of the Oxford Mobility Study   Later work by Kellner and Wilby (1980) shows that the claim made by Goldthorpe was not equally true for all social classes. They drew up a 1:2:4 rule of relative hope. This states that, over the period covered (the middle to latter part of the twentieth century), whatever the chance of a working-class boy moving up to the service class, a boy from the intermediate class had twice the chance to make this move, and one from the service class itself had four times the chance. Therefore, they concluded that UK society has seen no significant increase in openness.

Another major problem with Goldthorpe's study is that, although it suggested easier entry to the service class as a whole, it did not explore what might be called elite self-recruitment. Feminists would rightly argue that the study ignored a large part of the workforce – namely, women. In a later work, Goldthorpe and Payne (1986) attempted to address this issue. They found that however women were included in the study (whether by including them in their husband's class, by assigning the family a class based on the higher wage-earner, or by assigning women their own class), very little difference was made to relative mobility rates.

Works by Stanworth (1984), Heath (1981) and Payne and Abbott (1990) suggest that women from all social classes are more likely to be downwardly socially mobile and less likely to be upwardly social mobile than men, and that women born into classes 1 and 2 were very likely to fall to class 3. Of the number from the lower classes who were socially mobile, very few ended up in the top two classes. It could be argued that, by ignoring women, the picture of social mobility in the UK is inaccurate and incomplete. The study of women would suggest that mobility is somewhat less than previously thought and that, for women, downward mobility is as likely as upward mobility.

The Essex Study

The Essex Study of social mobility in the 1980s attempted to consider both male and female mobility, and both inter- and intragenerational mobility. Marshall et al. (1988) found that, as a result of the expansion of white-collar work, there had been fairly high rates of upward mobility, but the rates were lower for women. This study found that the class of origin has a strong effect on subsequent job opportunities. They interviewed people who had begun their working careers in the service class and looked at how many of them had managed to stay in this class over a period of time. Of the men who had been born into the service class, 84 per cent were still there at the time of being interviewed (that is, there had been no inter- or intragenerational mobility).

However, only 64 per cent of the men born into the working class were still employed in the service class. For women, the figures were 77 per cent and 43 per cent. It could be argued that even when some social mobility is achieved early in life, it is not always maintained, and that life chances at birth may have a part to play in the ultimate destination of an individual.

Goldthorpe and Jackson (2007) argue that because service sector jobs have probably now reached a peak, the chances of upward mobility from the working class are now very low. The levels of mobility found in Goldthorpe's earlier work are unlikely to be repeated over the next decade, and social mobility patterns are likely to be much more static.

The Sutton Trust

Studies by the Sutton Trust (2007) have looked at more recent changes in intergenerational mobility based on educational attainment at the age of 23. The main findings are in the box.

The Sutton Trust

In 2005 the Sutton Trust commissioned a report which highlighted the fall in intergenerational mobility for children born in the UK in 1970 compared with those born in 1958. This revealed that the adult earnings of the 1970 cohort were more closely linked to the income of their parents when compared with those in the 1958 cohort. Most notably, the proportion of people from the poorest fifth of families obtaining a degree increased from 5 per cent to 7 per cent, while the graduation rates for the richest fifth rose from 20 per cent to 37 per cent. The research also found that social mobility in the UK and the US was lower than all other advanced nations for which there was comparable data during this period.

This study tries to gauge the levels of social mobility for children born between 1970 and 2000. The research focuses on information gathered for the children (born on average in 1985) of the 1958 cohort and the children (born on average in 1999) of the 1970 cohort.

Partly because of a lack of survey data for children born in the 1980s, the 2005 study investigates the link between the income of parents and the intermediate outcomes of their offspring, rather than their adult earnings. These outcomes include acquiring a degree by the age of 23, cognitive test scores during the early years and parents' reports of behaviour during childhood. A key assumption is that, as demonstrated by previous studies, earlier educational and behaviourial outcomes for children are a good (and reasonably constant) predictor of their future earnings as adults.

So inequalities in intermediate outcomes between children from poorer and richer households provide an indication of future mobility for children growing up in Britain today and in the recent past. The evidence from more recent surveys suggests that the association between family income and intermediate outcomes has held constant for children born in the period 1970–2000 – parental background continues to have a significant influence on children's academic progress.

Degree acquisition

For those graduating in 2002, there was a slight widening of educational inequality in graduation rates compared with those acquiring degrees in the 1990s. The proportion of people acquiring degrees among the poorest income groups dropped from 11 to 10 per cent, while the proportion acquiring degrees among the richest groups grew by 4 percentage points, from 40 per cent to 44 per cent.

Compiled from The Sutton Trust 2005

The Sutton Trust findings would seem to show that social mobility in the UK has actually declined as the higher social classes have maintained their hold on educational success, allowing them to maintain their social position, while the poorer groups, by failing in education, cannot rise from their class of origin.

Activity

Answer the following question in an essay of two or three pages:
'To what extent has social mobility changed in the past 20 years?'

Social mobility and ethnic minorities

Platt (2005) argues that longitudinal studies concerning the social mobility of ethnic minorities show that some groups have been more upwardly mobile than others, particularly Afro-Caribbean, black African, Indian and Chinese people. Their mobility patterns appeared to be linked to their educational success. She distinguished between migrants and non-migrants, looking at the generation differences when the parents had arrived in the UK. Migrants were more likely than non-migrants to be upwardly socially mobile, with 60 per cent of migrants and 70 per cent of non-migrants remaining in the same social class as their parents. However, middle-class migrants were more likely to suffer downward mobility than upward. There were religious differences within ethnicities, with Hindus more likely to be upwardly mobile than Muslims or Sikhs. Gender also affected mobility, with women more likely to remain in the same social class throughout their lives.

The maintenance of class differences

When looking at whether social mobility matters in the formation of class solidarity or of class-consciousness, different arguments will have to be made for different classes. It would appear that those members of the working class who are not upwardly mobile might develop a form of solidarity, since, for the past 50 years or so, there has been relatively little downward mobility into that class. However, for those classes in which there has been much inward and outward mobility, the chances of class-consciousness would seem slight. For Marxists, it could be argued that this talk of increased social mobility is nothing but a smokescreen, since, as has been seen, social closure at the top means that most mobility is only between the working and lower-middle class, and merely serves to disguise the fact that none of these people own or control the means of production.

The persistence of inequality in contemporary society

Some sociologists suggest that British society is no longer unequal, others that the inequalities may have altered slightly, but still persist. This disagreement can best be resolved by looking at various areas of life. Some of you will have studied different areas during the course of the year. However, all these areas show different links to the effects of stratification. There follow some brief examples of how stratification and differentiation are linked to the various topics you may have studied for AS and A2 Sociology, to give you an idea of how these themes tie into one another.

Culture and identity

Many forms of social differentiation are crucial to the formation of identity. The very way in which people differentiate themselves from others is central to their self-perception. Gender, age, social class, ethnicity and sexuality are crucial to how people view themselves.

The idea of what constitutes culture can be affected by class: for example, consumption of high culture such as opera or theatre needs a disposable income not enjoyed by everyone. Class will influence the way in which parents socialize their children. Even such things as whether one is breast-fed or smacked as a child are often a reflection of the social class one is born into.

Families and households

The higher the social class, the more likely it is that parents will be married or in a very stable relationship: they will be less likely to be separated or divorced. The chances of same-sex parents are also higher in the upper and middle classes than in the working class.

Ethnicity may affect the likelihood of being in a one-parent family: recent figures from the Department for Children, Schools and Families show that 57 per cent of Afro-Caribbean children live in lone-parent families, while only 12 per cent of Asian children do so, compared to 25 per cent of white children.

However, single parenthood has different causes and these vary between classes. 'Single-through-choice' is more frequent among the middle and professional classes, 'single-through-desertion' more prevalent among the working classes. Up-to-date figures on divorce and single parent families can be found at www.ons.gov.uk.

The number of children in a family is also influenced by class and ethnicity. Large families tend to be found among the very rich and the poor, among ethnic minorities rather than among white groups, and among Catholics and Muslims rather than other religions.

Wealth, poverty and welfare

On the whole, women earn less than men during their working lives and suffer greater poverty in retirement. Women are more likely than men to be in receipt of welfare benefits such as Income Support or Working Tax Credits during their 'working' life and Pension Credits in their retirement. This becomes doubly true if they are from an ethnic minority, and even more true if they are disabled or in ill health.

Poverty and social exclusion are similarly linked to forms of differentiation such as age, gender, ethnicity, disability or locality. An elderly, childless widow living in a country village with no post office, bus service, doctor or shop may be socially excluded even if she is relatively wealthy, whereas her counterpart in a big city may be less socially excluded because she has access to many services.

Putnam (2000) has suggested a link between social exclusion and social capital. Social capital refers to a person's social networks of friends and relatives. High social capital can, to some extent, lessen the problems of social exclusion experienced by different groups. For example, a newly arrived Bangladeshi woman speaking little English living as part of the only Asian family in the village will have less social capital and experience higher social exclusion than if she lives in a multicultural town with an enclave of other Asian families.

Education

In the UK, where there is a multiplicity of schools, run by the state and by charities and private companies, selection either by price or ability is a growing factor. Private education, which educates only 6–7 per cent of the age group, is only accessible to those with either money or the ability to win a scholarship. Access to state-run schools is becoming increasingly selective. City academies, faith schools and others now have the right to select some pupils. The 1988 Education Act introduced the idea of parental choice, where parents had the right to choose a school for their child. The reality is that the school decides. Those children seen as more desirable are more likely to gain entry, and class prejudices have an effect on the chances of entry.

Ethnicity also has a bearing on academic achievement. The latest figures can be found on the Department for Children, Schools and Families (DCSF) website (www.dcsf.gov.uk). Specific figures for ethnic minorities from the Ethnic Minority Achievement Unit show that between 2004–6:

- Chinese, Indian, Irish and mixed white and Asian pupils consistently performed above the national average for all pupils;
- black, Pakistani, Bangladeshi and mixed white and black Caribbean pupils consistently performed below the national average for all pupils;
- Gypsy/Roma and Traveller pupils had extremely low levels of attainment; moreover, many children from these groups were not recorded in the Annual School Census, were not present during Key Stage assessments and/or did not continue in education up until Key Stage 4.

Specific figures for the achievement of girls and boys are also available from the DCSF and show that girls as a whole do better than boys, and are now more likely to attend university than boys. Indeed, the largest single group studying medicine in the UK is Asian girls.

Health

Access to healthcare is greatly affected by aspects of stratification. Class determines much access. Tudor-Hart's '**Inverse Care Law**' (1971) states that those living in areas with the greatest need receive the least care, and those with the least need receive the greatest provision of health facilities. Working-class access to GPs may be affected adversely by their working hours and, when access is achieved, consultation times are shorter for working-class patients than for middle-class patients. The latter are also more likely to be referred for further specialist treatment. The middle classes are more likely to be able to gain access to private healthcare either through their employer or through their own insurance provision.

The **inverse care law** means that those whose need is least get the most resources, while those in greatest need get the fewest resources.

Other physical factors must also be taken into account when looking at poor health. Bad housing, badly maintained local areas, lack of open spaces to exercise and high traffic pollution all add to the likelihood of ill health. Poor diet caused by lack of money, or living far away from shops that sell fresh fruit and vegetables also have an effect. Such factors are more likely to be experienced by the working classes than by the middle classes.

The working conditions of different classes and of males and females also affect health. Working in a warm, temperature-controlled office has far fewer health risks than working on a building site in cold, wet, windy or stiflingly hot weather. Women and the middle classes are more likely to be found in the former situations, working-class men in the latter.

Figure 7.5 Some key social influences on health

Ethnic minorities often have problems with access to National Health Service facilities for a variety of reasons, including:

- cultural reasons, the need for Muslim women to see female doctors or be chaperoned by a male relative when visiting the doctor;
- language barrier;
- racism in health provision.

As the number of British-born and trained Asian doctors grows, it is to be hoped that many of these problems will disappear.

> ### Activity
>
> Look at figure 7.5 and answer the following questions:
> 1 Describe the ways in which the factors identified might be affected by a person's class.
> 2 Describe the ways in which the factors identified might be affected by a person's sex.
> 3 Describe the ways in which the factors identified might be affected by ethnicity.
> 4 Write an essay on the following: 'Assess the extent to which social differentiation affects the health and the life chances of the individual.'

Beliefs in society

It could be argued that theories concerning social differentiation underlie many of the theories concerning ideology and belief in all societies. There are clear connections to the works of Marx and the neo-Marxists such as Gramsci (1971) when considering the role of **ideology** and the creation of false consciousness. Feminist theories consider the role of religion and ideology in maintaining patriarchy, while **liberation theologists** attempt to alter the class basis of religious teaching in the Roman Catholic Church.

Membership of different groups, such as churches, denominations, sects, cults, new religious movements (NRMs) and New Age movements (NAMs) varies widely across the genders, social classes and different ethnic groups. The middle-class, white population is more likely to belong to longer-established churches or denominations, whereas chapel-goers are more commonly members of the lower-middle and upper-working class. Afro-Caribbeans and Africans are more likely to be among the congregation of evangelical NRMs than among older more traditional churches such as the Church of England. Women are found to be more religious than men, and older people are more likely to attend a place of worship than the young. This however, is not necessarily true of Islam or the NRMs.

Leadership of nearly all religious organizations is in the hands of men rather than women, and middle- or upper-class men rather than those from the working class. This seems particularly true of the older established religions such as Judaism, Islam, Shintoism and Christianity, especially the Roman Catholic Church and the Church of England. Women are more likely to be found in some leadership roles in Reformed Judaism, denominations such as Methodism and NRMs and NAMs. This is particularly true of Wicca (sometimes known by its practitioners as white witchcraft), where

An **ideology** is a set of ideas, values and beliefs that represent the outlook, and justify the interests, of a social group.

Liberation theologists are a group within the Roman Catholic Church whose members preach that the good things in life should be shared here on earth in an equal fashion.

nearly all the participants are women. It should be pointed out that very few long-lasting religious movements have ever been founded by women, the most notable exception being the Christian Science Movement founded by Mary Baker.

In recent times, sociologists have become interested in the move to **fundamentalism**_and how this might affect and be affected by class, gender, ethnicity, age and disability. It has been suggested that fundamentalism is often found among those who feel socially excluded and left out from the main stream of society. However, if that were entirely true, then one might expect the old, the poor and rural communities to be more fundamentalist than others, but the growth of radical fundamentalism is more likely to be found among the young and those living in cities. In many societies, sexuality is also a major concern. Many Islamic and African countries treat homosexuality as a crime.

> **Fundamentalism** means a return to the literal meaning of religious texts and associated behaviour.

Global development

It is impossible to look at global issues without being aware of the vast discrepancies of wealth and income between different parts of the globe. Even within the poorest, least developed societies, there are different levels of wealth and access to income, and great social differences between groups, even if it is only between men and women, young and old, healthy and unhealthy. The United Nations, in particular the Millennium Development Goals section, has the latest figures on a variety of social differences between groups and societies (see www.un.org).

Activity

1 Using the figures from table 7.5, name the *five* poorest countries in the world in terms of income per capita.
2 Which are the *five* richest?
3 List *three* things that each of these groups have in common.
4 Using your own knowledge, list *three* factors, apart from wealth, that differ between these two groups.

The mass media

In the area of the mass media the key areas to consider in relation to social differentiation are:

- ownership and control of the media;
- the role of the media in maintaining the ideology of the ruling class;
- representation within the media;
- moral panics and the groups likely to be scapegoated on the basis of class, gender, ethnicity, disability, sexuality or age;
- audience diversity;
- new media and their impact on different groups.

Table 7.5: Indicators on income and economic activity

Country or area	Year	Per capita GDP (US$)	Adult (15+) economic activity rate		
			Total	Men	Women
Afghanistan	2006	319	65	88	40
Bangladesh	2006	437	70	86	52
Bolivia	2006	1,101	74	84	63
Brazil	2006	5,640	68	79	57
Canada	2006	39,004	66	72	61
Chad	2006	634	72	78	66
China	2006	2,055	75	82	69
Cuba	2006	4,650	59	73	44
Ethiopia	2006	164	80	89	71
France	2006	35,375	55	61	48
India	2006	784	59	82	34
Indonesia	2006	1,592	68	85	51
Iraq	2006	1,647	49	78	20
Israel	2006	20,601	55	59	51
Japan	2006	34,661	60	73	48
Liechtenstein	2006	102,605	...	...	...
Nepal	2006	290	64	78	50
Norway	2006	71,525	68	73	64
Pakistan	2006	913	59	83	33
South Africa	2006	5,133	62	79	46
Tanzania, United Republic of	2006	335	88	90	86
Tunisia	2006	3,003	52	75	29
Turkey	2006	5,307	52	76	28
Uganda	2006	346	83	86	80
Ukraine	2006	2,287	56	64	50

Table 7.5 (continued)

Country or area	Year	Per capita GDP (US$)	Adult (15+) economic activity rate		
			Total	Men	Women
United Arab Emirates	2006	42,890	78	93	41
United Kingdom	2006	39,207	62	69	55
United States	2006	43,562	66	73	60
Yemen	2006	853	53	75	30
Zambia	2006	938	78	91	66
Zimbabwe	2006	133	74	85	64

Source: Compiled from figures produced by the United Nations

Ownership

Like most other businesses, mass media enterprises tend to be owned by white, middle-class men rather than women, ethnic minorities or the working class. A high proportion of owners have a privileged, university-educated background.

Ideology

Work by the Sutton Trust (2006) shows that leading news and current affairs journalists are more likely than not to have been to an independent (private) school. Since those who decide what is important and **newsworthy** come from such a privileged background, they are likely to reflect their interests in what is shown to the rest of the population. They maintain what Gramsci (1971) would call **hegemonic control**.

Newsworthy items are those items selected by editors and journalists as being of importance and thus which should be reported.

Representation

This hegemony is also maintained by the stereotypes found in the media. Women, ethnic minorities, the young, the old and the disabled are portrayed in ways that shape how they are viewed by the rest of society. Ethnic minorities are disproportionately mentioned in relation to crime, usually as criminals rather than victims, whereas, in reality, ethnic minorities are more likely to be victims than criminals.

Women, ethnic minorities, the old and the disabled are are disproportionately underrepresented and are all less likely to be seen on TV, films and in the newspapers than men.

Hegemonic control is a form of dominance in which the ruling class convinces the rest of society that their own ideas are the truth and should not, therefore, be questioned.

Moral panics

A **moral panic** is a wave of public concern about some exaggerated or imaginary threat to society, stirred up by exaggerated and sensationalized reporting in the mass media.

Moral panics occur when the mass media take an event and create a drama, such as 'all teenagers are hoodies', and create **scapegoats** to blame for all social ills. (For more on moral panics, see chapter 6, pages 407–9.) The groups so chosen are usually:

- working rather than middle class (social security scroungers rather than middle class tax evaders);
- male rather than female;
- in the case of gun and knife crime, ethnic minority rather than white;
- young rather than old – teenagers riding bikes on the pavement rather than electric-scooter-riding old age pensioners.

Audiences

A **scapegoat** is an individual who is picked out to blame for an action or event whether or not he or she is innocent or guilty. The term is usually applied to those who are innocent.

Class, gender, age and ethnicity all influence the way in which audiences use the media and receive media messages. Blumler and McQuail (1968) say that people use the media for different reasons. Soap-opera viewers who are young may watch them for relationship advice; older viewers may watch them for companionship. The cultural effects model (see chapter 3, pages 213–16) suggests that people from varying backgrounds will interpret what they see or hear in the light of their own past experience.

New media

The newer forms of the mass media are more accessible and available to some people than to others. Older people and those from lower social classes are less likely to have access to computers, for example. Access to fast broadband Internet services is also dependent upon where you live in the country, and whether you live in a city or in a rural community. Up to now, more men than women have undertaken computer courses at further and higher education level.

Power and politics

It should now be clear that social differentiation is at the base of all systems of power distribution and thus is the basis of all politics. In the UK, most power still resides in the hands of men rather than women, whether it be obvious power in the hands of politicians or the less obvious power wielded by big business. Arguably, business has more power than politicians. Transnational corporations can make decisions that affect the lives of millions – for example when they shift production from one country to another. In these circumstances, there is little the domestic politician can do to alter the situation.

Politicians are still drawn mainly from a privileged and educated group. There are only a very few parliaments in the world in which women are represented in proportion to their population size; Wales is one and Iceland, Sweden and Finland have quite high numbers of women in Parliament. So too do many Islamic countries – for example, Bangladesh and Afghanistan. Indeed, there have been more female prime ministers in Bangladesh and Sri Lanka than anywhere else in the world. Youth, however, seems to be a bar to political power. Prime ministers, presidents and other heads of state are rarely under 50. Given that half the world's population is under 16, it appears that power is not something given to the majority.

In the UK, ethnicity does have an effect on the chance of being elected to any public body. Ethnic minorities are not well represented at any level of government, not even on local councils in areas where they form a high proportion of the population.

When looking at who gets elected in a democracy, it is worth also looking both at the selection panels and the electorate. In order to be a candidate, one must be selected by a political party, or fund the cost oneself. Costs are high, which prevents most people from standing as independents. Thus selection by the political party concerned is essential. For parliamentary elections, the major parties have an approved list of candidates from whom the local party can pick. Most of this list is made up of white, middle-class and British-born men who tend to be over 40 and married with children. Very few candidates are disabled. The selection panels, drawn from party members in a given locality, are also predominantly middle class, middle-aged and white. Thus class, ethnicity and gender are factors that affect a person's chance of entering politics in a formal way.

Voters are also more likely to be older than the average, with those in the higher classes most likely to use their vote. Men and women appear to vote in general elections in similar proportions; for local elections the picture is less clear. Those who *abstain* from voting may do so deliberately or from sheer apathy. The apathetic group appears to be younger and more likely to be suffering from social exclusion. The active abstainers are usually more politically aware and use other means such as protest groups, pressure groups and other tactics to put across their political message. This group is more likely to consist of younger, well-educated, middle-class people. There are also disabled lobby groups and women's groups.

Crime and deviance

Everyone or anyone may break the law, but the word 'criminal' is reserved for those who have been caught. On that basis, it can be said that the majority of criminals are young, male, working-class urban-dwellers, and, for some offences, disproportionately black.

Laws in the UK are passed by Parliament; some laws from the European Union may override domestic law. In either case, when looking at the law-making process, it can be seen that most of those involved are male, middle class and from the ethnic majority in their own country. It is widely suggested that British laws are more concerned with the protection of property than anything else. Certainly, the sentences for burglary are higher than those for causing death by dangerous driving, for example, and of course most property belongs to the higher classes.

While crime involves breaking the law, deviance concerns the breaking of social conventions and thus is more difficult to measure. Who decides what is deviant? The groups most likely to be perceived or portrayed as deviant are the young, the working class, the ethnic minorities and the disabled. Women will be seen as deviant if they stray outside the confines of what is perceived to be conventional female behaviour. It is suggested that when women appear in court cases they are more likely to be treated leniently if they conform to 'feminine' stereotypes rather than presenting themselves as strong, independent and capable of looking after themselves.

The persistence of inequality: concluding remarks

From the discussions above, it would seem that whatever politicians and other social commentators may say about the inherent fairness of modern society, where all are treated equally, the reality is somewhat different. The life chances enjoyed by an individual are determined by his or her social class of birth, sex or gender, ethnicity and state of health. Moreover, being born in an affluent country such as the UK is far preferable to being born in, for example, sub-Saharan Africa.

Despite the recent tendency of sociologists and social commentators to suggest that social class is dying, Chapman (2008) and Reay (2007), amongst others, would suggest that it is still the major determinant of life chances in the UK and this is unlikely to change in the immediate future.

Activity

Consider the following pairs of photographs and discuss what inequalities exist in society based on each form of differentiation.

Ethnicity

Age

Disability

Adherence to particular religious practices

Sexuality

Research methods and social stratification and differentiation

This section assumes that chapter 5 has already been studied, and that you have a good grasp of the sociological methods studied at AS. If you haven't yet studied chapter 5, or you need to brush up on your AS methods, you are advised to return to this section once you have done so.

The aim of this section is to get you to apply your knowledge and understanding of sociological research to the study of social differentiation and stratification. Many methods have been used in studying this area of sociology. What follows is to get you thinking about some of these issues as well as some of the theoretical, ethical and practical difficulties in using the different research methods.

Information on all forms of social stratification and differentiation can be collected in a variety of ways:

- primary research, which you do yourself;
- secondary research: material that already exists;
- quantitative methods: those involving numbers such a structured questionnaire, the Census, etc.;
- qualitative methods: those involving the discovery of more subjective feelings, such as in-depth interviews;
- valid methods, which release the truth;
- reliable methods, which, if repeated, will collect the same information;
- sampling: by using a proportion of the target population, information can be col-

lected that reflects that which would have been given by the whole target population.

Research might consist of a snapshot (looking at a single moment in time) or it might be longitudinal (following a group or comparing statistics over a long period of time). Among the methods that might be used in studying stratification and differentiation are:

- comparison of official statistics;
- longitudinal social surveys;
- observational methods, both participant and non-participant;
- questionnaires;
- interviews, both formal and informal.

Activity

Consider each of the following ways of collecting data:
- in-depth interviews about subjective class assignment
- interviews about what it is like to be a woman
- questionnaires about current and previous occupation
- questionnaires about earnings
- surveys comparing a woman's occupation with that of her husband
- standardized mortality ratios by social class, ethnicity, geography and sex
- surveys on father's occupation and son's educational achievement
- memoirs from being a slave

1 Say whether they are quantitative or qualitative.
2 Say whether they are likely to be representative, giving reasons for your choice.
3 Decide whether they may be valid or reliable or both, giving reasons for your answer.

In what follows are two different pieces of research, both taken from the field of health. It does not matter whether you have studied this area or not; what you will be asked to do is answer the questions concerning the practicalities and ethics of using these methods rather than others.

Unequal in death: geographical areas and life expectancy

Where a child is born in Britain today is more important than ever in determining that child's life chances, particularly his or her chances of survival. Such a finding is the opposite to common preconceptions of relatively even life chances across the country. This inequality has arisen partly because absolute mortality rates have fallen steadily over the years, but mainly because those improvements have not been distributed evenly amongst the population as a whole. For instance, an infant girl in Leeds is now more than twice as likely to die in the first year of life as an infant girl growing up in a town in Dorset. Proportionately, eight times as many boys aged between 1 and 4 years died in Manchester as compared to rural Gloucestershire between 1990 and 1992. . . These are not the most extreme discrepancies but they are places in which the long-term trend is worsening. We are becoming less equal in death.

Using comparable 1951 local authority boundaries, the three areas with the highest mortality ratios in the 1990s (Oldham, Salford and Greenock) had mortality ratios only a fifth higher than the national average in the early 1950s. Their rates are now rising towards being a third higher than the national rate. Almost 1,000 deaths a year would be avoided, were the mortality ratios not excessive in just these three places. 'Excess deaths' are calculated as deaths above the average rate, not deaths above the lowest rate, which would have produced far higher numbers of 'avoidable' mortalities. Nationally there were 77,000 excess deaths in the 1990–2 period, representing about 4 per cent of all mortality. Because mortality statistics require census statistics, this is the latest date for which reliable local estimates can be made for small areas.

Source: Quoted from Danny Dorling, *Changing Mortality Ratios in Local Areas of Britain, 1950s–1990s* (Joseph Rowntree Foundation, August 1997)

Activity

Read the excerpt in the box above and, either individually or as a group, answer the following questions:
1 What research method was used?
2 Give three reasons why this particular research method might have been used.
3 What are the difficulties with using this method?
4 Give three other methods that might have been used to gather similar data.
5 Describe the advantages and disadvantages of each of these methods.
6 As an individual, write an essay of two or three pages assessing the usefulness of the method used in the 'Unequal in death' excerpt. Much of the work you have already done either as an individual or as a group will help you frame your answer.

Poverty, ethnicity and long-term ill health

This study explored the relationship between long-term health conditions and poverty across a diverse population. Poverty was broadly conceived and covered three domains: financial hardship, lack of participation in employment and limited social participation. Combining investigation of large-scale nationally representative surveys with in-depth qualitative work in a deprived area of London, the study explored people's experiences of long-term ill health and how they managed this, and its relationship with poverty and identity. The study included individuals with a range of health conditions, and concentrated on working-age individuals who had acquired their condition during adult life and who identified themselves as belonging to one of four ethnic groups: Pakistani, Ghanaian, Bangladeshi and white English. . . . [The study] explored both constraints and coping strategies and identified points of similarity and difference across the four ethnic groups. . . .

The study was carried out between February 2005 and July 2006, by researchers at the University of Sheffield, Sheffield Hallam University, University of Essex, the London School of Hygiene and Tropical Medicine and Social Action for Health. It was based upon secondary analysis of the Labour Force Survey 2001–5; the Citizenship Survey 2001;

published tables from the 2001 Census; and an extended period of fieldwork in the East End of London between April 2004 and February 2006, which had three phases: rapid assessment, 86 in-depth interviews and community feedback.

Source: Quoted from Sarah Salway et al., *Long-term Ill Health, Poverty and Ethnicity* (Joseph Rowntree Foundation, April 2007).

Activity

Read the excerpt in the box above, then answer the following questions:
1   How many different methods were used in this research?
2   Which method do you think added reliability to the research and which added validity?
3   Which methods were most likely to be representative?
4   Why do you think so many methods were used? Give *three* reasons for using this many methods.
5   Discuss the practical and ethical dilemmas that might have occurred in the in-depth interviews.
6   Draw up an interview schedule of 10 questions to explore the link between poverty and ill-health (you can assume that your respondents are suffering from long-standing ill health, but not that they are necessarily poor – so one of the questions may need to uncover whether they are poor, or at least whether they consider themselves poor).
7   What problems might there be with these questions? Think of practical, ethical and theoretical problems.
8   What other methods might have been used to gather the information concerning coping strategies?
9   What advantages and disadvantages would one of the alternative methods listed above have had? You can choose which one to consider. Write your answer as a short essay, discussing at least *three* advantages and *three* disadvantages. This will help you answer questions in the exam that ask you to 'assess the usefulness' of a given concept/ method etc.

CHAPTER SUMMARY

After studying this chapter you should be able to:

- describe the different forms of differentiation, inequality and stratification;

- describe the different theories of stratification, by social class, by ethnicity and by gender;

- explain and criticize the different theories of stratification such as functionalist, Marxist, interactionist, feminist and postmodernist;

- explain the problems in defining and measuring class;

- explain and criticize theories concerning the defining and measuring of class;

- use evidence about different classes to assess theories of stratification;

- describe changes in the structure of inequality and stratification;

- describe the patterns of social mobility;

- explain and criticize theories about social mobility, what it signifies and whether it exists;

- describe the connections between methodology and the study of differentiation and stratification;

- explain and criticize the usefulness of specific sociological methods in studying differentiation and stratification;

- explain and criticize the usefulness of specific sociological theories in studying differentiation and stratification.

KEY TERMS

age-set	fundamentalism	lifestyle	repressive state
apartheid	gender	lumpenproletariat	apparatus
bourgeoisie	hegemonic control	malestream	reserve army of labour
bureaucracy	hydraulic society	matrilocal	scapegoats
class-consciousness	ideal type	meritocracy	social closure
closed system/society	ideological state	meta-analysis	social construction
consumption patterns	apparatus	newsworthy	social exclusion
culture	ideology	norms	social mobility
deskilling	immediate gratification	open system/society	socialization
elite	income	party	social solidarity
embourgeoisement:	Industrial Revolution	patriarchy	status
ethnicity	institutional racism	patrilocal	teenagers
ethnocentrism	instrumental attitude	present-time orientation	trade union
expressive role	instrumental role	professions	underclass
false consciousness	inverse care law	proletarianization	values
fatalistic	liberation theologists	proletariat	wealth
feudal system	life chances	racism	

EXAM QUESTIONS

SECTION B: STRATIFICATION AND DIFFERENTIATION

Answer **all** the questions from this section

You are advised to spend approximately 45 minutes on Question 4

You are advised to spend approximately 30 minutes on Question 5

You are advised to spend approximately 45 minutes on Question 6

Time allowed: 2 hours   **Total for this section: 90 marks**

4 Read **Item C** below and answer the question that follows.

Item C

In the late 1980s the relative chance of being a member of the service class, according
to Kellner and Wilby, was 1:2:4, for those born into the unskilled working class: for
those born into the skilled manual working class: for those born into the service class.
This situation had changed only slightly from earlier mobility studies. Entry into the
elite groups in British industry, such as the managing directors of companies quoted on   5
the London Stock Exchange, was even less likely to happen. This was probably due to a
form of social closure practised by those already there. For women and ethnic minorities,
the chances of upward mobility were lower than for white men. Other studies showed
that for some women, those born into the higher classes in particular, downward social
mobility was a distinct possibility   10

(a) Examine some of the reasons for the mobility patterns outlined in **Item C**.   *(12 marks)*

(b) Assess sociological explanations for the status differences between men and women.

(21 marks)

5   This question requires you to **apply** your knowledge and understanding of sociological
research methods to the study of this **particular** issue in stratification and differentiation.
Read **Item D** below and answer parts (a) and (b) that follow.

Item D

In studying the long-term changes in the social differentiation in UK society, official
statistics, particularly those based on the 10-yearly Census and the Register of Births
Marriages and Deaths, have been of great importance. They allow us to map regional
variations in changes in certain aspects of modern life, such as increased life expectancy,
the decline in infant mortality and the rising age of first marriage. However, there are   5
many areas of differentiation which they are unable to reveal.

While the occupation of the parents is noted on the birth certificate, and the occupation of the bridal pair is noted on a marriage certificate, and are likely to be accurate, the
occupation most frequently noted on death certificates in the past was 'retired'. Thus,
patient analysis of an individual's life using these documents might show his or her   10
changing status at two or three points in his or her lifetime, but it will reveal nothing
about changes that might have occurred between these key events.

(TURN OVER)

(a) Identify *three* aspects of life that the official statistics outlined in **Item D** cannot reveal and suggest *one* way in which data on **each** of your named aspects might be collected.

(9 marks)

(b) Using material from **Item D** and elsewhere, assess the strengths and weaknesses of using official statistics to provide an accurate description of life in modern Britain. *(15 marks)*

6 Assess the contribution of feminist theories and research to our understanding of society.

(33 marks)

Glossary

Agenda-setting The media's influence over the issues that people think about because the agenda, or list of subjects, for public discussion is laid down by the mass media.

Age-set Groups of people of a similar age, who have shared status and roles. The transition from one age status to the next is often accompanied by a rite of passage.

Aid Economic, military, technical and financial assistance given (or loaned) to developing countries.

Alienation A lack of power, control, fulfilment and satisfaction experienced by workers in a capitalist society where the means of producing goods are privately owned and controlled.

Anomie A sense of normlessness, confusion and uncertainty over social norms, often found in periods of rapid social change and other disruptions of the routines and traditions of everyday social life.

Anti-capitalist movement A collectivity of a wide range of groups, united in their stand against the social inequality and exploitation fostered by capitalism.

Anti-globalization movement A loose network of groups and organizations globally opposing neo-liberal economic globalization (but using globalized communications).

Apartheid A system whereby society is divided on the basis of ethnic grouping, more especially, skin colour. Found in South Africa until the mid-1990s.

Authoritarian A system of rule which emphasizes the authority of a particular person, leading party or the state in general over the people.

Beliefs Ideas about things we hold to be true.

Bias A subject presented in a one-sided way, favouring one point of view over others, or ignoring, distorting or misrepresenting issues.

Bilateral aid Aid involving only the donor and recipient, usually government to government.

Biodiversity The number and variety of species in ecosystems that are threatened by human activity.

Bio-piracy The appropriation, generally by means of patents, of legal rights over indigenous knowledge – particularly indigenous biomedical knowledge – without compensation to the indigenous groups who originally developed such knowledge.

Bottom billion Collier's term for the poorest billion of the world's population; also known as 'Africa plus'.

Bourgeoisie In Marxist theory, the class of owners of the means of production.

Bretton Woods   The place where an agreement in 1944 set up the International Monetary Fund (IMF), the World Bank and what became the World Trade Organization (WTO).

Bureaucracy   A term derived from the works of Weber. A system of organization in which there is a hierarchy of officials, each with a different level of authority. All officials must stick to the rules, and detailed records are kept of every action.

Capitalism An economic system in which investment in and ownership of the means of production, distribution and exchange of wealth is made and maintained chiefly by private individuals or corporations, whose primary aim is to make profits.

Capitalists   The class of owners of the means of production in industrial societies whose primary purpose is to make profits.

Cash crops   Crops that are grown for sale in the market, and especially for export; colonialism imposed cash crop cultivation as the main form of agriculture in many colonies.

Circulation of elites   This describes how social change may occur where there is a single unitary elite holding power, suggesting that the only possibility for change is the replacement of one elite for another. Also, a circulation of elites may be a gradual process whereby younger members gradually replace older members within the existing elite.

Class-consciousness   An awareness in members of a social class of their real interests.

Cleavages   Groups in society that are distinguishable from each other by their different patterns of consumption.

Closed system/society   A society in which there is very little social mobility. Usually members of this society are likely to spend their whole lives in the class/group into which they were born. Status is therefore ascribed rather than achieved.

Collective conscience   The shared beliefs and values which form moral ties binding communities together, and regulate individual behaviour.

Colonialism   A system in which European powers had direct political control over most of today's developing countries.

Communism   An equal society, without social classes or class conflict, in which the means of production are the common property of all.

Conditionality   The setting of conditions on aid, so that it will be withheld if those conditions are not met.

Conservative force   One that maintains, or seeks to restore, traditional beliefs and customs and maintains the status quo (the way things are currently organized in society). This may sometimes involve supporting social change in order to return to traditional values and ways of life which are at risk of disappearing, or have already disappeared.

Constant sum view of power   A situation where some groups benefit to the detriment of others.

Consumption patterns   Ways in which people spend their money. Some sociologists, such as Giddens, suggest this is as important as class in demonstrating identity.

Corporate crime   Offences committed by large companies, or by individuals on behalf of large companies, which directly profit the company rather than individuals.

Crime   Behaviour which is against the criminal law – law-breaking.

Cultural homogenization   The idea that cultural differences are erased, with world cultures becoming increasingly the same. Often linked to the ideas of globalization and cultural imperialism.

Cultural imperialism   The imposition of Western, and especially American, cultural values on non-Western cultures, and the undermining of local cultures and cultural independence. Often linked to media imperialism.

Culture   The languages, beliefs, values and norms, customs, roles, knowledge and skills which combine to make up the way of life of any society.

Culture jamming   Subverting the messages transmitted by large corporations about the desirability of their brand.

Debt boomerang   George's term to describe the ways in which the debt crisis has negative effects in the developed world.

Debt crisis   Caused by the inability (and sometimes refusal) of indebted countries to pay interest on loans or to repay the original loan; debt repayments hold back development by diverting money and resources.

Delinquency   Crime committed by those under age 17, though the term 'delinquency' is often used to describe any anti-social or deviant activity by young people, even if it isn't criminal.

Democracy   A system of rule based on the equal treatment of all citizens and offering them all an opportunity to be involved in their own governance.

Demographic transition   In demography, the change from high birth and death rates to low birth and death rates.

Deforestation   The fall in the amount of land covered by forest as a result of human activity.

Dependency theory   Alternative Marxist-influenced theory to modernization, focused on external factors which impede development, including relationships with developed countries.

Desacrilization   The loss of the capacity to experience a sense of sacredness and mystery in life.

Desertification   The spread of deserts, as land on the edges of deserts loses its vegetation and top soil.

Deskilling   A situation in which the skills and knowledge previously needed to do a job are no longer required. A good example would be in printing photographs which used to need four specialized workers, but can now be done by a computer operated by a relatively unskilled person.

Determinism   The idea that people's behaviour is moulded by their social surroundings, and that they have little free will, control or choice over how they behave.

Development   The process by which societies change; a controversial term, with different writers having different conceptions of what processes are involved and what the outcome should be.

Development state   A state which sees its main purpose as development and leads the country's development programme.

Deviance   Rule-breaking behaviour of some kind, which fails to conform to the norms and expectations of a particular society or social group.

Deviancy amplification   The way the media may actually make worse or create the very deviance they condemn by their exaggerated, sensationalized and distorted reporting of events and their presence at them.

Deviant career   Where people who have been labelled as deviant find conventional opportunities blocked to them, and so are pushed into committing further deviant acts.

Deviant voters   Those who would seem to be voting for a political party which does not, on the face of it, seem to best reflect their class interest, such as a working-class Conservative.

Digital divide   The gap between those people with effective access to the digital and information technology making up the new media and those who lack such access.

Disability   A physical or mental impairment which has a substantial and long-term adverse effect on a person's ability to carry out normal day-to-day activities.

Discourses   Frameworks for thinking, bodies of ideas, which exist at particular times and in particular places. Discourses can be used as mechanisms for exerting power over people; they are often backed up by institutions.

Disenchantment   The process whereby the magical and mystical elements of life are eroded, as understandings of the world based on religion, faith, intuition, tradition, magic and superstition are displaced by rational argument, science and scientific explanation.

Dominant ideology   A set of ideas which justifies the social advantages of wealthy, powerful and influential groups in society, and justifies the disadvantages of those who lack wealth, power and influence.

Dysfunction   A part of the social structure which does not contribute to the maintenance and well-being of society, but creates tensions and other problems.

Ecofeminism   Feminist theory based on the idea that women's relationship with nature and the environment is different from that of men.

Economic growth   The growth of national income, usually measured by Gross National Product.

Elite   A small group holding great power and privilege in society.

Embourgeoisement   The notion that working-class manual workers were adopting more middle-class norms and values.

Empirical evidence   Observable evidence collected in the physical or social world.

Epidemiologic transition   In health, the change from the main problem in a society being infectious diseases to it being degenerative 'diseases of affluence' such as cancer and heart disease.

Ethnic identity   One where individuals assert their identity primarily in terms of the ethnic group and culture to which they belong.

Ethics   This involves the morality and standards of behaviour when carrying out research. These include the informed consent of those being studied, avoiding physical, social and mental harm to those helping with research, respecting confidentiality, and giving accurate and honest reports of findings.

Ethnicity   The shared culture of a social group which gives its members a common identity in some ways different from other social groups.

Ethnocentrism   A view of the world in which other cultures are seen through the eyes of one's own culture with a devaluing of the others.

Exhaustible resources   Those resources that can be renewed, but can also be exhausted and destroyed if overused, for example, fish stocks and forests.

Export-oriented industrialization   An industrialization strategy based on production for export.

Export processing zones   Areas in developing countries where the normal workplace regulations are relaxed to encourage transnational corporations (TNCs) to invest.

Expressive role   The nurturing, caring and emotional role, often linked by functionalists to women's biology and seen as women's 'natural' role in the family.

Fair trade   A movement to try to alter the terms of trade so that producers in developing countries receive a higher proportion of the profit.

False consciousness   The failure by members of a social class to recognize their real interests.

Fatalism   A state of mind where someone believes there is nothing they can do to alter their situation or circumstances.

Feudal system   A society in which the hierarchy of power and prestige is closely tied to the ownership of land.

Floating voters   Those who change the political party they vote for from election to election.

Folk devils   Individuals or groups posing an imagined or exaggerated threat to society.

Functional prerequisites   The basic needs that must be met if society is to survive.

Fundamentalism   A return to the literal meaning of religious texts and associated behaviour.

Future generations   The concept of sustainable development requires consideration of the future of today's children, and also of people not yet born, even though there is no established way of representing their interests.

Gate-keeping   The power of some people, groups or organizations to limit access to something valuable or useful. For example, the mass media have the power to refuse to cover some issues and therefore not allow the public access to some information.

Gender   The culturally created differences between men and women which are learnt through socialization.

Global civil society (GCS)   A loose collection of non-governmental organizations (NGOs), activist groups and others, overlapping with the anti-globalization movement; there is a debate as to whether there is a coherent GCS or whether the organizations are too different and lack any common focus.

Global culture   The way cultures in different countries of the world have become more alike, sharing increasingly similar consumer products and ways of life. This has arisen as globalization has undermined national and local cultures.

Global decision-making   Globalization has created problems which states acting alone cannot solve and so they work together through international governmental organizations (IGOs) to take decisions at a global level.

Global Schools Programme   Part of the British government's development education programme and of Millennium Development Goal 8 (MDG8), as a result of which many British schools have partnerships with schools in developing countries.

Global village   The way that the mass media and electronic communications now operate on a global scale so that the world has become like one village or community.

Global warming   The rise in global temperatures now acknowledged to be caused mainly by human activity, likely to lead to severe consequences such as rising sea levels and increased desertification.

Globalists   In the globalization debates, those who argue that globalization is a positive and irreversible force from which all will eventually benefit, associated with neo-liberalism.

Globalization   The growing interdependence of societies across the world, with the spread of the same culture, consumer goods and economic interests across the globe.

Green Revolution   Scientific and technological developments that improved agricultural yields, enabling more food to be produced in developing countries but creating some environmental problems because of heavy use of pesticides and insecticides.

Gross Domestic Product (GDP)   The total value of goods and services produced by a country in a particular year.

Hawthorne effect   When the presence of a researcher, or a group's knowledge that it has been specially selected for research, changes the behaviour of the group, raising problems of the validity of social research.

Hegemonic control   A form of dominance in which the ruling class convinces the rest of society that the ideas of the ruling class are the truth and should not, therefore, be questioned.

Hegemonic masculinity   A male gender identity that defines what is involved in being a 'real man', and is so dominant that those who don't conform to it are seen as odd or abnormal in some way.

Hegemony   The dominance in society of the ruling class's set of ideas over others, and acceptance of and consent to them by the rest of society.

Heterosexuality   A sexual orientation towards people of the opposite sex.

Hierarchy of credibility   The greatest importance being attached by journalists to the views and opinions of those in positions of power, like government ministers, political leaders, senior police officers or wealthy and influential individuals.

High culture   Specialist cultural products, seen as of lasting artistic or literary value, which are particularly admired and approved of by intellectual elites and predominantly the upper and middle class.

Highly Indebted Poor Countries Initiative (HIPC)   A system by which heavily indebted countries can apply to have debt written off provided they keep to conditions.

Homogenization   The removal of cultural differences, so that all cultures are increasingly similar.

Human capital   The theory that a country's people are a potential source of wealth; by educating its people, a country can increase its human capital.

Human Development Index   A composite measure of social and economic indicators, giving a statistical value to the level of development.

Hybridization   The creation of 'third cultures' when aspects of two different cultures encounter each other.

Hydraulic society   A society in which power is related to the control over access to water.

Hyperreality   The idea that, as a result of the spread of electronic communication, there is no longer a separate 'reality' to which news coverage, for example, refers. Instead, what we take to be 'reality' is created for us by such communication itself.

Ideal types   A view of a phenomenon built up by identifying the essential characteristics of many factual examples of it. The purpose of an ideal type is not to produce a perfect category, but to provide a measure against which real examples can be compared.

Ideological state apparatuses   Agencies which spread the dominant ideology and justify the power of the dominant social class.

Ideology   A set of ideas, values and beliefs that represent the outlook, and justify the interests, of a social group.

Immediate gratification   A desire to have rewards now rather than waiting to acquire them in the future, which is known as deferred gratification.

Impairment   Some abnormal functioning of the body or mind, either that one is born with or arising from injury or disease.

Imperialism   The process of empire-building associated with the colonial system.

Import substitution industrialization   An industrialization strategy based on domestic production of consumer goods to replace imported ones.

Income   An inward flow of money over time. For most people this consists of wages or salary, but other sources are benefits, pensions, interest on savings and dividends from shares.

Industrial Revolution   A phrase coined by Tawney in the 1880s to describe the process by which the UK had developed from an agricultural society into a society based on manufacturing.

Industrialized   Countries are industrialized if their economies are based on industry rather than agriculture or extraction.

Informal sector   An employment sector, characterized by lack of regular work and wages, including petty trading, self-employment, casual work and so on; the dominant sector in cities in developing countries.

Insider groups   Pressure groups which have an active relationship with governments, offering representatives the opportunity to sit in on government committees or act as consultants on government policy.

Institutional racism   Patterns of discrimination based on ethnicity that have become structured into existing social institutions.

Instrumental role   The provider/breadwinner role in the family, often associated by functionalists with men's role in family life.

Instrumental attitude   Having an attitude in which wages/money are the most important aspect of work.

International governmental organizations (IGOs)   These are established by states; examples include the International Monetary Fund (IMF), the World Bank and World Trade Organization (WTO).

International Monetary Fund (IMF)   A key IGO, which gives loans to members and which has helped to spread neo-liberal economic globalization.

Interpretivism   An approach emphasizing that people have consciousness involving personal beliefs, values and interpretations, and these influence the way they act. People have choices and do not simply respond to forces outside them. To understand society it is therefore necessary to understand the meanings people give to their behaviour, and how this is influenced by the behaviour and interpretations of others.

Interviewer bias This occurs when the answers given in an interview are influenced or distorted in some way by the presence or behaviour of the interviewer.

Inverse care law   Those whose need is least get the most resources, while those in greatest need get the fewest resources.

Iron law of oligarchy   A phrase coined by Michels referring to the principle that all organizations eventually end up being ruled by a few individuals.

Islamophobia   An irrational fear and/or hatred of or aversion to Islam, Muslims or Islamic culture.

Labour power   People's capacity to work. In Marxist theory, people sell their labour power to the employer in return for a wage; the employer buys only their labour power, not the whole person.

Laissez-faire   A philosophy of society in which government has only a minimal role; it suggests that the most efficient and free society is one in which the state provides only the most basic of society's needs.

Latent function   The unrecognized or unintended outcome of the action of an individual or institution.

Left-wing   In the political spectrum, those ideas and organizations that tend to be critical of existing social arrangements. These historically include democratic parties such as the Labour Party in Britain, as well as authoritarian anti-democratic parties such as the Communists.

Liberation theologists   A group within the Roman Catholic Church that preach that the good things in life should be shared here on earth in an equal fashion.

Life chances   The chances of obtaining those things defined as desirable and of avoiding those things defined as undesirable in a society.

Lifestyle   The way in which people live, usually indicating something about their disposable income.

Lumpenproletariat   A term used by Marx to describe the group of unorganized working class. Now seen as synonymous with the underclass by many commentators.

Malestream   A word coined by feminists to describe the type of sociology that concentrates on men, is mostly carried out by men and then assumes that the findings can be applied to women as well.

Manifest function   The recognized and intended outcome of the action of an individual or institution.

Marginality   Where some people are pushed to the margins or edges of society by poverty, lack of education, disability, racism and so on, and face social exclusion.

Master status   A status which overrides all other features of a person's social standing, and a person is judged solely in terms of one defining characteristic.

Matrilocal   Describes family systems in which the husband is expected to live near the wife's parents.

McDonaldization   Ritzer's term for the ways in which the organizing principles of a fast-food restaurant chain are coming to dominate and standardize many aspects of economic and cultural life globally.

Means of production   The key resources necessary for producing society's goods, such as land, factories and machinery.

Media imperialism   The suggestion that the new media, particularly satellite television and global advertising, have led to the Westernization of other cultures, with Western, and especially American, cultural values being forced on non-Western cultures, and the undermining of local cultures and cultural independence. Often linked to cultural imperialism.

Media representations   The categories and images that are used to present groups and activities to media audiences, which may influence the way we think about these activities and groups.

Meritocracy   A social system in which rewards are allocated on the basis of merit or ability.

Meta-analysis   A statistical technique of collating many different research findings and testing the reliability of the results by controlling the variables within each individual study.

Metanarrative   A broad all-embracing 'big theory' or explanation for how the world and societies operate.

Methodological pluralism   The use of a variety of methods in a single piece of research.

Metropolis   In dependency theory, the centre of economic activity, profiting from an exploitative relationship with satellites (dependent, underdeveloped countries).

Micro credit   Schemes to allow poor people to borrow small sums of money.

Millenarianism   The belief that existing society is evil, sinful or otherwise corrupt, and that supernatural or other extra-worldly forces will intervene to completely destroy existing society and create a new and perfect world order.

Millennium Development Goals (MDGs)   A set of eight targets set by the United Nations to achieve progress in development.

Minority ethnic group   A social group that shares a cultural identity which is different from that of the majority population of a society, such as African Caribbean, Indian Asian and Chinese ethnic groups in Britain.

Modern world system   In world systems theory, the global capitalist system.

Modernization theory   Dominant development theory of the 1960s, based on factors internal to Third World countries inhibiting their development.

Modernity   The condition of society from the Enlightenment of the seventeenth century to the middle of the twentieth century. It includes a rational outlook on social issues and highlights the role of science as a basis for understanding.

Moral entrepreneur   A person, group or organization with the power to create or enforce rules and impose their definitions of deviance.

Moral panic   A wave of public concern about some exaggerated or imaginary threat to society, stirred up by exaggerated and sensationalized reporting in the mass media.

Moral regulation   The control or regulation by social values of the actions and desires of individuals

Multilateral aid   Donors contribute to a shared fund, from which aid is then given to recipients.

Multinational corporations (MNCs)   Sometimes used interchangeably with transnational corporations (TNCs), but more usefully used to mean corporations that have some global aspects but are still clearly based in one nation.

Nation-state   A state with its own political apparatus over a specific territory, whose own citizens are backed by their military and with a nationalistic identity.

Need for achievement   In modernization theory, the desire to be entrepreneurial and to make money, essential for modernization.

Neo-colonialism   This is the continuation of past economic domination of former colonial powers over ex-colonies.

Neo-liberal economic theory   The dominant theory in influencing development policies in the 1980s and 1990s, based on a minimal role for states and liberalization of trade to allow the free market (capitalism) to work without restrictions.

Neo-Malthusian   modern followers of Malthus's main argument, that population growth will overtake food supply.

New Barbarism   Kaplan's theory, a variant of Malthusian theory, that overpopulation and exhaustion of resources were leading to civil wars in developing countries.

New International Division of Labour (NIDL)   The new global economic order said to be produced by factory production moving from the developed world to some developing countries.

New professions   These are distinguishable from the traditional professionals such as lawyers and doctors – one example is management consultants, who monitor and regulate the work of other professionals.

New Social Movements (NSMs)   Much looser informal and less organized coalitions of groups or individuals pushing a cause or broad interest, compared to more traditional pressure groups which are generally much more focused and organized. They are often global in scope and scale. Examples include the women's movement, the green movement and the anti-war movement.

Newly industrializing countries (NICs)   Those countries that seemed to make rapid progress in the late twentieth century, notably the 'Asian tigers'.

News values   The values and assumptions held by editors and journalists which guide them in choosing what is 'newsworthy' – what to report and what to leave out, and how what they choose to report should be presented.

Newsworthy   Those items selected by editors and journalists as being of importance and thus which should be broadcast.

Non-governmental organizations (NGOs)   Non-profit groups which are independent of the state; they are largely funded by private contributions and are mostly involved in humanitarian activities.

Norms   Social rules which define what is expected behaviour for an individual in a given society or situation.

Norm-setting   The way the mass media emphasize and reinforce conformity to social norms, and seek to isolate those who do not conform by making them the victims of unfavourable media reports.

North   The world's richer countries – developed nations; sometimes known as the 'global North' or the 'first world'.

Objectivity   Approaching topics with an open mind, avoiding bias, and being prepared to submit research evidence to scrutiny by other researchers.

Official Development Assistance (ODA)   The foreign aid programmes of the Organization for Economic Cooperation and Development (OECD) countries.

Oligarchy   Control by a small elite.

Open system   A social system in which it is possible for an individual to move from the social group in which he or she was born into a different social group.

Outsider groups   Pressure groups which, for whatever reason, do not have everyday operational links with governments.

Paradigm   A set of values, ideas, beliefs and assumptions providing a model or framework within which scientists operate, and providing guidelines for the conduct of research. These are rarely called into question until the evidence against them is overwhelming.

Parastatals   State-run organizations such as marketing boards, which played a leading role in the development policies of many states before neo-liberal policies were enforced.

Partisan dealignment   The idea that fewer and fewer individuals are strongly lining themselves up with a particular party and remaining loyal to that party over long periods of time.

Partisan self-image   A person with a view of themselves as a supporter of a particular political party.

Party   A term used by Weber to describe any group of individuals who organize for the pursuit of power based on their shared backgrounds, aims or interests.

Patriarchal ideology   A set of ideas that supports and justifies the power of men.

Patriarchy   Power and authority held by males.

Patrilocal   Describes family systems in which the wife is expected to live near the husband's parents.

Pluralism   A view that sees power in society spread among a wide range of interest groups and individuals, with no group or individual having a monopoly of power.

Pluralist ideology   A set of ideas that reflects the pluralist view of the distribution of power, with no one particular ideology able to dominate others, and with the prevailing ideas in society reflecting the interests of a wide range of social groups and interests.

Politics   The struggle for power between individuals and groups.

Polysemic   Used to describe a sign (such as a media message, picture or headline) which can be interpreted in different ways by different people.

Popular culture/mass culture   Cultural products that are produced as entertainment for sale to the mass of ordinary people, involving mass-produced, standardized, short-lived products of no lasting value, which are seen to demand little critical thought, analysis or discussion.

Positivism   The view that the logic, methods and procedures of the natural sciences, as used in subjects like physics, chemistry and biology, can be applied to the study of society with little modification.

Post-materialism   The theory that the need to acquire material goods is declining in importance as people give higher priority to non-material values, such as freedom, justice and personal improvement.

Power   The capacity of individuals or groups to get their own way in any given situation.

Power elite   The group that dominates society through its ability to control the important institutional positions in society. The elite is composed of those at the top of the great institutions of society, such as the government, the military, universities and industry.

Predatory state   A state that preys upon its own people, through appropriation and corruption, preventing development.

Present-time orientation   Concentrating on today without much consideration for the future or the past.

Pressure groups   Organizations that try to put pressure on those with power in society to implement policies they favour.

Primary definers   Powerful individuals or groups whose positions of power give them greater access to the media than others, and therefore put them in a more privileged position to influence what and how journalists define the news.

Primary deviance   Deviance that has not been publicly labelled as such.

Primary sources   Information that is gathered by researchers themselves.

Privatization   A government policy which is centred on reducing the public sector as much as possible through the transfer of industries and utilities from state ownership and control into the hands of private shareholders.

Privatized nuclear family   A nuclear family, cut off from extended kin, whose main concerns are focused on the home.

Professions   Types of occupation which are self-governing and usually of relatively high status.

Proletarian traditionalist   A member of the proletariat/working class who espouses the notions of solidarity which were supposedly found amongst long-established working-class communities.

Proletarianization   the process whereby other groups take on the attributes and characteristics of the proletariat.

Proletariat   The social class of workers who have to work for wages as they do not own the means of production.

Psephology   The study of voting patterns. It comes from the ancient Greek word *psepho* meaning pebble – voting in Athens took place by the casting of pebbles to decide issues.

Pull factors The advantages of city life which attract people to move there from rural areas.

Push factors The disadvantages of rural life which push people into moving to cities.

Qualitative data Information concerned with descriptions of the meanings and interpretations people have about some issue or event.

Quantitative data Information that can be expressed in statistical or number form or can be 'measured' in some way.

Racism Treating people differently on the basis of their ethnic origin.

Radicals In globalization debates, those who argue that globalization is a powerful negative force; associated with dependency theory and neo-Marxists.

Reflexivity The way the knowledge people gain about society can affect the way they behave in it, as people (and institutions) reflect on what they do and how they do it.

Relations of production The forms of relationship between those people involved in production, such as cooperation or private ownership and control.

Relative autonomy The idea in neo-Marxist theory that the superstructure of society has some independence from the economy, rather than being directly determined by it.

Relative deprivation The sense of lacking something compared to the group with which people identify and compare themselves.

Reliability This refers to whether another researcher, if repeating or replicating the research using the same method for the same research on the same group, would achieve the same results.

Religiosity The extent of importance of religion, religious beliefs and feelings in people's lives.

Religious pluralism A situation where there are a variety of different religions, different groups within a religious faith, and a range of beliefs of all kinds, with no one religious belief or organization reasonably able to claim to hold a monopoly of truth or to have the support of most members of society.

Repressive state apparatus The parts of the state concerned with mainly repressive, physical means of keeping a population in line, such as the army, police, courts and prisons.

Resacrilization The renewal and continuing vitality of religious beliefs.

Reserve army of labour This refers to a group of people not normally in the paid workforce who can be called on in time of need. Marx saw them as members of the Lumpenproletariat; feminists see them as married women and mothers.

Right wing Along the political spectrum, the ideas and organizations which generally favour the existing social arrangements and more traditional values. The right generally includes democratic parties such as the British Conservative Party, or 'Tories', and authoritarian anti-democratic parties or movements such as the British National Party (BNP).

Sanctions The rewards and punishments by which social control is achieved and conformity to norms and values enforced. These may be either positive sanctions, rewards of various kinds, or negative sanctions, various types of punishment.

Satellite   In dependency theory, the deformed and dependent economies of the underdeveloped countries.

Scapegoat   An individual picked out to be blamed for an action or event whether or not he or she is guilty. Very often applied to those who are innocent.

Secondary deviance   Deviance that follows once a person has been publicly labelled as deviant.

Secondary sources   This is data which already exists and which researchers haven't collected themselves.

Secularization   The process whereby religious thinking, practice and institutions lose social significance.

Selective biomedical intervention   in healthcare, interventions such as immunization campaigns to try to prevent the spread of disease.

Sexual orientation   The type of people that individuals are either physically or romantically attracted to, such as those of the same or opposite sex.

Sexuality   People's sexual characteristics and their sexual behaviour.

Shared resources   These are those resources that are not privately owned and whose use is freely shared – for example air, water (unless you choose to buy bottled water) and parts of the countryside. They are also sometimes referred to as 'public goods'.

Simulacra   Images or reproductions and copies which appear to reflect things in the real world but have no basis in reality.

Situational deviance   Acts which are only defined as deviant in particular contexts.

Social capital   The social networks of influence and support that people have.

Social construction   The way something is created through the individual, social and cultural interpretations, perceptions and actions of people. Official statistics, notions of health and illness, deviance and suicide are all examples of social phenomena that only exist because people have constructed them and given these phenomena particular labels.

Social control   This refers to the various methods used to persuade or force individuals to conform to the dominant social norms and values of a society or group.

Social control   The various methods used to persuade or force individuals to conform to the dominant social norms and values of a society or group.

Social closure   A system whereby members of a group can act to prevent others from joining the group.

Social exclusion   Being excluded from full participation in education, work, community life and access to services and other aspects of life seen as part of being a full and participating member of mainstream society.

Social facts   Phenomena which exist outside individuals and independently of their minds, but which act upon them in ways that constrain or mould their behaviour.

Social integration   The integration of individuals into social groups, binding them into society and building social cohesion.

Social policy   The packages of plans and actions adopted by national and local government or various voluntary agencies to solve social problems or achieve other goals that are seen as important.

Social problem   Something that is seen as being harmful to society in some way, and needs something doing to sort it out.

Social solidarity The integration of people into society through shared values, a common culture, shared understandings and social ties that bind them together.

Socialization The process by which we learn the accepted ways of behaving in our society.

Social mobility The movement of individuals or groups from one social class to another, both upwardly and downwardly.

Societal deviance Acts that are seen by most members of a society as deviant.

Sociological problem Any social or theoretical issue that needs explaining.

South The world's poorer countries, those which are developing; sometimes known as the 'global South'.

Spin doctor A label given to those who are seen as manipulating news coverage in such a way as to emphasize positive events, for the government, for example, and sideline negative news.

Stages of economic growth In Rostow's version of modernization, the five stages through which societies pass as they move from being traditional to fully developed.

State A central authority which has legitimate control over a set territory.

Status The amount of prestige or social importance a person has in the eyes of other members of a group or society.

Status frustration This is a sense of frustration arising in individuals or groups because they are denied status in society.

Stigmatized identity An identity that is in some way undesirable or demeaning, and stops an individual or group being fully accepted by society.

Structural Adjustment Programme A set of policies imposing neo-liberal policies on governments used by international governmental organizations (IGOs), especially the International Monetary Fund (IMF).

Structural differentiation The way new, more specialized social institutions emerge to take over functions that were once performed by a single institution.

Structural violence Galtung's term for the way in which, even in an apparently peaceful society, a group can be exploited by the systematic denial of their rights.

Structuralism A perspective that is concerned with the overall structure of society, and sees individual behaviour moulded by social institutions like the family, the education system, the mass media and work.

Structuration The two-way process by which people are constrained or shaped by society and social institutions, but they can at the same time take action to support, shape and change them.

Subsistence farming Farming to produce crops and livestock for consumption by the family rather than for sale in the market.

Surplus value The extra value added by workers to the products they produce, after allowing for the payment of their wages, and which goes to the employer in the form of profit.

Sustainability This refers to something that can continue at the same level indefinitely; for example, using trees from a forest for fuel is sustainable only if the wood is taken at the rate that the trees grow, so that the number of trees in the forest remains constant.

Sustainable development Development that sustains the natural environment, thereby ensuring that future generations can have the same level of development.

Symbol Something, like an object, word, expression or gesture, that stands for something else and to which individuals have attached some meaning.

Symbolic annihilation The lack of visibility, under-representation and limited roles of women or other groups in media representations, as they are omitted, condemned or trivialized in many roles.

Take-off In Rostow's five stages of economic growth, the third stage at which societies achieve a momentum that ensures development.

Tautology Something that is explained by the same thing that it seeks to explain.

Techniques of neutralization Justifications used to excuse acts of crime and deviance.

Teenage years A phrase first coined in about 1950 to describe the time of life between childhood and adulthood; the teenager's status is often ambiguous and changes from one situation to another, which reflects the confusion felt by teenagers themselves as to their exact status.

Terrorism In war and conflict, the use of tactics intended to persuade the opponents, or civilians, not to resist.

Theodicy An explanation for the contradiction between the existence of a God who is assumed to be all-powerful and benevolent, while at the same time there is widespread suffering and evil in the world.

Theodicy of disprivilege A religious explanation and justification for social inequality and social deprivation, explaining the marginalization (or disprivilege) of believers, often used as a test of faith with the promises of compensating rewards in a future after death.

Third way A political philosophy, pioneered by New Labour, that is committed to retaining the values of socialism, while supporting market policies for generating wealth and reducing inequalities.

Third World A term used to describe the world's poorer countries, distinct from the First World (developed capitalist) and Second World (developed communist, or, today, ex-communist).

Totem A sacred object representing and having symbolic significance and importance for a group.

Trade liberalization Removal of barriers to free trade, such as tariffs and subsidies.

Trade union An organization of workers whose aim is to protect the interests of their members and improve their life chances.

Transformationalists In the globalization debates, those who see globalization as a force, whose outcomes are uncertain, but which can be controlled and used to promote development.

Transnational capitalist class Associated with the radical view of globalization; globalization has created a new transnational class of business leaders, politicians and others who increasingly share common interests.

Transnational corporations (TNCs) Large business enterprises which produce and sell globally and have global supply chains.

Triangular trade The slave trade linking West Africa, Europe and the Americas.

Triangulation   This is the use of two or more research methods in a single piece of research to check the reliability and validity of research evidence.

Two faces of power   The idea that power can be exercised not only by getting your own way against opposition (the first face) but also by preventing an issue from ever being raised as controversial in the first place (the second face of power).

Typology   A generalization used to classify things into groups or types according to their characteristics, which do not necessarily apply in every real world example.

Underclass   A concept developed by Murray to describe a group considered to be outside the mainstream of society, below the working class. See also Lumpenproletariat.

Underdevelopment   Used by dependency theorists, the process of exploitation by which the North became and stayed rich at the expense of the South.

Universe of meaning   A set of ideas and values about the meaning of life which helps people make sense of and give meaning to the world, and enables them to give life some focus, order and meaning.

Urbanization   The process by which a growing proportion of people live in towns and cities, and the social and other changes which accompany this process.

Validity   This is concerned with notions of truth – how far the findings of research actually provide a true, genuine or authentic picture of what is being studied.

Value consensus   A widespread agreement around the main values of a society.

Value-freedom   The idea that the beliefs and prejudices of a researcher should not influence the way research is carried out and evidence interpreted.

Values   Ideas or beliefs which govern the way individuals behave. There is often an ethical dimension to this concept.

Variable sum view of power   A situation whereby everyone generally benefits from the exercise of power.

Verstehen   The idea of understanding human behaviour by putting yourself in the position of those being studied, and trying to see things from their point of view.

Victimology   The study of victims of crime and patterns of victimization.

Voter volatility   The chances of voters changing the political party they vote for.

Washington Consensus   A set of neo-liberal policies which were argued to be essential for reforming economies and promoting development.

Wealth   The total value of the possessions held by an individual or society.

Weltanschauung   The framework of ideas and beliefs through which an individual interprets the world and interacts with it.

White-collar crime   Offences committed by middle-class individuals who abuse their work positions within organizations for personal gain at the expense of the organization or clients of the organization.

World Bank   A key international governmental organization (IGO) which gives aid and loans to members to fight poverty; often accused of spreading neo-liberal economic globalization.

World Economic Forum   An annual gathering of the world's business and political leaders.

World Social Forum   An annual gathering of the anti-globalization movement.

References

Adler, F. (1975) *Sisters in Crime: The Rise of the New Female Criminal.* New York: McGraw-Hill.

Adonis, A. and Pollard, S. (1997) *A Class Act: Myth of Britain's Classless Society.* London: Hamish Hamilton.

Ahmed, L. (1992) *Women and Gender in Islam.* New Haven: Yale University Press.

Albrow, M. (1996) *The Global Age.* Cambridge: Polity.

Aldridge, A. (2007) *Religion in the Contemporary World.* Cambridge: Polity.

Allen, T. and Thomas, A. (2000) 'Agencies of Development', in T. Allen and A. Thomas (eds), *Poverty and Development Into the Twenty-first Century.* Oxford: Oxford University Press.

Althusser, L. (1969) *For Marx.* Harmondsworth: Penguin.

Althusser, L. (1971) *Lenin and Philosophy and Other Essays.* London: New Left Books.

Alvarado, M., Gutch, R. and Wollen, T. (1987) *Learning the Media: Introduction to Media Teaching.* London: Palgrave Macmillan.

Amin, S. (1976) *Unequal Development.* New York: Monthly Review Press.

Anderson, C. A. et al. (2003) 'The Influence of Media Violence on Youth', *Psychological Science in the Public Interest* 4: 81–110.

Anwar, M. (1981) *Between Two Cultures: A Study of Relationships Between Generations in the Asian Community in Britain.* London: Commission for Racial Equality.

Ariès, P. (1973) *Centuries of Childhood.* Harmondsworth: Penguin.

Atkinson, J. Maxwell (1971) 'Societal Reactions to Suicide: The Role of Coroners' Definitions', in S. Cohen (ed.), *Images of Deviance.* Harmondsworth: Penguin.

Atkinson, J. Maxwell (1983) *Discovering Suicide: Studies in the Social Organization of Sudden Death.* Basingstoke: Palgrave Macmillan.

Ayoob, M. (2001) 'State Making, State Breaking and State Failure', in C. Crocker et al. (eds), *Turbulent Peace.* Washington DC: US Institute of Peace.

Bachrach, P. and Baratz, M. (1970) *Power and Poverty: Theory and Practice.* Oxford: Oxford University Press.

Bagdikian, B. H. (2004) *The New Media Monopoly.* Boston: Beacon Press.

Bales, K. (2002) 'Because She Looks Like A Child', in B. Ehrenreich and A. Hochschild (eds), *Global Woman: Nannies, Maids and Sex Workers in the New Economy.* London: Granta.

Bandura, A., Ross, D. and Ross, S. A. (1961) 'Transmission of Aggression Through Imitation of Aggressive Models', *Journal of Abnormal and Social Psychology* 63: 575–82.

Barber, B. (1963) 'Some Problems in the Sociology of Professions', *Daedalus* 92/4.

Barker, E. (1984) *The Making of a Moonie.* Oxford: Blackwell.

Barker, E. (1989) *New Religious Movements: A Practical Introduction.* London: Stationery Office Books.

Barnes, C. (1992) *Disabling Imagery and the Media.* Halifax: Ryburn Publishing.

Barrett, L. (1977) *The Rastafarians: The Dreadlocks of Jamaica.* Kingston, Jamaica: Sangster Books.

Baudrillard, J. (1988) *The Ecstasy of Communication*, trans. Bernard and Caroline Schutze. New York: Semiotext.

Baudrillard, J. (2001) *Selected Writings*, ed. M. Poster. Cambridge: Polity

Bauer, P. (1995) 'Foreign Aid: Central Component of World Development?' in S. Corbridge (ed.), *Development Studies: A Reader.* London: Arnold.

Bauman, Z. (1992) *Intimations of Postmodernity.* London: Routledge & Kegan Paul.

Bauman, Z. (1996) 'From Pilgrim to Tourist – or, A Short History of Identity', in S. Hall and P. du Gay (eds), *Questions of Cultural Identity*. London: Sage.

Bauman, Z. (2007) *Consuming Life*. Cambridge: Polity.

Beall, J. (2000) 'Life in the Cities', in T. Allen and A. Thomas (eds), *Poverty and Development Into the Twenty-first Century*. Oxford: Oxford University Press.

de Beauvoir, S. (1953) *The Second Sex*. London: Jonathan Cape.

Beck, U. (1992) *Risk Society: Towards a New Modernity*. London: Sage.

Becker, H. (1950) *Through Values to Social Interpretation*. Durham, NC: Duke University Press.

Becker, H. (1971) 'Social Class Variations in the Teacher–Pupil Relationship', in B. Cosin et al. (eds), *School and Society*. London: Routledge & Kegan Paul.

Becker, H. S. (1967) 'Whose Side Are We On?', *Social Problems* 14/3.

Becker, H. S. (1997 [1963]) *Outsiders: Studies in the Sociology of Deviance*. New York: Free Press.

Belson, W. A. (1978) *Television Violence and the Adolescent Boy*. Westmead: Saxon House.

Berger, P. L. (1990) T*he Sacred Canopy: Elements of a Sociological Theory of Religion*. New York: Anchor Books.

Berger, P. L. (2001) 'Reflections on the Sociology of Religion Today', *Sociology of Religion* 62: 443–54.

Beynon, H. (1973) *Working for Ford*. Harmondsworth: Penguin.

Beynon, H. (1992) 'The end of the industrial worker', in N. Abercrombie and A. Warde (eds), *Social Change in Contemporary Britain*. Cambridge: Polity.

Bhaskar, R. (1998) *The Possibility of Naturalism: A Philosophical Critique of the Contemporary Human Sciences*. London: Routledge & Kegan Paul.

Biggs, S. (1993) *Understanding Ageing: Images, Attitudes and Professional Practice*. Milton Keynes: Open University Press.

Blanchflower, K. (2008) 'Another Poor Year for Overseas Aid', *Guardian*, 5 April.

Blumer, H. (1969) *Symbolic Interactionism: Perspective and Method*. Englewood Hills, NJ: Prentice-Hall.

Blumler, J. G. and McQuail, D. (1968) *Television in Politics: Its Uses and Influence*. London: Faber & Faber.

Bonnett, T. (1994) *A New Vocabulary for Governing in the 1990s: A Lexicon for Governors' Policy Advisors*. Washington DC: Georgetown University Press.

Booth, C. (1902–3) *Life and Labour of the People of London*. London: Macmillan.

Booth, D. (1985) 'Marxist Sociology: Interpreting the Impasse', *World Development* 13: 761–87; repr. in S. Corbridge (ed.), *Development Studies: A Reader*. London: Edward Arnold, 1995.

Boudon, R. (1974) *Education, Opportunity and Social Inequality*. New York: Wiley & Sons.

Bourdieu, P. (1971) 'Systems of Education and Systems of Thought', in M. Young (ed.), *Knowledge and Control*. London: Collins.

Bowling, B. and Phillips, C. (2002) *Racism, Crime and Justice*. Harlow: Pearson Education.

Box, S. (1983) *Power, Crime and Mystification*. London: Routledge & Kegan Paul.

Boyle, R. (2007) 'The "now" media generation', *Sociology Review* 17/1: September.

Bradley, H. (1996) *Fractured Identities: Changing Patterns of Inequality*. Cambridge: Polity.

Brandt, W. (1980) *North, South: A Programme for Survival*. Report of the Independent Commission on International Development (The Brandt Report). London: Pan.

Brantingham, P. and Brantingham, P. (1995) 'Criminality of Place: Crime Generators and Crime Attractors', *European Journal of Criminal Policy and Research* 3/3.

Braverman, H. (1974) *Labor and Monopoly Capital: The Degradation of Work in the Twentieth Century*. New York: Monthly Review Press.

Brennan, R. et al. (2008) *Mortality in the Democratic Republic of Congo: An Ongoing Crisis*. International Rescue Committee. Available at http://news.bbc.co.uk/1/shared/bsp/hi/pdfs/22_1_08congomortality.pdf.

Broadcasting Standards Commission (2003) *Ethnicity and Disability on Television, 1997 to 2002*. Briefing update. London: Broadcasting Standards Commission.

Bruce, S. (1995) *Religion in Modern Britain*. Oxford: Oxford University Press.

Bruce, S. (1996) *Religion in the Modern World: From Cathedrals to Cults*. Oxford: Oxford University Press.

Bruce, S. (2001) 'Christianity in Britain, RIP', *Sociology of Religion* 62/2.

Bruce, S. (2002a) 'God and Shopping', *Sociology Review* (November).

Bruce, S. (2002b) *God is Dead: Secularization in the West*. Oxford: Blackwell.

Bruce S. (2008) *Fundamentalism*, 2nd edn. Cambridge, Polity.

Bryman, A. (1999) 'The Disneyization of Society', *Sociological Review* 47 (February): 25–47.

Bunting, M. (2005) 'A Hall of Mirrors', *Guardian* (17 January).

Butler, C. (1995) 'Religion and Gender: Young Muslim Women in Britain', *Sociology Review* 4/2.

Butler, D. and Stokes, D. (1974) *Political Change in Britain*. London: Macmillan.

Callinicos, A. (2003) *Anti-Capitalist Manifesto*. Cambridge: Polity.

Cameron, D. (2007) *The Myth of Mars and Venus*. Oxford: Oxford University Press.

Carlen, P. (1988) *Women, Crime and Poverty*. Milton Keynes: Open University Press.

Carroll, R. (2002) 'The Eton of Africa', *Guardian* (25 November).

Chang, Ha Joon (2003) 'Kicking Away the Ladder: Infant Industry Promotion in Historical Perspective', *Oxford Development Studies* 31/1: 21–32.

Chapman, S. (2008): 'Any Dream Will Do: Equality of Opportunity in 2008', *Social Science Teacher* 37/3.

Charlesworth, S. (2000) A Phenomenology of Working-class Experience. Cambridge: Cambridge University Press.

Children Now (1999) *Boys to Men: Media Messages About Masculinity*. Children Now. Three related reports are available at: www.childrennow.org/issues/media/.

Cicourel, A. (1976) *The Social Organisation of Juvenile Justice*. London: Heinemann.

Clark, J. and Crichter, C. (1995) *The Devil Makes Work: Leisure in Capitalist Britain*. Basingstoke: Palgrave Macmillan.

Clarke, R. V. (2005) 'Seven Misconceptions of Situational Crime Prevention', in N. Tilley (ed.), *Handbook of Crime Prevention and Community Safety*. Cullompton: Willan.

Cloward, R. and Ohlin, L. (1960) *Delinquency and Opportunity: A Theory of Delinquent Gangs*. New York: Free Press.

Coates, K. and Silburn, R. (1970*): Poverty, The Forgotten Englishman*. Harmondsworth: Penguin.

Cochrane, A. and Pain, K. (2004) 'A Globalizing Society?' in D. Held (ed.), *A Globalizing World: Culture, Economics, Politics*, 2nd edn. London: Routledge & Kegan Paul.

Cohen, A. K. (1971) *Delinquent Boys: The Culture of the Gang*. New York: Free Press.

Cohen, R. (2006) *Migration and its Enemies: Global Capital, Migrant Labour and the Nation-State*. Aldershot: Ashgate.

Cohen, R. and Kennedy, P. (2007) *Global Sociology*, 2nd edn. Basingstoke: Palgrave Macmillan.

Cohen, R. and Rai, S. M. (2000) *Global Social Movements*. London: Althone Press.

Cohen, S. (2002 [1972]) *Folk Devils and Moral Panics*. London: Routledge & Kegan Paul.

Collier, P. (2007) *The Bottom Billion: Why the Poorest Countries are Falling Apart and What Can Be Done About It*. Oxford: Oxford University Press.

Connell, R. W. (1987) *Gender and Power: Society, the Person and Sexual Politics*. Cambridge: Polity.

Connell, R. W. (2005) *Masculinities*, 2nd edn. Cambridge: Polity.

Coontz, S. and Henderson, P. (eds) (1986) *Women's Work, Men's Property*. London: Verso.

Cornish, D. and Clarke, R. V. (1986) *The Reasoning Criminal*. New York: Springer-Verlag.

Corrigan, P. (1981) *Schooling the Smash Street Kids*. London: Macmillan.

Cottle, S. (2000) *Ethnic Minorities and the Media: Changing Cultural Boundaries*. Buckingham: Open University Press.

Coyle, D. (2001) 'Trade: The Great Debate', *Developments* 15.

Crewe, I. (1986) 'On the Death and Resurrection of Class Voting: Some Comments on How Britain Votes', *Political Studies* 34: 620–38.

Crewe, I. and Thompson, K. (1999) 'Party Loyalties: Dealignment or Realignment?' in G. Evans and P. Norris (eds), *Critical Elections: British Parties and Voters in Long-term Perspective*. London: Sage.

Croall, H. (2001) *Understanding White-collar Crime*. Buckingham: Open University Press.

Crompton, R. and Jones, G. (1984) *White-collar Proletariat: Deskilling and Gender in Clerical Work*. London: Macmillan.

Crow, B. (2000) 'Understanding Famine and Hunger', in T. Allen and A. Thomas (eds), *Poverty and Development Into the Twenty-first Century*. Oxford: Oxford University Press.

Cudworth, E. (2003) *Environment and Society*. London: Routledge & Kegan Paul.

Cuddy, A. J. C. and Fiske, T. S. (2004) 'Doddering But Dear: Process, Content, and Function in Stereotyping of Older Persons' in T. D. Nelson (ed.), *Ageism: Stereotyping and Prejudice Against Older Persons*. Cambridge, MA: Bradford Books/MIT Press.

Cumberbatch, G. (1994) *Video Violence: Villain or Victim?* Video Standards Council.

Cumberbatch, G. (2004) 'Legislating Mythology: Video Violence and Children', *Journal of Mental Health* 3: 485–94.

Cumberbatch, G. and Negrine, R. M. (1992) *Images of Disability on Television*. London: Routledge & Kegan Paul.

Curran (2005) *Culture Wars: The Media and the British Left*. Edinburgh: Edinburgh University Press.

Dahl, R. A. (1961) *Who Governs?* New Haven: Yale University Press.

Dahrendorf, R. (1959) *Class and Class Conflict in an Industrial Society*. London: Routledge & Kegan Paul.

Davie, G. (1994) *Religion in Britain Since 1945: Believing Without Belonging*. Oxford: Blackwell.

Davie, G. (2000) *Religion in Modern Europe*. Oxford: Oxford University Press.

Davie, G. (2002) *Europe: The Exceptional Case*. London: Darton, Longman and Todd Ltd.

Davies, T. (2008) 'Sociology and Social Policy', *Sociology Review* 17/3 (February).

Davis, K. and Moore, W. E. (1945) 'Some Principles of Stratification', repr. in R. Bendix and S. M. Lipset (eds), *Class, Status and Power*. London, Routledge & Kegan Paul, 1967.

Deem, R. (1990) 'All Work and No Play – Women, Work and Leisure', in *Social Studies Review* 5/4.

Dench, G., Gavron, K. and Young, M. (2006) *The New East End: Kinship, Race and Conflict*. London: Profile Books.

Dennis, N., Henriques, F. and Slaughter, C. (1956) *Coal is Our Life*. London: Eyre & Spottiswood.

Denscombe, M. (2001) 'Uncertain Identities and Health-risking Behaviour: The Case of Young People and Smoking in Late Modernity', *British Journal of Sociology* 52/1.

Devine, F. (1992) *Affluent Workers Revisited*. Edinburgh: Edinburgh University Press.

DfES (2006) *Ethnicity and Education*. London, DfES.

Dicken, P. (1992) *Global Shift: The Internationalisation of Economic Activity*. London: Paul Chapman.

Dorling, D. et al. (2007) *Poverty, Wealth and Place in Britain 1968-2005*. London, Joseph Rowntree Foundation.

Douglas, J. D. (1967) *The Social Meanings of Suicide*. Princeton, NJ: Princeton University Press.

Douglas, J. W. B. (1964) *The Home and the School*. London: MacGibbon & Kee.

Douglas, M. (1966) *Purity and Prayer*. London: Routledge & Kegan Paul.

Dowden, R. (2006) 'In Africa It's Good to Talk – Even Better to Sell', *Society Matters* 9: 10.

Dowling, T. (2007) 'They come over here . . .', *Guardian* (22 November).

Downes, D. and Rock, P. (2007) *Understanding Deviance*. Oxford: Oxford University Press.

Duncombe, J. and Marsden, D. (1995) 'Women's 'Triple Shift': Paid Employment, Domestic Labour and "Emotion Work"', *Sociology Review* 4/4.

Dunning, J. (1993) *The Globalisation of Business*. London: Routledge & Kegan Paul.

Durkheim, E. (1982 [1895]) *The Rules of Sociological Method*. London: Palgrave Macmillan.

Durkheim, E. (2001[1912]) *The Elementary Forms of the Religious Life*. Oxford: Oxford University Press.

Durkheim, E. (2002 [1897]) *Suicide: A Study in Sociology*. London: Routledge & Kegan Paul.

Easterley, W. (2006) *The White Man's Burden*, Oxford: Oxford University Press.

Edgell, S. (1993) *Class*. London: Routledge & Kegan Paul.

Edinger, L. and Searing, D. (1967) 'Social Background in Elite Analysis: A Methodological Inquiry', *American Political Science Review* 61 (June): 428–45.

Eduardo, F. (2000). 'International Money Information Network for Money Laundering Investigators', *Journal of Money Laundering Control*. New York: Cambridge University Press.

Ehrenreich, B. and Hochschild, A. (eds) (2002) *Global Woman: Nannies, Maids and Sex Workers in the New Economy*. London: Granta.

El Saadawi, N. (1980) *The Hidden Face of Eve: Women in the Arab World*. London: Zed Books.

Engels, F. (1972 [1891]) *The Origins of the Family, Private Property and the State*. London: Lawrence & Wishart.

Evans, G., Heath, A. and Payne, C. (1999) 'Class: Labour as a Catch-all Party?' in G. Evans and P. Norris (eds), *Critical Elections: British Parties and Voters in Long-term Perspective*. London: Sage.

Evans, P. B, (1989) 'Predatory, Developmental and Other Apparatuses: A Comparative Political Economy Perspective on the Third World State', *Sociological Forum* 4/4: 561–87.

Fanon, F. (1963) *The Wretched of the Earth*. Harmondsworth: Penguin.

FAO (2006) *The State of Food and Agriculture 2006*. Available at: www.fao.org/docrep/009/a0800e/a0800e00.htm.

Feilzer, M. and Hood, R. (2004) *Differences or Discrimination: Minority Ethnic Young People in the Youth Justice System*. London: Youth Justice Board.

Felson, M. and Clarke, R. V. (1998) *Opportunity Makes the Thief: Practical Theory for Crime Prevention*, Home Office Police Research Series Paper 98, London: Home Office. Available at: www.homeoffice.gov.uk/rds/prgpdfs/fprs98.pdf.

Fenton, N. (1999) 'Mass Media', in S. Taylor (ed.), *Sociology: Issues and Debates*. Basingstoke: Macmillan.

Ferguson, M. (1983) *Forever Feminine: Women's Magazines and the Cult of Femininity*. London: Heinemann.

Findlay, M. (2000) *The Globalisation of Crime*. London: Cambridge University Press.

Finkelstein, V. (1980) *Attitudes and Disabled People: Issues for Discussion*. New York: World Rehabilitation Fund.

Firestone, S. (1972) *The Dialectics of Sex*. London: Paladin.

Flew, T. (2002) *New Media: An Introduction*. Oxford: Oxford University Press.

Forero, J. and Goodman, P. S. (2007) 'Continental Drift Towards Venezuela's Economic Alternatives', *Guardian Weekly* (30 March – 5 April 2007).

Foucault, M. (1991) *Discipline and Punish: The Birth of the Prison*. Harmondsworth: Penguin.

Fox, K. (2005) *Watching the English*. London, Hodder & Stoughton.

Frank, A. G. (1969) *Capitalism and Underdevelopment in Latin America*. Harmondsworth: Penguin.

Frank, A. G. (1966) 'The Development of Underdevelopment', *Monthly Review* (September 1966).

Fukuyama, F. (1992) *The End of History and the Last Man*. London: Profile Books.

Gallie, D. (1988) *Employment in Britain*. Oxford: Blackwell.

Gallie, D. (1994) 'Are the Unemployed an Underclass?' in *Sociology* 28/3.

Galtung, J. and Ruge, M. H. (1970). 'The Structure of Foreign News: The Presentation of the Congo, Cuba and Cyprus Crises in Four Foreign Newspapers', in J. Tunstall, (ed.), *Media Sociology: A Reader*. London: Constable.

Garfinkel, H. (1984 [1967]) *Studies in Ethnomethodology*. Cambridge: Polity.

Garrod, J. (2004) 'What is Reality TV and Why Do We Like It?', *Sociology Review* (February).

Gauntlett, D. (1998) 'Ten Things Wrong With the "effects model"'. in R. Dickinson, R. Harindranath and O. Linné (eds), *Approaches to Audiences – A Reader*. London: Arnold; also available at www.theory.org.uk/david/effects.htm.

Gauntlett, D. (2002) *Media, Gender and Identity: An Introduction*. London: Routledge & Kegan Paul.

George, S. (1991) *The Debt Boomerang: How Third World Debt Harms Us All*. London: Pluto.

Gershuny, J. (1992) 'Changes in the Domestic Division of Labour in the UK, 1975–1987', in N. Abercrombie and A. Warde (eds), *Social Change in Contemporary Britain*. Cambridge: Polity.

Giddens, A. (1973) *The Class Structure of the Advanced Societies*. London: Hutchinson.

Giddens, A. (1986) *The Constitution of Society: Outline of the Theory of Structuration*. Cambridge: Polity.

Giddens, A. (1990) *The Consequences of Modernity*. Cambridge: Polity.

Giddens, A. (1991) *Modernity and Self-identity: Self and Society in the Late Modern Age*. Cambridge: Polity.

Giddens, A. (1994) *Beyond Left and Right: The Future of Radical Politics*. Cambridge: Polity.

Giddens, A. (1998) *The Third Way: The Renewal of Social Democracy*. Cambridge: Polity.

Giddens, A. (2006) *Sociology*, 5th edn. Cambridge: Polity (6th edn 2009).

Gilmore, D. (1991) *Manhood in the Making: Cultural Concepts of Masculinity*. London: Yale University Press.

Gilroy, P. (1982) 'Police and Thieves', in Centre for Contemporary Cultural Studies, *The Empire Strikes Back: Race and Racism in '70s Britain*. London: Hutchinson.

Gilroy, P. (2002) 'The End of Anti-racism', in J. Donald and A. Rattansi (eds), *Race, Culture and Difference*. London: Sage.

Glasgow University Media Group (1976) *Bad News*. London: Routledge & Kegan Paul.

Glasgow University Media Group (1980) *More Bad News*. London: Routledge & Kegan Paul.

Glass, D. (1954) *Social Mobility in Britain*. London: Routledge & Kegan Paul.

Glendinning, T. and Bruce, S. (2006) 'New Ways of Believing or Belonging: Is Religion Giving Way to Spirituality?', *The British Journal of Sociology* 57/3.

Glock, C. Y. and Stark, R. (1965) *Religion and Society in Tension*. Chicago, Rand McNally.

Godrej, D. (2004) 'Smoke Gets in Your Eyes', *New Internationalist* 369.

Goldthorpe, J (1980) *Social Mobility and Class Structure in Modern Britain*. Oxford: Clarendon Press.

Goldthorpe, J. & Payne, C. (1986) 'On the Class Mobility of Women', *Sociology* 20.

Goldthorpe, J. (1987) *Social Mobility and Class Structure in Modern Britain*, 2nd edn. Oxford: Clarendon Press.

Goldthorpe, J. (1995) 'The Service Class Revisited', in T. Butler and M. Savage (eds), *Social Change and the Middle Classes*. London: UCL Press.

Goldthorpe, J. and Jackson, M. (2007) 'Intergenerational Class Mobility in Contemporary Britain: Political Concerns and Empirical Findings', *British Journal of Sociology* 58/4.

Goldthorpe, J. H., Lockwood, D., Bechhofer, F. and Platt, J. (1969) *The Affluent Worker in the Class Structure*. Cambridge, Cambridge University Press.

Gottfredson, M. R. and Hirschi, T. (1990) *A General Theory of Crime*. Stanford: Stanford University Press.

Gouldner, A. W. (1971) *The Coming Crisis of Western Sociology*. London: Heinemann.

Gramsci, A. (1971) *Selections from the Prison Notebooks*. London: Lawrence & Wishart.

Grant, W. (2000) *Pressure Groups and British Politics*. Houndmills: Macmillan Press.

Grant, W. and Marsh, D. (1977) *The Confederation of British Industry*. London: Hodder & Stoughton.

Green, P. and Ward, T. (2004) *State Crime: Governments, Violence and Corruption*. London: Pluto Press.

Greer, C. (2003) *Sex Crime and the Media: Sex Offending and the Press in a Divided Society*. Cullompton: Willan.

Greer, C. (2005) 'Crime and Media: Understanding the Connections', in C. Hale, K. Hayward, A. Wahidin and E. Wincup (eds), *Criminology*. Oxford: Oxford University Press.

Gross, L. (1991) 'Out of the Mainstream: Sexual Minorities and the Mass Media', *Journal of Homosexuality* 21:19–46.

Grusky, D. (1996) 'Theories of Stratification and Inequality', in D. B. Grusky, J. N. Barron and D. J. Treiman (eds), *Social Differentiation and Inequality*. Boulder, CO: Westview Press.

Hagemann, F., Diallo, Y., Etienne, E. and Mehran, F. (2006) *Global Child Labour Trends 2000 to 2004*. Geneva: International Labour Office.

Hall, S. (2002) 'The Whites of Their Eyes: Racist Ideologies and the Media', in G. Dines and J. M. Humez (eds), *Gender, Race, and Class in Media: A Text-Reader*. London: Sage.

Hall, S., Critcher, C., Jefferson, T., Clarke, J. and Roberts, B. (1978) *Policing the Crisis: Mugging, the State and Law and Order*. London: Macmillan.

Hall, S. et al. (eds) (1992) *Modernity and Its Futures*. Cambridge: Polity.

Halloran, J. D. (1970) *The Effects of Television*. London: Panther.

Hallsworth, S. (1994) 'Understanding New Social Movements', *Sociology Review* 4/1.

Halman, L. and Draulans, V. (2006) 'How Secular is Europe?' *The British Journal of Sociology* 57/2.

Halsey, A. H, Heath, A. and Ridge, J. M. (1980) *Origins and Destinations*. Oxford: Clarendon Press.

Hanlon, J. (2006a) '200 Wars and the Humanitarian Response', in H. Yanacopulos and J. Hanlon (eds), *Civil War, Civil Peace*. Oxford: James Currey.

Hanlon, J. (2006b) 'External Roots of Internal War', in H. Yanacopulos and J. Hanlon (eds), *Civil War, Civil Peace*. Oxford: James Currey.

Hardt, A. and Negri, M. (2001) *Empire*. Cambridge, MA: Harvard University Press.

Hardt, A. and Negri, M. (2004) *Multitude*. New York: Penguin Press.

Hargrave, A. M. (ed.) (2002) *Multicultural Broadcasting: Concept and Reality*. London: Broadcasting Standards Commission.

Harris, N. (1995) *The New Untouchables: Immigration and the New World Worker*. London: Penguin.

Harrop, M. and Scammell, M. (1997) 'The Press', in D. Butler and D. Kavanagh, *The British General Election of 1997*. London and Basingstoke: Macmillan.

Hartmann, P. and Husband, C. (1974) *Racism and the Mass Media*. London: Davis-Poynter.

Harvey, D. (1990) *The Condition of Postmodernity*. Oxford: Blackwell.

Hawley J. S. (1994) *Fundamentalism and Gender*. Oxford: Oxford University Press.

Hayter, T. (1971) *Aid as Imperialism*. Harmondsworth: Penguin.

Heath, A. (1981) *Social Mobility*. Glasgow: Fontana.

Heath, A. and Britten, N. (1984) 'Women's Jobs Do Make a Difference', *Sociology* 18/4.

Heath, A., Jowell, R. and Curtice, J. (1985) *How Britain Votes*. Oxford: Pergamon Press.

Heath, A., Jowell, R. and Curtice, J. (1994) 'Can Labour Win?', in A. Heath, R. Jowell and J. Curtice, with B. Taylor (eds), *Labour's Last Chance*. Aldershot: Dartmouth Publishing.

Heelas, P. (1996) *The New Age Movement: the Celebration of the Self and the Sacralization of Modernity*. Oxford: Blackwell.

Heelas, P. (1998) 'Introduction', in Heelas, P. (ed.), *Religion, Modernity and Postmodernity*. Oxford: Blackwell.

Heelas, P., Woodhead, L., Seel, B., Szerszynski, B. and Tusting, K. (2004) *The Spiritual Revolution: Why Religion is Giving Way to Spirituality*. Oxford: Blackwell.

Heidensohn, F. (1996) *Women and Crime*. Basingstoke: Macmillan.

Henn, M. Weinstein, M. and Forrest, S. (2005) 'Uninterested Youth? Young People's Attitudes Towards Party Politics in Britain', *Political Studies* 53/3: 556–78.

Henry, S. and Milovanovic, D. (1996) *Constitutive Criminology: Beyond Postmodernism*. London: Sage.

Herberg, W. (1960) *Protestant – Catholic – Jew: An Essay in American Religious Sociology*. New York: Anchor Books.

Hester, M. and Westmarland, N. (2006) *Service Provision for Perpetrators of Domestic Violence*. Bristol: University of Bristol.

Hewitt, C. J. (1974) 'Elites and the Distribution of Power in British Society', in P. Stanworth and A. Giddens (eds), *Elites and Power in British Society*. Cambridge: Cambridge University Press.

Hewitt, T. (2000) 'Half a Century of Development', in T. Allen and A. Thomas (eds), *Poverty and Development Into the Twenty-first Century*. Oxford: Oxford University Press.

Hewitt, T. and Smyth, I. (2000) 'Is the World Overpopulated?', in T. Allen and A. Thomas (eds), *Poverty and Development Into the Twenty-first Century*. Oxford: Oxford University Press.

Hill, S. (1976) *The Dockers*. London: Heinemann.

Himmelweit, H. T., Oppenheim, A. N. and Vince, P. (1958) *Television and the Child*. Oxford: Oxford University Press.

Hirschi, T. (1969) *Causes of Delinquency*. Berkeley: University of California Press.

Hirst, P. and Thompson, G. (1999) *Globalization in Question*, 2nd edn. Cambridge: Polity.

Hobbs, D., Hadfield, P., Lister, S. and Winlow, S. (2003) *Bouncers: Violence and Governance in the Night-time Economy*. Oxford: Oxford University Press.

Hollowell, P. G. (1968) *The Lorry Driver*. London: Routledge & Kegan Paul.

Holm J. and Bowker, T. (1994) *Women in Religion*. London: Pinter Publishers.

Holm, J. (1994) 'Introduction: Raising the Issues', in J. Holm and T. Bowker, *Women in Religion*. London: Pinter Publishers.

Hoogvelt, A. (2005) 'Intervention as Management of Exclusion', in *OU Course Readings: War, Intervention and Development* (TU875). Milton Keynes: The Open University.

Hoselitz, B. F. (1952) 'Non-economic Barriers to Economic Development', repr. in S. Corbridge (ed.), *Development Studies: A Reader*. London: Edward Arnold, 1995.

Humphreys, L. (1970) *The Tearoom Trade: A Study of Homosexual Encounters in Public Places*. London: Duckworth.

Hunt, P. (1966) *Stigma: The Experience of Disability*. London, Geoffrey Chapman.

Hyman, H. H. (1967) 'The Value Systems of Different Classes', in R. Bendix and S. M. Lipset (eds), *Class, Status and Power*. London: Routledge & Kegan Paul.

Jackson, B. & Marsden, D. (1965) *Education and the Working Class*. London: Pelican.

Jacobs, E. and Worcester, R. (1994) *Britain under the MORI-scope*. London: Wiedenfeld and Nicholson.

Jacobson, J. (1998) *Islam in Transition: Religion and Identity Among British Pakistani Youth*. London: Routledge & Kegan Paul.

Jewkes, Y. (2004) *Media and Crime*. London: Sage.

Johal, S. (1998) 'Brimful of Brasia', *Sociology Review* (November).

Johnson, P. (1981) 'The Seven Deadly Sins of Terrorism', in B. Netanyahu (ed.), *International Terrorism: Challenge and Response*. New Brunswick, NJ: Transaction Books.

Jones, A. (2006) *Dictionary of Globalization*. Cambridge: Polity.

Jones, S. (1994) *The Language of the Genes*. London: Flamingo.

Kaldor, M. (1999) *New and Old Wars*. Cambridge: Polity.

Kaplan, A. (1973) *The Conduct of Inquiry: Methodology for Behavioral Science*. New York: Chandler Publishing.

Kaplan, R. (1994) 'The Coming Anarchy: How Scarcity, Crime, Overpopulation and Disease Are Rapidly Destroying the Social Fabric of our Planet', *Atlantic Monthly* (February): 44–76.

Karofi, U. A. and Mwanza, J. (2006) 'Globalisation and Crime', *Bangladesh e-Journal of Sociology* 3/1 (January).

Katz, E. and Lazarsfeld, P. F. (1955) *Personal Influence: The Part Played by People in the Flow of Mass Communication*. New York: Free Press.

Katz, J. (1988) *Seductions of Crime*. New York: Basic Books.

Kellner, P. and Wilby, P. (1980) 'The 1:2:4 rule of class in Britain', *Sunday Times* (13 January).

Kinsey, R., Lea, J. and Young, J. (1986) *Losing the Fight Against Crime*. Oxford: Blackwell.

Klapper, J. T. (1960) *The Effects of Mass Communication*. New York: Free Press.

Klein, J. (1965) *Samples from English Culture*. London: Routledge & Kegan Paul.

Klein, N. (2000) *No Logo: No Space, No Choice, No Jobs*. London: Flamingo.

Klein, N. (2007) *The Shock Doctrine: The Rise of Disaster Capitalism*. Harmondsworth: Penguin.

Klug, F. (2001) 'The Human Rights Act: A "Third Way" or "Third Wave" Bill Of Rights,' *European Human Rights Law Review* 4: 361–72.

Kuhn, T. S. (1962) *The Structure of Scientific Revolutions*. Chicago: University of Chicago Press.

Kunstler, J. H. (2005) 'Globalization is an Anomaly and Its Time Is Running Out', *Guardian* (24 August).

Lacey, C. (1972) *Hightown Grammar: The School as a Social System*. Manchester: Manchester University Press.

Lane, T. and Roberts, K. (1971) *Strike at Pilkington's*. London: Fontana.

Lash, S. and Urry, J. (1994) *Economics of Signs and Space*. London: Sage.

Laslett, P. (1983) *The World We Have Lost*, 3rd edn. London: Routledge & Kegan Paul.

Lea, J. (1998) 'Criminology and Postmodernity', in P. Walton and J. Young (eds.), *The New Criminology Revisited*. Basingstoke: Palgrave Macmillan.

Lea, J. and Young, J. (1984) *What is to be Done About Law and Order?* London: Penguin Books.

Lee, N. (2005) *Childhood and Human Value*. London: Open University Press.

Leftwich, A. (1995) 'Bringing Politics Back In: Towards a Model of the Development State', *Journal of Development Studies* 31/3: 400–27.

Lemert, E. M. (1972) *Human Deviance, Social Problems and Social Control*. Englewood Cliffs, NJ: Prentice Hall.

Leonard, M. (2003) 'Women and Development: Examining Gender Issues in Developing Countries', in G. McCann and S. McCloskey (eds), *From the Global to the Local*. London: Pluto.

Lister, M., Dovey, J., Giddings, S., Grant, I. and Kelly, K. (2003) *New Media: A Critical Introduction*. London: Routledge & Kegan Paul.

Lloyd, J. (2004) *What the Media are Doing to Our Democracy*. London: Constable.

Lloyd, P. (1979) *Slums of Hope? Shanty Towns of the Third World*. Harmondsworth: Penguin.

Lockwood, D. (1958) *The Black-coated Worker*. London: Allen & Unwin.

Lukes, S. (2005) *Power: A Radical View*, 2nd edn. Basingstoke: Palgrave Macmillan.

Lull, J. (1990) *Inside Family Viewing: Ethnographic Research on Television's Audiences*. London: Routledge & Kegan Paul.

Lull, J. (1995) *Media, Communication, Culture*. Cambridge: Polity.

Lupton, T. and Wilson, S. (1974) 'The Social Background of Top Decision-makers', in J. Wakeford and J. Urry (eds), *Power in Britain*. London: Heinemann.

Luttwak, E. (1999) 'Give War A Chance', *Foreign Affairs* 78/4: 36–44.

Lynch, G. (2008) 'Understanding the Sacred', *Sociology Review* 17/2 (November).

Lyng, S. (1990) 'Edgework: A Social Psychological Analysis of Voluntary Risk-taking', *American Journal of Sociology* 95 (4).

Lyon, D. (2000) *Jesus in Disneyland: Religion in Postmodern Times*. Cambridge: Polity.

Lyotard, J.-F. (1984) *The Postmodern Condition: A Report on Knowledge*. Manchester: Manchester University Press.

Mac an Ghaill, M. (1994) *The Making of Men: Masculinities, Sexualities and Schooling*. Buckingham: Open University Press.

Maguire, M. (2002) 'Crime Statistics: The 'Data Explosion' and its Implications', in M. Maguire, R. Morgan and R. Reiner (eds), *The Oxford Handbook of Criminology*, 3rd edn. Oxford: Oxford University Press.

Maguire, M. (2007) 'Crime Data and Statistics' in M. Maguire, R. Morgan and R. Reiner (eds), *The Oxford Handbook of Criminology*, 4th edn. Oxford: Oxford University Press.

Malik, S. (2002) *Representing Black Britain: Black and Asian Images on Television*. London: Sage.

Malinowski, B. (2004 [1926]) *Magic, Science and Religion and Other Essays*, ed. Robert Redfield. Whitefish: Kessinger Publishing.

Mannheim, K. (1985 [1936]) *Ideology and Utopia: An Introduction to the Sociology of Knowledge*, trans. L. Wirth and E. Shils. San Diego, CA: Harcourt Brace.

Manning, P. (1999) 'Who Makes the News?' *Sociology Review* (September).

Marshall, B. and Johnson, S. (2005) *Crime in Rural Areas: A Review of the Literature for the Rural Evidence Research Centre*. London: Jill Dando Institute of Crime Science.

Marshall, G. et al. (1988) *Social Class in Modern Britain*. London: Hutchinson.

Marsland, D. (1994) 'Sociologists and Social Policy: The Need for Intelligent Involvement', *Sociological Notes* No. 21. London: Libertarian Alliance.

Martin, D. (1969) *The Religious and the Secular*. London: Routledge & Kegan Paul.

Martin, G. (2004) 'Sea Change: The Modern Terrorist Environment in Perspective', in George Ritzer (ed.), *Handbook of Social Problems*. Thousand Oaks, CA: Sage.

Matza, D. (1964) *Delinquency and Drift*. New York: Wiley.

Mayhew, H. (1851) *London Labour and the London Poor*. Harmondsworth: Penguin; repr. 1985.

McClelland, D. (1961) *The Achieving Society*. Princeton: Princeton University Press.

McGiffen, P. (2002) *Globalisation*. Harpenden: Pocket Essentials.

McGrew, A. (2000) 'Sustainable Globalization?', in T. Allen and A. Thomas (eds), *Poverty and Development Into the Twenty-first Century*. Oxford: Oxford University Press.

McGrew, A. (2004) 'Power Shift: From National Government to Global Governance?' in D. Held (ed.), *A Globalizing World: Culture, Economics, Politics*, 2nd edn. London: Routledge & Kegan Paul.

McGuire, M. B. (2001) *Religion: The Social Context*, 5th edn. London: Wadsworth.

McKenzie, Stuart et al. (2006): 'All That Is Solid'. *Sociology* 40/5.

McLuhan, H. M. (1962) *The Gutenberg Galaxy: The Making of Typographic Man*. Toronto: University of Toronto Press.

McNeill, P. (1986) 'Social Research', in P. McNeill and C. Townley (eds), *Fundamentals of Sociology*. London: Hutchinson.

McQuail, D. (1972) *The Sociology of Mass Communications*. Harmondsworth: Penguin.

McRobbie, A. (1994) *Postmodernism and popular culture*. London: Routledge & Kegan Paul.

McRobbie, A. and Garber, J. (1976) 'Girls and Subcultures: An Exploration', in S. Hall, and T. Jefferson (eds), *Resistance Through Rituals*. London: Hutchinson.

McRobbie, A. and Thornton, S. (1995) 'Rethinking 'Moral Panic' for Multi-mediated Social Worlds', *British Journal of Sociology* 46/4.

Mead, M. (1935) *Sex and Temperament in Three Primitive Societies*. New York: Harper Collins.

Merton, R. K. (1968 [1957]) *Social Theory and Social Structure*. New York: Free Press.

Messerschmidt, J.M. (1993) *Masculinities and Crime: Critique and Reconceptualization of Theory*, Lanham, MD: Rowman & Littlefield.

Michels, R. (1962) *Political Parties*, trans. Eden and Cedar Paul. New York: Free Press.

Miliband, R. (1973) *The State in Capitalist Society*. London: Quartet Books.

Miller, A. S, and Hoffmann, J. P. (1995) 'Risk and Religion', *International Journal of the Addictions* 30/10: 1207–41.

Miller, W. B. (1962) 'Lower-class Culture as a Generating Milieu of Gang Delinquency', in M. E. Wolfgang, L. Savitz and N. Johnson (eds), *The Sociology of Crime and Delinquency*. New York: Wiley.

Millett, K. (1970) *Sexual Politics*. New York: Doubleday.

Mills, C. W. (1951) *White Collar: The American Middle Classes*. New York: Oxford University Press.

Mills, C. W. (1970) *The Sociological Imagination*. Harmondsworth: Penguin.

Mirza, H. (1992) *Young, Female and Black*. London: Routledge & Kegan Paul.

Mirza, M. (2008) 'Religious Extremism and British Muslims', *Sociology Review* 17/4 (April).

Mirza, M., Senthilkumaran, A. and Ja'far, Z. (2007) *Living Apart Together: British Muslims and the Paradox of Multiculturalism*. London: Policy Exchange.

Mitsos, E. and Browne, K (1998) 'Gender Differences in Education: The Underachievement of Boys', *Sociology Review* 8/1.

Modood, T., Beishon, S. and Virdee, S. (1994) *Changing Ethnic Identities*. London: Policy Studies Institute.

Monbiot, G. (2008) 'The Great Green Land Grab', *Guardian* (13 February).

Moore, B. (1967) *Social Origins of Dictatorship and Democracy: Lord and Peasant in the Making of the Modern World*. Hardmondsworth: Penguin.

Murdock G. P. (1949) *Social Structure*. New York, Macmillan.

Murray, C. (1984) *Losing Ground*. New York: Basic Books.

Myhill, A. and Allen J. (2002) *Rape and Sexual Assault of Women: Findings from the British Crime Survey*. London: Home Office.

Naidoo, K. (2008) 'Let's Change the Climate', *Developments* 40: 14.

Newburn, T. (2007) *Criminology*. Cullompton: Willan.

Newburn, T. and Hagell, A. (1995) 'Violence on Screen: Just Child's Play?', *Sociology Review* 4/3.

Newson, E. (1994) 'Video Violence and the Protection of Children', *Journal of Mental Health* 3: 221–6.

Niebuhr, H. R. (1957 [1929]) *The Social Sources of Denominationalism*. New York: Meridian Books.

Nordlinger, E. A. (1981) *On the Anatomy of the Democratic State*. Cambridge, MA: Harvard University Press.

Norris, P. (1991) 'Traditional, Revised and Radical Models of Women's Political Participation in Britain', *Government and Opposition* 26/1: 56–74.

Norris, P. (1999) 'Gender: A Generation Gap?' in G. Evans and P. Norris (eds), *Critical Elections: British Parties and Voters in Long-term Perspective*. London: Sage.

Norris, P. (2001) (ed.) *Britain Votes*. Oxford: Oxford University Press.

Oakley, A (2002) *Gender on Planet Earth*. Cambridge: Polity.

Oakley, A. (1974a) *Housewife*. London: Allen Lane.

Oakley, A. (1974b) *The Sociology of Housework*. Oxford: Martin Robertson.

Oakley, A. (1981) *Subject Women*. Oxford: Martin Robertson.

Ofcom (2005) *The Representation and Portrayal of People with Disabilities on Analogue Terrestrial Television*. London: Office for Communications.

Ohmae, K. (1994) *The Borderless World*. London: Harper Collins.

Oliver, M. (1990) *The Politics of Disablement*. London: Macmillan.

Ollocks, B. (2008) 'Subtextual Discourse and Postconceptualist Metaphors in Baudrillardian Prenarratives', in W. Schlangekraft (ed.), *Mental Debility, Recursive Transition and the Mystification of Postmodernist Obscurantism*. Little Compton: Zorograstrian Publications.

Ortner, S. (1974) 'Is Female to Males as Nature is to Culture', in M. Z. Rosaldo (ed.), *Women, Culture and Society*. Stanford: Stanford University Press.

Orton, M. and Rowlingson, K. (2007) *Public Attitudes to Economic Inequality*. London: Joseph Rowntree Foundation.

Oxfam (2002) Briefing Paper 34: *Milking the CAP*. Available at: www.oxfam.org.uk/what_we_do/issues/trade/downloads/bp34_cap.pdf.

Oxfam (2007) Briefing Paper 99: *Pricing Farmers out of Cotton*. Available at: www.oxfam.org.uk/resources/policy/debt_aid/downloads/bp99_cotton.pdf.

Pakulski, J. and Waters, M. (1996) *The Death of Class*. London: Sage.

Parker, S. (1971) The Future of Work and Leisure. London: MacGibbon & Kee.

Parker, S. (1976) 'Work and Leisure', in E. Butterworth and D. Weir (eds), *The Sociology of Work and Leisure*. London: Allen & Unwin.

Parkin, F. (1968) *Middle-class Radicalism*. Manchester: Manchester University Press.

Parry, N. and Parry, J. (1976) *The Rise of the Medical Profession*. London: Croom Helm.

Parsons, T. (1951) *The Social System*. New York: Free Press.

Parsons, T. (1964) *Social Structure and Personality*. London: Collier-Macmillan.

Parsons, T. (1967) *Sociological Theory and Modern Society*. New York: Free Press.

Parsons, T. (1969) *Politics and Social Structure*. New York: Free Press.

Patrick, J. (1973) *A Glasgow Gang Observed*. London: Eyre Methuen.

Payne, G. and Abbott, P. (1990) *The Social Mobility of Women*. Basingstoke: Falmer Press.

Pearson R. (2000) 'Rethinking Gender Matters in Development', in T. Allen and A. Thomas (eds), *Poverty and Development Into the Twenty-first Century*. Oxford: Oxford University Press.

Peston, R. (2008) *Who Runs Britain? How Britain's New Elite Are Changing Our Lives*. London: Hodder & Stoughton.

Philo, G. and Berry, M. (2004) *Bad News from Israel*. London: Pluto Press.

Platt, L. (2005) 'Intergenerational Social Mobility of Minority Ethnic Groups', *Sociology* 39/3.

Platt, L. (2007) *Poverty and Ethnicity in the UK*. London: Joseph Rowntree Foundation.

Plummer, K. (1979) 'Misunderstanding Labelling Perspectives', in D. Downes and P. Rock (eds), *Deviant Interpretations: Problems in Criminological Theory*. Oxford: Martin Robertson.

Polsby, N. (1963) *Community Power and Political Theory*. Yale: Yale University Press.

Popper, K. R. (2002) *The Logic of Scientific Discovery*. London: Routledge & Kegan Paul.

Postman, N. (1994) *The Disappearance of Childhood*. New York: Vintage Books.

Potter, D. (2000a) 'The Power of Colonial States', in T. Allen and A. Thomas (eds), *Poverty and Development Into the Twenty-first Century*. Oxford: Oxford University Press.

Potter, D. (2000b) 'Democratization, 'Good Governance' and Development', in T. Allen and A. Thomas (eds), *Poverty and Development Into the Twenty-first Century*. Oxford: Oxford University Press.

Poulantzas, N. (1969) 'The Problem of the Capitalist State' *New Left Review* 58.

Pryce, K. (1979) *Endless Pressure: A Study of West Indian Lifestyles in Bristol*. Harmondsworth: Penguin.

Putnam, R. (2000) *Bowling Alone*. New York: Simon and Schuster.

Puttick, K. (1997) *Women in New Religions: In Search of Community, Sexuality and Spiritual Power*. London: Sage.

Quinton, P. and Miller, J. (2003) *Promoting Ethical Policing: Summary Findings of Research on New Misconduct Procedures and Police Corruption*, Home Office Online Report. London: Home Office.

Ransom, D. (2006) *The No-nonsense Guide to Fair Trade*. Oxford: New Internationalist.

Reay, D. (2007) 'Class Out of Place', in L. Weis (ed.), *The Way Class Works: Readings on School, Family and the Economy*. New York: Routledge & Kegan Paul.

Reay, D. (2007) 'Education and Social Class', *Sociology Review* 17/2.

Reiner, R. (2000) *Politics of the Police*. Oxford: Oxford University Press.

Reiner, R. (2007) 'Media Made Criminality: The Representation of Crime in the Mass Media', in M. Maguire, R. Morgan and R. Reiner (eds), *The Oxford Handbook of Criminology*, 4th edn. Oxford: Oxford University Press.

Richards, P. (1996) *Fighting for the Rain Forest: War, Youth and Resources in Sierra Leone*. Oxford: James Currey.

Ritzer, G. (2008) *The McDonaldization of Society*, 5th edn. London: Pine Forge Press.

Robinson, L. (2001) 'When Will Revolutionary Movements Use Religion?' in S. Monahan, W. A. Mirola and M. O. Emerson (eds), *Sociology of Religion: A Reader*. Englewood Cliffs, NJ: Prentice Hall.

Rodney, W. (1972) *How Europe Underdeveloped Africa*. London: Bogle-L'Ouverture Publications.

Roe, S. and Ashe, J. (2008) *Young People and Crime: Findings from the 2006 Offending, Crime and Justice Survey*, Home Office Statistical Bulletin (September). London: Home Office.

Roof, W.C. (2001) *Spiritual Marketplace: Baby Boomers and the Remaking of American Religion*. Princeton, NJ: Princeton University Press.

Rosaldo M. Z. (1974) *Women, Culture and Society*. Stanford, CA: Stanford University Press.

Rostow, W. W. (1960) *The Stages of Economic Growth: A Non-Communist Manifesto*. Cambridge: Cambridge University Press.

Sachs, J. (2005) *The End of Poverty*. London: Penguin.

Saggar, S. and Heath, A. (1999) 'Race: Towards a Multicultural Electorate?' in G. Evans and P. Norris (eds), *Critical Elections: British Parties and Voters in Long-term Perspective*. London: Sage.

Sancho, J. (2003) *Disabling Prejudice: Attitudes Towards Disability and Its Portrayal on Television*.

London: The British Broadcasting Corporation, the Broadcasting Standards Commission and the Independent Television Commission.

Sarlvick, B. and Crewe, I. (1983) *Decade of Dealignment*. Cambridge: Cambridge University Press.

Saul, J. R, (2004) 'The Collapse of Globalism and the Rebirth of Nationalism', *Harper's Magazine* (March).

Saunders, P. (1990) *Social Class and Stratification*. London: Routledge & Kegan Paul.

Saunders, P. (1999) 'Capitalism and the Environment,' in M. J. Smith (ed.), *Thinking Through the Environment*. London: Routledge & Kegan Paul.

Savage, M., Barlow, J., Dickens, P. and Fielding, T. (1992) *Property, Bureaucracy and Culture: Middle Class Formation in Contemporary Britain*. London: Routledge & Kegan Paul.

Sayer, A. (1992) *Method in Social Science: A Realist Approach*. London: Routledge & Kegan Paul.

Scammell, M. (1995) *Designer Politics: How Elections are Won*. London: Macmillan.

Schuurman, F. J. (2002) 'The Impasse in Development Studies', in V. Desai and R. B. Potter (eds), *The Companion to Development Studies*. London: Arnold.

Seagar, A. and Lewis, J. (2007) 'How Top London Law Firms Help Vulture Funds Devour Their Prey', *Guardian* (17 October).

Shakespeare, T. (1994) 'Cultural Representations of Disabled People', *Disability and Society* 9/3.

Shakespeare, T. (1998) *The Disability Reader: Social Science Perspectives*. London: Cassell.

Sharma, A. (1987) *Women in World Religion*. Albany: State University of New York Press.

Sharp, C. and Budd, T. (2005) *Minority Ethnic Groups and Crime: Findings from the Offending, Crime and Justice Survey 2003*, online report. London: Home Office.

Shaw, C. R. and McKay, H. D. (1931) *Social Factors in Juvenile Delinquency*. Washington, DC: Government Printing Office.

Shaw, C. R. and McKay, H. D. (1942) *Juvenile Delinquency and Urban Areas*. Chicago: University of Chicago Press.

Sklair, L. (1995) *Sociology of the Global System*, 2nd edn. Hemel Hempstead: Prentice Hall.

Skocpol, T. (1985) 'Bringing the State Back In: Strategies and Analysis in Current Research', in P. Evans, D. Rueschemeyer and T. Skocpol (eds), *Bringing the State Back In*. Cambridge: Cambridge University Press.

Slapper, G. and Tombs, S. (1999) *Corporate Crime*. Harlow: Longman.

Slatterthwaite, D. (2007) 'Humanity Crosses Urban Milestone', *Society Matters* 10.

Smart, C. (1976) *Women, Crime and Criminology: A Feminist Critique*. London: Routledge & Kegan Paul.

Southerton, D. (2002) 'Class, Mobility and Identification in a New Town', *Sociology* 36/1.

Spencer, H. (1996 [1885]) *The Study of Sociology*. London: Routledge & Kegan Paul.

Stanworth, M. (1984) 'Women and Class Analysis', *Sociology* 18/2.

Stanworth, P. and Giddens, A. (eds) (1971) *Elites and Power in British Society*. Cambridge: Cambridge University Press.

Stark, R. (1999) 'Secularization, RIP', *Sociology of Religion* 60/3.

Stark, R. and Bainbridge, W. S. (1985) *The Future of Religion: Secularization, Revival and Cult Formation*. Berkeley: University of California Press.

Stark, R. and Bainbridge, W. S. (1996) *A Theory of Religion*. New Brunswick, NJ: Rutgers University Press.

Stark, R. and Glock, R. (1968) *American Piety. The Nature of Religious Commitment*. Berkeley: University of California Press.

Stewart, A., Prandy, K. and Blackburn, R. M. (1980) *Social Stratification and Occupations*. London: Macmillan.

Stiglitz, J. (2002) *Globalization and its Discontents*. London: Penguin.

Storey, A. (2003) 'Measuring Development', in G. McCann and S. McCloskey (eds), *From the Global to the Local*. London: Pluto.

Strinati, D. (1995) *An Introduction to Theories of Popular Culture*. London: Routledge & Kegan Paul.

Sugarman, B. (1970) 'Social Class, Values and Behaviour in Schools', in M. Craft (ed.), *Family, Class and Education: A Reader*. London: Longman.

Sutcliffe, B. (2001) *100 Ways of Seeing An Unequal World*. London: Zed Books.

Sutcliffe, S. J. (2003) *Children of the New Age: A History of Spiritual Practices*. London: Routledge & Kegan Paul.

Sutherland, E. H. (1949) *Principles of Criminology*. Philadelphia: J. B. Lippincott.

Sutton Trust (2005) *The Educational Background of Members of the House of Commons and the House of Lords*. London: The Sutton Trust.

Sutton Trust (2006) *The Educational Backgrounds of Leading Journalists*, London: Sutton Trust.

Sutton Trust (2007) *Recent Changes in Intergenerational Mobility in the UK*. London: Sutton Trust.

Swain, J. (2007) 'Performing masculinities', *Sociology Review* 17/2.

Swift, R. (1998) 'The Cocoa Chain', *New Internationalist* 304 (August).

Szmigin, I. and Carrigan, M. (2000) 'Does Advertising in the UK Need Older Models?', *Journal of Product and Brand Management* 9/2.

Szreter, S. (1998) 'Social Capital, the Economy and the Third Way'. Available at: www.netnexus.org/events/july98/talks/szreter.htm.

Taylor, I., Walton, P. and Young, J. (1973) *The New Criminology: For a Social Theory of Deviance*. London: Routledge & Kegan Paul.

Taylor, S. (1982) *Durkheim and the Study of Suicide*. London: Macmillan.

Taylor, S. (1988) *Suicide*. London: Longman.

Taylor, S. (1990) 'Beyond Durkheim: Sociology and Suicide', *Social Studies Review* (November).

Thekaekara, M. M. (2005) 'Tsunami Business', *New Internationalist* 383 (October).

Thiel, D. (2008) *Policing Terrorism: A Review of the Evidence*. London: Policing Foundation.

Thomas, A. (2000) 'Meanings and Views of Development', in T. Allen and A. Thomas (eds), *Poverty and Development Into the Twenty-first Century*. Oxford: Oxford University Press.

Thomas, W. I. and Thomas D. S. (1928) *The Child in America: Behavior Problems and Programs*. New York: Knopf.

Tierney, J. (1996) *Criminology: Theory and Context*. London: Harvester Wheatsheaf.

Tiger, L. and Fox, R. (1972) *The Imperial Animal*. London: Secker & Warburg.

Timmer, D. A. and Eitzen, S. (1989) *Crime in the Streets and in the Suites*. Boston, MA: Allyn and Bacon.

Tönnies, F. (2001) *Community and Civil Society*, ed. J. Harris. Cambridge: Cambridge University Press.

Townsend, P. (1963) *The Family life of Old People*. London: Allen Lane/Pelican.

Townsend, P. (1979) *Poverty in the United Kingdom*. Harmondsworth: Penguin.

Toynbee, P. and Walker, D. (2008) *Unjust Rewards*. London: Granta Books.

Troeltsch, E. (1992 [1931]) *The Social Teaching of the Christian Churches*. Louisville, KY: Westminster John Knox Press.

Tuchman, G., Daniels, A. K. and Benet, J. W. (eds) (1978) *Hearth and Home: Images of Women in the Mass Media*. Oxford: Oxford University Press.

Tudor-Hart, J. (1971) 'The Inverse Care Law' *The Lancet* 1.

Tumin, M. (1953) 'Some Principles of Stratification: A Critical Analysis', repr. in R. Bendix and S. M. Lipset (eds), *Class, Status and Power*. London: Routledge & Kegan Paul, 1967.

Tunstall, J. (1962) *The Fishermen*. London: MacGibbon & Kee.

Turner, B. (1993) *Religion and Social Theory*. London: Sage.

UN (2005) *Millennium Development Goals*. Available at: www.un.org/millenniumgoals/pdf/mdg 2007.pdf.

UN Department of Economic and Social Affairs, Population Division (2006) *World Urbanization Prospects: The 2005 Revision*. Available at: www.un.org/esa/population/publications/WUP2005/2005wup.htm.

UN Development Programme, Human Development Report (1999). *Globalization with a Human Face*. New York: Oxford University Press.

UNIFEM (2006) *Progress of the World's Women 2005: Women, Work and Poverty*. United Nations: www.un.org.

Uvin, P. (1998) *Aiding Violence: The Development Enterprise in Rwanda*. West Hartford: Kumarian Press.

van Dijk, T. (1991) *Racism and the Press*. London: Routledge & Kegan Paul.

Voas, D. and Crockett, A. (2005) 'Religion in Britain: Neither Believing Nor Belonging', *Sociology* 39/1.

Walby, S. (1990) *Theorizing Patriarchy*. Oxford: Blackwell.

Walker, A. (1990) 'Why Are Most Churchgoers Women?' *Vox Evangelica* 20: 73–90.

Walklate, S. (1996) 'Community and Crime Prevention' in E. McLaughlin and J. Muncie (eds), *Controlling Crime*. London: Sage.

Walklate, S. (2004) *Gender, Crime and Criminal Justice*, 2nd edn. Cullompton: Willan.

Wallerstein, I. (2004) 'The Rise and Future Demise of the World Capitalist System', in F. Lechner and J. Boli (eds), *The Globalization Reader*, 2nd edn. Oxford: Blackwell.

Walliman, I., Rosenbaum, H., Tatis, N. and Zito, G. (1980) 'Misreading Weber: The Conept of '*Macht*', *Sociology* 14: 261–75.

Wallis, R. (1974) 'Ideology, Authority and the Development of Cultic Movements', *Social Research* 41.

Wallis, R. (1984) *The Elementary Forms of the New Religious Life*. London: Routledge & Kegan Paul.

Wallis, R. and Bruce, S. 1992 'Secularization: The Orthodox Model', in S. Bruce (ed.), *Religion and Modernization. Sociologists and Historians Debate the Secularization Thesis*. Oxford: Oxford University Press.

Walter, T. and Davie, G. (1998) 'The Religiosity of Women in the Modern West', *British Journal of Sociology* 49/4.

Ware, H. (ed) (2006) *The No-nonsense Guide to Conflict and Peace*. Oxford: New Internationalist.

Warren, B. (1980) *Imperialism: Pioneer of Capitalism*. London: New Left Books.

Watson, H. (1994) 'Women and the Veil: Personal Responses to Global Process', in A. S. Ahmed and H. Donnan, *Islam, Globalization and Postmodernity*. London: Routledge & Kegan Paul.

Webber, R. (2008) 'Postcodes and Social Class: Which Tells Us More?' *Social Science Teacher* 37/2.

Weber, M. (1922 [1978]) 'The Soteriology of the Underprivileged', in W. G. Runciman, *Max Weber: Selections in translation*. Cambridge: Cambridge University Press.

Weber, M. (1947) *The Theory of Social and Economic Organization*, trans. A. R. Henderson and T. Parsons. London: William Hodge.

Weber, M. (1993 [1920]) *The Sociology of Religion*. Boston, Beacon Press.

Weber, M. (2001 [1904]) *The Protestant Ethic and the Spirit of Capitalism*. Chicago: Fitzroy Dearborn.

Weisbrot, M., Baker, D., Kraev, E. and Chen, J. (2001) *The Scorecard on Globalization 1980-2000: Twenty Years of Diminished Progress*. Available at: www.cepr.net/documents/publications/globalization_2001_07_11.pdf.

Westergaard, J. and Resler, H. (1975) *Class in a Capitalist Society*. London: Heinemann.

Wield, D. and Chataway, J. (2000) 'Unemployment and Making a Living', in T. Allen and A. Thomas (eds), *Poverty and Development Into the Twenty-first Century*. Oxford: Oxford University Press.

Williams, H. (2006) *Britain's Power Elites: The Rebirth of a Ruling Class* London: Constable.

Willis, P. (1977) *Learning to Labour: How Working-class Kids get Working-class Jobs*. Farnborough: Saxon House.

WHO (2008) *Closing the Gap in a Generation: Health Equity Through Action on the Social Determinants of Health*. Geneva: World Health Organization.

Wilson, B. R. (1959) 'An Analysis of Sect Development', *American Sociological Review*.

Wilson, B. R. (1966) *Religion in Secular Society: A Sociological Comment*. London: Watts.

Wilson, B. R. (1970) *Religious Sects: A Sociological Study*. London: Weidenfeld & Nicholson.

Wilson, B. R. (1982) *Religion in Sociological Perspective*. Oxford: Oxford University Press.

Wilson, D., Sharpe, C. and Patterson, A. (2006) *Young People and Crime: Findings from the 2005 Offending, Crime and Justice Survey*, Home Office Statistical Bulletin 17/06. London: Home Office.

Wilson, J. Q. (1985) *Thinking About Crime*, rev. edn. New York: Vintage.

Wilson, J. Q. and Kelling, G. L. (1982) *The Police and Neighborhood Safety: Broken Windows*. Available at: www.manhattan-institute.org/pdf/_atlantic_monthly-broken_windows.pdf.

Winlow, S. (2001) *Badfellas: Crime, Tradition and New Masculinities*. Oxford: Berg.

Wittfogel, K. (1957) *Oriental Despotism: A Comparative Study of Total Power*. New York: Vintage Books.

Woodhouse, P. (2000) 'Environmental Degradation and Sustainability', in T. Allen and A. Thomas (eds), *Poverty and Development Into the Twenty-first Century*. Oxford: Oxford University Press.

Worsley, P. (1978) *Introducing Sociology*. Harmondsworth: Penguin.

Wright, E. O. (1978) *Class, Crisis and the State*. London: New Left Books.

Yanacopulos, H. and Hanlon, J. (eds) (2006) *Civil War, Civil Peace*. Oxford: James Currey.

Young, J. (1971) 'The Role of the Police as Amplifiers of Deviancy, Negotiators of Reality and Translators of Fantasy', in S. Cohen (ed.), *Images of Deviance*. Harmondsworth: Penguin.

Young, M. (1958) *The Rise of the Meritocracy*, London: Allen Lane/Pelican.

Young. M. and Willmott, P. (1962) *Family and Kinship in East London*. London: Pelican.

Index

Using the index

If you are looking for general topics, it is best to refer first to the contents pages at the beginning of this book, or those at the beginning of each chapter. If you can't find what you want there, or want to find a particular item of information, look it up in this index. If you can't find the item, think of other headings it might be given under: the same references are often included several times under different headings. This index includes only the largest or most significant references found in this book, rather than every single occurrence of the theme. It is sensible always to check the largest references first, such as pages 437–41, before 165, 283 or 332. The chances are that what you're looking for will be in the largest entry, and this will save you time wading through a lot of smaller references. Numbers in *italics* refer to entries in the glossary.